THE AMERICAN PAGEANT

7th Edition

The American Pageant

A HISTORY OF THE REPUBLIC

VOLUME I

Thomas A. Bailey
Stanford University

David M. Kennedy
Stanford University

D. C. HEATH AND COMPANY
Lexington, Massachusetts   Toronto

Preface

This seventh edition of *The American Pageant* carries forward the collaboration we began on the sixth edition, which was the most thorough revision of the book since it first appeared in 1956. We have once again gone over the book carefully, enlivening the existing text in many places, and incorporating new material that reflects recent scholarship and the evolving concerns of our fellow historians. As before, we have enriched the *Pageant* by combining our diverse yet complementary areas of expertise—Thomas A. Bailey's in political, diplomatic, constitutional, and military history; David M. Kennedy's in social, economic, cultural, and intellectual history.

Readers will find substantially new treatment of several topics, including American Indian life in the pre-Columbian era, the Spanish impact on the New World, colonial social and economic history (particularly in the Chesapeake region), 19th-century immigration and social mobility, and the First World War. We have also added much material on changes in the structure of the family and the roles of women in the 19th Century, and on the implications of emancipation for masters and slaves alike. In addition, we have extensively recast the section on the Gilded Age, in order to highlight the important political changes of that period. We have similarly rewritten the chapters on the 1920s, to emphasize the extraordinary cultural and economic developments of that era. An entirely new chapter on the Carter administration and the beginning of the Reagan presidency brings the account fully up to date.

We have made other improvements as well. All bibliographies have been updated, as have charts and tables, where appropriate. We have added explanatory material to virtually every map, and to many of the illustrations. Parallel changes have been made in the accompanying *Guidebook* and *Quizbook*.

Readers often tell us that *The American Pageant* is one of the few textbooks with a personality, and we have preserved that personality in this edition. Believing that the way to hold the attention of students is to present the subject in an engaging way, we have worked to make this edition, like its predecessors, as lively as possible without distorting the often sobering reality of the past. As in previous editions, we have maintained a strong chronological narrative and a writing style that emphasizes clarity, concreteness, and a measure of wit. We hope that readers of this book will enjoy learning from it, and will come to share our enjoyment of the study of American history.

THOMAS A. BAILEY
Department of History
Stanford University
Stanford, California

DAVID M. KENNEDY
Department of History
Stanford University
Stanford, California

Contents

16
Shaping the National Economy, 1790–1860
274

The coming of the factory system. Capitalists and workers.
The ripening of commercial agriculture. The transportation
revolution. The emergence of a continental economy. America
and the Atlantic economy. Clipper ships and the Pony Express.

17
Creating an American Character, 1790–1860
293

Pioneer democracy. European immigration. The Germans and
the Irish. Religious revivals. The Mormons. Educational
advances. The changing American family.

18
The Ferment of Reform and Culture, 1790–1860
313

Scientific achievements. Reform stirrings. Temperance.
Women's roles and women's rights. Utopian experiments.
Art and architecture. A national literature.

19
The South and the Slavery Controversy
329

The Cotton Kingdom. The white South. The black South. The
"peculiar institution." Abolitionists. The Southern response.

24
The Ordeal of Reconstruction
429

The defeated South.   The freed slaves.   Andrew Johnson versus the Radical Republicans.   Military Reconstruction, 1867–1877. "Black Reconstruction."   Impeachment.   The legacy of Reconstruction.

Maps

Charts and Tables

Sail, sail thy best, ship of Democracy,
Of value is thy freight, 'tis not the Present only,
The Past is also stored in thee,
Thou holdest not the venture of thyself alone, not of
*   the Western continent alone,*
Earth's résumé entire floats on thy keel, O ship, is
*   steadied by thy spars,*
With thee Time voyages in trust, the antecedent
*   nations sink or swim with thee,*
With all their ancient struggles, martyrs, heroes, epics,
*   wars, thou bear'st the other continents,*
Theirs, theirs as much as thine, the destination-port
*   triumphant....*

WALT WHITMAN
Thou Mother with Thy Equal Brood, 1872

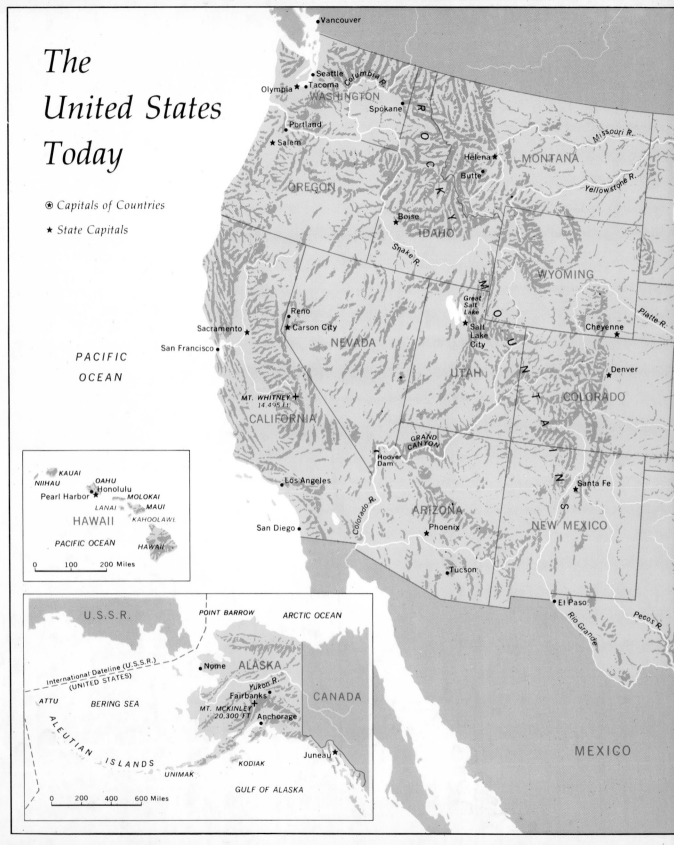

The United States Today

⊛ *Capitals of Countries*

★ *State Capitals*

PACIFIC OCEAN

Vancouver

Seattle
Olympia ★ Tacoma
WASHINGTON
Spokane
Portland
Salem
OREGON

Helena ★ MONTANA
Butte

Columbia R.
Missouri R.
Yellowstone R.

ROCKY

Boise ★
IDAHO

Snake R.

WYOMING

Reno
Carson City ★
Sacramento ★
San Francisco
NEVADA

Great Salt Lake
Salt Lake City ★
UTAH

Cheyenne ★
Platte R.

Denver ★
COLORADO

MOUNTAINS

MT. WHITNEY 14,495 ft.
CALIFORNIA

GRAND CANYON
Hoover Dam

Los Angeles

Colorado R.

ARIZONA

Phoenix ★

Santa Fe ★
NEW MEXICO

San Diego

Tucson

El Paso
Rio Grande
Pecos R.

HAWAII inset

KAUAI
NIIHAU   OAHU
Honolulu
Pearl Harbor ★
LANAI   MOLOKAI
MAUI
KAHOOLAWE
HAWAII

HAWAII

PACIFIC OCEAN

0   100   200 Miles

ALASKA inset

U.S.S.R.   POINT BARROW   ARCTIC OCEAN

International Dateline (U.S.S.R.)
(UNITED STATES)

ATTU   BERING SEA

Nome   ALASKA

Yukon R.
Fairbanks
MT. McKINLEY 20,300 FT.
Anchorage

CANADA

ALEUTIAN ISLANDS

UNIMAK   KODIAK

Juneau ★

GULF OF ALASKA

0   200   400   600 Miles

MEXICO

CANADA

Lake of the Woods

LAKE SUPERIOR

Quebec

St. Lawrence R.

MAINE
Eastport

Ottawa R.

Montreal

NORTH DAKOTA

Bismarck

Duluth

Ottawa

Montpelier

Augusta

MINNESOTA

St. Paul

LAKE HURON

VT. N.H.

Portland

Concord

LAKE MICHIGAN

Toronto

LAKE ONTARIO

NEW YORK

Rochester

Albany

Boston

SOUTH DAKOTA

Pierre

Minneapolis

WISCONSIN

Madison

Milwaukee

MICHIGAN

Lansing

Grand Rapids

Detroit

Buffalo

LAKE ERIE

Hartford

Providence, R.I.

MASS.

CONN.

R.I.

Hudson R.

NEBRASKA

IOWA

Des Moines

Chicago

South Bend
Ft. Wayne

Toledo

Cleveland

PENNSYLVANIA

Harrisburg

Pittsburgh

New York

Trenton

NEW JERSEY

Philadelphia

Omaha

OHIO

Columbus

MD.

Dover

DELAWARE

Missouri R.

Lincoln

ILLINOIS

Springfield

INDIANA

Indianapolis

Cincinnati

WEST VIRGINIA

Charleston

Baltimore

Annapolis

Washington, D.C.

Mississippi R.

Kansas City

Kansas City

St. Louis

Ohio R.

Frankfort

Louisville

VIRGINIA

Richmond

Norfolk

Topeka

KANSAS

Wichita

MISSOURI

Jefferson City

KENTUCKY

APPALACHIAN MOUNTAINS

ROANOKE ISLAND

CAPE HATTERAS

Arkansas R.

Tulsa

Knoxville

Nashville

Tennessee R.

NORTH CAROLINA

Raleigh

Oklahoma City

TENNESSEE

Charlotte

OKLAHOMA

ARKANSAS

Little Rock

Memphis

Columbia

SOUTH CAROLINA

Red R.

Mississippi R.

Birmingham

Atlanta

Savannah R.

Charleston

Ft. Worth

Dallas

MISSISSIPPI

Jackson

ALABAMA

Montgomery

GEORGIA

Savannah

TEXAS

Sabine R.

LOUISIANA

Pearl R.

Mobile

Jacksonville

Tallahassee

Colorado R.

Austin

Baton Rouge

New Orleans

ATLANTIC OCEAN

Houston

San Antonio

FLORIDA

Tampa

Rio Grande

Miami

0   100   200   300   400   500 Miles

1

New World Beginnings

...For I shall yet live to see it [*Virginia*] *an Inglishe nation.*

SIR WALTER RALEIGH, 1602

Planetary Perspectives

Several billion years ago that whirling speck of dust known as the earth, fifth in size among the planets, came into being.

About six thousand years ago—only the day before yesterday geologically—recorded history of the Western world began. Certain peoples of the Middle East, developing a primitive culture, gradually emerged from the haze of the past.

Nearly five hundred years ago—only yesterday—the American continents were stumbled on by Europeans. This epochal achievement, one of the most dramatic in the chronicles of mankind, opened breathtaking new vistas, and forever altered the future of both the Old World and the New.

The two new continents eventually brought forth a score of sovereign republics. By far the

1

most influential of this brood—the United States—was born a pygmy and grew to be a giant. It was destined to leave a deep imprint upon the rest of the world as a result of its refreshingly liberal ideals, its revolutionary democratic experiment, and its boundless opportunities for the common folk of foreign lands. The enormous output of its robust economy ultimately made it a decisive weight in the world balance of power. Its achievements in science, technology, and culture shaped people's lives in every corner of this planet.

Fascinating though it is, the pageant of the American people does not loom large on the time chart of man's known past. But the roots of the United States reach down into the subsoil of the formative colonial years more deeply than is commonly supposed.

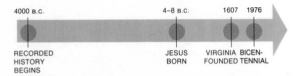

4000 B.C.   4–8 B.C.   1607   1976

RECORDED HISTORY BEGINS   JESUS BORN   VIRGINIA FOUNDED   BICENTENNIAL

The American Republic, which is still relatively young when compared with the Old World, was from the outset richly favored. It started from scratch on a vast and virgin continent, which was so sparsely peopled by Indians that they could be eliminated or shouldered aside. Such a magnificent opportunity for a great democratic experiment may never come again, for no other huge, fertile, and relatively uninhabited areas are left in the temperate zones of this crowded planet.

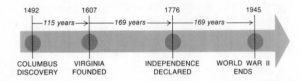

1492   1607   1776   1945

←—115 years—→ ←——169 years——→ ←——169 years——→

COLUMBUS DISCOVERY   VIRGINIA FOUNDED   INDEPENDENCE DECLARED   WORLD WAR II ENDS

Despite its marvelous development, the United States will one day reach its peak, like Greece and Rome. It will ultimately fall upon evil days, as they did. But whatever uncertainties the future may hold, the past at least is secure and will richly repay examination.

Indirect Discoverers of the New World

The American continents were slow to yield their virginity. The all-conquering Romans, a half century after the birth of Christ, expanded their empire northwestward as far as Britain. But for nearly fifteen hundred years thereafter, the New World lay unknown and unsuspected to Europeans, awaiting its discoverers. It is true that about the year A.D. 1000, blond-bearded Norsemen from Scandinavia chanced upon the northeastern shoulder of North America, at a place abounding in wild grapes, which they named Vinland. But their settlements were soon abandoned, and the discovery was forgotten, except in Scandinavian saga and song.

America was to be a child of Europe, not of a specific country, such as England. One must seek in the Old World that momentous chain of events which led to a drive toward the Far East—and a completely accidental discovery of the New World.

Christian Crusaders must take high rank among the indirect discoverers of America. Tens of thousands of these European warriors, clad in shining armor, invaded Palestine from the 11th to the 14th Century. Whatever their true motives, they were avowedly attempting to wrest the Holy Land from the polluting hand of the Moslem infidel. Foiled in their repeated assaults, these Christian soldiers did manage to come into closer contact with the exotic delights of Asia—delights already introduced to Europe on a limited scale. European "barbarians" learned more fully the value of spices for spoiled and monotonous food; of silk for rough skins; of drugs for aching flesh; of perfumes for unbathed bodies; and of colorful draperies for gloomy castles.

But the luxuries of the Far East were almost too expensive in Europe. They had to be transported enormous distances from the Spice Islands (Indonesia), China, and India, in creaking ships and on swaying camel back, to the ports of the eastern Mediterranean. Moslem middlemen exacted a heavy toll en route. By the time the strange-smelling goods reached the Italian merchants at

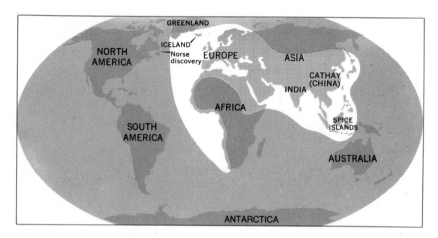

THE WORLD KNOWN TO
EUROPE, 1492

Venice and Genoa, they were so costly that purchasers and profits alike were narrowly limited. Consumers and distributors of Western Europe were naturally eager to find a less costly route to the riches of Eastern Asia—one that would also break the monopoly of the Italian cities.

European appetites were further whetted when foot-loose Marco Polo, an Italian adventurer, returned to Europe in 1295, after a stay of nearly twenty years in China. Several years later, while a war prisoner, he dictated a classic account of his travels. He too must be regarded as an indirect discoverer of the New World, for his book, with its descriptions of rose-tinted pearls and golden pagodas, stimulated European desires for a cheaper route to the treasures of the Indies.

An urge to find a shortcut waterway to Eastern Asia was strong, but success awaited new horizons and new facilities. Fortunately the Renaissance, which dawned in the 14th Century, shot hopeful rays of light through the mists of the Middle Ages. Better maps reduced superstitious fears of the unknown. The mariner's compass, possibly borrowed from the Arabs, eliminated some of the uncertainties of navigation. Printing presses, introduced about 1450, facilitated the spread of scientific knowledge. An atmosphere of rebirth also accompanied the Renaissance and created a healthy spirit of optimism, self-reliance, and venturesomeness.

Portuguese Pathfinders

As the kings gradually subordinated the nobles, the modern national state emerged in Western Europe from the feudalism of the Middle Ages. This new type of government alone had the unity, power, and resources to shoulder the formidable tasks of discovery, conquest, and colonization.

The first nations to unite were the first to flourish as colonial empire builders—Portugal, Spain, England, France, and the Netherlands. Those countries that did not achieve unity until the 19th Century, notably Germany and Italy, were left with crumbs dropped by the early feasters.

Little Portugal took the lead in discovering what came to be the coveted water route to the Indies. A courageous band of Portuguese navigators, edging cautiously down the pistol-handle coast of Africa, pushed southeasterly in the general direction of Asia. In 1488, four years before Columbus chanced upon America, Bartholomeu Diaz rounded the southernmost tip of the Dark Continent. Complete success crowned Portuguese efforts in 1498 when Vasco da Gama finally reached India (hence the name "Indies," given to all the mysterious lands of the Orient). He coaxed few jewels and spices from the natives, but later voyagers reaped lush profits from this treasure trove.

Portuguese empire builders ultimately estab-

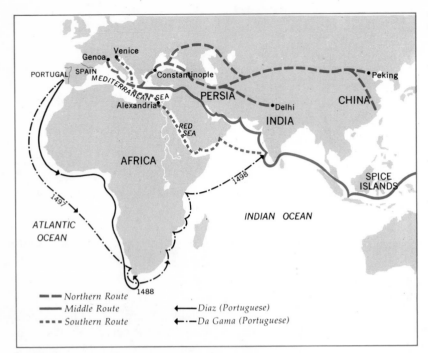

TRADE ROUTES WITH THE EAST
Goods on the early routes were passed through so many hands along the way that their ultimate source remained mysterious to Europeans.

lished flourishing trading stations in India, Africa, China, and the East Indies. Immense wealth flowed to European coffers from these varied ventures. In turn, the ballooning prices of Asian products collapsed, and the monopolistic grip of the Italian commercial cities was broken.

Brazil, by sheer accident, was unveiled in 1500. An India-bound Portuguese navigator, Pedro Cabral, touched upon the giant bulge of South America eight years after the first voyage of Columbus. Portugal subsequently erected a huge empire in the Brazilian wilderness. But the net return from this New World outpost was only a small fraction of the profits that the Portuguese garnered from exploiting their water route to the riches of the Indies.

Columbus Stumbles Upon a New World

The Kingdom of Spain became united—an event pregnant with destiny—late in the 15th Century. This new unity resulted primarily from the marriage of two sovereigns, Ferdinand and Isabella,

and from the brutal expulsion of the "infidel" Moslem Moors. Glorying in their new strength, the Spaniards were eager to outstrip their Portuguese rivals in the race for the fabled Indies.

Christopher Columbus, a skilled Italian seaman, now stepped upon the stage of history. A man of vision, energy, resourcefulness, and courage, he finally managed, after heartbreaking delays, to gain the ear of the Spanish rulers. Like all of his informed contemporaries, he was convinced that the world was round. Then why not find the way to East Asia by sailing directly westward into the darkness of the Atlantic, instead of eastward for unnecessary miles around Africa?

The Spanish monarchs at last decided to gamble on the persistent mariner. They helped outfit him with three tiny but seaworthy ships, manned by a motley crew. Daringly, he spread the sails of his cockleshell craft. Winds were friendly and progress was rapid, but the superstitious sailors, fearful of sailing over the edge of the world, grew increasingly mutinous. Nearly six long weeks passed and failure loomed ahead when, on October 12, 1492, land was sighted—an island in the Bahamas. A new world thus swam within the vision of Europeans.

Columbus's sensational achievement has obscured the fact that he was one of the most successful failures of history. Seeking a new water route to the fabled Indies of the East, he had in fact bumped into an enormous land barrier blocking the ocean pathway. For decades thereafter explorers strove to get through it—or around it. The truth gradually dawned that sprawling new continents had been discovered. Yet Columbus stubbornly maintained until his death in 1506 that he had skirted the rim of the "Indies." So certain was he that he called the near-naked natives "Indians," a gross geographical misnomer that somehow stuck.

Ironically, the remote ancestors of these Native Americans were the true discoverers of America. Some 10,000 to 20,000 years earlier they had ventured across the narrow waters from Asia to what is now Alaska. From there they roamed slowly southward as far as South America. Over the centuries they had split into hundreds of tribes and language groups. Some of these aboriginal peoples had evolved stunning civilizations. Incas in Peru, Aztecs in Mexico, and Mayans in Central America

developed advanced agricultural practices, based on the cultivation of corn (a gift from the Indians to the Old World), that supported populations of millions. They erected bustling, elaborately carved stone cities, rivaling in size those of contemporary medieval Europe. They carried on far-flung commerce, studied mathematics, and made strikingly accurate astronomical observations.

Indian life in North America was cruder, though high levels of cultural development were found among the Pueblos in the Southwest, the Creeks in the Southeast, and the Iroquois in the Northeast. Most native settlements were small, scattered, and often impermanent. So thinly spread across the land was the North American Indian population that large areas were virtually uninhabited, with whispering, primeval forests and sparkling, virgin waters. Perhaps one million Indians dwelled in all of the present-day United States at the time of Columbus's discovery. They ate corn, fish, wild game, nuts, and berries. Private property, especially private landholding, was a concept almost unknown to the Indians until the white Europeans moved in on them. Political organization was equally unfamiliar; loose, independent tribal structures served the Indians well until they clashed with the powerful governments

NORTH AMERICAN INDIAN TRIBES AT THE TIME OF EUROPEAN COLONIZATION This map illustrates the great diversity of the Indian population—and suggests the inappropriateness of identifying all the Native American peoples with the single label "Indian." The more than 200 tribes were deeply divided by geography, language, and life-style.

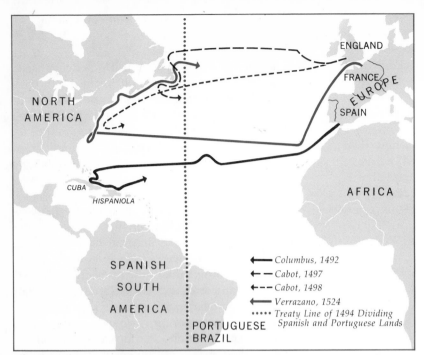

←— Columbus, 1492
← — Cabot, 1497
←--- Cabot, 1498
←— Verrazano, 1524
•••• Treaty Line of 1494 Dividing Spanish and Portuguese Lands

of the whites. Europeans encountered only a handful of Indian institutions larger than the tribal unit, such as the Iroquois Confederacy in the region of present-day New York, and the Powhatan Confederacy in Virginia.

The Spanish Conquistadores

Gradually the realization sank in that the American continents held rich prizes of their own—especially the glittering gold of the advanced Indian civilizations in the southern continent. Spain secured its claim to Columbus's discoveries in the Treaty of Tordesillas (1494), dividing with Portugal the "heathen lands" of the New World. The lion's share went to Spain, but Portugal received compensating territory in Africa and Asia, and also title to lands that would one day be Brazil.

Spain now became the dominant exploring and colonizing power in the 1500s. Love of God joined with the lure of gold in spurring the Spaniards on, as zealous priests sought to convert the pagan natives to Catholic Christianity. On Spain's long roster of heroic deeds two spectacular exploits must

be headlined. Vasco Nuñez Balboa, hailed as the discoverer of the Pacific Ocean, waded into the foaming waves off Panama in 1513 and claimed for his King all the lands washed by that sea! Ferdinand Magellan started from Spain in 1519 with five tiny ships. After discovering the storm-lashed strait off South America that bears his name, he was slain by the natives in the Philippines, but his one remaining vessel creakily completed the first circumnavigation of the globe in 1522.

Exploratory beginnings were launched by other adventuresome Spaniards in what was destined to be the United States. In 1513 Juan Ponce de León discovered Florida, which he thought an island. Debauched by high living, he was seeking the mythical Fountain of Youth. He found instead death—from an Indian arrow. Francisco Coronado, in quest of golden cities that turned out to be primitive pueblos, wandered in 1540–1542 with a clanking cavalcade through Arizona and New Mexico as far east as Kansas. His expedition discovered en route two impressive natural wonders: the Grand Canyon of the Colorado and enormous herds of buffalo (bison).

Hernando de Soto, with six hundred armor-

Typical Spanish *Conquistador.*
By Frederic Remington, artist of the West.

plated men, undertook a fantastic gold-seeking expedition during 1539–1542. Floundering through marshes and pine barrens, from Florida westward, he discovered and crossed the majestic Mississippi north of the Arkansas River. After cruelly misusing the Indians with iron collars and fierce dogs, he at length died of fever and wounds. His remains were secretly buried at night in the Mississippi, lest the Indians abuse the dead body of their abuser.

All these meanderings had little impact upon the events that gave birth to the United States, with two noteworthy exceptions. Hernando Cortés, with seven hundred men and eighteen horses (which awed the horseless natives), tore open the coffers of the Mexican Aztecs in 1519–1521. Francisco Pizarro, an iron-fisted conqueror, crushed the Peruvian Incas in 1532, and added another incredible hoard of gold and silver to the loot from Mexico. The Spanish invaders not only robbed the Indians, but subsequently enslaved them and put them to work digging up precious metals. By 1600, Spain was swimming in New World silver, mostly from the fabulously rich mines at Potosi, Peru.

The Spanish conquerors (*conquistadores*), curiously enough, were indirect founding fathers of the United States. Their phenomenal success excited the envy of Englishmen, and helped spur some of the early attempts at colonization. Moreover, the dumping of the enormous Indian treasure chests upon Europe inflated the currency and drove prices upward. The pinch further distressed underpaid English toilers, many of whom in turn were later driven to the New World. There,

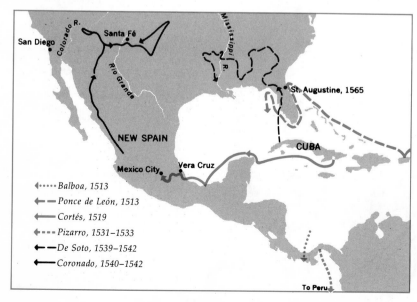

Balboa, 1513
Ponce de León, 1513
Cortés, 1519
Pizarro, 1531–1533
De Soto, 1539–1542
Coronado, 1540–1542

PRINCIPAL SPANISH EXPLORATIONS AND CONQUESTS
Note that Coronado traversed northern Texas and Oklahoma. In present-day eastern Kansas he found, instead of the great golden city he sought, a drab encampment, probably of Wichita Indians.

ironically, they challenged Spanish supremacy.

These plunderings by the Spaniards unfortunately obscured their substantial colonial achievements, and helped give birth to the "Black Legend." This false concept meant that the conquerors merely tortured and butchered the Indians ("killing for Christ"), stole their gold, infected them with smallpox, and left little but misery behind. The Spanish invader did kill thousands of natives and exploit the rest, but he intermarried with them as well, creating a distinctive South American culture of *mestizos*—people of mixed Indian and European heritage. He erected a colossal empire, sprawling from California and the Floridas to Tierra del Fuego. He transplanted and engrafted his culture, laws, religion, and language, and laid the foundations for a score of Spanish-speaking nations.

The bare statistics of Spain's colonial empire are alone impressive. By 1574, thirty-three years before the first primitive English shelters in Virginia, there were about two hundred Spanish cities and towns in North and South America. A total of 160,000 Spanish inhabitants, mostly men, had subjugated some 5 million Indians—all in the name of the gentle Jesus. Majestic cathedrals dotted the land, printing presses were turning out books, and literary prizes were being awarded. Two distinguished universities were chartered in 1551, one at Mexico City and the other at Lima, Peru. Both of them antedated Harvard, the first college established in the English colonies, by eighty-five years.

It is clear that the Spaniards, who had more than a century's head start over the English, were genuine empire builders in the New World. As compared with their Anglo-Saxon rivals, their colonial establishment was larger and richer, and it lasted more than a quarter of a century longer.

The Gilbert and Raleigh Fiascos

Feeble indeed were the efforts of England in the 1500s to compete with the sprawling Spanish empire. Sir Humphrey Gilbert tried to plant a colony

North Carolina Indians "Sitting at Meate."   Painted by John White, a member of Sir Walter Raleigh's second expedition, 1585. Indians such as these may have absorbed the more than one hundred "lost colonists" from Sir Walter Raleigh's ill-starred venture on Roanoke Island. In one nearby county of present-day North Carolina, blue-eyed and fair-haired characteristics have persisted among the Indians, along with Elizabethan words and the family names of forty-one Roanoke colonists. (Library of Congress.)

Sir Walter Raleigh (c. 1552–1618). Here he is shown "drinking tobacco," as smoking was first called. He is credited with introducing both tobacco and the potato into England. A dashing courtier, he launched important colonizing failures in the New World. After seducing (and marrying) one of Queen Elizabeth's maids of honor, he fell out of favor and was ultimately beheaded for treason.

on the bleak coast of Newfoundland, but lost his gamble and his life in 1583, when his ship sank in a storm. Sir Walter Raleigh, Gilbert's gallant half-brother, attempted in the 1580s to establish a colony in warmer climes. The settlers chose North Carolina's Roanoke Island, which lay just off the coast of Virginia—a vague region named by the Virgin Queen Elizabeth in honor of herself. With Raleigh busy at home, the ill-starred Roanoke colony mysteriously vanished, swallowed up by the wilderness. Most probably disease and hostile Indians wiped out many of the colonists. Among them was Virginia Dare, the first of many millions of babies of English blood to be born in the New World. Her known life lasted nine days.

The Anglo-Saxons were plainly losing out. When the reign of "Good Queen Bess" ended in 1603, England did not have a single permanent habitation in all the Americas. Her backwardness contrasted strikingly with the imperial achievements of both Spain and Portugal.

Huge empires cannot be erected on shoestrings. The failures of lone wolves like Gilbert and Raleigh merely proved that the risky business of colony building was beyond the resources of a single private purse. But the child must creep before he can walk, and these discouraging setbacks taught badly needed lessons.

A Troubled England on the Eve of Empire

By the early 1600s the English were ready to enter the colonial scramble in dead earnest. Why?

Economic motivations were strong. A vigorous middle class had risen, challenging the social position of the nobles, and providing an active group of merchants who could furnish business leadership and wealth for colonial enterprises. Moreover, the joint-stock company—forerunner of the modern corporation—was now perfected. It had the virtue of enabling a considerable number of investors ("adventurers") to pool their capital—an advantage that the luckless Gilbert and Raleigh had not enjoyed.

England was also burdened with a surplus population. At least she thought she was, even though her 4 million inhabitants totaled only about half those of London in the mid-20th Century. The woolen industry was experiencing boom days, and farms were being turned into grazing lands, with the sheep displacing many soil tillers. Catholic monasteries and nunneries, which had formerly cared for the poor, had been seized by the anti-papal Crown. Penniless souls, in a period of increasingly hard times, were being turned loose on the country. In the late 1500s the land swarmed with "sturdy beggars and paupers," who engaged in "lewd and naughty practices" and who might well be dumped on America.

English colonization was also profoundly influenced by the Protestant Reformation. Martin Luther, a German who dramatically launched his reformist attack on the Church of Rome in 1517, was another indirect founding father of the United States. Much-married Henry VIII of England, using the Reformation for his own devices and divorces, broke with Rome and made himself head of the Church of England. Unhappy Protes-

The Tudor Rulers of England
(SEE P. 28 FOR CONTINUATION OF TABLE.)

Name, Reign	Relation to America
Henry VII, 1485–1509	Cabot voyages, 1497, 1498
Henry VIII, 1509–1547	English Reformation begun
Edward VI, 1547–1553	Strong Protestant tendencies
"Bloody" Mary, 1553–1558	Catholic reaction
Elizabeth, 1558–1603	Break with Rome final; Drake; Spanish Armada defeated

tants, especially those who felt that their king had not parted company completely with the Papacy, came to look upon America as a desirable haven for people of their faith. Many persecuted Catholics, who believed that their sovereign had gone too far, likewise began to regard America as a possible refuge.

International religious rivalry, in addition, spurred English colonization. The King of England ruled the leading Protestant nation; the King of Spain ruled the leading Catholic nation. A bitter contest between these two powers for the spoils of North America was, curiously, to take on some of the features of a religious crusade extended to the New World. English America was in some degree a child of Catholic-Protestant strife.

Sir Francis Drake and the Spanish Armada

Hardy English freebooters swarmed out upon the shipping lanes in the mid-1500s. They sought to promote the twin goals of Protestantism and plunder by seizing Spanish treasure ships, even though England and Spain were technically at peace. The most famous of these semi-piratical "sea dogs" was the courtly Francis Drake. He plundered his way around the planet, and returned in 1580 with his ship heavily ballasted with Spanish silver and gold. The venture netted profits of about 4,600

Elizabeth I (1533–1603).   Although accused of being vain, fickle, prejudiced, and miserly, she proved to be an unusually successful ruler. She never married ("The Virgin Queen"), although various royal matches were projected. (National Portrait Gallery, London.)

percent to his financial backers, among whom, in secret, was Queen Elizabeth I. Defying the protests of Spain, she brazenly knighted Drake on the deck of his barnacled ship. Seldom has patriotic piracy been so handsomely rewarded. Elizabeth further outraged the Spanish Crown by sending English troops to the Netherlands, where they helped the partially Protestant Dutch to wrest their independence from Catholic Spain.

A showdown came in 1588 when Philip II of

Spain, self-anointed foe of the Protestant Reformation, amassed his "Invincible Armada" of some 130 ships bearing troops for an invasion of England. The English sea dogs fought back. They inflicted heavy damage in four running engagements, using craft that were swifter, more maneuverable, more numerous, and better armed. Then devastating storms took over, causing even greater damage. About half of the crippled Spanish fleet finally crept back into port. Spanish prestige, and with it the Catholic cause, had suffered a humiliating blow.

The defeat of the Spanish Armada was a red-letter event in American history. It dampened the fighting spirit of Spain, and gave further proof of the decline in her power, though by no means its end. The triumph also helped to insure England's naval dominance in the North Atlantic. It started her well on her way to becoming Mistress of the Seas—a fact of enormous importance to the American people. Control of the watery highways enabled England, with relative ease, not only to plant her colonies but to supply and protect them as well. Specifically, the victory helped clear the way for the English to settle on the Atlantic coast as far south as Virginia. This area was regarded by

Ark Royal, **the English Flagship Used in the Defeat of the Spanish Armada.** (Reproduced by courtesy of the Trustees of the British Museum.)

Spain as her own private preserve, for there she had already planted a Jesuit missionary outpost in 1570 which had soon been wiped out by Indians.

England's rocky road to settlement in America was further smoothed in 1603, when Queen Elizabeth died. She carried her personal feud with Spain to her grave, and the next year the two rivals signed an uneasy peace.

A wondrous flowering of the English national spirit also followed the crippling of the Spanish Armada. A golden age of literature dawned in this exhilarating atmosphere, with Shakespeare, who was at the forefront, making occasional poetical reference to England's American colonies. Englishmen were seized with restlessness, with thirst for adventure, and with curiosity regarding the unknown. Everywhere there blossomed a new spirit of self-confidence, of vibrant patriotism, and of boundless faith in the future of the English nation.

England Plants the Jamestown Seedling

In 1606, two years after peace with Spain, the hand of destiny beckoned toward Virginia. A joint-stock company, known as The Virginia Company of London, received a charter from King James I of England for a settlement in the New World. The main attraction was the promise of gold, although there was also a strong desire to convert the Indians to Christianity and to find a passage through America to the Indies. Like most joint-stock companies of the day, The Virginia Company was intended to endure for only a few years, after which its stockholders hoped to liquidate it for a profit. This arrangement put severe pressure on the luckless colonists, who were threatened with abandonment in the wilderness if they did not quickly strike it rich on the company's behalf. Few of the investors thought in terms of long-term colonization. Apparently no one even faintly suspected that the seeds of a mighty nation were being planted.

The charter of the Virginia Company is a significant document in American history. It guaranteed to the overseas settlers the same rights of

◻║

> King James I had scant enthusiasm for the Virginia experiment, partly because of his hatred of tobacco smoking, which had been introduced into the Old World by the Spanish discoverers. In 1604 he published the pamphlet *A Counterblast to Tobacco:* "A custom loathsome to the eye, hateful to the nose, harmful to the brain, dangerous to the lungs, and in the black stinking fume thereof, nearest resembling the horrible Stygian smoke of the pit [Hades] that is bottomless."

◻║

Englishmen that they would have enjoyed if they had stayed at home. This precious boon was gradually extended to the other English colonies, and became a foundation stone of American liberties.

Unluckily, the site selected in 1607 for the tiny colony was Jamestown, on the wooded and malarial banks of the James River, named in honor of King James I. Although mosquito-infested and unhealthful, the spot was easy to defend.

The early years at Jamestown proved to be a nightmare for all concerned—except the buzzards. Forty would-be colonists perished during the initial voyage in 1606–1607. Another expedition in 1609 lost its leaders and many of its precious supplies in a shipwreck in Bermuda. Of the 400 settlers who managed to make it to Virginia, only 60 survived the "starving time" winter of 1609–10. Ironically, the woods rustled with game and the rivers flopped with fish, but the greenhorn settlers wasted valuable time grubbing for nonexistent gold when they should have been gathering provisions. Diseased and despairing, the colonists dragged themselves aboard homeward-bound ships in the spring of 1610–only to be met at the mouth of the James River by a relief party, which ordered them back to Jamestown.

Disease continued to reap a gruesome harvest among the Virginians, and Indian raids added to the death toll. One Indian uprising in 1622 left 347 settlers dead. By 1625, Virginia contained only some 1200 hard-bitten survivors of the nearly 8000 adventurers who had tried to start life anew in the ill-fated colony.

Virginia was saved from collapse at the start largely by the leadership and resourcefulness of an incredible young adventurer, Captain John Smith. Taking over in 1608, he whipped the gold-hungry colonists into line with the rule, "He who will not work shall not eat." The brown-skinned Indian maiden Pocahontas may not have saved his life, as he dramatically related, by suddenly interposing her head between his and the war clubs of his Indian captors. But there can be little doubt that she contributed to the salvation of the colony by helping to preserve peace and provide foodstuffs. At times of scarcity the settlers were forced to eat "dogges, Catts, Ratts, and Myce." One hungry man killed, salted, and ate his wife, for which misbehavior he was executed.

Virginia: Child of Tobacco

John Rolfe, who married Pocahontas in 1613 and became father of the tobacco industry, was also an economic savior of the Virginia colony. By 1616 he perfected methods of raising and curing the pungent weed (another Indian gift to Europe) which eliminated much of the bitter tang. Tobacco-rush days began, as crops were planted even

Pochantas (c. 1595–1617). Taken to England by her husband, she was received as a princess. She died when preparing to return, and her infant son ultimately reached Virginia, where hundreds of his descendants have lived, including the second Mrs. Woodrow Wilson. (National Portrait Gallery, Smithsonian Institution, Washington, D.C.)

in the streets of Jamestown and between the numerous graves. So heavy was the concentration on the yellow leaf that some foodstuffs had to be imported.

Virginia's prosperity was finally built on tobacco smoke. This "bewitching weed" played a vital role in putting the colony on firm foundations, and in setting an example for other successful colonizing experiments. But tobacco—King Nicotine—was something of a tyrant. It was ruinous to the soil when greedily planted in successive years, and it enchained the prosperity of Virginia to the fluctuating price of a single crop. Finally, tobacco promoted the broad-acred plantation system, and with it a brisk demand for slave labor.

In 1619, the year before the Plymouth Pilgrims landed in New England, what was described as a Dutch warship appeared off Jamestown and sold some twenty black Africans. (The scanty record does not reveal whether they were purchased as lifelong slaves or as servants committed to limited years of servitude.) Yet black slaves were too costly for most of the hard-pinched white colonists to acquire, and for decades they were imported only in driblets. Virginia counted but 300 blacks in 1650, although by the end of the century blacks made up approximately 14 percent of the colony's population.

Representative self-government was also born in primitive Virginia, in the same cradle with slavery and in the same year—1619. The London Company authorized the settlers to summon an

assembly, known as the House of Burgesses. A momentous precedent was thus feebly established, for this assemblage was the first of many miniature parliaments to mushroom from the soil of America.

"Cavalier" Virginia and Bacon's Rebellion

As time passed, James I grew increasingly hostile to Virginia. He detested tobacco and he distrusted the representative House of Burgesses, which he branded a "seminary of sedition." In 1624 he arbitrarily revoked the charter of the bankrupt Virginia Company, thus making Virginia a royal colony directly under his control. He next planned to abolish the House of Burgesses; but he died the next year, and in the subsequent change-over the newborn assembly was allowed to continue.

To add to the confusion, civil wars convulsed England in the 1640s. The personal rule of King Charles I, supported by his loyal "Cavaliers," was openly challenged by the Parliamentarians ("Roundheads"). They ultimately found their great leader in Oliver Cromwell. The Virginians showed surprising loyalty to the distant Crown, and when the Parliamentarians triumphed and Charles I was beheaded, a sprinkling of the vanquished Cavaliers fled to hospitable Virginia. Only a handful of them were of noble birth; most of them were Cavaliers only by sentiment or political attachment. But the tradition of aristocratic origins spread rapidly in Virginia—later "the Cavalier State"—and the belief that many of its founders were exiled noblemen came to have a profound impact on the Southern mind.

Cavalier or not, class and sectional tensions quickly jelled in colonial Virginia. Lace-bedecked gentry monopolized the rich tidewater lands of the coastal areas; the Byrd family alone eventually amassed 179,000 acres. Poorer folk were forced into the wild and dangerous back country. There, though unrepresented or underrepresented in the House of Burgesses, they were compelled to bear the full brunt of the Indian attacks.

The wife of a Virginia governor wrote to her sister in England in 1623 of her voyage: "For our Shippe was so pestered with people and goods that we were so full of infection that after a while we saw little but throwing folkes over board: It pleased god to send me my helth till I came to shoare and 3 dayes after I fell sick but I thank god I am well recovered. Few else are left alive that came in that Shippe. . . ."

Rebellion was clearly in the making. Autocratic old Governor Berkeley, who was allegedly involved in fur trade with the Indians, was unwilling to antagonize them by fighting back. About a thousand angry back-country men broke out of control in 1676, under the leadership of a twenty-nine-year-old planter, Nathaniel Bacon, whose overseer had been slain. They chastised the Indians, friendly and hostile alike, routed Governor Berkeley, and burned Jamestown. In the hour of victory Bacon suddenly died, amid rumors that he had been poisoned by the Berkeleyites. The governor thereupon crushed the uprising with needless cruelty, hanging in all more than twenty rebels. Back in England Charles II complained, "That old fool has put to death more people in that naked country than I did here for the murder of my father."

Bacon's ill-fated rebellion was symptomatic of much that was to be American. It highlighted the cleavage between the old order of aristocracy and special privilege, on the one hand, and the emerging new order of free enterprise and equal opportunity, on the other. The outburst arrayed the despised commoners against the lordly governing class, and the back-country frontier against the tidewater aristocracy. Bacon and his followers showed at this early date that aroused colonists would unite and die for what they regarded as their rights as free men.

Maryland: Catholic Haven

Maryland—the second plantation colony but the fourth English colony to be planted—was founded in 1634 by Lord Baltimore, of a prominent English Catholic family. He embarked upon the venture partly to reap financial profits and partly to create a refuge for his co-religionists. Protestant England was still persecuting Roman Catholics; among numerous discriminations, a couple seeking wedlock could not be legally married by a Catholic priest.

Absentee proprietor Lord Baltimore hoped that the 200 settlers who founded Maryland at St. Mary's, on Chesapeake Bay, would be the vanguard of a vast new feudal domain. Huge estates

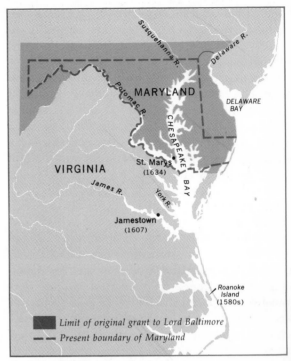

EARLY MARYLAND AND VIRGINIA

were to be awarded to his largely Catholic relatives, and gracious manor houses, modeled on those of England's aristocracy, were intended to sprout from the fertile forests. But colonists proved willing to come only if offered the right to acquire land of their own. Soon they were dispersed around the Chesapeake region on modest farms, and the haughty land barons, mostly Catholic, were surrounded by resentful back-country planters, mostly Protestant. Resentment flared into open rebellion near the end of the century, and the Baltimore family for a time lost its proprietary rights.

Despite these tensions, Maryland prospered. Like Virginia, it blossomed forth in acres of tobacco. Like Virginia, it depended for labor in its early years mainly on white indentured servants—penniless persons who bound themselves to work for a number of years to pay their passage. In both colonies it was only in the later years of the 17th Century that black slaves began to be imported in large numbers—a response to the rising price of white labor, and perhaps to fears of further troubles with rebellious white settlers like Nathaniel Bacon. At the same time, laws began to appear on the books that formally decreed the iron conditions of black slavery. These earliest "slave codes" made blacks and their children the property for life of their white masters. Not even conversion to Christianity could qualify a slave for freedom. Thus did the God-fearing whites put the fear of God into their hapless black laborers.

Lord Baltimore, a canny soul, permitted unusual freedom of worship at the outset. He hoped that he would thus purchase toleration for his own fellow worshipers. But the heavy tide of Protestants threatened to submerge the Catholics and place severe restrictions on them, as in England. Faced with disaster, the Catholics of Maryland threw their support behind the famed Act of Toleration, which was passed in 1649 by the local representative assembly.

Maryland's new religious statute guaranteed toleration to all Christians. But it decreed the death penalty for those, like Jews and atheists, who denied the divinity of Jesus. The law thus sanctioned less toleration than had previously existed in the settlement, but it did extend a temporary cloak of protection to the uneasy Catholic minority. One result was that when the colonial era ended, Maryland probably sheltered more Roman Catholics than any other English-speaking colony in the New World.

A North Carolina Indian. A painting by John White, who was a member of the Raleigh expedition of 1585. (Library of Congress.)

Cecelius Calvert (Lord Baltimore), c. 1605–1675. Inheriting the land grant from his father, he served as the first proprietor of Maryland, named after the English queen. He never saw his colony but governed through deputies. The present Anne Arundel county, embracing Annapolis and Baltimore, was named after his wife. (Enoch Pratt Free Library. Photograph from the Maryland Historical Society.)

Colonizing the Carolinas

The Carolinas were formally created in 1670, after Charles II had granted to eight of his court favorites—Lords Proprietors—an expanse of wilderness ribboning across the continent to the Pacific. These aristocratic founders hoped to make their fortunes in this warm climate by producing non-English products, such as silk, wine, and olive oil.

South Carolina started auspiciously. There was no "starving time," as in Virginia, though the first fleet was on short rations when it arrived. Moss-festooned Charles Town—named after

The Thirteen Original Colonies

Name	Founded by	Year	Charter	Made Royal	1775 Status
1. Virginia	London Co.	1607	1606 1609 1612	1624	Royal (under the Crown)
Plymouth	Separatists	1620	None		(Merged with Mass., 1691)
Maine	F. Gorges	1623	1639		(Bought by Mass., 1677)
2. New Hampshire	John Mason and others	1623	1679	1679	Royal (absorbed by Mass., 1641–1679)
3. Massachusetts	Puritans	c.1628	1629	1691	Royal
4. Maryland	Lord Baltimore	1634	1632	——	Proprietary (controlled by proprietor)
5. Connecticut	Mass. emigrants	1635	1662	——	Self-governing (under local control)
6. Rhode Island	R. Williams	1636	1644 1663	——	Self-governing
New Haven	Mass. emigrants	1638	None		(Merged with Conn., 1662)
7. N. Carolina	Virginians	1653	1663	1729	Royal (separated informally from S.C., 1691)
8. New York	Dutch	c.1613			
	Duke of York	1664	1664	1685	Royal
9. New Jersey	Berkeley and Carteret	1664	None	1702	Royal
10. S. Carolina	Eight nobles	1670	1663	1729	Royal (separated formally from N.C., 1712)
11. Pennsylvania	William Penn	1681	1681	——	Proprietary
12. Delaware	Swedes	1638	None	——	Proprietary (merged with Penn., 1682; same governor, but separate assembly, granted 1703)
13. Georgia	Oglethorpe and others	1733	1732	1752	Royal

King Charles II—rapidly became the most important seaport of the South. Many high-spirited younger sons of English noble families, deprived of an inheritance, came to the Charleston area and lent it a rich aristocratic flavor. The village also became a melting-pot community, to which French Protestant refugees and others were attracted by religious toleration.

South Carolina prospered and gradually developed close economic and cultural ties with the flourishing British West Indies. In a broad sense, the mainland colony was but the most northwesterly of these islands. Rice and the indigo plant, which then provided the most important blue dyestuff, were grown profitably on large plantations. The hot sun and swampy land combined to create a strong demand for African slaves; by 1776 South Carolina was the only colony in which blacks outnumbered whites, by nearly two to one.

Nearby, in Florida, the Catholic Spaniards bitterly resented the intrusion of these English heretics. South Carolina's frontier was often aflame. Spanish-incited Indians brandished their tomahawks, and armor-clad warriors of Spain attacked or were attacked during the successive Anglo-Spanish wars. But by 1700 South Carolina was too strong to be wiped out.

The wild northern expanse of the huge Carolina grant bordered on Virginia. From the older colony there drifted down a motley group of poverty-stricken outcasts and religious dissenters. Many of them had been repelled by the rarefied atmosphere of Virginia, dominated as it was by big-plantation aristocrats belonging to the Church of England. North Carolinians, as a result, have been called "the quintessence of Virginia's discontent." The newcomers, who frequently were "squatters" without legal right to the soil, raised their tobacco and other crops on small farms, with little need for slaves.

Distinctive traits developed rapidly in North Carolina. The poor but sturdy inhabitants, regarded as riffraff by their snobbish neighbors, earned a reputation for being irreligious and hospitable to pirates. Isolated from neighbors by raw wilderness and stormy Cape Hatteras, "graveyard of the Atlantic," the North Carolinians developed a strong spirit of resistance to authority. Their location between aristocratic Virginia and aristocratic South Carolina caused the area to be dubbed "a vale of humility between two mountains of conceit." Following much friction with governors, North Carolina was officially separated from South Carolina in 1712, and subsequently each segment became a royal colony.

North Carolina shares with tiny Rhode Island

EARLY CAROLINA AND
GEORGIA SETTLEMENTS

several distinctions. These two outposts were the most democratic, the most independent-minded, and the least aristocratic of the original thirteen English colonies.

Late-Coming Georgia: The Buffer Colony

Pine-forested Georgia, with the harbor of Savannah nourishing its chief settlement, was formally founded in 1733. It proved to be the last of the thirteen colonies to be planted—fifty-two years after Pennsylvania. Chronologically it belongs elsewhere, but geographically it may be grouped with its Southern neighbors.

Georgia was valued by the English Crown chiefly as a buffer. It would serve to protect the more valuable Carolinas from inroads by vengeful Spaniards from Florida, and by hostile Frenchmen from Louisiana. Georgia in truth suffered much buffeting, especially when wars broke out between Spain and England in the European cockpit. As a vital link in imperial defense, the exposed colony received monetary subsidies from the British government at the outset—the only one of the "original thirteen" to enjoy this boon in its founding stage.

Named in honor of George II of England, Georgia was launched by a high-minded group of philanthropists. Aside from producing silk and wine, and strengthening the empire, they were determined to create a haven for wretched souls imprisoned for debt. The ablest of the founders was the dynamic soldier-statesman James Oglethorpe, who became keenly interested in prison reform after one of his friends had died in a debtors' jail. As an able military leader, Oglethorpe repelled savage Spanish attacks. As an imperialist and a philanthropist, he saved "the Charity Colony" by his energetic leadership and by mortgaging heavily his own personal fortunes.

The hamlet of Savannah, like Charleston, was a melting-pot community. German Lutherans and kilted Scots Highlanders, among others, added color to the pattern. Religious toleration was extended to all Christian worshipers except

Catholics. The early days of the colony were vexed by the presence of too many religious prima donnas, some of whom came for missionary work among debtors and Indians. Prominent among them was young John Wesley, who, after various adventures and misadventures, returned to England and later founded the Methodist Church.

Georgia grew with painful slowness and at the end of the colonial era was perhaps the least populous of the colonies. Prosperity through a large-plantation economy was thwarted by an unhealthful climate, by early restrictions on black slavery, and by demoralizing Spanish attacks.

The Plantation Colonies

Certain distinctive features were shared by England's Southern mainland colonies: Maryland, Virginia, North Carolina, South Carolina, and Georgia.

Broad-acred, these outposts of empire were all in some degree dominated by a plantation economy. Profitable staple crops were the rule, notably tobacco, rice, and indigo, though to a lesser extent in small-farm North Carolina. Immense acreage in the hands of a favored few fostered a strong aristocratic atmosphere, except in North Carolina and to some extent in debtor-tinged Georgia. The wide scattering of plantations and farms, often along stately rivers, made the establishment of churches and schools both difficult and expensive. In 1671 testy Governor Berkeley, who had become something of a tyrant, thanked God that no free schools existed in Virginia, though there were then actually two.

All the plantation colonies were agitated by an underprivileged back-country element, which was seeking a larger voice in government. This was again less true of North Carolina, which from the beginning had attracted a poorer class of people.

All the plantation colonies were in some degree expansive. "Soil butchery" by excessive growing of tobacco drove men westward, and the long, lazy rivers invited penetration of the continent.

All the plantation colonies permitted some religious toleration. The tax-supported Church of England became the dominant faith, though weakest of all in non-conformist North Carolina. The Calvinistic Puritanism of New England, with its rather gloomy outlook on life, did not flourish in the sunny South. Many of the people, especially the wealthy landowners, were much more interested in racing horses and chasing foxes than in fighting the Devil and listening to lengthy hell-fire sermons.

VARYING VIEWPOINTS

The history of discovery and the earliest colonization raises perhaps the single most fundamental question about all American history. Should it be understood as the extension of European civilization into the New World, or as the gradual development of a uniquely "American" culture? An older school of thought tended to emphasize the Europeanization of America. Historians of that persuasion thus paid close attention to the situation in Europe, particularly in England and Spain, in the 15th and 16th Centuries. They also focused on the various means by which the values and institutions of the Mother Continent were exported to the new lands in the Western sea. Some European writers have varied this general question by asking what transforming effect the discovery of America had on Europe itself. But both of these approaches are Eurocentric. More recently, historians have concentrated on the distinctive aspects of America, especially the Americanization of Europeans and the interactions among various races that have been among the noteworthy characteristics of the American experience.

SELECT READINGS

Edward Cheyney ably describes *The European Background of American History, 1300–1600* (1904). The immediate English backdrop is colorfully presented in Peter Laslett, *The World We Have Lost* (1965), and in Carl Bridenbaugh, *Vexed and Troubled Englishmen, 1590–1642* (1968). A modern classic is Wallace Notestein, *The English People on the Eve of Colonization, 1603–1630* (1954). See also A. L. Rowse, *Elizabethans and America* (1959). Early English relations with the New World are treated in David B. Quinn, *England and the Discovery of America, 1481–1620* (1974). The ablest summation of the Spanish experience is Charles Gibson, *Spain in America* (1966); James Lang, *Conquest and Commerce: Spain and England in the Americas* (1975), is a comparative chronicle of colonial rivalries. A fascinating brief synthesis of early European contact with the Americas is J. H. Elliott, *The Old World and the New, 1492–1650* (1970). Samuel E. Morison has written several masterful accounts of the discoveries; among the best are *Admiral of the Ocean Sea* (2 vols., 1942; condensed as *Christopher Columbus, Mariner*, 1956), *The European Discovery of America: The Northern Voyages,* A.D. *500–1600* (1971), and *The European Discovery of America: The Southern Voyages,* A.D. *1492–1616* (1974). An excellent brief account of the process of discovery is J. H. Parry, *The Establishment of the European Hegemony, 1415–1715* (1961). The impact on Europe is given in Earl J. Hamilton, *American Treasure and the Price Revolution in Spain, 1501–1650* (1934), a seminal work that inspired much later scholarship. Recent studies that pursue the same theme are C. Cipolla, *European Culture and Overseas Expansion* (1970), and I. Wallerstein, *The Modern World-System: Capitalist Agriculture and the Origins of the European World-Economy in the Sixteenth Century* (1974). A marvelous volume, richly illustrated, portraying the impact of America on the European imagination is Hugh Honour, *The New Golden Land* (1975). A good introduction to early American conditions is C. L. Ver Steeg, *The Formative Years: 1607–1763* (1964). The best general discussion of the Southern colonies is W. F. Craven, *The Southern Colonies in the Seventeenth Century, 1607–1689* (1949). Virginia's story is found in P. L. Barbour, *The Three Worlds of Captain John Smith* (1964), and in Alden Vaughan, *American Genesis: Captain John Smith and the Founding of Virginia* (1975). The Chesapeake region has recently received much fresh attention, especially in Aubrey C. Land, et al., *Law, Society, and Politics in Early Maryland* (1977); T. W. Tate and D. L. Ammerman, eds., *The Chesapeake in the Seventeenth Century* (1979); and Paul G. E. Clemens, *The Atlantic Economy and Colonial Maryland's Eastern Shore* (1980). The role of slavery in early colonial society gets perceptive treatment in Edmund S. Morgan, *American Slavery, American Freedom* (1975). See also Winthrop Jordan's monumental *White Over Black* (1968), and Peter Wood's account of South Carolina, *Black Majority* (1974). Gary Nash analyzes relations among all three races in *Red, White, and Black: The Peoples of Early America* (1974). Native Americans get special attention in W. E. Washburn, *The Indian in America* (1975), and in Francis Jennings, *The Invasion of America* (1975). See also Karen Ordahl Kupperman, *Settling with the Indians: The Meeting of English and Indian Cultures in America, 1580–1640* (1980), and Bernard W. Sheehan, *Savagism and Civility: Indians and Englishmen in Colonial Virginia* (1980). Nathan Wachtel presents the Indians' view of the Spanish conquest in *The Vision of the Vanquished* (1977). Nathaniel Bacon is somewhat downgraded in W. E. Washburn, *The Governor and the Rebel* (1957).

2

Completing the Thirteen Colonies

*God hath sifted a Nation that he might send
Choice Grain into this Wilderness.*

WILLIAM STOUGHTON [of Massachusetts Bay], 1669

Calvinism Conceives Puritanism

Little did the religious reformer John Calvin know, when he fled his native France in 1534, that he was to shape the destinies of a yet unheralded nation. Arriving in Switzerland, this radical young zealot gave the Protestant Reformation a twist that profoundly affected the thinking and character of generations of Americans yet unborn. Calvinism, ultimately somewhat watered down, became the basic theology of the dominant Puritan group in New England. It was also the creed of the Scottish Presbyterians, the French Huguenots, and communicants of the Dutch Reformed Church. The members of all these sects, as immigrants, played an influential role in American moral and spiritual life.

The awesome doctrine of predestination was a distinguishing feature of Calvinism. God in His infinite wisdom had predestined a mass of sinners, including babes in the womb, to be tortured in hell for an eternity. The Almighty had also chosen a selected few—the "elect"—to enjoy eternal bliss. Nothing that the damned could do would save them, whether faith, repentance, or good deeds. The complexities of Calvinism were later summed up by a rhymester:

> You can and you can't,
> You will and you won't.
> You'll be damned if you do,
> You'll be damned if you don't.

Calvinists were a peculiar lot, partly because no believers could be completely sure that they were of the "elect." A gnawing doubt led to much soul searching and Scripture reading. It also led to a denial of the pleasures of this earth in a preoccupation with the satisfactions of a future life. Even though a Calvinist might be convinced that he was of the "elect," he could not be certain that his neighbors were, and this curiosity led to much Puritanical prying into the lives of others. Nor was toleration tolerated by the extreme Calvinists; anyone who denied the truth of Calvinism was clearly a heretic.

The Puritans of Old England, even before 1620, were unhappy over the snail-like progress of the Protestant Reformation. They were especially eager to de-Catholicize further the Church of England. To them it was still "popish" and "idolatrous," with its Roman creed and ritual, and with its long black robes and other vestments.

Puritan reformers fell into two general groups. The first consisted of the Non-conformists, who sought to change the Church of England by boring from within. Devoted and sincere though they were, they constituted a difficult and militant minority. The second type of Puritans were Separatists. They wished to separate entirely from the Church of England and its "Romish" practices, in order that they might worship God and combat the Devil in their own way.

King James I, a shrewd Scotsman, was head of both the state and the church in England. He

Pilgrims on *Mayflower* Leave England

quickly perceived that if his subjects could defy him as their spiritual leader, they might one day defy him as their political leader, as in fact they later defied his son, Charles I. He therefore threatened to harass the more bothersome Separatists out of the land.

The Pilgrims End Their Pilgrimage at Plymouth

The most famous congregation of Separatists, fleeing royal wrath, departed for Holland in 1608. During the ensuing twelve years of toil and poverty, they were increasingly distressed by the "Dutchification" of their children. They longed to find a haven where they could live and die as Englishmen. America was the logical refuge, despite the early ordeals of Jamestown, and despite tales of cannibals roasting steaks from their white victims before open fires.

A group of the Separatists in Holland, after negotiating with the Virginia Company, at length secured rights to settle under its jurisdiction. But their crowded *Mayflower*, sixty-five days at sea, missed its destination and arrived off the rocky coast of New England in 1620, with a total of 102 persons. One had died en route—an unusually short casualty list—and one had been born and appropriately named Oceanus. Fewer than half

NEW ENGLAND SETTLEMENTS ABOUT 1650

of the entire party were Separatists. Prominent among the non-belongers was a peppery and stocky soldier of fortune, Captain Myles Standish, dubbed by one of his critics "Captain Shrimp." He later rendered indispensable service as an Indian fighter and negotiator.

The Pilgrims did not make their initial landing at Plymouth Rock, as commonly supposed, but undertook a number of preliminary surveys. They finally chose for their site the shore of inhospitable Plymouth Bay. This area was outside the domain of the Virginia Company, and consequently the settlers became squatters. They were without legal right to the land, and without specific authority to establish a government.

Before disembarking, the Pilgrim Fathers drew up and signed the brief Mayflower Compact. Though setting an invaluable precedent for later written constitutions, this document was not a constitution at all. It was a simple agreement to form a body politic, and to submit to the will of the majority under the regulations agreed upon. The Compact was signed by forty-one adult males, eleven of them with the exalted rank of "mister," though not by the servants and two seamen. The pact was a promising step toward genuine self-government, for soon the adult male settlers were assembling to make their own laws in open-discussion town meetings—a great laboratory of liberty.

The winter of 1620–1621 was a bone-chilling one, with cold and disease taking a grisly toll. Only 44 out of the 102 survived. At one time only seven were well enough to lay the dead in their frosty graves. Yet when the *Mayflower* sailed back to England in the spring, not a single one of the courageous band of Separatists left. As one of them wrote, "It is not with us as with other men, whom small things can discourage." The Pilgrim Mothers endured the same hardships as the Pilgrim Fathers, plus others, including childbearing.

God prospered His children, so the Pilgrims believed. The next autumn, that of 1621, brought bountiful harvests, and with them the first Thanksgiving Day in New England. In time the frail colony found sound economic legs in fur, fish, and lumber. But the beaver and the Bible were the early mainstays: the one for the sustenance of the body, the other for the sustenance of the soul. Plymouth proved that Englishmen could maintain themselves in this uninviting region.

The Pilgrims were extremely fortunate in their leaders. Prominent among them was the cultured

The Pilgrims Land, 1620. (Scribner's "History of the United States.")

IOIIOIIOIIOIIOIIOIIOIIOIIOIIOIIOIIOIIOIIOIIOIIOIIOIIOIIOIIO

> William Bradford wrote in *Of Plymouth Plantation,* ''Thus out of small beginnings greater things have been produced by His hand that made all things of nothing, and gives being to all things that are; and, as one small candle may light a thousand, so the light here kindled hath shone unto many, yea in some sort to our whole nation.''

IOIIOIIOIIOIIOIIOIIOIIOIIOIIOIIOIIOIIOIIOIIOIIOIIOIIOIIOIIO

William Bradford, a self-taught scholar who read Hebrew, Greek, Latin, French, and Dutch. He was chosen governor thirty times in the annual elections. His descendants are now numbered by the thousands, and the descendants of Priscilla and John Alden, who were immortalized by Longfellow's "Courtship of Myles Standish," by the tens of thousands.

Quiet and quaint, the little colony of Plymouth was never important economically or numerically. It claimed only seven thousand souls by 1691, when, still charterless, it merged with its giant neighbor, the Massachusetts Bay Colony. But the tiny settlement of Pilgrims was big both morally and spiritually.

Aye, call it holy ground,
  The soil where first they trod!
They have left unstained what there they found—
  Freedom to worship God!*

The Bay Colony Bible Commonwealth

Bustling fishing villages and other settlements gradually sprouted to the north, on the storm-lashed shores of Massachusetts Bay, where many people were as much interested in cod as God. In 1629 an energetic group of non-Separatist Puritans in England, organizing the Massachusetts Bay Company, secured a charter from the Crown. Prompted by both economic and religious motives, they proposed to plant a settlement in the infertile

---

*Felicia D. Hemans, "The Landing of the Pilgrim Fathers."

Massachusetts area, with Boston soon becoming its hub. Stealing a march on both King and Church, the newcomers brought their charter with them. For many years they used it as a kind of constitution, out of immediate reach of royal authority. They steadfastly denied that they wanted to separate from the Church of England, only from its impurities. But back in the Mother Country the highly orthodox Archbishop Laud snorted that the Bay Colony Puritans were "swine which rooted in God's vineyard."

The Massachusetts Bay enterprise was singularly blessed. The massive expedition of 1630, with eleven vessels and hundreds of colonists, started the establishment off on a larger scale than any of the other English colonies. Another distinctive feature was the large proportion of fairly prosperous members of the middle class, including an unusual number of university graduates. "Dukes don't emigrate," the saying goes, for if men enjoy wealth and security they do not ordinarily expose their lives in the wilderness. The power of deep religious convictions is further attested by the presence in Massachusetts of well-to-do pillars of English society, notably Governor John Winthrop.

Puritan settlers on Massachusetts Bay, despite their preoccupation with things of the spirit, gave conscientious attention to earning a livelihood. Their settlements grew marvelously, as fur trading, fishing, and shipbuilding blossomed into important industries, especially fish and ships. The Massachusetts Bay Colony rapidly shot to the fore as not only the biggest but the most influential of the New England outposts.

Additional and enriching waves of Puritans were tossed upon the shores of Massachusetts in the 1630s. Persecution of Puritans at home by Archbishop Laud, arbitrary rule by Charles I, and economic insecurity in England resulted in the "Great Puritan Migration" of 1629–1640. Altogether, about 75,000 refugees left the Motherland. But not all of them were Puritans, and only about one-third came to the English mainland of North America. Many were attracted by the warm and fertile West Indies, especially by the sugar-rich island of

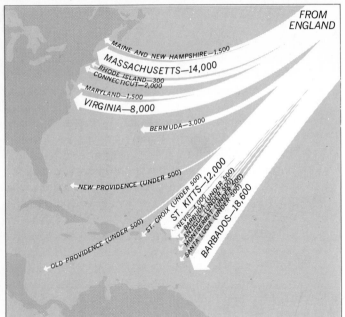

FROM ENGLAND

MAINE AND NEW HAMPSHIRE—1,500
MASSACHUSETTS—14,000
RHODE ISLAND—300
CONNECTICUT—2,000
MARYLAND—1,500
VIRGINIA—8,000
BERMUDA—3,000
NEW PROVIDENCE (UNDER 500)
OLD PROVIDENCE (UNDER 500)
ST. CROIX (UNDER 500)
ST. KITTS—12,000
NEVIS—4,000
BARBUDA (UNDER 500)
ANTIGUA (UNDER 500)
MONTSERRAT (UNDER 500)
SANTA LUCIA (UNDER 500)
BARBADOS—18,600

Barbados. More Puritans came to this Caribbean islet, rather surprisingly, than to all Massachusetts.

At first the Bay Colony was a "Bible Commonwealth." For more than fifty years no resident of the colony could vote in provincial elections unless he belonged to the Puritan Church, which in time was generally called the Congregational Church. On this basis, only about one-fifth of the adult white males enjoyed the ballot. The other males, as non-church members, were voteless, as were women. Yet they were taxed—an early instance of "taxation without representation." And the principal duty of the government was always to enforce "God's laws."

Religious leaders or "theocrats" also wielded much unofficial authority in the Bay Colony. Prominent among the "Saints" was fiery John Cotton, whose zeal sometimes prompted him to preach and pray as much as six hours in a single day. Such men exercised great influence through their spiritual leadership, as well as through their prestige as ministers of a church intimately associated with the government.

But the power of the preachers was not absolute; they were barred from holding formal political office. Puritans in England had suffered too much at the hands of a "political" Anglican clergy

to permit in the New World another unholy union of religious and governmental power. In a limited way, the Bay Colonists thus endorsed the idea of the separation of church and state.

Religious Intolerance in Massachusetts

The age was not tolerant, whether in Europe or America, and the early religious leaders of Massachusetts Bay were not tolerant. Newcomers either conformed to the established Puritan Church, kept quiet, or departed—sometimes in haste. As custodians of the "true light," the Puritan emigrants from England, themselves the victims of intolerance, had little tolerance for other dissenters. Quakers, who flouted the authority of the Massachusetts rulers, were persecuted with fines, floggings, and banishment. Four Quakers who defied expulsion, one of them a woman, were hanged on the Boston Common. But this was an extreme case.

The age was not democratic—and the early Massachusetts leaders, often branded "blue-nosed bigots" by later generations, were not democrats. Holding unusual power in their own hands, they strove, like aristocrats in the other colonies, to

I□I□I□I□I□I□I□I□I□I□I□I□I□I□I□I□I□I□I□I□I□I

> Colonel Robert E. Lee (later General) reflected a common Southern view when he wrote to his wife in 1856, "Is it not strange that the descendants of those Pilgrim Fathers who crossed the Atlantic to preserve their own freedom of opinion have always proved themselves intolerant of the spiritual liberty of others?"

I□I□I□I□I□I□I□I□I□I□I□I□I□I□I□I□I□I□I□I□I□I

keep it from falling into the hands of the rabble. "If the people be governors," queried the Reverend John Cotton, "who shall be governed?" The able John Winthrop feared and distrusted the "commons" as the "meaner sort," and thought that democracy was the "meanest and worst" of all forms of government.

Yet the religious and political leaders of the Bay Colony, try as they would, could not completely choke the rising voice of the masses. Beginnings of popular rule may be discerned in the charter of the colony; in the self-governing and hence democratic congregations of the Congregational Church; and above all in the "direct" or "pure" democracy of the town meeting. There the qualified voters enjoyed the priceless boon of publicly discussing local issues, often with much heat, and of voting on them by a majority-rule show of hands.

□I□I□I□I□I□I□I□I□I□I□I□I□I□I□I□I□I□I□I□I□I

> The arbitrary nature of Anne Hutchinson's trial is reflected in the record of the court:
> GOVERNOR WINTHROP: Mrs. Hutchinson, you hear the sentence of the Court. It is that you are banished from out of our jurisdiction as being a woman not fit for our society. And you are to be imprisoned till the Court send you away.
> MRS. HUTCHINSON: I desire to know wherefore I am banished.
> GOVERNOR WINTHROP: Say no more. The Court knows wherefore, and is satisfied.

I□I□I□I□I□I□I□I□I□I□I□I□I□I□I□I□I□I□I□I□I□I

A sharp challenge to the authority of the clergymen of Massachusetts came from Mistress Anne Hutchinson. She was an intelligent, strong-willed, and talkative woman, ultimately the mother of fourteen children. Boasting a more intimate contact with God than even the Puritan clergy could claim, she committed the "sin" of interpreting their sermons to others. Banished as a "leper" after a farcical trial in 1638, she set out on foot for Rhode Island, though pregnant. She finally moved to New York, where she and all but one of her household were murdered by the Indians. Back in the Bay Colony, the pious John Winthrop saw "God's hand" in her fate.

The Trial of Anne Hutchinson. Mistress Hutchinson (1591–1643) was not only a religious leader but one of the earliest American feminists. A kindly soul, she not only held unorthodox religious discussions in her home but also committed the sin of invading the domain of the clergy, a calling hitherto reserved for the male sex.

More dangerous to the Puritan leaders was a fellow clergyman, Roger Williams, a young man with radical ideas and an unrestrained tongue. Among various alarming proposals, he defended Indian claims to the soil, and he agitated—horrifying thought to the ruling caste!—for a complete separation of church and state. He argued that religious groups should be supported by voluntary contributions of members, rather than by taxes imposed upon the population at large. He was accused of inciting others to cut the cross out of an English flag, and he branded the state-connected sects as "ulcered and gangrened."

Their patience exhausted by 1635, the Bay Colony authorities found Williams guilty of disseminating "newe & dangerous opinions," and ordered him banished. He was permitted to remain several months longer because of illness, but he kept up his criticisms. The outraged magistrates, fearing that he might organize a rival colony of malcontents, then planned to exile him to England.

The Rhode Island "Sewer"

Aided by friendly Indians, Roger Williams fled to the Rhode Island area in 1636, in the midst of a bitter winter. But he found, as he wrote, that

> God makes a path, provides a guide,
> And feeds in wilderness!

At Providence, the courageous and far-visioned Williams built a Baptist church, probably the first in America. He established complete freedom of religion, even for Jews and Catholics. In this respect he was not only far ahead of his age, but ahead of any of the other English settlements in the New World. He demanded no oaths regarding one's religious beliefs, no compulsory attendance at worship, no taxes to support a state church. He even sheltered the abused Quakers, although disagreeing sharply with their views.

Those outcasts who clustered about Roger Williams enjoyed additional blessings. They exercised simple manhood suffrage from the start, though this boon was later modified by a property qualification. Opposed to special privilege of any sort, the doughty Rhode Islanders managed to achieve remarkable freedom of opportunity.

Other scattered settlements soon dotted Rhode Island. They consisted largely of malcontents and exiles, some of whom could not bear the stifling theological atmosphere of the Bay Colony. Many of these restless souls in "Rogues' Island" were neither democratic nor tolerant, including Anne Hutchinson, who had little in common with Roger Williams—except banishment. The Puritan clergy back in Boston sneered at Rhode Island as "that sewer" in which the "Lord's debris" had collected and rotted.

Planted by dissenters and exiles, Rhode Island became strongly individualistic and stubbornly independent. With good reason "Little Rhody" was later known as "the traditional home of the otherwise minded." Begun as a squatter colony in 1636 without legal standing, it finally established rights to the soil when it secured a charter from Parliament in 1644. A huge bronze statue of the "Independent Man" appropriately stands today on the dome of the state house in Providence.

New England Spreads Out

The smiling valley of the Connecticut River, one of the few highly fertile expanses of any size in all New England, had meanwhile attracted a sprinkling of Dutch and English settlers. Hartford was founded in 1635. The next year witnessed a spectacular beginning of the centuries-long westward movement across the continent. An energetic group of Boston Puritans, led by the Reverend Thomas Hooker, swarmed as a body into the Hartford area, with Mrs. Hooker riding a horse litter.

Three years later, in 1639, the settlers of the new Connecticut River colony drafted in open meeting a trail-blazing document known as the Fundamental Orders. It was in effect a modern constitution, which established a regime democratically controlled by the "substantial" citizens. Essential features of the Fundamental Orders

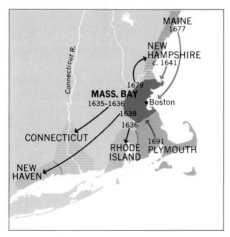

MASSACHUSETTS BAY,
THE HUB OF NEW ENGLAND
All earlier colonies grew into it; all later colonies grew
out of it.

were later borrowed by Connecticut for her colonial charter, and ultimately for her state constitution.

Another flourishing Connecticut settlement began to spring up at New Haven in 1638. It was a prosperous group, containing many souls who could not endure the overbearing Puritan rulers of the Bay Colony. Themselves overbearing, they contrived to set up an ironclad regime which was even more autocratic than that of Boston. Although only squatters without a charter, the colonists dreamed of making New Haven a flourishing seaport. But they fell into disfavor with Charles II, as a result of having sheltered two of the judges who had condemned his father, Charles I, to death. In 1662, to the acute distress of the New Havenites, the Crown granted a charter to Connecticut which merged New Haven with the more democratic settlements in the Connecticut Valley.

Far to the north, enterprising fishermen and fur traders had been active on the coast of Maine for a dozen or so years before the founding of Plymouth. After disheartening attempts at colonization in 1623 by Sir Ferdinando Gorges, this

land of lakes and forests was absorbed by Massachusetts Bay after a formal purchase in 1677 from the Gorges heirs. It remained a part of Massachusetts for nearly a century and a half, and then became a separate state.

Granite-ribbed New Hampshire also sprang from the fishing and trading activities along her narrow coast. She was absorbed in 1641 by the grasping Bay Colony, under a strained interpretation of the Massachusetts charter. The King, annoyed by this display of greed, arbitrarily separated New Hampshire from Massachusetts in 1679, and made her a royal colony.

Seeds of Colonial Unity and Independence

A path-breaking experiment in union was launched in 1643, when four colonies banded together to form the New England Confederation. Old England was then deeply involved in civil wars, and hence the colonials were thrown upon their own resources. The primary purpose of the Confederation was defense against foes or potential foes, notably the Indians, the French, and the Dutch. Purely intercolonial problems, such as runaway servants and criminals who had fled from one colony to another, also came within the jurisdiction of the Confederation. Each member, regardless of size, wielded two votes—an arrangement highly displeasing to the most populous one, Massachusetts Bay.

The Confederation was essentially an exclusive Puritan club. It consisted of the two Massachusetts colonies (the Bay Colony and bantam-sized Plymouth) and the two Connecticut colonies (New Haven and the scattered Valley settlements). The Puritan leaders blackballed Rhode Island, as well as the Maine outposts. These places, it was charged, harbored too many heretical or otherwise undesirable characters. Shockingly, one of the Maine towns had made a tailor its mayor, and had even sheltered an excommunicated minister of the gospel.

Weak though it was, the Confederation was

"Philip, King of Mount Hope."   Philip was not only shot and killed but, as a "traitor" to the King, beheaded, drawn, and quartered. His head was exhibited at Plymouth for many years. (An engraving by Paul Revere, Courtesy of The American Antiquarian Society.)

valuable experience in delegating their votes to properly chosen representatives.

The New England Confederation functioned usefully during the bloody war in 1675–1676 with the Indian chieftain King Philip, whose followers struck back at encroachments by whites on their lands. Several hundred settlers were killed and dozens of towns were burned, but the whites finally emerged victorious. If the Confederation had been continued and strengthened, it almost certainly would have spared the colonials much grief in their subsequent conflicts with the French and Indians.

Back home in England, the King paid little attention to the American colonies during the early years of their planting. They were allowed, in effect, to become semi-independent republics. This era of "salutary neglect" was further prolonged when the Crown, struggling to retain its power, became involved during the 1640s in civil wars with the Parliamentarians. A climax came in 1649 when Charles I was beheaded. Meanwhile the American colonists, like children neglected by their parents, became increasingly impatient of overseas restraints.

Following the restoration of the English Crown in 1660, the royalists (including the Church of England element) were once more firmly in the saddle. Hopes of purifying the established faith fled. A renewed stream of embittered Puritans departed for America, where they added to the festering groups of malcontents already there and to the future sources of friction with the King.

the first notable milestone on the long and rocky road toward colonial unity. The delegates took tottering but urgently needed steps toward acting together on matters of intercolonial importance. Rank-and-file colonists, for their part, received

The Stuart Dynasty in England
(SEE P. 10 FOR PREDECESSORS; P. 46 FOR SUCCESSORS.)

Name, Reign	Relation to America
James I, 1603–1625	Va., Plymouth founded; Separatists persecuted
Charles I, 1625–1649	Civil Wars, 1642–1649; Cavalier tradition; Mass., Md. founded
(Interregnum, 1649–1660)	Commonwealth; Protectorate (the Cromwells)
Charles II, 1660–1685	The Restoration; Carolinas, Penna., N.Y. founded; Conn. chartered
James II, 1685–1688	Catholic trend; Glorious Revolution, 1688
William & Mary, 1689–1702	King William's War, 1689–1697
(Mary died 1694)	

Deepening colonial defiance was nowhere more glaringly revealed than in Massachusetts. One of the King's agents in Boston was mortified to find that royal orders had no more effect than old issues of the London *Gazette.* Punishment was soon forthcoming. As a slap at Massachusetts, Charles II granted to rival Connecticut in 1662 a sea-to-sea charter grant, which legalized the squatter settlements. The very next year the outcasts in Rhode Island received a new charter, which gave kingly sanction to the most democratic government yet devised in America. A final and crushing blow fell on the stiff-necked Bay Colony in 1684, when her precious charter was revoked by the London authorities.

Sir Edmund Andros (1637–1714). An able but iron-fisted administrator, Andros was three times recalled from North American colonial posts because of local resentment at his rule. He ended his career as governor of the tiny island of Guernsey, in the English Channel.

Andros Promotes the First American Revolution

Massachusetts suffered further humiliation in 1686, when the Dominion of New England was created by royal authority. Unlike the homegrown New England Confederation, it was imposed from London. Embracing at first all New England, it was expanded two years later to include New York and East and West Jersey. The Dominion also aimed at bolstering colonial defense in the event of war with the Indians, and hence from the imperial viewpoint of London was a statesmanlike move.

More importantly, the Dominion of New England was designed to promote urgently needed efficiency in the administration of the English Navigation Laws. Those laws, reflecting the intensifying colonial rivalries of the 17th Century, sought to stitch England's overseas possessions more tightly to the Motherland. Like colonial peoples everywhere, the Americans chafed at such confinements, and smuggling became an increasingly common and honorable occupation.

At the head of the new Dominion stood autocratic Sir Edmund Andros, an able English military man, conscientious but tactless. Establishing headquarters in Puritanical Boston, he generated much hostility by his open affiliation with the despised Church of England. The colonials were also outraged by his noisy and Sabbath-profaning soldiers, who were accused of teaching the people "to drink, blaspheme, curse, and damn."

Andros was prompt to use the mailed fist. He ruthlessly curbed the cherished town meetings, and laid heavy restrictions on the courts, the press, and the schools. Dispensing with the popular assemblies, he taxed the people without the consent of their duly elected representatives. He also strove to enforce the unpopular Navigation Laws and suppress smuggling. Liberty-loving colonials, accustomed to unusual privileges during long decades of neglect, were goaded to the verge of revolt.

The people of Old England, likewise resisting oppression, stole a march on the people of New England. In 1688–1689 they engineered the memorable Glorious (or Bloodless) Revolution. Dethroning the despotic and unpopular Catholic James II, they enthroned the Protestant rulers of the Netherlands, the Dutch-born William III and his English wife, Mary, daughter of James II.

When the news of the Glorious Revolution reached America, the ramshackle Dominion of New England collapsed like a house of cards. A Boston mob, catching the fever, rose against the existing regime. Sir Edmund Andros attempted to flee in woman's clothing, but was betrayed by

ANDROS'S DOMINION OF
NEW ENGLAND

boots protruding beneath his dress. He was then shipped off to England.

Massachusetts, though rid of the despotic Andros, did not gain as much from the upheaval as she had hoped. In 1691 she was arbitrarily made a royal colony, with a new charter and a new royal governor. The permanent loss of the ancient charter was a staggering blow to the proud Puritans, who never fully recovered. Worst of all, the privilege of voting, once a monopoly of church members, was now to be enjoyed by all qualified male property holders.

England's Glorious Revolution had a far-flung impact, for unrest erupted from New England to the Carolinas. The upheaval resulted in a permanent abandonment of many of the objectionable features of the Andros system, as well as a temporary breakdown of the new imperial policy of enforcing the Navigation Laws.

Molding the New England Conscience

Oddly enough, the story of early New England was largely written by rocks. The heavily glaciated soil was strewn with countless stones, many of which were forced to the surface after the winter freeze. In a sense the Puritan fathers did not possess the soil; it possessed them by reshaping their character. Scratching a living from the protesting earth was an early American success story. Back-bending toil put a premium on industry and pennypinching frugality, as in Scotland. Traditionally sharp Yankee traders, some of them palming off wooden nutmegs, made their mark. Connecticut in time came to be called good-humoredly "the Nutmeg State." Cynics exaggerated when they said that the three stages of progress in New England were "to get on, to get honor, to get honest."

The grudging land also left colonial New England less ethnically mixed than its southern neighbors. European immigrants were not attracted in great numbers to a site where the soil was so stony—and the religion so sulfurous.

Climate likewise molded character. New England summers were often uncomfortably hot, and the winters were cruelly cold. This combination of soil, climate, and Calvinism made for energy, purposefulness, sternness, stubbornness, self-reliance, and resourcefulness.

> New England says, "Make do, or go without,"
> So they make do.*

Connecticut, not surprisingly, was known as "the Land of Steady Habits." Yet there were a great many Puritans—legend to the contrary—who enjoyed simple pleasures: they ate plentifully, drank heartily, sang songs occasionally, and made love discreetly.

Yet life was serious business, and hell-fire was real—a hell where sinners shriveled and shrieked for divine mercy. An immensely popular poem in New England, selling one copy for every twenty persons, was clergyman Michael Wigglesworth's "Day of Doom" (1662). Especially horrifying were his descriptions of the fate of the damned:

> They cry, they roar for anguish sore,
>   and gnaw their tongues for horrour.
> But get away without delay,
>   Christ pitties not your cry:
> Depart to Hell, there may you yell,
>   and roar Eternally.

---

*Bianca Bradbury, "Rule of Thumb."

Religious tolerance was generally slow to appear. The Puritan oligarchy tried to prod sinful people into saintliness by the famous "blue laws." These regulations, among other restraints, required rigid observance of the Sabbath and the repression of certain harmless human instincts. All other colonies passed similar laws, but those of New England were the most severe. In New Haven, for example, a young unmarried couple was fined twenty shillings for the crime of kissing, and in later years Connecticut came to be dubbed "the Blue Law State."

New England's tense and repressive atmosphere ultimately found a frightening outlet. In Salem, Massachusetts, a hysterical witchcraft delusion brought about the legal lynching in 1692 of twenty persons, nineteen of whom were hanged and one of whom was pressed to death. Two dogs were also hanged. Larger-scale witchcraft persecutions were common in Europe, and several outbreaks had already flared forth in the colonies. But the reign of horror in Salem reached an all-time peak in American experience, and seriously weakened the prestige of the Puritan clergy, some of whom had supported it.

On the positive side, the Puritan stress on unity of purpose also stimulated the growth of self-government. Democracy in Congregational Church government led logically to democracy in political government. The town meeting, in which the free-

Witches Hanged in England as in America.

The Sacred Cod. As displayed in the Boston State House. (George M. Cushing.)

men met together and each man voted, exhibited democracy in its purest form. It was, observed Thomas Jefferson, "the best school of political liberty the world ever saw."

Righteous Puritans also prided themselves on being God's chosen people. They long boasted that Boston was "the Hub of the Universe"—at least spiritually. A famous jingle of later days ran:

> I come from the city of Boston,
> The home of the bean and the cod,
> Where the Cabots speak only to Lowells,
> And the Lowells speak only to God.

New England's impact on the rest of the nation has been incalculable. Countless tens of thousands of New Englanders, ousted by their sterile soil, were destined to pull up stakes and re-create New England towns all the way to Oregon and Hawaii. A people courageous, conscientious, and willing to sacrifice for their beliefs, they made the idealism represented by Plymouth Rock a national symbol. As flinty as their stones, as stiff as their cuffs and collars, they cross-fertilized innumerable other communities with their ideals and democratic practices. The New England conscience added something indispensable to the fiber and backbone of the American people.

The soil and climate of New England encouraged a diversified agriculture and industry. Staple products like tobacco did not flourish, as in the South. Black slavery, although tried, could not exist profitably on small farms, especially where the surest crop was stones. No broad, fertile hinterland, comparable to that of the South, beckoned men inland. The mountains ran fairly close to the shore, and the rivers were generally short and rapid.

Repelled by the rocks, the hardy New Englanders turned instinctively to their fine natural harbors. Hacking timber from their dense forests, they became proficient in shipbuilding and commerce. They were also ceaselessly active in exploiting the inexhaustible and self-perpetuating codfish lode off the coast of Newfoundland—the fishy "gold mines of New England," which have yielded more wealth than all the treasure chests of the Aztecs. During colonial days the wayfarer seldom got far from the sound of the ax and hammer, or the swift rush of the ship down the ways to the sea, or the smell of rotting fish. As a reminder of the importance of fishing, a handsome replica of the "sacred cod" is proudly displayed to this day in the Massachusetts State House in Boston.

Puritan Textbooks.   A page from the *New England Primer;* and the hornbook for children, so called because the printing was protected by transparent horn.

The New England Way of Life

Sturdy New Englanders evolved a compact social structure, the basis of which was small farms and villages. This development was but natural in a people who were partially anchored by geography and hemmed in by Indians, Frenchmen, and Dutchmen. Calvinism, combined with a closely knit community life, likewise made for unity of purpose, and also for nosiness regarding the affairs of one's neighbors. It was no accident that the later crusade for abolishing black slavery—with Massachusetts agitators in the forefront—sprang in some degree from the New England conscience, with its Puritanical and Calvinistic coloration.

In the Chesapeake region the expansion of settlement was somewhat random and was usually undertaken by lone-wolf planters on their own initiative, but New England society grew in a more orderly fashion. New towns were legally chartered by the colonial authorities, and the distribution of land was entrusted to the steady hands of sober-minded town fathers. Towns of more than fifty families were required to provide elementary education, and as early as 1636 the Massachusetts Puritans established Harvard College, today the oldest corporation in America, to train local boys for the ministry.

Yet worries plagued the God-fearing pioneers of these tidy settlements. The pressure of population was gradually dispersing the Puritans onto outlying farms, away from the control of church and neighbors. The passage of time was depleting the first generation's religious zeal. About the middle of the 17th Century a new form of sermon began to be popular in Puritan pulpits—the "jeremiad." Taking their cue from the doom-saying Old Testament prophet Jeremiah, sober preachers scolded parishioners for their waning piety. Especially alarming was the apparent decline in "conversions"—testimonials by individuals that they had received God's grace and therefore deserved to be admitted to the church as members of the "elect." Troubled ministers in 1662 announced a new formula for church membership, the "Half-Way Covenant." It offered partial membership rights to persons not yet "converted."

The "Half-Way Covenant" dramatized the difficulty of maintaining at fever pitch the religious fervor of the founding generation. Jeremiads continued to thunder from the pulpits, but as time went on the doors of the Puritan churches swung fully open to all comers, whether converted or not. This widening of church membership gradually erased the distinction between the "elect" and other members of society, and it tended to water down the burning theology of the earliest days.

Old Netherlanders at New Netherland

Late in the 16th Century, the oppressed people of the Netherlands unfurled the standard of rebellion against Catholic Spain. After bloody and protracted fighting, they finally succeeded, with the aid of Protestant England, in winning their independence.

The 17th Century—the era of Rembrandt and other famous artists—was a golden age in Dutch history. This vigorous little lowland nation finally emerged as a major commercial and naval power, and then ungratefully challenged the supremacy of her former benefactor, England. Three great Anglo-Dutch naval wars were fought in the 17th Century, with as many as a hundred ships on each side. The sturdy Dutchmen dealt blows about as heavy as they received.

Holland also became a leading colonial power, with by far her greatest activity in the East Indies. There she maintained an enormous and profitable empire for over three hundred years. The Dutch East India Company was virtually a state within a state, and at one time supported an army of 10,000 men and a fleet of 190 ships, forty of them men-of-war.

Seeking greater riches, this enterprising com-

Henry Hudson (?–1611). An English explorer of little known antecedents, he made two famous voyages. The first, for the Dutch East India Company, resulted in the discovery of the Hudson River in 1609; the second, for some English merchants, in the discovery of Canada's Hudson Bay in 1610. His crew, suffering from extreme cold and other hardships, finally mutinied and set him adrift to die with his small son and seven others.

pany employed an English explorer, Henry Hudson. Disregarding orders to sail northeast, he ventured into Delaware Bay and New York Bay in 1609 and then ascended the Hudson River, hoping that at last he had chanced upon the coveted shortcut through the continent. But, as the event proved, he merely filed a Dutch claim to a magnificently wooded and watered area.

Much less powerful than the mighty Dutch East India Company was the Dutch West India Company, which maintained profitable enterprises in the Caribbean. At times it was less interested in trading than in raiding, and at one fell swoop in 1628 captured a fleet of Spanish treasure ships laden with loot worth $15 million. The company also established outposts in Africa and a flourishing sugar industry in Brazil, which for several decades was its principal center of activity in the New World.

New Netherland, in the beautiful Hudson River area, was planted in 1623–1624 on a permanent basis. Established by the Dutch West India Company for its quick-profit fur trade, it was never more than a secondary interest of the founders. The company's most brilliant stroke was to buy Manhattan Island from the Indians (who did not actually "own" it) for trinkets worth about $24— 22,000 acres of what is now perhaps the most valuable real estate in the world for one-tenth of a cent an acre.

New Amsterdam—later New York City—was a company town. It was run by and for the Dutch company, in the interests of the stockholders. The investors had no enthusiasm for religious toleration, free speech, or democratic practices; and the governors appointed by the company as directors-general were usually harsh and despotic. In response to repeated protests by the colonists, a semi-representative body was at length reluctantly granted. Religious dissenters who opposed the official Dutch Reformed Church were looked upon with suspicion, and for a while Quakers were savagely abused.

This picturesque Dutch colony took on a strongly aristocratic tinge, and retained it for generations. Vast feudal estates fronting the Hudson

EARLY SETTLEMENTS IN THE
MIDDLE COLONIES

erected a stout wall, from which Wall Street derived its name.

New England was hostile to the growth of its Dutch neighbor, and the people of Connecticut finally ejected intruding Hollanders from their verdant valley. Three of the four member colonies of the New England Confederation were eager to wipe out New Netherland with military force. But Massachusetts, which would have had to provide most of the troops, vetoed the proposed foray.

The Swedes in turn trespassed on Dutch preserves, from 1638 to 1655, by planting the anemic colony of New Sweden on the Delaware River.

River, known as patroonships, were granted to promoters who would settle fifty persons on them. One of the largest in the Albany area was slightly larger than the later state of Rhode Island.

Colorful little New Amsterdam attracted a cosmopolitan population, as is common in seaport towns. A French Jesuit missionary, visiting in the 1640s, noted that eighteen different languages were being spoken in the streets. The later babel of immigrant tongues was thus foreshadowed.

Friction with English and Swedish Neighbors

Vexations of various sorts beset the Dutch company-colony from the beginning. The directors-general were generally incompetent, though Washington Irving's later characterization of one of them as "a beer barrel on skids" is unfair. Company shareholders demanded their dividends, even at the expense of the colony's welfare. The Indians, infuriated by Dutch cruelties, retaliated with horrible massacres. As a defense measure, the hard-pressed settlers on Manhattan Island

Peter Stuyvesant (1602–1682). Despotic in government and intolerant in religion, he lived in a constant state of friction with the prominent men of New Netherland. When protests arose, he replied that he derived his power from God and the Company, not the people. He opposed popular suffrage on the grounds that "the thief" would vote "for the thief" and "the rogue for the rogue."

This was the golden age of Sweden, during and following the Thirty Years' War of 1618–1648, in which her brilliant King Gustavus Adolphus had carried the torch for Protestantism. This outburst of energy in Sweden caused her to enter the costly colonial game in America, albeit on something of a shoestring.

Resenting the Swedish intrusion on the Delaware, the Dutch dispatched a small military expedition in 1655. It was led by the ablest of the directors-general, the energetic and hotheaded Peter Stuyvesant, who was dubbed "Father Wooden Leg" by the Indians. The main fort fell after a bloodless siege, whereupon Swedish rule came to an abrupt end. The colonists were absorbed by New Netherland.

New Sweden was never important. It faded away, leaving behind in later Delaware a sprinkling of Swedish place names and Swedish log cabins (the first in America), as well as an admixture of Swedish blood.

Dutch Residues in New York

The days of the Dutch on the Hudson were numbered, for the English regarded them as intruders. In 1664, after Charles II had granted the area to his brother, the Duke of York, a strong English squadron appeared off the decrepit defenses of New Amsterdam. A fuming Peter Stuyvesant, short of all munitions except courage, was forced to surrender without firing a shot. New Amsterdam was thereupon renamed New York, in honor of the Duke of York. England won a splendid harbor, strategically located in the middle of the mainland colonies, and a stately Hudson River penetrating the interior. The English banner now waved triumphantly, with the removal of this foreign wedge, over a solid stretch of territory from Maine to the Carolinas.

As the neglected stepchild of a trading company, New Netherland was destined from the beginning to be English. Lacking vitality, and representing only a secondary commercial interest of the Dutch, it lay under the shadow of the vigorous English colonies to the north. In addition, it was honeycombed with New England immigrants. Numbering about one-half of New Netherland's 10,000 souls in 1664, they might in time have seized control from within.

The conquered Dutch province tenaciously retained many of the illiberal features of earlier days. An autocratic spirit survived, and the aristocratic element gained strength when certain corrupt English governors granted immense acreage to their favorites. Influential landowning families —such as the Livingstons and the De Lanceys— wielded disproportionate power in the affairs of colonial New York. These monopolistic land policies, combined with the lordly atmosphere, discouraged many European immigrants from coming. The physical growth of New York was correspondingly retarded.

The short-lived Dutch colony contributed little of major significance, whether to democracy, government, education, toleration, or literature.

New Amsterdam (New York) in 1673. (The J. Clarence Davies Collection, Museum of the City of New York.)

A possible exception would be the Knickerbocker themes that Washington Irving developed in the 19th Century with such charm. The Dutchmen peppered place names over the land, including Harlem (Haarlem), Brooklyn (Breuckelen), and Hell Gate (Hellegat). They likewise left their imprint on the gambrel-roofed architecture. As for social customs and folkways, no other foreign group of comparable size has made so colorful a contribution. Noteworthy were Easter eggs, Santa Claus, waffles, sauerkraut, bowling, sleighing, skating, and kolf (golf)—a dangerous game played with heavy clubs and forbidden in settled areas.

Diluted Dutch blood from New Netherland runs through the veins of many of America's "best families," including a host of "vans" and "velts." Three Presidents of the United States traced their ancestry back to the precarious colony: Martin Van Buren, Theodore Roosevelt, and Franklin D. Roosevelt. The last of the trio, when inclined to be stubborn, would speak of getting his "Dutch" up.

Penn's Holy Experiment in Pennsylvania

A remarkable group of dissenters, commonly known as Quakers, arose in England during the mid-1600s. Their name derived from the report that they "quaked" when under deep religious emotion. Officially they were known as the Religious Society of Friends.

Quakers were especially offensive to the authorities, both religious and civil. They refused to support the established Church of England with taxes. They built simple meetinghouses, without a paid clergy, and "spoke up" in meeting themselves when moved. Believing that they were all children in the sight of God, they kept their broad-brimmed hats on in the presence of their "betters," and addressed others with simple "thees" and "thous," rather than with conventional titles. They would take no oaths, because Jesus had said, "Swear not at all." This peculiarity often embroiled them with government officials, for "test oaths" were

Quakers Abused in England.   New England persecutions were similarly harsh.

still required to establish the fact that a person was not a Roman Catholic.

The Quakers, beyond a doubt, were a people of deep conviction. They abhorred strife and warfare, and refused military service. As advocates of passive resistance, they would turn the other cheek and rebuild their meetinghouse on the site where their enemies had torn it down. Their courage and devotion to principle finally triumphed. Though at times they seemed stubborn and unreasonable, they were a simple, devoted, democratic people, contending in their own odd way for religious and civic freedom.

William Penn, a well-born and athletic young Englishman, was attracted to the Quaker faith in 1660, when only sixteen years old. His father, disapproving, administered a sound flogging. After various adventures in the army (the best portrait of the peaceful Quaker has him in armor), the youth firmly embraced the despised faith and suffered much persecution. The courts branded him a "saucy" and "impertinent" fellow. Several hundred of his less fortunate co-religionists died of cruel treatment, and thousands more were fined, flogged, or cast into "nasty stinking prisons."

Penn's thoughts naturally turned to the New World, where a sprinkling of Quakers had already fled, notably to Rhode Island, North Carolina, and New Jersey. Eager to establish an asylum for his people, he also hoped to experiment with liberal ideas in government, and at the same time make a profit. Finally, in 1681, he managed to secure from the King an immense grant of fertile land, in consideration of a monetary debt owed to his deceased father by the Crown. The King called the area Pennsylvania ("Penn's Woodland") in honor of the sire. But the modest son, fearing that critics would accuse him of naming it after himself, sought unsuccessfully to change the name.

Pennsylvania was by far the best advertised of all the colonies. Its founder—the "first American advertising man"—sent out paid agents and distributed countless pamphlets printed in English, Dutch, French, and German. Unlike the lures of many another American real estate promoter, then and later, Penn's inducements were generally truthful. He especially welcomed forward-looking spirits and substantial citizens, including industrious carpenters, masons, shoemakers, and other manual workers. His liberal land policy, which encouraged substantial holdings of land, was instrumental in attracting a heavy inflow of immigrants.

Quaker Pennsylvania and Her Neighbors

Penn formally launched his colony in 1681. His task was simplified by the presence of several thousand "squatters"—Dutch, Swedes, English, Welsh—who were already scattered along the banks of the Delaware River. Philadelphia, meaning "brotherly love" in Greek, was more carefully planned than most colonial cities, and consequently enjoyed wide and attractive streets. Penn farsightedly bought land from the Indians, including Chief Tammany, later patron saint of New York's political Tammany Hall. His treatment of the red men was so fair that the Quaker "Broad Brims" went among them unarmed, and even employed them as baby tenders.

Penn's new proprietary regime was unusually liberal, and included a representative assembly elected by the landowners. There was no tax-supported state church. Freedom of worship was guaranteed to all residents, although Penn, under pressure from London, was forced to deny Catho-

William Penn (1644–1718). He wrote in 1682, "Any government is free to the people under it where the laws rule and the people are a party to the laws." Penn was among the few English colonizers who learned to speak an Indian tongue.

lics and Jews the privilege of voting or holding office. The death penalty was imposed only for treason and murder, as compared with some two hundred capital crimes in England.

Among other noteworthy features, no provision was made by the peace-loving Quakers of Pennsylvania for a military defense. No restrictions were placed on immigration, and naturalization was made easy. The humane Quakers early developed a strong dislike of black slavery, and in the genial glow of Pennsylvania some progress was made toward social reform.

With its many liberal attractions, Pennsylvania attracted a richly mixed racial group. The lot included numerous religious misfits who were repelled by the harsh practices of neighboring colonies. This Quaker haven boasted a surprisingly modern atmosphere in an unmodern age, and to an unusual degree afforded economic opportunity, civil liberty, and religious freedom. Even so, there were some "blue laws" aimed at "ungodly revelers," stage plays, playing cards, dice, May games, and excessive hilarity.

Under such generally happy auspices, Penn's brainchild grew lustily. The Quakers were shrewd businessmen, and in a short time the settlers were exporting grain and other foodstuffs. Within two years Philadelphia claimed 300 houses and 2,500 people. Within nineteen years—by 1700—the colony was surpassed in population and wealth only by long-established Virginia and Massachusetts.

William Penn, who altogether spent about four years in Pennsylvania, was never fully appreciated by his colonists. His governors, some of them incompetent and tactless, quarreled bitterly with the people, who were constantly demanding greater political control. Penn himself became too friendly with James II, the deposed Catholic King. Thrice arrested for treason, thrust for a time into a debtors' prison, and racked by apoplectic fits, he died full of sorrows. His enduring monument was not only a noble experiment in government but also a new commonwealth. Based on civil and religious liberty, and dedicated to freedom of conscience and worship, it held aloft a hopeful torch in a world of semi-darkness.

Smaller Quaker settlements flourished next door to Pennsylvania. New Jersey was started in 1664, when two noble proprietors received the area from the Duke of York. A substantial number of New Englanders, including many whose weary soil had petered out, flocked to the new colony. One of the proprietors sold West New Jersey in 1674 to a group of Quakers, who here set up a sanctuary even before Pennsylvania was launched. East New Jersey was also acquired in later years by the Quakers, whose wings were clipped in 1702 when the Crown combined the two Jerseys in a royal colony.

Swedish-tinged Delaware consisted of only three counties—two at high tide, the witticism goes—and was named after Lord de la Warr. Har-

boring some Quakers, and closely associated with Penn's flourishing colony, Delaware was granted its own assembly in 1703. But until the American Revolution it remained under the governor of Pennsylvania.

The Middle Way in the Middle Colonies

The Middle Colonies—New York, New Jersey, Delaware, and Pennsylvania—enjoyed certain features in common.

In general, the soil was fertile and the expanse of land was broad, unlike rock-bestrewn New England. Pennsylvania, New York, and New Jersey came to be known as the "Bread Colonies," by virtue of their heavy exports of grain.

Rivers also played a vital role. Broad, languid streams—notably the Susquehanna, the Delaware, and the Hudson—tapped the fur trade of the interior and beckoned adventuresome spirits into the back country. The rivers had few cascading waterfalls, unlike New England's, and hence presented little inducement to manufacturing with water-wheel power.

A surprising amount of industry, nonetheless, flourished in the Middle Colonies. Virginal forests abounded for lumbering and shipbuilding. The presence of deep river estuaries and landlocked harbors stimulated commerce and the growth of seaports, such as New York and Philadelphia. Even Albany, more than a hundred miles up the Hudson, was a port of some consequence in colonial days.

The Middle Colonies were in many respects midway between New England and the Southern plantation group. Except in aristocratic New York, the land holdings were generally intermediate in size—smaller than in the big-acreage South but larger than in small-farm New England. Local government lay somewhere between the personalized town meeting of New England and the diffused county government of the South. There were fewer industries in the Middle Colonies than in New England, more than in the South.

Yet the Middle Colonies, which in some ways were the most American part of America, could claim certain distinctions in their own right. Generally speaking, the population was more racially mixed than that of other settlements. The people were blessed with an unusual degree of religious toleration and democratic control. Earnest and devout Quakers, in particular, made a contribution to human freedom out of all proportion to their numbers. Desirable land was more easily acquired in the Middle Colonies than in New England or in the tidewater South. One result was that a considerable amount of economic and social democracy prevailed, though less so in aristocratic New York.

Modern-minded Benjamin Franklin, entering Philadelphia as a seventeen-year-old youth with a roll of bread under each arm, found a congenial home in the urbane atmosphere of the city. It is true that he was born a Yankee in Puritanical Boston, but, as one Pennsylvanian later boasted,

First Church in Philadelphia

"He came to life at seventeen, in Philadelphia."

Long before 1760 the thirteen colonies as a group revealed striking similarities, even though they had developed wide differences. They were all basically English. They all exercised certain priceless Anglo-Saxon freedoms. They all possessed some measure of self-government, though by no means complete democracy. They all enjoyed some degree of religious toleration and educational opportunity. They all afforded unusual advantages for economic and social self-development. Finally—and perhaps most significantly—they were all separated from home authority by a billowing ocean moat 3,000 miles wide.

VARYING VIEWPOINTS

Not only New England, but New Englanders—from William Bradford in the 17th Century to Samuel Eliot Morison in the 20th Century—have dominated our understanding of the colonial era. Their traditional histories stressed the religious character of the "Puritan experiment," and usually emphasized the slow secularization of colonial life. More recent scholars have begun to move away from this exclusive focus on intellectual history. They have suggested that the decline in piety that so worried the Puritans and so preoccupied their patriotic chroniclers was but one aspect of a general disintegration of traditional social forms. Local histories, using sophisticated quantitative techniques and relying on modern demographic theories, illustrate the innumerable stresses that a rough wilderness existence put upon transplanted Europeans. These stresses strained religious faiths, family life, economic organization, and landholding patterns.

SELECT READINGS

New England has received more scholarly attention than any other colonial region. A rich contemporary account is William Bradford, *Of Plymouth Plantation,* available in an edition edited by S. E. Morison in 1952. See also Morison's sweeping survey, *Builders of the Bay Colony* (1930), and J. E. Pomfret, *Founding the American Colonies, 1583–1660* (1970). An incisive short account is Edmund S. Morgan, *The Puritan Dilemma: The Story of John Winthrop* (1958). A brilliant and complex intellectual history is Perry Miller, *The New England Mind* (2 vols., 1939, 1953), a work that has long been a landmark for other scholars. Robert Middlekauff focuses on *The Mathers: Three Generations of Puritan Intellectuals, 1596–1728* (1971), and Larzer Ziff, on *The Career of John Cotton* (1962). David Levin deals with his subject's youthful years in *Cotton Mather* (1978). See also Ziff's *Puritanism in America* (1973). Sacvan Bercovitch traces the heritage of the New England temperament in *The Puritan Origins of the American Self* (1975). Edmund S. Morgan describes the crisis that beset the original Puritans when their children displayed a lesser degree of religiosity in *Visible Saints* (1963). Social structure and politics are analyzed in R. E. Brown, *Middle-Class Democracy and the Revolution in Massachusetts, 1691–1780* (1955). Economic questions receive critical attention from Bernard Bailyn in *The New England Merchants in the Seventeenth Century* (1955). Some less attractive features of the New England experience are treated in Chadwick Hansen, *Witchcraft at Salem* (1969), and Paul Boyer and Stephen Nissenbaum, *Salem Possessed: The Social Origin of Witchcraft* (1974). Family life and local history are imaginatively scrutinized in Edmund S. Morgan, *Puritan Family* (1944), B. Bailyn, *Education in the Forming of American Society* (1960), S. C. Powell, *Puritan Village* (1963), D. Rutman, *Winthrop's Boston* (1965), J. Demos, *A Little Commonwealth: Family Life in Plymouth Colony* (1970), P. Greven, *Four Generations: Population, Land, and Family in Colonial Andover, Massachusetts* (1970), K. Lockridge, *New England Town: Dedham* (1970), Roger Thompson, *Women in Stuart England and America* (1974), Lyle Koehler, *A Search for Power: The "Weaker Sex" in Seventeenth-Century New England* (1980), and P. Greven, *The Protestant Temperament* (1977), which analyzes child-rearing practices. Religious issues are discussed in Sidney Mead, *The Lively Experiment* (1963), and in the early portions of Sidney Ahlstrom's monumental *Religious History of the American People* (1972). J. T. Ellis pays special attention to such issues in *Catholics in Colonial America* (1965), and O. E. Winslow, in *Master Roger Williams* (1957). Areas outside New England are dealt with in T. J. Wertenbaker, *The Founding of American Civilization: The Middle Colonies* (1938). Michael Kammen describes *Colonial New York* (1975). Pennsylvania is treated in E. B. Bronner, *William Penn's 'Holy Experiment'* (1962), Mary Maples Dunn, *William Penn: Politics and Conscience* (1967), and Gary Nash, *Quakers and Politics: Pennsylvania, 1681–1726* (1971). Comprehensive are David Grayson Allen, *In English Ways* (1981), a comparative study of England and Colonial America, and T. H. Breen, *Puritans and Adventurers* (1980), which discusses "localism" in both New England and Virginia.

3

The Duel for North America

A torch lighted in the forests of America set all Europe in conflagration.

FRANÇOIS VOLTAIRE, c. 1756

France Finds a Foothold in Canada

France was another latecomer in the scramble for New World real estate, like England and Holland, and for basically the same reasons. She was convulsed during the 1500s by foreign wars and domestic strife, including the frightful clashes between the Roman Catholics and the Protestant Huguenots. On St. Bartholomew's Day, 1572, over 10,000 Huguenots—men, women, and children—were butchered in cold blood.

A new era dawned in 1598 when the Edict of Nantes, issued by the Crown, granted limited toleration to the French Protestants. Religious wars ceased, and in the 1600s France blossomed into the mightiest and most-feared nation in Europe. Leadership of a high order was provided by a series of brilliant ministers, and by the vainglorious King Louis XIV. *Le Grand Monarque*

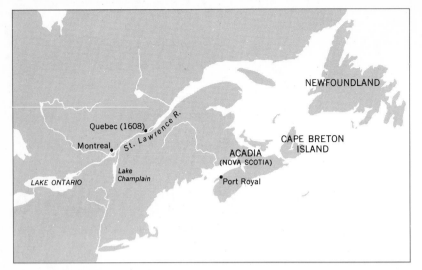

reigned majestically, beginning as a five-year-old boy, for an incredible seventy-two years (1643–1715). Though involved with a glittering court and numerous mistresses, he was deeply interested in overseas colonies, and bestirred himself to promote their welfare.

Even earlier, while the religious wars were still raging in the mid-1500s, the French had planted a few colonial seedlings. Noteworthy were the short-lived Catholic settlements on the St. Lawrence River, and the havens which the harassed Huguenots strove to create in Brazil, Florida, and South Carolina. But all these feeble experiments collapsed, either of their own weight or under the sword of Catholic enemies, whether Portuguese or Spaniards.

Success finally crowned the exertions of France in the New World. In 1608, the year after Jamestown, the permanent beginnings of a vast empire were established at Quebec, a rocky sentinel commanding the St. Lawrence River. The leading figure was Samuel de Champlain, an intrepid soldier

Champlain Fights the Iroquois, 1609. This illustration commemorates the battle on Lake Champlain. Champlain's explorations extended French claims as far inland as Wisconsin. He was fittingly buried in Quebec. (By permission of the Houghton Library, Harvard University.)

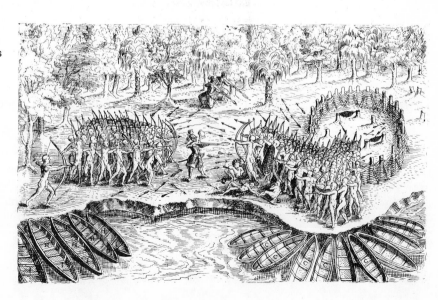

and explorer whose energy and leadership fairly earned for him the title "Father of New France."

Champlain entered into friendly relations—a fateful friendship—with the nearby Huron Indian tribes. Yielding to their entreaties, he joined them in battle against their feathered foes, the federated Iroquois tribes of the upper New York area. Two shots from the "lightning sticks" of the whites routed the terrified Indians, who left behind three dead and one wounded. France, to her sorrow, thus earned the lasting enmity of the Iroquois tribes. These painted warriors hampered French penetration of the Ohio Valley, ravaged French settlements, and served as allies of the British in the prolonged struggle for supremacy on the continent.

Old Feudalism in New France

The government of New France (Canada) finally fell under the direct control of the King, after various commercial companies had faltered or failed. This royal regime was almost completely autocratic. There were no popularly elected assemblies, as in the English colonies; there was no trial by jury—merely the decision of the magistrate.

Feudalism was dying out in Europe, but some of its most picturesque trappings were transplanted to New France. Noteworthy were the huge feudal estates, fronting the river highways, and the medieval customs, including the annual dues to the lord in chickens and other produce. The peasants (*habitants*) were little more than serfs. The autocracy thus established in the wilderness, unlike the regime in the English colonies, was ideal for military defense. It insured unity of purpose, speed of action, precision of movement, and a maximum concentration of meager resources.

Population in Catholic New France grew with painful slowness: as late as 1750 there were only 60,000 or so whites. Wintry blasts did not appeal to the peasants of sunny France, and the stubborn soil was uninviting. Protestant Huguenots were not allowed refuge in the raw colony, although some 400,000 were driven from their home-

land by the termination of the Edict of Nantes in 1685. They would have added a thrifty and industrious element, but they no doubt would have caused internal friction.

Officials in New France, unable to recruit more than a dribble of immigrants, tried with some success to stimulate the birthrate. Bachelors were subjected to heavy restrictions. Fathers of unmarried daughters of sixteen were fined, and a small number of well-chaperoned "King's girls" were imported and married, following whirlwind courtships on the docks.

All things considered, the importance of New France was secondary to Old France. In the 1600s and 1700s the scattered French islands in the Caribbean, rich in sugar and rum, comprised a much more profitable enterprise than the snow-cloaked wilderness of the northern colony.

Red Men and Black Robes in Canada

Fur was the big "money crop" of New France. Lush pelts, especially beaver, were popular in Europe for their warmth, adornment, and proof of social position. More than 100,000 beaver skins were trapped in the best years, and the Indian fur flotilla which reached Montreal in 1693 numbered four hundred canoes.

But the fur-trapping business had fatal drawbacks. It was cannibalistic, for it ate up its own capital. Retreating animals had to be followed into the interior, and the lure of the sharp-toothed beaver dangerously diluted the already scanty vanguard of French inhabitants. English settlers, on the other hand, were dammed up east of the Allegheny barrier, and did not finally flow over the mountains in numbers until they had first been pressed together into a compact social structure.

Indians who trapped the furs were jerked from the stone age to the iron age almost overnight. Bows and arrows gave way to firearms. Red men became different creatures as they were debauched by the white man's diseases and alcohol—"bottled suicide"—sometimes adulterated with pepper. French Catholic missionaries tried desperately

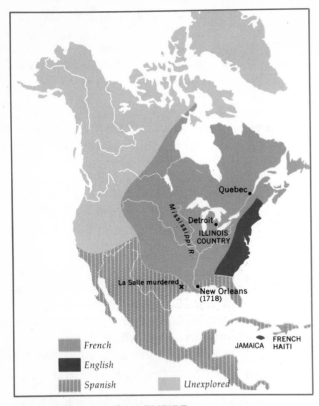

FRANCE'S AMERICAN EMPIRE
AT GREATEST EXTENT, 1700

French
English
Spanish
Unexplored

Father Jogues (1607–1646). With a hand mutilated by the Mohawks, he escaped and was granted special dispensation by the Pope to celebrate mass. He returned to the Mohawks, who tortured and then killed him. The Pope canonized him in 1930.

It is true that they made few permanent converts, despite their heroic sacrifices in establishing missions. But in the capacity of explorers, geographers, and teachers they did much to publicize New France in Old France, and thus helped to save the colony.

New France Fans Out

Daring French explorers and traders were inevitably drawn deeper and deeper into the heart of the continent. They walked, rode, snowshoed, sailed, or paddled amazing distances. They were eager to find a shorter waterway to the Indies; to discover fabulous mines like those uncovered by the Spaniards in Mexico; to check Spanish penetration into the region of the Gulf of Mexico; and to thwart English traders pushing into the Ohio Valley. Partly for this last purpose Antoine Cadillac founded Detroit, "The City of Straits," in 1701.

Most famous of all the French explorers was the haughty but far-visioned La Salle. In 1682 he floated down the mighty Mississippi to the point where it mingles with the Gulf, and named the interior basin "Louisiana," in honor of his sovereign, Louis XIV. Dreaming of empire, La Salle proceeded to fit out a colonizing expedition of four ships in France. But he landed in Spanish Texas,

to block the sale of "firewater." But they were met with the crushing rebuttal that a denial of French brandy would force the Indian to exchange his furs for the rum of the English and Dutch traders, who were Protestant heretics.

French Catholic missionaries, notably the Jesuits, labored zealously to save both the bodies and souls of the heathen Indians. The Black Robes were at odds with the fur traders, whose chief purpose was to get the red man drunk and rob him of his peltries for a few strings of beads. Some of the Jesuit missionaries, their efforts unappreciated, suffered unspeakable tortures at the hands of the Indians. Conspicuous among the martyrs were Father Isaac Jogues and the giant Jean de Bréboeuf, who is said to have kissed the stake at which he was burned, and whose skull is still preserved as a relic in Quebec.

The role of the Jesuits was vital to New France.

after missing the delta of the Mississippi, and in 1687 was murdered by his own men.

Undismayed, French officials persisted in their efforts to forestall Spain on the Gulf of Mexico. They planted several fortified posts in present-day Mississippi and Louisiana, the most important of which was New Orleans (1718). Commanding the outlet of the Mississippi River, this strategic outpost also tapped the fur trade of the great interior basin. The fertile Illinois country, where missions and trading-post forts were firmly established, became the garden of France's North American empire. Surprising amounts of grain were floated down the Mississippi for transshipment to the West Indies and to Europe.

French explorers were lured still farther inland by the siren call of the unknown. They ranged in a gigantic arc from the border of Texas northward through the valleys of the Arkansas, Missouri, and Platte Rivers into Saskatchewan and Manitoba of present-day Canada. In 1743 a party of Frenchmen, though preceded some years earlier by Spaniards, glimpsed the Rocky Mountains.

Robert De La Salle (1643–1687). This Frenchman envisioned a North American empire for France.

But French influence was buttered too thin over a vast continent, and its lasting effect, except in Canada, was not great. French Canadians served as explorers and traders and, in the role of backwoods engineers, as trailblazers and city founders. Far-ranging *coureurs de bois* ("runners of the woods") were also runners of risks—two-fisted drinkers, free spenders, free livers, and free lovers ("squaw men"). Singing, paddle-swinging French *voyageurs* left behind a brood of half-breeds, and peppered the land with scores of place names, including Baton Rouge (red stick), Terre Haute (high land), and Des Moines (some monks).

Other French impacts were significant, if less direct. The character of the English colonists to the south and east was toughened by a series of bitter wars with the French, prolonged throughout three-fourths of a century. New France also diverted a considerable stream of Huguenots to English America by barring her own gates to them. Among these refugees were the ancestors of such distinguished Americans as the diplomat John Jay, the abolitionist poet John Greenleaf Whittier, and the silversmith-horseman Paul Revere, originally Revoire.

The Clash of Empires in Two Hemispheres

As the 17th Century neared its sunset, a titanic struggle was shaping up for mastery of the North American continent. It involved three civilizations: English, French, and Spanish.

Large-scale armed conflict was avoided until 1689. Why? At first there was enough elbowroom for all. Hundreds of miles of trackless forest separated the English from the French in the north and west, and from the Spaniards in the west and south. Rivalry for the furs taken by the Indians could be kept within bounds.

International politics and intrigue also promoted peace. The Stuart kings of England who reigned from 1660 to 1688—Charles II and James II—not only had strong Catholic leanings toward France but also were striving to build up a despotism at

English Caricature of Louis XIV. This French "Sun King," shown here with and without royal regalia, was feared and hated in England.

home. Finding Parliament stingy, they secured secret monetary subsidies from Louis XIV of France. And who bites the hand that feeds him? But the picture changed sharply in 1689, when the Catholic Louis XIV backed the exiled Catholic King of England, James II, against the two imported Protestants from Holland, William and Mary. War erupted in that year—the first of a series in a duel unto death.

In Europe, the two antagonists were fairly well matched. England boasted the stronger navy, France the stronger army, largely because of some 20 million inhabitants, as compared with only 5.5 million English people.

But in America, when the final showdown came in 1754, the English settlers enjoyed an overwhelming advantage in population of about 1.5 million to 60,000. Colonists under the British flag,

Later English Kings
(SEE PP. 10, 28 FOR EARLIER ONES.)

Name, Reign	Relation to America
William III, 1689–1702	War of Spanish Succession begun
Anne, 1702–1714	Queen Anne's War, 1702–1713
George I, 1714–1727	Navigation Laws laxly enforced ("salutary neglect")
George II, 1727–1760	Ga. founded; King George's War; French and Indian War
George III, 1760–1820	American Revolution, 1775–1783

though of mixed racial and national origins, were predominantly English. They were also relatively compact, confined to the Eastern seaboard by the ramparts of the Alleghenies and by unfriendly Frenchmen, Spaniards, and Indians.

Yet the population of New France, though sparse and diffuse, was far stronger than mere numbers would indicate. Being French Catholic, it was less racially mixed than its southern neighbor. New France also contained a higher proportion of arms-bearing men than the English colonies, especially Pennsylvania, where the Quakers condemned war.

Government in Canada was well designed for war making. It was tightly unified, highly centralized, heavily paternalistic, and sternly autocratic. The full might of the French Canadians could more easily be mobilized and manipulated by a few leaders.

In contrast, the numerical superiority of the English colonies was largely offset by loose governmental control, both at home and from London. As a result of the numerous religious sects and extensive popular rule, authority was widely decentralized and diluted. Andros's limited Dominion of New England, which would have provided some unity, had collapsed. Squabbling between the locally elected assemblies and the London-appointed governors was incessant. At times the colonials seemed more interested in fighting their royal governors than in fighting their French and Indian foes. There was also much intercolonial friction over boundaries and other local disputes. All these discords contributed to a high degree of disunity, and to a general unwillingness to assist neighbors in a common cause.

Yet elements of strength flowed from these apparent weaknesses in the English colonies. The existence of popular government and extensive democratic control encouraged individualism, self-reliance, and resourcefulness. These qualities were invaluable assets to the English settlers in the prolonged series of Anglo-French clashes.

England's colonies, moreover, possessed an overwhelming economic advantage. They enjoyed

Canadiens en Raquette allant en guerre sur la nege

Canadian Dressed for Winter Warfare. (Boston Public Library.)

The French, who also enlisted painted allies, were blessed with front-rank military leaders. Towering among them were the Comte de Frontenac and the Marquis de Montcalm, who were able to work wonders with scanty tools. The English at first were cursed with inept generals, but finally secured able ones by costly methods of trial and error—chiefly error.

Colonial Pawns on the European Chessboard

The four Anglo-French intercolonial wars, from 1689 to 1763, were in a sense American backwashes of European conflicts. Each of the first three erupted in Europe and spread to America, where there was a reciprocal open season on Frenchmen and Englishmen. The bulk of the English settlers, especially in these early frays, were not eager to start butchering their neighbors when dynastic rivalry in Europe led to shooting. But the colonials, as vanguards of empire, were caught in a squeeze. To a large extent the New World settlements were regarded by Europeans as puppets whose strings could be pulled by overseas monarchs.

All four of these Anglo-French conflicts, which involved groupings of the powers, were world wars. They resulted in a death struggle for European mastery of the seas, and were fought in the waters and on the soil of two hemispheres. Counting these first four clashes, there have been nine world wars since 1688. The American people, whether as British subjects or American citizens, were unable to stay out of a single one of them. Isolation from the broils of Europe was all too often a hope rather than a reality.

The first of the Anglo-French collisions was known in America as King William's War, and it grew in part from the opposition of the French monarch to the expulsion of James II and the seating of William III. Fierce fighting was waged mainly in the various theaters of Europe, as well as in India, North and South America, and the Caribbean.

a wide diversification of industry, with all that this meant in self-sufficiency. But French Canada was weak economically. It rested uneasily on the back of the westward-retreating beaver and, except for furs, lacked a profitable overseas commerce. The frigid Canadian colony never produced enough grain for its own use, and was forced to import large quantities of foodstuffs for its military and civilian personnel.

Other military advantages were unevenly distributed. England's colonies enjoyed the direct shield of the potent British navy, and the indirect shield of the formidable Iroquois Confederacy.

BRITISH TERRITORY AFTER TWO WARS, 1713

Map legend:
- English
- French
- Spanish
- Unexplored

a virtual draw, and by the terms of the treaty of peace in 1697 all captured territory was returned.

An uneasy truce ending King William's War lasted a scant four years. In 1701 hostilities broke out anew, following the brazen attempt of Louis XIV to eliminate the traditional boundary of the Pyrenees Mountains by seating his grandson on the throne of Spain. England could not and would not tolerate this dangerous unbalancing of the balance of power.

The subsequent struggle, known as the War of Spanish Succession, was the most far-flung yet fought in Europe: England and her European allies were banded together against France, Spain, and their allies. Though extending to the Caribbean, the fighting occurred principally in Europe, where England captured and retained the defiant Rock of Gibraltar.

This roaring conflagration spread rapidly to America. Spain was now on the side of France, so the South Carolinians engaged in bloody but inconclusive skirmishes with the Spaniards in Florida. War cries of the French-led Indians, as before, split the night air along the northern frontier, notably at Deerfield, Massachusetts. The ill-trained colonials, happily combining pluck with luck, again captured the French fortress of Port Royal in Acadia.

Peace terms, signed in 1713, revealed how badly France and her Spanish ally had been beaten. England was rewarded with Acadia (renamed Nova Scotia or New Scotland), Newfoundland,

In America the fortunes of battle seesawed. War-whooping Indians, led by Frenchmen, ravaged with torch and tomahawk the frontiers of New England, and wiped out the village of Schenectady, New York. The English colonials, after failing miserably in attempts to capture Quebec and Montreal, temporarily seized the stronghold of Port Royal in Acadia. The war abroad ended in

The Nine World Wars

Dates	In Europe	In America
1688–1697	War of the League of Augsburg	King William's War, 1689–1697
1701–1713	War of Spanish Succession	Queen Anne's War, 1702–1713
1740–1748	War of Austrian Succession	King George's War, 1744–1748
1756–1763	Seven Years' War	French and Indian War, 1754–1763
1778–1783	War of the American Revolution	American Revolution, 1775–1783
1793–1802	Wars of the French Revolution	Undeclared French War, 1798–1800
1803–1815	Napoleonic Wars	War of 1812, 1812–1814
1914–1918	World War I	World War I, 1917–1918
1939–1945	World War II	World War II, 1941–1945

> The Duke of Marlborough's triumph inspired Robert Southey's "The Battle of Blenheim" (1798):
>
> "And everybody praised the Duke,
> Who this great fight did win."
> "But what good came of it at last?"
> Quoth little Peterkin.
> "Why, that I cannot tell," said he;
> "But 'twas a famous victory."

and the bleak Hudson Bay region. These immense areas applied the pincers to the St. Lawrence settlements of France, and foreshadowed their ultimate doom. Except for Nova Scotia, the English colonials themselves had not captured any of these spoils. The final New World transfers were actually determined by the successes of British arms in the Old World. In Germany the Duke of Marlborough, for example, scored a notable victory against the French at Blenheim (1704). A generation of peace ensued, during which Britain provided her American colonies with decades of "salutary neglect"—fertile soil for the roots of independence.

European Wars Create American Sideshows

By the treaty of 1713 the British had won limited trading rights in Spanish America, but these later involved much friction over smuggling. Ill feeling flared up when an English Captain Jenkins, encountering Spanish revenue authorities, had one ear sliced off by a sword. The Spanish commander reportedly sneered, "Carry this home to the King, your master, whom, if he were present, I would serve in like fashion." The victim, with a tale of woe on his tongue and a shriveled ear in his hand, aroused furious resentment when he reached England.

The War of Jenkins' Ear, curiously named, broke out in 1739 between the English and the Spaniards. It was confined to the Caribbean Sea and to the much buffeted buffer colony of Georgia and its environs, where the philanthropist-soldier James Oglethorpe fought his Spanish foe to a standstill.

This small-scale scuffle with Spain in America soon merged with the large-scale War of Austrian Succession in Europe. It exploded with full fury in 1740, when Frederick the Great of Prussia treacherously seized the province of Silesia from his Austrian neighbor, the young and beautiful Maria Theresa. The talented empress fought back with all the fury of a woman scorned, and when Spain and France joined the Prussians, England entered the fray on the side of Austria.

As usual, the War of Austrian Succession was waged mainly in Europe, although sideshow skirmishes erupted in the Caribbean and along the thinly manned English colonial frontier in North America. The French had built a reputedly impregnable fortress, Louisbourg, on Cape Breton Island, commanding the Gulf of St. Lawrence and serving as a pistol pointed at the heart of New England. An expedition of rustic New Englanders was organized to seize it. With the support of a British fleet, and with incredibly good luck, the raw and sometimes drunken recruits blundered into victory and captured the prize in 1745.

But the peace terms of 1748 were determined by the global balance sheet. In Europe, the fighting had again proved inconclusive, except that Frederick of Prussia retained the rich province he had faithlessly wrested from his queenly neighbor. The British had lost Madras in India to France, and in regaining this valuable foothold in the general restoration, they handed back Louisbourg to their foe. The victorious New Englanders were outraged. Taking a narrowly provincial stand, they felt that their interests had been sacrificed to the imperial selfishness of Old Englanders. Although they were finally reimbursed in part for the expenses of their expedition, money did not completely salve their pride or quiet their fears. France was still powerful and unappeased.

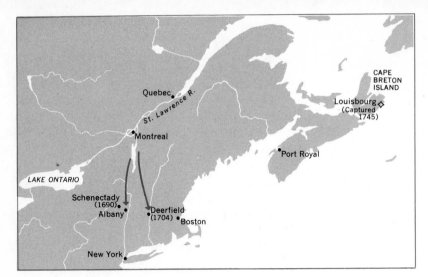

George Washington Inaugurates War with France

As the drama unfolded in the New World, the Ohio Valley became the chief bone of contention between the French and British. The Ohio country was the critical area into which the westward-pushing English would inevitably penetrate. It was the key to the continent which the French had to retain, particularly if they were going to link their Canadian holdings with those of the lower Mississippi Valley. By the mid-1700s the English colonials, painfully aware of these basic truths, were no longer so reluctant to bear the burdens of empire. Alarmed by French land-grabbing and cutthroat fur-trade competition in the Ohio Valley, they were determined to fight for their economic security and for the supremacy of their way of life in North America.

Rivalry for the lush lands of the upper Ohio Valley brought tensions to the snapping point. In 1749 a group of English colonial speculators, chiefly influential Virginians including the Washington family, had secured rights to some 500,000 acres in this region. In the same disputed wilderness the French were in the process of erecting a chain of forts commanding the strategic Ohio River.

In 1753 the governor of Virginia ushered George Washington, a twenty-one-year-old surveyor and fellow Virginian, onto the stage of history. The tall, athletic youth was commissioned to warn the French that they must leave the Ohio Valley; and while delivering the message he was to spy out their armed strength. Already marked out as an able and ambitious young man of promise, Washington completed this dangerous mission, after several brushes with death. But the French were not going to be ejected by mere words. They tightened their hold on the Ohio Valley by building a strong outpost, Fort Duquesne, at the strate-

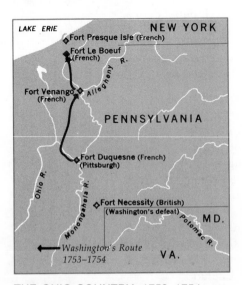

THE OHIO COUNTRY, 1753–1754

gic point where the Monongahela and Allegheny Rivers join to form the Ohio—the later site of Pittsburgh.

In 1754, shortly after his hazardous errand, Washington was sent to the Ohio country as a lieutenant-colonel in command of about 150 Virginia militiamen. Encountering a small detachment of French troops in the forest about forty miles from Fort Duquesne, the Virginians opened fire—the first shots of the globe-girdling new war. The French leader was killed and his men retreated. An exultant Washington wrote: "I heard the bullets whistle, and believe me, there is something charming in the sound." It soon lost its charm.

The French promptly returned with reinforcements, which surrounded Washington behind his hastily constructed breastworks, Fort Necessity. After a ten-hour siege he was forced to surrender his entire command in July 1754—ironically the Fourth of July. But he was permitted to march his men away with the full honors of war.

With the shooting already started and in danger of spreading, the British authorities in Nova Scotia took vigorous action. Understandably fearing a stab in the back from the French Acadians, whom England had acquired in 1713, the British brutally uprooted some 4,000 of them in 1755. These unhappy French deportees were scattered as far south as Louisiana, where the descendants of the French-speaking Acadians are now called "Cajuns" and number perhaps half a million.

Global War and Colonial Disunity

The first three Anglo-French colonial wars had all started in Europe, but the tables were now reversed. A fourth struggle, known as the French and Indian War, began in America. Touched off by George Washington in the wilds of the Ohio Valley in 1754, it rocked along on an undeclared basis for two years, and then widened into the most titanic conflict the world had yet seen—the Seven Years' War. It was fought not only in America but in Europe, in the West Indies, in the

Philippines, in Africa, and on the ocean. The Seven Years' War was a seven seas war.

In Europe the principal adversaries were England and Prussia on one side, arrayed against France, Spain, Austria, and Russia on the other. The bloodiest theater was in Germany, where Frederick the Great deservedly won the title of "Great" by repelling French, Austrian, and Russian armies, often with the manpower odds three to one against him. The London government, unable to send him effective troop reinforcements, liberally subsidized him with gold. Luckily for the English colonials, the French wasted so much strength in this European bloodbath that they were unable to throw an adequate force into the New World. "America was conquered in Germany," declared Britain's great statesman William Pitt.

In previous intercolonial clashes, the Americans had revealed an astonishing lack of unity. Colonists who were nearest the shooting had responded much more generously with volunteers and money than those enjoying the safety of remoteness. Even the Indians had laughed at the inability of the colonials to pull together. With bullets already whining in the Ohio country, the crisis called for concerted action.

In 1754 the British government summoned an intercolonial Congress to Albany, New York, near the Iroquois Indian country. Travel-weary delegates from only seven of the thirteen colonies showed up. The immediate purpose was to keep the scalping knives of the Iroquois tribes loyal to the British in the spreading war. The chiefs were harangued at length and then presented with thirty wagon loads of gifts, including guns.

The longer-range purpose at Albany was to achieve greater colonial unity, and thus bolster the common defense against France. A month before the Congress assembled, ingenious Benjamin Franklin published in his *Pennsylvania Gazette* the most famous cartoon of the colonial era. Showing the separate colonies as parts of a disjointed snake, it broadcast the slogan, "Join, or Die."

Famous Cartoon by Benjamin Franklin. Delaware and Georgia were omitted.

Franklin himself, a wise and witty counselor, was the leading spirit of the Albany Congress. His outstanding contribution was a well-devised scheme for colonial home rule. It was unanimously adopted by the Albany delegates, but was spurned by the individual colonies and by the London regime. To the colonials, it did not seem to give enough independence; to the British officials, it seemed to give too much. The disappointing result confirmed one of Franklin's sage observations: all people agreed on the need for union, but their "weak noddles" were "perfectly distracted" when they attempted to agree on details.

Braddock's Blundering and Its Aftermath

The opening clashes of the French and Indian War went badly for the English colonials. Haughty and bull-headed General Braddock, a sixty-year-old officer experienced in European warfare, was sent to Virginia with a strong detachment of British regulars. After gathering scanty supplies from the reluctant colonists, he set out in 1755 with some 2,000 men to capture Fort Duquesne. A considerable part of his force consisted of ill-disciplined colonial militiamen ("buckskins"), whose behind-the-tree methods of fighting Indians won "Bulldog" Braddock's professional contempt.

Braddock's expedition, dragging heavy artillery, moved slowly. Axmen laboriously hacked a path through the dense forest, thus opening a road that was later to be an important artery to the West. A few miles from Fort Duquesne, Braddock encountered a much smaller French and Indian army. At first the enemy force was repulsed, but it quickly melted into the thickets and poured a murderous fire into the ranks of the Redcoats. George Washington, an energetic and fearless aide to Braddock, had two horses shot from under him and four bullet holes in his coat, and Braddock himself was mortally wounded. The entire force was routed after appalling losses.

Inflamed by this easy victory, the Indians took to a wider warpath. The whole frontier from Pennsylvania to North Carolina, left virtually naked by Braddock's bloody defeat, felt their fury. Scalping forays occurred within eighty miles of Philadelphia, and in desperation the local authorities offered bounties for Indian scalps: $50 for a squaw and $130 for a brave. George Washington, with only 300 men, did heroic work in helping to defend the scorched frontier.

The British launched a full-scale invasion of Canada in 1756, now that the undeclared war in America had at last merged into a world conflict. But they unwisely tried to attack a number of exposed wilderness posts simultaneously, instead of throwing all their strength at Quebec and Montreal. If these strongholds had fallen, all the outposts to the west would have withered on the vine for lack of river-borne supplies. But the British ignored such sound strategy, and defeat after defeat tarnished their arms, both in America and in Europe.

General Edward Braddock (1695–1755). Braddock was buried in the road of retreat so that his grave could not be detected by the enemy. His last, futile words were reported to be, "We shall know better how to deal with them next time."

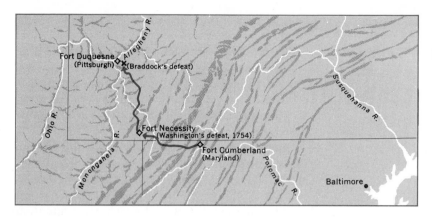

BRADDOCK'S MARCH, 1755

Pitt's Palms of Victory

In the hour of crisis Britain brought forth, as she repeatedly has, a superlative leader—William Pitt. A tall and imposing figure, whose flashing eyes were set in a hawk-like face, he was popularly known as the "Great Commoner." Pitt drew much of his strength from the common people, who admired him so greatly that on occasion they kissed his horses. A splendid orator endowed with a majestic voice, he believed passionately in his cause, in his country, and in himself.

In 1757 Pitt became a foremost leader in the London government. Throwing himself headlong into his task, he soon earned the title "Organizer of Victory." He wisely decided to soft-pedal assaults on the French West Indies, which had been bleeding away much British strength, and to concentrate on the vitals of Canada—the Quebec-Montreal area. He also picked young and ener-

EVENTS OF 1755–1760

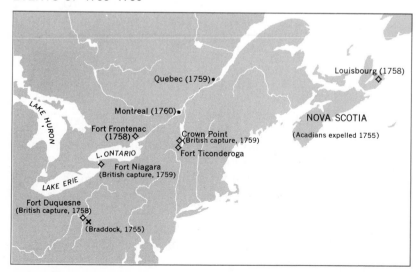

William Pitt (1708–1778). He opposed the King's stubborn policies against the colonies but never favored complete independence.

NORTH AMERICA BEFORE 1754

English
French
Spanish
Russian
Unexplored

FRENCH HAITI
BR. HONDURAS

NORTH AMERICA AFTER 1763
(after French losses)

English
French
Spanish
Russian
Unexplored

FRENCH HAITI
BR. HONDURAS

getic leaders, thus bypassing incompetent and cautious old generals.

Pitt first dispatched a powerful expedition in 1758 against Louisbourg. The frowning fortress, though it had been greatly strengthened, fell after a blistering siege. Wild rejoicing swept England, for this was the first significant British victory of the entire war.

Quebec was next on Pitt's list. For this crucial expedition he chose the thirty-two-year-old James Wolfe, who had been an officer since the age of fourteen. Though slight and sickly, Wolfe combined a mixture of dash with painstaking attention to detail. The British attackers were making scant progress when Wolfe, in a daring move, sent a detachment up a poorly guarded part of the rocky eminence protecting Quebec. This vanguard scaled the cliff, pulling itself upward by the bushes and showing the way for the others. In the morning the two armies faced each other on the Plains of Abraham on the outskirts of Quebec, one under Wolfe and the other under Montcalm. Both commanders fell fatally wounded, but the French were defeated and the city surrendered.

The battle of Quebec ranks as one of the most significant engagements in British and American history. Yet it was only one of the bumper crop of victories in 1759, known in British history as "the wonderful year." The English writer Horace Walpole noted, "We were forced to ask every morning what victory there is, for fear of missing one."

Yet the triumph at Quebec was not completely decisive. Winter descended, ice-locking the St. Lawrence River, and leaving the scurvy-ridden and outnumbered British army facing heavy attacks from Montreal. But with spring, the ice broke and reinforcements arrived. Montreal fell in 1760, and the French flag waved in Canada for the last time. Even so, the war continued globally for three more years. France and Spain were lucky to escape as well as they did, but the bad beating they received was reflected in severe peace terms.

By the peace settlement at Paris (1763), French

power was thrown completely off the continent of North America, leaving behind a fertile French population that is to this day a strong minority in Canada. This bitter pill was sweetened somewhat when the French were allowed to retain several small but valuable sugar islands in the West Indies, and two never-to-be-fortified islets in the Gulf of St. Lawrence for fishing stations. A final blow came when the French, to compensate their luckless Spanish ally for her losses, ceded to Spain all trans-Mississippi Louisiana, plus the outlet of New Orleans. Spain, for her part, turned Florida over to England in return for Cuba, where Havana had fallen to British arms.

Great Britain thus emerged as the dominant power in North America, while taking her place as the leading naval power of the world.

Mother-and-Daughter Friction

England's colonials, baptized by fire, emerged with increased confidence in their military

Anti-Quaker Cartoon. Non-combatant Pennsylvania Quakers traded with the French, and in this cartoon (c. 1760) Franklin points out that the Quaker (with fox's head) will flourish, regardless of who wins. (The Historical Society of Pennsylvania.)

strength. They had borne the brunt of battle at first; they had fought bravely beside the crack British regulars; and they had gained valuable experience, officers and men alike. In the closing days of the conflict some 20,000 American recruits were under arms.

The French and Indian War, while bolstering colonial self-esteem, simultaneously shattered the myth of British invincibility. On Braddock's bloody field the "buckskin" militia had seen the demoralized regulars huddling helplessly together or fleeing their unseen enemy.

Ominously, friction had developed during the war between arrogant English officers and the raw colonial "boors." Displaying the contempt of the professional soldier for amateurs, the British refused to recognize any American militia commission above the rank of captain—a demotion humiliating to "Colonel" George Washington. They also showed the usual condescension of snobs from the civilized Old Country toward the "scum" who had confessed failure by fleeing to the "outhouses of civilization." General Wolfe referred to the colonial militia, with exaggeration, as "in general the dirtiest, most contemptible, cowardly dogs that you can conceive." Energetic and hardworking American settlers, on the other hand, sensed that they were the cutting edge of British civilization. They believed that they deserved credit rather than contempt for risking their lives to erect a New World empire.

British officials were further distressed by the reluctance of the colonials to support the common cause wholeheartedly. American shippers, using fraudulent papers, developed a golden traffic with the enemy ports of the Spanish and French West Indies. This treasonable trade in foodstuffs actually kept some of the hostile islands from starving at the very time when the British navy was trying to subdue them. In the last year of the war the British authorities, forced to resort to drastic measures, forbade the export of all supplies from New England and the Middle Colonies.

Nor had the conduct of other colonials been

The Reverend Andrew Burnaby, an observant Church of England clergyman who visited the colonies in the closing months of the French and Indian War, scoffed at any possibility of unification (1760): ". . . for fire and water are not more heterogeneous than the different colonies in North America. Nothing can exceed the jealousy and emulation which they possess in regard to each other. . . . In short . . . were they left to themselves there would soon be a civil war from one end of the continent to the other, while the Indians and Negroes would . . . impatiently watch the opportunity of exterminating them all together."

praiseworthy. Self-centered and regarding the war as remote, large numbers of them had been loath to provide men and money for the conflict. They demanded the rights and privileges of Englishmen, without the duties and responsibilities of Englishmen. Not until Pitt had offered to reimburse the colonies for a substantial part of their expenditures—some £900,000—did they move with some enthusiasm. If the Americans had to be bribed to defend themselves against a relentless and savage foe, would they ever unite to strike the Mother Country?

The curse of intercolonial disunity, present from early days, had continued throughout the recent hostilities. It had been caused mainly by enormous distances; by geographical barriers like rivers; by conflicting religions, from Catholic to Quaker; by varied national backgrounds, from German to Irish; by differing types of colonial governments; by numerous boundary disputes; and by the resentment of the crude back-country democracy against the aristocratic bigwigs. Many of the colonials felt much more kindly toward Englishmen in England than they did toward Englishmen next door.

Yet unity received some encouragement during the French and Indian War. When soldiers and statesmen from widely separated colonies met around common campfires and council tables, they were often agreeably surprised by what they found. Despite deep-seated jealousy and suspicion, they discovered that they were all fellow Americans who generally spoke the same language and shared common ideals. Barriers of disunity began to melt, although a long and rugged road lay ahead before a nation could emerge.

American Men of Destiny

The removal of the French menace in Canada profoundly affected American attitudes. While the French hawk had been hovering in the North and West, the colonial chicks had been forced to cling close to the wings of the mother hen. Now that the hawk was killed, they could range far afield with a new spirit of independence.

Frenchmen, humiliated by the British and saddened by the fate of Canada, consoled themselves with one wishful thought. Perhaps the loss of their American empire would one day result in Britain's loss of her American empire. In a sense the history of the United States began with the fall of Quebec and Montreal; the infant republic was cradled on the Plains of Abraham.

The Spanish and Indian menaces, in like manner, were removed by the recent war. Spain was eliminated from Florida, although now entrenched in Louisiana and New Orleans. And the Indian allies of France were left in the lurch. A violent post-war flare-up against the white men occurred in the Ohio Valley and Great Lakes region in 1763, with the vengeful chieftain Pontiac as the principal leader. Catching the British napping, the red men wiped out a number of their posts. But the whites, rallying in superior numbers, crushed the uprising and pacified the frontier, temporarily.

Land-hungry American colonials were now free to burst over the dam of the Appalachian Moun-

SETTLED AREAS AT END OF FRENCH AND INDIAN WAR, 1763
This map, showing the colonies thirteen years before the Declaration of Independence, helps to explain why the British would be unable to conquer their offspring. The Colonials were spreading rapidly into the backcountry, where the powerful British navy could not flush them out. During the Revolutionary War, the British at one time or another captured the leading colonial cities—Boston, New York, Philadelphia, and Charleston; but the more remote interior remained a sanctuary for rebels.

tains, and flood out over the grassy Western lands. A tiny rivulet of men like Daniel Boone had already trickled into Tennessee and Kentucky; other courageous pioneers were preparing for the long trek over the mountains.

Then, out of a clear sky, the London government issued its Proclamation of 1763. It flatly prohibited settlement in the area beyond the Appalachian Mountains, pending further adjustments. The truth is that this hastily drawn document was not designed to oppress the colonials at all, but to work out the Indian problem fairly in the interests of the fur traders and the other groups concerned.

But countless Americans, especially land speculators, were dismayed and angered. Was not the land beyond the mountains their birthright? Had they not, in addition, bought it with their blood in the recent war? In complete defiance of the paper Proclamation, they clogged the westward trails. In 1765 an estimated 1,000 wagons rolled through the town of Salisbury, North Carolina, on their way "up west." This wholesale flouting of royal authority boded ill for the longevity of British rule in America.

The French and Indian War also caused the colonials to develop a new vision of their ultimate destiny. With the path cleared for the conquest of a continent, with their birthrate high and their energy boundless, they sensed that they were a potent people on the march. And they were in no mood to be restrained.

Lordly Britons, whose suddenly swollen empire had tended to produce swollen heads, were in no mood for back talk. Puffed up over their recent victories, they were already annoyed with their unruly colonials. The stage was set for a violent family quarrel.

VARYING VIEWPOINTS

The duel for North America was but one episode in the epochal story of the worldwide expansion of European commerce and culture after 1500. Scholarly inquiry has revolved around four principal questions: How did New World developments fit into the overall pattern of rivalries among the great European powers? What were the relative strengths and weaknesses of the British and French imperial systems that spelled the final triumph of the British and the defeat of the French? How well or poorly did the British Empire function? Finally, were the Americans well or badly treated in the British imperial system? In short, how economically justifiable was the eventual American Revolution?

SELECT READINGS

The workings of the British mercantile system are detailed in G. L. Beer, *The Origins of the British Colonial System* (1908), and *The Old Colonial System* (2 vols., 1912). See also C. M. Andrews' vast *Colonial Period of American History* (4 vols., 1935–1938), and L. Gipson's still more ambitious *British Empire before the American Revolution* (15 vols., 1936–1970). Recent efforts to analyze the colonial empire are M. Hall, *Edward Randolph and the American Colonies, 1676–1703* (1960), J. Henretta, *"Salutary Neglect": Colonial Administration under the Duke of Newcastle* (1972), and Michael Kammen's especially interesting *Empire and Interest* (1970). The French colonial effort is described in G. M. Wrong, *The Rise and Fall of New France* (2 vols., 1928), and in S. Morison, *Samuel de Champlain: Father of New France* (1972). The Anglo-French struggle is recounted in H. H. Peckham, *The Colonial Wars, 1689–1762* (1964), and in Max Savelle, *The Origins of American Diplomacy: The International History of Angloamerica, 1492–1763* (1967). Classic accounts are Francis Parkman's several volumes, including *Count Frontenac and New France under Louis XIV* (1877), *Montcalm and Wolfe* (2 vols., 1884), and *A Half-Century of Conflict* (1892). Parkman's tomes are condensed, without serious loss of flavor, in *The Battle for North America* (ed. John Tebbel, 1948) and *The Parkman Reader* (ed. S. E. Morison, 1955). A recent military history is C. P. Stacey, *Quebec, 1759: The Siege and the Battle* (1959). An impressive biography is D. S. Freeman, *Young Washington* (2 vols., 1948), a subject treated in less detail in J. T. Flexner, *George Washington: The Forge of Experience* (1965). See also B. Knollenberg's revealing *George Washington: The Virginia Period* (1965).

4

Colonial Society on the Eve of Revolution

*Driven from every other corner of the earth,
freedom of thought and the right of private
judgment in matters of conscience direct their
course to this happy country as their last asylum.*

SAMUEL ADAMS, 1776

Conquest by the Cradle

The common term "thirteen original colonies" is misleading. There were thirty-two colonies under British rule in North America by 1775, including Canada, the Floridas, and the various islands of the Caribbean. But only thirteen of them unfurled the standard of revolt. A few of the nonrebels, such as Canada and Jamaica, were larger, wealthier, or more populous than some of the thirteen. And even among the revolting thirteen, dramatic differences in economic organization, social structure, and ways of life were evident.

All the eventually rebellious colonies did have one outstanding feature in common: their population was growing by leaps and bounds. In 1700 they contained fewer than 300,000 souls, about 20,000 of whom were black. By 1775, 2.5 million

Early Advertising. Appeal in England for American colonists.

their own rattlesnakes. This was especially true in New England, where the people were fertile even if the soil was not. Lower population densities slowed the spread of contagious microbes, making American death rates lower than those of the relatively crowded Old World. Simply put, America was a healthier place than Europe, though the southern colonies remained deathtraps until late in the 17th Century. Even the captive black population of the Chesapeake region reached the point of sustained natural increase sometime around 1720—about two generations later than the southern white settlers—making it one of the few slave societies in history to perpetuate itself by its own natural reproduction.

persons inhabited the thirteen colonies, of whom about half a million were black. White immigrants made up nearly 400,000 of the increased number, and black "forced immigrants" accounted for almost as many again. But most of the spurt stemmed from the remarkable natural fertility of all Americans, white and black. To the amazement and dismay of Europeans, the colonists were doubling their numbers every twenty-three years. Unfriendly Dr. Samuel Johnson, back in England, growled that the Americans were multiplying like

Early marriage encouraged the booming birthrate. Women were scarce and seldom stayed single for long. An unwed girl of twenty-one could be labeled "an antique virgin." In the courtship stages and in places where heating was a problem, "bundling" was occasionally permitted; that is, the young couple would cuddle together in bed fully clothed. Unwanted pregnancies sometimes re-

Graveyard Art.   These New England colonists evidently died in the prime of life. Carving likenesses on grave markers was a common way of commemorating the dead. (American Antiquarian Society.)

sulted, although one New England rhymester defended the practice:

> Since in a bed a man and maid
>   May bundle and be chaste,
> It doth no good to burn up wood;
>   It is a needless waste.

Babies arrived with sometimes frightening frequency. Benjamin Franklin was one of seventeen by two mothers; William Phips, a Massachusetts governor was one of twenty-seven—all by the same mother. Ceaseless child-bearing drained the vitality of many pioneer women, as the weather-eroded colonial tombstones eloquently reveal, and a number of the largest families were borne by several mothers. Yet these maternal sacrifices had political consequences. In 1700 there were twenty Englishmen for each American colonist. By 1775 the English advantage in numbers had fallen to three-to-one—setting the stage for a momentous shift in the balance of power between colonies and the mother country.

The bulk of the population was cooped up east of the Alleghenies, although by 1775 a vanguard of pioneers had trickled into the stump-studded clearings of Tennessee and Kentucky. The most populous colonies in 1775 were Virginia, Massachusetts, Pennsylvania, North Carolina, and Maryland—in that order. There were only four communities that might properly be called cities: Philadelphia, including suburbs, was first with about 34,000, while New York, Boston, and Charleston were strung out behind. About 90 percent of the people lived in rural areas.

A Mingling of the Races

Colonial America was a melting pot, and had been from the outset. The population, although basically English in stock and language, was picturesquely mottled with sizable foreign groups.

Heavy-accented Germans constituted about 6 percent of the total population, or 150,000, by 1775. Fleeing religious persecution, economic oppression, and the ravages of war, they had flocked to America in the early 1700s, and had settled chiefly in Pennsylvania. Known popularly but erroneously as the Pennsylvania Dutch (a corruption of the German word *Deutsch*), they totaled about one-third of the colony's population. In Philadelphia the street signs were painted in both German and English.

These German newcomers moved into the back country of Pennsylvania, where their splendid stone barns gave—and still give—mute evidence of industry and prosperity. Not having been brought up as Englishmen, they had no deep-rooted loyalty to the British Crown, and they clung tenaciously to their German language and customs. But as permanent settlers they became the forebears of many distinguished Americans, including George Herman ("Babe") Ruth, the home-run king, and President Dwight D. Eisenhower.

The Scotch-Irish, who in 1775 numbered about 175,000, or 7 percent of the population, were an important non-English group, although English-speaking. They were not Irish at all, but turbulent Scots Lowlanders. Over a period of many decades, they had first been transplanted to Northern Ireland, where they had not prospered. The Irish Catholics already there, hating Scotch Presbyterianism, resented the intruders, and still do. The economic life of the Scotch-Irish was severely hampered, especially when the English government placed burdensome restrictions on their production of linens and woolens.

A young Frenchman named Crèvecoeur wrote about 1770 of the mixed population. "They are a mixture of English, Scotch, Irish, French, Dutch, Germans, and Swedes. From this promiscuous breed, that race now called Americans have arisen. . . . I could point out to you a family whose grandfather was an Englishman, whose wife was Dutch, whose son married a French woman, and whose present four sons have now four wives of different nations."

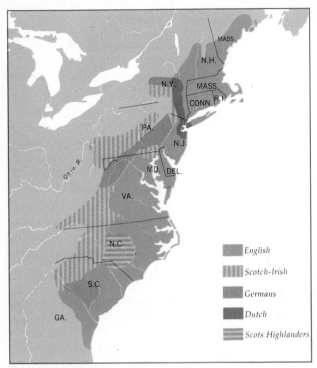

NATIONALITIES IN 1775

- English
- Scotch-Irish
- Germans
- Dutch
- Scots Highlanders

Early in the 1700s tens of thousands of embittered Scotch-Irish finally pulled up stakes and came to America, chiefly to tolerant and deep-soiled Pennsylvania. Finding the best acres already taken by Germans and Quakers, they pushed out onto the frontier. There many of them illegally but defiantly squatted on the unoccupied lands, and quarreled with both red and white owners. It was said, somewhat unfairly, that the Scotch-Irish kept the Sabbath—and all else they could lay their hands on. Pugnacious, lawless, and individualistic, they brought with them the Scottish secrets of whiskey distilling and proceeded to set up their own stills. Already experienced colonizers and agitators in Ireland, they proved to be superb frontiersmen and Indian fighters. They cherished no love for the British government which had uprooted them, and many of them—including the youthful Andrew Jackson—joined the embattled American Revolutionists. All told, about a dozen future Presidents were of Scotch-Irish descent.

Approximately 5 percent of the multi-colored colonial population consisted of other foreign groups. These embraced French Huguenots, Welsh, Dutch, Swedes, Jews, Irish, Swiss, and Scots Highlanders—as distinguished from the Scotch-Irish. Except for the Scots Highlanders, such hodgepodge elements felt little loyalty to the British Crown.

By far the largest single non-English group was African. Perhaps 400,000 blacks were carried in chains to colonial North America, yet they were only a tiny fraction of the millions brought to the New World as a whole in the centuries preceding the American Revolution. The small and struggling colonial economy did not at first provide an attractive market for slave traders. Most of the early human cargoes taken from West Africa's "slave coast" on the Gulf of Guinea went to South America or the West Indies. Throughout most of the 17th Century, nearly half the slaves brought to mainland America came by way of the West Indies, not directly from Africa. They had originally been captured in Africa by African coastal tribes, who traded them in crude markets on the shimmering tropical beaches to itinerant European flesh merchants. The captives were herded aboard sweltering ships for the gruesome "middle passage," on

Estimated Population Elements, 1790*

(BASED ON FAMILY NAMES)

Ethnic Groups	Number	Percentage
English and Welsh	2,605,699	66.3%
Scotch (including Scotch-Irish)	221,562	5.6
German	176,407	4.5
Dutch	78,959	2.0
Irish	61,534	1.6
French	17,619	0.4
All other whites	10,664	0.3
Black	757,181	19.3
GRAND TOTAL	3,929,625	

*Rossiter, *A Century of Population Growth* (1909). Later estimates by Barker and Hansen (1931) are not used here because they are confused by the inclusion of Spanish and French elements *later* a part of the United States.

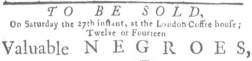

A Pennsylvania Advertisement for Slaves in the 1760s.
Note that the slaves are said to have had smallpox and to
be able to speak English. (Rare Book Division, The New
York Public Library, Astor, Lenox and Tilden Foundations.)

which death rates ran as high as 20 percent. Terrified survivors were eventually shoved onto auction blocks in New World ports.

Slave imports to the American colonies mounted rapidly after about 1690, as white labor became more expensive. In 1698 the Royal African Company lost its crown-granted monopoly on carrying slaves to the colonies. Enterprising Americans then rushed to cash in on the lucrative slave trade. "Guinea ships," mostly from New England, plied the grim course directly from Africa to America. Newport, Rhode Island, became a main port of entry, though it was dwarfed by the giant slave market at Charleston, South Carolina.

The population of the thirteen colonies, though mainly Anglo-Saxon, was perhaps the most mixed to be found anywhere in the world. The South, holding about 90 percent of the slaves, already displayed its historic black-and-white racial composition. New England, mostly staked out by the original Puritan migrants, showed the least ethnic diversity. The middle colonies, especially Pennsylvania, received the bulk of later white immigrants, and boasted an astonishing variety of peoples. Of the fifty-six signers of the Declaration of Independence in 1776, eighteen were non-English, and eight had been born outside the colonies.

Frontier Patricians

Crude frontier life did not permit the flagrant display of class distinctions, and 17th-Century colonial society had a certain simple sameness to it. Yet many settlers, who considered themselves of the "better sort," tried to re-create on a modified scale the social structure they had known at home. To some extent, they were successful, though yeasty democratic forces frustrated their full triumph. The most remarkable feature of the social ladder was the rags-to-riches ease with which an ambitious colonial, even a former indentured servant, might rise from a lower rung to a higher one, quite unlike in Old England.

Would-be American bluebloods resented the pretensions of the "meaner sort" and passed laws to keep them in their place. Massachusetts in 1651 prohibited poorer folk from "wearing gold or silver lace," and in 18th-Century Virginia a tailor was fined and jailed for arranging to race his horse—"a sport only for gentlemen."

Elites feathered their nests more finely in the 18th Century. People came to be seated in churches and schools according to their social rank. (Future President John Adams was placed fourteenth in a class of twenty-four at Harvard, where ability also affected one's standing.) At the top of the social ladder in the New England and Middle colonies roosted the merchant princes. Many of them laid the foundations of their fortunes with profits made as military suppliers during the wars of the 1690s and early 1700s. In the Southern colonies, land-holding was the passport to power, prestige, and wealth. The Virginia gentry proved remarkably able to keep its lands in a small circle of families over several generations—largely because they parceled out their huge holdings among several children, rather than just to the eldest son, as was the custom in England. A clutch of extended clans, such as the Fitzhughs, the Lees, and the Washingtons, owned amongst them vast tracts of Virginia real estate, and together they dominated Virginia politics. Just before the Revolutionary War, 70 percent of the leaders of the

House of Burgesses came from families established in Virginia before the 1690s—the famed "First Families of Virginia," or "FFV's."

The power of the great planters was also bolstered by their disproportionate ownership of slaves. The riches created by the swelling slave population in the 18th Century were not distributed evenly among the whites. Wealth tended to concentrate in the hands of the largest slave owners—thus widening the gap between the prosperous gentry and the "poor whites," with relatively few whites in between. In all the colonies, the ranks of the upper crust were further enhanced by the more successful professional men, the clergy of the established churches, and the well-dressed British officials, including the governors and other "ruffle-shirted Anglicans."*

The Lower Rungs of Society

Below the aristocracy was the middle class—the backbone of the colonies. Largest in New England, it consisted chiefly of the small farmers, often clad in buckskin breeches, who owned modest holdings and tilled them with their own hands and

Franklin's Press. Benjamin Franklin, a many-sided Philadelphian, was the best known and most prosperous colonial printer. He rose to hobnob with European royalty.

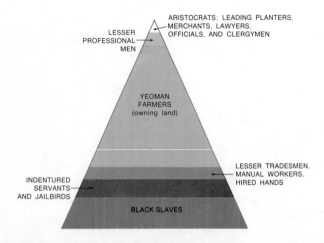

ARISTOCRATS: LEADING PLANTERS, MERCHANTS, LAWYERS, OFFICIALS, AND CLERGYMEN

LESSER PROFESSIONAL MEN

YEOMAN FARMERS (owning land)

LESSER TRADESMEN, MANUAL WORKERS, HIRED HANDS

INDENTURED SERVANTS AND JAILBIRDS

BLACK SLAVES

THE COLONIAL SOCIAL PYRAMID, 1775
(an approximation)

horses. Closely associated with this group were the skilled artisans, with their well-greased leather aprons, and the smaller tradesmen. America's most famous printer, Benjamin Franklin, was never fully accepted by the snobs of his adopted Philadelphia. The son of a Boston candlemaker, he was looked down upon as a social climber—a person in "trade."*

Below the prosperous middle class were "hired hands" and other landless poor whites. Happily, the ne'er-do-wells were not numerous; extreme poverty and extreme wealth were both rather rare.

Even lower on the social ladder were the indentured servants, of whom perhaps 250,000 had arrived by 1775. These "white slaves" were mainly persons who could not afford to pay their passage across the Atlantic. In return for transportation, they voluntarily mortgaged the sweat of their bodies for a period of years, usually four or more. Their lot was often harsh, and runaways were common.

Indentured servants, upon serving their time, frequently were given or otherwise secured land, and the more enterprising souls often became prosperous. Nor did any serious social stigma attach to them. Some even broke into the upper crust of aristocracy, and two became signers of the Declaration of Independence. The inden-

---

*See Gilbert Stuart's painting of "The Skater," color portfolio, for a rendition of an elegantly clad Revolutionary-era aristocrat.

*For a portrait of another famous Colonial craftsman, Paul Revere, see John Singleton Copley's painting in the color portfolio.

tured-servant system admittedly inflicted much hardship, but it did give tens of thousands of impoverished people a chance to start anew in the Land of Opportunity.

Far less desirable than the voluntary indentured servants were the paupers and convicts who were involuntarily shipped over as indentured servants. Altogether, about 50,000 "jayle birds" were dumped on the American colonies by the London authorities. This riffraff crowd, including robbers, rapists, and murderers, was generally sullen and undesirable, and not bubbling over with good-will for the King's government. But many convicts were the unfortunate victims of circumstances and of a viciously unfair penal code that included about 200 capital crimes. Some of the deportees, in fact, came to be highly respected citizens.

Colonial Slavery

Luckless black slaves remained in society's basement. Enchained in all the colonies, the blacks were heavily concentrated in the South, where their numbers rose dramatically throughout the 18th Century. Blacks accounted for nearly half the population of Virginia by midcentury. In South Carolina they outnumbered whites two to one. There the climate was hostile to health and the labor was life draining. Isolated rice and indigo plantations were lonely hells-on-earth where gangs of mostly male blacks toiled and perished. Only fresh imports could sustain the slave population in the deep South. In 1739 more than fifty resentful blacks in South Carolina exploded in revolt and tried to march to Spanish Florida, but were stopped by the local militia.

Blacks in the tobacco-growing Chesapeake region had a somewhat easier lot. Farms were closer together, permitting more frequent contact with friends and relatives, and tobacco was a less physically demanding crop than those of the deeper South. By about 1740 the proportion of females in the slave population had begun to rise, making family life possible. The increasing presence of native-born Afro-Americans also contributed to

Slave-Catcher Advertisment. Runaway slaves were so numerous in colonial days that newspapers kept on hand stock woodcuts like those here reproduced. One Virginia owner offered five pounds reward for the return of Toby, a fourteen-year-old mulatto boy "with a scar on the right side of his throat", and with "an old brown jacket, tow shirt and check trousers, which are supposed to be worn out by this time."

the growth of a stable and distinctive slave culture, a mixture of African and American elements of speech, religion, and folkways.

Fears of black rebellion plagued the whites. Some of the colonial legislatures, notably South Carolina's in 1760, sensed the dangers present in a heavy concentration of rebellious slaves, and attempted to restrict or halt their importation. But the British authorities vetoed all such efforts. Many colonials looked upon this veto as a callous disregard of their welfare, although it was done primarily in the interests of imperial policy and of the British and New England slave trade. Thomas Jefferson, himself a slaveholder, assailed such vetoes in an early draft of the Declaration of Independence, but his proposed clause was finally dropped, largely out of regard for Southern sensibilities.

A few of the blacks had been freed, but the vast majority were condemned to a life under the lash. The universal passion for freedom vented itself during the colonial era in numerous cases of arson, murder, and insurrection or near-insurrection. A slave revolt erupted in New York City in 1712 which cost the lives of a dozen whites and caused the execution of twenty-one blacks, some of them burned at the stake over a slow fire. Yet the Africans made a significant contribution to America's early development through their labor, chiefly the sweaty toil of clearing swamps, grubbing out trees, and other menial tasks. A few of them were permitted to become artisans—carpenters, bricklayers, tanners—thus refuting the common prejudice that black people lacked the intelligence to perform skilled labor.

Clerics, Physicians, and Jurists

Most honored of the professions was the Christian ministry. In 1775 clergymen wielded less influence than in the early days of Massachusetts, when fanaticism had burned more fiercely. But they still occupied a position of high prestige.

Most physicians, on the other hand, were poorly trained and not highly esteemed. Not until 1765 was the first medical school established, although European centers attracted some students. Aspiring young doctors served for a while as apprentices to older practitioners, and were then turned loose on their "victims." Bleeding was a favorite and often fatal remedy; when the physician was not available, a barber was often summoned.

Plagues were a constant nightmare. Especially dreaded was smallpox (one of Europe's "gifts" to the New World), which afflicted one out of five persons, including the heavily pockmarked George Washington. A crude form of inoculation was introduced in 1721, despite the objections of many physicians and some of the clergy, who opposed tampering with the will of God. Powdered dried toad was a favorite prescription for smallpox. Diphtheria was also a deadly killer, especially of young people. One epidemic in the 1730s took the lives of thousands. This grim reminder of their mortality may have helped to prepare many colonists in their hearts and minds for the religious revival that was soon to sweep them up.

At first the law profession was not favorably regarded. In this pioneering society, which required much honest manual labor, the parties to a dispute often presented their own cases in court. Lawyers were commonly regarded as noisy windbags or troublemaking rogues; an early Connecticut law classed them with drunkards and brothel keepers. When future President John Adams was a young law student, the father of the woman whom he eventually married frowned upon him as a suitor.

By about 1750, seaboard society had passed the pioneering stage, and trained attorneys were generally recognized as useful. Able to defend colonial rights against the Crown on legal grounds, lawyers like the eloquent James Otis and the flaming Patrick Henry took the lead in the agitation that led to revolt. Other lawyer-orators played hardly less important roles in forging new constitutions and in serving in representative bodies.

Workaday America

Agriculture was the leading industry, involving about 90 percent of the people. Cheap land continued to attract farmers. An acre of virgin soil cost about what an American carpenter could earn in one day as wages, which were roughly three times those of his European counterpart. Tobacco continued to be the staple crop in Maryland and Virginia. The fertile Middle ("Bread") Colonies produced large quantities of grain, and by 1759 New York alone was exporting 80,000 barrels of flour a year. Seemingly the farmer had only to tickle the soil with a hoe and it would laugh with a harvest.

On doctors and medicine Benjamin Franklin's *Poor Richard's Almanack* offered some homely advice:

"God heals and the doctor takes the fee."

"He's the best physician that knows the worthlessness of most medicines."

"Don't go to the doctor with every distemper, nor to the lawyer with every quarrel, nor to the pot for every thirst."

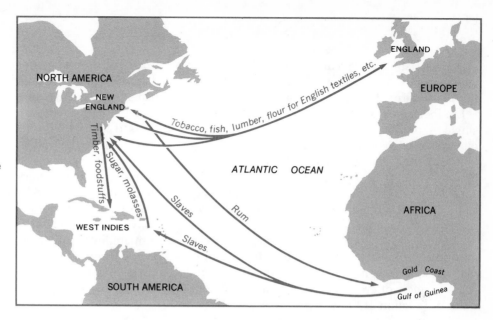

COLONIAL TRADE PATTERNS, c. 1770

Future President John Adams noted about this time that "the commerce of the West Indies is a part of the American system of commerce. They can neither do without us, nor we without them. The Creator has placed us upon the globe in such a situation that we have occasion for each other."

Fishing (including whaling), though ranking far below agriculture, was rewarding. Pursued in all the colonies, this harvesting of the sea was a major industry in New England, which exported smelly shiploads of dried cod to the Catholic countries of Europe. The fishing fleet also stimulated shipbuilding and served as a nursery for the seamen who manned the navy and merchant marine.

A bustling commerce, both coastwise and overseas, enriched all the colonies, especially the New England group, New York, and Pennsylvania. Commercial ventures and land speculation, in the absence of later get-rich-quick schemes, were the surest avenues to speedy wealth. Yankee seamen were famous in many climes not only as skilled mariners but as tight-fisted traders.* They provisioned the Caribbean sugar islands with food and forest products. They hauled Spanish and Portuguese gold, wine, and oranges to London, to be exchanged for industrial goods, which were then sold for a juicy profit in America.

The so-called triangular trade was infamously profitable, though small in relation to total colonial commerce. A skipper, for example, would leave a New England port with a cargo of rum and sail to the Gold Coast of Africa. Bartering the fiery liquor with African chiefs for captured African slaves, he would proceed to the West Indies with his screaming and suffocating cargo sardined below deck. There he would exchange the survivors for molasses, which he would then carry to New England, where it would be distilled into rum. He would then repeat the trip, making a handsome profit on each leg of the triangle.

Manufacturing in the colonies was of only secondary importance, although there was a surprising variety of small enterprises. As a rule, workmen could get ahead faster in soil-rich America by tilling the land. Huge quantities of "kill devil" rum were distilled in Rhode Island and Massachusetts; and even some of the "elect of the Lord" developed an overfondness for it. Handsome beaver hats were manufactured in quantity, despite British restrictions. Smoking iron forges, including Pennsylvania's Valley Forge, likewise dotted the land, and in fact were more numerous in 1775, though generally smaller, than those of England. In addition, household manufacturing, including spinning and weaving by womenfolk, added up to an impressive output. As in all pioneering countries, strong-backed laborers and

---

*Sea-going Yankees also found time for play, as shown in John Greenwood's painting of "Sea Captains Carousing in Surinam" in the color portfolio.

skilled craftsmen were scarce and highly prized. In early Virginia a carpenter who had committed a murder was freed because he was needed.

Lumbering was perhaps the most important single manufacturing activity. Countless cartloads of virgin timber were consumed by shipbuilders, at first chiefly in New England, and then elsewhere in the colonies. By 1770 about 400 vessels of assorted sizes were splashing down the ways each year, and about one-third of the British merchant marine was American-built.

Colonial naval stores—such as tar, pitch, rosin, and turpentine—were highly valued, for Britannia was anxious to gain and retain a mastery of the seas. London offered generous bounties to stimulate production of these items; otherwise Britain would have to turn to the uncertain and possibly hostile Baltic areas. Towering trees, ideal as masts for His Majesty's Navy, were marked with the King's broad arrow for future use. The luckless colonial who was caught cutting down this reserved timber was subject to a fine. Even though there were countless unreserved trees and the ones marked were being saved for the common defense, this shackle on free enterprise engendered considerable bitterness.

Americans held an important flank of a thriving, many-sided Atlantic economy by the dawn of the 18th Century. Yet strains appeared in this complex network as early as the 1730s. Fast-breeding Americans demanded more and more English products—yet the slow-growing English population early reached the saturation point for absorbing imports from America. How, then, could the colonists sell the goods to make the money to buy what they wanted in the mother country? The answer was obvious: by seeking foreign (non-English) markets.

By the eve of the revolution the bulk of Chesapeake tobacco was filling pipes in France and other continental countries, though it passed through the hands of English re-exporters, who took a slice of the profits. More important was the trade with the West Indies, especially the French islands. West Indian purchases of North American timber and foodstuffs provided the crucial cash for the colonists to continue to make their own purchases in England. In 1733, bowing to pressure from influential British West Indian planters, Parliament passed the Molasses Act, aimed at squelching North American trade with the *French* West Indies. If successful, this scheme would have struck a crippling blow to American international trade, and to the colonists' standard of living. American merchants responded by bribing and smuggling their way around the law. Thus was foreshadowed the impending imperial crisis, when headstrong Americans would revolt rather than submit to the dictates of a far-off Parliament, apparently bent on destroying their very livelihood.

Horsepower and Sailpower

All sprawling and sparsely populated pioneer communities are cursed with oppressive problems of transportation. America, with a scarcity of both money and manpower, was no exception.

Not until the 1700s were there roads connecting even the major cities, and these dirt thoroughfares were treacherously poor. A wayfarer could have rumbled along more rapidly over the Roman highways in the days of Julius Caesar, nearly 2,000 years earlier. It actually took twenty-nine days for the news of the Declaration of Independence—the story of the year—to reach Charleston from Philadelphia.

Roads were often clouds of dust in the summer and quagmires of mud in the winter. Stagecoach travelers braved such additional dangers as tree-strewn roads, rickety bridges, carriage overturns, and runaway horses. A man venturesome

Stagecoach Advertisement, 1781

Early Colonial Mail Carrier Trumpeting His Arrival

Religious Ferment and the Great Awakening

Religion still had a fiery grip on the people. Sunday customs generally were observed with rigidity, church attendance was faithful (though often compulsory), and long-winded sermons were absorbed with rapt attention. The Bible was almost universally read as the infallible word of God, supplemented by such religious books as Bunyan's *Pilgrim's Progress* and Baxter's *Call to the Unconverted*. The famed *New England Primer* pounded home such precepts as:

> Christ crucify'd,
> For Sinners dy'd.

Yet the life of the spirit was not the all-absorbing concern in 1775 that it had been in the heyday of the Puritan fathers. Existence in the 1600s had been harsh, and religion had taken on the stern character of its pioneer surroundings. But as men attained more ease and luxury, the appeal of a fire and brimstone religion became less attractive, and fanaticism faded. Decidedly more liberal doctrines were sharply challenging Calvinism. They proclaimed that human beings were not necessarily predestined to damnation, but might save themselves by repentance and good works. Many of the unorthodox worshipers even argued that a spiritual conversion was not necessary for church

enough to journey from Philadelphia to New York, for example, would not think it amiss to make his will and assemble his family for prayers before departing.

Where man-made roads were wretched, heavy reliance was placed on God-grooved waterways. Population tended to cluster along the banks of navigable rivers. There was also much coastwise traffic, and although it was slow and undependable, it was relatively cheap and pleasant.

Taverns sprang up along the main routes of travel, as well as in the cities. Their attractions customarily included such items as bowling alleys, pool tables, bars, and gambling equipment. Before a cheerful, roaring log fire all social classes would mingle, including the village loafers and drunks. The tavern was yet another cradle of democracy.

Gossips also gathered at the taverns, which were clearinghouses of information, misinformation, and rumor—frequently stimulated by alcoholic refreshment and impassioned political talk. A successful politician, like the wire-pulling Samuel Adams, was often a man who had a large alehouse acquaintance in places like Boston's Green Dragon Tavern. Taverns were important in crystallizing public opinion, and proved to be hotbeds of agitation as the Revolutionary movement gathered momentum.

An intercolonial postal system was established by the mid-1700s, although private couriers remained. Some mail was handled on credit. Service was slow and infrequent, and secrecy was problematical. Mail carriers, serving long routes, would sometimes pass the time by reading the letters entrusted to their care.

Franklin's *Poor Richard's Almanack* contained such thoughts on religion as:

"A good example is the best sermon."

"Many have quarreled about religion that never practiced it."

"Serving God is doing good to man, but praying is thought an easier service, and therefore more generally chosen."

"How many observe Christ's birthday; how few his precepts! O! 'tis easier to keep holidays than commandments."

membership, and some of the orthodox churches grudgingly made concessions to this new heresy.

In the 1730s and 1740s a reaction to this move away from hell-fire religion exploded into the Great Awakening—a rousing series of mass revivals that began in Europe and spread throughout America. Revivalist theologians (or "New Lights," as they were called) dwelt on man's evil and helpless nature. Revivalist ministers developed an electrifying new style of preaching, heaping abuse on sinners and scaring enormous audiences with emotional appeals. One preacher cackled hideously in the faces of hapless wrongdoers. Another, naked to the waist, leaped frantically about in the light of flickering torches.

The foremost Great Awakener in America was a tall, delicate, and intellectual Massachusetts theologian and preacher, Jonathan Edwards ("the Artist of Damnation"). He proclaimed with burning conviction the need for a complete conversion from sin to righteousness. Warming to his subject, he would paint in lurid detail the landscape of hell and the eternal torments of the damned. "Sinners in the Hands of an Angry God" was the title of one of his most famous sermons. He believed that hell was "paved with the skulls of unbaptized children."

George Whitefield, a former alehouse attendant, was a less intellectual but more emotional English pulpit-thumper. His magnificent voice could be heard by many thousands of enthralled listeners in an open field, and his eloquence caused the skeptical and thrifty Benjamin Franklin to empty his pockets into the collection plate. During these

George Whitefield (1714–1770). A great open-air revivalist, he was a leader in England of the Calvinistic Methodist Church. He made seven trips to America.

Jonathan Edwards preached hell-fire, notably in one famous sermon: "The God that holds you over the pit of hell, much as one holds a spider or some loathsome insect over the fire, abhors you, and is dreadfully provoked. His wrath toward you burns like fire; he looks upon you as worthy of nothing else but to be cast into the fire."

roaring revival meetings, countless sinners professed conversion, while hundreds of the "saved" groaned, shrieked, or rolled in the snow from religious excitement.

The Great Awakening touched off the first significant battle in America between fundamentalist evangelism and liberalism in religion. The more cautious "Old Light" clergy were deeply skeptical of the theatrical antics of the new revivalists. Congregationalists and Presbyterians split over this issue, and many of the believers in religious conversion went over to the Baptists and other more emotional sects. This denominational spin-off, which weakened the hold of the old-line clergy, also made for more democratic control.

Significantly, the Great Awakening was the first spontaneous mass movement of the American people. As such, it tended to break down sectional boundaries as well as denominational lines. It foreshadowed revolutionary new departures elsewhere, even in governmental control. The King would have done well to keep a more careful eye on his colonies.

Estimated Religious Census, 1775

Name	Number	Chief Locale
Congregationalists	575,000	New England
Anglicans	500,000	N.Y., South
Presbyterians	410,000	Frontier
German Churches (incl. Lutheran)	200,000	Penn.
Dutch Reformed	75,000	N.Y., N.J.
Quakers	40,000	Penn., N.J., Del.
Baptists	25,000	R.I., Penn., N.J., Del.
Roman Catholics	25,000	Md., Penn.
Methodists	5,000	Scattered
Jews	2,000	N.Y., R.I.

ESTIMATED TOTAL MEMBERSHIP 1,857,000
ESTIMATED TOTAL POPULATION 2,493,000
PERCENTAGE CHURCH MEMBERS 74%

ments, like Virginia fox hunting, were less frowned upon. So dismal was the reputation of the Anglican clergy in 17th-Century Virginia that the College of William and Mary was founded in 1693 to train a better class of clerics.

The influential Congregational Church, which had grown out of the Puritan Church, was formally established in all the New England colonies, except independent-minded Rhode Island. At first Massachusetts taxed all residents to support Congregationalism, but later relented and exempted members of other well-known denominations. Presbyterianism, though closely associated with Congregationalism, was never made official in any of the colonies.

Ministers of the gospel, turning from the Bible to this sinful world, increasingly grappled with burning political issues. As the early rumblings of

Dominant Denominations

Two "established" or tax-supported churches were conspicuous in 1775: the Anglican and the Congregational. A considerable segment of the population, surprisingly enough, did not worship in any church. And in those colonies where there was an "established" religion, only a minority of the people belonged to it.

The Church of England, whose members were commonly called Anglicans, became the official faith in Georgia, North and South Carolina, Virginia, Maryland, and a part of New York. Established also in England, it served in America as a major prop of kingly authority. British officials naturally made vigorous efforts to impose it on additional colonies, but they ran into a stone wall of opposition.

In America the Anglican Church fell distressingly short of its promise. Secure and self-satisfied, like the parent establishment in England, it clung to a faith that was less fierce and more worldly than the religion of Puritanical New England. Sermons were shorter; hell was less scorching; and amuse-

Established (Tax-Supported) Churches in the Colonies, 1775

Colonies	Churches	Year Disestablished
Mass. (incl. Me.)	Congregational	1833
Connecticut		1818
New Hampshire		1819
New York	Anglican (in N.Y. City and three neighboring counties)	1777
Maryland	Anglican	1777
Virginia		1786
North Carolina		1776
South Carolina		1778
Georgia		1777
Rhode Island	None	
New Jersey		
Delaware		
Pennsylvania		

Note the persistence of the Congregational establishment in New England.

revolution against the British Crown could be heard, sedition flowed freely from pulpits. Presbyterianism, Congregationalism, and Rebellion were triplets. Many of the leading Anglican clergymen, aware of what side their tax-provided bread was buttered on, naturally supported their King.

Anglicans in the New World were seriously handicapped by not having a resident bishop, whose presence would be convenient for the ordination of young ministers. American students of Anglican theology had to travel to England to be ordained. On the eve of the Revolution there was serious talk of creating an American bishopric, but the scheme was violently opposed by many non-Anglicans, who feared a tightening of the royal reins. This controversy poured holy oil on the smoldering fires of rebellion.

Religious toleration had indeed made enormous strides in America, at least when compared with halting steps abroad. Roman Catholics were still generally discriminated against, as in England, even in office holding. But there were fewer Catholics in America, and hence the anti-papist laws were less severe and less strictly enforced. In general, a man could worship—or not worship—as he pleased.

Schools and Colleges

A time-honored English ideal regarded education as a boon reserved for the aristocratic few, not for the unwashed many. Education should be for

---

IOIIOIIOIIOIIOIIOIIOIIOIIOIIOIIOIIOIIOIIOIIOIIOIIOIIOIIOI

John Adams, the future second President, once wrote to his wife:

"The education of our children is never out of my mind. Train them to virtue. Habituate them to industry, activity, and spirit. . . . For God's sake make your children *hardy, active*, and *industrious*; for strength, activity, and industry will be their only resource and dependence."

IOIIOIIOIIOIIOIIOIIOIIOIIOIIOIIOIIOIIOIIOIIOIIOIIOIIOIIOI

---

leadership, not citizenship, and primarily for the male sex. Only slowly and painfully did the colonials break the chains of these ancient restrictions.

Puritan New England, largely for religious reasons, was more zealously interested in education than any other section. Dominated by the Congregational Church, it stressed the need for Bible reading by the individual worshiper. The primary goal of the clergy was to make good Christians rather than good citizens. A more secular approach was evident late in the 18th Century, when some children were warned:

> He who ne'er learns his A.B.C.
> Forever will a blockhead be.
> But he who learns his letters fair
> Shall have a coach to take the air.

Education, principally for boys, flourished almost from the outset in New England. Population was compact and boasted an impressive number of graduates from the English universities, especially Cambridge, the intellectual center of England's Puritanism. New Englanders, at a relatively early date, established primary and secondary schools, which varied widely in the quality of instruction and in the length of time· that their doors remained open each year. Back-straining farm labor drained much of the youth's time and energy.

Fairly adequate primary and secondary schools were also hammering knowledge into the heads of reluctant "scholars" in the Middle Colonies and in the South. Some of these institutions were tax-supported; others were privately operated. The South, with its white and black population diffused over wide areas, was severely handicapped in attempting to establish an effective school system. Wealthy families leaned heavily on private tutors.

The general atmosphere in the colonial schools and colleges continued grim and gloomy. Most of the emphasis was placed on religion and on the classical languages, Latin and Greek. The stress was not on experiment and reason, but on doctrine and dogma. The age was one of orthodoxy, and independence of thinking was discouraged. Disci-

For purposes of convenience and economy, nine local colleges were planted during the colonial era. Student bodies were small, numbering about 200 boys at the most; and at one time a few lads as young as eleven were admitted to Harvard. Instruction was poor by present-day standards. The curriculum was still heavily loaded with theology and the "dead" languages, although by 1750 there was a distinct trend toward "live" languages and other modern subjects. A significant contribution was made by Benjamin Franklin, who had a large hand in launching what became the University of Pennsylvania, the first American college free from denominational control.

Harvard College About 1770. Engraving by Paul Revere, Boston silversmith of "midnight ride" fame. (Harvard University.)

pline was severe, with many a mettlesome lad being sadistically "birched" with a switch cut from a birch tree. Sometimes punishment was inflicted by an indentured-servant teacher, who could himself be whipped for his failures as a worker, and who therefore was not inclined to spare the rod.

College education was regarded—at least at first in New England—as more important than instruction in the ABCs. Churches would wither if a new crop of ministers was not trained to lead the spiritual flocks. Many well-to-do families, especially in the South, sent their boys abroad to English institutions.

Culture in the Backwoods

The dawn-to-dusk toil of pioneer life left little vitality or aptitude for artistic effort. Americans were too busy chopping down trees to sit around painting landscapes, especially when a hostile Indian might burst from a nearby bush. There was no strong esthetic tradition; many clergymen, in fact, regarded art as an invention of the Devil.

As the colonists gradually acquired some wealth and leisure, their surplus energy went into religious and political leadership, not art. The materialistic atmosphere was not favorable to artistic endeavor. One famous painter, John

Colonial Colleges

Name	Original Name (If Different)	Location	Opened or Founded	Denomination
1. Harvard		Cambridge, Mass.	1636	Congregational
2. William and Mary		Williamsburg, Va.	1693	Anglican
3. Yale		New Haven, Conn.	1701	Congregational
4. Princeton	College of New Jersey	Princeton, N.J.	1746	Presbyterian
5. Pennsylvania	The Academy	Philadelphia	1751	Nonsectarian
6. Columbia	King's College	New York City	1754	Anglican
7. Brown	Rhode Island College	Providence, R.I.	1764	Baptist
8. Rutgers	Queen's College	New Brunswick, N.J.	1766	Dutch Reformed
9. Dartmouth (begun as an Indian missionary school.)		Hanover, N.H.	1769	Congregational

Trumbull of Connecticut (1756–1843), was discouraged in his youth by his father with the chilling remark, "Connecticut is not Athens." Charles W. Peale (1741–1827), best known for his portraits of George Washington, ran a museum, stuffed birds, and practiced dentistry. Gifted Benjamin West (1738–1820) and precocious John S. Copley* (1738–1815) succeeded in their ambition to become famous painters, but they had to go to England to complete their training. Only there could they find subjects who had the leisure to sit for their portraits, and the money to pay handsomely for them. Copley was regarded as a Loyalist during the Revolutionary War, while West, a close friend of George III and official court painter, was buried in London's St. Paul's Cathedral.

Architecture was largely imported from the Old World, and modified to meet the peculiar climatic and religious conditions of the New World. Even the lowly log cabin was apparently borrowed from Sweden. The red-bricked Georgian style, so common in the pre-Revolutionary decades, was introduced about 1720, and is best exemplified by the beauty of now-restored Williamsburg, Virginia.

Colonial literature, like art, was generally undistinguished, and for much the same reasons. Among numerous handicaps, it was dominated by theology, although many sermons had literary quality. What little writing emerged is known only to specialists, with several noteworthy exceptions.

Of unusual interest is the precocious black poetess Phillis Wheatley (c. 1753–1784), a slave girl brought to Boston at age eight and never formally educated. Taken to England when twenty years of age, she published a book of verse, and subsequently wrote other polished poems that revealed the influence of Alexander Pope. She died when about thirty. Her verse compares favorably with the best of the poetry-poor colo-

*See color portfolio for painting by Copley.

nial period, but the remarkable fact is that, considering her grave handicaps, she could write any poetry at all.

Greatest of the "Great Awakeners" was Jonathan Edwards, who customarily arose at four o'clock to put in a fourteen-hour day. His religious writings were as numerous as they were hairsplitting, and established him as the finest theological mind ever produced in America. Some of his treatises, rivaling those of John Calvin in explaining Calvinism, were widely read in Presbyterian Scotland. His most famous work, *On the Freedom of the Will*, was perhaps the first American book of world importance. It was translated into many languages, including Arabic.

Many-sided Benjamin Franklin, often called "the first civilized American," also shone as a literary light. Although his autobiography is now a classic, he was best known to his contemporaries for *Poor Richard's Almanack*, which he edited from 1732 to 1758. This famous publication, containing many pithy sayings culled from the thinkers of the ages, emphasized such homespun virtues as thrift, industry, morality, and common sense. Examples are: "What maintains one vice would bring up two children"; "Plough deep while sluggards sleep"; "Honesty is the best policy"; and "Fish and visitors stink in three days." "Poor Richard" was well known in Europe and was more widely read in America than anything else, except the Bible. As a teacher of both old and young, Franklin's influence in shaping American character was incalculable. His down-to-earth approach to life did much to offset the influence of clergymen like Jonathan Edwards.

Science, rising above the shackles of theology and superstition, was making some progress, though lagging behind the Old World. A few botanists, mathematicians, and astronomers had won some repute, but Benjamin Franklin was perhaps the only first-rank scientist produced in the American colonies. His spectacular but dangerous experiments with electricity, including the kite-flying episode, won him numerous honors in Europe. But his mind had a practical turn, and among his numerous inventions were bifocal spectacles and the highly efficient Franklin stove. His lightning rod, not surprisingly, was condemned by the less liberal clergy as "presuming on God" by attempting to control the "artillery of the heavens."

Pioneer Presses

Stump-grubbing Americans were too poor to buy quantities of books and too busy to read them. One South Carolina merchant in 1744 advertised the arrival of a shipment of "printed books, Pictures, Maps, and Pickles." A few private libraries of fair size could be found, especially among the clergy. The Byrd family of Virginia enjoyed perhaps the largest collection in the colonies, consisting of about 4,000 volumes. Bustling Benjamin Franklin established in Philadelphia the first privately supported circulating library in America; and by 1776 there were about fifty public libraries and collections supported by subscription.

Hand-operated printing presses were active in running off pamphlets, leaflets, and journals. On the eve of the Revolution there were about forty colonial newspapers, chiefly weeklies which consisted of a single large sheet folded once.

Andrew Hamilton concluded his eloquent plea in the Zenger case with these words: "The question before the court and you, gentlemen of the jury, is not of small nor private concern. It is not the cause of a poor printer, nor of New York alone, which you are now trying. No! It may, in its consequence, affect every freeman that lives under a British government on the main[land] of America. It is the best cause. It is the cause of liberty."

Columns ran heavily to dull essays, frequently signed with such pseudonyms as Cicero, Philosophicus, and Pro Bono Publico (for the public good). The "news" often lagged many weeks behind the event, especially in the case of overseas happenings, in which the colonials were deeply interested. Newspapers proved to be a powerful agency for airing colonial grievances and building up opposition to British control.

A celebrated legal case, in 1734–1735, involved John Peter Zenger, a newspaper printer. Significantly, the case arose in New York, reflecting the tumultuous give-and-take of politics in the middle colonies, where so many different ethnic groups jostled against one another. Zenger's newspaper had assailed the corrupt royal governor. Charged with seditious libel, the accused was haled into court, where he was defended by a distinguished Philadelphia lawyer, Andrew Hamilton, then nearly eighty. Zenger argued that he had printed the truth, while the bewigged royal chief justice ruled that the mere fact of printing, irrespective of the truth, was enough to convict. Yet the jury, swayed by the eloquence of Hamilton, defied the red-robed judges and daringly returned a verdict of "not guilty." Cheers burst from the spectators.

The Zenger decision was epochal. It pointed the way to the kind of freedom of expression required by the diverse society that was colonial New York, and that all America was to become. Though contrary to existing law and not accepted by other royal judges, in time it helped set a precedent against judicial tyranny in libel suits. Newspaper editors had something of a burden lifted from their backs, even though complete freedom of the press was unknown during the pre-Revolutionary era.

The Great Game of Politics

American colonials may have been backward in natural or physical science, but they were making noteworthy contributions to political science.

The thirteen colonial governments presented a varied structure. By 1775, eight of the colonies had royal governors, who were appointed by the King. Three were under proprietors who themselves chose the governors—Maryland, Pennsylvania, and Delaware. And two—Connecticut and Rhode Island—elected their own governors under self-governing charters.

Practically every colony utilized a two-house legislative body. The upper house, or council, was normally appointed by the Crown in the royal colonies, and by the proprietor in the proprietary colonies. It was chosen by the voters in the self-governing colonies. The lower house, as the popular branch, was elected by the people—or rather by those persons who owned enough property to qualify as voters. In several of the colonies, the back-country elements were seriously underrepresented, and they hated the ruling colonial clique perhaps more than they did kingly authority. Legislatures, in which the people enjoyed direct representation, voted such taxes as they chose for the necessary expenses of colonial government. Self-taxation through representation was a precious privilege which Americans had come to cherish above most others.

Governors appointed by the King were generally able men, sometimes outstanding figures, and their households were an important outcropping of Europe's cultural frontier. But the appointees were sometimes incompetent or corrupt, and included broken-down politicians badly in need of jobs. The worst of the group was impoverished Lord Cornbury, first cousin of Queen Anne, who was made governor of New York and New Jersey in 1702. He proved to be a drunkard, a spendthrift, a grafter, an embezzler, a religious bigot, and a vain fool, especially when he appeared in public dressed like a woman. Even the best of the King's appointees had trouble with the colonial legislatures, basically because the royal governor embodied a bothersome transatlantic authority some 3,000 miles away.

But the colonial assemblies were by no means defenseless. Some of them employed the trick of withholding the governor's salary unless he

Junius, the pseudonym for a critic (or critics) of the British government from 1768 to 1772, published a pointed barb in criticizing one new appointee: "It was not Virginia that wanted a governor but a court favorite that wanted a salary."

yielded to their wishes. He was normally in need of money—otherwise he would not have come to this God-forsaken country—so the power of the purse usually forced him to terms. But one governor of North Carolina died with his salary eleven years in arrears.

The London government, in leaving the colonial governor to the tender mercies of the legislature, was guilty of poor administration. In the interests of simple efficiency the British authorities should have arranged to pay him from independent sources. As events turned out, control over the purse by the colonial legislatures led to prolonged bickering, which proved to be one of the persistent irritants that generated a spirit of revolt.*

Administration at the local level was also varied. County government remained the rule in the plantation South; town-meeting government predominated in New England; and a modification of the two developed in the Middle Colonies. In the town meeting, with its open discussion and open voting, direct democracy functioned at its best. In this unrivaled cradle of self-government, Americans learned to cherish their privileges and exercise their duties as citizens of the New World commonwealths.

Yet the ballot was by no means a birthright.

---

*Parliament finally arranged for separate payment of the governors through the Townshend taxes of 1767, but by then the colonials were in such an ugly mood over taxation that this innovation only added fresh fuel to the flames.

Heated Public Gathering. The spirit of the New England town meeting. (Library of Congress.)

By 1775 America was not yet a true democracy—socially, economically, or politically. But it was far more democratic than England and Europe. Colonial institutions were giving freer rein to the democratic ideals of tolerance, educational advantages, equality of economic opportunity, freedom of speech, freedom of the press, freedom of assembly, and representative government. And these democratic seeds, planted in rich soil, were to bring forth a lush harvest in later years.

Colonial Folkways

Everyday life in the colonies may now seem glamorous, especially as reflected in antique shops. But judged by modern standards, it was drab and tedious. For the mass of the people, the labor was heavy and constant—from daybreak to backbreak.

Food was plentiful, though the diet could be coarse and monotonous. Americans probably ate more bountifully, especially of meat, than any people in the Old World. Lazy or sickly was the man who could not manage to fill his stomach.

Basic comforts now taken for granted were lacking. Churches were not heated at all, except for charcoal foot-warmers which the womenfolk carried. During the frigid New England winters, the preaching of hell-fire may not have seemed altogether unattractive. Drafty homes were poorly heated, chiefly by inefficient fireplaces. There was no running water in the houses, no plumbing, and probably not a single bathtub in all colonial America. Flickering lights were inadequate, for illumination was provided by candles and whale-oil lamps. Garbage disposal was primitive. Long-snouted hogs customarily ranged the streets to consume refuse, while buzzards, protected by law, flapped greedily over tidbits of waste.

Amusement was eagerly pursued where time and custom permitted. The militia assembled periodically for "musters," which consisted of several days of drilling, liberally interspersed with merrymaking and eyeing the girls. On the frontier,

Religious or property qualifications for voting, with even stiffer qualifications for office holding, existed in all the colonies in 1775. The privileged upper classes, fearful of democratic excesses, were unwilling to grant the ballot to every "biped of the forest." Perhaps half of the adult white males were thus disfranchised. But because of the ease of acquiring land and thus satisfying property requirements, the right to vote was not beyond the reach of most industrious and enterprising colonials.

pleasure was often combined with work at house-raisings, quilting bees, husking bees, and apple parings. Funerals and weddings everywhere afforded opportunities for social gatherings, which customarily involved the swilling of much strong liquor.

Winter sports were common in the North, while in the South card playing, horse racing, cock-fighting, and fox hunting were favorite pastimes. George Washington, not surprisingly, was a superb rider. In the non-Puritanical South, dancing was the rage—jigs, square dances, the Virginia reel—and the agile Washington could swing his fair partner with the best of them.

Other diversions beckoned. Lotteries were universally approved, even by the clergy, and were used to raise money for churches and colleges, including Harvard. Stage plays became popular in the South, but were disapproved in the Quaker and Puritan colonies, and in some places were even forbidden by law. Many New England clergymen regarded play-acting as time-consuming and immoral; they preferred religious lectures, from which their flocks derived much spiritual satisfaction.

Holidays were everywhere celebrated, but Christmas was frowned upon in New England as an offensive reminder of "Popery." "Yuletide is fooltide" was a common Puritan sneer. Thanksgiving Day came to be a truly American festival, for it combined thanks to God with an opportunity for jollification, gorging, and guzzling.

Early lumbering. An 18th Century sawmill in colonial New York. (The William L. Clements Library.)

England's American colonists in 1775 were a remarkable people: restless, energetic, ambitious, resourceful, ingenious, and independent-minded. With every passing year they were less willing to bow their necks to the yoke of overseas authority. They were like a fast-growing and well-muscled farm boy who is coming of age, and who expects to be treated as an adult and not as a lackey. With a boundless continent before them, with impressive pioneer achievements behind them, and with an astonishing fertility within them, they had caught a vision of their destiny and were preparing to grasp it. Woe unto him who should try to thwart them!

VARYING VIEWPOINTS

It has always been difficult to view the history of the 18th Century in any way other than as a prelude to the Revolution of 1776. Historians of the "imperial school" used to emphasize the transatlantic economic motifs of the period as an overture to revolution. But as in so many other areas of American history, recent scholars have increasingly stressed social history. They now want to know the "preconditions" of American society in the mid-18th Century so as to answer the key question: Just how "revolutionary" was the Revolution? Thus issues like social structure, extent of the suffrage, and distribution of wealth have in recent years taken on increased significance.

SELECT READINGS

Social history is painted with broad strokes in J. Henretta, *The Evolution of American Society, 1700–1815* (1973), in D. Boorstin, *The Americans: The Colonial Experience* (1958), and in L. B. Wright, *The Cultural Life of the American Colonies, 1607–1763* (1957). Richard Hofstadter takes a suggestive snapshot view in *America at 1750* (1971). Indispensable as well as entertaining is Benjamin Franklin's classic *Autobiography;* "Poor Richard's" best biographer is still C. Van Doren, *Benjamin Franklin* (1938). Population trends are detailed in E. B. Greene and V. Harrington, *American Population before the Federal Census of 1790* (1932), and in R. V. Wells, *The Population of the British Colonies in America before 1776* (1975). Black "immigrants" are studied in P. Curtin, *The African Slave Trade: A Census* (1969), indentured servants, in A. E. Smith, *Colonists in Bondage* (1947), and colonial immigration in general, in the early portions of Maldwyn Jones, *American Immigration* (1960). J. T. Main astutely analyzes *The Social Structure of Revolutionary America, 1763–1788* (1965). Access to the ballot is scrutinized in C. Williamson, *American Suffrage: From Property to Democracy, 1760–1860* (1961). C. Bridenbaugh looks closely at social history in *Myths and Realities* (1952), *Cities in the Wilderness* (1938), and *Cities in Revolt* (1955). See the same author's *Fat Mutton and Liberty of Conscience* (1976). The toiling classes are probed in R. B. Morris, *Government and Labor in Early America* (1946), and in G. W. Mullin, *Flight and Rebellion: Slave Resistance in Eighteenth-Century Virginia* (1972). Large-scale economic patterns are traced in R. Davis, *Rise of the Atlantic Economies* (1973), and in Stuart Bruchey, *The Roots of American Economic Growth, 1607–1861* (1965). Transatlantic cultural relations are treated in Michael Kraus, *The Atlantic Civilization: Eighteenth-Century Origins* (1949). Religious revivalism is chronicled in E. S. Gaustad, *The Great Awakening in New England* (1957), and the broad social implications of the Awakening are analyzed in R. L. Bushman, *From Puritan to Yankee: Character and Social Order in Connecticut, 1690–1765* (1967). Consult also J. M. Bumsted and J. E. Van de Wetering, *What Must I Do To Be Saved?*

(1976). Cultural history is imaginatively presented in H. M. Jones, *O Strange New World: American Culture in the Formative Years* (1964). Comprehensive is Henry May, *The Enlightenment in America* (1976). The sometimes heroic dedication to education is portrayed by L. Cremin, *American Education: The Colonial Experience, 1607–1783* (1970), and the general social implications of the early educational system are studied in J. Axtell, *School upon a Hill* (1974). Colonial politics are interpreted in a most suggestive way in B. Bailyn, *The Origins of American Politics* (1965). More fine-grained local studies are R. E. and B. K. Brown, *Virginia 1705–1786: Democracy or Aristocracy?* (1964), P. Bonomi, *A Factious People: Politics and Society in Colonial New York* (1971), James T. Lemon, *The Best Poor Man's Country* (1972), which deals with Pennsylvania, and Daniel Blake Smith, *Inside the Great House: Planter Family Life in Eighteenth-Century Chesapeake Society* (1980). Broader is Richard B. Davis, *Intellectual Life in the Colonial South, 1585–1763* (3 vols., 1978).

5

The Road to Revolution

The Revolution was effected before the war commenced. The Revolution was in the minds and hearts of the people.

JOHN ADAMS, 1818

The Deep Roots of Revolution

In a broad sense, the American Revolution was not the same thing as the American War of Independence. The war itself lasted only eight years. But the revolution lasted over a century and a half, and began when the first permanent English settlers set foot on the new continent. Insurrection of thought usually precedes insurrection of deed. And over the years such a ferment occurred in the thinking of the colonists that the revolution was partially completed in their minds before the musket balls began to fly. America was a revolutionary force from the day of its discovery.

England's colonies were settled largely by emigrants who were discontented or rebellious in spirit—by people who had failed to adjust themselves to their harsh lot in the Old World. Most of

NOVA BRITANNIA.

OFFERING MOST

Excellent fruites by Planting in
VIRGINIA.

Exciting all such as be well affected
to further the same.

LONDON
Printed for SAMVEL MACHAM, and are to be sold at
his Shop in Pauls Church-yard, at the
Signe of the Bul-head.
1609.

Advertisement of a Voyage
to America, 1609

starving men fought over the bodies of vermin. As a sailor's song ran:

> We ate the mice, we ate the rats,
> And through the hold we ran like cats.

Such a perilous crossing left many emotional scars. Survivors who staggered ashore on the Promised Land were, as a rule, isolated spiritually from the faraway Old World. They were more than ever aware that the long arm of the London government, enfeebled by 3,000 miles of ocean, could not reach them nearly so effectively as at home. Distance weakens authority; great distance weakens authority greatly.

America's lonely wilderness likewise stimulated ideas of independence. Back in England some villagers had lived near graveyards that contained the bones of their ancestors for a thousand years past. Born into such conservative surroundings, the poor plowman did not question the social rut in which he found himself. But in the New World he was not held down by the scowl of his overlords.

In America all was strange, crude, different. Dense forests and the rugged pioneering conditions changed patterns of living, and consequently habits of thought. Those wretched settlers perished who could not adapt themselves to their raw surroundings, and hundreds of the early Virginia colonists paid the supreme penalty. Before long, men were eating Indian corn, wearing Indian moccasins and buckskin, and in extreme instances on the frontier uttering the war whoop as they scalped their fallen red foe. Hacking a home out of the wildwood with an ax developed strength, self-confidence, individualism, and a spirit of independence.

As the Americans matured, they acquired privileges of self-government enjoyed by no other colonial peoples. They set up thirteen parliaments of their own, and aped the parliamentary methods of the Mother Country. Ultimately they came to regard their own legislative bodies as more or less on a footing with the great Mother of Parliaments in London. One governor of Rhode Island

them had not been able to get along, whether socially, politically, economically, or religiously. Some of them were tired of taking off their hats and standing bareheaded in the presence of their "betters." Others wanted a larger share in government, or a richer portion of this world's goods, or an opportunity to worship God in their own peculiar way.

The nightmare of crossing the Atlantic normally lasted about six to eight weeks, often much longer. Ships were frequently turned into "floating coffins" by food shortages or epidemics of disease; in one extreme case 350 of 400 passengers and crew perished. Cannibalism was not unknown, and would wear no wig unless it had been made in England and was exactly like that worn by the Speaker of the British House of Commons.

The Mercantile Theory

Britain's empire was acquired in a "fit of absent-mindedness," as the old saying goes, and there is much truth in it. Not one of the original thirteen colonies, except Georgia, was formally planted by the British government. The actual founding was done haphazardly by trading companies, religious groups, land speculators, and others. Authorities in London did not even dream that a new nation was being born. And the colonials themselves, busy chopping down trees, were no less short-visioned.

Machinery in Britain for controlling the colonies was relatively simple. As it had evolved by 1696, the principal agency was the Board of Trade, joined in an advisory capacity by certain other prominent officials. With the passage of time, interest in the board flagged, and membership on it became something of a joke. Yet the recommendations of the board regarding the colonies were often made into law, either by act of Parliament or in regulations adopted by the Privy Council (the King's advisers).

The theory that shaped and justified English exploitation of the American colonies was mercantilism. According to this doctrine the colonies existed for the benefit of the Mother Country;

Adam Smith, the Scottish "Father of Modern Economics," frontally attacked mercantilism in 1776: "To prohibit a great people, however, from making all that they can of every part of their own produce, or from employing their stock and industry in the way that they judge most advantageous to themselves, is a manifest violation of the most sacred rights of mankind."

---

they should add to its wealth, prosperity, and self-sufficiency. Otherwise why go to all the trouble and expense of governing and protecting them? The settlers were regarded more or less as tenants. They were expected to produce tobacco and other products needed in England, and not to bother their heads with dangerous experiments in agriculture or self-government.

Specifically, how were the American colonies to benefit the Mother Country? First of all, they were to insure Britain's naval supremacy by furnishing ships, ships' stores, seamen, and trade. In addition, they were to provide a profitable consumer's market for the English manufacturers at home. Finally, they were to keep gold and silver money within the empire by growing products, such as sugar, that otherwise would have to be bought from foreigners. The ideal of "Buy British" would thus be promoted in a manner that foreshadowed later protective tariffs.

Mercantilist Trammels on Trade

Numerous measures were passed by Parliament to enforce the mercantile system. Most famous were the Navigation Laws. The first of these, enacted in 1650, was aimed at rival Dutch shippers who were elbowing their way into the American carrying trade. These Navigation Laws, as finally perfected, restricted commerce to and from the colonies to English vessels. Such regulation not only kept money within the empire but bolstered the British—and colonial—merchant marine, which in turn was an indispensable auxiliary to the Royal Navy.

An alert Parliament from time to time enacted additional laws favorable to the Motherland. European goods consigned to America had to be landed first in England, where customs duties could be collected and where the British middleman would get his cut of the profit. Still other curbs required certain "enumerated" products, notably tobacco, to be shipped to England and not to a foreign market, though prices in Europe might be higher.

IO

> As the *Boston Gazette* declared in 1765, "A colonist cannot make a button, a horseshoe, nor a hobnail, but some snooty ironmonger or respectable buttonmaker of Britain shall bawl and squall that his honor's worship is most egregiously maltreated, injured, cheated, and robbed by the rascally American republicans."

IOIOIOIOIOIOIOIOIOIOIOIOIOIOIOIOIOIOIOIOIOIOIOIO

In the interests of the empire, settlers were even restricted in what they might produce at home. They were forbidden to manufacture for export certain products, such as woolen cloth and beaver hats, because the colonies were supposed to complement and not compete with English industry.

Americans also felt the pinch in the area of currency. No banks existed in the colonies, and the money problem on the eve of the Revolution was acute. Industrious colonials were now busily buying more goods from England than they were selling to her, so the difference had to be made up in hard cash. Every year gold and silver money, much of it in quaint Spanish coins from the West Indies, was drained out of the colonies. The colonials simply did not have enough left for the convenience of everyday purchases. Barter became necessary, and even butter, nails, pitch, and feathers were used for purposes of exchange.

Currency problems came to a boil when dire need finally forced many of the colonies to issue paper money, which unfortunately depreciated. British merchants and creditors, understandably worried, squawked so loudly that Parliament was forced to act. It restrained the colonial legislatures from printing paper currency and from passing lax bankruptcy laws—practices that might result in defrauding British merchants. The Americans, who felt that their welfare was again being sacrificed, reacted angrily. Another burning grievance was thus heaped upon the pile of combustibles already smoldering.

London officialdom naturally kept a watchful

The Female Combatants. Britain is symbolized as a lady of fashion, and her rebellious daughter as an Indian princess. (Lewis Walpole Library, Farmington.)

eye on the legislation passed by the colonial assemblies. If such laws conflicted with British regulations or policy, they were declared null and void by the Privy Council—just as the Supreme Court of the United States today declares some laws unconstitutional.

This "royal veto" was necessary for efficient government, but it was used rather sparingly—469 times in connection with 8,563 laws. The colonies naturally took a narrower view. Some of them were aggrieved when, in the interests of the Mother Country, they were forbidden to make reforms that they deemed desirable, such as curbing the degrading trade in African slaves.

The Merits of Mercantilism

Red-blooded Americans have long regarded the British mercantile system as thoroughly selfish

John Hancock (1736–1793). A merchant prince, he was the wealthiest New Englander on the Patriot side during the Revolution. Attaining popularity through the lavish expenditure of money, he served as president of the Continental Congress when independence was declared in 1776. His signature is the first, largest, and boldest on the famous Declaration, penned, it was said, so that George III could read Hancock's name without his glasses.

and deliberately oppressive, if not downright malicious. The truth is that until 1763 the Navigation Laws imposed no intolerable burden, partly because they were laxly enforced. Ingenious colonial merchants early learned to disregard or evade restrictions that they found vexatious. In fact, some of the early American fortunes were amassed by wholesale smuggling. Wealthy and vain John Hancock of Massachusetts came to be known as the "King of Smugglers," though his illicit activity was greatly exaggerated.

Americans, in addition, were fortunate enough to reap direct benefits from the mercantile system. London paid liberal bounties or price supports to those colonials who produced ships' parts and ships' stores, even though English competitors complained heatedly. When independence came, the bounties dried up and many of these American producers were forced to the wall.

Virginia tobacco planters, in particular, enjoyed valuable privileges. While forbidden to ship their pungent yellow leaf to any place other than England, they were guaranteed a monopoly of the British market. Tobacco growing was also outlawed in England and Ireland, although the plant had already been raised in England with some success.

American colonials additionally fared well in other fields. They enjoyed the undiluted rights of Englishmen, as well as unusual opportunities for self-government. They were not compelled to tax themselves to support a professional army and navy for protection against the French, Dutch, Spaniards, Indians, and pirates. Although the colonists went to some little expense in "training" militiamen, they enjoyed the shield of a strong army of British Redcoats and the mightiest navy in the world—without a penny of cost. After independence, the Americans would themselves be required to pay the costs of maintaining a tiny army and navy, both of which afforded inadequate protection.

In manufacturing and trade the New World settlers did not fare badly. They were denied the privilege of fabricating specified articles for export, notably fur hats, but this regulation worked no serious hardships, because it was laxly enforced and because other pursuits were usually more profitable. Americans were forced to deal with the British middleman, but they would have done so anyhow, owing to a common language, standard pounds and shillings, liberal credit arrangements, and familiar business methods.

"Prosperity trickles down" is a common saying; and in truth the Americans enjoyed a generous share of Britain's profits under the time-honored mercantile system. The average American was probably better off economically than the average Englishman at home. If the colonies existed for the benefit of the Mother Country, it was hardly less true that the Mother Country existed for the benefit of the colonies. The well-meaning officials in London were working for the welfare of the empire as a whole, and they gave overall unity to its policies. A wise man does not disembowel or starve the goose that lays the golden eggs. Mistakes were made by the British authorities, but they were not, until revolt was precipitated, the mistakes of malice.

Mercantilism had sufficient merit to be widely adopted and long perpetuated. All other colonial nations of that age, including Spain and France, embraced mercantilistic principles completely and enforced them ironhandedly. Mercantilism has endured to the present century, even in the United States. Interested groups of Americans seek to insure prosperity for manufacturers and wage earners by protective tariffs, and to bolster the national defense by subsidies to shipbuilders. American Navigation Laws—shades of the 17th Century!—are still designed to prevent foreign shippers from encroaching on coastwise trade, even that between Hawaii and the mainland.

The Menace of Mercantilism

Even when painted in its rosiest colors, the mercantile system burdened the colonials with annoying liabilities. Economic initiative was stifled because Americans were not at complete liberty to buy, sell, ship, or manufacture under conditions that they found most profitable. Southern colonies, as "pets," were generally favored over the Northern ones, chiefly because they grew non-English products like tobacco, sugar, and rice. Revolution was one seed that sprouted vigorously from the stony soil of New England, for the proud sons of the Puritans resented being treated like unwanted relatives.

One-crop Virginians, despite London's preference for Southern colonies, also nursed rankling grievances. Forced to sell their tobacco in England, they were at the mercy of British merchants, who often gouged them. Many of the fashionable Virginia planters were plunged into

---

English statesman Edmund Burke warned in 1775: "Young man, there is America—which at this day serves for little more than to amuse you with stories of savage men and uncouth manners; yet shall, before you taste of death, show itself equal to the whole of that commerce which now attracts the envy of the world."

---

debt by the falling price of tobacco, and were forced to buy their necessities in England by mortgaging future crops. Some debts, becoming hereditary, were bequeathed by father to son.

Impoverished Virginia vied for leadership with restless Massachusetts in agitating for revolt against England; and unfriendly critics sneered that her cry, "Liberty or Death," might better have been "Liberty or Debt." While this charge was unfair in many cases, countless Virginians welcomed the opportunity to end their economic bondage to the Mother Country.

Finally—and of supreme importance—mercantilism was debasing to the Americans. The colonies, many of them felt, were being used or milked, as cows are milked. They were to be kept in a state of perpetual economic adolescence, and never allowed to come of age. As Benjamin Franklin wrote in 1775:

We have an old mother that peevish is grown;
She snubs us like children that scarce walk alone;
She forgets we're grown up and have sense of our own.

Revolution broke out, as Theodore Roosevelt later remarked, because England failed to recognize an emerging nation when she saw one.

The Stamp Tax Uproar

The costly Seven Years' War, which ended in 1763, marked a new relationship between Britain and her transatlantic colonies. A revolution in British colonial policy precipitated the American Revolution.

Victory-flushed Britain emerged from the conflict possessing one of the biggest empires in the world—and also, less happily, the biggest debt. It amounted to £140 million, about half of which had been incurred in defending the American colonies. British officials wisely had no intention of asking the colonials to help pay off this crushing burden. But London felt that the Americans should be asked to defray one-third the cost of maintaining a garrison of some 10,000 Redcoats, presumably for their own protection.

Prime Minister George Grenville, an honest and able financier not noted for tact, moved vigorously. Dedicated to efficiency, he aroused the resentment of the colonials in 1763 by ordering the British navy to enforce the Navigation Laws. He also secured from Parliament the so-called Sugar Act of 1764, the first law ever passed by that body for raising revenue in the colonies for the Crown. Among various provisions, it increased the duty on foreign sugar imported from the West Indies. After bitter protests from the colonials, the duties were lowered substantially, and the agitation died down. But resentment was kept burning by the Quartering Act of 1765. It required certain colonies to provide food and quarters for British troops.

Then in the same year, 1765, Grenville proposed the most ominous measure of all: a stamp tax, to raise revenues to support the new military force. The Stamp Act required the use of stamped paper or the affixing of stamps, certifying payment of tax. Involved were about fifty trade items and certain types of commercial and legal documents, including playing cards, pamphlets, newspapers, diplomas, bills of lading, and marriage licenses.

Grenville regarded all these measures as reasonable and just. He was simply asking the Americans to pay their fair share for colonial defense, through taxes that were already familiar in England. In fact, Englishmen for two generations

A Royal Stamp. The motto in French is translated "Shame to him who evil thinks."

A Parody of the "Fatal Stamp"

had endured a stamp tax far heavier than that passed for the colonies.

Yet the Americans were angrily aroused at what they regarded as Grenville's fiscal aggression. The new laws did pinch their pocketbooks. Earlier parliamentary imposts on the colonies had been mostly indirect taxes, designed primarily to regulate trade. They had been more or less painlessly levied at the customs house, then passed on to consumers in higher prices. But the stamp tax was a direct tax, offensively obvious to the consumer and clearly aimed to raise revenue.

The colonists sensed that more than their livelihood was threatened. Grenville's legal looting, they grumbled, menaced the local liberties they had come to assume as a matter of right. Thus some colonial assemblies defiantly refused to comply with the Quartering Act or voted only a fraction of the supplies that it called for. Angry throats raised the cry, "No taxation without representation." There was irony in the slogan, because the seaports and tidewater towns that were most wrathful against Grenville had long denied full representation to their own "back-country" pioneers. But now the agitated colonials took the high ground of principle. They scoffed at Grenville's theory of "virtual representation," which claimed that every member of Parliament represented all British subjects, even those in Boston or in Charleston who had never voted for a member of the London Parliament.

Worse still, Grenville's noxious legislation seemed to menace the basic rights of the colonists as Englishmen. Both the Sugar Act and the Stamp Act provided for trying offenders in the hated admiralty courts, where juries were not allowed. The burden of proof was on the defendant, who was assumed to be guilty unless he could prove himself innocent. Trial by jury and the doctrine of "innocent until proved guilty" were ancient privileges that Englishmen everywhere, including Americans, held most dear. And why was a British army needed at all in the colonies, now that the French were vanquished and Pontiac's red men crushed? Could its real purpose be to whip rebellious colonials themselves into line? Many Americans began to sniff the strong scent of a conspiracy to strip them of all their historic liberties. They lashed back violently, and the Stamp Act soon became a magnet that drew their most ferocious fire.

Many colonials did not really want direct representation in Parliament. If they had obtained it, any gouty member of the House of Commons could have proposed an oppressive tax bill for the colonies, and the American representatives could have been heavily outvoted. In these circumstances the colonists preferred taxation without representation to taxation with representation.

What the colonials really wanted was a return to the "good old days" before the French and Indian War. Then the Navigation Laws had been only laxly enforced, and the Americans had suffered no taxation, except by their own elected assemblies. Betraying a quite human preference for benefits without burdens, the colonists were

Nicholas Cresswell, a Tory, observed in 1774: "The New Englanders by their canting, whining, insinuating tricks have persuaded the rest of the Colonies that the Government is going to make absolute slaves of them."

The famous circular letter from the Massachusetts House of Representatives (1768) stated: ". . . considering the utter impracticability of their ever being fully and equally represented in Parliament, and the great expense that must unavoidably attend even a partial representation there, this House think that a taxation of their constituents, even without their consent, grievous as it is, would be preferable to any representation that could be admitted for them there."

unwilling to shoulder the new responsibilities that went with being part of a great empire.

Parliament Forced to Repeal the Stamp Act

Colonial outcries against the hated stamp tax took various forms. The most conspicuous assemblage was the Stamp Act Congress of 1765, which brought together in New York City twenty-seven distinguished delegates from nine colonies. After dignified debate, the members drew up a statement of their rights and grievances, and besought the King and Parliament to repeal the odious legislation.

The Stamp Act Congress, which was largely ignored in England, made little splash at the time in America. But it did do something to break down sectional suspicions, for it brought together around the same table leading men from the different and rival colonies. It was one more halting but significant step toward intercolonial unity.

More effective than the Congress was the widespread adoption of non-importation agreements against British goods. Woolen garments of homespun became fashionable, and the eating of lamb chops was discouraged lest wool-bearing sheep not be allowed to mature. Non-importation agreements were in fact a promising stride toward

Hanging John Huske in Effigy. A Paul Revere engraving showing the fate in America of an alleged supporter of the Stamp Act. (American Antiquarian Society.)

turers suffered from the colonial non-importation agreements, and hundreds of laborers were thrown out of work. Loud demands converged on Parliament for repeal of the Stamp Act. But many of the members could not understand why 7.5 million Britons had to pay heavy taxes to protect the colonies, while some 2 million colonials refused to pay for only one-third of the cost of their own defense.

After a stormy debate, and as a matter of expediency and not of right, Parliament in 1766 reluctantly repealed the Stamp Act. At the same time, and by an overwhelming vote, it saved face by passing the Declaratory Act. This futile measure proclaimed that Parliament had the right "to bind" the colonies "in all cases whatsoever." A bare assertion of this right was but a feeble victory for parental authority, for the unruly colonials had proved that the London government could be forced to yield to boycotts and mob action.

America forthwith burst into an uproar of rejoicing. Grateful residents of New York erected a leaden statue to King George III—a tribute which was later melted into thousands of bullets to be fired at his own troops.

union; they spontaneously united the American people for the first time in common action.

Violence also attended colonial protests. Groups of ardent spirits, known as Sons of Liberty and backed by Daughters of Liberty, took the law into their own hands. Crying "Liberty, Property, and No Stamps," they enforced the non-importation agreements against violators, often with a generous coat of tar and feathers. Houses of unpopular officials were ransacked, their money was stolen, and stamp agents were hanged on Liberty Poles, albeit in effigy.

Shaken by violence, the machinery for collecting the tax broke down. On that dismal day in 1765 when the new act was to go into effect, the stamp agents had all been forced to resign, and there was no one to sell the stamps. While flags flapped at half-mast, the law was openly and flagrantly defied—or rather, nullified.

England was hard hit. Merchants and manufac-

Boycott Handbill

WILLIAM JACKSON,

an *IMPORTER*; at the

BRAZEN HEAD,

North Side of the TOWN-HOUSE,

and *Opposite the Town-Pump, in*

Corn-hill, BOSTON.

It is desired that the Sons and DAUGHTERS of *LIBERTY,* would not buy any one thing of him, for in so doing they will bring Disgrace upon *themselves,* and their *Posterity,* for *ever* and *ever,* AMEN.

The Townshend Tea Tax and the Boston "Massacre"

Control of the British ministry was now seized by the gifted but erratic "Champagne Charley" Townshend, who could deliver brilliant speeches in Parliament while drunk. Rashly promising to pluck feathers from the colonial goose with a minimum of squawking, he persuaded Parliament in 1767 to pass the Townshend Acts. The most important of these new regulations was a light import duty on glass, white lead, paper, and tea. Townshend deferred to the sensitive colonials by making this tax, unlike the Stamp Act, an indirect customs duty payable at American ports.

Flushed with their recent victory over the stamp tax, the colonists were in a rebellious mood. The impost on tea was especially irksome, for an estimated 1 million persons drank "the cup that cheers" twice a day, and even tipplers used it when alcohol was not available.

The new Townshend revenues, worse yet, would be used to pay the salaries of the royal governors and judges in America. From the standpoint of efficient administration by London, this was a reform long overdue. But the ultra-suspicious Americans, who had beaten the royal governors into line by controlling the purse, regarded Townshend's tax as another attempt to enchain them. Their worst fears took on greater reality when the London government, after passing the Townshend taxes, suspended the legislature of New York for failure to comply with the Quartering Act in 1767.

Non-importation agreements, previously potent, were quickly revived against the Townshend Acts. But they proved less effective than those devised against the Stamp Act. The colonials, again enjoying prosperity, took the new tax less seriously than might have been expected, largely because it was light and indirect. They found, moreover, that they could secure smuggled tea at a cheap price, and consequently smugglers increased their activities, especially in Massachusetts.

Redcoats Landing in Boston

British officials, faced with a breakdown of law and order, landed two regiments of troops in Boston in 1768. Many of the soldiers, as might be expected, were drunken and profane characters. Liberty-loving colonials, resenting the presence of the red-coated "ruffians," taunted the "bloody backs" unmercifully.

A clash was inevitable. On the evening of March 5, 1770, a crowd of some sixty townspeople set upon a squad of about ten "bloody backs," one of whom was hit by a club and another of whom was knocked down. Acting apparently without orders but under extreme provocation, the troops opened fire and killed or wounded eleven "innocent" citizens. One of the first to die was Crispus Attucks, described by contemporaries as a powerfully built runaway "mulatto" and as a leader of the mob. Both sides were in some degree to blame, and in the subsequent trial only two of the soldiers could be found guilty of manslaughter. They were released after being branded on the hand.

The so-called Boston Massacre—"the Boston Brawl" rather than a "massacre"—further inflamed the colonials against the British, especially after the conviction spread that the Americans had been wholly unoffending. Paul Revere, the artist-horseman, wrote:

Unhappy Boston! see thy sons deplore
Thy hallowed walks besmear'd with guiltless gore.

Massacre Day was observed in Boston as a patriotic holiday until 1776, when the more glorious Fourth of July eclipsed it.

The Seditious Committees of Correspondence

By 1770 King George III, then only thirty-two years old, was strenuously attempting to restore the declining power of the British monarchy. He was a good man in his private morals, but he proved to be a bad ruler. Earnest, industrious, stubborn, lustful for power, and plagued with periodic fits of supposed madness, he surrounded himself with cooperative "yes men," notably his corpulent Prime Minister, Lord North.

The ill-timed Townshend Acts had failed to produce revenue, though producing near rebellion. Net proceeds from the tax in one year were £295, and during that time the annual military costs to Britain in the colonies had mounted to £170,000. Non-importation agreements, though feebly enforced, were pinching British manufacturers. The government of Lord North, bowing to various pressures, finally persuaded Parliament to repeal the Townshend revenue duties. But the three-pence tax on tea was retained to keep alive the principle of parliamentary taxation.

Flames of discontent in America continued to be fanned by numerous incidents, including the redoubled efforts of the British officials to enforce the Navigation Laws. Resistance was further whipped up by a master propagandist

and engineer of rebellion, Samuel Adams of Boston, a cousin of John Adams. Unimpressive in appearance (his hands trembled), he had failed miserably in private life. His friends had to buy him a presentable suit of clothes when he left Massachusetts on intercolonial business. But zealous, tenacious, and courageous, he was ultrasensitive to infractions of colonial rights. Cherishing a deep faith in the common man, he appealed effectively to what was called his "trained mob." Skillful also as a pamphleteer, he soon became known as the "Penman of the Revolution."

Samuel Adams's signal contribution was to organize in Massachusetts the local committees of correspondence. After he had formed the first one in Boston during 1772, some eighty towns in the colony speedily set up similar organizations. Their chief function was to spread propaganda and information by interchanging letters, and thus keep alive opposition to British policy. One critic referred to the committees as "the foulest, subtlest, and most venomous serpent ever issued from the egg of sedition." No more effective device for stimulating resistance could have been contrived, and modern Communist revolutionists have adopted some of its underground techniques in establishing "cells."

Intercolonial committees of correspondence were the next logical step. Virginia led the way in 1773 by creating such a body as a standing committee of the House of Burgesses. Within a short time every colony had established a central committee through which it could exchange ideas and information with other colonies. These intercolonial groups, which were supremely significant in stimulating and disseminating sentiment in favor of united action, evolved directly into the first American Congresses.

Tea Parties at Boston and Elsewhere

Thus far—that is, by 1773—nothing had happened to make rebellion inevitable. Non-importation was weakening. Increasing numbers of colonials were reluctantly paying the tea tax, because the

Public Punishment. Boston customs official, John Malcolm, paraded after being tarred and feathered, January 25, 1774. (Detail from an English cartoon. Harvard College Library.)

legal tea was now cheaper than the smuggled tea, and cheaper than tea in England. Even John Adams on one occasion hoped that the tea he was drinking was smuggled Dutch tea, but he could not be sure and did not want to know.

A new ogre entered the picture in 1773. The powerful British East India Company, overburdened with 17 million pounds of unsold tea, was facing bankruptcy. If it collapsed, the London government would lose heavily in tax revenue. The ministry therefore decided to assist the company by awarding it a complete monopoly of the American tea business. The terms thus granted would enable the giant corporation to sell the coveted leaves more cheaply than ever before, even with the threepence tax added. But to many American consumers, principle was more important than price.

Violence was inevitable, for the new tea monopoly had many features that were hateful to the colonials. Above all, it seemed like a shabby attempt to trick the Americans, with the bait of cheaper tea, into acceptance of the detested tax. Once more the colonials rose in their wrath. Not a single one of the several thousand chests of

tea shipped by the company reached the hands of the consignees. At Annapolis, the Marylanders burned both the cargo and the vessel, while proclaiming "Liberty and Independence or death in pursuit of it." At Boston, which was host to the most famous tea party of all, a band of white townsfolk, disguised as Indians, boarded the three tea ships on December 16, 1773. They smashed open 342 chests and dumped the "cursed weed" into the harbor, while a silent crowd watched approvingly from the wharves as salty tea was brewed for the fish.

Reactions varied. Extremists in America rejoiced; conservatives shuddered. This wanton destruction of private property was going too far. The British at home were outraged; even friends of America hung their heads. Punishment and coercion were the only possible responses of the London authorities, as long as the mercantilist philosophy prevailed and the colonials refused to accept responsibility. The granting of some kind of home rule to the Americans might have prevented rebellion, but the Britons of that age were not blessed with such vision. Edmund Burke, a friend of America in Parliament, declared, "To tax and to please, no more than to love and be wise, is not given to men."

Parliament Passes the "Intolerable Acts"

An outraged Parliament responded speedily to the Boston Tea Party with measures that brewed a revolution. By huge majorities in 1774 it passed a series of "Repressive Acts," which were designed to chastise Boston in particular, Massachusetts in general. They were branded in America as "the Massacre of American Liberty."

Most drastic of all was the Boston Port Act. It closed the tea-stained harbor until damages were paid and order could be assured. By other "Intolerable Acts"—as they were called in America—many of the chartered rights of colonial Massachusetts were swept away. Restrictions were likewise placed on the precious town meet-

QUEBEC BEFORE AND AFTER 1774

Young Alexander Hamilton voiced the fears of many colonists when he warned that the Quebec Act of 1774 would introduce "priestly tyranny" into Canada, making that country another Spain or Portugal. "Does not your blood run cold," he asked, "to think that an English Parliament should pass an act for the establishment of arbitrary power and Popery in such a country?"

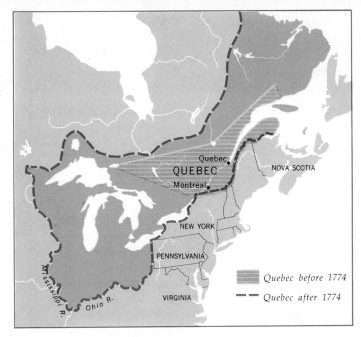

Quebec before 1774
- - - Quebec after 1774

ings. Contrary to previous practice, enforcing officials who killed colonials in line of duty could now be sent to England for trial. There, suspicious Americans assumed, they would be likely to get off scot-free.

By a fateful coincidence, the "Intolerable Acts" were accompanied in 1774 by the Quebec Act. Passed at the same time, it was erroneously regarded in English-speaking America as one of the "repressive" measures. Actually, the Quebec Act was a good law in bad company. For many years the British government had debated how it should administer the 60,000 or so conquered

French subjects in Canada, and it had finally framed this farsighted and statesmanlike measure. The French were guaranteed their Catholic religion. They were also permitted to retain many of their old customs and institutions, which did not include a representative assembly or trial by jury in civil cases. In addition, the old boundaries of the Province of Quebec were now extended southward all the way to the Ohio River.

The Quebec Act, from the viewpoint of the French Canadians, was a shrewd and conciliatory measure. If England had only shown as much foresight in dealing with her English-speaking colonies, she might not have lost them.

But from the viewpoint of the American colonials as a whole, the Quebec Act was the most intolerable of the "Intolerable Acts." All the other "repressive" laws slapped directly at Massachusetts, but this one had a much wider range. It seemed to set a dangerous precedent in America against jury trials and popular assemblies. It alarmed land speculators, who were distressed to see the huge trans-Allegheny area snatched from their grasp. It aroused the host of anti-Catholics, who were shocked by the extension of Roman Catholic jurisdiction southward into a huge region that had once been earmarked for Protestantism—a region about as large as the thirteen original colonies. One angry Protestant cried that there ought to be a "jubilee in hell" over this enormous gain for "popery."

The Continental Congress and Bloodshed

American dissenters, outraged by the Quebec Act, responded sympathetically to the plight of Massachusetts. She had put herself in the wrong by the wanton destruction of the tea cargoes; now the Mother Country had put herself in the wrong by brutal punishment that did not seem to fit the crime. Flags were flown at half-mast throughout the colonies on the day that the Boston Port Act went into effect, and sister colonies rallied to send food to the stricken city. Rice was shipped even from faraway South Carolina.

Most memorable of the responses to the "Intolerable Acts" was the summoning of a Continental Congress in 1774. It was to meet in Philadelphia to consider ways of redressing colonial grievances. Twelve of the thirteen colonies, with Georgia alone missing, sent fifty-five distinguished men, among them Samuel Adams, John Adams, George Washington, and Patrick Henry. Intercolonial frictions were partially melted away by social activity after working hours; in fifty-four days George Washington dined at his own lodgings only nine times.

The First Continental Congress deliberated for seven weeks, September 5 to October 26, 1774. It was not a legislative but a consultative body; it was a convention rather than a Congress. John Adams played a stellar role. Eloquently swaying his colleagues to a revolutionary course, he helped defeat by the narrowest of margins a proposal by the moderates for a species of American home rule under British direction. After prolonged argument, the Congress drew up several dignified papers. These included a ringing Declaration of Rights, as well as solemn appeals to other British American colonies, to the King, and to the British people.

Samuel Adams (1722–1803). A second cousin of John Adams, he contributed a potent pen and tongue to the American Revolution as a political agitator and organizer of rebellion. He was the leading spirit in hosting the Boston Tea Party. A failure in the brewing business, he was sent by Massachusetts to the First Continental Congress of 1774. He signed the Declaration of Independence and served in Congress until 1781. (Courtesy, Museum of Fine Arts, Boston. Deposited by the City of Boston.)

The most significant action of the Congress was the creation of The Association. Unlike previous non-importation agreements, this one called for a *complete* boycott of British goods: non-importation, non-exportation, and non-consumption. A document known as The Association, by providing for concerted action, was the closest approach to a written constitution that the colonies as a unit had yet devised. But still there was no genuine drive toward independence—merely an effort to bring about a repeal of the offensive legislation and a return to the happy days before parliamentary taxation. If colonial grievances were redressed, well and good; if not, the Congress was to meet again in May 1775.

But the deadly drift toward war continued. The petitions of the Continental Congress were rejected, after considerable debate, by strong majorities in Parliament. In America chickens squawked and tar kettles bubbled as violators of The Association were tarred and feathered.

Muskets were being collected, men were openly drilling, and a clash seemed imminent.

In April 1775, the British commander in Boston sent a detachment of troops to nearby Lexington and Concord. They were to seize stores of colonial gunpowder, and also to bag the "rebel" ringleaders, Samuel Adams and John Hancock. At Lexington, the colonial "Minute Men" refused to disperse rapidly enough, and shots were fired which killed eight Americans and wounded several more. The affair was more the "Lexington Massacre" than a battle. The Redcoats pushed on to Concord, whence they were forced to retreat by the homespun Americans, whom Emerson immortalized:

> By the rude bridge that arched the flood,
> Their flag to April's breeze unfurled,
> Here once the embattled farmers stood,
> And fired the shot heard round the world.*

The bewildered British, fighting off murderous fire from militiamen crouched behind thick stone walls, finally regained the sanctuary of Boston. Licking their wounds, they could count about 300 casualties, including some 70 killed. England now had a war on her hands.

Imperial Strength and Weakness

Aroused Americans had brashly rebelled against a mighty empire. The population odds were about three to one against the rebels—some 7.5 million Britons to 2.5 million colonials. The odds in monetary wealth and naval power were overwhelmingly in favor of the Mother Country.

Black people were only a partial asset to the American cause, for they could hardly be expected to fight for a society that had enslaved them. Still, about 5,000 saw military service, whether as freemen or as slaves promised freedom, and in a number of engagements fought bravely. Even larger numbers, often guaranteed freedom with no strings attached, fled to enemy lines and left the country when the British departed.

*Ralph Waldo Emerson, "Concord Hymn."

Britain then boasted a professional army of some 50,000 men, as compared with the numerous but wretchedly trained American militia. George III, in addition, had the money with which to hire foreign soldiers, and some 30,000 Germans—so-called Hessians—were ultimately employed. The British enrolled about 50,000 American Loyalists and enlisted the services of many Indians, who though unreliable fair-weather fighters, ravaged long stretches of the frontier. One British officer boasted that the war would offer no problems that could not be solved by an "experienced sheep herder."

Yet the Mother Country was weaker than she seemed at first glance. Oppressed Ireland was a latent volcano, and British troops had to be detached to watch her. France, bitter from her recent defeat, was awaiting an opportunity to stab Britain in the back. The London government was confused and inept. There was no William Pitt, "Organizer of Victory," only the stubborn George III and his pliant Lord North.

Many earnest and God-fearing Britons had no desire whatever to kill their American cousins. William Pitt withdrew a son from the army rather than see him thrust his sword into fellow Anglo-Saxons struggling for liberty. The English Whig factions, opposed to Lord North's Tory factions,

Privately (1776) General Washington expressed his distrust of militia: "To place any dependence upon militia is assuredly resting on a broken staff. . . . The sudden change in their manner of living . . . brings on sickness in many, impatience in all, and such an unconquerable desire of returning to their respective homes that it not only produces shameful and scandalous desertions among themselves, but infuses the like spirit in others. . . . If I was called upon to declare upon oath whether the militia have been most serviceable or hurtful upon the whole, I should subscribe to the latter."

Lord North (1732–1792). A staunch Tory and a loyal supporter of George III, he served as Prime Minister from 1770 to 1782, when his plan to reconquer America had evidently failed. His overreaction to the Boston Tea Party (1773) did much to precipitate the American Revolution.

openly cheered American victories—at least at the outset. Aside from trying to embarrass the Tories politically, many Whigs believed that the battle for English freedom was being fought in America. If George III triumphed, his rule at home might become tyrannical. This outspoken sympathy in England, though plainly that of a minority, greatly encouraged the Americans. If they continued their resistance long enough, the Whigs might come into power and deal generously with them.

Britain's army in America had to operate under endless difficulties. The generals were second-rate; the soldiers, though generally capable, were brutally treated. There was one extreme case of 800 lashes on the bare back for striking an officer. Provisions were often scarce, rancid, and wormy. On one occasion a supply of biscuits, captured some fifteen years earlier from the French, was softened by dropping cannon balls on them.

Other handicaps loomed. The Redcoats had to conquer the Americans; a draw would be a victory for the colonials. Britain was operating some 3,000 miles (4,830 kilometers) from her home base, and distance added greatly to the delays and uncertainties arising from storms and other mishaps. Military orders were issued in London which, when received months later, would not fit the changing situation.

America's geographical expanse was enormous: roughly 1,000 by 600 miles (1,600 by 970 kilometers). The United Colonies had no urban nerve center, like France's Paris. British armies captured every city of any size, yet like a boxer punching a feather pillow, they made little more than a dent in the entire country. The Americans wisely traded space for time. Benjamin Franklin calculated that during the prolonged campaign in which the Redcoats captured Bunker Hill and killed some 150 Yankees, about 60,000 American babies were born.

American Pluses and Minuses

The Revolutionists were blessed with outstanding leadership. George Washington was a giant among men; Benjamin Franklin was a master among diplomats. Open foreign aid, theoretically possible from the start, eventually came from France. Numerous European officers, many of them unemployed and impoverished, volunteered their swords for pay. In a class by himself was a wealthy young French nobleman, the Marquis de Lafayette. Fleeing from boredom, loving glory and ultimately liberty, at age nineteen the "French gamecock" was made a major general in the colonial army. His commission was largely a recogni-

General Lafayette (1757–1834). He gave to America not only military services but some $200,000 of his private funds. He returned to France after the American Revolution to play a conspicuous but disappointing role in the French Revolution.

tion of his family influence and political connections, but the services of this teenage general in securing further aid from France were invaluable.

Other conditions aided the Americans. They were fighting defensively, with the odds, all things considered, favoring the defender. In agriculture, the colonies were mainly self-sustaining, like a kind of Robinson Crusoe's island. Colonial "buckskins," moreover, were a tough, self-reliant people. As marksmen, they far outshone the British, who often pointed rather than aimed their muskets. A competent American rifleman could hit a man's head at 200 yards (183 meters).

In addition, the Americans enjoyed the moral advantage that came from belief in a just cause. The historical odds were not impossible. Other peoples had triumphed in the face of greater obstacles: the Greeks against Persians, the Swiss against Austrians, the Dutch against Spaniards.

Yet the American rebels were badly organized for war. From earliest days they had been almost fatally lacking in unity, and the new nation lurched forward uncertainly like an uncoordinated centipede. Even the Continental Congress, which directed the conflict, was hardly more than a debating society, and it grew feebler as the struggle dragged on. "Their Congress now is quite disjoint'd," jibed an English satirist, "Since Gibbits (gallows) [are] for them appointed." Disorganized colonials fought almost the entire war before adopting a written constitution—the Articles of Confederation—in 1781.

Jealousy everywhere raised its hideous head. Individual states, proudly regarding themselves as sovereign, resented the attempts of Congress to exercise its weak powers. Sectional jealousy boiled up over the appointment of military leaders; some distrustful New Englanders almost preferred British officers to Americans from other sections.

Economic difficulties were well-nigh insuperable. Metallic money had already been heavily drained away. A cautious Continental Congress, unwilling to raise anew the explosive issue of taxation, was forced to print "Continental" paper money profusely. As this currency poured from the presses, it depreciated until the expression became current, "not worth a Continental." One barber contemptuously papered his shop with the almost worthless dollars. The confusion worsened when the individual states were compelled to issue depreciated paper money of their own.

Inflation of the currency inevitably skyrocketed prices. Families of the soldiers at the fighting front were hard hit, and hundreds of anxious husbands and fathers deserted. Debtors easily acquired handfuls of the semi-worthless money and gleefully paid their debts "without mercy"—sometimes with the bayonets of the authorities to back them up.

A Thin Line of Heroes

Basic military supplies in the colonies were dangerously scanty, especially firearms and powder. Benjamin Franklin seriously proposed going back to the bow and arrow. Even where food was accumulated, wagons were often not available to haul it. At Valley Forge, in the winter of 1777–1778, the shivering American soldiers were without bread for three successive days. In one Southern campaign some men fainted for lack of food.

Manufactured goods were generally in short supply in agricultural America, and clothing and shoes were appallingly scarce. The path of the patriot fighting men was often marked by bloody snow. At frigid Valley Forge, during one anxious period, 2,800 men were barefooted or nearly naked. Woolens were desperately needed against the wintry blasts; and in general the only real uniform of the colonial army was uniform raggedness. During a grand parade at Valley Forge some of the officers appeared wrapped in woolen bed covers. One Rhode Island unit was known as the "Ragged, Lousy, Naked Regiment."

American militiamen were numerous but highly unreliable. Able-bodied American males—perhaps several hundred thousand of them—had received rudimentary training, and many of these recruits served for short terms in the rebel armies. But poorly trained plowboys, though better shots, could not stand up in the open field against professional British troops advancing with bare bayonets. Many of these undisciplined warriors would, in the words of Washington, "fly from their own shadows."

A few thousand regulars—perhaps 7,000 or 8,000 at war's end—were finally whipped into shape by stern drillmasters. Notable among these officers was an organizational genius, the salty German Baron von Steuben. He spoke no English when he reached America, but he soon taught his men that bayonets were not for broiling beefsteaks over open fires. As they gained experience, these soldiers of the Continental Line could hold their own in open battle against crack British troops.

Morale in the Revolutionary army was badly undermined by American profiteers. These grasping gentry, putting profits before patriotism, sold to the British because the invader could pay in gold. Speculators forced prices sky-high; and some Bostonians made profits of 50 percent to 200 percent on army clothing while the American army was freezing at Valley Forge. Washington never had as many as 20,000 effective

> General Washington's disgust is reflected in a diary entry for 1776: "Chimney corner patriots abound; venality, corruption, prostitution of office for selfish ends, abuse of trust, perversion of funds from a national to a private use, and speculations upon the necessities of the times pervade all interests."

troops in one place at one time, despite bounties of land and other inducements. Yet if the rebels had thrown themselves into the struggle with Revolutionary zeal, they could easily have raised many times that number.

The brutal truth is that only a select minority of the American colonials attached themselves to the cause of independence with a spirit of selfless devotion. These were the dedicated souls who bore the burden of battle and the risks of defeat; these were the freedom-loving patriots who deserved the gratitude and esteem of generations yet unborn. Seldom have so few done so much for so many.

VARYING VIEWPOINTS

Historians once assumed that the Revolution was just another chapter in the unfolding story of human liberty—a kind of divinely ordained progress toward perfection in human affairs. This approach is often called the Whig view of history. Around the beginning of this century, the concept was sharply challenged by the so-called progressive historians, who argued that not God but a sharp struggle among different social groups brought about change. "Progressives" thus saw the Revolution as stemming from class conflict and ending in a truly transformed social order. As one of them put it, the Revolution was not only about home rule, but about "who should rule at home." Since World War II, scholars have questioned this interpretation.

They have uncovered evidence that the British imperial system really was not unduly burdensome to the colonists, and more important, that colonial society was *already* fairly democratic before 1776 (at least as regards white people).

Two questions naturally arise: What really caused the divorce of Mother Country and colonists, and precisely how "revolutionary" was the Revolution? Interestingly, recent scholarship has tended to emphasize not economic or political friction, but ideological and even psychological factors. The root causes of the Revolution may well have been the felt need to defend existing political liberties, combined with an exaggerated fear of conspiracy against them.

SELECT READINGS

Edmund S. Morgan, *The Birth of the Republic, 1763–1789* (1956), is among the best brief accounts of the Revolutionary era. It stresses the happy coincidence of the Revolutionaries' principles and their interests. L. Gipson, *The Coming of the Revolution, 1763–1775* (1954), summarizes his 15-volume masterwork (cited in Chapter 3). Merrill Jensen, *The Founding of a Nation* (1968), is a more recent effort at a general synthesis, as is Page Smith's massive *A New Age Now Begins: A People's History of the American Revolution* (1976). R. R. Palmer, *The Age of the Democratic Revolution: A Political History of Europe and America, 1760–1800* (2 vols., 1959, 1964), masterfully places American events in the larger context of Western history. Two enlightening collections of essays are J. P. Greene, ed., *The Reinterpretation of the American Revolution, 1763–1789* (1968), and A. F. Young, ed., *The American Revolution* (1976), which generally represents a "new left" revisionist view. An interesting effort to blend British and American perspectives is I. R. Christie and B. W. Labaree, *Empire or Independence, 1760–1776* (1976). The sources of American dissatisfaction with the British imperial system can be traced in C. Ubbelohde, *The American Colonies and the British Empire, 1607–1763* (1968), and T. C. Barrow, *Trade and Empire: The British Customs Service in Colonial America* (1967). O. M. Dickerson, *The Navigation Acts and the American Revolution* (1951), concludes that the navigation system did not put undue burdens on the colonies. B. Knollenberg examines the effects of the British tightening of the imperial system in the 1760s in *Origin of the American Revolution, 1759–1766* (1960), as does Michael Kammen in *Empire and Interest* (1970). John Shy imaginatively explores an important aspect of the imperial system's effect on America in *Toward Lexington: The Role of the British Army in the Coming of the American Revolution* (1965). A perceptive short account of the American reaction to British initiatives is E. S. and H. M. Morgan, *The Stamp Act Crisis* (1953). B. W. Labaree discusses another instance of American reaction in *The Boston Tea Party* (1964). P. Maier focuses on the crucial role of the "mob" in *From Resistance to Revolution: Colonial Radicals and the Development of American Opposition to Britain, 1756–1776* (1972). The British side is told in P. D. G. Thomas, *British Politics and the Stamp Act Crisis* (1975). Light is shed on the same subject and others in J. Brooke, *King George III* (1972). C. Bridenbaugh, *Mitre and Sceptre* (1962), explains the colonial fears of a British-imposed Anglican episcopate. A. Heimert, *Religion and the American Mind from the Great Awakening to the Revolution* (1966), seeks to find connections between the religious upheavals of the early 18th Century and the political uprising of 1776. C. Rossiter, *Seedtime of the Republic* (1953), stresses the importance of ideas in pushing the Revolution forward, as does B. Bailyn's seminal *Ideological Origins of the American Revolution* (1967), which also emphasizes the colonists' fears of a conspiracy against their liberties. Helpful biographies of key Revolutionary figures include J. C. Miller, *Sam Adams* (1936), R. D. Meade, *Patrick Henry* (1957), M. Peterson, *Thomas Jefferson and the New Nation* (1970), Dumas Malone, *Jefferson and His Time* (5 vols., 1948–1974), and P. Maier, *The Old Revolutionaries: Political Lives in the Age of Samuel Adams* (1980). Imaginative cultural history is found in Robert A. Gross, *The Minutemen and Their World* (1976). Gary B. Nash emphasizes class conflict in *The Urban Crucible: Social Change, Political Consciousness, and the Origins of the American Revolution* (1979). Two recent books take a psychological approach to the problem of the revolutionary generation's assault on established authority: Kenneth S. Lynn, *A Divided People* (1977), and Jay Fliegelman, *Prodigals and Pilgrims: The American Revolution against Patriarchal Authority, 1750–1800* (1982).

6

America Secedes from the Empire

These are the times that try men's souls. The summer soldier and the sunshine patriot will, in this crisis, shrink from the service of their country; but he that stands it now, *deserves the love and thanks of man and woman.*

THOMAS PAINE, December 1776

Congress Drafts George Washington

Bloodshed at Lexington and Concord, in April 1775, was a clarion call to arms. About 20,000 musket-bearing "Minute Men" swarmed around Boston, there to coop up the outnumbered British.

The Second Continental Congress met in Philadelphia the next month, on May 10, 1775; and this time the full slate of thirteen colonies was represented. The conservative element in Congress was still strong, despite the shooting in Massachusetts. There was no real sentiment for independence—merely a desire to continue fighting in the hope that King and Parliament would consent to a redress of grievances. Congress hopefully drafted new appeals to the British people and

King—appeals that were spurned. Anticipating a possible rebuff, the delegates also adopted measures to raise money and to create an army and navy.

Perhaps the most important single action of the Congress was to select George Washington, one of its members already in officer's uniform, to head the hastily improvised army besieging Boston. This choice was made with considerable misgivings. The tall, powerfully built, dignified, blue-eyed Virginia planter, then forty-three, had never risen above the rank of a colonel in the militia. His largest command had numbered only 1,200 men, and that had been some twenty years earlier. Falling short of true military genius, he was actually destined to lose more pitched battles than he won.

But the distinguished Virginian was gifted with outstanding powers of leadership and immense strength of character. He radiated patience, courage, self-discipline, and a sense of justice. He was a great moral force rather than a great military mind—a symbol and a rallying point. Men instinctively trusted him; they sensed that when he put himself at the head of a cause, he was prepared, if necessary, to go down with the ship. He insisted on serving without pay, though he kept a careful expense account amounting to more than $100,000. Later he sternly reprimanded his steward at Mount Vernon for providing the enemy, under duress, with supplies. He would have preferred to see the enemy put the torch to his mansion.

The Continental Congress, though dimly perceiving Washington's qualities of leadership, chose more wisely than it knew. His selection, in truth, was largely political. Americans in other sections, already jealous, were beginning to distrust the large New England army being collected around Boston. Prudence suggested a commander from Virginia, the largest and most populous of the colonies. As a man of wealth, both by inheritance and by marriage, Washington could not be accused of being a fortune seeker. As an aristocrat, he could be counted on to check the excesses of the masses.

Martha Washington (1732–1802). Destined to be the first First Lady, she was the daughter of a prominent Virginia planter. Her first husband died, leaving her a wealthy young widow with two children. Two years later she married George Washington. Known as "Lady Washington" for her charm and aristocratic graciousness, she brought considerable status to the Patriot cause. She bore Washington no children. It was said that fate had ordained that he was to be only the Father of his Country.

Bunker Hill and Hessian Hirelings

The clash of arms continued on a strangely contradictory basis. On the one hand, the Americans were emphatically affirming their loyalty to the King, and earnestly voicing their desire to patch up existing difficulties. On the other hand, they were raising armies and shooting down His Majesty's soldiers. This curious war of inconsistency was fought for fourteen long months—from April 1775 to July 1776—before the fateful plunge into independence was taken.

Gradually the tempo of warfare increased. In May 1775, a tiny American force, under Ethan Allen and Benedict Arnold, surprised and captured the British garrisons at Ticonderoga and Crown Point, on the scenic lakes of upper New York. A priceless store of powder and artillery for the siege of Boston was thus secured. In June

1775, the colonials seized a hill, now known as Bunker Hill (actually Breed's Hill), from which they menaced the enemy in Boston. The British, instead of cutting off the retreat of their foes by flanking them, blundered bloodily when they launched a frontal attack with 3,000 men. Sharp-shooting Americans, numbering 1,500 and strongly entrenched, mowed down the advancing foe with frightful slaughter. But their scanty store of powder finally gave out, and they were forced to abandon the hill in disorder. With two more such victories, remarked the French foreign minister, the British would have no army left in America.

Following Bunker Hill, the King slammed the door on all hope of reconciliation. In August 1775, he formally proclaimed the colonies in rebellion, with all that this implied in the way of future hangings. The next month he further widened the chasm when he completed arrangements for hiring thousands of German troops (so-called Hessians) to help crush his rebellious subjects. Six German princes involved in the transaction needed the money (one reputedly had seventy-four children); George III needed the men.

News of the Hessian deal shocked the colonials. The quarrel, they felt, was within the family. Why bring in outside mercenaries, especially fiercely mustached foreigners, who had an exaggerated reputation for butchery and bestiality?

Hessian hirelings proved to be good soldiers in a mechanical sense, but many of them were more interested in booty than in duty. For good reason they were dubbed "Hessian flies." Seduced by American promises of land, hundreds of them finally deserted and remained in the United States to become respected citizens.

The Abortive Conquest of Canada

The unsheathed sword continued to take its toll. In October 1775, on the eve of a cruel winter, the British burned Falmouth (Portland), Maine. In that same autumn the rebels daringly undertook a two-pronged invasion of Canada. American leaders believed, erroneously, that the conquered French were explosively restive under the British yoke. A successful assault on Canada would add a fourteenth colony, while depriving Britain of a valuable base for striking at the colonies in revolt. But this large-scale attack, involving some 2,000 American troops, contradicted the claim of the colonials that they were merely fighting defensively for a redress of grievances. Invasion northward was undisguised offensive warfare.

This bold stroke for Canada narrowly missed success. One invading column under the Irish-born General Richard Montgomery, formerly of the British army, pushed up the Lake Champlain route and captured Montreal. He was joined at Quebec by the bedraggled army of General Benedict Arnold, whose men had been reduced to eating dogs and shoe leather during their grueling march through the Maine woods. An assault on Quebec, launched on the last day of 1775, was beaten off. The able Montgomery was killed; the dashing Arnold was wounded in one leg. Scattered remnants under his command retreated up the St. Lawrence River, reversing the way Montgomery had come. French-Canadian leaders, who had been generously treated by the British in the Quebec Act of 1774, showed no real desire to welcome the plundering anti-Catholic invaders.

General Benedict Arnold, Hero-Traitor (1741–1801). He died in England twenty years after fleeing the country. Legend has him repenting on his deathbed, "Let me die in my old uniform. God forgive me for ever putting on any other."

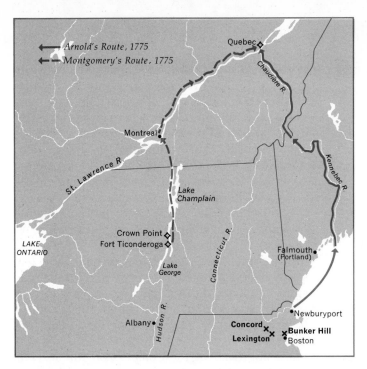

REVOLUTION IN THE NORTH, 1775–1776
Benedict Arnold's troops were described as "pretty young men" when they sailed from Massachusetts. They were considerably less pretty on their arrival in Quebec, after eight weeks of struggling through wet and frigid forests, often without food. "No one can imagine," one of them wrote, "the sweetness of a roasted shot-pouch [ammunition bag] to the famished appetite."

Bitter fighting continued in the colonies, though the Americans still disclaimed all desire for independence. In January 1776, the British set fire to the Virginia town of Norfolk. In March they were finally forced to evacuate Boston, taking with them the leading friends of the King. (Evacuation Day is still celebrated annually in Boston.) In the South the rebellious colonials won two victories in 1776; one in February against some 1,500 Loyalists at Moore's Creek Bridge, in North Carolina; and the other in June against an invading British fleet at Charleston harbor.

Thomas Paine Preaches Common Sense

Why did Americans continue to deny any intention of independence? Loyalty to the empire was deeply ingrained; colonial unity was poor; and open rebellion was dangerous, especially against a formidable Britain. Irish rebels of that day were customarily hanged, drawn, and quartered. American rebels might have fared no better. As late as January 1776—five months before independence was declared—the King's health was being toasted by the officers of Washington's mess near Boston. "God save the King" had not yet been replaced by "God save the Congress."

Gradually the Americans were shocked into an awareness of their inconsistency. Their eyes were opened by harsh British acts like the burning of Falmouth and Norfolk, and especially by the hiring of the Hessians. Early in 1776 came the publication of *Common Sense*, one of the most potent pamphlets ever written. Its author was the radical Thomas Paine, once an impoverished corset-maker's apprentice, who had come over from England a year earlier. His tract became a whirlwind best seller, and within a few months reached the astonishing total of 120,000 copies.

Paine flatly branded the shilly-shallying of the colonials as contrary to "common sense." Why not throw off the cloak of inconsistency? Nowhere in the physical universe did the smaller heavenly body control the larger one. Then why should the tiny island of England control the vast continent of America? As for the King, whom the Americans professed to revere, he was nothing but "the Royal Brute of Great Britain." America

IO

Paine rose to heights of eloquence in *Common Sense:* "O! ye that love mankind! Ye that dare oppose not only the tyranny but the tyrant, stand forth! Every spot of the Old World is overrun with oppression. Freedom hath been hunted round the globe. Asia and Africa have long expelled her. Europe regards her as a stranger and England hath given her warning to depart. O! receive the fugitive and prepare in time an asylum for mankind."

IOIOIOIOIOIOIOIOIOIOIOIOIOIOIOIOIOIOIOIOIOIOIOI

had a sacred mission—a moral obligation to the world—to set herself up as an independent, democratic republic, untainted by association with corrupt and monarchical Britain.

Paine's passionate protest was simple and somewhat shallow, but it was direct and persuasive. It was both high-class journalism and high-class propaganda. Thousands of American waverers, their eyes jolted open, were prodded into going the whole way. They not only perceived the folly of their position, but—perhaps most important—they realized that they could not hope for open aid from France as long as they swore allegiance to the King. The French Crown was interested in the destruction of the British Empire, not in its reconstruction under a plan of reconciliation.

Jefferson's "Explanation" of Independence

Members of the Philadelphia Congress, instructed by their respective colonies, gradually edged toward a clean break. On June 7, 1776, fiery Richard Henry Lee of Virginia moved that "These United Colonies are, and of right ought to be, free and independent states. . . ." After considerable debate, the motion was adopted nearly a month later, on July 2, 1776.

The passing of Lee's resolution was the formal "declaration" of independence by the American colonies, and technically this was all that was needed to cut the British tie. John Adams wrote confidently that ever thereafter July 2 would be celebrated annually with fireworks. But something more was required. An epochal rupture of this kind called for some formal explanation to "a candid world." An inspirational appeal was also needed to enlist other English colonies in the Americas, to invite assistance from foreign nations, and to rally resistance at home.

Shortly after Lee made his memorable motion on June 7, Congress appointed a committee to prepare an appropriate statement. The task of drafting it fell to Thomas Jefferson, a tall, freckled, sandy-haired Virginia lawyer of thirty-three. Despite his youth, he was already recognized as a brilliant writer, and he measured up splendidly to his opportunity. After some debate and amendment, the Declaration of Independence was formally approved by the Congress on July 4, 1776. It might better have been called "the Explanation of Independence" or, as one contemporary described it, "Mr. Jefferson's advertisement of Mr. Lee's resolution."

Jefferson's pronouncement, couched in a lofty style, was magnificent. He gave his appeal universality by invoking the "natural rights" of mankind —not just British rights. He argued persuasively that because the King had flouted these rights, the colonials were justified in cutting their connection. He then set forth a long list of the presumably tyrannous misdeeds of George III. The overdrawn bill of indictment included imposing taxes without consent, dispensing with trial by jury, abolishing valued laws, establishing a military dictatorship, maintaining standing armies in peacetime, cutting off trade, burning towns, hiring mercenaries, and inciting savage Indians.*

Jefferson's withering blast was admittedly onesided. But he was in effect the prosecuting attorney, and he took certain liberties with historical truth. He was not writing history; he was making it through what has been called "the world's

_____
*For an annotated text of the Declaration of Independence, see Appendix.

George III (1738–1820). America's last king, he was a good man, unlike some of his scandal-tainted brothers and sons, but a bad king. Doggedly determined to regain arbitrary power for the Crown, he antagonized and then lost the thirteen American colonies. During much of his sixty-year nominal reign, he seemed to be insane, but recently medical science has found that he was suffering from a rare metabolic and hereditary disease called porphyria. (Reproduced by courtesy of the Trustees of the British Museum)

greatest editorial." He owned many slaves, and his affirmation that "all men are created equal" was to haunt him and his countrymen for generations.

The formal declaration of independence cleared the air as a thundershower does on a muggy day. Foreign aid could be solicited with greater hope of success. Those patriots who defied the King were now rebels, not loving subjects shooting their way into reconciliation. They must all hang together, Franklin is said to have grimly remarked, or they would all hang separately. Or, in the eloquent language of the Great Declaration, "We mutually pledge to each other our lives, our fortunes and our sacred honor."

Jefferson's defiant Declaration of Independence had a universal impact unmatched by any other American document. This "shout heard round the world" has been a source of inspiration to countless revolutionary movements against arbitrary authority. Lafayette hung a copy on a wall in his home, leaving beside it room for a future French Declaration of the Rights of Man—a declaration that was officially born thirteen years later.

Patriots and Loyalists

The War of Independence, strictly speaking, was a war within a war. Colonials loyal to the King (Loyalists) fought the American rebels (Patriots), while the rebels also fought the British Redcoats. Loyalists were derisively called "Tories" after the dominant political factions in England, while Patriots were called Whigs after the opposition factions in England. A popular definition of a Tory among the Patriots betrayed bitterness: "A Tory is a thing whose head is in England, and its body in America, and its neck ought to be stretched."

Like many revolutions, the American Revolution was a minority movement. Roughly one-third of the people were apathetic or neutral, including those Byrds of Virginia who sat on the fence. Perhaps somewhat more than one-third were in varying degrees rebellious; probably somewhat fewer than one-third were Loyalists who remained true to their King. Families were often split over the issue of independence: Benjamin Franklin supported the Patriot side, while his handsome illegitimate son, William Franklin (the last royal governor of New Jersey), upheld the Loyalist cause.

The Loyalists were tragic figures. For generations Englishmen in the New World had been taught fidelity to their King. Loyalty is ordinarily

The American signers had reason to fear for their necks. In 1802, twenty-six years later, George III approved this death sentence for seven Irish rebels: ". . . you are to be hanged by the neck, but not until you are dead; for while you are still living your bodies are to be taken down, your bowels torn out and burned before your faces, your heads then cut off, and your bodies divided each into four quarters, and your heads and quarters to be then at the King's disposal; and may the Almighty God have mercy on your souls."

regarded as a major virtue—loyalty to one's family, one's friends, one's country. If the King had triumphed, as he seemed likely to do, the Loyalists would have been acclaimed patriots, and defeated rebels like Washington would have been disgraced, severely punished, and probably forgotten.

Conservative Americans generally remained loyal—the people of education and wealth, of culture and caution. These moderate souls were satisfied with their lot, and believed that any violent change would only be for the worse. They feared that the "dirty rabble," inflamed by violence, might break out of control. "If I must be devoured," moaned one aristocrat, "let me be devoured by the jaws of a lion, and not gnawed to death by rats and vermin." Loyalists were also more numerous among the older generation. Young men make revolutions, and from the outset energetic, purposeful, and militant young men surged forward—figures like the sleeplessly scheming Samuel Adams and the impassioned Patrick Henry. His flaming outcry before the Virginia Assembly—"Give me liberty or give me death!"—still quickens patriotic pulses.

Loyalists also included the King's officers and other beneficiaries of the Crown—men who knew which side their daily bread came from. The same was generally true of the Anglican clergy and a large portion of their flocks, all of whom had long been taught obedience to the King.

Usually the Loyalists were most numerous where the Anglican Church was strongest. A notable exception was Virginia, where the debt-burdened Anglican aristocrats flocked into the rebel camp. The King's followers were well entrenched in aristocratic New York City and Charleston, and also in Quaker Pennsylvania and New Jersey, where General Washington felt that he was fighting in "the enemy's country." While his men were starving at Valley Forge, nearby Pennsylvania farmers were selling their produce to the British for the King's gold.

Loyalists were least numerous in New England, where self-government was especially strong and mercantilism especially weak. Rebels were the most numerous where Presbyterianism and Congregationalism flourished, notably in New England. Invading British armies vented their contempt and anger by using Yankee churches for pigsties.

The Loyalist Exodus

Before the Declaration of Independence in 1776, persecution of the Loyalists was relatively mild. Yet they were subjected to some brutality, including tarring and feathering and riding astride fence rails.

After the Declaration of Independence, which sharply separated Loyalists from Patriots, harsher methods prevailed. The rebels naturally desired a united front. Putting loyalty to the colonies first, they regarded their opponents, not themselves, as

Tory Suspended, While Goose is Plucked for Coat of Feathers. (The Bettmann Archive, Inc.)

traitors. Loyalists were roughly handled; hundreds were imprisoned; and a few noncombatants were hanged. But there was no wholesale reign of terror comparable to that which later bloodied both France and Russia. For one thing, the colonials reflected Anglo-Saxon regard for order; for another, the leading Loyalists were prudent enough to flee to the British lines.

About 80,000 loyal supporters of George III were driven out or fled, but several hundred thousand or so of the mild Loyalists were permitted to stay. The estates of many of the fugitives were confiscated and sold—a relatively painless way of helping to finance the war. Confiscation often worked great hardship, as, for example, when two aristocratic old ladies were forced to live in their former chicken house.

Some 50,000 Loyalist volunteers at one time or another bore arms for the British. They also helped the King's cause by serving as spies, by inciting the Indians, and by keeping Patriot soldiers at home to protect their families. Ardent Loyalists had their hearts in their cause, and a major blunder of the haughty British was not to make full use of them in the fighting.

General Washington at Bay

With Boston evacuated in March 1776, the British concentrated on New York as a base of operations. Here was a splendid seaport, centrally located, where the King could count on cooperation from the numerous Loyalists. An awe-inspiring British fleet appeared off New York in July 1776. It consisted of some 500 ships and 35,000 men—the largest armed force to be seen in America until the Civil War. General Washington, dangerously outnumbered, could muster only 18,000 ill-trained troops with which to meet the crack army of the invader.

Disaster befell the Americans in the summer and fall of 1776. Outgeneraled and outmaneuvered, they were routed at the Battle of Long Island, where panic seized the raw recruits. By the narrowest of margins, and thanks to a favoring

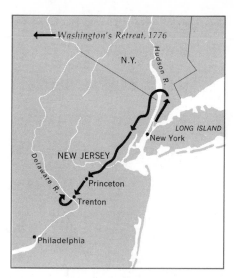

NEW YORK AND NEW JERSEY, 1776–1777

wind and fog, Washington escaped to Manhattan Island. Retreating northward, he crossed the Hudson River to New Jersey, and finally reached the Delaware River with the British close at his heels. Tauntingly, enemy buglers sounded the fox-hunting call, so familiar to Virginians of Washington's day. The Patriot cause was at low ebb when the rebel remnants fled across the river, after collecting all available boats to forestall pursuit.

The wonder is that Washington's adversary, General William Howe, did not speedily crush the demoralized American forces. But he was no military genius, and he well remembered the horrible slaughter at Bunker Hill, where he had commanded. The country was rough, supplies were slow in coming, and as a professional soldier Howe did not relish the rigors of winter campaigning. He evidently found more agreeable the bedtime company of his mistress, the wife of one of his subordinates—a scandal with which American satirists had a good deal of ribald fun.

Washington, now almost counted out, stealthily recrossed the ice-clogged Delaware River. At Trenton, on December 26, 1776, he surprised and captured a thousand Hessians who were sleeping off the effects of their Christmas celebration. A

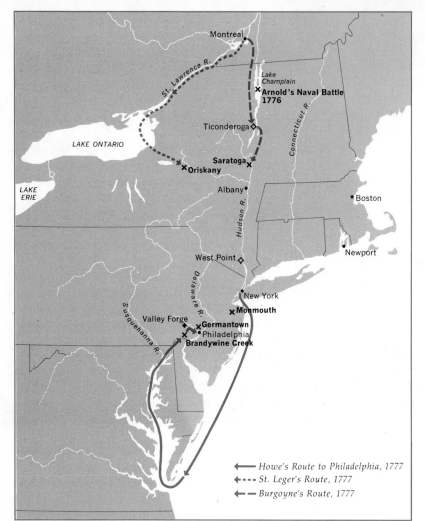

NEW YORK–PENNSYLVANIA THEATER, 1777–1778
Distinguished members of the Continental Congress fled from Philadelphia in near-panic as the British army approached. Thomas Paine reported that at three o'clock in the morning the streets were "as full of Men, Women, and Children as on a Market Day." John Adams had anticipated that "I shall run away, I suppose, with the rest," since "we are too brittle ware, you know, to stand the dashing of balls and bombs." Adams got his chance to decamp with the others into the interior of Pennsylvania, and tried to put the best face on things. "This tour," he commented, "has given me an opportunity of seeing many parts of this country which I never saw before."

← *Howe's Route to Philadelphia, 1777*
←---- *St. Leger's Route, 1777*
←- - - *Burgoyne's Route, 1777*

week later, leaving his campfires burning as a ruse, he slipped away and inflicted a sharp defeat on a smaller British detachment at Princeton. This brilliant New Jersey campaign, crowned by these two lifesaving victories, revealed "Old Fox" Washington at his military best.

Burgoyne's Blundering Invasion

London officials adopted an intricate scheme for capturing the vital Hudson River Valley in 1777. If successful, the British would sever New England from the rest of the states and paralyze the American cause. The main invading force, under an actor-playwright-soldier, General ("Gentleman Johnny") Burgoyne, would push down the Lake Champlain route from Canada. General Howe's troops in New York, if needed, could advance up the Hudson River to meet Burgoyne near Albany. A third and much smaller British force, commanded by Colonel St. Leger, would come in from the west by way of Lake Ontario and the Mohawk Valley.

British planners did not reckon with General Benedict Arnold. After his repulse at Quebec in 1775, he had retreated slowly along the St. Lawrence River back to the Lake Champlain area, by heroic efforts keeping an army in the field. The

British had pursued his tattered force to Lake Champlain in 1776. But they could not move farther south until they had won control of the lake, which, in the absence of roads, was indispensable for carrying their supplies.

Tireless, Arnold assembled a small fleet, and the British had to stop to construct a larger one. His tiny flotilla was finally destroyed after desperate fighting, but winter was descending and the British were forced to retire to Canada. General Burgoyne had to start anew from this base the following year. If Arnold had not contributed his daring and skill, the British invaders of 1776 almost certainly would have penetrated as far south as Fort Ticonderoga. If Burgoyne had started from this springboard in 1777, instead of Canada, he almost certainly would have succeeded in his venture. (At long last the apparently futile American invasion of Canada in 1775 was beginning to pay rich dividends.)

General Burgoyne began his fateful invasion with 7,000 regular troops. He was encumbered by a heavy baggage train and a considerable number of women, many of whom were wives of his officers. Progress was painfully slow, for sweaty axmen had to chop a path through the forest, while American militiamen began to gather like hornets on Burgoyne's flanks.

General Howe, meanwhile, was causing astonished eyebrows to rise. At a time when it seemed obvious that he should be starting up the Hudson River from New York to join his slowly advancing colleague, he deliberately embarked with the main British army for an attack on Philadelphia, the rebel capital. As scholars now know, he wanted to force a general engagement with Washington's army, destroy it, and leave the path wide open for Burgoyne's thrust. Howe apparently assumed that he had ample time to assist Burgoyne directly, should he be needed.

General Washington, keeping a wary eye on the British in New York, hastily transferred his army to the vicinity of Philadelphia. There, late in 1777, he was defeated in two pitched battles, at Brandywine Creek and Germantown. Pleasure-loving General Howe then settled down comfortably

The Generals in America Doing Nothing, or Worse Than Nothing. British satire on the sloth and indifference of General Burgoyne. After playing solitaire and drinking heavily, he falls asleep as his plea to General Howe for help drops to the floor. Meanwhile Burgoyne's army is surrendering.

in the lively capital, leaving Burgoyne to flounder through the wilds of upper New York. Benjamin Franklin, recently sent to Paris as an envoy, truthfully jested that Howe had not captured Philadelphia but that Philadelphia had captured Howe. Washington finally retired to winter quarters at Valley Forge, a strong hilly position some twenty miles northwest of Philadelphia, and there his frost-bitten and hungry men were short of about everything except misery. This rabble was nevertheless whipped into a professional army by the recently arrived Prussian drillmaster, the profane but patient Baron von Steuben.

Burgoyne meanwhile had begun to bog down north of Albany, while a host of American militiamen, scenting the kill, swarmed about him. In a series of sharp engagements, in which General Arnold was again shot in the leg wounded at Quebec, the British army was trapped. Meanwhile the Americans had driven back St. Leger's force at Oriskany. Unable to advance or retreat, Burgoyne was forced to surrender his entire command at Saratoga, on October 17, 1777, to the American General Gates.

Saratoga ranks high among the decisive battles of both American and world history. The victory immensely revived the faltering colonial cause. Even more important, it made possible the urgently needed foreign aid from France which in turn helped insure American independence.

Strange French Bedfellows

France, thirsting for revenge, was eager to inflame the quarrel that had broken out in America. The New World colonies were by far Britain's most valuable overseas possessions, and if they could be wrested from her, she presumably would cease to be a front-rank power. France might then regain her former position and prestige, the loss of which in the recent Seven Years' War rankled deeply.

America's cause rapidly became something of a fad in France. The bored aristocracy, which had developed some interest in the writings of liberal French thinkers like Rousseau, was rather intrigued by the ideal of American liberty. Hard-headed French officials, on the other hand, were not prompted by a love for America but by a realistic concern for the interests of France. Any marriage with the United States would be strictly one of convenience.

After the shooting at Lexington, in April 1775, the French agents undertook to blow on the embers. They secretly provided the Americans with lifesaving amounts of powder and other munitions, chiefly through a sham company rigged up for that purpose. About 90 percent of all the gunpowder used by the Americans in the first two and a half years of the war came from French arsenals.

The Horse *America* Throwing His Master.   The rider is Lord North, British Prime Minister, represented with a whip of swords. Note the Frenchman in the background. (A British cartoon in the New York Public Library.)

Secrecy enshrouded all these French schemes. Open aid to the American rebels might provoke England into a declaration of war; and France, still weakened by her recent defeat, was not ready to fight. She feared that the American rebellion might fade out, for the colonies were proclaiming their desire to patch up differences. But the Declaration of Independence in 1776 showed that the Americans really meant business; and the smashing victory at Saratoga seemed to indicate that they had an excellent chance of winning their freedom.

After the humiliation at Saratoga in 1777, the British Parliament belatedly passed a measure which in effect offered the Americans home rule within the empire. This was essentially all that the colonials had ever asked for—except independence. If the French were going to break up the British Empire, they would have to bestir themselves. Wily and bespectacled old Benjamin Franklin, whose simple fur cap and witty sayings had captivated the French public, played skillfully on France's fears of reconciliation.

The French King, Louis XVI, was reluctant to intervene. Although somewhat stupid, he was alert enough to see grave dangers in aiding the Americans openly and incurring war with Britain. But his ministers at length won him over. They argued that hostilities were inevitable, sooner or later, to undo the victor's peace of 1763. If England should regain her colonies, she might join with them to seize the sugar-rich French West Indies, and thus secure compensation for the cost of the recent rebellion. The French had better fight while they could have an American ally, rather than wait and fight both Britain and her reunited colonials.

So France, in 1778, offered the Americans a treaty of alliance. It promised everything that Britain was offering—plus independence. Both allies bound themselves to wage war until the United States had won its freedom, and until both agreed on terms with the common foe.

This was the first entangling military alliance in the experience of the Republic, and one that later caused prolonged trouble. The American

I◻I◻II◻I◻II◻I◻II◻I◻II◻I◻II◻I◻II◻I◻II◻I◻II◻I◻II◻I◻II◻I◻II◻I◻II◻I◻II◻I

> After concluding the alliance, France sent a minister to America, to the delight of one Patriot journalist: "Who would have thought that the American colonies, imperfectly known in Europe a few years ago and claimed by every pettifogging lawyer in the House of Commons, every cobbler in the beer-houses of London, as a part of their property, should to-day receive an ambassador from the most powerful monarchy in Europe."

I◻I◻II◻I◻II◻I◻II ◻I◻II◻I◻II◻I◻II◻I◻II◻I◻II◻I◻II◻I◻II◻I◻II◻I◻II◻I◻II◻I

people, with ingrained isolationist tendencies, accepted the French entanglement with distaste. They were painfully aware that it involved a hereditary foe which was also a Roman Catholic power. But when one's house is on fire, one does not inquire too closely into the background of those who carry the water buckets.

The Colonial War Becomes a World War

England and France thus came to blows in 1778, and the shot fired at Lexington rapidly widened into a global conflagration. Spain entered the fray against Britain in 1779, as did Holland. Combined Spanish and French fleets outnumbered those of England, and on two occasions the British Isles seemed to be at the mercy of hostile warships.

The weak maritime neutrals of Europe, who had suffered from Britain's dominance over the seas, now began to demand more respect for their rights. In 1780 the imperious Catherine the Great of Russia took the lead in organizing the Armed Neutrality, which she later sneeringly called the "Armed Nullity." It lined up almost all the remaining European neutrals in an attitude of passive hostility toward England. The war was now being fought not only in Europe and North America, but also in South America, the Caribbean, and Asia.

To say that America, with some French aid, defeated England is like saying, "Daddy and I killed the bear." To the Mother Country, struggling for her very life, the scuffle in the New World became secondary. The Americans deserve credit for having kept the war going until 1778, with secret French aid. But they did not achieve their independence until the conflict erupted into a multi-power world war that was too big for Britain to handle. From 1778 to 1783, France provided the rebels with large sums of money, immense amounts of equipment, about one-half of America's regular armed forces, and practically all of the new nation's naval strength.

Britain Against the World

Britain and Allies		*Enemy or Unfriendly Powers*

Great Britain
Some Loyalists and Indians
30,000 hired Hessians
(*Total population on
  Britain's side: c. 8 million*)
	Belligerents
	(*Total population:
	  c. 39.5 million*)
		{ United States, 1775–1783
		France, 1778–1783
		Spain, 1779–1783
		Holland, 1779–1783
		
		Ireland (restive)

	Members of the Armed Neutral- ity (with dates of joining)	{ Russia, 1780 Denmark–Norway, 1780 Sweden, 1780 Holy Roman Empire, 1781 Prussia, 1782 Portugal, 1782 Two Sicilies, 1783 (after peace signed)

France's entrance into the conflict forced the British to change their basic strategy in America. Hitherto they could count on blockading the colonial coast and commanding the seas. Now the French had powerful fleets in American waters, chiefly to protect their own valuable West Indian islands, but in a position to jeopardize Britain's blockade and lines of supply. The British therefore decided to evacuate Philadelphia and concentrate their strength in New York City.

In June 1778, the withdrawing Redcoats were attacked by General Washington at Monmouth, New Jersey, on a blisteringly hot day. Scores of men collapsed or died from sunstroke. But the battle was indecisive, and the British escaped to New York, although about one-third of their Hessians deserted. Henceforth, except for the Yorktown interlude of 1781, Washington remained in the New York area hemming in the British.

Blow and Counterblow

In the summer of 1780 a powerful French army of 6,000 regular troops, commanded by the Comte de Rochambeau, arrived in Newport, Rhode Island. The Americans were somewhat suspicious of their former enemies; in fact, several ugly flare-ups, involving minor bloodshed, had already occurred between the new allies. But French gold and goodwill melted restraints. Dancing parties were arranged with the prim

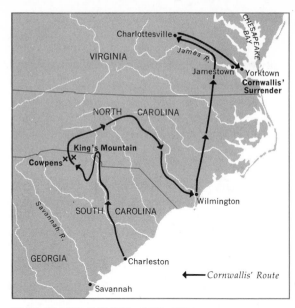

WAR IN THE SOUTH, 1780–1781

Puritan maidens; and one French officer related, doubtless with exaggeration, "The simple innocence of the Garden of Eden prevailed." No real military advantage came immediately from this French reinforcement, although preparations were made for a Franco-American attack on New York.

Improving American morale was staggered later in 1780, when General Benedict Arnold turned traitor. A leader of undoubted dash and brilliance, he was ambitious, greedy, unscrupulous, and suffering from a well-grounded but petulant feeling that his valuable services were not fully appreciated. He plotted with the British to sell out the key stronghold of West Point, which commanded the Hudson River, for £6,300 and an officer's commission. By the sheerest accident the plot was detected in the nick of time, and Arnold fled to the British. "Whom can we trust now?" cried General Washington in anguish.

The British meanwhile had devised a plan to roll up the colonies, beginning with the South, where the Loyalists were numerous. Georgia was ruthlessly overrun in 1778–1779; Charleston, South Carolina, fell in 1780. The surrender of the city to the British involved the capture of 5,000 men and 400 cannon, and was a heavier loss to the

Comte de Rochambeau (1735–1807). He got along so well with Washington that one observer said that the Comte was created to understand the American general. A statue of Rochambeau, a gift from France in 1902, was placed in Lafayette Square, across from the White House in Washington, D.C. (National Portrait Gallery, Smithsonian Institution, Washington, D.C.)

Americans, in relation to existing strength, than that of Burgoyne was to the British.

Warfare now intensified in the Carolinas, where Patriots bitterly fought their Loyalist neighbors. It was not uncommon for prisoners on both sides to be butchered in cold blood after they had thrown down their arms. A turn of the tide came late in 1780 and early in 1781, when American riflemen wiped out a British detachment at King's Mountain, and then defeated a smaller force at Cowpens. In the Carolina campaign of 1781, General Nathanael Greene, a Quaker-reared tactician, distinguished himself by his strategy of delay. Standing and then retreating, he exhausted his foe, General Cornwallis, in vain pursuit. By losing battles but winning campaigns, the "Fighting Quaker" finally succeeded in clearing most of Georgia and South Carolina of British troops.

The Land Frontier and the Sea Frontier

The West was ablaze during much of the war. Indian allies of George III, hoping to protect their land, were busy with torch and tomahawk; they were egged on by British agents branded as "hair buyers" because they allegedly paid bounties for American scalps. Fateful 1777 was known as "the Bloody Year" on the frontier. Yet the human tide of westward-moving pioneers did not halt its flow. Eloquent testimony is provided by place names in Kentucky, such as Lexington (named after the battle) and Louisville (named after America's new ally, Louis XVI).

In the wild Illinois country the British were vulnerable to attack, for they held scattered posts which they had captured from the French. An audacious frontiersman, George Rogers Clark, conceived the idea of seizing these forts by surprise. With the blessing of Virginia and £1,200 in depreciated currency, he floated down the Ohio River with about 175 men and captured in quick succession Kaskaskia, Cahokia, and Vincennes. These daring forays no doubt helped quiet the Indians. But Clark's admirers have also assumed, without positive proof, that his occupation of

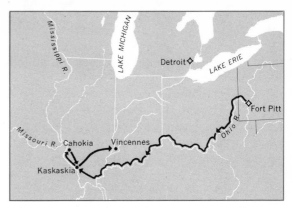

GEORGE ROGERS CLARK'S CAMPAIGN, 1778–1779

the southwest corner of the great area north of the Ohio River forced the British to cede the whole region to the United States at the peace table in Paris.

America's infant navy had meanwhile been laying the foundations of a brilliant tradition. The naval establishment consisted of only a handful of nondescript ships, commanded by daring officers, the most famous of whom was a hard-fighting young Scotsman, John Paul Jones. As events turned out, this tiny naval force never made a real dent in Britain's thunderous fleets. Its chief contribution was in destroying British merchant shipping, and thus carrying the war into the waters around the British Isles. An English song of the time, critical of the Royal Navy, began:

The tradesmen stand still, and the merchant bemoans
The losses he meets with from such as Paul Jones.

More numerous and damaging than ships of the regular American navy were swift privateers. These craft were privately owned armed ships—legalized pirates in a sense—specifically author-

Early American Naval Flag. The flag is shown with a yellow background and a rattler striking.

ized by Congress to prey on enemy shipping. Altogether over 1,000 American privateers, responding to the call of patriotism and profit, sallied forth with about 70,000 men ("sailors of fortune"). They captured some 600 British prizes, while British warships captured about as many American merchantmen and privateers.

Privateering was not an unalloyed asset. It had the unfortunate effect of diverting manpower from the main war effort and involving Americans, including Benedict Arnold, in speculation and graft. But the privateers brought in urgently needed gold, harassed the enemy, and raised American morale by providing victories at a time when victories were few. British shipping was so badly riddled by privateers and by the regular American navy that insurance rates skyrocketed. Merchant ships were compelled to sail in convoy, and British shippers and manufacturers brought increasing pressure on Parliament to end the war on honorable terms.

Yorktown and the Final Curtain

One of the darkest periods of the war was 1780–1781, before the last decisive victory. Inflation of the currency was continuing at full gallop. Not only was the government virtually bankrupt but Congress had been forced to repudiate its financial obligations, in part, on a forty-to-one basis. Despair was prevalent; disunion was increasing among the states; and mutiny over back pay was spreading in the army.

Meanwhile the British General Cornwallis was blundering into a trap. After futile operations in Virginia, he had fallen back to Chesapeake Bay at Yorktown, there to await seaborne supplies and reinforcements. He assumed that Britain would continue to control the sea. But these few fateful weeks just happened to be one of the brief periods during the war in America when British naval superiority slipped away.

The French were now prepared to cooperate energetically in a brilliant stroke. Admiral de Grasse, operating with a powerful fleet in the West Indies, advised the Americans that he was free to join with them in an assault on Cornwallis at Yorktown. Quick to seize this opportunity, General Washington made a swift march of more than 300 miles (483 kilometers) to the Chesapeake from the New York area. Accompanied by Rochambeau's French army, he beset the British by land, while De Grasse blockaded them by sea after beating off the British fleet. Completely cornered, Cornwallis surrendered his entire force of 7,000 men, on October 19, 1781, as his band appropriately played "The World Turn'd Upside Down." The triumph was no less French than American: the French provided essentially all the seapower and about half of the regular troops in the besieging army of some 16,000 men.

Stunned by news of the disaster, Prime Minister Lord North cried, "Oh God! It's all over! It's all over!" But it was not. George III stubbornly planned to continue the struggle, for England was far from being crushed. She still had 54,000 troops in North America, including 32,000 in the United States. Washington returned with his army to New York, there to continue keeping a vigilant eye on the British force of 10,000 men.

Fighting actually continued for more than a year after Yorktown, with Patriot-Loyalist warfare in the South especially savage. "No quarter for Tories" was the common battle cry. One of Washington's most valuable contributions was to keep the languishing cause alive, the army in the field, and the states together during these

Lord George Germain, secretary of state for the colonies and a chief architect of war plans, swelled with confidence after Yorktown: "So very contemptible is the Rebel Force now in all Parts, and so vast is Our Superiority everywhere, that no resistance on their [Americans'] Part is to be apprehended, that can materially obstruct the Progress of the King's Army in the Speedy Suppression of the Rebellion."

Benjamin Franklin (1706–1790). He left school at age ten, and became a wealthy businessman; a journalist; an inventor; a scientist; a legislator; and pre-eminently a statesman-diplomatist. He was sent to France in 1776 as the American envoy at age seventy, and he remained there until 1785, negotiating the alliance with the French and helping to negotiate the treaty of peace. His fame had preceded him, and when he discarded his wig for the fur cap of a simple "American agriculturist," he took French society by storm. The ladies, with whom he was a great favorite, honored him by adopting the high *coiffure à la Franklin* in imitation of his cap.

critical months. Otherwise a satisfactory peace treaty might never have been signed.

Peace at Paris

After Yorktown, the war-weary British were increasingly ready to come to terms. They had suffered heavy reverses in India and in the West Indies. The island of Minorca in the Mediterranean had fallen; the Rock of Gibraltar was tottering. Lord North's ministry collapsed in March 1782, temporarily ending the personal rule of George III. A Whig ministry, rather favorable to the Americans, replaced the Tory regime of Lord North.

Three American peace negotiators had meanwhile gathered at Paris: the aging but astute Benjamin Franklin; the flinty John Adams, vigilant for New England interests; and the impulsive John Jay of New York, deeply suspicious of Old World intrigue. The three envoys had explicit instructions from Congress to make no separate peace, and to consult with their French allies at all stages of the negotiations. But the American representatives chafed under this directive. They well knew that it had been written by a subservient Congress, with the French Foreign Office indirectly guiding the pen.

France was in a painful position. She had induced Spain to enter the war on her side, in part by promising to deliver British-held Gibraltar. Yet the towering rock was defying frantic joint assaults by Frenchmen and Spaniards. Spain also coveted the immense trans-Allegheny area, on which restless American pioneers were already settling.

France, ever eager to smash Britain's empire, desired an independent United States, but one feebly independent. She therefore schemed to keep the new republic cooped up east of the Allegheny Mountains. A weak America—like a horse gentle enough to plow but not vigorous enough to kick—would be easier to manage in promoting French interests and policy. France was paying a heavy price in men and treasure to win America's independence, and she wanted to get her money's worth.

But John Jay was unwilling to play France's game. Suspiciously alert, he perceived that the French could not satisfy the conflicting ambitions of both Americans and Spaniards. He saw signs—or thought he did—which indicated that the Paris Foreign Office was about to betray America's trans-Allegheny interests to satisfy those of Spain. He therefore secretly made separate overtures to London, contrary to his instructions from Congress. The hard-pressed British, eager to entice one of their enemies from the alliance, speedily came to terms with the Americans. A preliminary treaty of peace was signed in 1782; the final peace, the next year.

UNITED STATES IN 1783

By the Treaty of Paris of 1783, the British formally recognized the independence of the United States. In addition, they granted generous boundaries, stretching majestically to the Mississippi on the west, to the Great Lakes on the north, and to Spanish Florida on the south. (Spain had recently captured Florida from Britain.) The Yankees, though now divorced from the Empire, were to retain a share in the priceless fisheries of Newfoundland. The Canadians, of course, were profoundly displeased.

The Americans, on their part, had to yield important concessions. Loyalists were not to be further persecuted, and Congress was to *recommend* to the state legislatures that confiscated Loyalist property be restored. As for the debts long owed to British creditors, the American states were bound to put no lawful obstacles in the way of their collection. Unhappily for future harmony,

I□II□II□II□II□II□II□II□II□II□II□II□II□II□II□II□II□II□I

Blundering George III, a poor loser, wrote this of America: "Knavery seems to be so much the striking feature of its inhabitants that it may not in the end be an evil that they become aliens to this Kingdom."

I□II□II□II□II□II□II□II□II□II□II□II□II□II□II□II□II□II□I

the assurances regarding both debts and Loyalists were not carried out in the manner hoped for by London.

A New Nation Legitimized

Britain's terms were liberal almost beyond belief. The enormous trans-Allegheny area was thrown in as a virtual gift, for George Rogers Clark had captured only a small segment of it. Why the generosity? Had the United States beaten the Mother Country to her knees?

The key to the riddle may be found in the Old World. At the time the peace terms were drafted, England was trying to seduce America from her French alliance, so she made the terms as alluring as possible. The shaky Whig ministry, hanging on by its fingernails for only a few months, was more friendly to the Americans than were the

The Reconciliation Between Britannia and Her Daughter America. America (represented by an Indian) is invited to buss (kiss) her mother. (Detail from an English cartoon. New York Public Library.)

Tories. It was determined, by a policy of liberality, to salve recent wounds, reopen old trade channels, and prevent future wars over the coveted trans-Allegheny region. This far-visioned policy was regrettably not followed by the successors of the Whigs.

In spirit, the Americans made a separate peace—contrary to the French alliance. In fact, they did not. The Paris Foreign Office formally approved the terms of peace, though disturbed by the lone-wolf course of its American ally. France was immensely relieved by the prospect of bringing the costly conflict to an end, and of freeing herself from her embarrassing promises to the Spanish Crown.

America alone gained from the world-girdling war. The British, though soon to stage a comeback, were battered and beaten. The French gained sweet revenge, but plunged headlong down the slippery slope to bankruptcy and revolution. In truth, Dame Fortune smiled benignly on the Americans. Snatching their independence from the furnace of world conflict, they began their national career with a splendid territorial birthright and a priceless heritage of freedom. Seldom, if ever, has any people been so favored.

VARYING VIEWPOINTS

The consequences of the Revolution have recently been re-examined in much the same way as its causes. Scholars used to think that the conflict brought sweeping changes in social life and political institutions. Some historians now consider that view greatly exaggerated. They tend to agree with John Adams, who once said that history had already made radicals out of the Americans—and that the Revolution, therefore, was a conservative protest to maintain existing liberties. But this emphasis does not necessarily deny the real radicalism of the Revolution. There were sweeping changes, modern scholars conclude, but not so much in daily life as in people's minds. Democratic and egalitarian ideas had been current in the colonial period but always surrounded by a certain air of illegitimacy and impermanency. Now they could be seen as fully legitimate, correct, and successful. This sense of rightness began to spill over into many areas of life, creating pressures for social change in later movements of American history, such as Jacksonian democracy and the drive to abolish slavery. But problems remain with this persuasive view. What, for example, are historians to make of the Loyalists, supposedly arch-conservatives, if in fact we regard the Patriots themselves as conservative defenders of existing conditions?

SELECT READINGS

The war is sketched briefly in H. H. Peckham, *The War for Independence* (1958); more fully in J. R. Alden, *A History of the American Revolution* (1969). An excellent military history is D. Higginbotham, *The War of American Independence: Military Attitudes, Policies and Practice, 1763–1789* (1971). A highly original essay is John Shy, *A People Numerous and Armed: Reflections on the Military Struggle for American Independence* (1976). Highly imaginative is Charles Royster, *A Revolutionary People at War: The Continental Army and the American Character* (1980). The conflict is considered in its European setting in Piers Mackesy, *The War for America, 1775–1783* (1964). Carl Becker's classic *The Declaration of Independence* (1922) is masterful; on the same subject, see also David Hawke, *A Transaction of*

Free Men (1964). Propaganda is analyzed in Carl Berger, *Broadsides and Bayonets* (1961). The role of the Loyalists is treated in W. H. Nelson, *The American Tory* (1961), W. Brown, *The Good Americans: The Loyalists in the American Revolution* (1969), R. Calhoon, *The Loyalists in Revolutionary America* (1973), and B. Bailyn's unusually sensitive biography of the governor of colonial Massachusetts, *The Ordeal of Thomas Hutchinson* (1974). A general treatment of an often neglected subject is B. Quarles, *The Negro in the American Revolution* (1961). See also D. MacLeod, *Slavery, Race and the American Revolution* (1974), and D. B. Davis, *The Problem of Slavery in the Age of Revolution, 1770–1823* (1975), an able, gracefully written book. International implications are developed in S. F. Bemis, *The Diplomacy of the American Revolution* (1935), W. C. Stinchcombe, *The American Revolution and the French Alliance* (1969), J. H. Hutson, *John Adams and the Diplomacy of the American Revolution* (1980), and in R. B. Morris, *The Peacemakers: The Great Powers and American Independence* (1965). See also the same author's *The American Revolution Reconsidered* (1967). Gary Wills has trenchantly reexamined the Declaration in *Inventing America: Jefferson's Declaration of Independence* (1980). Attention to the social history of the Revolution has been largely inspired by J. F. Jameson's seminal *The American Revolution Considered as a Social Movement* (1926). J. R. Main, *The Social Structure of Revolutionary America* (1969), takes the exploration further along the same lines, with conclusions somewhat at variance with Jameson's. See also James Hutson and S. Kurz, *Essays on the American Revolution* (1973). Interesting biographies are S. E. Morison's swashbuckling *John Paul Jones* (1959); E. Foner's *Tom Paine and Revolutionary America* (1976); O. Aldridge's study of the same subject, *Man of Reason* (1959); J. T. Flexner, *George Washington in the American Revolution, 1775–1783* (1968); and R. Burlingame, *Benjamin Franklin: Envoy Extraordinary* (1967). British troubles are laid bare in G. S. Brown, *The American Secretary: The Colonial Policy of Lord George Germain, 1775–1778* (1963), and in W. B. Willcox, *Portrait of a General: Sir Henry Clinton in the War of Independence* (1964). Women are the subject of Linda K. Kerber, *Women of the Republic: Intellect and Ideology in Revolutionary America* (1980), and Mary Beth Norton, *Liberty's Daughters: The Revolutionary Experience of American Women* (1980). Jack N. Rakove has provided a masterful history of the Continental Congress in *The Beginnings of National Politics* (1979). An excellent guide to the scholarly controversies about the period is Jack P. Greene, ed., *The Reinterpretation of the American Revolution* (1968). Michael Kammen brilliantly evokes the ways the Revolution has been enshrined in the national memory in *A Season of Youth: The American Revolution and the Historical Imagination* (1978).

7

The Confederation and the Constitution

This example of changing the constitution by assembling the wise men of the state, instead of assembling armies, will be worth as much to the world as the former examples we have given it.

THOMAS JEFFERSON, 1787

The Residue of Revolution

The American Revolution was not a revolution in the sense of a radical or total change. It was not a sudden and violent overturning of the political and social framework, such as later occurred in France and Russia, when both were already independent nations. Significant changes were ushered in, but they were not breathtaking. What happened was accelerated evolution rather than outright revolution. During the conflict itself people went on working and praying, marrying and playing. Most of them were not seriously disturbed by the actual fighting, and many of the more isolated communities scarcely knew that a war was on.

IＩＯＩＩＯＩＩＯＩＩＯＩＩＯＩＩＯＩＩＯＩＩＯＩＩＯＩＩＯＩＩＯＩＩＯＩＩＯＩＩＯＩＩＯＩＩＯＩＩＯＩ

> The impact of the American Revolution was worldwide. About 1783 a British ship stopped at some islands off the East African coast, where the natives were revolting against their Arab masters. When asked why they were fighting they replied, "America is free. Could not we be?"

IＩＯＩＩＯＩＩＯＩＩＯＩＩＯＩＩＯＩＩＯＩＩＯＩＩＯＩＩＯＩＩＯＩＩＯＩＩＯＩＩＯＩＩＯＩＩＯＩＩＯＩＩＯ

America's War of Independence heralded the birth of three modern nations. One was Canada, which received its first large influx of English-speaking population from the thousands of Loyalists who fled there from the United States. Another was Australia, which became a convict dumping ground, now that America was no longer available for jailbirds. The third newcomer (by far the most important)—the United States—based itself squarely on republican principles.

Yet even the political overturn was not so revolutionary as one might suppose. In some states, notably Connecticut and Rhode Island, the war largely ratified a colonial self-rule already existing. Hated British officials, everywhere ousted, were replaced by a home-grown governing class, which promptly sought a local substitute for King and Parliament.

After the shooting started, the thirteen independent states were forced to devise new constitutions. For a time the manufacturing of governments was more pressing than the manufacturing of gunpowder. In the cases of Connecticut and Rhode Island, the yellowing charters were kept essentially intact but were retouched a bit to conform to new conditions. Significantly, none of the state constitutions was a radical departure from what the people had been accustomed to in the older colonial charters.

The newly forged state constitutions enjoyed many features in common. Their similarity, as it turned out, made easier the drafting of a workable federal charter when the time was ripe. Some of the state constitutions included bills of rights, specifically guaranteeing long-prized liberties. Most of them required the annual election of legislators, who were thus forced to toe the mark. All of them had weak executive and judicial branches, at least by present-day standards. The explanation is that the legislatures, now granted sweeping powers, were more directly representative of the people and hence more responsive to popular control. A generation of quarreling with His Majesty's officials had implanted a deep distrust of despotic governors and arbitrary judges.

At the end of the shooting, as before, none of the states enjoyed universal manhood suffrage, and only a few women were allowed to vote. In all of them a voter or officeholder was required to own property or pay taxes. During the war the restrictions on voting were eased in about half the states, but were increased in a few others.

Yet encouraging gains were registered for political democracy. More people—probably many more—could vote after the Revolution than before. This was especially true of the scorned back-country folk, notably the Germans and Scotch-Irish of Pennsylvania. Tories, quite understandably, had sneered:

> Down at night a bricklayer or carpenter lies,
> Next sun a Lycurgus, a Solon doth rise.

New Social Fabrics

Social changes were striking but not bewildering. The expulsion of some 80,000 substantial Loyalists robbed the new ship of state of valuable leadership as well as of needed conservative ballast. This loss also weakened the aristocratic upper crust, with all its culture and elegance, and produced a gain for democratic "leveling."

War inevitably breeds a loosening of moral standards, often manifested in a spirit of "eat, drink, and be merry, for tomorrow we die." Sixty distilleries had operated in Massachusetts during the war. Alarmists pointed to the sharp increase of juvenile delinquency, of Sabbath breaking, of absenteeism from churches, and of the spread of

French radical ideas, notably those of the free-thinking Voltaire.

Church buildings had suffered severely from the conflict. Many of them were destroyed or damaged by invading armies, which thus vented their wrath against Whiggish preachers of sedition. Old South Church in Boston, for example, was made into a riding school for British cavalry.

The Anglican Church, tainted by association with the British Crown, was ruined. A new, de-Anglicized American church had to be built on the ashes of the old one. The Protestant Episcopal Church was therefore launched shortly after the guns fell silent. This blow to the Anglican Church, combined with the feverish democratic spirit aroused by the war, encouraged the spread of other faiths, especially on the frontier. Conspicuous among them were the more zestful Baptists and Methodists, whose popularity resulted in part from their more democratic organization.

A protracted fight for separation of church and state resulted in spectacular gains. Although the well-entrenched Congregational Church continued to be legally established in some New England states, the Anglican Church was everywhere disestablished. The struggle for a complete divorce between religion and government proved to be bitterest in Virginia. It was prolonged to 1786, when free-thinking Thomas Jefferson and his co-reformers, including the lowly Baptists, won a complete victory. (See table of established churches, p. 71.)

Social democracy was further stimulated by the widening of the franchise and the growth of trade organizations for artisans and laborers. Citizens in many states, flushed with republican fervor, also sawed off the remaining shackles of medieval inheritance laws, such as primogeniture, which awarded all a father's property to the eldest son.

The Revolutionary War likewise weakened the institution of slavery. Hostilities had hampered the noxious trade in "black ivory," and most of the new state constitutions forbade its renewal. Several Northern states either abolished slavery outright or provided for the gradual emancipation of black

Charleston Slave Advertisement. *State Gazette of South Carolina*, 1787.

bondsmen. These laws codified the Declaration's concept that "all men are created equal," though laws against interracial marriage sprang up at the same time. Even in slave-burdened Virginia, a few idealistic masters freed their human chattels. In this revolution of sentiments, symbolized and inspired by the Declaration of Independence, were to be found the frail first sprouts of the later abolitionist movement.

Historians have searched with less success in the record of the Revolutionary era for the seeds of the feminist movement. Some women did serve (disguised as men) in the military, and New Jersey's new constitution in 1776 even temporarily gave women the vote. But though Abigail Adams teased her husband John Adams in 1777 that "the ladies" were determined "to foment a rebellion" of their own if they were not given political rights, most women were still doing traditional women's work.

Why in this dawning democratic age did abolition not go further and blot the evil of slavery from the fresh face of the new nation? The sad truth is that the fledgling idealism of the Founding Fathers was sacrificed to political expediency. A fight over the slavery issue would have fractured the fragile national unity that was so desperately needed. Nearly a century later, the same issue did wreck the Union—temporarily.

Education was temporarily blighted by the war, as schools were physically damaged, put on a part-time basis, or completely closed. Yet a refreshing spirit of liberalism began to suffuse the college curricula, partly as a result of the French alliance and the presence of French officers and troops in America. In 1782 Harvard College, one of the last holdouts, finally permitted the substitution of French for Hebrew.

Economic Crosscurrents

Economic changes begotten by the war were likewise noteworthy, but not overwhelming. States seized control of former Crown lands, and although rich speculators had their day, many of the large Loyalist holdings were confiscated and eventually cut up into small farms. Roger Morris' huge estate in New York, for example, was sliced into 250 parcels—thus accelerating the spread of economic democracy. The frightful excesses of the French Revolution were avoided, partly because cheap land was easily available. Men do not chop off heads so readily when they can chop down trees. It is highly significant that in the United States economic democracy, broadly speaking, preceded political democracy.

A sharp stimulus was given to manufacturing by the pre-war non-importation agreements, and later by the war itself. Goods that had formerly been imported from England were mostly cut off, and the ingenious Yankee was forced to make his own. Ten years after the Revolution the busy Brandywine Creek, south of Philadelphia, was turning the waterwheels of numerous mills along an 8-mile (13-kilometer) stretch. Yet America remained overwhelmingly a nation of soil-tillers.

Economically speaking, independence had drawbacks. Much of the coveted commerce of the Mother Country was still reserved for the loyal parts of the empire; and now that the Americans were aliens, they were forced to find new customers. Fisheries were disrupted, and bounties for ships' stores had abruptly ended. In some respects, the hated British Navigation Laws were

Thomas Jefferson, then minister to France, was not overjoyed by the prospect of much manufacturing. As he wrote (1784), "While we have land to labor then, let us never wish to see our citizens occupied at a work-bench, or twirling a distaff. . . . For the general operations of manufacture, let our workshops remain in Europe. . . . The mobs of great cities add just so much to the support of pure government, as sores do to the strength of the human body."

more disagreeable after independence than before.

New commercial outlets, fortunately, compensated partially for the loss of old ones. Americans could now trade freely with foreign nations, subject to local restrictions—a boon they had not enjoyed in the old days of mercantilism. Enterprising Yankee shippers ventured boldly—and profitably—into the Baltic and China seas. In 1784 the *Empress of China*, carrying a valuable weed (ginseng) that was highly prized by Chinese herb doctors as a cure for impotence, led the way into the East Asian markets.

Yet the general economic picture was far from being rosy. War had spawned demoralizing extravagance, speculation, and profiteering, with profits as indecently high as 300 percent. Runaway inflation had been ruinous to middle-class citizens on fixed incomes, and Congress had failed in its feeble attempts to curb economic laws by fixing prices. Probably the average citizen was worse off financially at the end of the shooting than he had been at the beginning.

The whole economic and social atmosphere was unhealthy. A newly rich class of profiteers was noisily conspicuous, while many once-wealthy people were left destitute. The controversy leading to the war had bred a keen distaste for taxes; and the wholesale seizure of Loyalist estates had encouraged disrespect for private property. John

Adams had been shocked when gleefully told by a horse-jockey neighbor that the courts of justice were all closed—a plight that proved to be only temporary.

A Shaky Start Toward Union

What would the Americans do with the independence they had so dearly won? London had dumped the responsibility of creating and operating a new central government squarely into their laps.

Prospects for erecting a lasting regime were far from bright. It is always difficult to set up a new government, doubly difficult to set up a new type of government. The picture was further confused in America by men preaching "natural rights" and looking suspiciously at all persons clothed with authority. America was more a name than a nation, and unity ran little deeper than the color on the map.

Disruptive forces stalked the land. The stabilizing Tory element had been tossed overboard. Patriots had fought the war with a high degree of disunity, but they had at least enjoyed the unifying cement of a common cause. Now even that was gone. It would have been almost a miracle if any government fashioned in all this confusion had long endured.

Hard times, the bane of all regimes, set in shortly after the war, and hit bottom in 1786. As if other troubles were not enough, British manufacturers, with dammed-up surpluses, began flooding the American market with cut-rate goods. War-baby American industries, in particular, suffered industrial colic from such ruthless competition. One Philadelphia newspaper in 1783 urged the use of ill-fitting homespun cloth:

> Of foreign gewgaws let's be free,
> And wear the webs of liberty.

Yet hopeful signs could be discerned. The thirteen sovereign states were basically alike in governmental structure, and functioned under similar constitutions. Americans enjoyed a rich political inheritance, derived partly from England and partly from their own homegrown devices for self-government. Finally, they were blessed with political leaders of a high order in men like George Washington, James Madison, John Adams, Thomas Jefferson, and Alexander Hamilton.

Creating a Confederation

The Second Continental Congress of Revolution days was little more than a conference of ambassadors from the thirteen states. It was totally without constitutional authority, and in general did only what it dared to do. In all respects the states were sovereign, for they coined money, raised armies and navies, and erected tariff barriers. The legislature of Virginia even ratified separately the treaty of alliance of 1778 with France.

Shortly before declaring independence in 1776, the Congress appointed a committee to draft a written constitution for the new nation. The finished product was the Articles of Confederation. Adopted by Congress in 1777, it was translated into French after the battle of Saratoga so as to convince France that America had a genuine government in the making. In due course this new constitution was sent out to the states for their

A View of the State House in Philadelphia.

Independence Hall. Here the Declaration of Independence, Articles of Confederation, and U.S. Constitution were signed. (Free Library of Philadelphia.)

WESTERN LANDS, 1783

WESTERN LANDS, 1802

approval. But final action was delayed for four years, until 1781, less than eight months before the decisive victory at Yorktown.

The chief apple of discord was western lands. Six of the jealous states, including Pennsylvania and Maryland, had no holdings beyond the Allegheny Mountains. Seven, notably New York and Virginia, were favored with enormous acreage, on the basis of earlier sea-to-sea charter grants. The six landless states argued that their more fortunate sisters would not have retained possession of this splendid prize if all the other states had not fought for it also. A major complaint was that the land-blessed states could sell their trans-Allegheny tracts, and thus pay off pensions and other debts incurred in the common cause. States without such holdings would have to tax themselves heavily to defray these obligations. Why not turn the whole western area over to the central government?

Unanimous approval of the Articles of Confederation by the thirteen states was required, and landless Maryland stubbornly held out until March 1, 1781. She at length gave in when New York sur-

rendered her western claims, and Virginia seemed about to do so. To sweeten the pill, Congress pledged itself to dispose of these vast areas for the "common benefit." It further agreed to carve from the new public domain not colonies but a number of "republican" states, which in time would be admitted to the Union on terms of complete equality with all the others. This extraordinary commitment faithfully reflected the anti-colonial spirit of the Revolution, and the pledge was later fully redeemed in the famed Northwest Ordinance of 1787.

Fertile public lands thus transferred to the central government proved to be an invaluable bond of union. The states that had thrown their heritage into the common pot had to remain in the Union if they were to reap their share of the advantages from the land sales. An army of westward-moving pioneers purchased their farms from the federal government, directly or indirectly, and they learned to look to the national capital, rather than to the state capitals—with a consequent weakening of local influence. Finally, a uniform national land policy was made possible.

The Articles of Confederation: America's First Constitution

The Articles of Confederation—some have said "Articles of Confusion"—provided for a loose confederation or "firm league of friendship." Thirteen independent states were thus linked together for joint action in dealing with common problems, such as foreign affairs. A clumsy Congress was to be the chief agency of government. There was no executive branch—George III had left a bad taste—and the vital judicial arm was left almost exclusively to the states, which remained sovereign.

Congress, though dominant, was closely hobbled. All bills dealing with specified subjects of importance required at least a two-thirds vote; any amendment of the Articles themselves required a unanimous vote. Unanimity was almost impossible, and this meant that the amending process, perhaps fortunately, was unworkable. If it had been workable, the Republic might have struggled along with a patched-up Articles of Confederation rather than adopting an effective new Constitution.

The shackled Congress was weak—and was purposely designed to be weak. Suspicious states, having just won control over taxation and commerce from Britain, had no desire to yield their newly acquired privileges to an American Parliament—even one of their own making.

Two handicaps of the Congress were crippling. It had no power to regulate commerce, and this weakness left the states free to establish conflictingly different laws regarding tariffs and navigation. Nor could the Congress enforce its tax-collection program. It established a tax quota for each of the states, and then asked them please to contribute their share on a voluntary basis. The central authority—a "government by supplication"—was lucky if in any year it received one-fourth of its requests.

The feeble national government in Philadelphia could advise and recommend and request. But in dealing with the independent states it could not command or coerce or enforce. It could not act directly upon the individual citizens of a sovereign

state; it could not even protect itself against gross indignities. In 1783 a dangerous threat came from a group of mutinous Pennsylvania soldiers who demanded back pay. After Congress had appealed in vain to the state for protection, the members were forced to move in disgrace to Princeton College in New Jersey. The new Congress, with all its paper powers, was even less effective than the old Continental Congress, with no constitutional powers at all.

Yet the Articles of Confederation, weak though they were, proved to be a landmark in government. They were for those days a model of what a loose *con*federation ought to be. Thomas Jefferson enthusiastically hailed the new structure as the best one "existing or that ever did exist." To compare it with the European governments, he thought, was like comparing "heaven and hell." But although the Confederation was praiseworthy as confederations went, the troubled times demanded not a loose *con*federation but a tightly knit federation. This involved the yielding by the states of their sovereignty to a completely new federal government, which in turn would leave them free to control their local affairs.

Despite their defects, the Articles of Confederation were a significant steppingstone toward the present Constitution. They clearly outlined the general powers that were to be exercised by the central government, such as making treaties and establishing a postal service. As the first written constitution of the Republic, the Articles kept alive the flickering ideal of union and held the

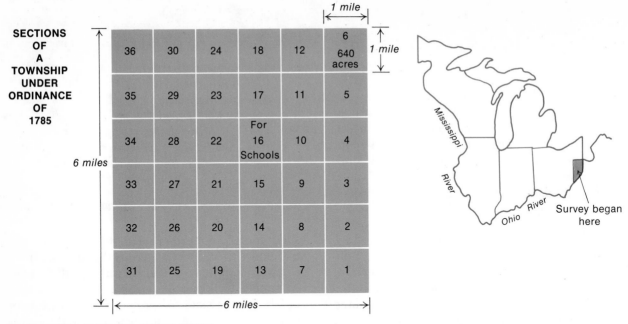

					1 mile
36	30	24	18	12	6 640 acres
35	29	23	17	11	5
34	28	22	For 16 Schools	10	4
33	27	21	15	9	3
32	26	20	14	8	2
31	25	19	13	7	1

SECTIONS OF A TOWNSHIP UNDER ORDINANCE OF 1785

6 miles

6 miles

1 mile

Mississippi River

Ohio River

Survey began here

SURVEYING THE OLD NORTHWEST

states together—until such time as they were ripe for a strong constitution by peaceful, evolutionary methods. The anemic Articles represented what the states regarded as an alarming surrender of their power. Without this intermediary jump, they probably would never have consented to the breathtaking leap from the old boycott Association of 1774 to the Constitution of the United States.

Landmarks in Land Laws

Handcuffed though the Congress of the Confederation was, it managed to pass two supremely farsighted pieces of legislation. These related to an immense part of the public domain recently acquired from the states, and commonly known as the Old Northwest. This area lay northwest of the Ohio River, east of the Mississippi River, and south of the Great Lakes.

The first of these red-letter laws was the Land Ordinance of 1785. It provided that the acreage of the Old Northwest should be sold, and that the proceeds should be used to help pay off the national debt. The vast area was to be surveyed be-

fore sale and settlement, thus forestalling endless confusion and lawsuits. It was to be divided into townships six miles square, each of which in turn was to be split into thirty-six sections of one square mile each. The sixteenth section of each township was set aside to be sold for the benefit of the public schools—a priceless gift to education in the Northwest.

Even more noteworthy was the Northwest Ordinance of 1787, which related to governing of the Old Northwest. This law came to grips with the problem of how a nation should deal with its colonial peoples—the same problem that had bedeviled the King and Parliament in London. The solution provided by the Northwest Ordinance was a judicious compromise: temporary tutelage, then permanent equality. First, there would be two evolutionary territorial stages, during which the area would be subordinate to the federal government. Then, when a territory could boast 60,000 inhabitants, it might be admitted by Congress as a state, with all the privileges of the thirteen charter members. (This is precisely what the Continental Congress had promised the states when they surrendered their lands in 1781.) The Ordinance also forbade slavery in the Old Northwest—a path-breaking gain for freedom.

The wisdom of Congress in handling this explosive problem deserves warm praise. If it had attempted to chain the new territories in permanent subordination, a second American Revolution almost certainly would have erupted in later years, fought this time by the West against the East. Congress thus neatly solved the seemingly insoluble problem of empire. The scheme worked so well that its basic principles were ultimately carried over from the Old Northwest to other frontier areas.

The World's Ugly Duckling

Foreign relations, especially with London, continued troubled during these anxious years of the Confederation. The Mother Country resented the stab in the back from her rebellious offspring, and for eight years she refused to send a minister to America's "backwoods" capital. She suggested, with barbed irony, that if she sent one she would have to send thirteen.

Britain flatly declined to make a commercial treaty or to repeal her ancient Navigation Laws. Lord Sheffield, whose ungenerous views prevailed, argued persuasively in a widely sold pamphlet that England would win back America's trade anyhow. Commerce, he insisted, would naturally follow old channels. So why go to the Americans hat in hand? The British also officially shut off their profitable West Indian trade from the United States, though the Yankees, with their time-tested skill in smuggling, illegally shared some of it nonetheless.

Scheming British agents were also active along the far-flung northern frontier. They intrigued with the disgruntled Allen brothers of Vermont, and sought to annex that troubled area to Britain. Along the northern border the Redcoats continued to hold a chain of trading posts on United States soil, and there they maintained their profitable fur trade with the Indians. One plausible excuse for remaining was the failure of the American states

to carry out the treaty of peace in regard to debts and Loyalists. But probably the main purpose of Britain in hanging on was to curry favor with the red men and keep their tomahawks lined up on the side of the King as a barrier against future American attacks on Canada.

All these grievances against England were maddening to patriotic Americans. Some citizens demanded, with more heat than wisdom, that the United States force the British into line by imposing restrictions on their imports to America. But Congress could not control commerce, and the states refused to adopt a uniform tariff policy. Some "easy states" deliberately lowered their tariffs in order to attract an unfair share of trade.

Ethan Allen (1738–1789). A Vermont leader, a Revolutionary hero, and a major-general in the local militia. On May 10, 1775, more than a year before independence was declared, Ethan Allen and his Green Mountain Boys captured the key British fort of Ticonderoga on Lake Champlain. Allen is reported to have demanded surrender "In the name of the Great Jehovah and the Continental Congress." Actually, he appears to have had no commission from either source.

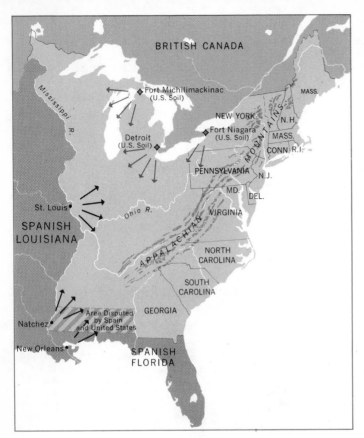

MAIN CENTERS OF SPANISH AND BRITISH INFLUENCE AFTER 1783

This map shows graphically that the United States in 1783 achieved complete independence in name only, particularly in the area west of the Appalachian Mountains. Not until twenty years had passed did the new republic, with the purchase of Louisiana from France in 1803, eliminate foreign influence from the area east of the Mississippi River.

Spain, though recently an enemy of England, was openly unfriendly to the new Republic. She controlled the mouth of the all-important Mississippi, down which the pioneers of Tennessee and Kentucky were forced to float their produce. The West was thus threatened with strangulation. Spain likewise claimed a large area north of the Gulf of Mexico, including Florida, granted to the United States by the British in 1783. At Natchez, on disputed soil, she held an important fort. She also intrigued with the neighboring red men to hem the Americans in east of the Alleghenies. Spain and England together, radiating their influence out among warlike Indian tribes, prevented America from exercising effective control over about half of its total territory.

Even America's French ally, now that she had humbled Britain, cooled off. She demanded the repayment of money loaned during the war; she restricted trade with her bustling West Indies and other ports.

Pirates of the North African states, including the arrogant Dey of Algiers, were ravaging America's Mediterranean commerce and enslaving Yankee seamen. The British purchased protection for their own subjects, and as colonials the Americans had enjoyed this shield. But as an independent nation the United States was too weak to fight and too poor to bribe. A few Yankee shippers engaged in the Mediterranean trade with forged British protection papers, but not all were so bold or so lucky.

John Jay, secretary for foreign affairs, derived some hollow satisfaction from these insults. He hoped they would at least humiliate the American people into framing a new government at home that would be strong enough to command respect abroad.

The Horrid Specter of Anarchy

Economic storm clouds continued to hang low in the mid-1780s. The requisition system of raising money was breaking down; some of the states refused to pay anything, while complaining bitterly about the tyranny of "King Congress." Interest on the public debt was piling up at home, while the nation's credit was evaporating abroad.

Individual states were getting out of hand. Several of them were quarreling over boundaries, which generated several minor pitched battles. Some of the states were levying duties on goods from their neighbors; New York, for example, taxed firewood from Connecticut and cabbages from New Jersey. A number of the states were again starting to grind out depreciated paper currency, and a few of them had passed laws sanctioning the semi-worthless "rag money." As a contemporary rhymester put it:

> Bankrupts their creditors with rage pursue;
> No stop, no mercy from the debtor crew.

An alarming uprising, known as Shays's Rebellion, flared up in western Massachusetts in 1786. Impoverished back-country farmers, many of them Revolutionary War veterans, were losing their farms through mortgage foreclosures and tax delinquencies. Led by Captain Daniel Shays, a veteran of the Revolution, these desperate debtors demanded cheap paper money, lighter taxes, and a suspension of mortgage foreclosures. Hundreds of angry men, again seizing their muskets, attempted to enforce their demands.

Massachusetts authorities responded with dras-

IOIIOIIOIIOIIOIIOIIOIIOIIOIIOIIOIIOIIOIIOIIOIIOIIOIIOI

Regarding popular disorders, Jefferson wrote privately in 1787: "A little rebellion, now and then, is a good thing, and as necessary in the political world as storms in the physical. . . . It is a medicine necessary for the sound health of government."

IOIIOIIOIIOIIOIIOIIOIIOIIOIIOIIOIIOIIOIIOIIOIIOIIOIIOI

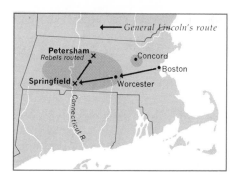

MAIN SHAYSITE CENTERS IN MASSACHUSETTS, 1786–1787
Disaffection existed in all parts of the state, but was concentrated in shaded areas.

tic action. Supported partly by contributions from wealthy citizens, they raised a small army under General Lincoln. Several skirmishes occurred—at Springfield three Shaysites were killed and one was wounded—and the movement collapsed. Daniel Shays, who believed that he was fighting anew against tyranny, was condemned to death but was later pardoned.

Shays's followers were crushed—but the nightmarish memory lingered on. The outbursts of these and other distressed debtors struck fear in the hearts of the propertied men, who began to suspect that the Revolution had raised up a Frankenstein's monster of "mobocracy." "Good God!" burst out George Washington, who felt that only a Tory or a Briton could have predicted such disorders. There was obviously a crying need for a stronger central government. A few panicky citizens even talked of importing a European monarch to carry on where George III had failed.

How critical were conditions under the Confederation? Conservatives, anxious to safeguard their wealth and position, naturally exaggerated the seriousness of the nation's plight. They were eager to persuade their countrymen to scrap the Articles of Confederation, under which the states were sovereign, in favor of a muscular central government, in which the federal authority would be sovereign. But the poorer states'-rights people, who favored at most a simple amending of the

Articles, pooh-poohed the talk of anarchy. Many of them were debtors who feared that a powerful federal government would force them to pay their creditors.

Yet friends and critics of the Confederation generally agreed that it needed strengthening. Popular toasts were "Cement to the Union" and "A hoop to the barrel." The chief differences arose over how this goal should be attained, and how a maximum amount of states' rights could be reconciled with a strong central government. America probably could have muddled through somehow with amended Articles of Confederation. But the adoption of a completely new constitution certainly spared the Republic much costly indecision, uncertainty, and turmoil.

The nationwide picture was actually brightening before the Constitution was drafted. Nearly half the states had not issued semi-worthless paper currency; and some of the monetary black sheep showed signs of returning to the sound-money fold. Congressional control of commerce was in sight, specifically by means of an amendment to the Articles of Confederation. Prosperity was beginning to emerge from the fog of depression. By 1789 overseas shipping had largely regained its place in the commercial world. If conditions had been as grim in 1787 as painted by foes of the Articles, the move for a new constitution would hardly have encountered such heated opposition.

A Convention of "Demi-Gods"

Control of commerce, more than any other problem, touched off the chain reaction that led to a constitutional convention. Interstate squabbling over this issue had become so alarming by 1786 that Virginia, taking the lead, issued a call for a convention at Annapolis, Maryland. Nine states appointed delegates, but only five were finally represented. With so feeble a showing, nothing could be done about the ticklish question of commerce. A classic-featured New Yorker, thirty-one-year-old Alexander Hamilton, brilliantly saved the convention from complete failure by engineering the adoption of his report. It called upon Congress to summon a convention to meet in Philadelphia the next year, not to deal with commerce alone but to bolster the entire fabric of the Articles of Confederation.

Congress, though slowly dying in New York City, was reluctant to take a step that might be the signing of its own death warrant. But after six of the states had seized the bit in their teeth and appointed delegates anyhow, Congress belatedly issued the call for a convention *"for the sole and express purpose of revising"* the Articles of Confederation.

Every state chose representatives, except independent-minded Rhode Island (still "Rogues' Island"), a stronghold of paper-moneyites. These statesmen were all appointed by the state legislatures, whose members had been elected by voters who could qualify as property holders. This double distillation inevitably brought together a select group of propertied men.

A quorum of the fifty-five emissaries from twelve states finally convened at Philadelphia on May 25, 1787, in the imposing red-brick statehouse. The smallness of the assemblage facilitated intimate acquaintance and hence compromise. Sessions were held in complete secrecy, with armed sentinels posted at the doors. Delegates knew that they would generate heated differences, and they did not want to advertise their own dissensions, or put crippling arguments into the mouths of the opposition.

The caliber of the participants was extraordinarily high—"demi-gods," Jefferson called them. The crisis was such as to induce the ablest men to drop their personal pursuits and come to the aid of their country. Most of the members were lawyers, and most of them fortunately were old hands at constitution-making in their own states.

George Washington, towering austere and aloof among the "demi-gods" was unanimously elected chairman. His enormous prestige, as "the Sword of the Revolution," served to quiet overheated tempers. Benjamin Franklin, then eighty-one, added the urbanity of an elder statesman, though

IOI

Alexander Hamilton clearly revealed his class-interest views of an aristocratic government in his Philadelphia speech (1787): "All communities divide themselves into the few and the many. The first are the rich and wellborn, the other the mass of the people. . . . The people are turbulent and changing; they seldom judge or determine right. Give therefore to the first class a distinct, permanent share in the government. They will check the unsteadiness of the second, and as they cannot receive any advantage by change, they therefore will ever maintain good government."

OIIOIIOIIOIIOIIOIIOIIOIIOIIOIIOIIOIIOIIOIIOIIOIIOIIOIIOIIOII

Alexander Hamilton (1755–1804). He was one of the youngest and most brilliant of the Founding Fathers, who might have become President but for his ultraconservatism, an adulterous scandal, and a duelist's bullet. (Copyright Yale University Art Gallery)

he was inclined to be indiscreetly talkative in his declining years. James Madison, then thirty-six and a profound student of government, made contributions so notable that he has been dubbed "the Father of the Constitution." Alexander Hamilton, then only thirty-two, was present as an advocate of a super-powerful central government. His five-hour speech in behalf of his plan, though the most eloquent of the convention, netted only one favorable vote—his own.

Most of the flaming Revolutionary leaders of 1776 were absent. Thomas Jefferson and Thomas Paine were in Europe; Samuel Adams and John Hancock were not elected by Massachusetts. Patrick Henry, ardent champion of states' rights,

was chosen as a delegate from Virginia but declined to serve, declaring that he "smelled a rat." It was perhaps well that these architects of revolution were absent. The time had come to yield the stage to statesmen interested in fashioning solid political systems.

Patriots in Philadelphia

The fifty-five delegates were a conservative, well-to-do body: lawyers, merchants, shippers, land speculators, and moneylenders. Not a single spokesman was present from the poorer, debtor groups.

Some forty of the fifty-five members owned depreciated securities of the existing regime. These men probably suspected that the value of their holdings would sharply increase if they succeeded in establishing a strong new government. Unfriendly critics of a later era have charged the Founding Fathers with having deliberately set out to feather their own nests. What is the truth about these so-called pocketbook patriots?

Many men in the Philadelphia assemblage, including the self-sacrificing Washington, were clearly prompted by patriotic motives, though some may not have been. The delegates realized that while they themselves might profit personally from a sounder government, so would the nation as a whole. If every man who stood to gain financially from a new constitution had bowed out, the

IOIIOIIOIIOIIOIIOIIOIIOIIOIIOIIOIIOIIOIIOIIOIIOIIOIIOIIOIIOI

Jefferson, despite his high regard for the statesmen at the Philadelphia convention, still was not unduly concerned about Shaysite rebellions. He wrote (November 1787): "What country before ever existed a century and a half without a rebellion? . . . The tree of liberty must be refreshed from time to time with the blood of patriots and tyrants. It is its natural manure."

IOIIOIIOIIOIIOIIOIIOIIOIIOIIOIIOIIOIIOIIOIIOIIOIIOIIOIIOIIOI

country would have been robbed of its key leadership, and there probably would have been no Constitution.

What were the Founding Fathers after? They desired above all else a firm, dignified, and respected government. In a broad sense the piratical Dey of Algiers, who drove the delegates to their work, was a Founding Father. They aimed to clothe the central authority with genuine power, especially in controlling tariffs, so that the United States could wrest satisfactory commercial treaties from foreign nations. The shortsighted hostility of the British mercantilists spurred the constitution-framers to their task, and in this sense the illiberal Lord Sheffield was a Founding Father.

Other motives were present in the stately Philadelphia hall. Delegates were determined to preserve the Union, forestall anarchy, and insure security of life and property against dangerous uprisings by the "mobocracy." The specter of the recent outburst in Massachusetts held them to their labors, and in this sense Daniel Shays was a Founding Father. Grinding necessity extorted the Constitution from a reluctant nation. Fear occupied the fifty-sixth chair.

Hammering Out a Bundle of Compromises

Some of the travel-stained delegates, when they first reached Philadelphia, decided upon a daring step. They would completely *scrap* the old Articles of Confederation, despite explicit instructions from Congress to *revise*. Technically, these bolder spirits were determined to overthrow the existing government of the United States by peaceful means. The sovereign states were in danger of losing their sovereignty.

A scheme proposed by populous Virginia, and known as "the large-state plan," was first pushed forward as the framework of the Constitution. Its essence was that representation in Congress should be based on population—an arrangement that would naturally give the larger states an advantage.

Tiny New Jersey, suspicious of Virginia, countered with "the small-state plan." This provided for equal representation in Congress by states, regardless of size and population, as under the existing Articles of Confederation. The weaker states feared that under the Virginia scheme the stronger states would band together and lord it over the rest. Angry debate, heightened by a stifling heat wave, led to deadlock. The danger loomed that the convention would break up in complete failure. Even skeptical old Benjamin Franklin seriously proposed that the daily sessions be opened with prayer by a local clergyman.

After bitter and prolonged debate, the "Great Compromise" of the convention was hammered out and agreed upon. A cooling of tempers came coincidentally with a cooling of the temperature. The larger states were conceded representation by population in the House of Representatives (Art. I, Sec. II, para. 3; see Appendix at end of this book), and their smaller sisters were appeased by equal representation in the Senate (see Art. I, Sec. III, para. 1). Each state, no matter how poor or small, would have two senators. The big states, which would have to bear the major burden of taxation, obviously yielded more. As a sop to them, the delegates agreed that every tax bill or revenue measure must originate in the House, where population counted the more heavily (see Art. I, Sec. VII, para. 1). This critical compromise broke the logjam, and from then on success seemed within reach.

Gouverneur Morris (1752–1816). A delegate from Pennsylvania to the Constitutional Convention of 1787, he spoke more frequently than any other member and served as principal draftsman of that superbly written document. A wealthy and rock-ribbed conservative, he had joined the Revolutionary movement with reluctance and to the end feared the "riotous mob." (The New York Historical Society)

The Constitution as drafted was a bundle of compromises; they stand out in every section. A vital compromise was the method of electing the President indirectly by the Electoral College, rather than by direct means (see Art. II, Sec. I, para. 2). One Virginia delegate insisted that to leave the choice to the people was like asking a blind man to choose colors.

Sectional jealousy also intruded. Should the voteless slave of the Southern states count as a person in apportioning direct taxes and also representation in the House of Representatives? The South, not wishing to be deprived of influence, answered "yes." The North replied "no," arguing that the North might as logically have additional representation based on its horses. As a compromise between total representation and none at all, it was decided that a slave might count as three-fifths of a person. Hence the memorable, if somewhat illogical, "three-fifths compromise" (see Art. I, Sec. II, para. 3), an idea seriously discussed four years earlier.

Most of the states wanted to shut off the African slave trade. But South Carolina and Georgia, requiring slave labor in their rice paddies and malarial swamps, raised vehement protests. By way of compromise the convention stipulated that the slave trade might continue until the end of 1807, at which time Congress could turn off the spigot (see Art. I, Sec. IX, para 1). It did so as soon as the prescribed interval had elapsed. Meanwhile all

the new state constitutions except Georgia's forbade overseas slave trade.

Safeguards for Conservatism

Heated clashes among the delegates have been overplayed. The area of agreement was actually large; otherwise the convention would have speedily disbanded. Economically, the members generally saw eye to eye; they demanded sound money and the protection of private property. Politically, they were in basic agreement; they favored a stronger government, with three branches and with checks and balances among them—what critics called a "triple-headed monster." Finally, the convention was virtually unanimous in believing that manhood-suffrage democracy—government by "democratick babblers"—was something to be feared and fought.

Daniel Shays, the prime bogeyman, still frightened the conservative-minded delegates. They deliberately erected safeguards against the excesses of the "mob," and they made these barriers as strong as they dared. The awesome federal judges were to be appointed for life. The powerful President was to be elected *indirectly* by the Electoral College; the lordly senators were to be chosen *indirectly* by state legislatures (see Art. I, Sec. III, para. 1). Only in the case of one-half of one of the three great branches—the House of Representatives—were qualified (propertied) citizens permitted to choose their officials by *direct* vote (see Art. I, Sec. II, para. 1).

Yet the new charter also contained democratic elements. Above all, it stood foursquare on the great principle that the only legitimate government was one based on the consent of the governed. "We the people," the Preamble began, in a ringing affirmation of the doctrine of popular sovereignty.

At the end of seventeen muggy weeks—May 25 to September 17, 1787—only forty-two of the original fifty-five members remained to sign the Constitution. Three of the forty-two, refusing to do so, returned to their states to resist ratification. The

Evolution of Federal Union

Years	Attempts at Union	Participants
1643–1684	New England Confederation	4 colonies
1686–1689	Dominion of New England	7 colonies
1754	Albany Congress	7 colonies
1765	Stamp Act Congress	9 colonies
1772–1776	Committees of Correspondence	13 colonies
1774	First Continental Congress (adopts The Association)	12 colonies
1775–1781	Second Continental Congress	13 colonies
1781–1789	Articles of Confederation	13 states
1789–1790	Federal Constitution	13 states

remainder, adjourning to the City Tavern, appropriately celebrated the occasion. They little suspected that one day an 18th Amendment would be added forbidding the manufacture and sale of alcoholic beverages.

No members of the convention were completely happy about the result. They were too near their work—and too weary. Whatever their personal desires, they finally had to compromise and adopt what was acceptable to the entire body, and what presumably would be acceptable to the entire country.

The Clash of Federalists and Anti-Federalists

The Framing Fathers early foresaw that nationwide acceptance of the Constitution would not be easy to obtain. A formidable barrier was unanimous ratification by all thirteen states, as required for amendment by the still-existent Articles of Confederation. But since absent Rhode Island was certain to veto the Constitution, the delegates boldly adopted a different scheme. They stipulated that when *two-thirds* of the states—that is, nine—had registered their approval through specially elected conventions, the Constitution would become the supreme law of the land in those states ratifying (see Art. VII).

This was extraordinary, even revolutionary. It was in effect an appeal over the heads of the Congress that had called the convention, and over the heads of the legislatures that had chosen its members, to the people—or those of the people who could vote. In this way the framers could claim greater popular sanction for their handiwork.

IOIIOIIOIIOIIOIIOIIOIIOIIOIIOIIOIIOIIOIIOIIOIIOIIOI

One of the Philadelphia delegates recorded in his journal a brief episode involving Benjamin Franklin, who was asked by a lady when the convention ended, ''Well, Doctor, what have we got, a republic or a monarchy?'' He answered, ''A republic, if you can keep it.''

IOIIOIIOIIOIIOIIOIIOIIOIIOIIOIIOIIOIIOIIOIIOIIOIIOI

Congress reluctantly submitted the document to the states on this basis, without recommendation of any kind.

People were somewhat shocked, so well had the secrets of the convention been kept. The public had expected the old Articles of Confederation to be patched up; now it was handed a frightening document in which, many thought, the precious jewel of state sovereignty was swallowed up. One of the hottest debates of American history forthwith erupted. The anti-federalists, who opposed the stronger federal government, were arrayed against the federalists, who naturally favored it.

A motley crowd gathered in the anti-federalist camp. It consisted primarily, though not exclusively, of the states'-rights devotees, the back-country men, the one-horse farmers, the work-soiled artisans, the ill-educated and illiterate—in general, the poorer classes. They were joined by paper-moneyites and debtors, many of whom feared that a potent central government would force them to pay off their debts—and at full value. Large numbers of anti-federalists suspected that something sinister was being put over on them by the aristocrats.

Silver-buckled federalists were more respectable; they generally embraced the cultured and propertied groups. Most of them lived in the settled areas along the seaboard, not in the raw back country. They were in outlook rather closely akin to the conservative Loyalist group of Revolutionary days. In fact, many of the remaining former Loyalists gave vigorous support to the Constitution; without them it might have failed of ratification.

Anti-federalists, their worst fears aroused, voiced vehement objections to the ''gilded trap'' known as the Constitution. They cried with much truth that it had been drawn up by the aristocratic elements, and hence was anti-democratic. They likewise charged that the sovereignty of the states was being swallowed up, and that the freedoms of the individual were jeopardized by the absence of a bill of rights. They decried the dropping of annual elections for congressmen; the setting up of a federal stronghold ten miles square (later the

Strengthening the Central Government

Under Articles of Confederation	Under Federal Constitution
A loose confederation of states	A firm union of people
1 vote in Congress for each state	2 votes in Senate for each state; representation by population in House (see Art. I, Secs. II, III)
⅔ vote (9 states) in Congress for all important measures	Simple majority vote in Congress, subject to presidential veto (see Art. I., Sec. VII, para. 2)
Laws executed by committees of Congress	Laws executed by powerful President (see Art. II, Secs. II, III)
No congressional power over commerce	Congress to regulate both foreign and interstate commerce (see Art. I, Sec. VIII, para. 3)
No congressional power to levy taxes	Extensive power in Congress to levy taxes (see Art. I, Sec. VIII, para. 1)
No federal courts	Federal courts, capped by Supreme Court (see Art. III)
Unanimity of states for amendment	Amendment less difficult (see Art. V)
No authority to act directly upon individuals, and no power to coerce states	Ample power to enforce laws by coercion of individuals and to some extent of states

District of Columbia); the creation of a standing army; the omission of any reference to God; and the highly questionable procedure of ratifying with only two-thirds of the states. A Philadelphia newspaper added that Franklin was "a fool from age," and Washington "a fool from nature."

The Great Debate in the States

Special elections, some apathetic but others hotly contested, were held in the various states for members of the ratifying conventions. Candidates—federalist or anti-federalist—were elected on the basis of their pledges for or against the Constitution.

The newly forged document was quickly accepted by four small states, for they had come off much better than they could have expected. Pennsylvania, number two on the list of ratifiers, was the first large state to act, but not until high-handed irregularities had been employed by the

federalist legislature in calling a convention. These included the forcible seating of two anti-federalist members, their clothes torn and their faces red with rage, in order to complete a quorum.

Massachusetts, the second most populous state, provided an acid test. If the Constitution had failed there, the entire movement might easily have bogged down. The Boston ratifying convention at first contained an anti-federalist majority. It included weather-beaten Shaysites and the suspicious Samuel Adams, that aging "Engineer of Revolution" who now distrusted change. The assembly buzzed with dismaying talk of summoning another constitutional convention, as though the nation had not already shot its bolt. Clearly the choice was not between this Constitution and a better one, but between this Constitution and the creaking Articles of Confederation. The absence of a bill of rights was especially alarming to the anti-federalists. But the federalists gave solemn assurances that the first Congress would add such

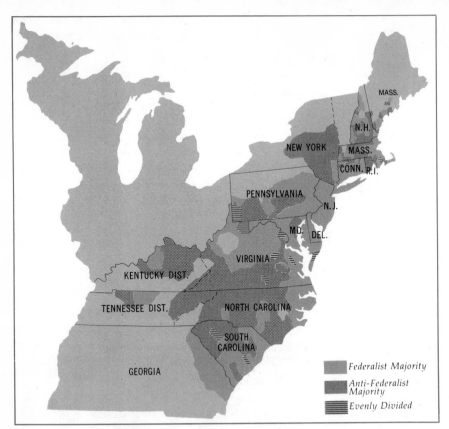

MASS.

N.H.

NEW YORK

MASS.

CONN. R.I.

PENNSYLVANIA

N.J.

MD. DEL.

VIRGINIA

KENTUCKY DIST.

TENNESSEE DIST.

NORTH CAROLINA

SOUTH CAROLINA

GEORGIA

Federalist Majority

Anti-Federalist Majority

Evenly Divided

a safeguard by amendment, and ratification was then secured in Massachusetts by the rather narrow margin of 187 to 168.

Three more states fell into line. The last of these was New Hampshire, whose convention at first had contained a strong anti-federalist majority. The federalists cleverly engineered a prompt adjournment, and then won over enough waverers to secure ratification. Nine states—all but Virginia,

▮口▮口▮口▮口▮口▮口▮口▮口▮口▮口▮口▮口▮口▮口▮口▮口▮口▮口▮口▮

In the Massachusetts ratifying convention, one member expressed distrust of the taxing power of the new government: "These lawyers, and men of learning, and moneyed men . . . expect to get into Congress themselves. . . . And then they will swallow up all us little folks . . . just as the whale swallowed up Jonah."

▮口▮口▮口▮口▮口▮口▮口▮口▮口▮口▮口▮口▮口▮口▮口▮口▮口▮口▮口▮

New York, North Carolina, and Rhode Island—had now taken shelter under the "new federal roof," and the document was officially adopted on June 21, 1788. Francis Hopkinson exulted in his song "The New Roof":

Huzza! my brave boys, our work is complete;
The world shall admire Columbia's fair seat.

But such rejoicing was premature so long as the four dissenters, conspicuously New York and Virginia, remained outside the fold.

The Four Laggard States

Proud Virginia, the biggest and most populous state, provided fierce anti-federalist opposition. There the college-bred federalist orators, for once, encountered worthy antagonists, including the fiery Patrick Henry. He professed to see in the fearsome parchment the death warrant of liberty. George Washington, James Madison, and John

Ratification of the Constitution

State	Date	Vote in Convention	Rank in Population	1790 Population
1. Delaware	Dec. 7, 1787	Unanimous	13	59,096
2. Pennsylvania	Dec. 12, 1787	46 to 23	3	433,611
3. New Jersey	Dec. 18, 1787	Unanimous	9	184,139
4. Georgia	Jan. 2, 1788	Unanimous	11	82,548
5. Connecticut	Jan. 9, 1788	128 to 40	8	237,655
6. Massachusetts (incl. Maine)	Feb. 7, 1788	187 to 168	2	475,199
7. Maryland	Apr. 28, 1788	63 to 11	6	319,728
8. South Carolina	May 23, 1788	149 to 73	7	249,073
9. New Hampshire	June 21, 1788	57 to 46	10	141,899
10. Virginia	June 26, 1788	89 to 79	1	747,610
11. New York	July 26, 1788	30 to 27	5	340,241
12. North Carolina	Nov. 21, 1789	195 to 77	4	395,005
13. Rhode Island	May 29, 1790	34 to 32	12	69,112

Marshall, on the federalist side, lent influential support. With New Hampshire about to ratify, the new Union was going to be formed anyhow, and Virginia could not very well continue comfortably as an independent state. After a close and exciting debate in the state convention, ratification carried, 89 to 79.

New York, which also experienced an uphill struggle, was the only state that permitted a manhood-suffrage vote for the members of the ratifying convention. The result was a heavy anti-federalist majority. Alexander Hamilton at heart favored a much stronger central government than that under debate, but he contributed his sparkling personality and persuasive eloquence to whipping up support. He also joined John Jay and James Madison in penning a masterly series of articles for the New York newspapers. Though designed as propaganda, these essays remain the most penetrating commentary ever written on the Constitution, and are still widely sold in book form as *The Federalist.*

New York finally yielded. Realizing that the state could not prosper apart from the Union, the convention ratified the document by the close count of 30 to 27. At the same time, it approved thirty-two proposed amendments and—vain hope—issued a call for yet another convention to modify the Constitution.

Last-ditch dissent developed in only two states. A hostile convention met in North Carolina, then adjourned without taking a vote. Rhode Island

REDEUNT SATURNIA REGNA.

On the erection of the Eleventh PILLAR of the great National DOME, we beg leave most sincerely to felicitate " OUR DEAR COUNTRY."

Rise it will.

☞ *The foundation good—it may yet be SAVED.*

A Triumphant Cartoon. It appeared in the *Massachusetts Centinel* on August 2, 1788. Note the two laggards, especially the sorry condition of Rhode Island.

Hamiltonian Frigate. A victory parade in New York City honoring Hamilton and the ratification of the Constitution. At the key New York ratifying convention at Poughkeepsie, Hamilton, by sheer eloquence and cogent argument, turned a two-thirds majority against the Constitution into a majority of three in favor of it. (Brown Brothers)

did not even summon a ratifying convention. The two most ruggedly individualist centers of the colonial era—homes of the "otherwise minded"—thus ran true to form. They were to change their course, albeit unwillingly, only after the new government had been in operation for some months.

The battle for ratification, despite much apathy, was close and extremely bitter in some localities. No lives were lost, but riotous disturbances broke out in New York and Pennsylvania, involving bruises and bloodshed. There was much behind-the-scenes pressure on delegates who had solemnly promised their constituents to vote against the Constitution. The last four states ratified, not because they wanted to, but because they had to. They could not safely exist apart from the Union.

A Conservative Triumph

The minority had triumphed—doubly. A militant minority of American radicals had engineered the military revolution which cast off the unwritten British constitution. A militant minority of conservatives—now embracing many of the earlier radicals—had engineered the peaceful revolution which overthrew the inadequate constitution known as the Articles of Confederation. Eleven states, in effect, had seceded from the Confederation, leaving two out in the cold.

A majority had not spoken. Only about one-fourth of the adult white males in the country, chiefly the propertied people, had voted for delegates to the ratifying conventions. Careful estimates indicate that if the new Constitution had been submitted to a manhood-suffrage vote, as in New York, it would have encountered much more opposition, probably defeat.

Conservatism was victorious. Safeguards had been erected against mob-rule excesses, and the democratic gains of the Revolution were conserved in the face of possible anarchy. Radicals like Patrick Henry, who had overthrown British

Referring to the belief that self-government is better than good government, Fisher Ames of Massachusetts, a Federalist member of the new Congress, is quoted as having said: "A monarchy is like a merchantman [merchant ship]. You get on board and ride the wind and tide in safety and elation but, by and by, you strike a reef and go down. But democracy is like a raft. You never sink, but, damn it, your feet are always in the water."

rule, had in turn been overthrown by American conservatives. The result was a kind of peaceful counter-revolution. It restored the economic and political stability of colonial years, and set the drifting ship of state on a more promising course. Yet if the architects of the Constitution were conservative, it is worth emphasizing that what they conserved was the principle of popular, democratic government, made forever sacred in the fires of the Revolution. One of the distinctive—and enduring—paradoxes of American history was thus revealed: in the United States, conservatives and radicals alike have championed the heritage of democratic revolutionism.

VARYING VIEWPOINTS

Charles Beard's book, *An Economic Interpretation of the Constitution of the United States* (1913), has long defined the area around which debate on the constitutional period has revolved. Beard described the Constitution as the "reactionary" phase of the Revolutionary era—a shrewd maneuver by conservative men of property to curtail the democratic excesses let loose in 1776. Most modern scholars, if they accept Beard's argument at all, accept it only with severe qualifications. The most recent discussions of the Constitution have been cast in terms of reflections on the ancient riddle of republicanism: Does republican self-government rest on the virtue of the people or on the formal political institutions which channel and control human behavior? Seen in this light, the men who made the Constitution appear more "radical" than their opponents. They trusted human nature enough to go forward with the bold experiment of a strong national government based on republican principles. The anti-federalists, on the other hand, so feared man's weakness for corruption that they shuddered at the prospect of putting powerful political weapons in his hands. In this sense, the Constitution represents a vote of confidence in human rationality—the fulfillment, not the repudiation, of the most advanced ideas of the Revolutionary era. Thus it was "radical"; but whether it was "right" is an issue that will be endlessly debated.

SELECT READINGS

John Fiske, in *The Critical Period of American History* (1888), portrayed America under the Articles of Confederation as a crisis-ridden country. His view has been sharply qualified by the work of Merrill Jensen, summarized in *The Making of the American Constitution* (1964). On the Constitutional Convention, see Clinton Rossiter, *1787: The Grand Convention* (1966). Especially learned is G. S. Wood's massive and brilliant *The Creation of the American Republic, 1776–1787* (1969). See also Willi Paul Adams, *The First American Constitutions* (1980). Charles A. Beard shocked conservatives with *An Economic Interpretation of the Constitution of the United States* (1913). It is seriously weakened by two blistering attacks: R. E. Brown, *Charles Beard and the Constitution* (1956), and Forrest McDonald, *We the People: The Economic Origins of the Constitution* (1958). See also the latter author's *E Pluribus Unum: The Formation of the American Republic, 1776–1790* (1965). J. T. Main, *The Anti-Federalists* (1961), partially rehabilitates Beard. S. Lynd explores another aspect of the topic in *Class Conflict, Slavery, and the United States Constitution* (1967). More detailed is H. J. Henderson, *Party Politics in the Continental Congress* (1974). See also L. Levy, *Essays on the Making of the Constitution* (1969). Sectionalism is developed in J. R. Alden, *The First South* (1961), and W. N. Chambers, *Political Parties in a New Nation* (1963). Finance is treated fully in C. P. Nettels, *The Emergence of a National Economy, 1775–1815* (1962). David Szatmary is perceptive on *Shays's Rebellion* (1980). Relevant biographical studies of merit are J. C. Miller, *Alexander Hamilton: Portrait in Paradox* (1959); and Irving Brant, *James Madison* (6 vols., 1941–1961).

8

Launching the New Ship of State

I shall only say that I hold with Montesquieu, that a government must be fitted to a nation, as much as a coat to the individual; and, consequently, that what may be good at Philadelphia may be bad at Paris, and ridiculous at Petersburg [Russia].

ALEXANDER HAMILTON, 1799

A New Ship on an Uncertain Sea

When the Constitution was launched in 1789, the Republic was continuing to grow at an amazing rate. Population was still doubling about every twenty-three years, and the first official census of 1790 recorded almost 4 million souls. Cities had blossomed proportionately: Philadelphia numbered 42,000; New York, 33,000; Boston, 18,000; Charleston, 16,000; and Baltimore, 13,000.

America's population was still about 90 percent rural, despite the flourishing cities; all but 5 percent lived east of the mountains. The trans-Allegheny overflow was concentrated chiefly in Kentucky, Tennessee, and Ohio, all of which were welcomed as states within fourteen years. (Vermont had preceded them, becoming the fourteenth state in 1791.) Foreign travelers everywhere looked down their noses at the roughness and crudity resulting from ax-and-rifle pioneering life. Yet, critical though they might be, they were impressed by evidences of energy, self-confidence, and material well-being.

The new ship of state, despite these promising signs of fair weather, did not spread its sails to the most favorable breezes. Within twelve troubled years the American people had risen up and thrown overboard their first two constitutions: the British constitution and the Articles of Confederation. A decade of constitution-smashing and law-breaking was not the best training for government-making. Americans had come to regard a central authority, replacing that of George III, as a necessary evil—something to be distrusted, watched, and curbed.

Men of the western waters, in the stump-studded clearings of Kentucky, Tennessee, and Ohio, were restive and dubiously loyal. The mouth of the Mississippi, their life-giving outlet, lay in the hands of unfriendly Spaniards. Smooth-tongued Spanish and British agents, jingling gold, moved freely among the settlers and held out seductive promises of independence.

Finances of the infant government were likewise precarious. The revenue had declined to a trickle, while the public debt, with interest heavily in arrears, was mountainous. Worthless paper money, both state and national, was as plentiful as metallic money was scarce.

The French statesman Turgot had high expectations for a *united* America: "This people is the hope of the human race. . . . The Americans should be an example of political, religious, commercial and industrial liberty. . . . But to obtain these ends for us, America . . . must not become . . . a mass of divided powers, contending for territory and trade."

The Americans, moreover, were brashly attempting to erect a republic on an immense scale. They ignored the fact that hitherto a democratic form of government had succeeded only on a tiny scale, notably in Switzerland. The eyes of a skeptical world were on the upstart United States, and the bejeweled monarchs of Europe in particular feared that the new Republic would provide a dangerous example for their long-oppressed subjects.

Washington's Pro-Federalist Regime

General Washington, the esteemed war hero, was unanimously drafted as President by the Electoral College in 1789—the only presidential nominee ever to be honored by unanimity. He would not run for the office; he would not run from the office. His presence was imposing: 6 feet 2 inches, 175 pounds (1.88m, 79.5kg), broad and sloping shoulders, strongly pointed chin, and pockmarks (from smallpox) on nose and cheeks. Much preferring the quiet of Mount Vernon to the turmoil of politics, he was perhaps the only President who

Washington Being Sworn in at Federal Hall, New York. Being the first President under the Constitution, Washington could neither cite precedents nor blame a predecessor. (Stokes Collection, New York Public Library.)

President-Elect Washington Honored in New Jersey. Before leaving home he wrote, "My movements to the chair of government will be accompanied by feelings not unlike those of a culprit who is going to the place of his execution." (Lithograph, Library of Congress.)

did not in some way angle for this exalted office. But his name and fame, which had spread throughout two hemispheres, made him an "indispensable man." Balanced rather than brilliant, he commanded men by strength of character rather than by the arts of the politician.

Washington's long journey from Mount Vernon to New York City, the temporary capital, was a triumphal procession. He was greeted by roaring cannon, pealing bells, flower-carpeted roads, and singing and shouting citizens. With appropriate ceremony, he solemnly and somewhat nervously took the oath of office on April 30, 1789, on a crowded balcony overlooking Wall Street, which some have regarded as a bad omen. A cold but able New Englander, John Adams, was sworn in as Vice-President—an office which Benjamin Franklin thought should have carried the title "His Superfluous Excellency."

The Constitution does not mention a Cabinet; it merely provides that the President "may require" written opinions of the heads of his departments (see Art. II, Sec. II, para. 1). But this system proved so cumbersome, and involved so much homework, that Cabinet meetings gradually evolved in the Washington administration. The President thus

secured an invaluable body of special advisers. Along with numerous other features not specifically authorized, the Cabinet has become an integral part of the "unwritten Constitution."

At first there were only three full-fledged department heads under the President: Secretary of State Thomas Jefferson, Secretary of the Treasury Alexander Hamilton, and Secretary of War Henry Knox. The last-named was a 300-pound (136-kg) Revolutionary general to whom were entrusted both the infant army and the newborn navy.

The shining star in this governmental galaxy was smooth-faced Alexander Hamilton, just thirty-four years old. He was once called the "bastard brat of a Scotch peddler," though the sneer was unfair. His parents could not legally marry because of a technicality connected with his mother's divorce from her first husband. Hamilton's genius was unquestioned, but doubts about his character and his loyalty to the democratic experiment always swirled about his head. He was said to have shocked Jefferson by exclaiming, "Your people, sir, are a Great Beast!"

Critics claimed that Hamilton loved his country more than he loved his countrymen. Born on a tiny island in the British West Indies, he never de-

Evolution of the Cabinet

Original Members	Added, 1798–1913	Added, 1947–1979
Secy. of State, 1789	Secy. of Navy, 1798 (Loses Cabinet status, 1947)	Secy. of Defense, 1947 (Subordinate to him, without Cabinet rank, are Secys. of Army, Navy, Air Force)
Secy. of Treasury, 1789	Postmaster General, 1829 (Loses Cabinet status, 1970)	
Secy. of War, 1789 (Loses Cabinet status, 1947)	Secy. of Interior, 1849	Secy. of Health, Education, and Welfare, 1953 (divided in 1979)
Attorney General, 1789 (Not head of Justice Dept. until 1870)	Secy. of Agriculture, 1889	Secy. of Housing and Urban Development, 1965
	Secy. of Commerce and Labor, 1903 (Office divided in 1913)	Secy. of Transportation, 1966
	Secy. of Commerce, 1913	Secy. of Energy, 1977
	Secy. of Labor, 1913	Secy. of Health and Human Services, 1979
		Secy. of Education, 1979

veloped that passionate state loyalty which dominated so many Americans. Hamilton regarded himself as a kind of prime minister in Washington's Cabinet, and on occasion thrust his hands into the affairs of other departments, including that of his arch-rival, Thomas Jefferson.

Other newly sawed governmental planks were nailed into place. Effective federal courts were created under the Judiciary Act passed by Congress in 1789. The first Congress likewise passed twelve amendments to the Constitution, of which ten were ratified by the states in 1791. Popularly known as the Bill of Rights, the new safeguards guaranteed the most precious of American principles. Among these are assurances against unreasonable search and the right to jury trial, as well as freedom of religion, freedom of speech, freedom of the press, freedom of assembly, and freedom of petition (see Amendments I–X).

Hamilton Revives the Corpse of Public Credit

Financial vexations, which had crippled the Articles of Confederation, were the most pressing. Alexander Hamilton, a financial wizard, sprang to the rescue. His plan was to shape the fiscal policies of the administration in such a way as to favor the wealthier groups. They, in turn, would gratefully lend the government monetary and moral support. The new federal regime would flourish, the propertied classes would grow fat, and prosperity would trickle down to the masses.

The youthful financier's first objective was to bolster the national credit. Without public confidence in the government, Hamilton could not secure the funds with which to float his risky schemes. He therefore boldly urged Congress to "fund" the entire national debt at par, and to assume completely the debts incurred by the states during the recent war.

"Funding at par" meant that the federal government would pay off its debts at face value, plus accumulated interest—a then enormous total of more than $54 million. So many people believed the infant Treasury incapable of meeting those obligations that government bonds had depreciated to ten or fifteen cents on the dollar. Yet speculators held fistfuls of them, and when Congress passed Hamilton's measure in 1790, they grabbed for more. Some of them galloped into rural areas ahead of the news, buying for a song the depreciated paper holdings of farmers, war veterans, and widows.

Hamilton was bitterly reproached for not having sought out the original holders of these securities. But such a course would have been impossible to carry out with complete fairness. Besides, Con-

|0|0|0|0|0|0|0|0|0|0|0|0|0|0|0|0|0|0|0|0|0|0|0|0|0|0|

One of the most eloquent tributes to Hamilton came from Daniel Webster in the Senate (1831): "He smote the rock of the national resources, and abundant streams of revenue gushed forth. He touched the dead corpse of public credit, and it sprung upon its feet."

|0|0|0|0|0|0|0|0|0|0|0|0|0|0|0|0|0|0|0|0|0|0|0|0|0|0|

President Washington's "White House" in Philadelphia, 1794. The first national capital was New York (1789–1791) followed by Philadelphia (1791–1800), and then Washington.

gress, with some speculators in its ranks, flatly rejected such a proposal.

Some cynics have dubbed the first congressmen "Funding Fathers," with reference to their pocket-lining practices. Yet many of these legislators were convinced that the success of the new government depended on their approval of Hamilton's schemes. They could hardly have been expected to vote "nay" just because principle and personal profit happened to coincide.

Assuming the State Debts

Hamilton was willing, even eager, to have the new government shoulder additional obligations. While pushing the funding scheme, he urged Congress to assume the debts of the states, totaling some $21.5 million.

The secretary made a convincing case for "assumption." The state debts could be regarded as a proper national obligation, for they had been incurred in the war for independence. But foremost in Hamilton's thinking was the belief that assumption would chain the states more tightly to the "federal chariot." Thus, the secretary's maneuver would shift the attachment of wealthy creditors from the states to the federal government. The support of the rich for the national administration was a crucial link in Hamilton's political strategy of strengthening the central government.

States that were burdened by heavy debts, like Massachusetts, were delighted by Hamilton's proposal. States that had small debts, or had taken energetic steps to pay them off, were less happy. They saw no good reason why they should be taxed by the central government to pull their less thrifty sisters out of a fiscal hole. The fight against assumption was vigorously led by Virginia, and took on the semblance of another North-South sectional struggle. In some of the states there was even irresponsible talk of leaving the Union.

The stage was set for some old-fashioned horse trading. Virginia did not want the state debts assumed, but she did want the forthcoming federal district*—now the District of Columbia—to be located on the Potomac River. She would thus gain in commerce and prestige. Hamilton persuaded a reluctant Jefferson, who had recently come home from France, to line up enough votes in Congress for assumption. In return, Virginia would have the federal district on the Potomac. The bargain was carried through in 1790, though Jefferson later claimed that he had been outwitted. It proved to be one of the earliest instances of congressional logrolling.†

Customs Duties and Excise Taxes

The new ship of state thus set sail dangerously overloaded. The national debt had swelled to $75 million owing to Hamilton's insistence on honoring the outstanding federal and state obligations alike. A man less determined to establish a healthy

---

*Authorized by the Constitution, Art. I, Sec. VIII, para. 17.
†On the frontier, heavy logs in clearings were rolled into place by enlisting the assistance of neighbors. Mutual aid in legislative bodies to pass laws for special interests came to be called logrolling—"an aye for an aye."

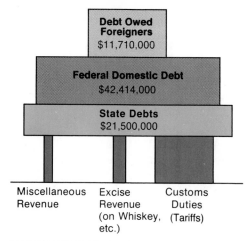

Debt Owed Foreigners
$11,710,000

Federal Domestic Debt
$42,414,000

State Debts
$21,500,000

Miscellaneous Revenue

Excise Revenue (on Whiskey, etc.)

Customs Duties (Tariffs)

HAMILTON'S FINANCIAL STRUCTURE
SUPPORTED BY REVENUES

public credit could have sidestepped $13 million in back interest, and could have avoided the state debts entirely.

But Hamilton, "Father of the National Debt," was not greatly worried. His objectives were as much political as economic. He believed that, within limits, a national debt was a "national blessing"—a kind of cement of union. The more creditors to whom the government owed money, the more people there would be with a personal stake in the success of his ambitious enterprise. His unique contribution was to make a debt—ordinarily a liability—an asset for vitalizing the financial system as well as the government itself.

Where was the money to come from to pay interest on this huge debt and to run the government? Hamilton's first answer was customs duties, derived from a tariff. Tariff revenues, in turn, depended on a vigorous foreign trade, another crucial link in Hamilton's overall economic strategy for the new Republic.

The first tariff law, a low one of about 8 percent on the value of dutiable imports, was speedily passed by the first Congress in 1789, even before Hamilton was sworn in. Revenue was by far the main goal, but the measure was also designed to erect a low protective wall around infant indus-

tries, which bawled noisily for more shelter than they received. Hamilton had the vision to see that the Industrial Revolution would soon reach America, and he argued strongly in favor of more protection for the well-to-do manufacturing groups—another vital element in his economic program. But Congress was still dominated by the agricultural and commercial interests, and it voted only two slight increases in the tariff during Washington's presidency.

Hamilton, with characteristic vigor, sought additional internal revenue, and in 1791 secured from Congress an excise tax on a few domestic items, notably whiskey. The new levy of seven cents a gallon was borne chiefly by the distillers who lived in the back country, where the wretched roads forced the farmer to reduce his bulky bushels of grain to horseback proportions. Whiskey flowed so freely on the frontier that it was used for money; a gallon of the fiery liquid passed for one shilling—or about twenty-five cents.

But Hamilton was not unduly bothered by the cries of outrage from the backwoods. The federal regime had to be bolstered, no matter how unpopular his measures. Besides, the excise would accustom the people, especially the reluctant states'-rights advocates, to a direct tax by the federal government. In any case, the secretary had little sympathy for the Western distillers, many of whom from the outset had opposed the powerful new Constitution and Hamilton's centralizing schemes.

Hamilton Battles Jefferson for a Bank

As the capstone of his financial system, Hamilton proposed a Bank of the United States. An enthusiastic admirer of most things English, he took as his model the Bank of England. Specifically, he proposed a powerful private institution, of which the government would be the major stockholder, and in which the Federal Treasury would deposit its surplus monies. The central government not only would have a convenient strongbox, but federal funds would stimulate business by remaining in circulation. The Bank would also print urgently needed paper money, and thus provide a sound and stable national currency, badly needed since the days when the Continental dollar was "not worth a Continental."

Ardent champions of states' rights, spearheaded by Secretary of State Jefferson, cried out against a giant Bank. They predicted that their cherished state banks could not survive competition from this monopolistic monster. More alarming, the states'-righters feared that their precious liberties would be jeopardized by a grasping banking colossus which, in fact, came to enjoy a virtual monopoly of the government's surplus funds.

Jefferson, whose written opinion Washington requested, argued vigorously against the Bank. There was, he insisted, no specific authorization in the Constitution for such a financial octopus. He was convinced that all powers not specifically granted to the central government were reserved to the states, as provided in the about-to-be-ratified Bill of Rights (see Art. X). He therefore concluded that the states, not Congress, had the power to charter banks. Believing that the Constitution should be interpreted "literally" or "strictly," Jefferson and his states'-rights disciples zealously embraced the theory of "strict construction."

Hamilton, also at Washington's request, prepared a brilliantly reasoned reply to Jefferson's arguments. He boldly invoked that clause of the Constitution which stipulates that Congress may pass any laws "necessary and proper" to carry out the powers vested in the various governmental agencies (see Art. I, Sec. VIII, para. 18). The government was explicitly empowered to collect taxes and regulate trade. In carrying out these basic functions, Hamilton argued, a national bank would be not only "proper" but "necessary." By inference or implication—that is, by virtue of "implied powers"—Congress would be fully justified in establishing the Bank of the United States. In short, Hamilton contended for a "loose" or "broad" interpretation of the Constitution. He and his federalist followers thus evolved the theory of "loose construction" by invoking the "elastic clause" of the Constitution—a precedent for enormous federal powers.

Hamilton's financial views prevailed. His eloquent and realistic arguments were accepted by Washington, who reluctantly signed the Bank

The First Bank of the United States. The first bank of the United States, established in Philadelphia, lasted from 1789 to 1811; the second, from 1816 to 1836. (Library of Congress.)

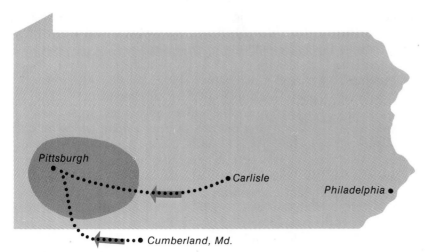

Hamilton regarded the "Whiskey Boys"
not as mere tax resisters but as traitors
scheming to detach the West from the
newborn union. Yet after sharp interroga-
tion of several captured rebels, the Treasury Secretary was forced to conclude
that no secessionist plot existed. Even so,
he wanted to leave an army of occupation
in the whiskey country, to stop "the political putrefaction of Pennsylvania." Washington vetoed this heavy-handed measure.

measure into law. This explosive issue had been
debated with much heat in Congress, where the
old North-South cleavage again appeared ominously. The most enthusiastic support for the Bank
naturally came from the commercial and financial
centers of the North, while the strongest opposition arose from the agricultural South.

The Bank of the United States, as created by
Congress in 1791, was chartered for twenty years.
Located in Philadelphia, it was to have a capital
of $10 million, one-fifth of it owned by the federal
government. Stock was thrown open to public
sale. To the agreeable surprise of Hamilton, a milling crowd oversubscribed in less than two hours,
pushing aside many would-be purchasers.

Mutinous Moonshiners in Pennsylvania

The Whiskey Rebellion, which flared up in southwestern Pennsylvania in 1794, sharply challenged
the new national government. Hamilton's excise
bore harshly on these homespun pioneer folk.
They regarded it not as a tax on a luxury but as a
burden on an economic necessity and a medium
of exchange. Even preachers of the gospel were
paid in "Old Monongahela rye." Defiant distillers
finally erected Whiskey Poles, similar to the Liberty Poles of anti–Stamp Tax days in 1765, and
raised the cry "Liberty and No Excise." Boldly

tarring and feathering revenue officers, they
brought collections to a halt.

President Washington, once a Revolutionist,
was alarmed by what he called these "self-created
societies." With the warm encouragement of
Hamilton, he summoned the militia of several
states. Anxious moments followed the call, for
there was much doubt as to whether men in other
states would muster to crush a rebellion in a sister
state. Despite some opposition, an army of about
13,000 rallied to the colors, and two widely separated columns marched briskly forth in a gor-
geous, leaf-tinted Indian summer, until knee-deep
mud slowed their progress. Washington accompanied the troops a part of the way; Hamilton all
the way.

The federal force was overpoweringly strong—
larger in fact than Washington's army during
much of the Revolutionary War. When the troops
reached the hills of western Pennsylvania, they
found no insurrection. The "Whiskey Boys" were
overawed, dispersed, or captured. Washington,
with an eye to healing old sores, pardoned the
two small-fry convicted culprits. Hamilton, disgusted by this turn of affairs, wanted to punish
the real ringleaders. Ironically, the cost of crushing the rebels cost more than three years' net
revenue from the excise.

The Whiskey Rebellion was small—some three

rebels were killed—but its consequences were large. George Washington's government, now substantially strengthened, commanded a new respect. Yet the numerous foes of the federalists condemned the administration for its brutal display of force—for having used a sledge hammer to crush a gnat. The ranks of the Jeffersonians were consequently enlarged. Back-country men, taught a harsh lesson, now saw the wisdom of forsaking the tar kettle for the ballot box—and voting for Jefferson.

The Hamiltonian Balance Sheet

Almost overnight Hamilton's fiscal feats had established the public credit. The Treasury was now able to secure needed funds in the Netherlands on terms more favorable than those being extended to any other borrowing nation.

The dynamic secretary, under the leadership of Washington, also strengthened the government politically while bolstering it financially. His major schemes—funding, assumption, the excise, the Bank—all encroached sharply upon states' rights. This trend, facilitated by "loose construction," was destined to continue its controversial course to the Civil War and beyond.

States'-rights people naturally condemned Hamilton in harsh terms. The Constitution had been ratified by a painfully narrow margin; and if the voters had foreseen how the states were going to be overshadowed by the federal colossus, they almost certainly would have voted it down. Hamilton in general believed that what the Constitution did not forbid it permitted; Jefferson in general believed that what it did not permit it forbade.

Though a skillful planner, Hamilton was at heart a gambler—a taker of calculated risks. He was playing for enormous stakes, and the outcome might be either a resounding success or a crashing failure. The huge debt, which he had so confidently urged Congress to assume, could be paid off only if ample receipts flowed into the customs-houses. Disaster would befall the nation if foreign trade languished, or if it were choked off by war with America's best customer, Great Britain.

Luck was with Hamilton. Returning prosperity preceded the Constitution, and floated it over the financial reefs. A full-blown foreign war was avoided for more than two decades, and by that time the experimental stage had passed. Even so, the race between mounting expenditures and increasing revenues was nip and tuck for about ten years.

Government by the Wellborn

Hamilton navigated skillfully on the sea of economic policy, but politically he encountered increasingly heavy weather. Out of the resentment against his revenue-raising and centralizing policies an organized opposition began to emerge.

National political parties, in the modern sense, were unknown to America when George Washington took the inaugural oath. There had been Whigs and Tories, federalists and anti-federalists, but these groups were factions rather than parties. They had sprung into existence over hotly contested special issues; they had faded away when their cause had triumphed or had become hopelessly lost.

American political parties date their birth from the bitter clashes between Hamilton and Jefferson, chiefly over fiscal policy and foreign affairs. By 1792–1793 two well-defined groupings had crystallized: the Hamiltonian Federalists and the Jeffersonian Republicans. The two-party system

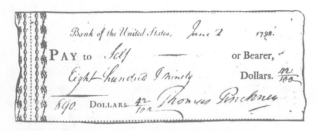

Check on the Bank of the U.S.   By Thomas Pinckney, minister to England.

> Jefferson, who became one of the ablest political organizers in American history, was distrustful of the evils spawned by parties. He wrote in 1789, "If I could not go to Heaven but with a party I would not go there at all."

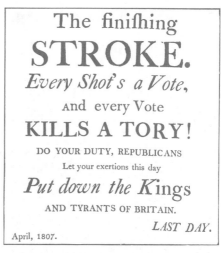

The finifhing
STROKE.
Every Shot's a Vote,
And every Vote
KILLS A TORY!
DO YOUR DUTY, REPUBLICANS
Let your exertions this day
Put down the Kings
AND TYRANTS OF BRITAIN.
LAST DAY.
April, 1807.

Jeffersonian Republican Leaflet. It treats Federalists as Tories as late as 1807.

has existed in the United States since that day, and has provided indispensable machinery for self-government. The party of the "outs" has traditionally played the invaluable role of both critic and brake—"the loyal opposition."

As might be expected, most federalists of the pre-Constitution period (1787–1789) became Federalists in the Washington era. By 1793 they were welded into an effective group, largely through the magnetic leadership and organizational genius of Alexander Hamilton.

Federalists openly advocated rule by the "best people." They believed in a government by the upper classes, with secondary attention to the masses. "Those who own the country," remarked Federalist John Jay, "ought to govern it." With their intellectual arrogance and Tory tastes, the Hamiltonians deplored democratic tendencies and distrusted the common man. They regarded democracy as the mother of all mischiefs, and feared the "swayability" of the crowd. Let the rich rule, insisted many Federalist leaders, for they had the leisure with which to study the problems of governing. They also enjoyed all the advantages of intelligence, education, and culture. The untutored masses would only throw monkey wrenches into the machinery; democracy was too important to be left to the people.

Hamiltonians likewise advocated a potent central government. It would maintain law and order, crush democratic excesses (like Shays's Rebellion), and protect the lives and estates of the wealthy. The foreign-born Hamilton, in pursuit of these goals, would subordinate the sovereignty-loving states.

Hamiltonian Federalists also believed that the national government should foster business, not interfere with it. This attitude was only natural in a group dominated by merchants, manufacturers, and shippers. The great majority of Federalists lived in the urban areas of the seaboard, where commerce and manufacturing flourished. If a gunner could have fired cannonballs 50 miles (80.5 kilometers) inland, he would have hit few Hamiltonians.

The Federalists, in addition, were at bottom pro-British. Though Americans first of all, they felt that the nation's foreign policy should be slanted toward friendship with England, above any other outside power. Foreign trade, especially with England, was a key element in Hamilton's entire fiscal machinery. Many Hamiltonians were mild Loyalists, leftovers from Revolutionary days. Basically conservative in their outlook, they welcomed the Federalist bias for the Mother Country, to which they retained much sentimental attachment.

Jeffersonian Idealism and Idealists

Leading the anti-Federalist forces was Thomas Jefferson. Lanky and relaxed in appearance, lacking personal aggressiveness, weak-voiced, and unable to deliver a rabble-rousing speech, he be-

Monticello, Jefferson's Self-Designed Architectural Marvel. A talented inventor, he installed a number of gadgets, including a device for pulling up chilled bottles of wine from the cellar to the dining table. (Virginia Chamber of Commerce, photo by D'Adamo.)

came a master political organizer through his ability to lead men rather than drive them. His strongest appeal was to the middle class and to the underprivileged—the "dirt" farmers, the laborers, the artisans, and the small shopkeepers.

Liberal-thinking Jefferson, with his aristocratic head set on a farmer's frame, was a bundle of inconsistencies. By one set of tests he should have been a Federalist, for he was a Virginia aristocrat and slaveowner who lived in an imposing hilltop mansion at Monticello. A so-called traitor to his upper class, Jefferson cherished uncommon sympathy for the common man, especially the downtrodden, the oppressed, and the persecuted. As he wrote in 1800, "I have sworn upon the altar of God eternal hostility against every form of tyranny over the mind of man."

Jeffersonian Republicans, or Democratic-Republicans, as they were called, demanded a weak central regime. They believed that the best government was the one that governed least. The bulk of the power, Jefferson argued, should be retained by the states. There the people, in intimate contact with local affairs, could keep a more vigilant eye on their public servants. Otherwise, a dictatorship might develop. Central authority—a kind of necessary evil—was to be kept at a minimum through a strict interpretation of the Constitution. The national debt, which Jefferson regarded as a curse illegitimately bequeathed to later generations, was to be paid off.

Jeffersonians, themselves primarily agrarians, insisted that there should be no special privileges for special classes, particularly manufacturers. Agriculture, to Jefferson, was the favored branch of the economy. He regarded farming as essentially ennobling; it kept men away from wicked cities, out in the sunshine and close to the sod—and God. Most of his followers naturally came from the agricultural South and Southwest.

Above all, Jefferson advocated the rule of the people. But he did not propose thrusting the ballot into the hands of *every* adult white male. He favored government *for* the people, but not by *all* the people—only by those men who were literate enough to inform themselves and wear the mantle of American citizenship worthily. Universal education would have to precede universal suffrage. The ignorant, he argued, were incapable of self-government. But he had profound faith in the reasonableness and teachableness of the masses, and in their collective wisdom when taught. His enduring appeal was to America's better self.

The open-minded Jefferson championed free speech, because without free speech the misdeeds of tyranny could not be exposed. He even went so far as to say that as between "a government without newspapers" and "newspapers without a government," he would choose the latter. No American statesman, except perhaps Lincoln, ever suffered more foul abuse from editorial pens; he might well have prayed for freedom *from* the Federalist press. Yet in 1801 he declared, "Error of opinion may be tolerated where reason is left free to combat it."

Jeffersonian Republicans, unlike the Federalist "British boot-lickers," were basically pro-French. They earnestly believed that it was to America's advantage to support the liberal ideals of the

French Revolution, rather than applaud the reaction of the English Tories. So it was that foreign policy and domestic politics became perilously intermingled, as the fledgling American Republic was caught up in the bloody international conflicts of the French Revolutionary era.

VARYING VIEWPOINTS

The Federalist era witnessed some of the sharpest political conflicts in American history. Certain critics see this period as virtually the *only* time in the nation's experience when major differences of ideology separated the main political leaders. In the clash between Hamiltonians and Jeffersonians, historians have generally sympathized with the liberal Virginian. Yet most scholars agree that it was fortunate for the Republic that the Federalists had the helm for a time. Their leaders put federal finances and foreign policy on a sound conservative foundation, thus permitting the later construction of a "liberal" Jeffersonian edifice.

SELECT READINGS

Perceptive introductions are provided by Marcus Cunliffe's succinct *The Nation Takes Shape, 1789–1837* (1959), and J. C. Miller's more detailed *The Federalist Era, 1789–1801* (1960). On administration, consult L. D. White, *The Federalists* (1948); on finance, D. F. Swanson, *The Origins of Hamilton's Fiscal Policies* (1963), and the book by Nettels cited in the previous chapter. See also those by Chambers on politics and the biographical studies by Brant, Miller, Mitchell, and Rossiter.

Also illuminating is Gerald Stourzh, *Alexander Hamilton and the Idea of Republican Government* (1970). A comprehensive biography is James T. Flexner, *George Washington and the New Nation, 1783–1793* (1969). Consult also Forrest McDonald, *The Presidency of George Washington* (1974). Of special interest is R. H. Kohn, *Eagle and Sword: The Federalists and the Creation of the Military Establishment in America, 1783–1802* (1975).

9

Federalists and Foreign Friction

And ne'er shall the sons of Columbia be slaves,
While the earth bears a plant, or the sea rolls its
waves.

POPULAR SONG BY ROBERT TREAT PAINE,
"Adams and Liberty," 1798

The Impact of the French Revolution

When Washington's first administration ended early in 1793, domestic controversies had already formed two political camps—Hamiltonian Federalists and Jeffersonian Republicans. As his second term began, issues of foreign policy brought differences to a fever pitch.

Only a few weeks after Washington's inauguration in 1789, the curtain had arisen on the first act of the French Revolution. Twenty-six years were to pass before the seething continent of Europe settled back into a peace of exhaustion. Few non-American events have left a deeper scar on American political and social life. In a sense, the French Revolution was misnamed: it was a *world* revolution that touched all civilized peoples.

In its early stages the upheaval was surprisingly

peaceful, involving as it did a successful attempt to impose constitutional shackles on Louis XVI. The American people, loving liberty and deploring despotism, were pleased. They were flattered to think that the outburst in France was but the second chapter of their own glorious revolution, as to some extent it was. Only a few ultra-conservative Federalists—fearing change, reform, and "leveling" principles—were from the outset dubious or outspokenly hostile to the "despicable mobocracy." The more ardent Jeffersonians were overjoyed.

The French Revolution entered upon a more ominous phase in 1792, when France declared war on hostile Austria. Powerful ideals and powerful armies alike were on the march. Late in that year the electrifying news reached America that French citizen armies had hurled back the invading foreigners, and that France had proclaimed herself a republic. American enthusiasm found expression in singing "The Marseillaise" and other French revolutionary songs, and in renaming thoroughfares. King Street in New York, for example, became Liberty Street, while in Boston Royal Exchange Alley became Equality Lane.

But centuries of pent-up poison could not be purged without baleful results. The guillotine was set up, the King was beheaded in 1793, Christianity was abolished, and the head-rolling Reign of Terror was begun. Back in America, God-fearing Federalist aristocrats nervously fingered their tender white necks and eyed the Jeffersonian masses apprehensively. Lukewarm Federalist approval of the early Revolution turned, almost overnight, to heated opposition to "blood-drinking cannibals."

Sober-minded Jeffersonians regretted the bloodshed. But they felt, with Jefferson, that one could not expect to be carried from "despotism to liberty in a feather bed," and that a few thousand aristocratic heads were a cheap price to pay for human freedom. When the news came of Louis XVI's beheading, the Pittsburgh *Gazette* brutally rejoiced, "Louis Capet has lost his caput."

Such gloating was shortsighted, for dire peril loomed ahead. The earlier battles of the French Revolution had not hurt America directly, but now

William Cobbett wrote of the frenzied reaction in America to the death of Louis XVI: "Never was the memory of any man so cruelly insulted as that of this mild and humane monarch. He was guillotined in effigy, in the capital of the Union [Philadelphia], twenty or thirty times every day, during one whole winter and part of the summer. Men, women and children flocked to the tragical exhibition, and not a single paragraph appeared in the papers to shame them from it."

Britain was sucked into the titanic conflict. The conflagration speedily spread to the New World, where it vitally affected the expanding young Republic. Thus was repeated the familiar story of every major European war, beginning with 1689, that involved a death struggle for control of the Atlantic Ocean. (See table on p. 48.)

Washington's Neutrality Proclamation

Ominously, the Franco-American alliance of 1778 was still on the books. By its own terms it was to last "forever." It bound the United States to help the French defend their West Indies against future foes; and the booming British fleets were certain to attack these strategic islands.

Many Jeffersonian Republicans favored honoring the alliance, though dubious about defending the French island outposts at the risk of war. Aflame with the liberal ideals of the French Revolution, red-blooded Jeffersonians were eager to enter the conflict against Britain, the recent foe, at the side of France, the recent friend. America owed France her freedom, they argued, and now was the time to pay the debt of gratitude.

But President Washington, level-headed as usual, was not swayed by the clamor of the crowd. Backed by Hamilton, he perceived that war had to be avoided at all costs. The nation in 1793 was militarily weak, economically wobbly, and politi-

The Contrast.   Adaptation of an English cartoon. C. C. Coffin, *Building a Nation*, 1882. (Boston Public Library.)

A contemporary later wrote, "Can it ever be forgotten what a racket was made with the citizen Genêt? The most enthusiastic homage was too cold to welcome his arrival; and his being the first minister of the infant [French] republic . . . was dwelt upon. . . . What hugging and tugging! What addressing and caressing!"

cally disunited. But solid foundations were being laid, and American cradles were continuing to rock a bumper crop of babies. Washington sagaciously reasoned that if America could avoid the broils of Europe for a generation or so, she would then be populous enough and strong enough to assert her maritime rights with vigor and success. Otherwise, she might invite disaster. This strategy of delay—of playing for time while the birthrate fought America's battles—was a cardinal policy of the Founding Fathers. Hamilton and Jefferson, often poles apart on other issues, were in agreement here.

Accordingly, Washington boldly issued his Neutrality Proclamation in 1793, shortly after the outbreak of war between Britain and France. This epochal document not only proclaimed the government's official neutrality in the widening conflict, but sternly warned American citizens to be impartial toward both armed camps. It was America's first formal declaration of aloofness from Old World quarrels, and as such proved to be a major prop of the spreading isolationist tradition.

The pro-French Jeffersonians were enraged by the Neutrality Proclamation; the pro-British Federalists were enheartened. A few days earlier an impetuous, thirty-year-old representative of the French Republic, Citizen Genêt, had landed at Charleston, South Carolina. With unrestrained zeal, he undertook to fit out privateers and otherwise take advantage of the existing Franco-American alliance. The giddy-headed envoy—all sail and no anchor—was soon swept away by his enthusias-

tic reception by the Jeffersonian Republicans. He foolishly came to believe that the Neutrality Proclamation did not reflect the true wishes of the American people, and he consequently embarked upon unneutral activity not authorized by the French alliance. After he had threatened to appeal over the head of "Old Washington" to the sovereign voters, the President demanded Genêt's withdrawal and the Frenchman was replaced by a less impulsive spokesman.

Washington's Neutrality Proclamation clearly illustrates the truism that self-interest is the basic cement of alliances. In 1778, both France and America stood to gain; in 1793, only France. Technically, the Americans did not flout their obligation, because France never officially called upon them to honor it. Her homeland, and especially her blockaded West Indian Islands, were urgently in need of Yankee foodstuffs. If the Americans had entered the war, the British fleets would have blockaded their coasts and cut off those desperately needed supplies. America was much more useful to France as a prosperous provider than as a prostrate partner.

Embroilments with Britain

President Washington's far-visioned policy of neutrality was sorely tried by the British. For ten long years they had been retaining the chain of northern frontier posts on United States soil, all in defiance of the peace treaty of 1783. There they openly sold firearms and firewater to the Indians, who continued to attack pale-faced pioneers invading their lands. When General "Mad Anthony" Wayne crushed the Northwest Indians at the Battle of Fallen Timbers on August 20, 1794, the fleeing foe left on the field British-made arms, as well as the corpses of a few British-Canadians. In the Treaty of Greenville in 1795, the Indians, finally abandoned by their red-coated friends, ceded their claims to a vast virgin tract in the Ohio country.

On the sea frontier, the British were eager to starve out the French West Indies, and naturally expected the United States to defend them under the Franco-American alliance. Hard-boiled commanders of the Royal Navy, acting under instructions from London in 1793, struck savagely. They seized about 300 American merchant ships in the West Indies, impressed scores of seamen into service on English vessels, and threw hundreds of others into foul dungeons.

These outrages were intolerable. A mighty outcry arose, chiefly from Jeffersonians, that America should once again fight George III in defense of her liberties. At the very least, she should cut off all supplies to her oppressor through a nationwide embargo.

But the Federalists stoutly resisted all demands for drastic action. War with Britain would be a lethal blow at the heart of the Hamiltonian financial system. About 90 percent of the revenue supporting the nation's still-shaky financial structure flowed from customs duties, and some 75 percent of all customs duties came from British imports. An armed clash with England would dry up this life-giving revenue.

John Jay Negotiates a Treaty

President Washington, in a last desperate gamble to avert war, decided to send John Jay to London in 1794. The Jeffersonians were acutely unhappy over the choice, partly because they feared that so notorious a Federalist and Britain-lover would sell out his country. Arriving in London, Jay gave the Jeffersonians further cause for alarm when, at the presentation ceremony, he routinely kissed the Queen's hand.

Unhappily, Jay entered the negotiations with weak cards, which were further weakened by Hamilton. The latter, fearful of war with England, secretly supplied the British with the details of America's bargaining strategy. Not surprisingly, Jay won few concessions. The British did promise to evacuate the chain of posts on United States soil—a concession that inspired little confidence, since it had been made before in Paris (to the same John Jay!) in 1783. In addition, Britain consented to pay damages for the recent seizures of American ships. But the British stopped short of pledging anything about *future* maritime seizures and impressments, or about Indian butcheries. And they forced Jay to give ground by binding the United States to pay the debts still owed to British merchants on pre-Revolutionary accounts.

AMERICAN POSTS HELD BY BRITISH
AFTER 1783

IOIOIIOIIOIIOIIOIIOIIOIIOIIOIIOIIOIIOIIOIIOIIOIIOIIOIIOIIOIIOI

Evidently satirizing Jay's obeisance to the British Queen, one American journal wrote, "Hear the voice of truth, hear and believe! John Jay, ah! the arch traitor—seize him, drown him, hang him, burn him, flay him alive! Men of America, he betrayed you with a kiss!"

IOIOIIOIIOIIOIIOIIOIIOIIOIIOIIOIIOIIOIIOIIOIIOIIOIIOIIOIIOIIOI

John Jay Burned in Effigy. (After a drawing by F. O. C. Darley.)

When the Jeffersonians learned of Jay's concessions, their rage was fearful to behold. The treaty seemed like an abject surrender to Britain, as well as a betrayal of the Jeffersonian South. Southern planters would have to pay the major share of the pre-Revolutionary debts, while rich Federalist shippers were collecting damages for recent British seizures. Jeffersonian mobs hanged, burned, and guillotined in effigy that "damn'd archtraitor, Sir John Jay." His unpopular pact, more than any other issue, vitalized the newborn Democratic-Republican party of Thomas Jefferson.

President Washington was now confronted with an agonizing decision. He realized that the treaty was highly disappointing, but he also perceived, as did Hamilton, that the choice was either this treaty or none. If it was none, war would almost certainly ensue. And war might well be ruinous, given America's financially overstrained condition. So Washington, in one of the most courageous acts of a courageous life, threw his immense prestige behind the pact.

The President's course was both condemned and condoned. "Damn George Washington," reportedly cried John Randolph of Virginia in a public toast. Other violent Jeffersonians guillotined the President in effigy. But the Senate, after a stormy debate, approved the treaty by the narrowest of margins. Thus war with Great Britain was averted for seventeen years.

A memorable pact with Spain was one of the aftermaths of Jay's Treaty, which in some ways was more important for its by-products than for its provisions. Spain feared that the Anglo-American pact foreshadowed an Anglo-American alliance—to her detriment. She therefore made haste to conclude with the United States the Pinckney Treaty of 1795. Unlike Jay's Treaty, it conceded virtually everything the Americans demanded. At long last Spain granted free navigation of the Mississippi; she yielded the large area north of Florida that had been in dispute for over a decade. (See map on p. 128.) America's totally unexpected diplomatic successes in this quarter were again a direct result of Spain's European distresses.

George Washington's Farewell

A weary Washington had hoped to retire in 1793, at the end of his first term. But his friends and advisers, including the arch-rivals Jefferson and Hamilton, begged him to stay. This was no time to turn from a leader of international eminence to one of sectional stature, like the disagreeably stiff New Englander, John Adams. Washington was unanimously re-elected, simply because the nation could not do without him. Many people could still sing "God save great Washington," to the tune of "God Save the King."

But two full terms were enough. Washington was not only exhausted physically, but he was weary of verbal abuse. Having lost his non-partisan standing when he became a Federalist, he was being assailed by political foes as an "American Caesar" and as the "Stepfather of His Country." Although he had no serious constitutional scruples against a third election, his decision to retire con-

IOIIOIIOIIOIIOIIOIIOIIOIIOIIOIIOIIOIIOIIOIIOIIOIIOIIOIIOI

Thomas Paine, then in France and resenting George Washington's anti-French policies, addressed the President in an open letter (1796) that reveals his bitterness: "And as to you, sir, treacherous in private friendship (for so you have been to me, and that in the day of danger) and a hypocrite in public life, the world will be puzzled to decide, whether you are an apostate or an imposter; whether you have abandoned good principles, or whether you ever had any."

IOIIOIIOIIOIIOIIOIIOIIOIIOIIOIIOIIOIIOIIOIIOIIOIIOIIOIIOI

tributed powerfully to establishing the two-term tradition.*

Washington's Farewell Address was not delivered orally, but was published in the newspapers of 1796. The bulk of the document, legend to the contrary, was not concerned with foreign affairs. About two-thirds of it was devoted to domestic problems, including a sage warning against partisan bitterness. Its admonition about alliances has been most misunderstood. Washington did not say that the nation should never make any alliances of any kind under any circumstances. As a military man, he favored "temporary alliances" for "extraordinary emergencies." But he strongly advised the avoidance of "permanent alliances," like the still-vexatious French Treaty of 1778.

Washington added still other words of paternal wisdom. With the pro-British Federalists and the pro-French Jeffersonians clearly in mind, he urged that the Republic avoid tying its political fortunes to the tail of a foreign kite. Subservience to overseas nations would cause America to become "in some degree a slave." With the plottings of Genêt and other French agents fresh in memory, Washington urged that the nation banish foreign intrigue from both domestic and diplomatic affairs.

---

*Not broken until 1940 by Franklin D. Roosevelt, and made a part of the Constitution in 1951 by the 22nd Amendment.

The Farewell Address was not received with unanimous acclaim. Jeffersonians, on fire to help the French ally, assailed Washington's impartial words as though they were a declaration of war on France. The truth is that the President, in urging no "permanent" foreign entanglements, was giving admirable advice to a weak and divided nation in the year 1796. But what is sound counsel for a growing boy may not apply later to a muscular giant.

Washington's contributions as President were enormous, even though the sparkling Hamilton at times seemed to outshine him. The central government, its fiscal feet now under it, was solidly established. The West was expanding. The merchant marine was plowing the seas. Above all, Washington had kept the nation out of both overseas entanglements and foreign wars. The experimental stage had passed, and the presidential chair could now be turned over to a less impressive figure. But republics are notoriously ungrateful. When Washington left office in 1797, he was showered with the brickbats of partisan abuse, quite in contrast with the bouquets that had greeted his coming. Though the vast majority of his countrymen honored his name, the more venomous Jeffersonians hailed his departure as ending tyranny and graft. "This day," cried journalist Benjamin Franklin Bache, a grandson of "Old Ben," "ought to be a jubilee in the United States."

"Bonny Johnny" Adams Becomes President

Who should succeed the exalted "Father of His Country"? Alexander Hamilton was the best-known member of the Federalist party, now that Washington had bowed out. But his financial policies, some of which had fattened the speculators, had made him so unpopular that he could not hope to be elected President. The Federalists were forced to turn to the experienced but ungracious John Adams, a rugged chip off old Plymouth Rock. The Democratic-Republicans natur-

John Adams, Flinty Second President. He was the first to move into the White House (1800), and his wife Abigail used the unfinished East Room for drying the family wash. An unusually intelligent woman, she was dubbed "Mrs. President" by critics who accused her of influencing her husband unduly.

ally rallied behind their master-organizer and leader, Thomas Jefferson.

Political passions ran feverishly high in the presidential canvass of 1796. The presence of Washington had hitherto imposed some restraints; now the lid was off. Cultured Federalists like Fisher Ames referred to the Jeffersonians as "fire-eating salamanders, poison-sucking toads." Federalists and Democratic-Republicans even drank their liquor in separate taverns. The issues of the campaign, as it turned out, focused heavily on personalities. But the Jeffersonians again assailed the too-forceful crushing of the Whiskey Rebellion and, above all, the negotiation of Jay's hated treaty.

John Adams, with most of his support in New England, squeezed through by the narrow margin of 71 votes to 68 in the Electoral College. The resulting taunt, "President by three votes," was galling to his pride, which was highly developed. Jefferson, as runner-up, became Vice-President.*

---

*The possibility of such an inharmonious two-party combination in the future was removed by the 12th Amendment to the Constitution in 1804. (See text in Appendix.)

> Jefferson wrote privately of John Adams in 1787, "He is vain, irritable, and a bad calculator of the force and probable effect of the motives which govern men. This is all the ill which can possibly be said of him. He is as disinterested as the Being who made him."

One of the ablest statesmen of his day, Adams at sixty-two was a stuffy figure. Sharp-featured, bald, short (5 feet 7 inches; 1.7 meters) and thickset ("His Rotundity"), he impressed observers as a man of stern principles who did his duty with stubborn devotion. Though learned and upright, he was a tactless and prickly intellectual aristocrat, with no appeal to the masses, and with no desire to cultivate any. Many citizens regarded him with "respectful irritation."

The crusty New Englander suffered from other handicaps. He had stepped into Washington's shoes, which no successor could hope to fill. In addition, Adams was hated by Hamilton, who had resigned from the Treasury in 1795, and who now headed the war faction of the Federalist party. The famed financier even secretly plotted with certain members of the Cabinet against the President, who had a conspiracy rather than a Cabinet on his hands. Most ominous of all, Adams inherited a violent quarrel with France—a quarrel which foreshadowed blazing gunpowder.

Unofficial Fighting with France

Frenchmen were infuriated by Jay's Treaty. They condemned it as the initial step toward an alliance with England, their relentless foe. They further assailed the pact as a flagrant violation of the Franco-American Treaty of 1778. French warships, in retaliation, began to seize defenseless American merchant vessels, altogether about 300 by mid-1797. Adding insult to outrage, the Paris regime haughtily refused to receive America's newly appointed envoy, and even threatened him with arrest.

President Adams kept his head, temporarily, even though the nation was mightily aroused. True to Washington's policy of steering clear of war at all costs, he tried again to reach an agreement with the French, and appointed a diplomatic commission of three men, including John Marshall, the future chief justice.

Adams' envoys, reaching Paris in 1797, hoped to meet Talleyrand, the crafty French foreign minister. They were secretly approached by three go-betweens, later referred to as X, Y, and Z in the published dispatches. The French spokesmen, among other concessions, demanded an unneutral loan of 32 million florins, plus what amounted to a bribe of $250,000 for the privilege of merely talking with Talleyrand.

These terms were intolerable. The American trio knew that bribes were standard diplomatic devices in Europe, but they gagged at paying a quarter of a million dollars for mere talk, without any assurances of a settlement. Negotiations quickly broke down, and John Marshall, on reaching New York in 1798, was hailed as a conquering hero for his steadfastness.

War hysteria swept the United States, catching up President Adams. The slogan of the hour became "Millions for defense, but not one cent for tribute." The song of the hour was "Hail Columbia," which was sung lustily in theaters and taverns:

> Immortal patriots, rise once more!
> Defend your rights, defend your shore.

The Federalists were delighted at this unexpected turn of affairs, while all except the most rabid Jeffersonians hung their heads over the misbehavior of their fine-feathered French friends.

War preparations in America were pushed feverishly, despite considerable Jeffersonian opposition in Congress. The Navy Department was created; the three-ship navy was expanded; the Marine Corps was established. A new army of 10,000 men was authorized (but never fully raised), to be headed by the redoubtable but aging General Washington. He reluctantly heeded the call of duty, but stipulated that the active command be

Preparation for War to Defend Commerce. The building of the frigate *Philadelphia*. In 1803 this frigate ran onto the rocks near Tripoli harbor, and about 300 officers and men were imprisoned by the Tripolitans. The ship was refloated for service against the Americans, but Stephen Decatur led a party of men that set her afire. (Prints Division, The New York Public Library, Astor, Lenox and Tilden Foundations.)

entrusted to the younger Alexander Hamilton, who became a major general. A frustrated military genius, Hamilton was intoxicated by dreams of conquest. He would lead a victorious American army, supported by the British navy, against the possessions of France's Spanish ally—specifically the Floridas, Louisiana, Mexico, and perhaps points south.

Bloodshed was confined to the sea, and principally to the West Indies. In two and one-half years of undeclared hostilities (1798–1800), American privateers and men-of-war of the new navy captured over eighty armed vessels flying the French colors, though several hundred Yankee merchantmen were lost to the enemy. Evidently only a slight push would plunge both nations into a full-dress war.

Adams Puts Patriotism Above Party

Embattled France, her hands full in Europe, wanted no war. An outwitted Talleyrand realized that to fight the United States would merely add one more foe to his enemies. The British, who were lending the Americans cannon and other war supplies, were actually driven closer to their wayward cousins than they were to be again for many years. Talleyrand therefore let it be known, through roundabout channels, that if the Americans would send a new minister, he would be received with proper respect.

This French furor brought to Adams a degree of personal acclaim that he had never known before—and was never to know again. The song "Adams and Liberty" was hardly less popular than "Hail Columbia." He doubtless perceived that a

---

Adams' firmness was revealed in his message to Congress (June 1798), "I will never send another minister to France without assurances that he will be received, respected, and honored as the representative of a great, free, powerful, and independent nation."

---

full-fledged war, crowned by the conquest of the Floridas and Louisiana, would bring new plaudits to the Federalist party—and perhaps a second term to himself. But the heady wine of popularity did not sway his final judgment. He realized full well, like other Founding Fathers, that war must be avoided while the country was relatively weak.

Adams unexpectedly exploded a bombshell when, early in 1799, he submitted to the Senate the name of a new minister to France. Hamilton and his war-hawk faction were enraged. But public opinion—Jeffersonian and reasonable Federalist alike—was favorable to one last try for peace.

America's envoys (now three) found the political skies brightening when they reached Paris early in 1800. The ambitious "Little Corporal," the Corsican Bonaparte, had recently seized dictatorial power. He was eager to free his hands of the American squabble so that he might continue to redraw the map of Europe, and perhaps create a New World empire in Louisiana. The distresses and ambitions of the Old World were again working to America's advantage.

After prolonged haggling, a memorable treaty known as the Convention of 1800 was signed in Paris. As finally amended, it brought about a mutually acceptable settlement. France agreed to grant a divorce from the twenty-two-year-old marriage of (in)convenience, but as a kind of alimony the United States itself agreed to pay the damage claims of American shippers. So ended the nation's only peacetime military alliance for a century and a half. Its troubled history does much to explain the traditional antipathy of the American people to foreign entanglements.

Adams, flinty to the end, deserves immense credit for his belated push for peace, even though moved in part by jealousy of Hamilton. He not only avoided the hazards of war, but unwittingly smoothed the path for the peaceful purchase of Louisiana three years later. He should indeed rank high among the forgotten purchasers of this vast domain. If America had drifted into a full-blown war with France in 1800, Napoleon would not have sold her Louisiana on any terms in 1803.

ロIロIロIロIロIロIロIロIロIロIロIロIロIロIロIロIロIロIロIロIロI

> In 1815 Adams wrote privately, "I will defend my missions to France, as long as I have an eye to direct my hand, or a finger to hold my pen. They were the most disinterested and meritorious actions of my life. I reflect upon them with . . . satisfaction."

ロIロIロIロIロIロIロIロIロIロIロIロIロIロIロIロIロIロIロIロIロI

President Adams, the bubble of his popularity pricked by peace, was aware of his signal contribution to the nation. He later suggested as the epitaph for his tombstone (not used): "Here lies John Adams, who took upon himself the responsibility of peace with France in the year 1800."

The Federalist Witch Hunt

Exulting Federalists had meanwhile capitalized on the anti-French frenzy to drive through Congress in 1798 a sheaf of laws designed to reduce or gag their Jeffersonian foes.

The first of these oppressive laws was aimed at supposedly pro-Jeffersonian "aliens." Most European immigrants, lacking wealth, were scorned by the aristocratic Federalist party. But they were welcomed as voters by the less prosperous and more democratic Jeffersonians. The Federalist Congress, hoping to discourage the "dregs" of Europe, erected a disheartening barrier. They raised the residence requirements for aliens who desired to become citizens from a tolerable five years to an intolerable fourteen. This drastic new law violated the traditional American policy of open-door hospitality and speedy assimilation.

Two additional Alien Laws struck heavily at undesirable immigrants. The President was empowered to deport dangerous foreigners in time of peace, and to deport or imprison them in time of hostilities. Though defensible as a war measure —and an officially declared war with France seemed imminent—this was an arbitrary grant of power contrary to American tradition and to the spirit of the Constitution.

But the Alien Laws were not so senseless as they may seem. Hundreds of foreign firebrands, fleeing the wrath of the homeland authorities, were pouring into America from France, England, and Ireland. Most of these outcasts joined the ranks of the Jeffersonians, where they naturally clamored for an anti-British policy. A few of them were French spies who should have been expelled; many were what President Adams called "foreign liars."

The stringent Alien Laws were never enforced. But they frightened out of the country certain foreign agitators, including a reported two shiploads of Frenchmen. In addition, an undetermined number of other foreigners were discouraged from sailing to the now not-so-promising Promised Land.

The "lockjaw" Sedition Act, the last of the harsh Federalist measures, was a direct slap at two priceless freedoms guaranteed in the Constitution by the Bill of Rights—freedom of speech and freedom of the press (1st Amendment). This law provided that anyone who impeded the policies of the government or falsely defamed its officials, including the President, would be liable to a heavy fine and imprisonment. Severe though the measure was, the Federalists believed that it was justified. The verbal violence of the day was unrestrained, and foul-penned editors, some of them exiled aliens, assailed Adams' anti-French policy in vicious terms.

Many outspoken Jeffersonian editors were indicted under the Sedition Act, but only ten were brought to trial. All of them were convicted, often by packed juries swayed by prejudiced Federalist judges. A few of the victims were harmless partisans, who should have been spared the notoriety of martyrdom. Among them was Congressman Matthew Lyon (the "Spitting Lion"), who had earlier gained fame by spitting in the face of a Federalist. He was sentenced to four months in jail for writing of President Adams' "unbounded thirst for ridiculous pomp, foolish adulation, and selfish avarice." Another culprit was lucky to get off with a fine of $100 after he had expressed the wish that the wad of a cannon fired in honor of

Congressional Pugilists. Satirical representation of Matthew Lyon's fight in Congress with the Federalist Representative Roger Griswold. (Courtesy of The New York Public Library, Astor, Lenox and Tilden Foundations.)

Adams had landed in the seat of the President's breeches.

The Sedition Act, at least in spirit, was in direct conflict with the Constitution. But the Supreme Court, dominated by Federalists, was of no mind to declare this Federalist law unconstitutional. (The law expired, in March 1801, to much rejoicing from Jeffersonians.) This attempt by the Federalists to crush free speech and silence the opposi-

lololllollolollolollollollollollollollollol

James Callender published in 1800 a pamphlet which assailed the President in this language: "The reign of Mr. Adams has, hitherto, been one continued tempest of *malignant* passions. As president, he has never opened his lips, or lifted his pen, without threatening and scolding. The grand object of his administration has been to exasperate the rage of contending parties, to caluminiate and destroy every man who differs from his opinions. . . . Every person holding an office must either quit it, or think and vote exactly with Mr. Adams." For such blasts Callender was prosecuted under the Sedition Act, fined $200, and sentenced to prison for nine months.

lololllollolollolollollollollollollollollol

tion party, high-handed as it was, undoubtedly made many converts for the Jeffersonians.

Yet the Alien and Sedition Laws, despite pained outcries from the Jeffersonians, commanded widespread popular support. Anti-French hysteria played directly into the hands of witch-hunting conservatives. In the congressional elections of 1798–1799 the Federalists, riding a wave of popularity, scored the most sweeping victory of their entire history.

The Virginia (Madison) and Kentucky (Jefferson) Resolutions

Resentful Jeffersonians naturally refused to take the Alien and Sedition Laws lying down. Jefferson himself feared that if the Federalists managed to choke free speech and free press, they would then wipe out other precious constitutional guarantees. His own political party might even be stamped out of existence. If this had happened, the country might have drifted into a dangerous one-party dictatorship.

As Vice-President under Adams, Jefferson was in an awkward position to protest openly against the Alien and Sedition Laws. Fearing prosecution for sedition, he secretly penned a series of resolutions, which the Kentucky legislature approved in 1798 and 1799. His friend and fellow Virginian, James Madison, drafted a similar but less extreme statement which was adopted by the legislature of Virginia in 1798.

Both Jefferson and Madison stressed the compact theory—a theory popular among English political philosophers in the 17th and 18th Centuries. As applied to America by the Jeffersonians, this concept meant that the thirteen sovereign states, in creating the federal government, had entered into a "compact" or contract regarding its jurisdiction. The national government was consequently the agent or creation of the states. Since water can rise no higher than its source, the individual states were the final judges of whether their agent had broken the "compact" by overstepping the authority originally granted. Invoking this logic, Jefferson's Kentucky resolutions concluded that the federal regime had exceeded its constitutional powers, and that with regard to the Alien and Sedition Acts "nullification" was the "rightful remedy."

If Federalists bent the bow too far in passing the Alien and Sedition Acts, Jefferson bent the bow too far in his reply. If the Federalist indiscretion had made many Jeffersonian voters, Jefferson's indiscretion made many Federalist voters. No other state legislatures, despite Jefferson's hopes, fell into line. Some of them flatly refused to endorse the Virginia and Kentucky resolutions. Others, chiefly in Federalist states, added ringing condemnations. Many Federalists argued that the people, not the states, had made the original com-

pact, and that it was up to the Supreme Court—not the states—to nullify unconstitutional legislation passed by Congress. This practice, though not specifically authorized by the Constitution, was finally adopted by the Supreme Court in 1803.

The Virginia and Kentucky resolutions were a brilliant formulation of the extreme states'-rights view regarding the Union. They were later used by Southerners to support nullification—and ultimately secession. Yet neither Jefferson nor Madison, as Founding Fathers of the Union, had any intention of breaking it up: they were groping for ways to preserve it. Their resolutions were basically campaign documents designed to crystallize opposition to the Federalist party, and to unseat it in the upcoming presidential election of 1800. The only real nullification that Jefferson had in view was the nullification of Federalist abuses.

Federalist and Republican Mudslingers

In the heated presidential contest of 1800, Adams and Jefferson were again the standard-bearers of their respective parties. The Federalists labored under heavy handicaps. Their Alien and Sedition Acts had aroused a host of enemies, although most of these critics were dyed-in-the-wool Jeffersonians anyhow. The Hamiltonian wing of the Federalist party, robbed of its glorious war with France, split openly with President Adams. Hamilton, a victim of arrogance, was so indiscreet as to attack the President in a privately printed pamphlet. Jeffersonians soon got hold of it and gleefully published it.

The most damaging blow to the Federalists was the refusal of Adams to give them a rousing fight with France. Their feverish war preparations had swelled the public debt and had required disagreeable new taxes, including a stamp tax. After all these unpopular measures, the war scare had petered out, and the country was left with an all-dressed-up-but-no-place-to-go feeling. The military preparations now seemed not only unnecessary but extravagant, as seamen for the "new navy" were called "John Adams' Jackasses."

The Providential Detection (Federalist Propaganda).
The American Eagle snatches the Constitution from Jefferson, who is about to burn it (together with the works of Voltaire, Paine, and others) on the altar to French revolutionary despotism. (Massachusetts Historical Society.)

IOI

The Reverend Timothy Dwight, president of Yale College, predicted that in the event of Jefferson's election ''the Bible would be cast into a bonfire, our holy worship changed into a dance of [French] Jacobin phrensy, our wives and daughters dishonored, and our sons converted into the disciples of Voltaire and the dragoons of Marat.''

IOIIOIIOIIOIIOIIOIIOIIOIIOIIOIIOIIOIIOIIOIIOIIOIIOIIOIIOIIOI

Adams himself was known as "The Father of the American Navy."

Thrown on the defensive, the Federalists concentrated their fire on Jefferson himself, who became the victim of one of the earliest "whispering campaigns." He was accused of having robbed a widow and her children of a trust fund, and of having fathered numerous mulatto children by his own slave women. As a liberal in religion, he had earlier incurred the wrath of the orthodox clergy, largely through his successful struggle to separate church and state in Virginia. From the New England stronghold of Federalism and Congregationalism, the preachers thundered against his atheism, although he did believe in God. Old ladies of Federalist families, fearing Jefferson's election, even buried their Bibles or hung them in wells.

The Jeffersonian "Revolution of 1800"

Jefferson won by a majority of 73 electoral votes to 65. But the colorless and presumably unpopular Adams polled more electoral strength than he had gained four years earlier—except for New York. The Empire State fell into the Jeffersonian basket, and with it the election, largely because Aaron Burr, a master wirepuller, turned New York to Jefferson by the narrowest of margins. The Virginian polled the bulk of his strength in the South and West, particularly in those states where manhood suffrage had been adopted.

Jeffersonians rejoiced wildly over the end of the "Federalist Reign of Terror." Some of them, with alcoholic enthusiasm, bawled the song "Jefferson and Liberty":

> Lord! how the Federalists will stare,
> At Jefferson, in Adams' chair!

But Jeffersonian joy was dampened by an unexpected deadlock. Through a technicality Jefferson, the presidential candidate, and Burr, his vice-presidential running mate, received the same number of electoral votes for the presidency. Under the Constitution the tie could be broken only by the House of Representatives (see Art. II, Sec. I, para. 2). This body was controlled for several more months by the lame-duck Federalists, who had been swept into office during the French war scare and who were eager to elect Burr.*

Voting in the House moved slowly to a climax. As ballots were taken in wearisome succession, congressmen snored in their seats; a sick member lay in an adjoining room. Historians used to think that Hamilton, bargaining secretly with Jefferson, played a decisive role. But the evidence indicates that the deadlock was broken when a few Federalists, despairing of electing Burr and hoping for moderation from Jefferson, refrained from voting. The election then went to the rightful candidate.

Jefferson later claimed that the election of 1800 was a "revolution" comparable in principle to that of 1776. In truth the outcome was not a mass upheaval or a popular mandate from anybody for anything. A switch of some 250 votes in New York would have defeated Jefferson. He did not—and could not—extend the suffrage. That was a privilege of the states. But he did persuade the apathetic and overawed marginal voter to go to the polls—the citizen who had just enough property to vote but who hesitated to speak up against his "betters." Above all, the electoral clash led to a peaceful transfer of power, remarkable in that

---

*A "lame duck" has been humorously defined as a politician whose political goose has been cooked at the recent elections. The possibility of another such tie was removed by the 12th Amendment in 1804 (for text, see Appendix). Before then, each elector had two votes, with the second-place finisher becoming Vice-President.

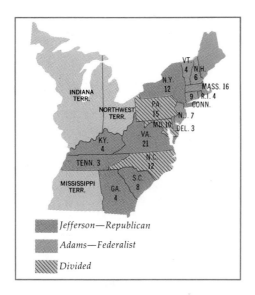

PRESIDENTIAL ELECTION OF 1800
(with electoral vote by state)
New York was the key state in this election, and Aaron Burr helped swing it away from the Federalists with tactics that anticipated the political "machines" of a later day. Federalists complained that Burr "travels every night from one meeting of Republicans to another, haranguing . . . them to the most zealous exertions. [He] can stoop so low as to visit every low tavern that may happen to be crowded with his dear fellow citizens." But Burr proved that the price was worth it. "We have beat you," Burr told kid-gloved Federalists after the election, "by superior *Management.*"

Map labels: VT 4, N.H. 6, N.Y. 12, MASS. 16, INDIANA TERR., 9, R.I. 4, NORTHWEST TERR., PA 15, CONN., N.J. 7, MD. 10, DEL. 3, KY. 4, VA. 21, N.C. 12, TENN. 3, MISSISSIPPI TERR., GA. 4, S.C. 8

Jefferson—Republican
Adams—Federalist
Divided

age, especially after all the partisan bitterness.

Yet the election was also in part a class struggle. Budding democracy was arrayed against entrenched aristocracy more openly than in any previous presidential election. The battle of the ballots resulted in a gratifying victory for the "forgotten man"—and clipped the wings of fine-feathered Federalist aristocrats.

The Federalist Finale

John Adams, as fate would have it, was the last Federalist President of the United States. His party sank slowly into the mire of political oblivion, and ultimately disappeared completely in the days of Andrew Jackson.

Whatever their shortcomings, the Federalists were of the elite. They boasted a much higher concentration of brains, talent, and ability than any other major American political party, past or present. Their political and financial leaders had built enduring foundations for the new government. Their diplomats, with a strong helping hand from Europe's distresses, had signed advantageous treaties with England, Spain, and France. Their statesmen had kept the peace during a crucial period when peace had to be kept.

After all the turmoil of the American Revolution, a conservative party served a needed function in preserving democratic gains and fending off anarchy. The Federalists provided a welcome breathing spell, a chance for the nation to get its bearings. They served, in the words of historian Henry Adams, great-grandson of John Adams, as the "half-way house between the European past and the American future."

But by 1800 the Federalists, blessed with more talent than wisdom, were out of place. The bustling new Republic knew instinctively where it was going. It was eager to take the high road over the mountains that would one day lead to the fulfillment of America's democratic experiment. The Federalists lost out because they were content to mark time, and failed to get in step with the westward march of progress. They were unable or unwilling to unbend and appeal to the common man. They could not adapt—so they died, like the dinosaur. Distinguished though their past service had been, it was no substitute for a capacity to grapple democratically with future problems. The victorious Jeffersonians were prepared to keep the Federalist edifice while ousting the Federalist architects.

VARYING VIEWPOINTS

Historians have rightly regarded the Federalist era as the seedtime of the nation's foreign policy. As debate continues over America's role abroad, so does argument still swirl about the diplomacy of the Federalists. Was George Washington the father of unreasoning "isolationism," or did he set forth a realistic policy for the infant nation to follow? Was that policy equally applicable when the infant nation had matured? What was the historical basis of Washington's ideas? Some scholars regard his policies as opportune rationalizations of the country's weak position. Others see them as high expressions of all the best Enlightenment thought about an ideal international order. This question—concerning the degree to which American foreign policy reflects self-interest or idealism—has continued to be argued from Washington's day to the present.

SELECT READINGS

Brief introductions are Marcus Cunliffe, *The Nation Takes Shape, 1789–1837* (1959), and his *George Washington* (1958). More detailed is J. C. Miller, *The Federalist Era, 1789–1801* (1960). Biographical studies of Hamilton and Madison listed for Chapter 7 are relevant. See also Dumas Malone, *Jefferson and the Rights of Man* (1951), and *Jefferson and the Ordeal of Liberty* (1962); also J. A. Carroll and M. W. Ashworth, *George Washington: First in Peace* (1957), and J. T. Flexner, *George Washington: Anguish and Farewell, 1793–1799* (1972). On the rise of parties consult N. E. Cunningham, *The Jeffersonian Republicans* (1958). On aspects of foreign policy, see Alexander De Conde, *Entangling Alliance* (1958), and his *The Quasi-War: The Politics and Diplomacy of the Undeclared War with France, 1797–1801* (1966); Gilbert Lycan, *Alexander Hamilton and American Foreign Policy* (1970); Jerald Combs, *The Jay Treaty* (1970); Lawrence S. Kaplan, *Colonies into Nation: American Diplomacy, 1763–1801* (1972); L. M. Sears, *George Washington and the French Revolution* (1960); P. A. Varg, *Foreign Policies of the Founding Fathers* (1963); Felix Gilbert, *To the Farewell Address* (1961); and Julian Boyd, *Number 7* (1964), on Hamilton's devious dealings with the British. For the view from across the Atlantic, see Charles R. Ritcheson, *Aftermath of Revolution: British Policy Toward the United States, 1783–1795* (1969). On Adams, consult Page Smith, *John Adams* (2 vols., 1962), and S. G. Kurtz, *The Presidency of John Adams* (1957). J. C. Miller, *Crisis in Freedom* (1951), and J. M. Smith, *Freedom's Fetters* (1956), treat the Alien and Sedition Laws, as does Leonard Levy, *Legacy of Suppression* (1960).

10

The Triumph of Jeffersonian Democracy

Timid men . . . prefer the calm of despotism to the boisterous sea of liberty.

THOMAS JEFFERSON, 1796

Responsibility Breeds Moderation

"Long Tom" Jefferson was inaugurated President on March 4, 1801, in the swampy village of Washington, the crude new national capital. Tall (6 feet 2.5 inches; 1.89 meters), with large hands and feet, reddish hair ("The Red Fox"), and prominent cheekbones and chin, he was an arresting figure. Believing that the customary pomp did not befit his democratic ideals, he spurned a horse-drawn coach and simply walked over to the Capitol from his boarding house.

The inaugural address, beautifully phrased, was a classic statement of democratic principles. Seeking to allay Federalist fears of a bull-in-the-china-closet overturn, Jefferson blandly stated, "We are all Republicans, we are all Federalists." As for foreign affairs, he pledged "honest friendship with all nations, entangling alliances with none."

Washington and Jefferson Contrasted. Note the emphasis on Jefferson's fondness for free-thinkers like Paine and Voltaire. Jefferson liked the democratic way of thinking and the aristocratic way of living. His personal wine bill at the White House ran to over $10,000. Widowed at thirty-nine, he is alleged to have fathered a half-dozen slave children by his mulatto woman Sally, but the charge has never been conclusively proved. (New York Historical Society.)

With its rustic setting, Washington lent itself admirably to the simplicity and frugality of the Jeffersonian Republicans. In this respect, it contrasted sharply with the elegant atmosphere of Federalist Philadelphia, the former temporary capital. Extending democratic principles to etiquette, Jefferson established the rule of pell-mell at official dinners—that is, seating without regard to rank. The resplendent British minister, who had enjoyed precedence among the pro-British Federalists, was insulted.

As a widower, Jefferson was shockingly unconventional. Having no wife to police his apparel, he would receive callers in sloppy attire—on one occasion in a dressing gown and heelless slippers.

IOIOIOIOIOIOIOIOIOIOIOIOIOIOIOIOIOIOIOIOIOIOIOI

Jefferson's toleration was reflected in his inaugural address: ''If there be any among us who would wish to dissolve this Union or to change its republican form, let them stand undisturbed as monuments of the safety with which error of opinion may be tolerated where reason is left free to combat it.''

IOIOIOIOIOIOIOIOIOIOIOIOIOIOIOIOIOIOIOIOIOIOIOI

He started the precedent, unbroken for 112 years, of sending messages to Congress to be read by a clerk. Personal appearances, in the Federalist manner, suggested too strongly a monarchical speech from the throne. Besides, Jefferson was painfully conscious of his weak voice and unimpressive platform presence.

As if plagued by an evil spirit, Jefferson was forced to reverse many of the political principles he had so vigorously championed. There were in fact two Thomas Jeffersons. One was the private citizen, who had philosophized in his study. The other was the public official, who made the disturbing discovery that bookish theories worked out differently in the noisy arena of practical politics. The open-minded Virginian was therefore consistently inconsistent; it is easy to quote one Jefferson to refute the other.

The triumph of Jefferson's Democratic-Republicans and the eviction of the Federalists marked the first party overturn in American history. The vanquished naturally feared that the victors would grab all the spoils of office for themselves. But Jefferson, in line with his conciliatory inaugural address, showed unexpected moderation. To the dismay of his office-seeking friends, the new Pres-

ΙΟΙΙΟΙΙΟΙΙΟΙΙΟΙΙΟΙΙΟΙΙΟΙΙΟΙΙΟΙΙΟΙΙΟΙΙΟΙΙΟΙΙΟΙΙΟΙΙΟΙΙΟΙΙΟΙ

President John F. Kennedy later greeted a large group of Nobel prizewinners as "the most extraordinary collection of talent, of human knowledge, that has ever been gathered together at the White House, with the possible exception of when Thomas Jefferson dined alone."

ΙΟΙΙΟΙΙΟΙΙΟΙΙΟΙΙΟΙΙΟΙΙΟΙΙΟΙΙΟΙΙΟΙΙΟΙΙΟΙΙΟΙΙΟΙΙΟΙΙΟΙΙΟΙΙΟΙ

ident dismissed few public servants for political reasons. Patronage-hungry Jeffersonians watched the Federalist appointees grow old in office, and grumbled that "few die, none resign."

Jefferson quickly proved himself an able politician. He was especially effective in the informal atmosphere of a dinner party. There he wooed Congressmen while personally pouring imported wines and serving the tasty dishes of his French cook.

In part, Jefferson had to rely on his personal charm because his party was so weak-jointed. Denied the power to dispense patronage, the Democratic-Republicans could not build a loyal political following. Opposition to the Federalists was the chief glue holding them together, and as the Federalists faded, so did Democratic-Republican unity. The era of well-developed, well-disciplined political parties still lay in the future.

Jeffersonian Reform Without Revolution

At the outset, Jefferson was determined to undo the Federalist abuses begotten by the anti-French hysteria. The hated Alien and Sedition Laws had already expired. The incoming President speedily pardoned the "martyrs" serving sentences under the Sedition Law, and the government returned many fines. Shortly after the Congress met, the Jeffersonians enacted the new naturalization law of 1802. It reduced the unreasonable requirement of fourteen years of residence to the former and more reasonable requirement of five years.

Jefferson actually kicked away only one sub-

stantial prop of the Hamiltonian system. He hated the excise tax, which bred bureaucrats and bore heavily on his farmer following, and he early persuaded Congress to repeal it. His devotion to principle thus cost the federal government about a million dollars a year in urgently needed revenue.

Swiss-born and French-accented Albert Gallatin, "Watchdog of the Treasury," proved to be as able a secretary of the treasury as Hamilton. Gallatin agreed with Jefferson that a national debt was a bane rather than a blessing, and by strict economy succeeded in reducing it substantially while balancing the budget.

Except for excising the excise tax, the Jeffersonians left the Hamiltonian framework essentially intact. They launched no attack on the Bank of the United States, and they did not repeal the mildly protective Federalist tariff. In later years they embraced Federalism to such a degree as to recharter a bigger Bank and to boost the protective tariff to higher levels.

The "Revolution of 1800," so far as it was a revolution, thus turned out to be largely one of men rather than of measures, especially in the national government. Generally speaking, the agrarian aristocrats of the Republican South and West—men like Jefferson—elbowed aside the commercial and manufacturing aristocrats of the Federalist northern seaboard.

The "Dead Clutch" of the Judiciary

The "death bed" Judiciary Act of 1801 was one of the last important laws passed by the expiring Federalist Congress. It created sixteen new federal judgeships and other judicial offices. President Adams remained at his desk until nine o'clock in the evening of his last day in office, allegedly signing the commissions of the Federalist "midnight judges." (Actually only three commissions were signed on his last day.)

This Federalist-sponsored Judiciary Act, though a long-overdue reform, aroused bitter resentment. "Packing" these lifetime posts with anti-Jeffersonian partisans was, in Republican eyes, a brazen attempt by the defeated party to entrench itself in one of the three powerful branches of government. Jeffersonians condemned the "midnight judges" in violent language. To them, the trickery of the Federalists was open defiance of the people's will, as recently expressed at the polls.

The newly elected Republican Congress bestirred itself to repeal the Judiciary Act of 1801 in the year after its passage. Jeffersonians thus swept sixteen benches from under the recently appointed "midnight judges." Frustrated Federalists, in turn, were acidly critical of this "assault" on the judicial arm.

Jeffersonians likewise had their knives sharpened for the scalp of Chief Justice John Marshall, whom Adams had appointed to the Supreme Court (as a fourth choice) in the dying days of his term. The lanky Marshall, with his rasping voice and steel-trap mind, was a cousin of Thomas Jefferson. As a Virginia Federalist, he was cordially disliked by the states'-rights Jeffersonians. He served for about thirty days under a Federalist administration, and thirty-four years under the administrations of the Jeffersonian Republicans and their successors. The Federalist party died out, but Marshall went on handing down Federalist decisions serenely for many more years. He probably did more than Hamilton to engraft the Hamiltonian concept of a powerful central government upon the American political and economic system.

One of the "midnight judges" of 1801 presented John Marshall with a historic opportunity. He was obscure William Marbury, whom President Adams had named a justice of the peace for the District of Columbia. When Marbury learned that his commission was being held up by the new secretary of state, James Madison, he sued for its delivery. Chief Justice John Marshall knew that his Jeffersonian rivals, entrenched in the executive branch, would hardly spring forward to enforce a writ to deliver the commission to his fellow Federalist Marbury. He therefore dismissed Marbury's suit, avoiding a direct political showdown. But the wily Marshall snatched a victory from the jaws of

> Jefferson referred privately to Marshall (1820) as "a crafty chief judge," and noted that "his twistifications in the case of Marbury, in that of Burr, and the Yazoo case show how dexterously he can reconcile law to his personal biases."

this judicial defeat. In explaining his ruling, Marshall said that the part of the Judiciary Act of 1789 on which Marbury tried to base his appeal was unconstitutional. The Act had attempted to assign to the Supreme Court powers that the Constitution had not foreseen.

In this self-denying opinion, Marshall greatly magnified the authority of the Court—and slapped at the Jeffersonians. Until the case of *Marbury* v. *Madison* (1803), controversy had clouded the question of who had the final authority to determine the meaning of the Constitution. Jefferson in the Kentucky resolutions (1798) had tried to assign that right to the individual states. But now his cousin on the Court had cleverly promoted the contrary principle of "judicial review"—that the black-robed tribunal of the Supreme Court alone had the last word on the question of constitutionality. In this epochal case, Marshall thus neatly inserted the keystone into the arch that supports the tremendous power of the Supreme Court in American life.*

Jefferson Threatens the Supremacy of the Supreme Court

Marshall's decision regarding Marbury spurred the Jeffersonians in their desire to lay rough hands on the Supreme Court through impeachment. Certain Federalist judges had become highly offensive, especially in Sedition Law cases, by de-

---

*The next invalidation of a federal law by the Supreme Court came fifty-four years later with the explosive Dred Scott decision (see p. 371).

Mad Tom in a Rage. A Federalist cartoon shows "Mad Tom" Jefferson, assisted by brandy and the Devil, trying to pull down the Federal edifice erected by Washington and Adams. (Houghton Library, Harvard.)

livering harangues from the bench against the Republican "mobocracy." Jefferson favored free speech, but not this kind of free speech. Accordingly, he urged action against an arrogant Supreme Court justice, Samuel Chase, who was so unpopular that Republicans named vicious dogs after him.

Early in 1804 impeachment charges against Chase were voted by the House of Representatives, which then passed the question of guilt or innocence on to the Senate. The indictment by the House was based on "high crimes and misdemeanors," as specified in the Constitution.* Yet the evidence was plain that the intemperate judge had not been guilty of "high crimes" but of bad manners, injudicious statements, and unrestrained partisanship. The Senate, after a determined prosecution, failed to muster enough votes to convict and remove Chase. The precedent thus established was fortunate. From that day to this, no really serious attempt has been made to reshape the Supreme Court by the impeachment weapon.

John Marshall viewed the attack on Chase with deep misgivings. He suspected, not unreasonably, that if it succeeded he would be next—and then his other Federalist colleagues. These fears were

*For impeachment, see Art. I, Sec. II, para. 5; Art. I, Sec. III, paras. 6, 7; Art. II, Sec. IV, in Appendix.

now laid to rest. Jefferson's ill-advised attempt at "judge breaking" was a reassuring victory for the independence of the judiciary, and for the separation of powers among the three branches of the federal government.

The Pacifist Jefferson Turns Warrior

As a passionate champion of freedom, Jefferson distrusted large standing armies as a standing invitation to dictatorship. Navies, though also suspect, were less to be feared: they could not march inland and "endanger liberties." Pinning his faith to the frail reed of an ill-trained militia, Jefferson reduced the military establishment to a mere police force of 2,500 officers and men. The Republicans, primarily agrarians, saw little point in protecting a few Federalist shippers with a costly navy that all the taxpayers would have to support. Pledged to rigid economy, Jefferson gladly reduced the navy to a peacetime footing, in accordance with legislation already passed by the outgoing Federalist Congress.

But harsh realities forced a penny-pinching Jefferson to change his tune on navies and war. Pirates of the North African states had long made a national industry of blackmailing and plundering merchant ships that ventured into the Mediterranean. Preceding Federalist administrations, in fact, had been forced to buy protection. At the time of the French crisis of 1798, when Americans were shouting, "Millions for defense, but not one cent for tribute," twenty-six barrels of blackmail dollars were being shipped to piratical Algiers.

At this price, war seemed cheaper than peace, and the showdown came in 1801. The Pasha of Tripoli, dissatisfied with his share of protection money, informally declared war on the United States by cutting down the flagstaff of the American consulate. A challenge was thus thrown squarely into the face of Jefferson—the noninterventionist, the pacifist, the critic of a big-ship navy, and the political foe of Federalist shippers. He reluctantly rose to the occasion by dispatching

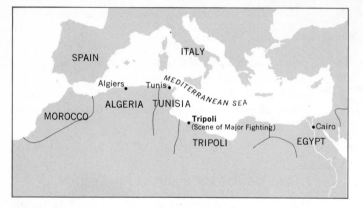

the infant navy to "the shores of Tripoli," as related in the song of the U.S. Marine Corps. After four years of intermittent fighting, marked by hair-raising exploits, Jefferson succeeded in extorting a treaty of peace from Tripoli in 1805. It was secured at the bargain price of only $60,000—a sum representing ransom payments for captured Americans.

With the pattern thus set, the punishment of other North African corsairs continued, off and on, until after the War of 1812. The navy reaped a rich harvest of experience, while strengthening its budding tradition. Foreign nations in general, and the Barbary cutthroats in particular, developed a wholesome respect for the United States—a nation willing and able to defend its rights with blazing guns.

Small gunboats, which the navy had used with some success in the Tripolitan War, fascinated Jefferson. Pledged to tax reduction, he advocated a large number of tiny coastal craft—"Jeffs" or the "mosquito fleet," as they were contemptuously called. He believed that these frail vessels would prove valuable in guarding American shores, although not in defending Federalist merchantmen on the high seas.

About two hundred tiny gunboats were constructed, democratically in small shipyards where votes could be made for Jefferson. Often mounting only one unwieldy gun, they were sometimes more of a menace to the crew than to the prospective enemy. During a hurricane and tidal wave at Savannah, Georgia, one of them was deposited eight miles (12.9 kilometers) inland in a cornfield, to the derisive glee of the Federalists. They drank toasts to American gunboats as the best in the world—on land. Jefferson's pinchpenny economizing backfired badly when the War of 1812 broke out and the whole swarm of gunboats proved virtually stingless. The money could have been much more wisely invested in a few frigates of the *Constitution* class.

Jefferson's One-Gun Gunboats, 1807
In June, 1813, fifteen of these gunboats, each with one heavy gun, attacked a becalmed British frigate near Norfolk, Va. Despite the superior numbers of American vessels, the frigate received only one or two shots in her hull. When the breeze arose, the British ship sailed away virtually unharmed—after killing one American and wounding two.

The Louisiana Godsend

A secret pact, fraught with peril for America, was signed in 1800. Napoleon Bonaparte induced the King of Spain to cede to France, for attractive considerations, the immense trans-Mississippi region of Louisiana, which included the New Orleans area.

Rumors of the transfer were partially confirmed in 1802, when the Spaniards at New Orleans withdrew the right of deposit guaranteed America by the treaty of 1795. Deposit privileges were vital to frontier farmers who floated their produce down the Mississippi to its mouth, there to await ocean-going vessels. A roar of anger rolled up the mighty river and into its tributary valleys. American pioneers talked wildly of descending upon New Orleans, rifles in hand. Had they done so, the nation probably would have been involved in war with both Spain and France.

Thomas Jefferson, both pacifistic and anti-entanglement, was again on the griddle. Louisiana in the senile grip of Spain posed no real threat; America could seize the territory when the time was ripe. But Louisiana in the iron fist of Napoleon, the pre-eminent military genius of his age, foreshadowed a dark and blood-drenched future. The United States would probably have to fight to dislodge him; and because it alone was not strong enough to defeat his armies, it would have to seek allies, contrary to the deepening anti-alliance policy.

Hoping to quiet the clamor of the West, Jefferson moved decisively. Early in 1803 he sent James Monroe to Paris to join forces with the regular minister there, Robert R. Livingston. The two envoys were instructed to buy New Orleans and

Toussaint L'Ouverture (c. 1774–1803). A self-educated ex-slave and military genius, L'Ouverture was finally betrayed by the French, who imprisoned him in a chilly dungeon in France, where he coughed his life away. By indirection he did much to set up the sale of Louisiana to the United States. (Library of Congress.)

> Explaining the Western outburst over the closing of the river, James Madison wrote to Pinckney, "The Mississippi is to them every thing. It is the Hudson, the Delaware, the Potomac, and all the navigable rivers of the Atlantic States, formed into one stream."

as much land to the east as they could get for a maximum of $10 million. If these proposals should fail and the situation should become critical, negotiations were to be opened with England for an alliance.

Nothing could better illustrate Jefferson's concern. Though a passionate hater of war and an enemy of entangling alliances, he was proposing to make an alliance with his old foe, England, against his old friend, France, with the object of waging a defensive war.

Napoleon now suddenly decided to sell all Louisiana and abandon his dream of a New World empire. He had failed in his efforts to reconquer the sugar-rich island of Santo Domingo, for which Louisiana was to serve as a granary. Infuriated ex-slaves, ably led by a gifted black, Toussaint L'Ouverture, had put up a stubborn resistance that was ultimately broken. Then the island's second line of defense—mosquitoes carrying yellow

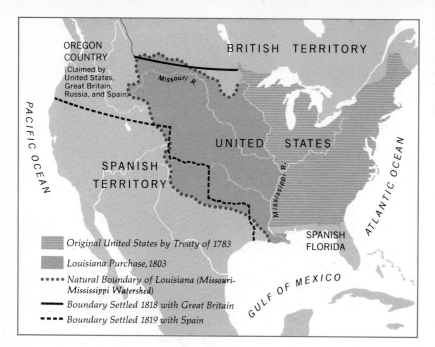

Map labels:
OREGON COUNTRY (Claimed by United States, Great Britain, Russia, and Spain)
BRITISH TERRITORY
Missouri R.
UNITED STATES
PACIFIC OCEAN
SPANISH TERRITORY
Mississippi R.
ATLANTIC OCEAN
SPANISH FLORIDA
GULF OF MEXICO

Legend:
Original United States by Treaty of 1783
Louisiana Purchase, 1803
•••• Natural Boundary of Louisiana (Missouri-Mississippi Watershed)
— Boundary Settled 1818 with Great Britain
- - - Boundary Settled 1819 with Spain

fever—had swept away thousands of crack French troops. Santo Domingo could not be reconquered, except perhaps at a staggering cost; hence there was no need for the granary. "Damn sugar, damn coffee, damn colonies!" burst out Napoleon.

Bonaparte was about to end the twenty-month lull in his deadly conflict with Britain. Because the British controlled the seas, he feared that he might be forced to make them a gift of Louisiana. Rather than drive America into the arms of England by attempting to hold the area, he decided to sell the huge wilderness to the Americans and pocket the money for his schemes nearer home. He hoped that the United States, strengthened by Louisiana, would one day grow up to be a military and naval power that would thwart the ambitions of the lordly British in the New World. The distresses of France in Europe were again paving the way for America's diplomatic successes.

Events now moved dizzily. The American Minister Livingston, pending the arrival of Monroe, was busily negotiating in Paris for a window on the Gulf of Mexico at New Orleans. Suddenly, out of a clear sky, the French foreign minister asked him how much he would give for all Louisiana. Scarcely able to believe his ears (he was partially deaf anyhow), Livingston nervously entered upon the negotiations. After about a week of haggling, while the fate of America trembled in the balance, treaties were signed, under the date April 30, 1803, ceding Louisiana to the United States for about $15 million.

The Devil and Napoleon. In England and among American Federalists, Napoleon came to be regarded as an anti-Christ, in league with the Devil. A contemporary French caricature.

Out-Federalizing the Federalists in Louisiana

When the news of the bargain reached America, Jefferson was startled. He had authorized his envoys to offer not more than $10 million for New Orleans, and as much to the *east* in the Floridas as they could get. Instead, they had signed three treaties which pledged $15 million for New Orleans, plus a vast wilderness entirely to the *west*—an area that would more than double the United States. They had bought a wilderness to get a city.

Once again the two Jeffersons wrestled with each other in private: the theorist and the former strict constructionist versus the realist and public official. Where in his beloved Constitution was the President authorized to negotiate treaties incorporating a huge new expanse into the union—an expanse containing some 50,000 red, white, and black inhabitants? There was no such clause.

Conscience-stricken, Jefferson secretly proposed that a constitutional amendment be passed. But his friends pointed out in alarm that in the interval Napoleon, for whom thought was action, might suddenly change his mind. So Jefferson shamefacedly submitted the treaties to the Senate, while privately admitting that the purchase was unconstitutional.

The senators were less finicky than Jefferson. Reflecting enthusiastic public support, they registered their prompt approval of the transaction. Land-hungry Americans were not disposed to split constitutional hairs when confronted with perhaps

IOIIOIIOIIOIIOIIOIIOIIOIIOIIOIIOIIOIIOIIOIIOIIOIIOIIOIIOI

In accepting the Louisiana Purchase, Jefferson thus compromised with conscience in a private letter: "It is the case of a guardian, investing the money of his ward in purchasing an important adjacent territory; and saying to him when of age, I did this for your good; I pretend to no right to bind you: you may disavow me, and I must get out of the scrape as I can: I thought it my duty to risk myself for you."

IOIIOIIOIIOIIOIIOIIOIIOIIOIIOIIOIIOIIOIIOIIOIIOIIOIIOIIOI

the most magnificent real estate bargain in history—828,000 square miles (2,144,520 square kilometers) at about three cents an acre.

If Louisiana made Jefferson a loose constructionist, it made many Federalists strict constructionists. (Hamilton, to his credit, was a partial exception.) Federalists argued vehemently that there was no constitutional warrant for the transfer. (Shades of the Federalists who had chartered the Bank of the United States!) Louisiana, so they claimed, was a worthless desert that would cost too much at a time when the Jeffersonians were pledged to rigid economy: $15 million in one pile of silver dollars would reach three miles into the air. (Shades of the Federalists who had cheerfully assumed Hamilton's debt of $75 million!)

What really worried the Federalists was that the signing of the Louisiana treaties was the signing of their own political death warrant. New states would be carved from the immense area—states that would outvote the thirteen charter members, including Federalist New England. The Jeffersonian agrarians would then become unassailable. At Williams College, in Massachusetts, a debating group voted fifteen to one that the purchase of Louisiana was undesirable. A few Federalist extremists even threatened to secede from the Union.

The purchase of Louisiana—the most glorious achievement of Jefferson as President—was a triumph for which neither he nor anyone else could claim much direct credit. Napoleon, for reasons purely selfish, dumped this rich prize into the laps of Livingston, Monroe, and Jefferson. Louisiana was so desirable that Jefferson found it less embarrassing to reverse himself on strict construction than to lose the magnificent windfall.

Louisiana in the Long View

Jefferson's bargain with France was epochal. By scooping up Louisiana, America secured at one bloodless stroke the western half of the richest river valley in the world, and further laid the foundations of a future major power. The ideal of a

An amazing Indian woman, Sacagawea, a Shoshone married to a Canadian interpreter, accompanied the Lewis and Clark expedition. She shared the hardships and privations with an infant strapped to her back. Without her assistance and the aid she obtained from the Shoshone Indians, Lewis and Clark might never have reached the Pacific Coast.

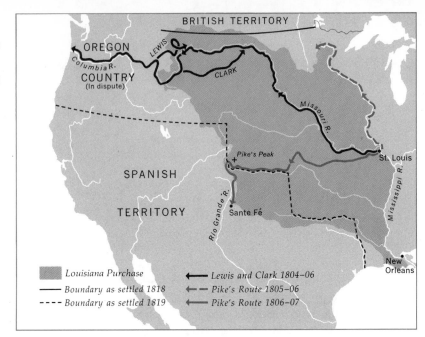

great agrarian democracy, as envisioned by Jefferson, would have elbowroom in the vast "Valley of Democracy." At the same time, the transfer established a precedent that was to be followed repeatedly: namely, the acquisition of foreign territory and peoples by purchase.

The extent of the huge new area was more fully unveiled by a series of explorations under the direction of Jefferson. He was keenly interested in

Lewis and Clark. A woodcut (1812) by Patrick Gass, a member of the expedition. (Rare Book Division, New York Public Library, Astor, Lenox and Tilden Foundations.)

the natural treasures of his purchase, including an enormous (and non-existent) mountain of salt. The expedition of Meriwether Lewis and William Clark ascended the "Great Muddy" Missouri River and struggled through the Rockies to the mouth of the Columbia River. This hazardous venture into the uncharted Western wilderness, from 1804 to 1806, bolstered America's claim to Oregon, while further opening the West to Indian trade and exploration. Zebulon M. Pike, in 1805–1806, explored the Louisiana territory near the headwaters of the Mississippi River, and in 1806–1807 ventured into Colorado and New Mexico, sighting the lofty peak that bears his name.

Jefferson's reluctant purchase of Louisiana proved to be a landmark in American foreign policy. Overnight he avoided a possible rupture with France, and the consequent entangling alliance with England. The nation was thus able to continue the non-interventionist policies of the Founding Fathers, though it later quarreled with Spain and Britain over the vague boundaries of Louisiana, north, south, and west. Not needing the navy of the Mother Country, the United States drifted away from her, and eventually fought her in 1812. But by that time the Republic was bigger

ioiioiioiioiioiioiioiioiioiioiioiioiioiioiioiioiioiioi

The French minister who negotiated the Louisiana Purchase treaties recalled that Minister Livingston had remarked at the signing, "We have lived long, but this is the noblest work of our whole lives. . . . From this day the United States take their place among the powers of the first rank. . . . The instruments which we have just signed will cause no tears to be shed: they prepare ages of happiness for innumerable generations of human creatures."

ioiioiioiioiioiioiioiioiioiioiioiioiioiioiioiioiioiioi

and stronger, and had Louisiana securely in its possession.

The Louisiana godsend likewise boosted national unity. Once-proud Federalists, now mere sectionalists, sank ever lower in public esteem as they were reduced to whining impotence. A few of their more extreme spokesmen attempted to plot with scheming Aaron Burr for the secession of New England and New York. But the intrigue failed, largely owing to the vigilance of Alexander Hamilton, who subsequently provoked Burr to a duel. The pistol that killed Hamilton in 1804 blew the brightest brain out of the Federalist party—and destroyed its one remaining hope of effective leadership.

A once-restive West, which now toasted the "immortal Jefferson," was more securely riveted to the Union by the purchase. Men of the western waters were grateful to the federal government for having safeguarded their interests, particularly in securing the mouth of the Mississippi. A new spirit of unity surged through the West.

Aaron Burr, turning his disunionist plottings to the trans-Mississippi West, was arrested in 1806 for treason. Tried the next year at Richmond, Virginia, he was freed after the presiding judge, Chief Justice Marshall, had infuriated the Jeffersonians by what seemed to be bias in favor of the accused. The government's case collapsed when two witnesses to the same overt act of treason could not be found, as required by the Constitu-

tion (see Art. III, Sec. III). Burr's schemes are still somewhat shrouded in mystery, but he apparently planned to separate the western part of the United States from the eastern and unite it with to-be-conquered Spanish territory west of the Louisiana Purchase. The very fact that so dashing a figure as Burr could muster only threescore followers was significant. It indicated, among other things, that the West was developing a deeper sense of loyalty to the Washington government.

America: A Nutcrackered Neutral

Jefferson was triumphantly re-elected in 1804, with 162 electoral votes to only 14 for his Federalist opponent. His success was not so much due to Republicanizing the Federalists, as he fondly supposed, as to Federalizing the Republicans. The iron hand of reality gradually forced him, quite unintentionally, to kill off the opposition party by stealing many of its principles and embracing them as his own. As was said, he caught the Federalists in bathing and made off with their clothes.

But the laurels of Jefferson's first administration soon withered under the blasts of the new storm that broke in Europe. After unloading Louisiana in 1803, Napoleon deliberately provoked a renewal of his war with Britain—a conflict that crashed to an awesome close eleven long years later.

For two years a maritime United States—the number one neutral carrier since 1793—enjoyed juicy commercial pickings. But a setback came in 1805. At the Battle of Trafalgar, one-eyed Lord Nelson achieved immortality by smashing the combined French and Spanish fleets off the coast

England (John Bull) Eats French Warships. Contemporary English caricature.

of Spain, thereby insuring Britain's supremacy on the seas. At the Battle of Austerlitz in Austria—the Battle of the Three Emperors—Napoleon crushed the combined Austrian and Russian armies, thereby insuring his mastery of the land. Like the tiger and the shark, France and Britain were supreme in their chosen elements. England ruled the waves and waived the rules.

Unable to hurt each other directly, the two antagonists were forced to strike indirect blows. The London government, beginning in 1806, issued a series of Orders in Council. As perfected, these edicts closed the ports under French continental control to foreign shipping, including American, unless the vessels first stopped at a British port. There they would pay the necessary fees and, if acceptable, secure clearance papers. Napoleon struck back savagely in a series of decrees. In effect, they ordered the seizure of all merchant ships, including American, that entered British ports.

Yankee skippers, like their predestined Calvinist ancestors, were seemingly damned if they did, damned if they did not. Even so, their trade prospered, because the greater the risk, the greater the profit. If only one vessel in three sailed over the reefs of French Decrees and past the shoals of British Orders in Council, the owner could make a comfortable gain.

British Man-Stealing

Even more galling to American pride than the seizure of wooden ships was the seizure of flesh-and-blood American seamen. Impressment—the forcible enlistment of sailors—was a crude form of conscription which the British, among others, had employed for over four centuries. Clubs and stretchers (for men knocked unconscious) were standard equipment of press-gangs from His Majesty's man-hungry ships.

The London authorities themselves set limits to this ugly practice. They claimed the right to impress only British subjects on their own soil, in their own harbors, or on merchant ships on

Intercourse or Impartial Dealings. A cartoon by "Peter Pencil" (1809) shows Jefferson being victimized by both England (*left*) and France (*right*). (Houghton Library, Harvard.)

the high seas. But many fair-skinned Americans looked like Englishmen, and the benefit of the doubt was seldom given to an experienced seaman in those short-handed days. The result was that some 6,000 bona fide United States citizens, according to the best estimates, were impressed by the "piratical man-stealers" of England from 1808 to 1811 alone. A number of these luckless souls died or were killed in the service, leaving their kinfolk and friends bereaved and embittered.

On their side, the British had counter-complaints. America's navy and merchant marine openly encouraged the enlistment of deserters from the "floating hells" of the British navy, where discipline was taught to the tune of the cat-o'-nine-tails. An expanding American merchant marine, also short of sailors, paid seductively high wages— "dollars for shillings." British deserters, conniving with ingenious Americans, would often secure fraudulent naturalization papers. (One resourceful female conniver had an oversized cradle in her shop so she could swear she had known the sailor "from the cradle.") But His Majesty's press-gangs laughed aside such documents, whether genuine or not, holding to the principle "Once an Englishman, always an Englishman." The King expected every free-born Briton to do his duty in time of crisis.

Britain had her back to the wall, and her desperate plight colored her views. If the Yankee "dollar grubbers" had not encouraged so much desertion, the British impressers might have been willing to make fewer mistakes in acquiring sailors. But England would not abandon her brutal practice of sailor-snatching at the behest of an upstart United States. Britons were making war; Americans were making money. The British feared that they would lose the war if they gave up their hoary method of conscription—and they would fight before they did.

Britain's determination was spectacularly highlighted in 1807. A royal frigate overhauled a United States frigate, the *Chesapeake*, about ten miles off the coast of Virginia. The British captain bluntly demanded the surrender of four alleged deserters. London had never claimed the right to seize men from a foreign warship, and the American commander, though totally unprepared to fight, refused the request. The British warship thereupon fired three devastating broadsides at close range, killing three Americans and wounding eighteen. Four deserters were dragged away, and the bloody hulk called the *Chesapeake* limped back to port.

An infuriated America—Federalists and Republicans alike—joined in an outburst of national

Regarding the *Chesapeake* affair, the Washington *Federalist* reported, "We have never, on any occasion, witnessed the spirit of the people excited to so great a degree of indignation, or such a thirst for revenge, as on hearing of the late unexampled outrage on the *Chesapeake*. All parties, ranks, and professions were unanimous in their detestation of the dastardly deed, and all cried aloud for vengeance."

wrath. Nothing like it had been seen since the French XYZ insults of 1797. Jefferson, the peace lover, could easily have had war if he had wanted it. As the event proved, if America were going to fight at all, she should have fought when the country was united.

Britain was clearly in the wrong, as the London Foreign Office admitted. But Jefferson unwisely attempted to use the *Chesapeake* outrage as a lever to force the British to renounce impressment altogether. This they flatly refused to do. The affair rankled for five years; and when reparation was finally made, it came too late to salve old wounds.

Jefferson's Backfiring Embargo

National honor would not permit a slavish submission to British and French mistreatment. Yet a large-scale foreign war was contrary to the settled policy of the new Republic—and in addition it would be futile. The navy was weak, thanks largely to Jefferson's anti-navalism; and the army was even weaker. A disastrous defeat would not improve America's plight.

The warring nations in Europe were heavily dependent upon the United States for raw materials and foodstuffs. In his eager search for an alternative to war, Jefferson seized upon this essential fact. He reasoned that if America voluntarily cut off her exports, the offending powers would be forced to come, hat in hand, and agree to respect her rights.

Responding to the presidential lash, Congress hastily passed the Embargo Act late in 1807. This rigorous law forbade the export of all goods from the United States, whether in American or in foreign ships. It was a compromise between submission and shooting.

Jefferson, the onetime strict constructionist, had once more flip-flopped into the camp of the loose constructionists. In the interests of the Federalist shippers, whom he disliked, he was rereading the Constitution with strange bifocals. To him, it now meant that Congress, under its authority to "regulate" commerce, could go so far as to stop

The Embargo (Ograbme).   As a snapping turtle, it halts overseas shipments. (Prints Division, New York Public Library, Astor, Lenox and Tilden Foundations.)

foreign trade altogether. Regulation thus became strangulation.

Federalist New England could well have prayed for relief from its newly found Virginia friend, "Mad Tom" Jefferson. Forests of dead masts gradually filled once-flourishing harbors; docks that had once rumbled were deserted (except for illegal trade); and soup kitchens cared for some of the hungry unemployed. Jeffersonian Republicans probably hurt the commerce of New England, which they avowedly were trying to protect, far more than Old England and France together were doing.

Farmers of the South and West, the strongholds of Jefferson, suffered no less disastrously than New England. They were alarmed by the mounting piles of exportable cotton, grain, and tobacco. Tart-tongued John Randolph of Virginia remarked that enacting the embargo was like cutting off one's toes to cure one's corns. Jefferson in truth seemed to be waging war on his fellow citizens, rather than on the offending belligerents.

The American people, from the days of the colonial Navigation Acts, have never submitted meekly to unpopular legislation. Though basically law-abiding, they habitually flout laws that are opposed by large numbers of the population. An enormous illicit trade mushroomed in 1808, especially along the Canadian border, where bands of armed Americans on loaded rafts overawed or overpowered federal agents. Irate citizens cynically transposed the letters of "Embargo" to read "O Grab Me," "Go Bar 'Em," and "Mobrage," while heartily denouncing the "Dambargo."

Jefferson nonetheless induced Congress to pass iron-toothed enforcing legislation. It was so inquisitorial and tyrannical as to cause some Americans to think more kindly of George III, whom Jefferson had berated in the Declaration of Independence. One indignant New Hampshire poet burst out in song:

> Our ships all in motion,
> Once whiten'd the ocean;
>   They sail'd and return'd with a Cargo;
> Now doom'd to decay
>   They are fallen a prey,
> To Jefferson, worms, and EMBARGO.

New England seethed with talk of secession; and Jefferson later admitted that he felt the foundations of government tremble under his feet.

An alarmed Congress, bowing to the storm of public anger, finally repealed the embargo, on March 1, 1809, three days before Jefferson's retirement. A half-loaf substitute was provided by the Non-Intercourse Act. This measure formally reopened trade with all the nations of the world, except the two most important, England and

A Federalist circular in Massachusetts against the embargo cried out, "Let every man who holds the name of America dear to him, stretch forth his hands and put this accursed thing, this *Embargo* from him. Be resolute, act like sons of liberty, of God, and your country; nerve your arm with vengeance against the Despot [Jefferson] who would wrest the inestimable germ of your independence from you—and you shall be *Conquerors!!!*"

France. Though thus watered down, economic coercion continued to be the policy of the Jeffersonians from 1809 to 1812, when the nation finally plunged into war.

The Wooden-Gun Embargo: A Successful Failure

Why did the embargo, Jefferson's most daring act of statesmanship, collapse after fifteen dismal months? First of all, he underestimated the bulldog determination of the British, as others have, and overestimated their dependence on America's trade. Bumper grain crops blessed the British Isles during these years, and the revolutionary Latin American republics unexpectedly threw open their ports for compensating commerce.

The hated embargo was not continued long enough or tightly enough to achieve the desired results. But a statesman must know the temper of his people, and Jefferson should have foreseen that such a self-crucifying weapon could not possibly command public support. The Americans, notoriously people of action, did not take kindly to the passive type of heroism. They much preferred commercial activity, with all its risks, to enforced inactivity, with no chance of profit.

A crestfallen Jefferson himself admitted that the embargo was three times more costly than war. The irony is that with only a fraction of its cost to the country, he could have built a fairly strong navy. Such a fighting force would have won more respect for American rights on the high seas, and might well have prevented the War of 1812.

The embargo further embroiled relations with both Britain and France. It embittered the British, partly because it hit them more forcibly than it did Napoleon. The French despot naturally applauded the embargo, for it was an indirect American blockade of his foe. He cynically helped enforce it by seizing scores of Yankee merchant ships in his ports; by the terms of the Embargo Act, he argued, these vessels should have been tied up at home. His "cooperation" merely rubbed salt into old sores.

A stoppage of exports hurt Federalist shipping, but revived the Federalist party. Gaining new converts, its leaders hurled their nullification of the embargo into the teeth of the "Virginia lordlings" in Washington. In 1804, the discredited Federalists had polled only 14 electoral votes out of 176; in 1808, the embargo year, the figure rose to 47 out of 175.

Curiously enough, New England plucked a new prosperity from the ugly jaws of the embargo. With shipping tied up and imported goods scarce, the resourceful Yankees reopened old factories and erected new ones. The real foundations of modern America's industrial might were laid behind the protective wall of the embargo, followed by non-intercourse and the War of 1812. Jefferson, the avowed critic of factories, may have unwittingly done more for American manufacturing than Alexander Hamilton, the outspoken friend of factories.

Jefferson's embargo, followed in modified form by non-intercourse, undeniably pinched England. Many British importers and manufacturers suffered severe losses, especially those dependent on American cotton. As thousands of factory workers were thrown out of jobs, agitation mounted for a repeal of the restrictions that had brought on the embargo. A petition to Parliament in 1812, from the city of Birmingham alone, bore 20,000 names on a sheet of parchment 150 feet long. So strong was public pressure that two days before Congress declared war in June 1812, the British foreign secretary announced that the offensive Orders in Council would be immediately suspended. The supreme irony is that Jefferson's policy of economic coercion did win in the end, but America was not patient enough to reap the reward of her sacrifices.

The Living Jefferson

Thomas Jefferson retained much of his popularity, even though it was severely tarnished by the embargo. One public toast ran: "May he receive from his fellow citizens the reward of his merit, a halter

IOI

Early in 1805 Jefferson privately foresaw the two-term 22nd Amendment (1951): "General Washington set the example of voluntary retirement after eight years. I shall follow it, and a few more precedents will oppose the obstacle of habit to anyone after a while who shall endeavor to extend his term. Perhaps it may beget a disposition to establish it by an amendment of the Constitution."

IOIIOIIOIIOIIOIIOIIOIIOIIOIIOIIOIIOIIOIIOIIOIIOIIOIIOIIOIIOI

[hangman's noose]." But his grip on his party was such that he could easily have won a third nomination and election. The international crisis was still acute; and although Jefferson was sixty-five years old, he was mentally alert and physically vigorous. He lived eighteen more years, glad to have escaped what he called the "splendid misery" of the presidential penitentiary.

Jefferson, rather than Washington, was the real father of the two-term tradition. Unlike the first President, who had no serious constitutional qualms, he feared that more than two terms might open the door to dictatorship. Yet Jefferson strongly favored the nomination and election of a kindred spirit, his friend and fellow Virginian, the quiet, intellectual, and unassuming James Madison.

Though bitterly assailed, Jefferson left office with the consolation that he had remained true to the guiding star of the other Founding Fathers. He had kept the country out of a serious foreign war. Despite numerous reversals of policy under the whiplash of practicality, he never lost his faith in democracy and in the common man. He brought a renovation rather than a revolution; the real revolution that did occur was in his own thinking. If the Federalists were the steppingstone between monarchical Europe and republican America, then the Jeffersonians were the steppingstone between aristocratic Federalism and democratic Jacksonianism.

Thomas Jefferson and John Adams died on the same day—appropriately the Fourth of July, 1826. The last words of Adams, then ninety-one, were: "Thomas Jefferson still survives." He was wrong, for three hours earlier Jefferson had breathed his last. But Thomas Jefferson still survives in the democratic ideals and liberal principles of the great nation which he risked his all to found, and which he served so long and faithfully.

VARYING VIEWPOINTS

The Jeffersonian era has long presented observers with a series of paradoxes: How did the pacifistic President lead the country so far down the path toward war? Why did America's most famous advocate of small government so greatly enlarge the federal domain and expand the power of the presidency? How did the man who proclaimed, "We are all Republicans, we are all Federalists," come to preside over one of the most bitterly partisan periods in American history? This last question has perhaps attracted the most attention from recent scholars. Many of them now view the Federalist and Jeffersonian decades as the seedbed of the modern system of political parties. How did the parties organize? How did the idea of *legitimate* opposition crystallize? On what basis were the people at large—the traditionally marginal masses—brought into the organized political system and infused with a sense of meaningful participation in national affairs?

SELECT READINGS

A monument of American historical writing is Henry Adams, *History of the United States during the Administrations of Jefferson and Madison* (9 vols., 1889–1891), available in a one-volume abridgment edited by Ernest Samuels. Especially fascinating are Adams' epilogue and prologue on the United States in 1800 and 1817. A brief introduction by a British scholar is Marcus Cunliffe, *The Nation Takes Shape, 1789–1837* (1959); greater detail is given in M. Smelser, *The Democratic Republic 1801–1815* (1968). Problems with the judiciary can be traced in A. J. Beveridge's still-respected *Life of John Marshall* (4 vols., 1919). A more recent and succinct analysis is R. E. Ellis, *The Jeffersonian Crisis: Courts and Politics in the New Republic* (1971). Politics are handled in N. E. Cunningham, *The Jeffersonian Republicans in Power* (1963), and treated in a broader, imaginative context in J. S. Young, *The Washington Community, 1800–1829* (1966)/ L. D. White brings administrative history to life in *The Jeffersonians* (rev. ed., 1959). Forrest McDonald is highly critical of his subject in *The Presidency of Thomas Jefferson* (1976). L. Levy debunks Jefferson's liberalism in *Jefferson and Civil Liberties* (1963), while B. W. Sheehan examines another important aspect of policy in *Seeds of Extinction: Jeffersonian Philanthropy and the American Indian* (1973). See also R. Horsman, *Expansion and American Indian Policy, 1783–1812* (1967). A first-class study of the negotiator of the Louisiana Purchase is G. Dangerfield, *Chancellor Robert R. Livingston of New York* (1960).

The development of political parties is dissected in W. N. Chambers, *Political Parties in a New Nation* (1963), and in Noble E. Cunningham, *The Jeffersonian Republicans: The Formation of Party Organization, 1789–1801* (1958). See also R. Buel, Jr., *Securing the Revolution* (1972), and Richard Hofstadter, *The Idea of a Party System* (1969), Lance Banning, *The Jeffersonian Persuasion* (1978), Drew McCoy, *The Elusive Republic: Political Economy in Jeffersonian America* (1980), and Robert E. Shalhope, *John Taylor of Caroline* (1980). Noble E. Cunningham, Jr., has carried his discussion forward in *The Process of Government under Jefferson* (1979). The standard scholarly biography is D. Malone, *Jefferson and His Time* (5 vols., 1948–1974). More compact is M. D. Peterson, *Thomas Jefferson and the New Nation: A Biography* (1970). Peterson has also scrutinized *The Jeffersonian Image in the American Mind* (1960). An expansionist thesis is fully developed in A. De Conde, *This Affair of Louisiana* (1976). The Embargo is treated in Burton Spivak, *Jefferson's English Crisis: Commerce, Embargo, and the Republican Revolution* (1979). D. Boorstin vividly evokes the intellectual climate of the age in *The Lost World of Thomas Jefferson* (1948). John C. Miller, *The Wolf by the Ears: Thomas Jefferson and Slavery* (1977), probes the third President's attitudes on an important question. I. Brant looks at *James Madison, Secretary of State* (1953), and F. E. Ewing examines Jefferson's powerful treasury secretary in *America's Forgotten Statesman: Albert Gallatin* (1959).

11

James Madison and the Second War for Independence

The Existing War—the Child of Prostitution. May no American Acknowledge it Legitimate.

A FEDERALIST TOAST DURING THE WAR OF 1812

Madison: Dupe of Napoleon

Scholarly James Madison took the presidential oath on March 4, 1809, as the awesome conflict in Europe was roaring to its climax. Small of stature (5 feet 4 inches; 1.62 meters), light of weight (about 100 pounds; 45 kilograms), bald of head, and weak of voice, he fell tragically short of providing vigorous executive leadership. Crippled also by factions within his Cabinet, he was unable to dominate his party, as Jefferson had once done.

The Non-Intercourse Act of 1809—the limited substitute for the embargo aimed solely at Britain and France—would expire in about a year. Congress, desperately attempting to uphold American rights, adopted in 1810 a bargaining measure known as Macon's Bill No. 2. While permitting American trade with all the world, it dangled an attractive lure. If either England or France repealed her commercial restrictions, America would restore non-importation against the non-repealing nation. In short, the United States would bribe the belligerents into respecting its rights.

This opportunity was made to order for Napoleon, a past master of deceit. He was eager to have non-importation clamped down once more on the British, because it would serve as a partial blockade which he would not have to raise a finger to enforce. He was hopeful that such a boycott would embroil the Americans in war with Britain, for then they would be serving as his indirect allies to weaken his arch-enemy. Accordingly, he blandly announced, in August 1810, that his objectionable decrees had been repealed. At the same time, he secretly ordered the sale of confiscated Yankee ships.

Responsible Americans, rising above self-delusion, should have examined the hollow-sounding French announcement with extreme caution. Napoleon, prince of liars, had no intention whatever of repealing his damaging decrees. But Madison, frantically seeking to wrest a recognition of American rights from England, accepted French bad faith as good faith. He formally announced, in November 1810, that France had complied with the terms of Macon's Bill No. 2, and that non-importation would consequently be re-established against Britain.

Madison's decision was fateful. Britons were angered by America's apparent willingness to be the dupe and partner of Napoleon. The wily Bonaparte, who continued to seize American merchantmen, was delighted by the success of his transparent scheme. Once Madison had aligned his nation against England commercially, he found himself gravitating toward France politically—and edging toward the whirlpool of war.

War Whoops Arouse the War Hawks

The complexion of the Twelfth Congress, which met late in 1811, differed markedly from that of its predecessor. Recent elections had swept away many of the older "submission men" and replaced

Henry Clay (1777–1852). A glamorous, eloquent, and ambitious member of the House and Senate for many years, Clay was thrice an unsuccessful candidate for the highest office in the land. "Sir," he declared in the Senate in 1850, "I would rather be right than be President." Right or wrong, he never made the grade but his devotion to the Union was inspirational. (Library of Congress)

them with young hotheads, chiefly from the South and West. The youthful newcomers—"the boys," John Randolph sneeringly called them—were on fire for a new war with the old enemy. Not having had a conflict in their own generation, these War Hawks were weary of hearing how their fathers had "whipped" the British single-handedly. They won control of the House of Representatives, and elevated to the speakership the tall (6 feet 2 inches; 1.88 meters), eloquent, and magnetic Henry Clay of Kentucky, the gallant "Harry of the West," then only thirty-four years old.

Western War Hawks, first of all, were eager to wipe out the renewed Indian resistance against the white settlers streaming steadily into the Western wilderness. As this white flood spread through the forests, more and more red men were pushed farther and farther toward the setting sun. Two

Tecumseh (1768?–1813). A Shawnee Indian born in the Ohio country, he was probably the most gifted organizer and leader of his people in U.S. history. A noted warrior, he fought the tribal custom of torturing prisoners and opposed the practice of permitting any one tribe to sell land that, he believed, belonged to all Indians.

remarkable Shawnee twin brothers, Tecumseh and the Prophet, knew that if this onrushing tide were ever to be stopped, that time had come. They began to weld together a far-flung confederacy of all the tribes east of the Mississippi. Their braves forswore firewater in order to be fit for the last-ditch battle with the "paleface" intruders. To make matters worse, the sturdy pioneers and their War Hawk representatives in Congress widely believed that the red men's firearms and scalping knives were being furnished by British "hair buyers" in Canada.

Only a few days after the War Hawk Congress convened in Washington, news of stirring events on the frontier further inflamed anti-Indian and anti-British feeling. General William H. Harrison, advancing with 1,000 men upon the Indian headquarters, repelled a surprise attack at Tippecanoe, in present Indiana, on November 7, 1811. He then put the torch to the settlement.

Harrison's onslaught broke the back of the red men's rebellion. It also made the blood course faster in the veins of the impetuous War Hawks. Men like Representative Felix Grundy of Tennessee, three of whose brothers had been murdered, cried that there was only one way to remove the menace of the Indians: wipe out their Canadian base.

Canada, in itself, was a lush prize. War Hawks made no bones about their desire to seize this enormous and richly wooded area, so near, so desirable, and apparently so defenseless. "On to Canada, on to Canada," was their ominous chant. Southern expansionists, less vocal, cast a covetous eye on Florida, then weakly held by Britain's ally, Spain.

A free sea, as well as free land, was a goal of the War Hawks. One of their most popular slogans ran, "Free Trade and Sailors' Rights." Yet why should men beyond the mountains, many of whom had never seen a body of salt water larger than a salt lick, want to fight for maritime rights?

Westerners, strange to relate, did have a vital interest in a free sea. They were proud, patriotic, and intensely nationalistic. The manhandling of an American sailor, though far away, struck these freedom-loving pioneers as outrageous. They might not have ships on the ocean, but they did have dammed-up agricultural products which, because of the odious British Orders in Council, could not be shipped to Europe. In short, Westerners, despite all their misleading clamor for Canada, did have a genuine emotional and financial stake in a free sea.

Militant War Hawks, with scattered but essential support from other sections, finally engineered a declaration of war in June 1812. The vote in the House was 79 to 49; in the Senate, 19 to 13. The close tally betrayed a dangerous degree of national disunity. Congressmen from the pro-British maritime and commercial centers of New England, as well as from the Middle Atlantic States, almost solidly opposed hostilities. Thus the West and Southwest, mostly landlocked, presented the sea-fronting East with a war for a free sea that the East vehemently resented.

Britain or Napoleon: A Choice of Foes

Why did the United States fight Britain and not France? Napoleonic seizures of Yankee ships since 1803 had numbered 558, as compared with 917 for Britain. Logically, the Americans should have fought both offenders, if the Republic were going to fight at all.

War Vote in House of Representatives, 1812
(SHOWING WESTERN AND SOUTHWESTERN WAR SENTIMENT)

States	Regions	For War	Against War
N.H.	Frontier New England	3	2
Vt.		3	1
Mass.	Maritime and Federalist New England; Mass. includes frontier Maine	6	8
R.I.		0	2
Conn.		0	7
N.Y.	Commercial and Federalist Middle States	3	11
N.J.		2	4
Del.		0	1
Penn.	Jeffersonian Middle States	16	2
Md.		6	3
Va.	Jeffersonian Southern States	14	5
N.C.		6	3
S.C.		8	0
Ga.		3	0
Ohio	The trans-Allegheny West—nest of the War Hawks	1	0
Ky.		5	0
Tenn.		3	0
		79	49

Why single out England? The Mother Country was the historic foe, and the Jeffersonian Republican party was traditionally anti-British and pro-French. This Gallic attachment partly explains why the Jeffersonians, disliking Federalist shippers, were ostensibly going to war to protect those shippers.

Nearness of offenses was also a vital factor. Napoleon had confiscated Yankee ships and imprisoned Yankee sailors, but his misdeeds were far away. British impressments and seizures, on the other hand, often took place within plain view. And on the frontier the Indian "hell hounds," bearing British arms, were smashing into the cabins of American pioneers.

To declare war on France would avail nothing, for she was not vulnerable. America had no border in common with her, and hence (fortunately) could not come to grips with Napoleon's armies. But a victorious war with England, aside from avenging grievances, would be profitable as well as patriotic. Her merchant marine, the richest in the world, would fall easy prey to swarming Yankee privateers. And Canada, the choicest prize of all, looked like a sitting duck.

Costly illusions beckoned from the north. The invasion of Canada, Americans fondly believed, would be absurdly simple—a "frontiersmen's frolic"; a "mere matter of marching," said Jefferson. The trick could be turned, boasted Henry Clay, "the Cock of Kentucky," by the militiamen of his state alone.

|ロ||ロ||ロ||ロ||ロ||ロ||ロ||ロ||ロ||ロ||ロ||ロ||ロ||ロ||ロ||ロ||ロ||ロ||ロ|

"The injuries received from *France*," insisted the editor of Niles's *Weekly Register* (June 27, 1812), "do not lessen the enormity of those heaped upon us by *England*. . . . In this 'straight betwixt two' we had an unquestionable right to select our enemy. We have given the preference to *Great Britain* . . . on account of her more flagrant wrongs."

|ロ||ロ||ロ||ロ||ロ||ロ||ロ||ロ||ロ||ロ||ロ||ロ||ロ||ロ||ロ||ロ||ロ||ロ||ロ|

Population odds justified such optimism. The United States numbered over 6 million whites, as compared with some 500,000 for Canada. A majority of the Canadians were Frenchmen, whose loyalty was dubious, and many of the rest were quite recent American emigrants, whose loyalty was even more dubious. England, bogged down in the Napoleonic War, could spare few troops for North America. Europe's distresses were again pointing the way to military successes.

The Northern mirage thus helped destroy America's last precious stores of patience. If Canada had not been so inviting and so helpless (seemingly), the administration probably would have endured British offenses a few more months. If it had done so, it would have learned of London's official announcement of the forthcoming repeal of her objectionable Orders in Council—an announcement made ironically two days *before* Congress voted war. If there had then been an Atlantic cable, the War Hawks probably could not have forced a formal declaration of hostilities through the Senate. A change of three votes would have brought a tie. But the tempting proximity of Canada turned American heads, and President Madison plunged into the conflict, contrary to the stall-for-time policy of the Founding Fathers.

American Allies of the Napoleonic Anti-Christ

New England, though fronting the sea, damned the declaration of war for a free sea. The news was greeted with muffled bells, flags at half-mast, and public fasting. One congressman, who had voted for war, was kicked through the streets of Plymouth, Massachusetts, by a frenzied mob.

Why the opposition? For one thing, violations of American rights were an old story; they had been continuing for about twenty years. The extent of impressment, though serious, had been exaggerated. Manufacturing in New England was mushrooming, and the luckier shippers, despite costly confiscations, were still raking in money. Profits dull patriotism. New England was also the tradi-

tional stronghold of pro-British Federalism, and it resented the pro-French favoritism of the "Virginia Dynasty" in Washington.

Federalist New England, moreover, had long been allied in sympathy with Old England. The Mother Country—"that fast-anchored isle"—was the last real bulwark of constitutional government left in the Old World. At a time when she was straining every nerve to defeat the despotism of Napoleon, the Federalists believed that Americans should be helping her. Instead the United States—the presumed friend of freedom and constitutionalism—was stabbing her in the back. Cold-bloodedly and calculatingly, Madison had concluded that Britain's war to the death with Napoleon, in indirect defense of American liberties, would enable America to seize some territory.

Nor did the sinfulness of the conflict, in Federalist eyes, end here. Not only had Madison treacherously pushed the Mother Country into the abyss of an unwanted war, but he had permitted himself to be tricked into it by her arch-enemy, Napoleon. More than that, Madison had become a virtual ally of the "Corsican butcher"—the "anti-Christ of the age."

The Present State of Our Country.   Partisan disunity over the War of 1812 threatens the nation's very existence. The pro-war Jeffersonian at the left is attacking the pillar of federalism; the anti-war Federalist at the right is trying to pull down Democracy. The spirit of Washington warns that the country's welfare depends upon all three pillars, including Republicanism. (A cartoon by William Charles. New York Public Library.)

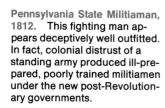

Pennsylvania State Militiaman, 1812. This fighting man appears deceptively well outfitted. In fact, colonial distrust of a standing army produced ill-prepared, poorly trained militiamen under the new post-Revolutionary governments.

Federalist charges of a quasi-alliance with France contained much distasteful truth. As the war in Europe ground on, Jeffersonian Republicans rejoiced over Napoleon's triumphs, while Federalists, no less loudly, acclaimed the victories of Britain and her allies over Bonaparte.

Federalists also condemned the War of 1812 because they opposed the acquisition of Canada. The seizure of this vast area, like the purchase of Louisiana, would merely add more agrarian states from the wild Northwest. These, in turn, would increase the voting strength of the Jeffersonians. Some New England Federalists feared the New West far more than they did Old England. They were determined, wrote one versifier,

> To rule the nation if they could,
> But see it damned if others should.

The bitterness of the New England Federalists against "Mr. Madison's War" led to treason or near treason. In a sense, America fought two enemies simultaneously: Old England and New England. Money holders of New England, possessing much of the nation's gold, probably lent more dollars to the British than to the Federal Treasury. Farmers of New England sent huge quantities of supplies north to Canada, including droves of cattle; and these foodstuffs enabled the British armies to invade New York. Governors of New England, thinking first of local defense, stubbornly refused to permit their militia to serve outside their states, though men were badly needed in the regular army.

Yet the disloyalty of New England has been overplayed. Jeffersonians in this section, comprising a substantial minority, vigorously opposed Federalist obstructionism. New England states actually contributed a surprising number of volunteers to the regular army; Massachusetts alone sent more than Virginia.

Unpreparedness and the Abortive Invasion of Canada

The War of 1812, largely because of widespread disunity, easily ranks as America's worst-fought major war. There was no burning national anger, as in 1807, following the *Chesapeake* outrage. War Hawks in Congress were no more than a zealous minority. President Madison, while supporting their aims, knew that there was serious disunity. But he made the near-fatal error of sponsoring a declaration of war in the hope that it would cause the nation to rally around the flag. New England and other Federalist centers were content to let the spangled banner fall into the mire.

America's manpower pool was deceptively large; there were at least a million males of arms-bearing age. But the government never mustered more than 7,000 men for any one battle. The supreme lesson of this conflict was the folly of leading a divided and apathetic people into war.

The Republic was dangerously unprepared, despite warnings going back nineteen years to the outbreak of the European war in 1793. The nation was still suffering from its own embargo and nonintercourse, which it had partially enforced for the better part of four years. Congress had shortsightedly permitted the Bank of the United States to expire in 1811, at a time when a powerful financial institution was needed. It was knifed largely by the jealousies of the competing state banks.

The regular army was scandalously inadequate, for it was ill-trained, ill-disciplined, and widely scattered. It had to be supplemented by the even more poorly trained militia, who were sometimes distinguished by speed of foot in leaving the battle-field. Some of the ranking generals were semi-senile heirlooms from the Revolutionary War, rust-ing on their laurels and lacking in vigor and vision. By a process of trial and error—chiefly costly error—the mossbacks were gradually weeded out by 1814. But by that time the golden prize of Canada had slipped from America's grasp.

Offensive strategy adopted in Washington was poorly conceived. Roads in Canada were few and bad, so the bulk of the population was scattered along the St. Lawrence, its tributary rivers, and the Great Lakes. Over these waterways all essential supplies had to be transported. Once Montreal was captured, everything to the west was bound to die, just as the leaves of a tree wither when the trunk is girdled. If the United States had thrown every-thing it had against Montreal when the defenders were heavily outnumbered, all of Canada probably would have fallen.

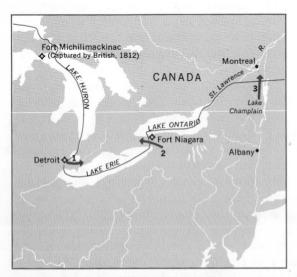

THE THREE U.S. THRUSTS OF 1812
Blue line delineates the Canadian border.

But instead of laying ax to the trunk, the Ameri-cans frittered away their strength in the three-pronged invasion of 1812. One thrust started from the wilderness outpost of Detroit, under General Hull. He quickly retired to his base, and then sur-rendered his entire army to a numerically inferior enemy without firing a shot. The second American invasion, launched across the Niagara River, was beaten back. New York's militia balked at crossing the Canadian line, while their countrymen on the other side were being shot down or forced to sur-render. A third force marched bravely for Mon-treal along the shores of Lake Champlain, but turned back when the state militia refused to cross the New York–Canada border.

By contrast, the British and Canadians from the outset displayed energy. Early in the war they captured the American fort of Michilimackinac, commanding the upper Great Lakes and a huge Indian-inhabited area to the south and west. In their brilliant defensive operations, the Canadians received vital help from a small but efficient force of professional British soldiers. Above all, they were blessed with an inspired British leader, General Isaac Brock, ably assisted (in the Amer-ican camp) by "General Mud" and "General Confusion."

Invasion in Reverse and War on the Lakes

In 1813 the several American invasions of Canada were again hurled back in disarray. The Cana-dians, many of them descended from the evicted American Loyalists of 1776–1783, fought bravely for their new homes and firesides. They had not impressed Yankee sailors or seized Yankee ships, and they regarded the invasion as a wanton attack—"the War of Defense," they called their side of it.

Control of the Great Lakes was vital for trans-porting military supplies westward, and an en-ergetic American naval officer, Oliver Hazard Perry, busied himself on the shores of Lake Erie. He managed to build a fleet of green-timbered ships, manned largely by even greener seamen, plus some Kentucky riflemen. In a furious engage-

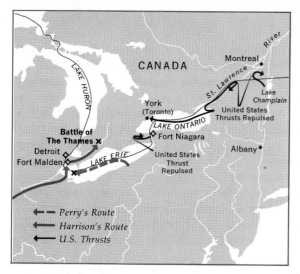

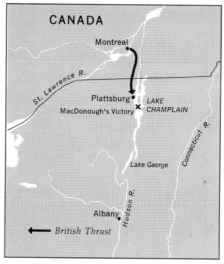

CAMPAIGNS OF 1813
Blue line denotes Canadian boundary.

BRITISH INVASION, 1814
Blue line denotes Canadian boundary.

ment on Lake Erie, he captured a less powerful British fleet. "We have met the enemy and they are ours," he reported to his superior, "two ships, two brigs, one schooner, and one sloop." His victory, combined with his slogan, infused new life into the drooping American cause.

With the control of Lake Erie firmly in American hands, the British holdings to the west, both at Malden and at captured Detroit, quickly withered. Forced to withdraw eastward into Canada, the retreating Redcoats were overtaken by General Harrison's army and beaten at the Battle of the Thames. There, in October 1813, the gifted Indian leader Tecumseh, now a brigadier general in the British army, lost his life.

Despite these successes, the Americans by late 1814, far from invading Canada, were grimly defending their own soil against the invading British. In Europe, the diversionary power of Napoleon was destroyed in mid-1814, and the dangerous despot was marooned on the Mediterranean isle of Elba. The United States, which had so brashly provoked war behind the protective skirts of Napoleon, was now left to face the music alone. As thousands of red-coated veterans began to pour into Canada, Europe's distresses, for once, failed the Americans.

Assembling some 10,000 crack troops, the British prepared in 1814 for a crushing blow into New York, along the familiar lake-river route. In the absence of roads, the invader was forced to bring his supplies over the Lake Champlain waterway. A weaker American fleet, commanded by the thirty-year-old Thomas Macdonough, challenged the British. The ensuing battle was desperately fought near Plattsburg, on September 11, 1814, on floating slaughterhouses. The American flagship at one point was in grave trouble. But Macdonough, unexpectedly turning his ship about with cables, confronted the enemy with a fresh broadside, and snatched victory from the fangs of defeat.

The results of this heroic naval battle were momentous. The invading British army, its supply line blocked, was forced to retreat, after having gained an initial minor success at Plattsburg over an outnumbered force of American recruits. Macdonough thus saved at least upper New York from conquest, New England from further disaffection, and the Union from possible dissolution. He also profoundly affected the concurrent negotiations of the Anglo-American peace treaty in Europe. The victories of Perry and Macdonough, though achieved on inland lakes, were by far the most decisive naval engagements of the war. The triumph of Macdonough, though the more important, is largely forgotten, partly because he devised no rousing slogan.

Washington Burned and New Orleans Defended

A second formidable British force, numbering about 4,000, landed in the Chesapeake Bay area in August 1814. Advancing rapidly on Washington, it easily dispersed some 6,000 panicky militia at Bladensburg ("the Bladensburg races"). The invaders then entered the capital and set fire to most of the public buildings, including the Capitol and the White House ("the Yankee Palace"). President Madison and his aides, chased into the surrounding hills like frightened rabbits, witnessed from afar the billowing smoke. The British fleet next appeared before Baltimore, a nest for privateers, but was beaten off by the doughty defenders at Fort McHenry, despite "bombs bursting in air." At the same time the American land defenders, though driven back at first, caused the attacking army to withdraw.

The wanton destruction of Washington reflected little credit on the British. They claimed that they had acted in retaliation for the unauthorized burning of certain public buildings by an American raiding party at York (Toronto) in 1813. But the deliberate application of the torch served only to inflame anti-British bitterness. The memory of the Chesapeake campaign was further kept alive when Francis Scott Key, a detained American anxiously watching the bombardment at Baltimore from a British ship, was inspired to write the words of "The Star-Spangled Banner." Set to the tune of a saucy old English tavern refrain, the song quickly attained popularity.

A third British blow of 1814, aimed at New Orleans, menaced the entire Mississippi Valley. Gaunt and hawk-faced Andrew Jackson, fresh from crushing the Southwest Indians at the Battle of Horseshoe Bend in what is now Alabama, was placed in command. His hodgepodge force consisted of 7,000 sailors, regulars, pirates, and Frenchmen, as well as militiamen from Louisiana, Kentucky, and Tennessee. Among the defenders were two Louisiana regiments of free black volunteers, numbering about 400 men. The Americans threw up their entrenchment, and

> Behind it stood our little force—
> None wished it to be greater;
> For ev'ry man was half a horse,
> And half an alligator.*

The overconfident British, numbering some 8,000 battle-seasoned veterans, blundered badly. They made the mistake of launching a frontal assault, on January 8, 1815, on the entrenched American riflemen and cannoneers. The attackers suffered the most devastating defeat of the entire war, losing over 2,000, killed and wounded, in half an hour, as compared with some 70 for the Americans. This slaughter was as useless as it was horrible, for the treaty of peace had been signed at Ghent, in Europe, two weeks earlier. But Jackson became more than ever the hero of the West. Was he not greater than Napoleon, for had he not

President James Madison (1751–1836). Though an eminent constitutionalist, legislator, and diplomatist, he was not a strong Chief Executive. Foolishly, he was the only President ever to go directly to the fighting front, but he quickly rode away as the British advanced on Washington in 1814.

---

*Popular song, "The Hunters of Kentucky." This song helped create the legend that the riflemen rather than the cannoneers inflicted the most damage.

THE SOUTHWEST, 1814–1815

Area captured by United States from Spain, 1812–1813

whipped the British veterans, who in turn had whipped Napoleon?

The smashing triumph at New Orleans was the only decisive American land victory that had not been set up by naval power. Yet if a nation is going to win only one such battle, a better aftertaste is left if it is the last one. The "glorious news" from New Orleans reached Washington early in February 1815, and about two weeks later came the tidings of the treaty of peace. Naive citizens promptly concluded that the British, beaten to their knees by Jackson, had hastened to make terms. More support was thus given to the legend that America soundly "thrashed" the British for a second time in the War of 1812—and with poorly trained militia at that.

Ship Duels and Privateer Prizes

Man for man and ship for ship the American navy did much better than the army. But the results of its heroism have been exaggerated.

Britain's navy in 1812 boasted more than 800 men-of-war. Of these oaken craft, 219 were ships-of-the-line of the 74-gun class, and 296 were frigates of roughly the 44-gun class. Little wonder that the motto of the British *Naval Register* was:

The winds and seas are Britain's wide domain,
And not a sail, but by permission, spreads.

America, by contrast, had only 16 ships in her entire navy, the largest of which were a few 44-gun frigates, unable to stand up to British ships-of-the-line. There could obviously be no saltwater fleet engagements in the slam-bang Trafalgar tradition; the only fleet battles were fought on the interior lakes.

American frigates and smaller sloops did clash with the enemy in a series of spectacular duels. In the frigate class, the Americans won four out of five of the single-ship contests, and in the sloop class, eight out of nine. American craft on the whole were more skillfully handled, had better gunners, and were manned by non–press-gang crews who were burning to avenge numerous indignities. The American frigates were specially designed super-frigates, notably the *Constitution* ("Old Ironsides"). They had thicker sides, heavier firepower, and larger crews, of which one sailor in six was a free black. These ships should have defeated their foes in the same category, and generally did, amid angry enemy charges that they were "disguised" ships-of-the-line.

The British were deeply humiliated by their naval defeats, all the more so because they had

Constitution and **Guerrière**, 1812.
The *Guerrière* was heavily outweighed
and outgunned, yet her British captain
eagerly—and foolishly—sought combat. His ship was totally destroyed.
Historian Henry Adams later concluded that this duel "raised the
United States in one half hour to the
rank of a first-class Power in the
world." (U.S. Naval Academy Museum.)

sneered at America's "few fir-built frigates, manned by a handful of bastards and outlaws." In a few months they lost more warships to the Yankees than the French and Spaniards together had captured in years of fighting.

After three straight losses in frigate duels, Englishmen rang the bells of London Tower in joy over one gratifying victory. The ill-starred American frigate *Chesapeake*, rashly taken into battle with an inexperienced crew, had been captured

ı□ıı□ıı□ıı□ıı□ıı□ıı□ıı□ıı□ıı□ıı□ıı□ıı□ıı□ıı□ıı□ı

> Smarting from wounded pride on the sea, the London *Times* urged chastisement for Americans: "The people—naturally vain, boastful, and insolent—have been filled with an absolute contempt of our maritime power, and a furious eagerness to beat down our maritime pretensions. Those passions, which have been inflamed by success, could only have been cooled by what in vulgar and emphatic language has been termed 'a sound flogging.'" (Dec. 30, 1814)

ı□ıı□ıı□ıı□ıı□ıı□ıı□ıı□ıı□ıı□ıı□ıı□ıı□ıı□ıı□ıı□ı

off Boston by the British frigate *Shannon* on June 1, 1813. From the dying lips of the American commander, Captain Lawrence, came the stirring slogan "Don't give up the ship. Blow her up." The British at length put an end to American single-ship frigate victories when they ordered their frigates to sail in pairs.

The loss of a dozen or so ships by the Royal Navy was negligible. But the victory-hungry Americans gathered from these triumphs a badly needed boost to their morale. When the conflict ended, there were only two or three ships of the American navy at large; Britain still had over 800. The United States obviously did not win the war on the sea. But the dramatic sloop and frigate duels gave further support to the legend that the navy had vanquished the British.

Swift and annoying American privateers—the "militia of the sea"—numbered about 500. They were in fact much more damaging than the regular navy, and had an important bearing on the coming of peace. Built to fly from stronger ships, rather than fight them, these speedy craft captured or destroyed some 1,350 British merchantmen, even pursuing them into the English Channel and the

Irish Sea. Assisted by fast-sailing sloops of the navy, Yankee privateers were so destructive that Lloyd's of London refused to insure unconvoyed British merchantmen crossing the Irish Sea. (At the same time British warships and privateers were capturing hundreds of American merchant ships.)

Yet the American privateers were not an unmixed blessing. They lost scores of their own craft, and diverted valuable manpower from the navy and army. But they brought urgently needed wealth into the country, boosted sagging morale, and slowed up British operations in Canada and elsewhere by capturing arms and supplies. More than that, the privateers brought the war home to British manufacturers, merchants, and shippers, who in turn exerted strong pressure on Parliament to end this costly war.

Its wrath aroused, the Royal Navy finally retaliated by throwing a ruinous naval blockade along America's coast, and by landing raiding parties almost at will. American economic life, including fishing, was crippled. Customs revenues were choked off, and near the end of the war the bankrupt Treasury was unable to meet its maturing obligations.

British Peace Demands at Ghent

Czar Alexander I of Russia, late in 1812, unexpectedly proposed mediation between the clashing Anglo-Saxon cousins. He was then hard-pressed by Napoleon's invading Grand Army, and did not wish to see his British ally fritter away its strength in America. Nothing came of the Czar's feeler immediately, but it set the machinery in motion which, in 1814, brought five American peacemakers to the quaint city of Ghent, now in Belgium. This bickering group was headed by the early-rising and puritanical John Quincy Adams, son of John Adams, who deplored the late-hour card playing of his high-living colleague Henry Clay.

Britain's envoys were instructed to make sweeping demands. Their position was bolstered by the knowledge that His Majesty's forces occupied

the eastern portion of Maine, and still held Fort Niagara. Britain, through her red allies, also loosely controlled a vast region between the Great Lakes and the Mississippi. The British negotiators therefore felt justified in demanding a neutralized Indian buffer state in this general area. Thrust between Canada and the United States, it would deprive the American pioneers of an immense field for future expansion.

The British diplomats further insisted upon control of the Great Lakes, so as to forestall a future invasion of Canada. With the defense of Canada also in mind, they demanded a substantial part of conquered Maine. They coveted this territory for a military road from Halifax to Quebec, to be employed during those months when the St. Lawrence River was ice-locked.

Such demands from London, harsh though they seemed, were not too far out of line with British military successes, past and prospective. But the American negotiators flatly rejected the proposed terms without even waiting to hear from the secretary of state.

Then, as if by magic, the atmosphere at Ghent changed. The British had presented their drastic proposals with complete confidence; they fully

"Bruin Becomes Mediator" or "Negotiation for Peace." The Russian Bear attempts to mediate between America and a chastened John Bull. America expresses concern over John Bull's horns, the Orders in Council. (A cartoon by William Charles. Courtesy of The New York Public Library, Astor, Lenox and Tilden Foundations.)

"A Wasp on a Frolic."   U.S. sloops-of-war *Wasp* and *Hornet* sting John Bull's pride. The *Wasp* captured the *Frolic.* Contemporary American cartoon.

expected that news would soon arrive of crushing victories. But when instead tidings came of the repulses in upper New York and at Baltimore, London was more willing to compromise. The Madison administration, for its part, was now reluctantly prepared to keep silent on the issue of impressment, even though it had originally insisted on abandonment of this infuriating practice.

In England, the atmosphere likewise changed. Irate Britons were impatient to humiliate the "insolent" and "treacherous" Yankees. But the "Iron Duke" of Wellington, conqueror of Napoleon, warned that the United States could not be successfully invaded without British control of the Great Lakes. Such control could be achieved only at a heavy cost, if at all; and England was debt-burdened and war-weary from her twenty-year clash with France. American sloops and privateers were taking their deadly toll. The Congress of Vienna, designed to unscramble the map of Europe, was at a critical stage. France was restive, and Napoleon might forsake nearby Elba to meet his Waterloo (which he soon did).

Revenge was sweet—but expensive. Much as the British yearned to thrash their upstart offspring, they finally decided that this satisfaction would cost too much, while involving them too deeply at a time when they had to keep a vigilant eye on France. The British lion unhappily resigned himself to licking his wounds. Once again the distresses of Europe were bringing diplomatic success, for the War of 1812 was largely "won" in Europe, so far as it was won at all by the United States.

The Gains of Ghent

The Treaty of Ghent, signed on Christmas Eve in 1814, was essentially an armistice. Both sides simply agreed to stop fighting and to restore conquered territory. No mention was made of those grievances for which America had ostensibly fought: the Indian menace, search and seizure, Orders in Council, impressment, and confiscations. These maritime omissions have often been cited as further evidence of the insincerity of the War Hawks. Rather, they are proof that the Americans did not defeat the British decisively. With neither side able to impose its will, the treaty negotiations—like the war itself—ended as a virtual draw.

Time—the great healer—solved certain problems that the negotiators could not untangle. Impress-

The War of 1812 won a new respect for America among many Britons. Michael Scott, a young lieutenant in the British navy, wrote: "I don't like Americans; I never did, and never shall like them. . . . I have no wish to eat with them, drink with them, deal with, or consort with them in any way; but let me tell the whole truth, *nor fight* with them, were it not for the laurels to be acquired, by overcoming an enemy so brave, determined, and alert, and in every way so worthy of one's steel, as they have always proved."

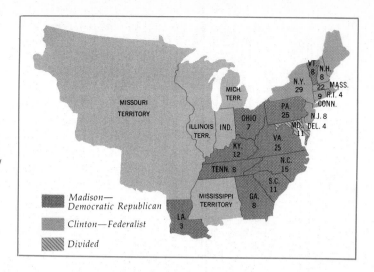

PRESIDENTIAL ELECTION OF 1812 (with electoral vote by state)
The Federalists showed impressive strength in the North, and their presidential candidate, DeWitt Clinton, the future "father of the Erie Canal," almost won. If the 25 electoral votes of Pennsylvania had gone to the New Yorker, he would have won, 114 to 103.

ment was never thereafter a burning issue. The British navy was reduced to a peace footing, and less brutal methods of enlistment were devised. The Peace of Ghent, like Jay's Treaty of 1794, was also a victory for arbitration: four boundary disputes were referred to arbitral commissions.

The "Truce of Ghent," which realistically swept problems under the rug, had one great merit. It was not a victor's peace; hence no territorial booty had to be won back. There were wounds—but not unhealable wounds. The treaty had done nothing, so nothing had to be undone. Therein lay the secret of its longevity.

The news from Ghent triggered an outburst of rejoicing in the United States. Many Americans had rather expected to lose some territory, so dark was the military outlook early in 1815. But when the treaty arrived, the public mood rocketed from gloom to glory. The popularity of the pact was so overwhelming that it was unanimously approved by the Senate. A slogan of the hour became "Not One Inch of Territory Ceded or Lost"—a watchword that contrasted strangely with "On to Canada" at the outset of the war.

Federalist Grievances and the Hartford Convention

Defiant New England remained a problem. She was by far the most prosperous section during the conflict, owing largely to illicit trade with the enemy in Canada and to the absence of a British blockade until 1814. But the embittered opposition of the Federalists to the war continued unabated. Late in 1812, when the first wartime presidential election was held, unhappy Federalists combined with disaffected Republicans and almost unseated President Madison. If the state of Pennsylvania alone had been transferred to their electoral column, they would have won.

As the war dragged on, New England extremists became more vocal. A small minority of them proposed secession from the Union, or at least a separate peace with England. Ugly rumors were afloat about "Blue Light" Federalists—treacherous New Englanders who supposedly flashed lanterns on the shore so that blockading British cruisers would be alerted to the attempted escape of American ships.

The most spectacular manifestation of Federalist discontent was the ill-omened Hartford Convention. Late in 1814, when the capture of New Orleans seemed imminent, Massachusetts issued a call for a convention at Hartford, Connecticut. The states of Massachusetts, Connecticut, and Rhode Island dispatched full delegations, while New Hampshire and Vermont sent partial representation. This group of prominent men, twenty-six in all, met in complete secrecy for about three weeks—December 15, 1814, to January 5, 1815—to discuss their grievances and to seek redress for their wrongs.

In truth, the Hartford Convention was less radical than alarmists supposed. Its immediate goal was to secure financial assistance from Washington, because the shores of New England were then being menaced by British blockading squadrons. A minority of the delegates gave vent to much wild talk of secession, but they were outvoted by the moderate Federalists. The report and resolutions adopted by the Convention, in fact, resemble a modern political platform.

The Hartfordites, resenting the war-bent policies of the administration, were eager to restore New England to her stellar role on the national stage. They recommended amendments to the Constitution aimed at hobbling Congress and restoring Federalist influence by a kind of minority veto. These proposals would require a two-thirds vote

"Three Wise Men of Gotham Went to Sea in a Bowl.—" This satirical anti-Federalist cartoon shows three Massachusetts men sailing precariously for Washington in a large chamber pot bearing Hartfordite demands. They are quieting their fears of sinking by exchanging off-color remarks. (Massachusetts Historical Society.)

before an embargo could be imposed, before new Western states could be admitted, and before war could be declared—except in case of invasion.

Three special envoys from Massachusetts, bearing demands of the Hartford Convention for financial support to promote defense, journeyed to the burned-out capital of Washington. The trio arrived just in time to be overwhelmed by the glorious news from New Orleans, followed by that from Ghent. Pursued by the sneers and jeers of the press, they slunk away into obscurity and disgrace.

The Hartford resolutions, as it turned out, were the death song of the Federalist party. In 1816, the next year, the Federalists nominated their last presidential candidate. He was lopsidedly defeated by James Monroe, yet another Virginian.

Unhappily, the stench of treason has clung to the Hartford Convention. The taint was not justified by its formal resolutions, which were an attempt of moderates to iron out rankling vexations by constitutional methods—in the American way. Yet if the war had not ended when it did, the Convention might well have paved the way for treasonable courses.

Federalist doctrines of disunity, which long survived the party, blazed a fateful trail. Until 1815, there was far more talk of nullification and secession in New England than in any other section, including the South. The outright flouting of the Jeffersonian embargo and the later crippling of the war effort were the two most damaging acts of nullification in America prior to the events leading to the Civil War.

The Second War for American Independence

The War of 1812 was a small war, involving about 6,000 Americans killed or wounded. It was but a footnote to the mighty European conflagration. In 1812, when Napoleon invaded Russia with about 500,000 men, Madison tried to invade Canada with about 5,000 men. But if the American conflict was globally unimportant, its results were highly important to the United States.

Oliver H. Perry's Battle Flag, 1813. Bearing Captain Lawrence's slogan, it now hangs conspicuously on a wall at the U.S. Naval Academy at Annapolis.

Americans wrested no formal recognition of their rights on the high seas, but informally they did. No longer did British aristocrats jeer at the "striped bunting" over "American cockboats." The Republic had shown that it would resent, sword in hand, what it regarded as grievous wrongs. Other nations developed a new respect for American fighting men. Naval officers like Perry and Macdonough were the most effective type of negotiators; the hot breath of their broadsides spoke the most eloquent diplomatic language. America's diplomats abroad were henceforth treated with less scorn. In a diplomatic sense, if not in a military sense, the conflict could be called the Second War for American Independence.

A new nation, moreover, was welded in the fiery furnace of armed conflict. Sectionalism, now identified with discredited New England Federalists, was given a black eye. The painful events of the war glaringly revealed, as perhaps nothing else could have done, the folly of sectional disunity. In a sense, the most conspicuous casualty of the war was the Federalist party.

The nation thrilled to the victories of its warriors. A brilliant naval tradition, already well launched, was strengthened by the exploits of the gallant seamen. Ineptitudes of insubordinate or fleeing militia were forgotten. The battle-singed regular army, which in the closing months of the war had fought bravely and well, had won its spurs. New war heroes emerged, men like Andrew Jackson, William Henry Harrison, and Winfield Scott. All three were to become presidential candidates, two of them successful.

Hostile Indians of the South had been crushed by Jackson at Horseshoe Bend (1814), and those of the North by Harrison at the Battle of the Thames (1813). Left in the lurch by their British friends at Ghent, the Indians were forced to make such terms as they could. They reluctantly consented, in a series of treaties, to relinquish vast areas of forested land north of the Ohio River.

Manufacturing increased behind the fiery wooden wall of the British blockade. In an economic sense, as well as in a diplomatic sense, the War of 1812 may be regarded as the Second War for American Independence. The industries that were thus stimulated by the fighting rendered America less dependent on the workshops of Europe.

Lingering Hates and Canadian Misgivings

Regrettably, the war revived and intensified bitterness toward the Mother Country. The uglier incidents of the conflict, notably the burning of Washington, added fuel to a century of Britain-hating and Britain-baiting. A contemporary American war song, "Johnny Bull," proclaimed:

> But if again he should be vain
>   Or dare to be uncivil,
> We'll let him know his rebel foe
>   Can thrash him like the D——.

Mutual suspicion and hate were perhaps the most enduring heritages of this frustrating little war. Few Americans could have guessed in 1815 that it was to be the nation's last armed conflict with England.

Canadian patriotism and nationalism, no less

than American patriotism and nationalism, received a powerful stimulus from the clash. The outnumbered Canadians, fighting bravely in defense of their homeland against the Yankee invader, won their full share of the laurels. Their stirring song, "The Maple Leaf," ringingly recalls these battles, including Chippewa and Lundy's Lane, which Americans regard as their victories.

All hope of annexing Canada, at least by nonforcible means, was given a deadly blow. Peaceful Yankee penetration might have won this rich prize, but caveman aggression defeated its own ends. It strengthened the arm of those Canadians, led by the sons of the Loyalists, who would die in the last ditch before they would live under the Stars and Stripes. The irony is that the Loyalists, whom America had defeated in her first war with England, helped thwart her in her second war with England.

Many Canadians, including Western fur traders, cried that they had been betrayed by the Treaty of Ghent. They were especially aggrieved by Britain's failure to secure the defensive bulwark of an Indian buffer state, or even mastery of the Great Lakes. Fully expecting the frustrated Yankee to come again, they felt naked in the face of their former enemy.

The U.S. Frigate *Constitution*. It was the pride of the scant American fleet.

Naval armament on the lakes continued to be inflammatory. When the war ended, the Americans and the British were both engaged in building powerful and costly warships. But economy-minded London officials, who perceived that such vessels were useless to the saltwater Royal Navy, finally became receptive to American proposals for arms limitation.

In 1817 Great Britain went so far as to negotiate with the United States the Rush-Bagot disarmament agreement. This memorable pact severely limited naval armament on the Great Lakes, despite Canadian misgivings and protests. The immediate fruits have been greatly overpraised, but the principle of disarmament was gradually extended to border fortifications, which disappeared in the 1870s. One happy result was that the United States and Canada ultimately came to share the longest unfortified boundary in the world—5,527 miles (8,899 kilometers) long, including Alaska.

Larger Anglo-American Legacies

Painful military lessons of the war went largely unheeded by the public, owing in part to overemphasis on spectacular naval duels. Forgotten were the perils of unpreparedness, the dangers of disunity, the muddlings of the militia. Americans assumed, mistakenly, that they had won the war decisively—without preparing for it. Then why go to all the expense of building an adequate military establishment if they could defeat their enemies without one? Unpreparedness was sanctified by seeming success.

Europe's finish-fight at Waterloo, in 1815, proved to be one of the decisive battles of American history. With a defeated Napoleon safely exiled on the island-rock of St. Helena, some 5,000 miles away, Europe slumped back into a peace of exhaustion. Deposed monarchs returned to battered thrones, as the Mother Continent prepared to take the rutted road back to conservatism, illiberalism, and reaction.

American citizens now experienced the joys of emancipation. Freed from the humiliating side blows of the belligerents, they no longer had to scan the Atlantic horizon for approaching sails—sails that might bring news of impending calamities. Americans thrilled to a new sense of nationality. They were like subject peoples attaining their majority, and for the first time shaking off the shackles of colonialism. Turning their backs on the Old World, they faced resolutely toward the untamed West. Unlike monarchy-cursed Europe, they were ready to take the high road toward democracy, liberalism, and freedom. The steady tramp, tramp, of the westward-moving pioneers came to be the giant drumbeat of a new destiny.

VARYING VIEWPOINTS

The causes and consequences of the War of 1812 have long sparked spirited debate. Was war the result of Western War Hawk expansionism or of British provocations on the high seas? Most recent historians emphasize the naval issue. The young nation's pride and independence, they argue, could not tolerate John Bull's repeated affronts. Perhaps more interestingly, scholars also have seen the first vague outlines of an American identity emerging from the smoke of the War of 1812. Henry Adams' magisterial *History* made this theme a central motif; Adams found evidence of a distinctive American character even in the tactics and techniques of Yankee seamen. The war does appear to have dissolved many localisms and to have begun to forge a genuine national consciousness—thus paving the way for the so-called Era of Good Feelings.

SELECT READINGS

Marcus Cunliffe, *The Nation Takes Shape, 1789–1837* (1959), provides a convenient introduction. More detailed are H. L. Coles, *The War of 1812* (1965), P. C. T. White, *A Nation on Trial: America and the War of 1812* (1965), J. M. Hitsman, *The Incredible War of 1812: A Military History* (1965), and R. Horsman, *The War of 1812* (1969). On causation, J. W. Pratt, *Expansionists of 1812* (1925), stresses Western pressures; Bradford Perkins, *Prologue to War: England and the United States, 1805–1812* (1961), and R. Horsman, *The Causes of the War of 1812* (1962), discuss free seas; R. R. Brown, *The Republic in Peril: 1812* (1964), emphasizes the need for saving the Republican form of government. The relevant volumes of Henry Adams' nine-volume *History of the United States* (1889–1891) still contain magnificent reading, both on the war and on the peace. For the general context of Anglo-American diplomacy, see B. Perkins, *Castlereagh and Adams: England and the United States, 1812–1823* (1964). An overall view can be found in J. K. Mahon, *The War of 1812* (1972). A popularized account of the Peace of Ghent is F. L. Engelman, *The Peace of Christmas Eve* (1962). Federalist reaction to Republican foreign policy is vividly etched in D. H. Fisher, *The Revolution of American Conservatism* (1965), and J. Banner, *To the Hartford Convention: The Federalists and the Origins of Party Politics in Massachusetts* (1970). Consult also James H. Broussard, *The Southern Federalists, 1800–1816* (1979). Irving Brant continues his strong pro-Madison bias in the relevant volumes of his six-volume work: *James Madison: The President, 1809–1812* (1956), and *James Madison: Commander-in-Chief, 1812–1836* (1961). See also Ralph Ketcham, *James Madison: A Biography* (1971). Other useful biographical studies are Bernard Mayo, *Henry Clay: Spokesman of the New West* (1937), G. G. Van Deusen, *The Life of Henry Clay* (1937) and Marquis James's spirited *Andrew Jackson: The Border Captain* (1933).

12

The Post-War Upsurge of Nationalism, 1815–1824

The American continents . . . are henceforth not to be considered as subjects for future colonization by any European powers.

JAMES MONROE, December 2, 1823

Nascent Nationalism

The most impressive by-product of the War of 1812 was a heightened nationalism—the spirit of nation-consciousness or national oneness. America may not have fought the war as one nation, but she emerged one nation. So exhilarating was the post-war era that President Madison, despite his blunders, enjoyed the unusual distinction of being more popular when he left the White House in 1817 than when he entered it in 1809.

A weak nationalism had existed since Revolutionary days, but the vibrant new nationalism was composed of many additional ingredients. It sprang partly from pride in recent victories, partly from the setback to Federalist sectionalism and states'-rightism, partly from a lessening of economic and political dependence on Europe, and partly from an exulting confidence in the future.

Swelling numbers of citizens—although probably not yet a majority—were coming to regard themselves as first of all Americans, and secondarily as citizens of their respective states.

The changed mood even manifested itself in the birth of a distinctively national literature. Washington Irving and James Fenimore Cooper attained international recognition in the 1820s, significantly as the nation's first writers of importance to use American scenes and themes. School textbooks, often British in an earlier era, were now being written by Americans for Americans. In the world of magazines, the highly intellectual *North American Review* saw the light of day in 1815—the year of the triumph at New Orleans. Even American painters increasingly celebrated the glories of American landscapes on their canvases.

A fresh nationalistic spirit could be recognized in many other areas. A more handsome national capital began to rise from the ashes of Washington —a capital fit to symbolize America's prospective greatness. The army was expanded to 10,000 men, though this number was inadequate for a serious emergency. Old fears that liberties might be crushed by a standing army largely melted away in the warm sun of emerging nationalism.

The navy, for a time at least, also received reasonably satisfactory financial support. It further covered itself with glory in 1815, when the naval heroes of the late war administered a thorough beating to the piratical plunderers of North Africa. These gratifying victories, inspired by the spirit of nationalism, further inflamed nationalism.

A rising tide of nation-consciousness also touched finance. The War of 1812 had demonstrated the folly of permitting the Bank of the United States to expire in 1811, on the very eve of hostilities. Weak state banks, responding to the vacuum, had seemingly sprung up beside every village tavern. The country was flooded with depreciated banknotes that, incidentally, had hampered the war effort.

A revived Bank of the United States, in response to these obvious needs, was voted by Congress in 1816. It was modeled on the first one but had a

Stephen Decatur (1779–1820). Decatur was a naval hero of the War of 1812 and the North African war. Reflecting and encouraging the post-war nationalism, he is best remembered for a famous toast: "Our country! In her intercourse with foreign nations may she always be in the right; but our country, right or wrong!"

total capital of $35 million—three and one-half times that of the original. Jeffersonian Republicans, taught a bitter lesson during the war, supported the revived institution. In fact, they cleverly but inconsistently borrowed the same arguments for a bank that Hamilton had used against Jefferson in 1791. The Federalist minority in Congress, opposing Republican measures with its dying gasps, no less inconsistently denounced the Federalist-spawned Bank as unconstitutional.

The Second Bank of the United States, unlike the first, started off on the wrong foot. Badly managed in its early years, it finally settled down and contributed richly to the economic life of the country. The "moneyed monster," as it was branded by its enemies, further broadened nationalism as it thrust its numerous branches out across state boundaries.

Industrial Nationalism and the Tariff

Nationalism likewise manifested itself in manufacturing. Patriotic Americans took pride in the factories that had recently mushroomed forth, largely as a result of the self-imposed embargoes and the war.

When hostilities ended in 1815, British competitors undertook to recover lost ground. They began to dump the contents of their bulging warehouses on the United States, often cutting their prices below cost in an effort to strangle the American war-baby factories in the cradle. The infant industries bawled lustily for protection. To many red-blooded Americans it seemed as though the British, having failed on the battlefield to crush Yankee fighters, were now seeking to crush Yankee factories.

A nationalist Congress, out-Federalizing the old Federalists, responded by passing the path-breaking Tariff of 1816. The legislators were impressed with the desirability of saving the new industries for the national defense, while at the same time promoting the general welfare. The Tariff of 1816, significantly, was the first in American history with aims that were primarily protective. Its rates—roughly 20 to 25 percent on the value of dutiable imports—were not high enough to provide completely adequate safeguards, but the law was a bold beginning. A strongly protective trend was started that stimulated the appetites of the protected for more protection.

The battle in Congress over the Tariff of 1816 reflected North-South sectional crosscurrents. Thirty-four-year-old Representative John C. Calhoun of South Carolina—slender, handsome, black-haired, intense, and intellectual—played a stellar role in the debates. A recent War Hawk and an ardent nationalist, he supported the tariff bill with all his eloquence and vigor. In 1816 there was some likelihood that the destiny of his native South lay in manufacturing, as well as in the intensive cultivation of cotton. But within a few years Calhoun became a relentless foe of a highly protective tariff. He sadly concluded that it was being used to enrich a few Yankee manufacturers, rather than to build up the economic self-sufficiency and well-being of the entire nation.

Calhoun encountered a worthy adversary in Daniel Webster of New Hampshire, also thirty-four. Stocky, bushy-browed, and dark-haired, "Black Dan." Webster eloquently opposed the highly protective duties of the Tariff of 1816. He took this stand even though he was later to be a zealous nationalist and an ardent champion of high protection. The explanation is simple. Manufacturing in New England had not yet pushed shipping into a back seat, and the shippers of Webster's New Hampshire district feared that a tariff would interfere with their carrying trade. New England, though favoring some protection, was not yet completely willing to exchange the mainsail for the loom—but that day was slowly dawning.

Nationalism was further highlighted by a grandiose plan of Henry Clay for developing a profitable home market. Still radiating the nationalism of War Hawk days, he threw himself behind an elaborate scheme known by 1824 as the American System. First, there would be the protective tariff, behind which Eastern manufacturing would flourish. Revenues gushing from the tariff would provide funds for roads and canals, especially in the fast-developing Ohio Valley. Through these new arteries of transportation would flow foodstuffs and raw materials from the South and West to the North and East. In exchange, a stream of manufactured goods would flow in the return direction.

A wedding of tariff revenues to internal improvements looked promising on paper. The entire country would prosper, while state boundaries would tend to become mere surveyors' lines. America would grow more self-sufficient, and under the

House Vote on Tariff of 1816

Regions	For	Against
New England	17	10
Middle States	44	10
West (Ohio)	4	0
South and Southwest	23	34
	88	54

NOTE: Even in South Carolina, Calhoun's state, the vote in favor of the bill was 4 to 3.

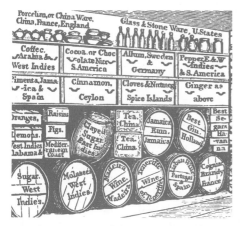

Pro-Tariff Woodcut Showing Foreign Goods on Shelves. Many Americans feared foreign goods more than foreign armies.

warm glow of prosperity the spirit of nationalism would deepen and broaden.

Roadblocks to Internal Improvements

Persistent and eloquent demands by Henry Clay and others for internal improvements struck a responsive chord with the public. The recent attempts to invade Canada had all failed partly because of oath-provoking roads—or no roads at all. Men who have dug wagons out of hub-deep mud do not quickly forget their blisters and backaches. An outcry for better transportation, rising most noisily in the road-poor West, was one of the most striking aspects of the nationalism inspired by the War of 1812.

Hope for more roads and canals came from an unexpected source. The Second Bank of the United States had been required to pay the federal government $1.5 million for its exclusive privileges. Calhoun, seeking to divert this sum to internal improvements, induced Congress in 1817 to pass the Bonus Bill, under which the Bank money would be parceled out to the states. But President Madison sternly vetoed this handout measure. In his view, the spending of federal funds for internal improvements within the individual states—but not

across state lines—violated the Constitution, as interpreted strictly.

This anti-improvement veto threw a wet blanket over the upsurging nationalism. Madison's successor, President Monroe, generally followed the same line of negative reasoning—with the same disheartening results. The individual states, though lacking sufficient funds, were forced to venture ahead with building programs of their own. The most notable of these was the Erie Canal, triumphantly completed by New York in 1825.

On the transportation question, the Jeffersonian Republicans were not consistently inconsistent. On all other important problems, they were at last prepared to gulp down the Hamiltonian doctrine of loose construction. Madison and Monroe, political heirs of Jefferson, could easily have argued that roads and canals solely within the states contributed to the welfare of the country as a whole, while bolstering the common defense. But instead they timidly recommended an appropriate constitutional amendment to permit internal improvements at federal expense. It was never enacted.

The enfeebled Federalists, now turncoat strict constructionists, could grudgingly applaud the vetoes of the Jeffersonian Republican Presidents. New England, in particular, strongly opposed federally constructed roads and canals, because such outlets would further drain away population and create competing states beyond the mountains.

The So-Called Era of Good Feelings

James Monroe—6 feet (1.83 meters) tall, somewhat stooped, courtly, and mild-mannered—was nominated for the presidency in 1816 by the Republicans. They thus undertook to continue the so-called Virginia Dynasty of Washington, Jefferson, and Madison. The fading Federalists ran a candidate for the last time in their checkered history, and he was crushed by 183 electoral votes to 34.

The death of the once-proud Federalist party was due to various diseases, shortcomings, and misfortunes. A list would include its disgraceful

President James Monroe (1758–1831). Monroe fought in the Revolution (suffering a wound), served as minister to France, became co-purchaser of Louisiana, and rose to the presidency in 1817. An excellent administrator, he presided over the Era of Good Feelings. His inaugural address declared: "National honor is national property of the highest value." His name is imperishably attached to the Monroe Doctrine and Monrovia, the capital city of Liberia in Africa. He had strongly backed the colonization there of ex-slaves. His wife and two daughters had expensive tastes and, like plantation-owner Jefferson, he died deeply in debt. (The Metropolitan Museum of Art, Bequest of Seth Low, 1929.)

war record; its inability to choke down the new nationalistic program; and the theft of its tenets by the Jeffersonians. Many Federalists followed their stolen principles into the opposition camp; others gradually crawled away to the political graveyard. The irony is that the original Hamiltonians, while the party of the "ins," had been conspicuously nationalistic; now, as the party of the "outs," they scorned the nationalism of the Republicans.

In James Monroe, the man and the times auspi-

ciously met. As the last President to wear an old-style cocked hat, he straddled two generations: the bygone age of the Founding Fathers and the emergent age of nationalism. Never brilliant, and perhaps not great, the serene Virginian with gray-blue eyes was in intellect and personal force among the least distinguished of the first eight Presidents. But the times called for sober administration, not heroics. And Monroe was an experienced, level-headed executive, with an ear-to-the-ground talent for interpreting popular rumblings.

Emerging nationalism was further cemented by a goodwill tour that Monroe undertook early in 1817, ostensibly to inspect military defenses. He pushed northward deep into New England, and then westward to Detroit, viewing en route the Niagara Falls. Even in Federalist New England, "the enemy's country," he received a heartwarming welcome; a Boston newspaper was so far carried away as to announce that an "Era of Good Feelings" had been ushered in. This happy phrase since then has been commonly used to describe the administrations of Monroe.

The Era of Good Feelings, unfortunately, was something of a misnomer. Considerable tranquillity and prosperity did in fact smile upon the early years of Monroe, but the period was a troubled one. The acute issues of the tariff, the Bank, internal improvements, and the sale of public lands were being hotly contested. Sectionalism was crystallizing, and the conflict over slavery was beginning to raise its hideous head.

Boston's *Columbian Centinel* was not the only newspaper to regard President Monroe's early months as the Era of Good Feelings. The Washington *National Intelligencer* observed in July 1817, "Never before, perhaps, since the institution of civil government, did the same harmony, the same absence of party spirit, the same national feeling, pervade a community. The result is too consoling to dispute too nicely about the cause."

A vanquished Federalist party was breathing its dying gasps, leaving the field to the triumphant Republicans and one-party rule. But where there is only one party, or where one of the parties enjoys a lopsided majority, the tendency is for factions to develop and fight among themselves. By the early 1820s there was an Era of Inflamed Feelings. Political giants—men like Clay, Calhoun, Jackson, and John Quincy Adams— were elbowing for power and championing the clashing economic interests of their respective sections.

The Panic of 1819 and the Curse of Hard Times

Much of the goodness went out of the good feelings in 1819, when a paralyzing economic panic descended. It brought deflation, depression, bankruptcies, bank failures, unemployment, soup kitchens, and overcrowded pesthouses known as debtors' prisons.

This was the first of the national financial panics since President Washington took office. It was to be followed by a succession of others every twenty or so years, in what seemed an inevitable cycle. Many factors contributed to the catastrophe of 1819, but looming large was overspeculation in frontier lands. The Bank of the United States, through its Western branches, had become deeply involved in this popular type of outdoor gambling.

Financial paralysis from the panic, which lasted in some degree for several years, gave a rude setback to the nationalistic ardor. Various parts of the country tended to drift back toward the old sectionalism, as they concentrated on bailing themselves out. The West was especially hard hit. When the pinch came, the Bank of the United States forced the speculative ("wildcat") Western banks to the wall, and foreclosed mortgages on countless farms. All this was technically legal but politically unwise. In the eyes of the Western debtor, the Bank soon became a kind of financial devil.

A more welcome child of the panic was fresh legislation for the public domain. The plight of the Western farmer, combined with the evils of land speculation, laid bare the defects of the Land Act of 1800, as amended in 1804. By its terms, the pioneer could buy a minimum of 160 acres at $2 an acre over a period of four years, with a down payment of $80. When hard times came, whole communities would default on their installments. An improved Land Act of 1820 lightened the burden somewhat, for it permitted the buyer to secure 80 virgin acres at a minimum of $1.25 an acre in cash—for a total cost of $100. There was less acreage but less outlay.

The Panic of 1819 also created backwashes in the political and social world. It hit especially hard the poorer classes—the one-suspender men—and hence helped cultivate the seedbed of Jacksonian democracy. It also directed attention to the inhumanity of imprisoning debtors. In extreme cases, often overplayed, mothers were torn from their infants for owing a few dollars. Mounting agitation against imprisonment for debt bore fruit in remedial legislation in an increasing number of states.

Growing Pains of the West

Beyond doubt the West, out of which had swooped the War Hawks of 1812, was by far the most nationalistic of the sections. Being new, it had no long-established states'-rights tradition. Moreover, it had early learned to lean on the national government, from which it had secured most of its land, directly or indirectly. It was a mixing bowl within the huge American melting pot, for people from all the sections rubbed elbows on the frontier.

Marvelous indeed had been the onward march of the West; nine frontier states had joined the original thirteen between 1791 and 1819. With an eye to preserving the North-South sectional balance, most of these commonwealths had been admitted alternately, free or slave. (See Admission of States, in Appendix.)

Why this explosive expansion? Fundamentally, there was the generations-old westward movement, which had been going on since early colonial days. In addition, the siren call of cheap lands— "the Ohio fever"—had a special appeal to European immigrants. Quaintly garbed newcomers from abroad were beginning to shuffle down the gangplanks in impressive numbers, especially after the war of embargoes and bullets. Land exhaustion in the older tobacco states, where the soil was "mined" rather than cultivated, likewise drove people westward. Glib-tongued speculators, accepting small down payments, made easier the purchase of new holdings.

The western boom was stimulated by additional developments. Acute distress during the embargo years turned many saddened faces toward the setting sun. The crushing of the Indians in the Northwest and South, by Generals Harrison and Jackson, soothed the frontier and opened up vast virgin tracts. The building of highways improved the land routes to the Ohio Valley. Noteworthy was the Cumberland Road, begun in 1811, which ran ultimately from western Maryland to Illinois. The employment of the first steamboat on Western waters, also in 1811, heralded a new era of upstream navigation.

But the West, despite the inflow of settlers, was still weak in population and influence. Not potent enough politically to make its voice heard, it was forced to ally itself with sister sections. Thus strengthened, it demanded cheap acreage, and partially achieved its goal in the Land Act of 1820. It demanded cheap transportation, and slowly got it, despite the constitutional qualms of the Presi-

Hard Times in Ohio. A satire on Western migration, from a pamphlet of 1819. (American Antiquarian Society, Worcester, Massachusetts.)

dents and the hostility of Easterners. Finally, the West demanded cheap money, issued by its own "wildcat" banks, and fought the powerful Bank of the United States to attain its goal.

Slavery and the Sectional Balance

Sectional tensions were nakedly revealed in 1819, when the territory of Missouri knocked on the doors of Congress for admission as a slave state. This fertile and well-watered area contained sufficient population to warrant statehood. But the House of Representatives threw a monkey wrench into the plans of the Missourians by passing the incendiary Tallmadge amendment. It stipulated that no more slaves should be brought into Missouri, and also provided for the gradual emancipation of children born to slave parents already there. A mounting roar of anger burst from slaveholding Southerners. They were joined by many depression-cursed pioneers who favored unhampered expansion of the West, and by many Northerners, especially diehard Federalists, who were eager to play politics.

Southerners saw in the Tallmadge amendment, which was defeated in the Senate, an ominous threat to the sectional balance. When the Constitution was adopted in 1788, the North and South were running ·neck and neck in wealth and population. But with every passing decade the North was becoming wealthier and more thickly settled—an advantage reflected in an increasing Northern majority in the House of Representatives. Yet in the Senate, with eleven states free and eleven slave, the Southerners had maintained equality. They were therefore in a good position to thwart any Northern effort to interfere with the expansion of slavery, and they did not want to lose this veto.

The future of the slave system caused Southerners profound concern. Missouri was the first state entirely west of the Mississippi River to be carved out of the Louisiana Purchase, and the Missouri emancipation amendment might set a damaging precedent for all the rest of the area. Even more disquieting was another possibility. If

Contemporary Anti-Slavery Propaganda.
This also appeared as "Am I Not a
Woman and a Sister?"

While the debate over Missouri was raging, Jefferson wrote to a correspondent: "I thank you for your information on the progress and prospects of the Missouri question. It is the most portentous one which ever yet threatened our Union. In the gloomiest moment of the revolutionary war I never had any apprehensions equal to what I feel from this source." He also wrote that the "question, like a firebell in the night, awakened and filled me with terror." With slavery, the aging ex-President declared, "we have the wolf by the ears, and we can neither hold him nor safely let him go."

an outcry against the evils of slavery. They were determined that the plague of human bondage should not spread further into the virgin territories.

The Uneasy Missouri Compromise

Deadlock in Washington was at length broken in 1820 by the time-honored American solution of compromise—actually a bundle of three compromises. Courtly Henry Clay of Kentucky, gifted conciliator, played a leading role. Congress, despite abolitionist pleas, agreed to admit Missouri as a slave state. But at the same time free-soil

Congress could abolish the "peculiar institution" in Missouri, might it not attempt to do likewise in the older states of the South? The wounds of the Constitutional Convention of 1787 were once more ripped open.

Ugly moral questions also protruded, even though the main issue was political and economic balance. A small but growing group of anti-slavery agitators in the North seized the occasion to raise

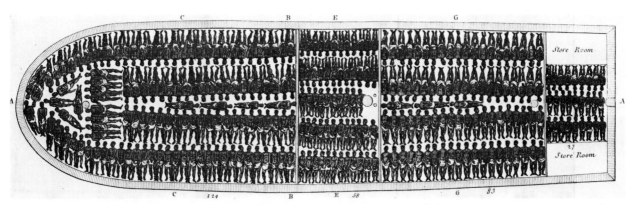

The "Middle Passage."   Human Cargo in the hold of a slave ship. (The Mariners Museum.)

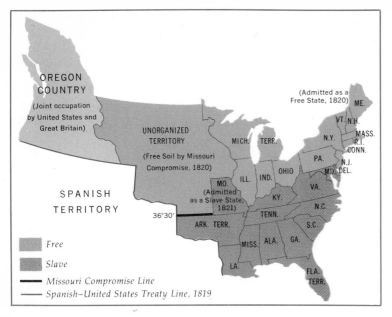

THE MISSOURI COMPROMISE AND
SLAVERY, 1820–1821
In the 1780s Thomas Jefferson had written of
slavery in America: "Indeed I tremble for my
country when I reflect that God is just; that his
justice cannot sleep forever; that . . . the Almighty has no attribute which can take side
with us in such a contest." Now, at the time of
the Missouri Compromise, Jefferson feared that
his worst forebodings were coming to pass. "I
considered it at once," he said of the Missouri
question, "as the knell of the Union."

Maine, which until then had been a part of Massachusetts, was admitted as a separate state. The
balance between North and South was thus kept
at twelve states each, and remained there for
fifteen years. Although Missouri was permitted to
retain slaves, all future bondage was prohibited
in the remainder of the Louisiana Purchase north
of the line of 36° 30′—the southern boundary of
Missouri.

This horse-trading adjustment was politically
evenhanded, though denounced by extremists on
each side as a "dirty bargain." Both North and
South yielded something; both gained something.
The South won the prize of Missouri as an unrestricted slave state. The North won the concession that Congress could forbid slavery in the
remaining territories. More gratifying to many
Northerners was the fact that the immense area
north of 36° 30′, except Missouri, was forever
closed to the blight of slavery. Yet the restriction
on future slavery in the territories was not unduly
offensive to the slaveowners, partly because the
northern prairie land did not seem adapted to
slave labor. Even so, a majority of Southern congressmen voted against the compromise.

Neither North nor South was acutely displeased,
although neither was completely happy. Fortunately, the Missouri Compromise lasted thirty-four
years—a vital formative period in the life of the
young Republic—and during that time it preserved
the shaky compact of the states. Yet the embittered dispute over slavery heralded the future
breakup of the Union. Ever after, the morality of
the South's "peculiar institution" was an issue
that could not be swept under the rug. The Missouri Compromise only ducked the question—it
did not resolve it. Sooner or later, Thomas Jefferson predicted, it will "burst on us as a tornado."

The Missouri dispute proved to be another
serious setback to nationalism, and a tremendous
stimulus to sectionalism—in the North, South, and
West. From this time forward the embattled South
began to develop a nationalism of its own—a kind
of sectional nationalism. Needing sectional reinforcements, it cast flirtatious eyes upon the ado-
lescent West, which in turn was seeking allies.

Hotheads in both the North and South, numbering only a tiny minority, clamored for secession or
a shooting showdown in 1820. But fortunately for
the Union, hostilities were postponed. With every
passing decade the North was becoming stronger
in population, wealth, industry, and transportation
—all of which added up to military strength.

Admittedly, the Missouri solution was a compromise—a partial surrender on both sides. Subsequent generations have tended to sneer at Henry Clay and the other architects of the settlement as weak men—"appeasers." Yet the fact should not be overlooked that compromise and statesmanship are often Siamese twins. In a free and peaceful association of once-sovereign states, no group of them could lord it over the others—that is, if they were all going to live together under the same roof. Without compromise there could have been no Constitution in 1787. Compromise made the Union in 1789; compromise saved the Union until 1860. When compromise broke down, the Union broke up.

The Missouri Compromise and the concurrent Panic of 1819 should have dimmed the political star of President Monroe. Certainly both unhappy events had a dampening effect on the Era of Good Feelings. But smooth-spoken James Monroe was so popular, and the Federalist opposition so weak, that in the presidential election of 1820 he received every electoral vote except one. Unanimity was an honor reserved for George Washington. Monroe, as it turned out, was the only President in American history to be re-elected after a term in which a major financial panic began.

John Marshall and Judicial Nationalism

Upsurging nationalism of the post-Ghent years, despite setbacks, was further reflected and strengthened by the Supreme Court.

The august tribunal was dominated by the tall, thin, and aggressive Chief Justice John Marshall, a "deathbed" Federalist appointee of John Adams' expiring administration. He had served at Valley Forge during the Revolution, and while suffering from cold and hunger had been painfully impressed with the drawbacks of feeble central authority. Before Marshall mounted the Supreme Bench in 1801, the judiciary had been the weakest and most timid of the three arms of the federal government. But he boldly asserted the doctrine of judicial review of congressional legislation in the case of *Marbury* v. *Madison* (1803).* And long before the end of his thirty-four years of service, he had made the judiciary, in some respects, the strongest branch of the national government.

Marshall, whose formal legal schooling had lasted only six weeks, was a judicial statesman rather than a strictly impartial judge. He examined a case through the colored lenses of his Federalist philosophy, and undertook to find legal precedents to support his Hamiltonian preconceptions. Sure of his ground, he wrote some of his most important decisions even before the lawyers had concluded their arguments.

In the vain hope of offsetting Marshall's Federalism, President Jefferson and his successors appointed Republicans to the Supreme Court. But

*See p. 170.

John Marshall (1755–1835). Born in a log cabin on the Virginia frontier, he attended law lectures for only a few months at the college of William and Mary—his only formal education. (National Portrait Gallery, Smithsonian Institution, Washington, D.C.)

by this time many Republicans had come to accept the Federalist ideal of a strong central government, and the masterful Marshall found it easy to lead his colleagues the rest of the way. The Jeffersonians raged, while Jefferson himself privately condemned the "twistifications" of his cousin, "the crafty chief judge." But Marshall pushed ahead inflexibly on his Federalist course, though bending slightly in his final years before the rising popular demands for a more democratic control of government.

For over three decades, the ghost of Alexander Hamilton spoke through the lanky, black-robed judge. As a shaper of the Constitution in the direction of a more potent central government, Marshall ranks as the foremost of the Molding Fathers. As a wealthy businessman and land speculator, he instinctively shared Hamilton's preference for the propertied class. As a Virginia aristocrat, he deplored democratic excesses, and opposed manhood suffrage and the rule of the unwashed masses.

The Supreme Court Curbs States' Rights

One group of Marshall's decisions—perhaps the most famous—resulted in bolstering the power of the federal government at the expense of the states. A notable case in this category was *McCulloch* v. *Maryland* (1819). The suit involved an attempt by the state of Maryland to destroy a branch of the Bank of the United States by imposing a tax on its notes. John Marshall, speaking for the Court, declared the Bank constitutional by invoking the Hamiltonian doctrine of implied powers (see p. 146). At the same time, he strengthened federal authority and slapped at state infringements when he denied the right of Maryland to tax the Bank. With ringing emphasis, he affirmed "that the power to tax involves the power to destroy," and "that a power to create implies a power to preserve."

In 1819, he gave the doctrine of "loose construction" its most famous formulation. The Constitution, he said, derived from the consent of the people and thus permitted the government to act for

their benefit. He further argued that the Constitution was "intended to endure for ages to come and, consequently, to be adapted to the various crises of human affairs." Finally, he declared: "Let the end be legitimate, let it be within the scope of the Constitution, and all means which are appropriate, which are plainly adapted to that end, which are not prohibited, but consist with the letter and spirit of the Constitution, are constitutional."

Two years later (1821) the case of *Cohens* v. *Virginia* gave Marshall one of his greatest opportunities. The Cohens, found guilty by the Virginia courts of illegally selling lottery tickets, appealed to the highest tribunal. Virginia won, in that the conviction of the Cohens was upheld. But she lost, in that Marshall resoundingly asserted the right of the Supreme Court to review the decisions of the state supreme courts in all questions involving powers of the federal government. The states'-rights people were aghast.

Hardly less significant in Marshall's career was the celebrated "steamboat case," *Gibbons* v. *Ogden* (1824). The suit grew out of an attempt by the state of New York to grant to a private concern a monopoly of waterborne commerce between New York and New Jersey. Marshall sternly reminded the upstart state that the Constitution conferred on Congress alone the control of interstate commerce (see Art. I, Sec. VIII, para. 3). He thus struck another blow at states' rights, while upholding the sovereign powers of the federal government. Interstate streams were thus cleared of this judicial snag, while the departed spirit of Hamilton may have applauded.

Judicial Dikes Against Democratic Excesses

Another sheaf of Marshall's decisions bolstered judicial barriers against democratic or demagogic attacks on property rights.

The notorious case of *Fletcher* v. *Peck* (1810) arose when a Georgia legislature, swayed by bribery, granted 35 million acres in the Yazoo River country (Mississippi) to private speculators. The next legislature, yielding to an angry public outcry,

Daniel Webster (1782–1852). Premier orator and states-man, he served many years in both Houses of Congress, and also as secretary of state. Often regarded as presidential timber, he was somewhat handicapped by an overfondness for good food and drink, and was often in financial difficulties. His devotion to the Union was inflexible. "One country, one constitution, and one destiny," he declaimed in 1837. (The Metropolitan Museum of Art, Gift of I. N. Phelps Stokes, Edward S. Hawes, Alice Mary Hawes, Marion Augusta Hawes, 1937)

most distinguished alumnus, Daniel Webster ('01). The "Godlike Daniel" reportedly pulled out all the stops of his tear-inducing eloquence when he declaimed, "It is, sir, as I have said, a small college. And yet there are those who love it."

Marshall needed no dramatics in the Dartmouth case. He put the states firmly in their place when he ruled that the original charter must stand. It was a contract—and the Constitution protected contracts against state encroachments. The Dartmouth decision had the fortunate effect of safeguarding business enterprise from domination by the states. But it had the unfortunate effect of creating a precedent which enabled chartered corporations, in later years, to escape the handcuffs of needed public control.

If John Marshall was a Molding Father of the Constitution, Daniel Webster was an Expounding Father. Time and again he left his seat in the Senate, stepped downstairs, and there expounded his federalistic and nationalistic philosophy before the Supreme Bench. The eminent chief justice, so Webster reported, approvingly drank in the familiar arguments as a baby sucks in its mother's milk. The two men dovetailed with each other. Webster's classic speeches in the Senate, challenging states' rights and nullification, were largely repetitions of the arguments that he had earlier presented before a sympathetic Supreme Court.

During Marshall's judicial reign, manhood suffrage was flowering and America was veering toward stronger popular control. The chief justice stoutly held the judicial dike against these upwashing democratic waves. Almost singlehandedly, he shaped the Constitution along conservative, centralizing lines that ran somewhat counter to the new spirit of the century.

Marshall's decisions are felt even today. In this sense his nationalism was the most tenaciously enduring of the era. Even after the masses had won control under President Andrew Jackson, they could not successfully assault the highest towers of the judicial fortress. While buttressing the federal union and nascent nationalism, Marshall checked the excesses of popularly elected state legislatures, and thus stabilized business.

canceled the crooked transaction. But the Supreme Court, with Marshall presiding, decreed that the legislative grant was a contract (even though fraudulently secured), and that the Constitution forbids state laws "impairing" contracts (Art. I, Sec. X, para. 1). The decision is perhaps most noteworthy as further protecting property rights against popular pressures. It is also one of the earliest clear assertions of the right of the Court to invalidate state laws conflicting with the federal Constitution.

A similar principle was upheld in the case of *Dartmouth College* v. *Woodward* (1819), perhaps the best-remembered of Marshall's decisions. The college had been granted a charter by King George III in 1769, but the democratic New Hampshire state legislature had seen fit to change it. Dartmouth appealed the case, employing as counsel its

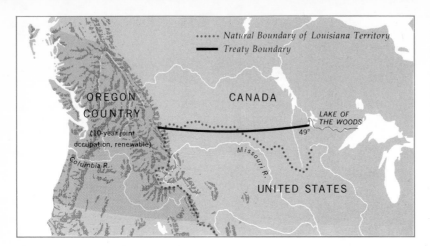

U.S.–BRITISH BOUNDARY SETTLEMENT, 1818

Note that the United States gained considerable territory by securing a treaty boundary rather than the natural boundary of the Missouri River watershed. The line of 49° was extended westward to the Pacific Ocean under the Treaty of 1846 with Britain (see p. 266).

Through him the conservative Hamiltonians triumphed from the tomb.

British Agreements and Spanish Friction

The yeasty nationalism of the years after the War of 1812 was likewise reflected in the shaping of foreign policy. To this end, the nationalistic President Monroe teamed with his nationalistic secretary of state, John Quincy Adams, the cold and scholarly son of the frosty and bookish ex-President. The younger Adams, a statesman of the first rank, happily rose above the ingrown Federalist sectionalism of his native New England and proved to be one of the great secretaries of state.

To its credit, the Monroe administration succeeded in negotiating with England the much underrated Treaty of 1818. This multi-sided agreement disposed of some of the unfinished business swept under the peace table at Ghent. For one thing, the Newfoundland fisheries quarrel had continued to bob up, and the new pact achieved a temporary settlement. The Americans were permitted to share again coveted fishing privileges with their Canadian cousins—privileges granted in 1783, and presumably ended by the War of 1812. In addition, the treaty makers agreed to define the vague northern limits of Louisiana, which henceforth would run along the 49th parallel to the Rocky ("Stony") Mountains.

The British-American negotiators of 1818 also discussed the possibility of running the same dividing line on to the Pacific. But agreement proved impossible. The Treaty of 1818 consequently provided for a ten-year joint occupation of the untamed Oregon Country, without surrender of the rights or claims of either America or Britain. With time on the side of an awesomely growing United States, the postponement of a decision foreshadowed a final settlement favorable to American demands.

To the south lay semi-tropical Spanish Florida, thrust like a giant thumb into the Gulf of Mexico. This coveted peninsula, many believed, occupied a part of the map which geography and Providence had destined for the United States. Already

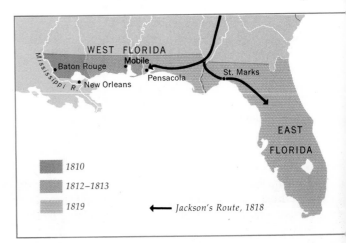

ACQUIRING THE FLORIDAS, 1810–1819

Americans had nibbled at West Florida, a region claimed by the federal government, rather flimsily, under the blanket of the Louisiana Purchase. Uninvited American settlers had moved into the area, and in 1810 rose to overthrow the hated Spanish flag. Congress formally ratified this grab in 1812 and added an even larger chunk to the east. During the War of 1812 with Britain (Spain's ally), a small American army seized the Mobile region, which the United States had already embraced (on paper). But the bulk of Florida remained, tauntingly, under Spain's flag.

When an epidemic of revolutions broke out in South America, Spain was forced to denude Florida of troops to fight the rebels. A chaotic situation rapidly developed in the swampy peninsula. Bands of Indians, runaway slaves, and white outcasts poured across the border into American territory, burning and scalping, and then fled to safety behind the surveyor's line.

General Andrew Jackson, idol of the West and scourge of the Indians, reappeared in 1817. The Monroe administration formally commissioned him to punish the Indians and, if necessary, to pursue them into Florida. But he was to respect all posts under the Spanish flag.

Early in 1818 Jackson swept across the Florida border with all the fury of an avenging angel. He hanged two Indian chiefs without ceremony and, after hasty military trials, executed two British subjects for assisting the Indians. He also seized the two most important Spanish posts in the area, St. Marks and then Pensacola, where he deposed the Spanish governor, who was lucky enough to escape Jackson's jerking noose.

Acquiring Florida from Spain

Jackson had clearly exceeded his instructions from Washington, unclear though they may have been. By dishonoring the Spanish flag, he had been guilty of a hostile act. By putting to death two British subjects who had a better right than he to be in Florida, he had caused a vengeful outcry for war to rise from British hotheads. With

Warrior Andrew Jackson, 1814. A self-taught and popularly elected major-general of the militia, Andrew Jackson became a major-general of the U.S. army in 1814. He was noted for his stern discipline, iron will ("Old Hickory"), and good luck.

difficulty a sane London government quieted the jingoes.

President Monroe in alarm consulted his Cabinet. Its members were for disavowing or disciplining the overzealous Jackson—all except the lone wolf John Quincy Adams, who refused to howl with the pack. An ardent patriot and nationalist, the flinty New Englander finally won the others over to his point of view. Far from apologizing, he took the offensive and emphatically informed Spain that she had violated the Spanish-American Treaty of 1795 by not suppressing the outlaws of Florida. He then insisted that the alternatives were for the Spaniards to control the area (a task which they admitted was impossible) or cede it to the

United States (a course which was galling to their pride).

Again Spain's distresses, both at home and in her rebellious Latin American colonies, operated to America's advantage. The Spaniards perceived that they were going to lose Florida anyhow. They wisely decided to dispose of the alligator-infested area while they could get something for it, rather than lose it after a humiliating and costly war.

The Florida Purchase Treaty of 1819, so called, was mislabeled. It involved much more than Florida. The western boundary of the Louisiana territory, hitherto vague, was made to zigzag along the Rockies to the 42nd parallel. The line then turned due west to the Pacific, to divide Oregon from Spanish holdings. Texas, although claimed by the United States under the elastic blanket of the Louisiana Purchase, was excluded from American jurisdiction. The vast plains of Texas were more important to Spain than was fast-slipping Florida; Florida was more immediately important to the United States. Texas could come later—and did.

In 1819 Spain, in effect, ceded Florida and her shadowy rights to Oregon in exchange for America's dubious pretensions to Texas. The United States also agreed to assume claims for damages to the extent of $5 million—seemingly uncollectible claims which American citizens had filed against the Spanish government. Spain lost Florida, but saved face.

When the Spanish-American pact of 1819 was signed, it seemed like a fair bargain, even though Western-minded American patriots decried the so-called surrender of Texas. By one stroke of the pen, the United States ended protracted friction with Spain, rounded out its continental domain, and gave another boost to swelling national pride.

The Menace of Monarchy in America

After the Napoleonic nightmare, the rethroned autocrats of Europe banded together in a kind of monarchical protective association. Determined

The successful invasion of Spain, so Secretary of State Adams recorded in his diary, caused panic in official Washington: "I find him [President Monroe] . . . alarmed, far beyond anything that I could have conceived possible, with the fear that the Holy Alliance [of European powers] are about to restore immediately all South America to Spain."

to restore the good old days, they undertook to stamp out the democratic tendencies that had sprouted from soil richly manured by the ideals of the French Revolution. The world must be made safe *from* democracy.

The crowned despots acted promptly. With complete ruthlessness, they smothered the embers of rebellion in Italy (1821) and in Spain (1823). According to the European rumor-factory, they were also gazing across the Atlantic. Russia, Austria, Prussia, and France, acting in partnership, would presumably send powerful fleets and armies to the revolted colonies of Spanish America, and there restore the autocratic Spanish King to his ancestral domains.

Many Americans were alarmed. Sympathetic to democratic revolutions everywhere, they had cheered when the Latin American republics rose from the ruins of monarchy. Americans feared that if the European powers intervened in the New World, the cause of republicanism would suffer irreparable harm. The physical security of the United States—the Mother Lode of democracy —would be endangered by the proximity of powerful and unfriendly forces.

The southward push of the Russian Bear, from the chill region now known as Alaska, had already publicized the menace of monarchy to North America. In 1821 the Czar of Russia issued a decree extending Russian jurisdiction over 100 miles (161 kilometers) of the open sea down to the line of 51°, an area which embraced most of the

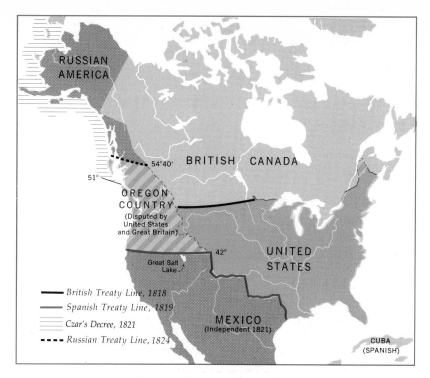

coast of present-day British Columbia. The energetic Russians had already established trading posts almost as far south as the entrance to San Francisco Bay, and the fear prevailed in the United States that they were planning to cut the Republic off from California, its prospective window on the Pacific.

Great Britain, still Mistress of the Seas, was now beginning to play a lone-hand role on the complicated international stage. In particular, she recoiled from joining hands with the Continental European powers in crushing the newly won liberties of the Spanish-Americans. These revolutionists had thrown open their monopoly-bound ports to outside trade, and British shippers, as well as Americans, had found the profits sweet.

Accordingly, in August 1823, George Canning, the haughty British foreign secretary, approached the American minister in London with a startling proposition. Would not the United States join with Britain in a joint declaration, specifically warning the European despots to keep their harsh hands off the Latin American republics? The American minister, lacking instructions, referred this fateful scheme to his superiors in Washington.

Mr. Monroe and His Doctrine

Reactions in America to the Canning proposal varied. The intimate advisers of President Monroe, including the aged Jefferson and Madison, recommended that the Republic lock arms with the hitherto distrusted Mother Country. The one notable exception was again the lone-wolf nationalist, Secretary Adams, who was hardheaded enough to beware of Britons bearing gifts. Why should the lordly British, with the mightiest navy afloat, need America as an ally—an America which had neither naval nor military strength? Such a union, argued Adams, was undignified—like a tiny American "cockboat" sailing "in the wake of the British man-of-war."

Adams, ever alert, thought that he detected the joker in the Canning proposal. The British feared that the aggressive Yankee would one day seize Spanish territory in the Americas—perhaps Cuba—

which would jeopardize England's possessions in the Caribbean. If Canning could seduce the United States into joining with him in support of the territorial integrity of the New World, America's own hands would be morally tied.

A self-denying alliance with Britain would not only hamper American expansion, concluded Adams, but it was unnecessary. He had good reason to suspect that the European powers had not agreed upon any definite plans for invading the Americas. In any event, the British navy would not permit hostile fleets to come, because the South American markets had to be kept open at all costs for English merchants. It was presumably safe for Uncle Sam, behind the protective wooden petticoats of the British navy, to blow a defiant, nationalistic blast at all Europe. The distresses of the Old World again set the stage for another American diplomatic coup.

The Monroe Doctrine was born late in 1823, when the nationalistic Adams won the nationalistic Monroe over to his way of thinking. The President, in his regular annual message to Congress of December 2, 1823, incorporated a stern warning to the European powers. Its two basic features were (1) non-colonization and (2) non-intervention.

Monroe first directed his verbal blast primarily at the lumbering Russian Bear in the Northwest. With emphatic tones he proclaimed, in effect, that the era of colonization in the Americas had ended, and that henceforth there would be a permanently closed season. What the great powers had they might keep, but neither they nor any other Old World powers could seize or otherwise acquire more. This lofty declaration was later resented by those nations, notably Germany and Italy, that were not unified and hence unable to take out colonial hunting licenses until late in the century.

At the same time Monroe sounded a trumpet blast against foreign intervention. He was clearly concerned with regions to the south, where fears were felt for the newly fledged Spanish-American republics. He bluntly warned the crowned heads of Europe to keep their hated monarchical systems out of this hemisphere. For its part, the

Czar Alexander I. The Russian leader of European monarchs, he was an inspirer of the Monroe Doctrine.

United States would not intervene in the war that the Greeks were then fighting against the Turks for their independence.

Monroe's Dictum Abroad

Monroe's ringing declaration quickened the patriotic pulse of nationalistic young America. The American people were thrilled, even though they had no effective army or navy, to shake their collective fists at all the European despots and loudly warn them to stay away. While gratifying national pride and striking a blow for democratic rule, Monroe was also striking a blow for the "Almighty Dollar," as represented by the freshly opened Latin American markets.

Reactions in England were mixed. The British press, likewise savoring the juicy Latin American markets, was generally favorable to Monroe's forceful warning. But Canning was irked, for he perceived that the Monroe Doctrine was aimed at possible land-grabbing by Britain, as well as by Europe. "Hands off" applied to all outside powers, including proud Britain.

The ermined monarchs of Europe were angered. Having resented the incendiary American experiment from the beginning, they were now deeply offended by Monroe's high-flown pronouncement—all the more so because of the gulf between America's loud pretensions and her weak military strength. But though offended by the upstart

IDIIDIIDIIDIIDIIDIIDIIDIIDIIDIIDIIDIIDIIDIIDI

> Prince Metternich, the Austrian chancellor, wrote bitterly of the "dangerous" new manifesto with its "unprovoked attacks . . . indecent declarations . . . evil doctrines and pernicious examples."

IDIIDIIDIIDIIDIIDIIDIIDIIDIIDIIDIIDIIDIIDIIDI

Yankee, the European powers found their hands tied, and their frustration increased their annoyance. Even if they had worked out plans for invading the Americas, they would have been helpless before the booming broadsides of the British navy.

Monroe's solemn warning, when issued, made little splash in the newly hatched republics to the south. Anyone could see that Uncle Sam was only secondarily concerned about his neighbors, because he was primarily concerned about defending himself against future invasion. Only a relatively few upper-class Latin Americans knew of the message, and they generally recognized that the British navy—not the paper pronouncement of James Monroe—stood between them and a hostile Europe.

In truth, Monroe's message actually did not have much contemporary significance. Americans applauded it, and then forgot it as they turned

Ruins of One of the Bastions at Russia's Fort Ross (c. 1890). Established just north of San Francisco Bay in 1811 without Spain's permission, this trading post seemed to be evidence of Russia's imperialistic ambitions on America's future Pacific Coast.

back to such activities as felling trees and Indians. Not until 1845 did President Polk revive it, and not until mid-century did it become an important national dogma.

The new doctrine was not even necessary, in a narrow sense, when given to the world. Secretary Adams, in firm diplomatic notes, had already warned Russia against trespassing on the Northwest Coast. Even before Monroe's stiff message, the Czar had decided to retreat. This he formally did in the Russo-American Treaty of 1824, which fixed his southernmost limits at the line of 54° 40'—the present southern tip of the Alaska panhandle.

Danger of an invasion of Latin America by the European powers was not imminent in 1823. But this does not mean that the monarchs, if unhampered, could not have drawn up a blueprint for conquest. Aside from the British navy, they were dissuaded from making incursions in later years by other attractions and deterrents. Among attractions were the richer and easier pickings of Asia and Africa; among deterrents was the growing strength of the United States and its neighbors.

Monroe's Self-Defense Doctrine in Retrospect

The Monroe Doctrine might more accurately have been called the Self-Defense Doctrine. President Monroe was concerned basically with the security of his own country—not of Latin America. The United States has never willingly permitted a powerful foreign nation to secure a foothold near its strategic Caribbean vitals. Yet in the absence of the British navy or other allies, the strength of the Monroe Doctrine has never been greater than America's power to eject the trespasser. The doctrine, as often noted, was just as big as the nation's armed forces—and no bigger. But attaching Monroe's name to the Self-Defense Doctrine has given it the prestige that comes from a distinguished personage.

Monroe and Adams must share about equally the credit for the authorship of the so-called Monroe Doctrine. But its basic principles, in one form or another, had been set forth earlier by Washington, Jefferson, Hamilton, and others. Monroe and Adams merely collected and codified existing ideas, giving them a new emphasis and slant.

The Monroe Doctrine has had a long career of ups and downs. It was never law—domestic or international. It was not, technically speaking, a pledge or an agreement. It was merely a simple, personalized statement of the policy of President Monroe. What one President says, another may unsay. And Monroe's successors have ignored, revived, distorted, or expanded the original version, chiefly by adding interpretations. Like ivy on a tree, it has grown with America's growth.

But the Monroe Doctrine in 1823 was largely an expression of the post-1812 nationalism energizing the United States. Although directed at a specific menace in 1823, and hence a kind of period piece, the doctrine proved to be the most famous of all the long-lived offspring of that nationalism. While giving vent to a spirit of patriotism, it simultaneously deepened the illusion of isolationism. Many Americans falsely concluded, then and later, that the Republic was in fact isolated from European dangers simply because it wanted to be, and because, in a nationalistic outburst, Monroe had publicly warned the Old World powers to stay away.

VARYING VIEWPOINTS

The Era of Good Feelings, not surprisingly, has generated little ill feeling among historians. They generally agree in seeing the period not in terms of conflict, but of consolidation. There were then few irreconcilable controversies, but rather a remarkable consensus on laying the new nation's institutional base. In effect, the era set up a political program for the future; defined the power of the Supreme Court and its relation to the other branches of government; stabilized national boundaries; established basic elements of foreign policy in the Monroe Doctrine; and drew up the battle lines on the explosive issues of the tariff and, especially, slavery.

SELECT READINGS

An excellent introduction is George Dangerfield, *The Awakening of American Nationalism, 1815–1828* (1965), which supplements his *The Era of Good Feelings* (1952). Consult also M. N. Rothbard, *The Panic of 1819* (1962); Glover Moore, *The Missouri Controversy, 1819–1821* (1953); E. S. Corwin, *John Marshall and the Constitution* (1919); and A. J. Beveridge, *The Life of John Marshall* (4 vols., 1916–1919). P. Miller, *The Life of the Mind in America* (1965), contains suggestive insights on legal thought and the role of the legal profession in the Marshall era. This and other topics are astutely placed in context by Lawrence Friedman, *A History of American Law* (1973). On the Monroe Doctrine the best single volume is Dexter Perkins, *A History of the Monroe Doctrine* (new ed., 1955). More recently, E. R. May has somewhat unconvincingly tied the doctrine to domestic politics, especially the impending election of 1824, in *The Making of the Monroe Doctrine* (1975). Related to the doctrine is J. A. Logan, Jr., *No Transfer: An American Security Principle* (1961). See also Harry Ammon, *James Monroe: The Quest for National Identity* (1971). On Calhoun consult M. L. Coit, *John C. Calhoun* (1950), and C. M. Wiltse's more detailed *John C. Calhoun, Nationalist, 1782–1828* (1944). See also G. M. Capers, *John C. Calhoun, Opportunist* (1960); R. N. Current, *John C. Calhoun* (1963); and S. F. Bemis, *John Quincy Adams and the Foundations of American Foreign Policy* (1949).

13

The Rise of Jacksonian Democracy

*The most disagreeable duty I have to perform is
the removals, and appointments to office. . . .
You will see from the public journals we have
begun reform, and that we are trying to cleans[e]
the Augean stables, and expose to view the corruption of some of the agents of the late administration.*

ANDREW JACKSON, 1829

The Spread of Manhood Suffrage

Democracy was something of a taint in the days of
the Federalist aristocrats. Martha Washington
(Mrs. George Washington), after a presidential
reception, was shocked to find a greasy smear on
the wallpaper, left there, she was sure, by an uninvited "filthy democrat."

But by the 1820s and 1830s, if not before, aristocracy was becoming a taint, and democracy was
becoming respectable. Lucky indeed was the aspiring politician who could boast of birth in a log
cabin. In 1840 Daniel Webster publicly apologized
for not being able to claim so lowly a birthplace,
though quickly adding that his brothers could.

The New Democracy, so called, was based on manhood suffrage rather than on the old property qualifications. Snobbish bigwigs, unhappy over the change, referred sneeringly to "coonskin congressmen" and to the enfranchised "bipeds of the forest." To them, the tyranny of King Numbers was no less offensive than that of King George.

The frontier state of Vermont, admitted in 1791, was the first to place the ballot in the hands of all adult white males. This trend continued, notably in the West, where land was so easily obtained as to render almost meaningless the old property qualifications. Property tests for office holding were also widely abolished, and even judges were now being popularly elected. The South trailed other regions in giving up property requirements.

Government *by* the masses—instead of government *of* the masses *by* the upper classes—was finally introduced at the national level in the days of Andrew Jackson. The common man was at last coming into his own: the sturdy American who donned plain trousers rather than silver-buckled knee breeches, who besported a plain haircut and a coonskin cap rather than an ornate wig, and who wore no man's collar, often not even one of his own. Instead of the old divine right of kings, America was now witnessing the divine right of the people.

The Reign of King Numbers

Debasement of the political tone was one nasty by-product of the New Democracy, commonly called Jacksonian democracy. A statesman was unable to elevate the unlettered masses to his own intellectual level. Rather, the masses dragged the politician down to the level of their own emotions and prejudices. Mudslinging frequently proved more effective than a sober discussion of issues. Candidates for office also made increasing use of banners, badges, parades, barbecues, free drinks, and baby-kissing. Yet competition for public favor did have the virtue of "bringing out the vote."

Successful politicians were now forced to unbend and curry favor with the voting masses.

David Crockett (1786–1836).   A semi-literate Tennesseean, he failed at farming but won distinction as a rifleman, soldier, scout, humorist, and three-time congressman. Rejected in politics, he left Tennessee to fight for Texas against the Mexicans and fell, bullet riddled, in the final assault on the Alamo.

Fatally handicapped was the candidate who appeared to be too clean, too well-dressed, too grammatical, too high-browishly intellectual, too conspicuously fit. The Western belief was spreading that a man was well qualified for high office if he was a superior militia commander or a victorious Indian fighter, like Andrew Jackson, or even an outstanding hunter. The semi-literate Davy Crockett was elected to the legislature of Tennessee, mainly on the basis of his prowess with the rifle. Later he killed 105 bears in a single season, and his constituents began to talk of running him for the presidency.

With the emergence of "nose-counting" democracy, the masses were demanding and securing a fuller measure of popular control. Jeffersonian democracy had proclaimed that the people should be governed as little as possible; Jacksonian democracy argued that the people might govern as much as they liked. Members of the Electoral College, to an increasing degree, were being chosen directly by the people, rather than by state legislatures. Presidential nominations by a congressional caucus, meeting secretly, were no longer in good odor. This procedure was now regarded as furtive, aristocratic, and subversive of good government. The delicate checks and balances among the three federal branches were weakened when the President was indirectly indebted to Congress for his exalted office.

New and more democratic methods of nominating presidential candidates would have to be found. In 1824 the voters, crying "The People Must Be Heard" and "Down with King Caucus," turned against the candidate (Crawford) who had been selected by the congressional clique. For a brief period nominations were made by some of the state legislatures. But these did not seem democratic either, and in 1831 the first of the circuslike national nominating conventions was held. Here the people appeared to exercise a higher degree of direct control, though their will was often thwarted by paunchy bosses in smoke-filled rooms.

Yet manhood suffrage, on balance, conferred incalculable benefits. It enhanced the dignity of the common man; and his greater personal responsibility led to a greater flowering of his talents. The national spirit was further unshackled for marvelous achievements. If the masses made mistakes, they made them themselves and were not the victims of aristocratic domination. If at times they stumbled, they stumbled forward.

The Adams-Clay "Corrupt" Bargaining

The woods were full of presidential timber in 1824. Four candidates towered above the others: Andrew Jackson of Tennessee, the tall, silver-maned, and hollow-cheeked "Old Hero" of New Orleans; Henry Clay of Kentucky, the gamey and gallant "Harry of the West"; William H. Crawford of Georgia, a giant of a man, able though ailing; and John Quincy Adams of Massachusetts, highly intelligent, experienced, and aloof.

All four rivals had much in common. They were all outstanding figures; they were all regarded as

Election of 1824

Candidates	Electoral Vote	Popular Vote	Popular Percentage
Jackson	99	153,544	42.16%
Adams	84	108,740	31.89
Crawford	41	46,618	12.95
Clay	37	47,136	12.99

strong nationalists; and they were all presumed to have similar views on such active issues as the tariff and internal improvements. A colorful note was injected when "Hickory Boys" whooped it up for "Old Hickory" Jackson.

The results of the noisy campaign were interesting but confusing. Jackson, the war hero, clearly had the strongest personal appeal, especially in the West. He polled almost as many popular votes as his next two rivals combined, but he failed to win a majority of the electoral vote. In such a deadlock the House of Representatives, as directed by the 12th Amendment (see Appendix), must choose among the top three candidates. Clay was thus eliminated, yet he still presided over the very chamber that had to pick the winner. Since he enjoyed all the influence of a popular speaker of the House, he was in a position to throw the election to the candidate of his choice.

Clay reached his fateful decision by a process of elimination. Crawford, recently felled by a paralytic stroke, was out of the picture. Clay hated the "military chieftain" Jackson, who in turn bitterly resented Clay's public denunciation of his Florida foray in 1818. The only candidate left was the puritanical Adams, with whom Clay—a free-living gambler and duelist—had never established cordial personal relations. But the two men had much in common politically: both were fervid nationalists and advocates of the American System. Shortly before the final balloting in the House, Clay met privately with Adams and assured him of his support.

Decision day came early in 1825. The House of Representatives met amid tense excitement, with sick members being carried in on stretchers. On the first ballot, thanks largely to Clay's behind-the-scenes influence, Adams was elected President. A few days later, the victor announced that Henry Clay would be the new secretary of state.

The secretaryship of state was then the prize plum, even more so than today. Three of the four preceding secretaries had reached the presidency, and the high Cabinet office was regarded as an almost certain runway to the White House. By allegedly dangling the secretaryship as a bribe before Clay, Adams, the second choice of the people, apparently defeated the first choice of the people, Andrew Jackson.

Masses of angered Jacksonians, most of them common folk, raised a roar of protest against the "Corrupt Bargain." The clamor continued for nearly four years. Jackson condemned Clay as the "Judas of the West," and John Randolph of Virginia publicly assailed the alliance between "the Puritan [Adams] and the black-leg [Clay]." Randolph also said of Clay, "He shines and stinks like rotten mackerel by moonlight." Clay, outraged, challenged Randolph to a duel, the bloodless outcome of which proved nothing, except perhaps shaky nerves and poor marksmanship.

No positive evidence has yet been unearthed to prove that Adams and Clay entered into a formal bargain, corrupt or otherwise. But appear-

---

Suspicions of a "Corrupt Bargain" have been strengthened by entries in Adams' diary. On January 1, 1825, after a public dinner, we find: "He [Clay] told me [in a whisper] that he should be glad to have with me soon some confidential conversation upon public affairs. I said I should be happy to have it whenever it might suit his convenience." The diary entry for January 9 reads in part: "Mr. Clay came at six, and spent the evening with me in a long conversation explanatory of the past and prospective of the future." Exactly a month later, with Clay's backing, Adams was elected.

---

ances were so damning as to render denials unconvincing. Even if a bargain had been struck, it was not necessarily corrupt, for "deals" of a similar nature are the stock-in-trade of politicians. But this "bargain" differed from others in its apparent flouting of the popular will by both Adams and Clay. Both men erred, the one by offering the post in circumstances sure to arouse suspicion, the other by accepting it. The best that can be said of them is that neither avoided the appearance of evil.

A Puritan Misfit in the Presidential Chair

John Quincy Adams was a chip off the old family glacier. Short (5 feet 7 inches; 1.7 meters), thickset, and billiard-bald, he was even more frigidly austere than his presidential father, John Adams. Shunning people, he often went for early morning swims, sometimes stark naked, in the then pure Potomac River. Essentially a closeted thinker rather than a politician, he was irritable, sarcastic, and tactless. Yet few men have ever come to the presidency with a more brilliant record in statecraft, especially in foreign affairs. He ranks as one of the most successful secretaries of state, yet one of the least successful Presidents.

A man of puritanical honor, Adams entered upon his four-year "sentence" in the White House smarting under charges of "bargain," "corruption," and "usurpation." Fewer than one-third of the voters had voted for him. As the first "minority President," he would have found it difficult to win popular support even under the most favorable conditions. Possessing almost none of the arts of the politician, he had achieved high office by commanding respect rather than by courting popularity. In an earlier era, an aloof John Adams could win the votes of propertied men by sheer ability. But with the raw New Democracy in the driver's seat, his cold-fish son could hardly hope for success at the polls.

Political spoilsmen annoyed Adams. Whether through high-mindedness or ineptitude, he re-

President John Quincy Adams (1767–1848). Adams wrote in his dairy, in June 1819, nearly six years before becoming President, "I am a man of reserved, cold, austere, and forbidding manners: my political adversaries say, a gloomy misanthropist, and my personal enemies, an unsocial savage."

solutely declined to oust efficient officeholders in order to create vacancies for political supporters. During his entire administration he removed only twelve public servants from the federal payroll. Such stubbornness caused countless Adams men to throw up their hands in despair. If the President would not reward party workers with political plums, why should they labor to keep him in office?

Adams' nationalistic views involved him in further woes. The old Jeffersonian Republican party was breaking into fragments, most of which tended to coalesce around a common hatred of the Adams-Clay partnership. The flinty President refused to recognize that the popular tide was turning away from the post-Ghent nationalism toward states' rights and sectionalism. Confirmed nationalist that he was, Adams urged upon Congress in his first annual message the construction of roads and canals. He renewed George Washington's proposal for a national university, and

went so far as to advocate federal support for an astronomical observatory, similar to Europe's more than 130 "lighthouses of the skies."

The public reaction to some of these proposals was prompt and unfavorable. To many workaday Americans grubbing out stumps, astronomical observatories seemed like a scandalous waste of public funds. The South in particular bristled up. If the federal government should take on such heavy financial burdens, it would have to continue the hated tariff duties. If it could meddle in local concerns like education and roads, it might even try to lay its hand on the "peculiar institution" of black slavery.

Adams' land policy likewise antagonized the Westerners. They clamored for wide-open expansion, and were angered by the President's well-meaning attempts to curb feverish speculation in the public domain. The fate of the Cherokee Indians, who were about to be evicted from their holdings in Georgia, generated additional bitterness. Ruggedly honest Adams, in attempting to deal fairly with the friendless Indians, further offended the West in general and the state of Georgia in particular. The governor, who threatened a resort to arms, successfully resisted the efforts of the Washington government to interpose federal authority on behalf of the Indians. Another fateful chapter was thus written in the nullification of the national will.

Adams Fumbles Foreign Affairs

If Adams was inept politically, he was deft diplomatically, and in foreign affairs he was expected to shine. But he quickly ran afoul of his old British adversary, George Canning. The clever foreign secretary, still smarting from Secretary Adams' rebuff at the time of the Monroe Doctrine, apparently took delight in thwarting his antagonist at every turn.

Trade with the British West Indies continued to be a thorny issue. Ever since the United States had broken away from the empire in 1776, this rich traffic had been officially closed, or subjected

IOI

The year after Secretary of State Adams stole a march on Foreign Secretary Canning by helping to frame the Monroe Doctrine, aimed in part at British influence in Latin America, the British government recognized the Spanish-American republics. Canning privately gloated, "The deed is done, the nail is driven, Spanish America is free; and if we do not mismanage our affairs badly, *she is English*." He was speaking, of course, of commercial ascendancy.

IOIOIOIOIOIOIOIOIOIOIOIOIOIOIOIOIOIOIOIOIOIOIOI

to annoying restrictions. When President Adams made a somewhat tactless attempt to induce the London government to reopen trade in 1826, Canning administered a stinging rebuff.

Another bitter cup was the Panama Congress of 1826. This assemblage of the American republics was summoned by Simón Bolívar, leading hero of the South American wars for independence. Its major purpose was to discuss common problems of defense and peaceful intercourse. Secretary Clay, a passionate pioneer of Pan-Americanism, eagerly accepted the invitation on behalf of the United States. President Adams thereupon appointed two delegates. But at the same time he unnecessarily and unwisely sought confirmation by the Senate, as well as expense money from Congress.

The ensuing debate in Congress was both windy and ill-tempered. Foes of Adams and Clay united to denounce the Panama scheme, while isolationists decried the dangers of foreign entrapments. The South, with an eye to its slave problem, was sensitive about sending delegates to a conference in which black South American representatives would be "putting on airs."

Adams finally won congressional approval, but his victory was little better than a defeat. One of the delegates died en route. The other reached Panama after the Congress, which had almost drowned in a sea of words, had adjourned without agreeing on anything of consequence. Hoots of

derision were showered upon Adams' head. The tragedy is that the foes of the administration sacrificed a splendid opportunity to assume leadership of the Pan-American movement at the very outset.

The Tricky Tariff of Abominations

The tariff issue provided yet another headache for Adams. Congress had come to grips with the problem in 1824, under President Monroe, when it increased the protective tariff of 1816. Formerly the general level had been 20 to 25 percent on the value of dutiable goods; the change boosted the charge to new heights of about 37 percent. But the woolen manufacturers, dissatisfied with their share of protection, bleated for higher barriers still.

Rabid Jacksonites, seeking to unhorse Adams, seized this opportunity to play politics with the Tariff of 1828. They rigged up a bill that was seemingly more concerned with manufacturing a President than with protecting manufacturers. A part of their scheme was to push the duties as high as about 45 percent on the value of certain manufactured items. At the same time, they would impose a heavy tariff on certain raw materials, notably wool. These materials were so urgently needed for manufacturing, especially in New England, that even this industrial section would presumably vote against the entire measure. Adams, whose stronghold was New England, would thus be given another political black eye, and Jackson would receive a boost, especially in the Middle States. There many voters were politically uncertain but protection-prone.

But the New Englanders spoiled this clever little game. Though disliking the proposed duties, they were anxious to continue the principle of protection. As a consequence, enough of them choked down the dishonest Tariff of 1828, as amended, to force its passage. Daniel Webster, who had earlier fought the mild Tariff of 1816, and John C. Calhoun, who had sponsored it, had by this time completely reversed their positions. The future of New England clearly lay in the

House Vote on Tariff of 1828 ("Tariff of Abominations")
(COMPARE 1816 TARIFF, P. 204.)

Regions	For	Against
New England	16	23
Middle States	57	11
West (Ohio, Ind., Ill., Mo.)	17	1
South (incl. La.)	3	50
Southwest (Tenn., Ky.)	12	9
TOTAL	105	94

factory, rather than on the waves, while the destiny of the South lay in the cotton fields.

Southerners, as heavy consumers of manufactured goods, were shocked by what they re-

John C. Calhoun (1782–1850). Calhoun was a South Carolinian, partially educated at Yale. Beginning as a strong nationalist and Unionist, he reversed himself and became the ablest of the sectionalists and disunionists in defense of the South and slavery. As a foremost nullifier and secessionist, he died trying to reconcile strong states' rights with a strong Union. In his last years he advocated a Siamese-twin presidency, probably unworkable, with one President for the North and one for the South. His former plantation home is now the site of Clemson University. (National Archives.)

garded as the outrageous rates of the Tariff of 1828. Hotheads promptly branded it the "Black Tariff" or the "Tariff of Abominations." Several Southern states adopted formal protests; in South Carolina flags were lowered to half-mast. "Let the *New* England beware how she imitates the *Old*," cried one eloquent Carolinian who remembered 1776.

Why did the South, especially South Carolina, react so angrily against the tariff? The Old South—the seaboard area first settled—was the least flourishing of all the sections. The bustling Northeast was experiencing a boom in manufacturing; the developing West was prospering from rising property values and a multiplying population; and the energetic Southwest was expanding into virgin cotton lands. Overcropped acres of the Old South were petering out, and the price of cotton was falling sharply. John Randolph of Virginia grimly quipped that masters would soon cease to advertise for their fugitive slaves, and slaves would advertise for their fugitive masters. So the Old South was seeking a scapegoat, and the tariff proved to be a convenient and plausible one.

The Tariff Yoke in the South

Southerners believed, not illogically, that the "Yankee tariff" discriminated against them. They sold their cotton and other farm produce in a world market completely unprotected by tariffs, and were forced to buy their manufactured goods in an American market heavily protected by tariffs.

The plight of the South may be illustrated by a hypothetical case. Let us suppose that in 1828 an English manufacturer could sell his shoes in South Carolina at $1.25 a pair, whereas a Massachusetts factory would have to charge $1.50 for a pair of equal quality. South Carolinians would naturally buy the British footwear. But if a tariff of fifty cents a pair were levied on foreign shoes at the Charleston customs house, the British shoes would cost $1.75 a pair. Southerners, if economy-minded, would be forced to buy the Yankee product at $1.50. They would thus be taxed twenty-five cents

Tariff Inequalities, North and South.   The protective tariff under which the North grows fat and prosperous brings economic hardship to the South. (*United States Weekly Telegram*, 1832.)

on each purchase to support Northern factories.

Towering tariff walls discourage imports. If a system of completely free trade had existed in 1828, the British would probably have bought more raw materials from those nations that consumed English manufactured goods. Rather than sail their ships away from American ports empty, they would have purchased more cotton, tobacco, and other products from the South. Little wonder that Southern leaders regarded the protective tariff as a foe of their economic development. On the other hand, many failed to appreciate that a prosperous manufacturing Northeast contributed to their prosperity by consuming their cotton and other farm produce.

South Carolinians took the lead in protesting against the "Tariff of Abominations." Their legislature went so far as to publish in 1828, though without formal endorsement, a pamphlet known as "The South Carolina Exposition." It had been secretly written by John C. Calhoun, one of the few top-flight political theorists ever produced by America. (As Vice-President, he was forced to conceal his authorship.) "The Exposition" boldly denounced the recent tariff as unjust and unconstitutional. Going a stride beyond the Kentucky

and Virginia resolutions of 1798, it bluntly and explicitly proposed that the states should nullify the tariff—that is, they should declare it null and void within their borders.

Calhoun found himself caught in an awkward straddle. Still a Unionist and a nationalist, he was also a Southern sectionalist. He therefore desperately sought a formula that would protect the minority in the South from the "tyranny of the majority" in the North and West. Seizing upon nullification, he undertook by this explosive device to preserve the Union and prevent secession. His aim was not to destroy the Union, but to salvage it by quieting the fears of those forces that might one day destroy it.

Calhoun's "Exposition," at least immediately, was a false alarm. No other state joined South Carolina in her heated anti-tariff protest. But the disruptive theory of nullification was further publicized, while the even more dangerous doctrine of secession was foreshadowed. South Carolina was not then prepared to force the controversy to a showdown. The election of Carolina-born Andrew Jackson to the presidency had occurred two weeks earlier, and the "Old Hero"—a fellow cotton planter and slaveowner—was expected to sympathize with the plight of the South.

Going "Whole Hog" for Jackson in 1828

The presidential campaign for Andrew Jackson had started early. It began on February 9, 1825, the day of John Quincy Adams' controversial election by the House, and continued noisily for nearly four years.

Even before the election of 1828, the temporarily united Republicans of the Era of Good Feelings had split into two camps. One was the National Republicans, with the ultra-nationalistic Adams as their standard-bearer. The other was the Democratic-Republicans, with the fiery Jackson heading their ticket. Rallying cries of the Jackson zealots were "Bargain and Corruption," "Huzza for Jackson," and "All Hail Old Hickory." Jacksonites planted hickory poles for their hickory-tough hero; "Adamites" adopted the oak as the symbol of their oakenly independent candidate.

"Shall the people rule?" was the chief issue of 1828, at least to Jacksonians. They argued that the will of the voters had been thwarted in 1825 by the backstairs "bargain" of Adams and Clay. The only way to right the wrong was to seat Jackson, who would then bring about "reform" by sweeping out the "dishonest" Adams gang. "Jackson and Reform" was a widely mouthed slogan, while hickory brooms were brandished as tokens of a forthcoming "clean sweep." Seldom has the public mind been so successfully poisoned against an honest and high-minded President.

Mudslinging reached a disgraceful level, partly as a result of the taste of the new mass electorate for bare-knuckle politics. Adams would not stoop to gutter tactics, but many of his backers were less squeamish. They described Jackson's mother as a prostitute; they printed black-bordered handbills, shaped like coffins, recounting his numerous duels and brawls and trumpeting his hanging of six mutinous militiamen. The "Old Hero" was also branded an adulterer. He had married an estimable woman, Rachel Robards, confident that her divorce had been granted. To the consternation of both, they discovered two years later that it had not been, and they made haste to correct the marital miscue.

Anti-Jackson Cartoon of 1828. The cartoon recalls his hanging of mutinous militiamen.

Mrs. Andrew Jackson. A devoted wife who did not live to become First Lady, she had unwittingly and hence innocently involved herself and her husband in scandal. (National Archives.)

Rachel Jackson was crushed by the vicious charges of bigamy and adultery. She lived to see her husband win the presidency, but she died—supposedly of a broken heart—before she could become First Lady. Jackson, devotedly attached to his wife, was convinced that his enemies had killed her. He never forgave them.

Jackson men also hit below the belt. President Adams had purchased, with his own money and for his own use, a billiard table and a set of chessmen. In the mouths of rabid Jacksonites, these items became "gaming tables" and "gambling furniture" for the "presidential palace." Criticism

One anti-Jackson newspaper declared, "General Jackson's mother was a Common Prostitute, brought to this country by the British soldiers! She afterwards married a MULATTO MAN with whom she had several children, of which number GENERAL JACKSON is one."

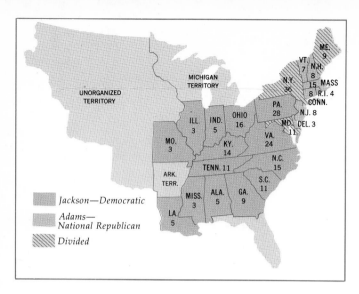

was also unfairly directed at the large sums that Adams had received over the years in federal salaries, well earned though they had been. He was even accused of having procured a servant girl for the lust of a Russian nobleman while minister to Russia—in short, of having served as a pimp.

The Jacksonian "Revolution" of 1828

General Jackson, victorious on the battlefields, was no less victorious at the ballot boxes. The popular tally was 647,286 votes for him to 508,064 for Adams, with an electoral count of 178 to 83. Support for Jackson came mainly from the West and South, and to a considerable extent from the sweat-stained laborers of the Eastern seaboard. Generally speaking, the common people—though by no means all of them—voted for the Hero of New Orleans. Adams won the backing of his own New England, as well as the propertied "better elements" of the Northeast.

The election of 1828 has often been called the "Revolution of 1828." Actually, as in 1800, there was no upheaval or landslide that swept out the incumbent. Adams, in fact, polled a respectable 44 percent of the popular vote. A considerable part of Jackson's support, moreover, was lined up by machine politicians, especially in New York and Pennsylvania, and not entirely among the leather-aproned artisans and other manual workers.

But the concept of a *political* revolution in 1828 is not completely farfetched. The increased turnout of voters proved that the common people, especially in the manhood-suffrage states, now had the vote and the will to use it for their ends. A discontented West, with its numerous rustics and debtors, generally voted for Jackson. The results show that the political center of gravity was continuing to shift away from the conservative seaboard East toward the emerging states across the mountains.

So in a broader sense the election was a "revolution," more than in 1800. It was a peaceful revolution, achieved by ballots instead of bullets, by counting heads instead of crushing them. "Shall the people rule?" cried the Jacksonians. The answering roar seemed to say, "The people shall rule!" In the struggle between the poorer masses and the entrenched classes, the homespun folk scored a resounding triumph. Rejecting the candidate who lacked the common touch, they rejoiced as though they had been delivered from some impending danger. Even so, there had been no mass turnout of voters; only about one-half the eligible persons balloted for a presidential candidate in 1828. But that proportion was already double the figure for 1824, and as the New Democracy infected the body politic, voter turnout rose dramatically. In the presidential election of

1840 ("Tippecanoe and Tyler too"), it reached 78 percent.

America hitherto had been ruled by an elite of brains and wealth, whether aristocratic Federalist shippers or aristocratic Jeffersonian planters. Jackson's victory accelerated the transfer of national power from the countinghouse to the farmhouse, from the East to the West, and from the snobs to the mobs. If Jefferson had been the hero of the gentleman farmer, Jackson was the hero of the dirt farmer. The plowholder was now ready to take over the government—*his* government.

Adams, though President-reject, was still destined for an enviable public career. Ever high-minded, he did not deem it beneath his dignity to accept election to the House of Representatives from Massachusetts. There he served with conspicuous success for seventeen fruitful years. Affectionately known as "Old Man Eloquent," he fought stalwartly for free government, free speech, free soil, and free men. A rough and savage debater, he finally was stricken on the job in 1848, at age eighty. His funeral was the greatest pageant of its kind that Washington had yet seen. Ironically, the popularity that had escaped him in life came to him in death.

The Advent of "Old Hickory" Jackson

Andrew Jackson cut a striking figure—tall (6 feet 1 inch; 1.86 meters), gaunt, and with bushy iron-gray hair brushed high above a prominent forehead, craggy eyebrows, and blue eyes. His irritability and emaciated condition (140 pounds; 64 kilograms) probably had resulted in part from long-term bouts with dysentery, malaria, tuberculosis, and lead poisoning from two bullets that he carried in his body from near-fatal duels. His autobiography was largely written in his lined face.

To a considerable degree, Jackson personified the New West. He reflected its individualism, its Jack-of-all-trades versatility, its opportunism, its energy, its directness, and its prejudices. He was a genuine folk hero—an uncommon common man. The backwoods preacher who cried that Jesus was

"just another Andrew Jackson" reflected a sentiment that did not seem out of place to some.

Jackson's upbringing was not of the best. Born in the Carolinas and early orphaned, "Mischievous Andy" grew up without parental restraints. As a youth, he displayed much more interest in brawling and cockfighting than in his scanty opportunities for reading and spelling. Although he ultimately learned to express himself in writing with vigor and clarity, his grammar was always rough-hewn and his spelling was often original, like that of many contemporaries. He sometimes misspelled a word two different ways in the same letter.

The youthful Carolinian had the foresight to emigrate "up West" to Tennessee, where a fighting man was more highly regarded than a writing man. There—through native intelligence, force of personality, and powers of leadership—he became a judge and a member of Congress. His passions were so terrible that on occasion he would choke into silence when he tried to speak. He won his greatest fame as a commander of militia troops, who dubbed him "Old Hickory" in honor of his toughness. Afflicted with a violent temper, he early became involved in numerous duels, stabbings, and other bloody frays. But, rough and forthright as democracy itself, he made things move.

The Hermitage.   Jackson's palatial Tennessee home. From an old print.

IロIIロIIロIIロIIロIIロIIロIIロIIロIIロIIロIIロIIロIIロIIロIIロI

In 1824, Jefferson said of Jackson: "When I was President of the Senate he was a Senator; and he could never speak on account of the rashness of his feelings. I have seen him attempt it repeatedly, and as often choke with rage. His passions are no doubt cooler now . . . but he is a dangerous man."

IロIIロIIロIIロIIロIIロIIロIIロIIロIIロIIロIIロIIロIIロIIロIIロI

The first President from the West, and the first without a college education, except Washington, Jackson was unique. His university was adversity. He had risen from the masses, but he was not one of them, except insofar as he shared many of their prejudices. Essentially a frontier aristocrat, he owned many slaves, cultivated broad acres, and lived in one of the finest mansions in America—the Hermitage, near Nashville, Tennessee. More Westerner than Easterner, more country gentleman than common clay, more courtly than crude, he was hard to fit into a neat category:

> He's none of your old New England stock,
> Or your gentry-proud Virginians,
> But a regular Western fighting-cock
> With Tennessee opinions.*

Contrary to legend, Jackson did not create the New Democracy. Before 1828, he had not contributed a single significant idea to it. As a clever and extremely lucky opportunist, he was the beneficiary of the New Democracy, and was tossed into office on the crest of its wave. He was the hero of the one-suspender man.

While President, Jackson proved to be a storm center. As a former military man, he demanded prompt and loyal support from his subordinates. If one was not for him, one was against him. Cherishing strong ideas as to his constitutional prerogatives, he ignored the Supreme Court on several conspicuous occasions. He likewise defied or

---

*"Andrew Jackson" from *A Book of Americans* by Rosemary & Stephen Vincent Benét. Copyright, 1933, by Rosemary & Stephen Vincent Benét. Copyright renewed ©, 1961, by Rosemary Carr Benét. Reprinted by permission of Brandt & Brandt Literary Agency, Inc.

dominated Congress as few Presidents have done. His six predecessors had wielded the veto ten times; during his two terms he employed it twelve times, sometimes on grounds of personal distaste rather than constitutional principle. Jackson's modest use of the veto axe was perfectly legitimate, but his numerous enemies condemned him as "King Andrew the First."

Jackson's inauguration symbolized the newly won ascendancy of the masses. "Hickoryites" poured into Washington from far places, sleeping on hotel floors or in hallways. They were curious to see their hero take office, and perhaps to pick up a well-paying office for themselves. Nobodies mingled with notables as the White House, for the first time, was thrown open to the multitude. A milling crowd of clerks, shopkeepers, hobnailed artisans, and grimy laborers surged in, wrecking the china and furniture, and threatening the "people's champion" with cracked ribs. Jackson was hastily spirited through a side door, and the White House miraculously emptied itself when the word was passed that huge bowls of well-spiked punch had been placed on the lawns. Such was "the inaugural brawl."

To conservatives, this orgy seemed like the end of the world. "King Mob" reigned triumphant as

"King Andrew the First." Jackson is here assailed as a tyrant who tramples underfoot the Constitution, the courts, and domestic welfare. (Houghton Library, Harvard.)

Jacksonian vulgarity replaced Jeffersonian simplicity. Old ladies of both sexes shuddered, drew their blinds, and recalled the opening scenes of the French Revolution.

Jackson Nationalizes the Spoils System

Under Jackson the spoils system—that is, rewarding political supporters with public office—was introduced into the federal government on a large numerical scale. On a percentage basis, Jefferson, with reluctance and discrimination, had already made about as large a beginning. Jackson, with more ruthlessness, extended it to more people, while complaining about those "clamoring for a public tit from which to suck the treasury."

The basic idea was as old as politics. Its name came later from Senator Marcy's classic remark in 1832, "To the victor belong the spoils of the enemy." The system had already secured a firm hold in New York and Pennsylvania, where well-greased machines were operating. Professional politicians, by ladling out the "gravy" of office, had been able to make politics a full-time business, rather than a sideline. The emphasis was more on spoils than on responsibilities.

A house-cleaning of some sort in Washington was clearly needed. No party overturn had occurred since the defeat of the Federalists in 1800, and even that had not produced wholesale evictions. During the ensuing twenty-eight years, festering evils had developed in the civil service. The old colonial-system ideal of holding office during good behavior had bred some incompetence and corruption, as well as considerable indifference and insolence ("uncivil servants"). A few office-holders, their commissions signed by President Washington, were lingering on into their eighties, drawing breath and salary but doing little else.

Jackson fully shared the view of the New Democracy that "every man is as good as his neighbor"—perhaps "equally better." As this was believed to be so, and as the routine of office was also thought to be simple enough for any upstanding American to learn quickly, why encourage the development of an aristocratic, bureaucratic, officeholding class? Experience, of course, had some value. But alertness and new blood had more—at least in the eyes of Jacksonians.

The New Democracy also trumpeted the ideal of "rotation in office"—or "a turn about is fair play." Since experience was discounted, and since officeholding provided valuable training for citizenship, let as many citizens as possible feed at the public trough for at least a short time. This was a polite way of saying "Throw the rascals out and put our rascals in."

More Victors than Spoils

Elected as a reformer, Jackson believed that the swiftest road to reform was to sweep out the Adams-Clay gang and bring in his own trusted henchmen. Furiously aroused against his foes, he agreed that the old Adams "barnacles" must "be scraped clean from the Ship of State."

The spoilsmen now had their inning. Office seekers hounded Jackson at every turn and even invaded his privacy: for every appointee there were seemingly ten disappointees. In view of such pressures, one may marvel that he removed so few incumbents rather than so many. During his eight years, only about one-fifth of the old civil servants were dismissed, leaving more than 9,000 out of the original 11,000. The "clean sweeps" were to come in later administrations.

Even so, a demoralizing practice was begun on a national scale. Insecurity replaced security and discouraged many able citizens from entering the

> One elderly postmaster, a Revolutionary war veteran, while personally appealing to Jackson not to evict him from office, removed his coat to display his war wounds. Jackson later exclaimed: "By the eternal! I will not remove the old man. Do you know that he carries a pound of British lead in his body?"

public service. Terrible hardships were worked on poor men with large families. One discharged employee cut his throat from ear to ear; another went raving mad. Fitness, merit, and the ideal of public service were subordinated, while offices were prostituted to political ends. The questions were not "What can he do for the country?" but "What has he done for the party?" or "Is he loyal to Jackson?"

Scandal inevitably accompanied the new system. Men were appointed to high office who had openly bought their posts by campaign contributions. Illiterates, incompetents, and plain crooks were given positions of public trust; they lusted for the spoils of office rather than the toils of office. Samuel Swartwout, despite ample warnings of his untrustworthiness, was awarded the high-salaried post of collector of the customs of the port of New York. Nearly nine years later he "Swartwouted out" for England, leaving his accounts more than a million dollars short—the first man to steal a million dollars from the Washington government.

Finally, the spoils system built up a potent, personalized political machine. Its delicate gears were lubricated by gifts from expectant party members, and by percentage levies on the salaries of office-holders—a kind of political job insurance. The system at length secured such a tenacious hold that more than half a century passed before its grip could be partially loosened.

Cabinet Crises and Nationalistic Setbacks

Jackson's Cabinet was mediocre; its members were used primarily as executive clerks. The only person of conspicuous ability was the smooth-tongued and keen-witted secretary of state, Dutch-descended Martin Van Buren of New York, who shone as a gifted conciliator and wire-puller. A balding, sharp-featured little man, he was affectionately addressed by Jackson as "Matty." But he was known to his enemies as the "Little Magician."

The official Cabinet of six was privately supplemented by an extra-official cabinet of about thir-teen ever-shifting members. It grew out of Jackson's informal meetings with his advisers, some of whom were newspapermen who kept him in touch with the fickle winds of public opinion. The enemies of the President branded these shirt-sleeved cronies "the Kitchen Cabinet." Subsequent generations have retained the picture of an uncouth clique gathering in the kitchen and spitting tobacco juice in the general direction of grimy spittoons. Actually, the group did not gather in the kitchen; it never met officially; its overall influence has been grossly exaggerated; and it was not unconstitutional. The President is free to consult with such unofficial advisers as he desires.

The regular Cabinet was wrecked in 1831, as a result of the "Eaton malaria." Secretary of War Eaton had married the daughter of a Washington boardinghouse keeper, pretty Peggy O'Neal, whom the tongue of scandal had perhaps unfairly linked with the male boarders. She was consequently snubbed by the ladies of Jackson's official family, conspicuously by the blue-blooded wife of Vice-President Calhoun. The President, whose own spouse had been victimized by scandalmongers, was chivalrously aroused in behalf of Mrs. Eaton's chastity. With a zeal worthy of a better cause, he tried to force the social acceptance of the black-haired beauty. But the all-conquering general finally had to acknowledge defeat in the "Petticoat War" at the hands of the female phalanx.

Peggy Eaton (1796–1879). Though scandal raised her to notoriety, she retained Jackson's favor. After her husband left the Cabinet, the President appointed him minister to Spain. For four years she basked in a brilliant Madrid society that had no prejudice against a woman with a past. (Library of Congress)

The Eaton scandal played directly into the hands of Secretary Van Buren. As a fancy-free widower, he further curried favor with Jackson by paying marked attention to Mrs. Eaton, whose physical charms lightened this self-imposed task. Jackson turned increasingly against Calhoun, and finally broke with him completely. Followers of the South Carolinian were purged from the Cabinet in 1831. Calhoun himself, resigning the vice-presidency the next year, entered the Senate as a champion of South Carolina.

It would be absurd to say that Peggy Eaton caused the Civil War. But up to this time Calhoun had publicly been a strong nationalist, despite his secret espousal of nullification in "The South Carolina Exposition" of 1828. As Vice-President, he thought himself in line for the presidency after Jackson had served one term. The open break with the incumbent, though foreshadowed earlier, blighted his hopes. He gradually abandoned his weakening nationalism and became an inflexible defender of Southern sectionalism. Seeking extreme medicines for protecting the states and preserving the Union, the "Great Nullifier" contributed to the almost fatal illness of the Union.

Jackson himself dealt nationalism a body blow by his hostility to localized roads and canals. It is true that he signed a number of measures which appropriated federal funds for ambitious internal improvements. But his states'-rights principles rebelled against spending money from the pinched Washington Treasury for roads built entirely within individual states and unrelated to an interstate network. He headlined his antagonism in 1830, when he vigorously vetoed a bill for improving the Maysville Road, which lay completely within Henry Clay's Kentucky (but which was connected with an interstate artery). This setback was incidentally a slap at the internal improvements aspect of the American System, so ardently championed by Clay, the "corrupt bargainer" whom Jackson never forgave. "Old Hickory's" veto was also a signal victory for Eastern and Southern states'-rightism in its struggle with Jackson's own West.

The Webster-Hayne Forensic Duel

Sectional jealousies found a spectacular outlet in the Senate during 1829–1830. Hidebound New England, resenting the marvelous expansion of the West, was determined to call a halt. The lavish distribution of Western acreage was draining off Eastern population, while further upsetting the political balance. Late in 1829, therefore, a New England senator introduced a resolution designed to curb the sale of public lands.

Sectional passions flared forth angrily in the Senate, as the Western senators sprang furiously to the defense of their interests. The South, seeking sectional allies in its controversies with the Northeast, promptly sided with the West. Its most persuasive spokesman was Robert Y. Hayne, of South Carolina, one of the silver-tongued orators of his generation.

Hayne's oratorical effort in the Senate was impressive. He roundly condemned the obvious disloyalty of New England during the War of 1812, as well as her selfish inconsistency on the protective tariff. Airing in detail the grievances of the South, he reserved his heavy fire for the "Tariff of Abominations" (1828). He then acclaimed Calhoun's dangerous doctrine of nullification as the only means of safeguarding the minority interests of his section. Hayne, like Calhoun, did not advocate a breakup of the Union; rather, he was seeking to protect Southern rights within the Union and under the Constitution. But his arguments were carefully stored up by nullifiers and secessionists for future use.

In 1839 Daniel Webster visited England, where his distinguished bearing and intellectual power made a great impression. The Reverend Sydney Smith, a merciless critic of America, reportedly remarked, "Daniel Webster struck me much like a steam-engine in trousers." He was also a "living lie, because no man on earth could be so great as he looked."

Webster challenged Hayne in these words: "The proposition that, in case of a supposed violation of the Constitution by Congress, the states have a constitutional right to interfere and annul the law of Congress is the proposition of the gentleman. I do not admit it. If the gentleman had intended no more than to assert the right of revolution for justifiable cause, he would have said only what all agree to. But I cannot conceive that there can be a middle course, between submission to the laws, when regularly pronounced constitutional, on the one hand, and open resistance, which is revolution or rebellion, on the other" (Jan. 26, 1830). Webster and Hayne thus clashed over the same question that had vexed Jefferson in the Kentucky resolutions and Marshall in *Marbury* v. *Madison*. Where did final authority to interpret the Constitution lie?

The "Godlike Daniel" Webster, spokesman for New England, now took the floor. Matchless orator and leader of the American bar, he awed audiences by his majestic presence, including craglike brows, flashing eyes, a sonorous voice, a noble head, and a well-chested frame. His life up to this point, including his frequent appearances before Chief Justice Marshall, had been a preparation for this nine-day running debate with Hayne in January of 1830.

After defending New England with vigor, if not complete candor, Webster, the ex-Federalist, passed on to the larger issue of Union. Insisting that the *people* and not the *states* had framed the Constitution (here he was on shaky historical ground*), he decried the insidious doctrine of

---

*The original preamble of the Constitution of 1787 had read: "We the people of the states of"—and then they were listed by name. But when it was objected that all the states might not ratify, the formula "We the people of the United States" was adopted. (For the text of the Preamble, see Appendix.)

nullification. Either the Supreme Court would judge the constitutionality of laws, or the Republic would be torn by revolution. If each of the twenty-four states was free to go its separate way in obeying or rejecting federal statutes, there would be no union but only a "rope of sand." Webster's concluding outburst, which brought tears to men's eyes, was a magnificent tribute to the Union, ending with those imperishable words: "Liberty and Union, now and forever, one and inseparable."

Websterian Cement for the Union

Webster did not overpower Hayne with his thunderous oratory; Hayne did not defeat Webster with his seductive eloquence. There were no official judges. The polished Southerner was sounder on historical and economic grounds; the impassioned New Englander was sounder on constitutional practicalities and common sense—on things as they were rather than as they had been. Each section was satisfied with its champion.

The impact of Webster's reply was spectacular. About 40,000 copies were printed in three months, and arguments for the Union were seared into the minds of countless Northerners. Among them was young Abraham Lincoln, just turning twenty-one and moving from Indiana to the Illinois frontier. Webster's inspirational peroration was printed in the school readers, and was memorized by tens of thousands of impressionable lads—the Boys in Blue who in 1861–1865 were willing to lay down their lives for the Union.

Webster, beyond a doubt, had a large hand in winning the Civil War. He probably did more than any other person to arouse the oncoming generation of Northerners to fight for the ideal of Union. His admirers have claimed that the nation was saved hardly less by the thunder of Webster's replies to Hayne than by the thunder of General Grant's replies to the cannonading of General Lee.

Hot-tempered "Old Hickory" had meanwhile been keeping strangely silent on Southern grievances. States'-rights leaders, at a Jefferson Day banquet in 1830, schemed to smoke him out. Their strategy was to devise a series of toasts in honor of Jefferson, onetime foe of centralization, that would lean toward states' rights and nullification. The plotters assumed that the "Old Hero"—a fellow Southerner—would be swept along by the tenor of the toasts and speak up in favor of states' rights.

Jackson, forewarned and inwardly fuming, had carefully prepared his response. At the proper moment he rose to his full height, fixed his eyes on Calhoun, and with dramatic intensity proclaimed:

> "Our Union: It must be preserved!"

The Southerners were dumbfounded, and Calhoun haltingly replied, in part:

> "The union, next to our liberty, most dear!"

Some seventy other anti-climactic toasts followed, but in effect the party was over.

Jackson's military ire was aroused. As commander-in-chief, he would stand for no back talk from the states, and particularly from the hated Calhoun. But, as fate decreed, the showdown with defiant South Carolina was postponed for over two years.

VARYING VIEWPOINTS

Aristocratic 19th-Century historians damned Jackson as a backwoods barbarian. They criticized Jacksonianism as democracy run riot—an irresponsible backcountry outburst that overturned the electoral system and raised hob with the national financial structure. Early-20th-Century "progressive" historians followed the lead of Frederick Jackson Turner in his famous 1893 essay, "The Significance of the Frontier in American History." They saw the frontier as the fount of democratic virtue, and they hailed Jackson as a popular hero sprung from the forests of the West. But with the publication of Arthur M. Schlesinger, Jr.'s *The Age of Jackson* in 1945, the focus of the debate on Jacksonianism shifted. Schlesinger argued that Jacksonians were strong in the urban East as well as in the Western woods. Ever since, the debate on Jacksonian democracy has tended to revolve around the question of social class rather than geographical section.

SELECT READINGS

The best general introductions are George Dangerfield, *The Awakening of American Nationalism, 1815–1828* (1965), and G. G. Van Deusen, *The Jacksonian Era, 1828–1848* (1959). A still-living classic treatise on the Jacksonian period is Alexis De Tocqueville, *Democracy in America* (1835, 1840). A. M. Schlesinger, Jr., in his pro-Jackson *The Age of Jackson* (1945), stresses the support of Eastern labor for Jackson, a view that has come under heavy attack in Lee Benson, *The Concept of Jacksonian Democracy: New York as a Test Case* (1961). See also Walter Hugins, *Jacksonian Democracy and the Working Class: A Study of the New York Workingmen's Movement, 1829–1837* (1960), and Marvin Meyers, *The Jacksonian Persuasion* (1957). More broadly conceived is J. W. Ward, *Andrew Jackson: Symbol for an Age* (1955). R. V. Remini has three revealing books: *Martin Van Buren and the Making of the Democratic Party* (1959); *The Election of Andrew Jackson* (1963); and *The Revolutionary Age of Andrew Jackson* (1976). On administrative aspects and the functioning of the spoils system consult L. D. White, *The Jacksonians* (1954), and S. H. Aronson, *Status and Kinship in the Higher Civil Service* (1964). See also Chilton Williamson, *American Suffrage from Property to Democracy, 1760–1860* (1960). S. F. Bemis, *John Quincy Adams and the Union* (1956), is the second and concluding volume of a distinguished biography. Robert Dalzell examines *Daniel Webster and the Trial of American Nationalism, 1843–1852* (1973). The standard work on the subject is Frank W. Taussig, *The Tariff History of the United States* (1931).

14

Jacksonian Democracy at Flood Tide

The vain threats of resistance by those who [in South Carolina] have raised the standard of rebellion shew their madness and folly. . . . In forty days, I can have within the limits of So. Carolina fifty thousand men. . . . The Union will be preserved.

ANDREW JACKSON, 1832

"Nullies" in South Carolina

The "abominable" Tariff of 1828 continued to rankle with hot-blooded South Carolinians. Some of them took to wearing ill-fitting homespun garments, untaxed by the hated Yankee tariff, while their slaves strutted about in discarded broadcloth. The nullifiers—"nullies," they were called—tried valiantly to muster the necessary two-thirds vote in the South Carolina legislature for nullification. But they were blocked by a determined minority of Unionists or "submission men."

Back in Washington, Congress touched off the fuse by passing the new Tariff of 1832, which fell far short of meeting all Southern demands. The measure did pare away the worst of the "abominations" of 1828, and it did lower the imposts to about the level of the moderate Tariff of 1824—roughly 35 percent, or a reduction of 10 percent. Yet the new law was frankly protective and to many Southerners it had a disquieting air of permanence.

South Carolina was now nerved for drastic action. Nullifiers and Unionists clashed head-on in the state election of 1832. "Nullies," defiantly wearing palmetto ribbons on their hats, emerged with more than a two-thirds majority. The state legislature then called for a special convention. Several weeks later the delegates, meeting in Columbia, solemnly declared the existing federal tariff to be null and void within South Carolina. The hotheaded assemblage also called upon the state legislature to undertake any necessary military preparations. As a final act of defiance, the convention threatened to take South Carolina out of the Union if the Washington regime attempted to collect the customs duties by force.

President-General Jackson, his military instincts rasped, reacted violently. Hating Calhoun and pledged to uphold the Union, he privately threatened to hang the nullifiers. But fortunately for compromise, he was much less pugnacious in public. He dispatched modest naval and military reinforcements to the Palmetto State, while quietly preparing a sizable army. He also issued a ringing proclamation against nullification, to which the governor of South Carolina, ex-Senator Hayne, responded with a counter-proclamation. If civil war was to be avoided, one side would have to surrender, or both would have to compromise.

Calhoun Criticized. This contemporary cartoon shows Calhoun reaching for power over the dead bodies of the Constitution and the Union. Jackson, at the far right, threatens to hang the nullifiers. (The New York Public Library, Astor, Lenox and Tilden Foundations)

Conciliatory Henry Clay of Kentucky, now in the Senate, stepped forward. An unforgiving foe of Jackson, he had no desire to see his old enemy win new laurels by crushing the Carolinians and returning with the scalp of Calhoun dangling from his belt. The gallant Kentuckian therefore threw his influence behind a compromise bill which would gradually reduce the Tariff of 1832 by about 10 percent over a period of eight years. By 1842 the rates would be at approximately the mildly protective level of 1816—that is, 20 percent to 25 percent on the value of dutiable goods.

House Vote on Tariff of 1832

Regions	For	Against	Explanations
New England	17	17	Divided on moderate tariff
Middle States	52	18	Pa., N.Y., protectionist strongholds
West (Ohio, Ind., Ill., Mo.)	18	0	Undeveloped West for tariff to support improvements
South (incl. La.)	27	27	Note division on moderate tariff
Southwest (Tenn., Ky.)	18	3	West favorable to tariff
TOTAL	132	65	

The vote was badly divided because the bill was really a compromise between extreme protection and free trade. Compare vote on 1828 tariff, p. 227.

House Vote on Compromise Tariff of 1833

Regions	For	Against	Explanations
New England	10	28 ⎱	Opposition in manufacturing centers to
Middle States	24	47 ⎰	lowered tariff
West	10	8	Divided on moderate tariff
South and Southwest	75	2	Strong Southern support for compromise
TOTAL	119	85	

The compromise Tariff of 1833 finally squeezed through Congress. Debate was bitter, with most of the opposition naturally coming from protectionist New England and the Middle States. Calhoun and the South favored the compromise, so it was evident that Jackson would not have to use firearms and rope. But at the same time, and partly as a face-saving device, Congress passed the Force Bill, known among Carolinians as the "Bloody Bill." It authorized the President to use the army and navy, if necessary, to collect federal tariff duties.

Militant South Carolinians welcomed this opportunity to extricate themselves without loss of face from a dangerously tight corner. To the consternation of the Calhounites, no other Southern states had sprung to their support, though Georgia and Virginia toyed with the idea. Moreover, an appreciable Unionist minority within South Carolina was gathering guns, organizing militia, and nailing the Stars and Stripes to flagpoles. Faced with civil war within and invasion from without, the Columbia convention met again and repealed the ordinance of nullification. As a final but futile gesture of fist-shaking, it nullified the unnecessary Force Act and adjourned.

Flag of South Carolina, with Palmetto Tree

A Victory for Both Union and Nullification

Neither Jackson nor the "nullies" won a clear-cut triumph. Admirers of "Old Hickory" insisted that he had avoided an armed clash, induced the South Carolinians to repeal their ordinance of nullification, and preserved the Union. On the other hand, the danger of disunion seems to have been exaggerated.

South Carolina actually emerged with colors flying. Although confronted with overwhelming odds, she had forced a reduction of the tariff to as reasonable a level as she could have expected. She had not only saved face but she had surrendered no principle. Unrepentant and defiant, she felt that she had won; and the people of Charleston—the "Cradle of Secession"—gave a gala "victory ball" for the volunteer troops. But ominously the South Carolinians gradually abandoned nullification in favor of the more extreme remedy of secession.

Later generations, gazing back through the smoke of the Civil War, have condemned the "appeasement" of South Carolina in 1833 as sheer folly. Unbloody and unbowed, she could have been voted the state most likely to secede. (In 1860 she was the first to go.) If Jackson had only strangled the serpent of secession in the cradle, so the argument runs, there might have been no costly Civil War. During the crisis of 1832 medals were struck off in honor of Calhoun bearing the words, "First President of the Southern Confederacy."

Yet force was the risky solution. The flare-up in South Carolina was no mere Whiskey Rebellion,

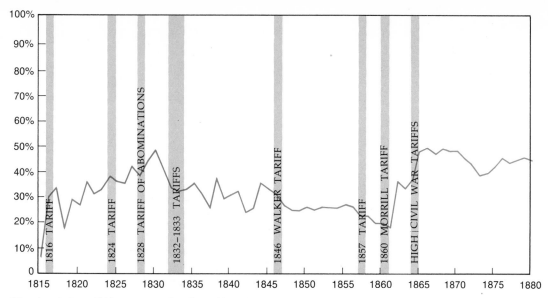

(The data before 1820 are approximations. Note that the effects of a tariff are often not immediately felt in the year of its passage.)

TARIFF LEVIES ON DUTIABLE IMPORTS, 1815–1880

and the nation was not yet ready to drink the cup of blood. Violence tends to beget violence. Armed invasion might have aroused other Southern states and touched off a civil war, at a time when the Unionists were even worse prepared for fighting than in 1861. Force is a confession that statesmanship has failed. Reasonable compromise was in the American tradition, and in 1833 any other course seemed unwise.

The Bank as a Political Football

President Jackson did not hate all banks and all businesses, but he distrusted monopolistic banking and over-big business, as did his followers. A man of violent dislikes, he came to share the prejudices of his own West against the "moneyed monster" known as the Bank of the United States (B.U.S.). He might have tolerated a renewal of its charter in 1836, with adequate safeguards. But hated Henry Clay aroused his ire by throwing himself behind a premature move in the Senate to recharter the Bank in 1832—four years early. "Gallant Harry" was the leading candidate of the National Republicans for the presidency, and with a

fateful blindness he looked upon the Bank issue as a surefire winner.

Clay's scheme was to ram a recharter bill through Congress, and then send it on to the White House. If Jackson signed it, he would alienate his worshipful Western followers. If he vetoed it, as seemed certain, he would presumably lose the presidency in the forthcoming election by alienating the wealthy and influential groups in the East. Clay seems not to have fully realized that the "best people" were now only a minority, and that they generally feared Jackson anyhow. The President growled privately, "The Bank . . . is trying to kill me, but I will kill it."

The recharter bill slid through Congress on greased skids, as planned, but was killed by a scorching veto from Jackson. The "Old Hero" assailed the plutocratic and monopolistic Bank as unconstitutional. Of course the Supreme Court had earlier declared it constitutional in the case of *McCulloch* v. *Maryland* (1819), but Jackson acted as though he regarded the executive branch as superior to the judicial branch. He had taken an oath to uphold the Constitution as he understood it, not as his foe, John Marshall, understood it.

Banker Biddle wrote to Henry Clay (August 1, 1832) expressing his satisfaction: "I have always deplored making the Bank a party question, but since the President will have it so, he must pay the penalty of his own rashness. As to the veto message, I am delighted with it. It has all the fury of a chained panther biting the bars of his cage. It is really a manifesto of anarchy . . . and my hope is that it will contribute to relieve the country of the domination of these miserable [Jackson] people."

Nicholas Biddle (1786–1844). A precociously brilliant linguist, writer, magazine editor, diplomat, legislator, and financier, he entered the University of Pennsylvania at age ten and completed the requirements for graduation at age thirteen. Drawn into high finance, he mastered the business and became president of the Bank of the United States. (Frick Art Reference Library)

Jackson's veto message went on to condemn the Bank as not only anti-Western but anti-American. A substantial minority of its stockholders were foreigners, chiefly Britons, for whom Americans still harbored a war-born hate. Thus, at one bold stroke, Jackson succeeded in mobilizing the prejudices of the West against the East. He was setting the log cabin against the business office, the apprehensive debtor against the steely-eyed creditor. More than that, he was arousing the "native" American against the foreigner, the states'-righter against the centralizer.

The gods continued to misguide Henry Clay. Delighted with the financial fallacies of Jackson's message, but blind to its political appeal, he arranged to have thousands of copies printed as a campaign document. The President's sweeping accusations may indeed have seemed demagogic to the moneyed men of the country, but they made good sense to the common men. The Bank issue was now thrown into the noisy arena of the Clay-Jackson presidential canvass of 1832.

Brickbats and Bouquets for the Bank

What of Jackson's vigorous charges? The Bank was undeniably anti-Western in its strong hostility to the wobbly "wildcat banks" that provided financial fuel—often volatile paper—for Western expansion. It had foreclosed on many Western farms, and had thus drained "tribute" into its Eastern coffers. For that era, it was a mammoth super-bank—a "monster monopoly"—and hence out of touch with the sweaty New Democracy. It was undeniably plutocratic, run by an elite moneyed aristocracy, headed by the able but high-handed Nicholas Biddle (dubbed "Czar Nicholas I"). The Bank was also in some degree autocratic and tyrannical, especially when it turned the screws on the weak "rag money" banks.

The charge that the Bank was a "hydra of corruption" contained much truth. Biddle cleverly lent funds where they would make influential friends. In 1831 alone, a total of fifty-nine members of Congress borrowed sums from "Biddle's Bank" totaling about a third of a million dollars. Even a dog does not ordinarily bite the hand that feeds him. During one period Daniel Webster was a director of the Bank, its chief paid counsel, its debtor in the sum of thousands of dollars, and a member of the United States Senate, where he eloquently battled for his employer's interests. Judicious loans by Biddle to newspaper editors likewise insured a "good press," and led to the sneer, "Emperor Nick of the Bribery Bank." Whomever he could not corrupt, it was believed, he crushed.

Yet the Bank had much to commend it. An eminently sound organization, it was the only national financial institution of its kind in American history. It kept the fly-by-night Western banks under some restraint—banks that often consisted of little more than a few chairs and a suitcase full of printed notes. It reduced bank failures and, at a time when the country was flooded with depreciated paper money, issued sound banknotes ("Old Nick's Money"). It helped the West expand by making credit and sound currency reasonably abundant. It was a safe depository for the funds of the Washington government, which it also served by transferring and disbursing money. Admittedly it had a monopoly of surplus federal funds, but that monopoly had been specifically authorized by the people's representatives in Congress.

The Bank, in short, was a highly important and useful institution which had fallen into the hands of a wealthy clique. Its officers were not only arrogant, but they were not fully aware of their responsibilities to society in the management of what amounted to a public utility.

"Old Hickory" Crushes Clay in 1832

Clay, as a National Republican, and Jackson, as a Democrat, were the chief gladiators in the presidential contest of 1832. The gaunt old general, who had earlier favored one term for a President and rotation in office, was easily persuaded by his cronies not to rotate himself out of office. Presidential power is a heady brew—and habit-forming.

The ensuing campaign was colorful and noisy. The "Old Hero's" adherents again raised the hickory pole and bellowed, "Jackson Forever: Go the Whole Hog." Admirers of Clay shouted, "Freedom and Clay," while his foes harped on his dueling, gambling, cockfighting, and fast living.

Novel features made the campaign of 1832 especially memorable. Americans witnessed for the first time nominations by national nominating conventions (three of them), which now took over from the state legislatures the function of naming candidates. The first national party platform was

"Race Over Uncle Sam's Course." Clay, with his American System, is supposed to gain the White House as Jackson, with his veto club and Van Buren as running mate, falls on the Bank issue in 1832. A falsely optimistic Whig cartoon. (Boston Public Library.)

also published. And for the first time a third-party ticket entered the field—the short-lived anti-Masonic group, which opposed the fearsome secrecy of the Masonic order. But on the whole the "hurrah" froth of the preceding campaign was subordinated to the solid issue of the Bank.

Henry Clay and his overconfident National Republicans enjoyed impressive advantages. Ample funds flowed into their campaign chest, including $50,000 in "life insurance" from the B.U.S. Most of the newspaper editors, some of them "bought" with Biddle's Bank loans, dipped their pens in acid when they wrote of Jackson. Oratorical big guns, including the incomparable Webster, were lined up on the side of Clay, as was true of the middle- and upper-income groups.

Yet Jackson won easily over the sparkling Kentuckian. The popular count stood at 687,502 to 530,189; the electoral count at 219 to 49. A Jacksonian wave swept over the West and South, washed into Pennsylvania and New York, and even broke into rock-ribbed New England.

Henry Clay, long bitten by the presidential bug, was crushed. Himself magnetically appealing, he had enlisted on his side the big money, the brilliant oratory, the "solid" citizenry, and the sound financial reasoning. But the peppery President, the idol of the masses, won because he had the votes. The poor always outnumber the rich—and in 1832, as in 1824 and 1828, the poor voted for "Old Andy" Jackson.

Badgering Biddle's Bank

A vindictive Jackson was not one to let the financial octopus die in peace. He was convinced that he now had a "mandate" from the voters, and he had good reason to fear that the slippery Biddle might try to manipulate the Bank (as he did) so as to force its recharter. Jackson therefore decided to "remove" the federal deposits gradually, thus cushioning the final shock when the Bank expired in four years. He would accomplish his objective by depositing no more funds with Biddle, and by

"The times are dreadfully hard," wrote a New York diarist, Philip Hone, Dec. 30, 1833. "The . . . act of tyranny which the President exercised in removing the deposits has produced a state of alarm and panic unprecedented in our city. . . . The truth is, we are smarting under the lash which the vindictive ruler of our destinies [Jackson] has inflicted upon us as a penalty for the sin which Nicholas Biddle committed in opposing his election. My share of the punishment amounts to $20,000, which I have lost by the fall of stocks in the last sixty days."

using existing deposits to defray the day-to-day expenses of the government.

"Removing" the deposits involved nasty complications. Jackson, his dander up, was forced to reshuffle his Cabinet before he could find a secretary of the treasury who would bend to his iron will. Surplus federal funds henceforth were placed in several dozen state institutions—the so-called pet banks or Jackson's pets. These new depositories were selected partly because of their pro-Jackson sympathies, but in general they were not nearly so weak as pictured by the President's enemies.

Biddle, for his part, was compelled to retrench after losing the federal deposits. But he called in loans with unnecessary severity, and evidently for the purpose of forcing a reconsideration of the charter by Congress. A number of the wobblier banks were driven to the wall by "Biddle's Panic," and the vengeful conduct of the dying "monster" seemed to justify the earlier accusations of its foes.

The teetering financial structure of the country received an additional shock in 1836, the year the Bank breathed its last. "Wildcat" currency had become so unreliable in the West that Jackson authorized the Treasury to issue a Specie Circular—a decree that required all public lands to be purchased with "hard" or metallic money. This drastic step was overdue, but coming at that time it gave the speculative bubble another sharp prick. Hard money brought hard feelings and hard times to the West.

Inflationary pressures nevertheless continued. By 1835 the national debt was finally liquidated for the first time, but additional funds still poured into the federal Treasury. This revenue flowed principally from the customs houses, which were benefiting from the high tariff duties and the heavy imports resulting from flush times. In 1836 a scheme passed Congress for distributing the surplus above $5 million to the states. When this transfer began, early in 1837, the risky speculative spiral was given another boost. Later that year the panic broke, and the bothersome problem of the surplus became the even more bothersome problem of a deficit.

Transplanting the Tribes

Wondrous indeed was the continued expansion of the American population. The unflagging fertility of the people, reinforced by immigration, brought the total figure to nearly 13 million by 1830—or more than three times that of 1790.* Most of the states east of the Mississippi had been admitted, leaving islands of red men marooned on lands coveted by their white neighbors.

President Jackson, the veteran Indian fighter known as "Big Knife," was convinced of the folly of continuing to regard the tribes as separate nations within the individual states. When Georgia attempted to exercise control over the Cherokees, and the Supreme Court thrice upheld the rights of the Indians, Jackson viewed continued defiance by the state with unaccustomed composure. A state might flout federal law if white men thereby profited at the Indians' expense. In a callous sneer at the red men's defender, Jackson reportedly snapped, "John Marshall has made his decision; now let him enforce it."

Yet Jackson also harbored protective feelings toward the Indians. Their present condition, he told Congress in 1829, "contrasted with what they once were, makes a most powerful appeal to our sympathies." Could not something be done, he implored, to preserve "this much injured race"? Jackson proposed a bodily removal of the remaining Eastern tribes—chiefly Cherokee, Creek, Choctaw, and Chickasaw—beyond the Mississippi. Individual Indians might remain if they adopted white men's ways. Emigration should be voluntary, since it would be "cruel and unjust to compel the aborigines to abandon the graves of their fathers."

Jackson's policy was high-sounding, but it led to the more or less forcible uprooting of more than 100,000 Indians in the 1830s. Many died on the "Trail of Tears" to the newly established Indian Territory (present Oklahoma), where they were to be "permanently" free of white encroachments. The Bureau of Indian Affairs was established in 1836 to administer relations with America's original inhabitants. But as the landhungry "palefaces" pushed west faster than anticipated, the government's guarantees went up in smoke. The "permanent" frontier lasted about fifteen years.

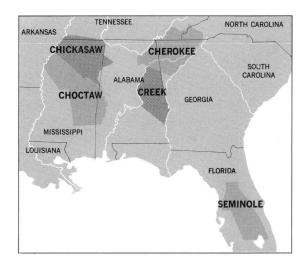

SOUTHERN TRIBES BEFORE TRANSPLANTING

---

*For population figures since 1790, see Appendix.

Black Hawk War, c. 1832. Resisting Indians in the Illinois country are dispatched by the white men's "fire sticks." (Rare Book Division, New York Public Library, Astor, Lenox and Tilden Foundations.)

Suspicious of white intentions from the start, braves from Illinois and Wisconsin, ably led by Black Hawk, resisted eviction. They were bloodily crushed in 1832 by regular troops, including Lieutenant Jefferson Davis of Mississippi, and by volunteers, including Captain Abraham Lincoln of Illinois.

In Florida the Seminole Indians, joined by runaway black slaves, retreated to the swampy Everglades. For seven years (1835–1842) they waged a bitter guerrilla war that took the lives of some 1,500 soldiers and proved to be the costliest Indian conflict in American experience. The spirit of the Seminoles was at last broken in 1837, when the American field commander treacherously seized their half-breed leader, Osceola, under a flag of truce. Some fled deeper into the Everglades, where their descendants now live, but about four-fifths of them were moved to present Oklahoma, where about 3,000 of the tribe survive.

Jackson's Brass-Knuckle Diplomacy

Trigger-tempered General Jackson was temperamentally unfitted for diplomacy. But in this field he turned out to be much more successful than President J. Q. Adams, his diplomatically seasoned predecessor.

How would Jackson get along with the British? Sober citizens had misgivings, for the fiery general had fought them in two wars. He had also borne on his head, since age fourteen, a sword scar brutally inflicted by an English officer. The problem of reopening trade with the British West Indies provided an acid test of Jackson's views. John Quincy Adams, the astute diplomat, had demanded reopening as a right. Jackson, with surprising moderation, requested it as a privilege. London, no doubt expecting a saber-rattling approach, was thrown off guard. Death had removed the imperious Foreign Secretary Canning from Downing Street, and the British were veering toward free trade, away from their ancient mercantilism. They therefore agreed to reopen this once-lucrative West Indian commerce, subject to the payment of normal customs duties.

As an international bill collector, Jackson proved equally successful, though much less velvet-gloved. In 1831 the Paris government belatedly agreed to pay the United States several million dollars, as compensation for American ships illegally seized during the Napoleonic upheaval. But partly because of political tensions in France, the initial payments were held back. Jackson, short on patience as usual, recommended in his annual message of 1834 that, if necessary, the federal government should seize French property in the United States and pay off the debt with the proceeds.

Gallic pride, traditionally thin-skinned, was hurt. The French closed their legation in Washington and ordered Chargé Alphonse Pageot home. He sailed with his American wife (whose father was a friend of Jackson) and his infant son, Andrew Jackson Pageot (whose godfather was the President). The American legation in Paris was likewise closed, as the buzz of war preparations increased on both sides. Jackson was urged by well-wishers to apologize, but he refused. "Apologize?" he reportedly burst out; "I'll see the whole race roasting in hell first!"

War with France seemed imminent. But the British, not wishing to see their French ally squander its strength in America, successfully mediated. Europe's distresses were still coming to America's aid. French officials, carefully rereading Jackson's messages to Congress, insisted that they now found in them a satisfactory apology—though Jackson loudly insisted that he had not apologized. At all events, arrangements were finally made to pay the debt; and Monsieur Pageot, Madame Pageot, and little Andrew Jackson Pageot sailed back to America.

Jackson had raised international blood pressures dangerously high over this relatively trifling affair. But he did get the money. He also ended a dispute that had explosive possibilities, and he

IOIIOIIOIIOIIOIIOIIOIIOIIOIIOIIOIIOIIOIIOIIOIIOIIOIIOIIOI

> Jackson defiantly declared in his annual message to Congress (Dec. 7, 1835), in relation to French claims, "The honor of my country shall never be stained by an apology from me for the statement of truth and the performance of duty; nor can I give any explanation of my official acts except such as is due to integrity and justice and consistent with the principles on which our institutions have been framed."

IOIIOIIOIIOIIOIIOIIOIIOIIOIIOIIOIIOIIOIIOIIOIIOIIOIIOIIOI

created a new respect in European capitals for the robust young Republic. The Henry Clayites condemned the verbal violence employed, while the President's admirers elatedly retorted, "Hurrah for Jackson!" "No Explanations! No Apologies!"

The Lone Star of Texas Flickers

Land-hungry Americans continued to covet the vast expanse of Texas, which the United States had abandoned to Spain when acquiring Florida in 1819. The Spanish authorities were desirous of populating this virtually unpeopled area, but before they could carry through their contemplated plans, the Mexicans won their independence. A new regime in Mexico City thereupon concluded arrangements in 1823 for granting a huge tract of land to Stephen Austin, with the understanding that he would bring in 300 American families. Immigrants were to be of the established Roman Catholic faith, and in addition were to become properly Mexicanized.

These two restrictions were largely ignored. Hardy Texan pioneers remained Americans at heart, resenting the trammels imposed by a "foreign" government. They were especially annoyed by the presence of Mexican soldiers, many of whom were ragged ex-convicts.

Virile and prolific, Texas-Americans numbered about 30,000 by 1835. Most of them were law-abiding, God-fearing men, but some of them had left the "states" only one or two jumps ahead of the sheriff. "G. T. T." (Gone to Texas) became current descriptive slang. Among the adventurers were Davy Crockett, the fabulous rifleman, and James Bowie, the presumed inventor of the murderous knife that bears his name. It was widely known in the Southwest as the "genuwine Arkansas toothpick." A distinguished latecomer and leader was an ex-governor of Tennessee, Sam Houston. His life had been temporarily shattered in 1829 when his bride of a few weeks left him and he took up transient residence with the Arkansas Indians, who dubbed him "Big Drink." He subsequently took the pledge of temperance.

The pioneer individualists who came to Texas were not easy to push around. Friction rapidly increased between Mexicans and Texans over such issues as slavery, immigration, and local rights. The explosion finally came in 1835, when dictator Santa Anna wiped out cherished rights guaranteed by the Mexican constitution of 1824.

Early in 1836 the liberty-loving Texans declared their independence and unfurled their Lone Star flag—with Sam Houston as commander-in-chief. Santa Anna, at the head of about 6,000 men, swept ferociously into Texas. Trapping a band of nearly 200 defiant Texans at the Alamo in San Antonio, he wiped them out to a man after a thirteen-day siege. Their commander, Colonel W. B. Travis, had heroically declared, "I shall never surrender nor retreat. . . . Victory or Death." The victims included Jim Bowie, who was shot as he lay sick and crippled on his cot, and Davy Crockett, whose body was found riddled with bullets and surrounded by enemy corpses. But the Mexican losses were extremely heavy. A short time later a band of about 400 surrounded and defeated American volunteers, having thrown down their arms at Goliad, were butchered as "pirates." All these operations further delayed the Mexican advance.

Texan war cries—"Remember the Alamo!" "Remember Goliad!" and "Death to Santa Anna!" —swept up into the United States. Scores of vengeful Americans seized their rifles and rushed to the aid of relatives, friends, and compatriots. But despite their efforts, the Lone Star was in grave danger of being dimmed forever as General Sam Houston's small army continued its thirty-seven-day eastward retreat.

But Houston proved equal to the occasion. A commanding figure of a man and a natural leader of the Texans, he lured the pursuers onward to San Jacinto, near the site of the city that now bears his name. The invaders numbered about 1,300 men; the Texans about 900. Suddenly, on April 21, 1836, Houston turned. Taking full advantage of the Mexican siesta hour, he wiped out the invading force and captured Santa Anna, who was

The Alamo. An abandoned mission at San Antonio, the Alamo occupies a glorious spot in Texas history. Known as "The Cradle of Texas Liberty," the Alamo was constructed as a Franciscan chapel in the days of Spanish colonization in the eighteenth century. It had been abandoned for some time prior to its famous use as a fort in 1836. Badly destroyed in the Mexican attack, the Alamo was purchased by the state of Texas in 1883 and subsequently restored. (Courtesy, Texas State Library.)

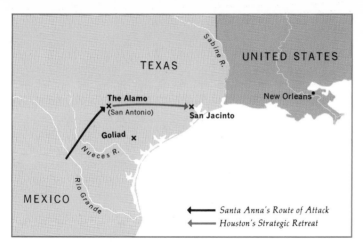

THE TEXAS REVOLUTION, 1835–1836
General Houston's strategy was to retreat and use defense in depth. His line of supply from the United States was shortened as Santa Anna's lengthened. The Mexicans were forced to bring up supplies by land because the Texas navy controlled the sea. This force consisted of only four small ships, but it was big enough to do the job.

found cowering in the tall grass near the battle-field. Confronted with thirsty Bowie knives, the quaking dictator was speedily induced to sign two treaties. By their terms he agreed to withdraw Mexican troops and to recognize the Rio Grande as the extreme southwestern boundary of Texas. When released, he repudiated the whole agreement as illegal and as extorted under duress.

Samuel Houston (1793–1863). After a promising career in Tennessee as a soldier, lawyer, congressman, and governor, Houston became the chief leader and hero of the Texas rebels. Elected to the U.S. Senate and the governorship of Texas, he was forced into retirement when his love for the Union caused him to spurn the Confederacy in the Civil War.

Texas: An International Derelict

Mexico no doubt had a genuine grievance against the United States. The Texans, though courageous, could hardly have won their independence without unneutral help in men and supplies from their American cousins. The Washington government, as the Mexicans bitterly complained, had a solemn obligation under international law to enforce its leaky neutrality statutes. But American public opinion, overwhelmingly favorable to the Texans, openly nullified the existing legislation. The federal authorities were powerless to act.

Jackson's heart was torn by the Texas issue. He disliked the Mexican overlords and admired the heroism of Sam Houston, his old comrade-in-arms against the Indians. But he was in no haste to recognize Texas formally as an independent republic. To do so would touch off the whole explosive issue of slavery, at a time when he was trying to engineer the election of his handpicked successor, Martin Van Buren. But after Van Buren had come safely under the wire, Jackson extended the right hand of recognition, the day before he left office in 1837.

Texas had every reason to expect a union with the United States, for what nation in its right mind would refuse so princely a dowry? The radiant Texan bride, officially petitioning for annexation in 1837, presented herself for marriage. But the expectant groom, Uncle Sam, was jerked back by the black hand of the slavery issue. Anti-slavery zealots in the North were opposing annexation with increasing vehemence; they contended that the whole scheme was merely a conspiracy cooked up by the Southern "slavocracy" to bring new slave pens into the Union.

At first glance, a "slavery plot" charge seemed plausible. Most of the early settlers in Texas, as well as American volunteers during the revolution, had come from the states of the South and Southwest. But scholars have concluded that the settlement of Texas was merely the normal and inexorable march of the westward movement. Most of the immigrants came from the South and Southwest simply because these states were closer. The explanation was proximity rather than conspiracy.

The jilted Texas bride was left in a dangerous predicament. Fearing the return of the "villain," Santa Anna, she understandably went so far as to flirt openly with Britain and France for support. An ugly situation, involving balance-of-power politics, began to develop below the underbelly of the United States. It could not be allowed to go on indefinitely.

The End of "King Andrew's" Reign

New parties were jelling as the 1830s lengthened. By 1834, the Democratic-Republicans of Andrew Jackson had unashamedly adopted the once-tainted name of "Democrats." National Republicans, glamorously led by Henry Clay, chose the time-honored name of Whig—a magic name closely associated with patriotism during the Revolutionary War. (See chart, p. 149.)

The Whig party was a hodgepodge of malcontents—"an organized incompatibility." Their guiding star at this time was opportunism; their chief cement was hatred of Jackson and hunger for the spoils of office. In the same political bed were gathered all kinds of Whigs: protectionists and free-traders, Southern nullifiers and Northern nationalists, rich Southern planters and poor Northern farmers.

As the presidential election of 1836 neared, the

Contemporary Election Parade. (Library of Congress.)

Whigs did not feel strong enough to beat the Jacksonian Democrats in a straight-out fight. Their strategy was to nominate several prominent "favorite sons," who would so scatter the vote that no candidate would get a majority. The deadlock would then have to be broken by the House of Representatives, where the Whigs had a chance. With Henry Clay bowing out of a near-hopeless race, the leading "favorite son" was heavy-jawed General William Henry Harrison of Ohio, so-called hero of the Battle of Tippecanoe.

Martin Van Buren of New York, a smooth-as-silk politician, was Jackson's choice for "appointment" as his successor. The hollow-cheeked Jackson, now nearing seventy, was too old and ailing to consider a third term. But he was not loath to try to serve a third term through Van Buren, something of a "yes man," who was unconvincingly called "Young Hickory." Leaving nothing to chance, the general carefully rigged the nominating convention and rammed his favorite down the throats of the delegates. Van Buren was supported by the Jacksonites without wild enthusiasm, even though he had promised "to tread generally" in the military-booted footsteps of his predecessor.

The finespun schemes of the Whigs availed nothing. Van Buren, the dapper "Little Van," squirmed into office by the close popular vote of 762,678 to 735,651, but by the comfortable margin of 170 votes to 73 in the Electoral College. Jackson could now step down.

In retrospect, the Jackson years were yeasty ones. It is true that they were marred by noise and bluster, as well as by bull-in-the-china-closet finance and diplomacy. Yet the rough-hewn general —through forthrightness, energy, and strength of character—did far better than might have been expected. He demonstrated anew the value of strong executive leadership; he led the common people into national politics; he united them into the powerful and long-lived Democratic party; and he proved that they could be trusted with both the vote and high office. Reasserting the prestige of the presidency, he amazed weak-kneed politicians by showing that the courageous course often wins the most votes.

The other side of the ledger is less satisfying. Jackson cannot escape blame for his encouragement of the spoils system and of unsound finance, with its heartbreaking legacy of a century of thousands of bank failures. No one can deny that the B.U.S. was a powerful and ultimately a corrupting monopoly, which needed to have its wings clipped. But chopping off its head instead of its wings was of dubious benefit to the entire nation.

Big Woes for the "Little Magician"

Martin Van Buren, eighth President, was the first to be born under the American flag. Bland of face, bald of head, slender of figure, the adroit little New Yorker has been described as "a first-class second-rate man." An accomplished wire-puller and spoilsman—"the wizard of Albany"—he was also a statesman of wide experience in both legislative and administrative life. In intelligence, education, and training, he was above the average of the Presidents since Jackson. The myth of his complete mediocrity sprouted from a series of misfortunes over which he had no control.

From the outset, the new politician-President labored under severe handicaps. As a machine-made candidate, he incurred the resentment of many Democrats—the men who objected to having a "bastard politician" smuggled into office beneath the tails of the old general's military coat.

Dandified Martin Van Buren (1782–1862). He has been generally underrated as a President because of his skill as a politician. It was said of him that he rowed toward his objectives "with muffled oars." Yet he was a politician with principles, as evidenced by his strong stand against slavery expansion and by his hopeless run for the presidency in his later years (1848) as candidate of the Free Soil party.

Jackson, the master showman, had been the dynamic type of executive whose administration had resounded with furious quarrels and cracked heads. Easygoing Martin Van Buren seemed to rattle about in the military boots of his testy predecessor. The people felt let down. Inheriting Jackson's mantle without his popularity, the polished New Yorker also inherited the ex-President's numerous and vengeful enemies.

Van Buren's four years overflowed with toil and trouble. A rebellion in Canada in 1837 stirred up ugly incidents along the northern frontier and threatened to trigger war with Britain. The President's attempt to play a neutral game led to the cry, "Woe to Martin Van Buren!" The anti-slavery agitators in the North were in full cry, and among other grievances were condemning the prospective annexation of Texas.

Worst of all, Van Buren inherited a searing depression from Jackson. Much of his energy had to be devoted to the purely negative task of battling the panic, and there were not enough rabbits in the "Little Magician's" tall silk hat. Hard times ordinarily blight the reputation of a President—and Van Buren was no exception.

Depression Doldrums and the Independent Treasury

The Panic of 1837 was a symptom of the financial sickness of the times. Its basic cause was evidently overspeculation, prompted by a mania of get-rich-quickism. Gamblers in Western lands were doing a "land-office business" on borrowed capital, much of it in the shaky currency of "wildcat banks." The speculative craze spread to canals, roads, railroads, and slaves.

But speculation alone did not cause the crash. Jacksonian finance, including the Bank War and the Specie Circular, gave an additional jolt to an already teetering structure. Failures of wheat crops, ravaged by the Hessian fly, deepened the distress. Grain prices were forced so high that mobs in New York City, three weeks before Van Buren took the oath, stormed warehouses and broke open flour barrels. The panic really began before Jackson left, but its full fury burst about Van Buren's bewildered head.

Financial stringency abroad likewise left its imprint on America. Late in 1836, while Jackson was still President, the failure of two prominent British banks created tremors and these in turn caused English investors to call in foreign loans. The resulting pinch in the United States, combined with other setbacks, heralded the beginning of the panic. Europe's economic distresses have often been America's distresses, for every major American financial panic has been affected by conditions overseas.

Hardship was acute and widespread. American banks collapsed by the hundreds, including some "pet banks," which carried down with them several millions in government funds. Commodity prices drooped, sales of public lands fell off, and customs revenues dried to a rivulet. Factories closed their doors; unemployed workers darkened the streets.

Philip Hone, a New York businessman, described in his diary (May 10, 1837) a phase of the financial crisis: "The savings-bank also sustained a most grievous run yesterday. They paid 375 depositors $81,000. The press was awful; the hour for closing the bank is six o'clock, but they did not get through the paying of those who were in at that time till nine o'clock. I was there with the other trustees and witnessed the madness of the people—women nearly pressed to death, and the stoutest men could scarcely sustain themselves; but they held on as with a death's grip upon the evidences of their claims, and, exhausted as they were with the pressure, they had strength to cry 'Pay! Pay!'"

Unhappily, the masses simply had to wait for the economic blizzard to blow itself out. The view prevailed, substantially unchanged until the 1930s, that the less governmental interference there was the better. Luckless Van Buren, shackled by this hands-off philosophy, could cope with the crisis only indirectly.

A perplexed President sought to bring some relief through his much-debated "Divorce Bill." Convinced that some of the financial fever had come from injecting government funds into politics, he championed the principle of "divorcing" the public revenue from private banks. The so-called Independent Treasury Bill is his chief claim to constructive statesmanship. The scheme was to lock the surplus federal money in government vaults, which would be located in the larger cities. Funds could be disbursed as needed, and they would not only be safe but completely divorced from politics. Yet they would also be denied to the banking system as reserves, thus shriveling available credit resources. The need for political purity triumphed over enlightened economics.

Van Buren's "divorce" scheme was never highly popular. It was supported only lukewarmly by his fellow Democrats, many of whom longed for the risky but lush days of the "pet banks." The new policy was condemned by the Whigs, primarily because it would dampen their hopes for a revived Bank of the United States. After a prolonged struggle, the Independent Treasury Bill passed Congress in 1840. Repealed the next year by the victorious Whigs, the sub-treasury scheme was re-enacted by the triumphant Democrats in 1846, and then continued until merged with the Federal Reserve System in the next century.

"Tippecanoe" Versus "Little Van"

Van Buren, though panic-tainted, was renominated by the Democrats in 1840, albeit without great enthusiasm. They had no acceptable alternative to what the Whigs called "Martin Van Ruin." Not to have run him again would have been a damaging admission that the party had foisted an unsound choice upon the country in 1836.

The Whigs, hungering for the spoils of office, scented victory in the breeze. Pangs of the panic

President William Henry Harrison (1773–1841). Harrison can claim several distinctions. At sixty-eight, he was the oldest man ever to be sworn in; he delivered the longest inaugural address (two hours); dying of pneumonia, he served the shortest term (thirty-one days); he obviously accomplished the least of any President; and he was responsible for the most progeny: 10 children; 48 grandchildren; 106 great-grandchildren. One of his grandchildren, Benjamin Harrison, became the 23rd President.

were still being felt; and voters blindly blamed their woes on the party in power. The Whigs turned again not to their ablest statesman—Clay or Webster—but to their presumably ablest vote-getter: General Harrison, a coarse-featured military chieftain, with a long, thin face and medium build (5 feet 8 inches; 1.72 meters).

The aging hero, nearly sixty-eight when the campaign ended, was a small-bore candidate. Despite an inflated reputation, he had been only moderately successful in civilian and military life, notably at the Battles of Tippecanoe (1811) and the Thames (1813). "Old Tippecanoe" was then living quietly in a sixteen-room mansion, located on a 3,000-acre farm near North Bend, Ohio. His views on current issues were only vaguely known. He was nominated primarily because he was issueless and enemyless—and a most unfortunate precedent was thus set. John Tyler of Virginia, an afterthought, was selected as his vice-presidential running mate.

The Whigs played this political game with the cards close to their vests. They published no platform, fearing to make bothersome commitments and unwilling to reveal the deep divisions within their own patchwork party. They hoped to sweep their hero in by a frothy huzza-for-Harrison campaign.

A dull-witted Democratic editor played directly into Whig hands. Stupidly insulting the West, he sneered at Harrison as an impoverished old farmer who would be content with a pension, a log cabin, and a barrel of hard cider—the poor Westerner's champagne. Whigs gleefully took up the challenge and, stressing the hard cider and log cabin theme, turned the campaign into a huge political revival meeting. Harrisonites portrayed their hero as the poor "Farmer of North Bend," who had been called from his plow and his log cabin to drive corrupt Jackson spoilsmen from the "presidential palace."

A non-existent candidate rapidly began to take shape in the hands of Whig mythmakers. The real Harrison was not lowborn, but from one of the F.F.V.'s (First Families of Virginia). He was not poverty-stricken; he did not live in a one-room log

Hard Cider Triumphant. A contemporary sketch.

cabin; he did not swill down gallons of hard cider (he evidently prefered whiskey); and he did not plow his fields with his own "huge paws."

Whig propagandists made merry with little "Matty" Van Buren, the "Flying Dutchman." Although reared in poverty, he was denounced as a supercilious aristocrat, who wore corsets and ate French food with golden teaspoons from golden plates. Jackson's rough-timbered Democratic party, deeply rooted in the West, was thus saddled with a simpering dandy from the aristocratic East. The aristocratic Whig party of Webster and Biddle, no less inconsistently, had come up with a backwoods nominee from the Democratic West—a reasonably good facsimile of wrinkled old General Jackson. As a jeering Whig campaign song proclaimed:

> Old Tip, he wears a homespun shirt,
>   He has no ruffled shirt, wirt, wirt.
> But Matt, he has the golden plate,
>   And he's a little squirt, wirt, wirt.

The Log Cabins and Hard Cider of 1840

Eager Democrats, who had hurrahed Jackson into the White House, now discovered to their chagrin that this was a game two could play. Acres of Whig audiences and miles of Whig marchers shouted

such slogans as: "Harrison, Two Dollars a Day and Roast Beef" and "With Tip and Tyler We'll Bust Van's Biler." Log cabins were dished up in every conceivable form. Bawling Whigs, stimulated by fortified cider, rolled huge inflated balls from village to village and state to state—balls that represented the snowballing majority for "Tip and Ty." As they pushed, they sang:

> Tippecanoe, and Tyler too.
> And with them we'll beat little Van, Van, Van,
>   Oh! Van is a used-up man.

Claptrap was king, as the electoral debauch reached an all-time intellectual low. There was little sober discussion of solid issues. Democrats inquired earnestly about the Bank, internal improvements, and the tariff. The replies were "log cabin," "hard cider," "Harrison is a poor man." Van Burenites, protesting futilely, were drowned in a tidal wave of apple juice as America experienced its first mass-turnout election.

Harrison won by the surprisingly close margin of 1,275,016 popular votes to 1,129,102, but by the overwhelming electoral count of 234 to 60. The hard-ciderites had seemingly received a mandate to go to Washington, tear down the White House, and erect a log cabin.

A Hard Road to Hoe! Jackson urges Van Buren toward the White House over a road littered with log cabins and hard cider. Van Buren, handicapped also by his unpopular sub-treasury policy, would evidently prefer the smoother road back to his Kinderhook home. A campaign cartoon of 1840. (Library of Congress.)

Basically, the vote was a protest against hard times—a thunderous shout of "Out with the old and in with the new." But the blatant buncombe and silly slogans set an unfortunate example for future campaigns. Democracy calls for hard thinking, not hard cider; for dignity, not delirium. Yet an able, well-organized, and well-entrenched political party, committed to solid principles, was hooted out of office by an inane hoopla campaign.

The Democrats were baffled. They complained with much bitterness and no little truth that they had been shouted down, sung down, lied down, and drunk down. Yet, though out-sloganed, they had kept their ranks intact. Even in defeat they were a stronger party than the Whigs. Though temporarily overdosed with hard cider, they would be heard from again.

VARYING VIEWPOINTS

The debate over Jacksonianism has shifted from a concern with geography to a concern with social class. Simultaneously, the question of Jackson's precise class position—and the class interests he represented—has moved to center stage. Arthur Schlesinger, Jr., had identified him with the working class and thus preserved Jackson's "popular" image. But other historians see "Old Hickory" as an aspiring frontier aristocrat, and they appraise Jacksonianism as a movement to liberate emerging capitalism from the restraints of an older "establishment." Jackson's war on the Bank, in this view, was less a popular crusade against the moneyed interests and more a blow by one segment of the business class against another segment of the business class. Indian policy, which has recently come in for renewed scrutiny, seems to reinforce the image of the Jacksonians as ambitious capitalists, motivated less by regard for human rights than by their own acquisitiveness.

SELECT READINGS

G. G. Van Deusen, *The Jacksonian Era, 1828–1848* (1959), is an excellent introduction. Colorful detail abounds in Marquis James, *Andrew Jackson: Portrait of a President* (1937). Incisive analysis can be found in Richard Hofstadter's essay on Jackson in *The American Political Tradition* (1948). Edward Pessen finds little to praise in *Jacksonian America: Society, Personality, and Politics* (1969). The opposing sides in the nullification crisis may be studied in C. M. Wiltse, *John C. Calhoun, Nullifier* (1951), and C. G. Sellers, *Andrew Jackson and the States-Rights Tradition* (1963). A superior monograph is W. W. Freehling, *Prelude to Civil War: The Nullification Controversy in South Carolina* (1966). Jacksonians are charged with ignorance and hypocrisy in Bray Hammond, *Banks and Politics in America, from the Revolution to the Civil War* (1957), and T. P. Govan defends *Nicholas Biddle: Nationalist and Public Banker* (1959). John McFaul looks at the broader picture in *The Politics of Jacksonian Finance* (1972). Jackson's Indian policies are scrutinized in four recent books: Arthur DeRosier, *The Removal of the Choctaw Indians* (1970), Thurman Wilkins, *Cherokee Tragedy* (1970), R. N. Satz, *American Indian Policy in the Jacksonian Era* (1975), and M. P. Rogin's heavily psychoanalytic *Fathers and Children: Andrew Jackson and the Subjugation of the American Indians* (1975). For an intriguing intellectual history of the same subject, see R. N. Pearce, *The Savages of America* (1965). Important political transformations are handled in R. P. McCormick, *The Second American Party System: Party Formation in the Jacksonian Era* (1966), and in R. Formisano, *The Birth of Mass Political Parties: Michigan, 1827–1861* (1971). Peter Temin interprets *The Jacksonian Economy* (1969). The color of the frothy presidential campaign of 1840 comes through in R. G. Gunderson, *The Log-Cabin Campaign* (1957). Daniel W. Howe provides a stimulating analysis of ideology in *The Political Culture of the American Whigs* (1980).

15

Manifest Destiny in the Forties

*Our manifest destiny [is] to overspread the
continent allotted by Providence for the free
development of our yearly multiplying millions.*

JOHN L. O'SULLIVAN, 1845*

The Accession of "Tyler Too"

A horde of hard-ciderites descended upon Washington early in 1841, clamoring for the spoils of office. Newly elected President Harrison, bewildered by the uproar, was almost hounded to death by Whig spoilsmen.

The real leaders of the Whig party regarded "Old Tippecanoe" as little more than an impressive figurehead. Daniel Webster, as secretary of state, and Henry Clay, the uncrowned king of the Whigs and their ablest spokesman in the Senate, would grasp the helm. The aging general was finally forced to rebuke the over-zealous Clay and

---

*Earliest known use of the term "manifest destiny," sometimes called "manifest desire."

pointedly remind him that William Henry Harrison was President of the United States.

Unluckily for Clay and Webster, their schemes soon hit a fatal snag. Before the new term had fairly started, Harrison came down with pneumonia. Wearied by official functions and plagued by office seekers, the enfeebled old warrior died after only four weeks in the White House—the shortest administration by far in American history, following by far the longest inaugural address.

The "Tyler too" part of the Whig ticket, hitherto only a rhyme, now claimed the spotlight. What manner of man did the nation now find in the presidential chair? Six feet (1.83 meters) tall, slender, blue-eyed, and fair-haired, with classical features and a high forehead, Tyler was a Virginia gentleman of the old school—gracious and kindly, yet stubbornly attached to principle. He had earlier resigned from the United States Senate, quite unnecessarily, rather than accept distasteful instructions from the Virginia legislature. Still a lone wolf, he had forsaken the Jacksonian Democratic fold for that of the Whigs, largely because he could not stomach the dictatorial tactics of Jackson.

Tyler's enemies accused him of being a Democrat in Whig clothing, but this charge was only partially true. The Whig party was something of a catchall, and the accidental President belonged to the minority wing, which embraced a number of Jeffersonian states'-righters. Tyler had in fact been put on the ticket partly to attract the vote of this influential group, many of whom were Southern gentry.

Yet Tyler, high-minded as he was, should never have consented to run on the ticket. Though the dominant Clay-Webster group had published no platform, every alert politician knew what the unpublished platform contained. And on virtually every major issue the obstinate Virginian was at odds with the majority of his Whig party, which was pro-Bank, pro–protective tariff, and pro–internal improvements. "Tyler too" rhymed with "Tippecanoe," but there the harmony ended. As events turned out, President Harrison, the Whig,

President John Tyler (1790–1862). The first "accidental President," he was faithful to his states'-rights convictions until death. A member of the Virginia secession convention in 1861, he served in the provisional congress of the Confederacy and was elected to a seat in the Confederate house of representatives. Invading Northern troops vengefully despoiled his beautiful Virginia estate, Sherwood Forest.

served for only four weeks, while Tyler, the ex-Democrat who was still largely a Democrat at heart, served for 204 weeks.

John Tyler: A President Without a Party

After their hard-won, hard-cider victory, the Whigs brought their secret platform out of Clay's waistcoat pocket. To the surprise of no one, it outlined a strongly nationalistic program.

Financial reform came first. The Whig Congress hastened to pass a law ending the Independent Treasury system, and President Tyler, disarmingly agreeable, signed it. Clay next drove through Congress a bill for a "Fiscal Bank," which would establish a new Bank of the United States.

Tyler's hostility to a centralized bank was notorious, and Clay—the "Great Compromiser"—would have done well to conciliate him. But the Kentuckian, robbed repeatedly of the presidency by lesser men, was in an imperious mood and riding for a fall. When the bank bill reached the presidential desk, Tyler flatly vetoed it on both practical and constitutional grounds. A drunken mob gathered late at night near the White House and shouted insultingly, "Huzza for Clay!" "A Bank! A Bank!" "Down with the Veto!"

The stunned Whig leaders tried once again.

Striving to meet Tyler's objections to a "Fiscal Bank," they passed another bill providing for a "Fiscal Corporation." But the President, still unbending, vetoed the offensive substitute. Democrats were jubilant: they had been saved from another financial "monster" only by the pneumonia that had felled Harrison.

Whig extremists, boiling with indignation, condemned Tyler as "His Accidency" and as an "Executive Ass." Widely burned in effigy, he received numerous letters threatening him with death. A wave of influenza then sweeping the country was called the "Tyler grippe." To the delight of Democrats, the stiff-necked Virginian was formally expelled from his party by a caucus of Whig congressmen, and a serious attempt to impeach him was made in the House of Representatives. His entire Cabinet resigned in a body, except Secretary of State Webster, who was then in the midst of delicate negotiations with England.

The proposed Whig tariff also felt the prick of the President's well-inked pen. Surprisingly enough, Tyler did sign a law passed in 1841 for bringing additional revenue to the depression-drained Treasury. But he looked with frosty eye on the major tariff scheme of the Whigs. It provided, among other features, for a distribution among the states of revenue from the sale of public lands in the West. Tyler could see no point in squandering federal money when the federal Treasury was not overflowing, and he again wielded an emphatic veto.

Chastened Clayites redrafted their tariff bill. They chopped out the offensive dollar-distribution scheme, and pushed down the rates to about the moderately protective level of 1832, roughly 32 percent on dutiable goods. Tyler had no fondness for a protective tariff, but realizing the need for additional revenue, he reluctantly signed the law of 1842. In subsequent months, the pressure for higher customs duties slackened as the country gradually edged its way out of the depression. The Whig slogan, "Harrison, Two Dollars a Day and Roast Beef," was rewritten by unhappy Democrats to read, "Ten Cents a Day and Bean Soup."

A War of Words with England

Hatred of England during the 19th Century came to a head periodically, and had to be lanced by treaty settlement or by war. The poison had festered ominously by 1842.

Anti-British passions were compounded of many ingredients. At bottom lay the bitter, red-coated memories of the two Anglo-American wars. In addition, the genteel pro-British Federalists had died out, eventually yielding to the boisterous Jacksonian Democrats. British travelers, sniffing with aristocratic noses at the crude scene, wrote acidly of American tobacco spitting, slave auctioneering, lynching, eye gouging, and other unsavory features of the rustic civilization. Travel books penned by these critics, whose views were avidly read on both sides of the Atlantic, stirred up angry outbursts in America.

But the literary fireworks did not end here. British magazines added fuel to the flames when, enlarging on the travel books, they launched sneering attacks on Yankee shortcomings. American journals struck back with "you're another" arguments, thus touching off the "Third War with

"Life In An American Hotel." An English caricature of American rudeness and readiness with the pistol. (*Punch*, 1856.)

England." Fortunately, it was fought with paper broadsides, and only ink was spilled. British authors, including Charles Dickens, entered the fray with gall-dipped pens, for they were being denied rich royalties by the absence of an American copyright law.*

Sprawling America, with expensive canals to dig and railroads to build, was a borrowing nation in the 19th Century. Imperial Britain, with her overflowing coffers, was a lending nation. The tight-fisted creditor is never popular with the debtor, and the phrase "bloated British bondholder" rolled bitterly from many an American tongue. When the Panic of 1837 broke, and several states defaulted on their bonds or repudiated them openly, honest Englishmen assailed Yankee trickery. One of them offered a new stanza for an old song:

> Yankee Doodle borrows cash,
> Yankee Doodle spends it,
>   And then he snaps his fingers at
> The jolly flat [simpleton] who lends it.

Troubles of a more dangerous sort came closer to home in 1837, when a short-lived insurrection erupted in Canada. It was supported by such a small minority of Canadians that it never had a real chance of success. Yet hundreds of hot-blooded Americans, hoping to strike a blow for freedom against the hereditary enemy, furnished military supplies or volunteered for armed service. The Washington regime tried arduously, though futilely, to uphold its weak neutrality regulations. But again, as in the case of Texas, it simply could not enforce unpopular laws in the face of popular opposition.

A provocative incident on the Canadian frontier brought passions to a boil in 1837. An American steamer, the *Caroline*, was engaged in carrying supplies to the insurgents across the swift Niagara River. It was finally attacked on the New York shore by a determined British force, which set the

vessel on fire. Lurid American illustrators showed the flaming ship, laden with shrieking souls, plunging over the Niagara Falls. The craft evidently sank short of the falls, and only one American was killed.

This unlawful invasion of American soil—a counter-violation of neutrality—had alarming aftermaths. The Washington officials lodged vigorous but ineffective protests. Three years later, in 1840, the incident was dramatically revived in the state of New York. A Canadian named McLeod, after allegedly boasting in a tavern of his part in the *Caroline* raid, was arrested and indicted for murder. The London Foreign Office, which regarded the *Caroline* raiders as members of an armed force and not as criminals, made clear that his execution would mean war. Fortunately, McLeod was freed after establishing an alibi. It must have been airtight, for it was good enough to convince a New York jury. The tension forthwith eased, but it snapped taut again in 1841, when British officials in the Bahamas offered asylum to 130 Virginia slaves who had rebelled and captured the American ship *Creole*.

Manipulating the Maine Maps

An explosive controversy of the early 1840s involved the Maine boundary dispute. The St. Lawrence River is icebound several months of the year, as the British, remembering the War of 1812, well knew. They were determined, as a defensive precaution against the Yankees, to build a road westward from the seaport of Halifax to Quebec. But the proposed route ran through disputed territory—claimed also by Maine under the misleading peace treaty of 1783. Tough-knuckled lumberjacks from both Maine and Canada entered the disputed no-man's-land of the tall-timbered Aroostook River Valley. Ugly fights flared up; both sides summoned the local militia. The small-scale lumberjack clash, dubbed the "Aroostook War," threatened to widen into a full-dress shooting war.

As the crisis deepened in 1842, the London Foreign Office took an unusual step. It sent to

---

*Not until 1891 did Congress extend copyright privileges to foreign authors.

Washington a non-professional diplomat, the conciliatory financier Lord Ashburton, who had married a wealthy American woman. He speedily established cordial relations with Secretary Webster, who had recently been lionized during a visit to England.

The two statesmen, their nerves frayed by protracted negotiations in the heat of a Washington summer, finally agreed to compromise on the Maine boundary. On the basis of a rough, split-the-difference arrangement, the Americans were to retain some 7,000 square miles (18,130 square kilometers) of the 12,000 square miles (31,080 square kilometers) of wilderness in dispute. The British got less land, but won the desired Halifax-Quebec route. During the negotiations the *Caroline* affair, dragged out since 1837, was patched up by an exchange of diplomatic notes.

The surrender of 5,000 square miles (12,950 square kilometers) of allegedly American soil to the British proved highly unpopular, especially among loyal Maine men. One irate United States senator branded the treaty a "solemn bamboozlement." But Webster had obtained an ancient map which indicated, ironically, that the British were entitled to the entire area in dispute. When he secretly displayed his find in Washington, the treaty quickly slipped through the Senate on greased skids.

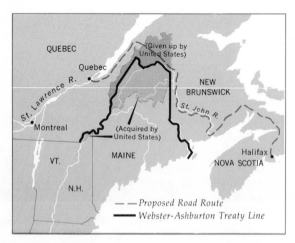

MAINE BOUNDARY SETTLEMENT, 1842

The London *Morning Chronicle* greeted the Webster-Ashburton treaty: "See the feeling with which the treaty has been received in America; mark the enthusiasm it has excited. What does this mean? Why, either that the Americans have gained a great diplomatic victory over us, or that they have escaped a great danger, as they have felt it, in having to maintain their claim by war."

British imperialists likewise condemned Lord Ashburton for his "capitulation." But their opposition also evaporated when the London officials turned up with another yellowing map: it proved that the *Americans* were entitled to the entire area in contention. Thus each party to the negotiation secretly held the other's trump card in the historic "Battle of the Maps."

Historians have since proved that the United States had a valid claim to the entire territory. This fact was not known at the time, perhaps fortunately, for the British were in no mood to give up the Halifax route. The yielding of 5,000 square miles (12,950 square kilometers) of pine-forested land, at least in 1842, seemed like a cheap price to pay for avoiding a senseless war.

An overlooked bonus was won in the same treaty when the British, in adjusting the boundary to the west, surrendered 6,500 square miles (16,835 square kilometers). The area was later found to contain the priceless Mesabi iron ore of Minnesota.

The Lone Star of Texas Shines Alone

The jilted Texan bride, during the uncertain eight years since 1836, had led a precarious existence. Mexico, refusing to recognize her independence, regarded the Lone Star Republic as a province in revolt, to be reconquered in the future. Mexican officials loudly threatened war if the American eagle should gather the fledgling republic under its protective wings.

General Santa Anna (1795–1876). Four-time president of Mexico, he lost California and the rest of the Mexican cession to the U.S. in 1848.

The Texans were forced to maintain a costly military establishment. Vastly outnumbered by their Mexican foe, they could not tell when he would strike again. Mexico actually did make two halfhearted raids which, though ineffectual, foreshadowed more fearsome efforts. Confronted with such perils, Texas was driven to open negotiations with England and France, in the hope of securing the defensive shield of a protectorate. In 1839 and 1840, the Texans concluded treaties with France, Holland, and Belgium.

Britain was intensely interested in an independent Texas. Such a republic would check the southward surge of the American colossus, whose bulging biceps posed a constant threat to nearby British possessions in the New World. A puppet Texas, dancing to strings pulled by Britain, could be turned upon the Yankees. Subsequent clashes would create a smoke-screen diversion, behind which foreign powers could move into the Americas and challenge the insolent Monroe Doctrine. French schemers were likewise attracted by the hoary game of divide and conquer. It would result, they hoped, in the fragmentation and militarization of America.

Dangers threatened from other foreign quarters. British abolitionists were busily intriguing for a foothold in Texas. If successful in freeing the few blacks there, they presumably would inflame the nearby slaves of the South. In addition, British merchants regarded Texas as a potentially important free-trade area—an offset to the tariff-walled United States. British manufacturers likewise perceived that those vast Texan plains constituted one of the great cotton-producing areas of the future. An independent Texas would relieve British looms of their fatal dependence on American fiber—a supply which might be cut off in time of crisis by embargo or war.

The Belated Texas Nuptials

Partly because of the fears aroused by British schemers, Texas became a leading issue in the presidential campaign of 1844. The foes of expansion assailed annexation, while Southern hotheads cried, "Texas or Disunion." The pro-expansion Democrats under James K. Polk finally triumphed over the Whigs under Henry Clay, the hardy perennial candidate. Lame-duck President Tyler thereupon interpreted the narrow Democratic victory, with dubious accuracy, as a "mandate" to acquire Texas.

Eager to crown his troubled administration with this splendid prize, Tyler deserves much of the credit for shepherding Texas into the fold. Many "conscience Whigs" feared that Texas in the Union would be red meat to nourish the lusty "slave power." Tyler despaired of securing the needed two-thirds vote for a treaty in the Senate, and he made haste to arrange for annexation by a joint resolution. This solution required only a simple majority in both houses of Congress. After a spirited debate, the resolution passed early in 1845, and Texas was formally invited to become the twenty-eighth star on the American flag. After some coyness, the waiting bride unpacked her mildewing wedding dress and was formally embraced as a full-fledged state.

Mexico angrily charged that the Americans had

Early Texas State House

despoiled her of Texas. This was to some extent true in 1836, but hardly true in 1845, for the area was no longer Mexico's to be despoiled of. As the years stretched out, realistic observers could see that the Mexicans would not be able to reconquer their lost province. Yet Mexico left the Texans dangling by denying their right to dispose of themselves as they chose.

By 1845, the Lone Star Republic had become a danger spot, inviting foreign intrigue that menaced the American people. Her continued existence as an independent nation threatened to involve the United States in a series of ruinous wars, both in America and in Europe. Americans were in a "lick all creation" mood when they sang "Uncle Sam's Song to Miss Texas":

> If Mexy back'd by secret foes,
>   Still talks of getting you, gal;
> Why we can lick 'em all you know
>   And then annex 'em too, gal.

What other power would have spurned the imperial domain of Texas? The bride was so near, so rich, so fair, so willing. Whatever the peculiar circumstances of the Texas revolution, the United States can hardly be accused of unseemly haste in achieving annexation. Nine long years were surely a decent wait between the beginning of the courtship and the consummation of the marriage.

Oregon Fever Populates Oregon

The so-called Oregon Country was an enormous wilderness. It sprawled magnificently west of the Rockies to the Pacific Ocean, and north of California to the line of 54° 40′—the present southern tip of the Alaska panhandle. All or substantial parts of this immense area were claimed at one time or another by four nations: Spain, Russia, Britain, and the United States.

Two claimants dropped out of the scramble. Spain, though the first to raise her banner in Oregon, bartered away her claims to the United States in the so-called Florida Treaty of 1819. The Russian Bear retreated to the line of 54° 40′ by the treaties of 1824 and 1825 with America and Britain. These two remaining rivals now had the field to themselves.

British claims to Oregon were strong—at least to that portion north of the Columbia River. They were based squarely on prior discovery and exploration, on treaty rights, and on actual occupation. The most important colonizing agency was the far-flung Hudson's Bay Company, which was trading profitably with the Indians of the Pacific Northwest for their furs.

Americans, for their part, could also point pridefully to exploration and occupation. Captain Robert Gray in 1792 had stumbled upon the majestic Columbia River, which he named after his ship; and the famed Lewis and Clark expedition of 1804–1806 had ranged overland through the Oregon Country to the Pacific. This shaky American toehold was ultimately strengthened by the presence of missionaries and other settlers, a sprinkling of whom reached the grassy Willamette River Valley, south of the Columbia, in the 1830s. These men of God, in saving the soul of the Indian, were instrumental in saving the soil of Oregon for the United States. They stimulated interest in a faraway domain which countless Americans had earlier assumed would not be settled for centuries.

Scattered American and British pioneers in Oregon continued to live peacefully side by side. At the time of negotiating the Treaty of 1818, the

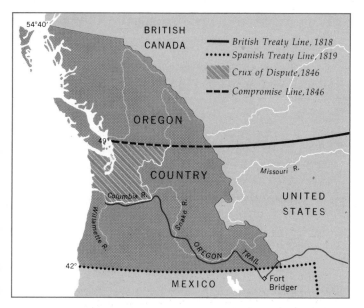

THE OREGON CONTROVERSY

In winning Oregon the Americans had great faith in their procreative powers. "Our people are spreading out," boasted one congressman in 1846, "with the aid of the American multiplication table. Go to the West and see a young man with his mate of eighteen; after the lapse of thirty years, visit him again, and instead of two, you will find twenty-two. That is what I call the American multiplication table."

United States had sought to divide the vast domain by the 49th parallel. But the British, who regarded the Columbia River as the St. Lawrence of the West, were unwilling to yield this vital artery. A scheme for peaceful "joint occupation" was thereupon adopted, pending a future settlement.

The handful of Americans in the Willamette Valley was suddenly multiplied in the early 1840s, when "Oregon fever" seized hundreds of restless pioneers. In increasing numbers their creaking covered wagons jolted over the 2,000-mile (3,200-kilometer) Oregon Trail as the human rivulet widened into a stream.* By 1846 there were about 5,000 American settlers south of the Columbia River, some of them tough "border ruffians," expert with Bowie knife and "revolving pistol."

The British, in the face of this rising torrent of humanity, could muster only 700 or so subjects

north of the Columbia. Losing out lopsidedly in the population race, they were beginning to see the wisdom of arriving at a peaceful settlement before being engulfed by their neighbors.

A curious fact is that only a relatively small segment of the Oregon Country was in actual controversy by 1845. The area in dispute consisted of the rough triangle between the Columbia River on the south and the 49th parallel on the north. Britain had repeatedly offered the line of the Columbia; America had repeatedly offered the 49th parallel. The whole fateful issue was now tossed into the presidential election of 1844.

A Mandate(?) for Manifest Destiny

The two major parties nominated their presidential standard-bearers in May 1844. Ambitious but often frustrated Henry Clay, easily the most popular man in the country, was enthusiastically chosen by the Whigs at Baltimore. The Democrats, meeting later in the same city, seemed hopelessly deadlocked. Finally the expansionists, dominated by the pro-Texas Southerners, trotted out and nominated James K. Polk of Tennessee, the nation's first "dark horse" or "surprise" presidential candidate.

Polk may have been a dark horse, but he was not an unknown or decrepit horse. Speaker of the House of Representatives for four years and governor of Tennessee for two terms, he was a determined, industrious, ruthless, and intelligent

---

*The average rate of progress in covered wagons was one to two miles an hour. This amounted to about 100 miles (161 kilometers) a week or about five months for the entire journey. Thousands of humans, in addition to horses and oxen, died en route. One estimate is seventeen deaths a mile for men, women, and children.

James K. Polk (1795–1849). Distinguished for both determination and deviousness, Polk added more territory to the U.S. (by questionable means) than any other President. In tenaciously pursuing his goals, he broke himself down with overwork and died 103 days after his single term ended. His childless wife (and secretary) had banned all drinking and dancing in the White House. (National Archives.)

public servant. Sponsored by Andrew Jackson, his friend and neighbor, he was rather implausibly built up by Democrats as yet another "Young Hickory." Whigs attempted to jeer him into oblivion with the taunt, "Who is James K. Polk?" They soon found out.

The campaign of 1844 was in part an expression of the mighty emotional upsurge known as Manifest Destiny. Countless citizens in the 1840s and 1850s, feeling a sense of mission, believed that Almighty God had "manifestly" destined the American people for a hemispheric career. They would irresistibly spread their uplifting and ennobling democratic institutions over at least the entire continent, and possibly over South America as well. Land greed and ideals were thus conveniently conjoined.

Expansionist Democrats were strongly swayed by the intoxicating spell of Manifest Destiny. They came out flat-footedly in their platform for the "Reannexation of Texas"* and the "Reoccupation of Oregon," all the way to 54° 40'. Outbellowing the Whig log-cabinites in the game of slogans, they shouted "All of Oregon or None." They also condemned Clay as a "corrupt bargainer," a dissolute character, and a slaveowner. (Their own candidate, Polk, owned slaves—a classic case of the pot calling the kettle black.)

The Whigs, as noisemakers, took no back seat. They countered with such slogans as "Hooray for Clay" and "Polk, Slavery, and Texas, or Clay, Union, and Liberty." They also spread the lie that a gang of Tennessee slaves had been seen on their way to a Southern market with the initials J. K. P. (James K. Polk) branded on them.

On the crucial issue of Texas, the acrobatic Clay tried to ride two horses at once. The "Great Compromiser" appears to have compromised away the presidency when he wrote a series of confusing letters. They seemed to say that while he personally favored annexing slaveholding Texas (an appeal to the South), he also favored postponement (an appeal to the North). He might have lost more ground if he had not "straddled," but he certainly alienated the more ardent anti-slaveryites.

In the stretch drive, "Dark Horse" Polk nipped Henry Clay at the wire, 170 to 105 in the Electoral College and 1,337,243 to 1,299,062 in the popular column. Clay would have won if he had not lost New York State by a scant 5,000 votes. There the tiny anti-slavery Liberty party absorbed nearly 16,000 votes, many of which would otherwise have gone to the unlucky Kentuckian. Ironically, the anti-Texas Liberty party, by helping to insure the election of pro-Texas Polk, hastened the annexation of Texas.

Land-hungry Democrats, flushed with victory, proclaimed that they had received a mandate from the voters to take Texas. But a presidential election is seldom, if ever, a clear-cut mandate on anything.

---

*The United States had given up its claims to Texas in the so-called Florida Purchase Treaty with Spain in 1819 (see p. 214). The slogan "Fifty-four forty or fight" was evidently not coined until two years later, in 1846.

The only way to secure a true reflection of the voters' will is to hold a special election on a given issue. The picture that emerged in 1844 is not one of mandate but of muddle. What else could there have been when the results were so close, the personalities so colorful, and the issues so numerous—including Oregon, Texas, the tariff, slavery, the Bank, and internal improvements? Yet this unclear "mandate" was interpreted by President Tyler as a clear mandate to annex Texas—and he signed the joint resolution three days before leaving the White House.

Polk the Purposeful

"Young Hickory" Polk, unlike "Old Hickory" Jackson, was not an impressive figure. Of middle height (5 feet 8 inches; 1.72 meters), lean, white-haired (worn long), gray-eyed, and stern-faced, he took life seriously and drove himself mercilessly into a premature grave. His burdens were increased by an unwillingness to delegate authority. Methodical and hardworking but not brilliant, he was shrewd, narrow, conscientious, and persistent. "What he went for he fetched," wrote a contemporary. Pur-

President Polk's Flimsy House of Cards. He appears to be hatching troublesome eggs relating to vexatious issues. (*Yankee Doodle.*)

House Vote on Tariff of 1846

Regions	For	Against
New England	9	19
Middle States	18	44
West and Northwest	29	10
South and Southwest	58	20
TOTAL	114	93

Compare vote on 1832 tariff, p. 239.

poseful in the highest degree, he developed a positive four-point program, and with remarkable success achieved it completely in less than four years.

One of Polk's goals was a lowered tariff. His secretary of the treasury, wispy Robert J. Walker, devised a tariff-for-revenue bill which reduced the average rates of the Tariff of 1842 from about 32 percent to 25 percent. With the strong support of low-tariff Southerners, Walker lobbied the measure through Congress, though not without loud complaints from the Clayites, especially in New England and the Middle States, that American manufacturing would be ruined. But these prophets of doom missed the mark. The Walker Tariff of 1846 proved to be an excellent revenue producer, largely because it was followed by boom times and heavy imports.

A second objective of Polk was the restoration of the Independent Treasury, unceremoniously dropped by the Whigs in 1841. Pro-Bank Whigs in Congress raised a storm of opposition, but victory at last rewarded the President's efforts in 1846.

The third and fourth points on Polk's "must list" were the acquisition of California and the settlement of the Oregon dispute.

"Reoccupation" of the "whole" of Oregon had been promised Northern Democrats in the campaign of 1844. But Southern Democrats, once they had "reannexed" Texas, rapidly cooled off. Polk, himself a Southerner, had no intention of insisting on the 54° 40′ pledge of his own platform. But feeling bound by the three offers of his predecessors to London, he again proposed the compromise line of 49°. The British minister in Washington, on

Ridiculous Exhibition. "Yankee noodle" putting his head into the British Lion's mouth. British view of American bluster on the Oregon issue. (*Punch,* 1846.)

his own initiative, brusquely spurned this olive branch.

The next move on the Oregon chessboard was up to Britain. Fortunately for peace, the ministry began to experience a change of heart. British anti-expansionists ("Little Englanders") were now persuaded that the Columbia River after all was not the St. Lawrence of the West, and that the turbulent American hordes might one day seize the Oregon Country. Why fight a hazardous war over this wilderness on behalf of an unpopular monopoly, the Hudson's Bay Company, which had already "furred out" much of the area anyhow?

Early in 1846 the British, hat in hand, came around and themselves proposed the line of 49°. Polk, irked by the previous rebuff, threw the decision squarely into the lap of the Senate. The senators speedily accepted the offer and approved the subsequent treaty, despite a few diehard shouts of "Fifty-four forty forever!" and "Every foot or not an inch!" The fact that the United States was then a month deep in the Mexican War doubtless influenced the final vote.

Satisfaction with the Oregon settlement among Americans was not unanimous. The Northwestern states, hotbed of Manifest Destiny and "fifty-four fortyism," joined the anti-slavery men in condemning what they regarded as a base betrayal by

the South. Why *all* of Texas and not *all* of Oregon? Because, sneered the expansionist Senator Benton of Missouri, "Great Britain is powerful and Mexico is weak."

So Polk, despite all the campaign bluster, got neither "fifty-four forty" nor a fight. But he did get something that in the long run was better: a reasonable compromise without shedding a drop of blood.

Misunderstandings with Mexico

Faraway California was another worry of Polk's. He and other disciples of Manifest Destiny had long coveted its verdant valleys, and especially the spacious bay of San Francisco. This splendid har-

Senator Benton Speaking at His Desk. Thomas Hart Benton (1782–1858), four-time Missouri senator, had grown up in Tennessee, where he had engaged in a tavern brawl with Andrew Jackson. The two became reconciled, and "Old Bullion" Benton loyally supported Jackson's hard-money ("Benton's Mint Drops") and anti-Bank policies.

AMERICAN LIFE IN PAINTING 1750-1865

Paul Revere, c. 1768
by John Singleton Copley
(1738–1815)

Copley, a Bostonian who pursued the major portion of his career in London, left an eloquent artistic record of colonial life. This painting of the Massachusetts silversmith-horseman, Paul Revere, challenged convention by portraying an artisan in working clothes admiring a teapot he had just finished. Note how Copley has depicted the serene confidence of the master craftsman and Revere's quiet pride in his work. *Courtesy Museum of Fine Arts, Boston* (Gift of Joseph W., William B., and Edward H. R. Revere).

Sea Captains Carousing in Surinam, 1757–1758, by John Greenwood (1727–1792)

This playful portrayal of Yankee sea captains far from home is often regarded as America's first "genre painting," or a painting realistically showing a scene from everyday life. The South American setting in Dutch Guiana is a reminder of the distant trade connections established by American shippers in the colonial era. The lively ale-house merriment suggests that not all seamen were sober-sided Puritans. *The St. Louis Art Museum.*

The Skater (Portrait of William Grant), 1782
by Gilbert Stuart (1755–1828)

Stuart, a Rhode Islander, is most famous for his
numerous portraits of the "American aristocracy."
(The current dollar bill bears one of Stuart's
several portraits of George Washington.) The
skater's easy equilibrium suggests the poise and
self-assurance of a well-to-do American gentleman
of the era. Like Copley's *Paul Revere,* Stuart's
skater is a model of self-confidence and individual
dignity. Compare these renditions of 18th-Century
people with George Tooker's portrayal of 20th-
Century life in *The Subway* (second color section).
National Gallery of Art, Washington (Andrew W. Mellon
Collection).

Fur Traders Descending the Missouri, 1844
by George Caleb Bingham
(1811–1879)

Bingham, a son of the Missouri frontier, achieved widespread popularity in his day with his paintings of scenes from the Western wilderness. Here he has portrayed a moment of calm in an obviously strenuous life. The fragile dugout canoe on the ominously placid water, the tethered animal in the bow, and the recently shot duck (contrasted with the flock in the distant sky) evoke the pioneer's constant battle with nature. *All rights reserved. The Metropolitan Museum of Art, Morris K. Jesup Fund, 1933.*

Winter Scene in Brooklyn, c. 1817–1820, by Francis Guy (1760–1820)

Life in the cities of the early Republic was devoid of many of the amenities that made urban living attractive to later generations of Americans. This painting of Brooklyn, near the site of the later Brooklyn Bridge, shows that city-dwellers, like their country counterparts, still had to split their own firewood, draw their own water, and brave the icy elements as they went about their daily business. *The Brooklyn Museum, Gift of the Brooklyn Institute of Arts and Sciences.*

The Old Plantation, Late 18th Century, artist unknown

This painting by an unknown artist reveals a frolicsome moment in the lives of slaves on a Southern plantation. The fancy clothing worn by the dancing blacks suggests that this scene may have been idealized. The painting also suggests that African art forms survived in America. The small drum on the right closely resembles the "gudu-gudu" drum used by the Yoruba peoples of West Africa. It is identifiable primarily by the small drumsticks the slave is using, made of rolled strips of stiff leather. *Abby Aldrich Rockefeller Folk Art Center, Williamsburg, Virginia.*

The Residence of David Twining, 1787, 1845–1848, by Edward Hicks (1780–1849)

A Quaker sign-painter from Bucks County, Pennsylvania, Hicks reproduced many scenes of farm life and of a tranquil nature where all manner of animals and children mingled peaceably with one another. Elements of that eloquent Quaker vision can be seen in this vivid painting of David Twining's well-maintained eastern Pennsylvania farm, where different breeds of animals, different generations, and different races live in fertile harmony. *Abby Aldrich Rockefeller Folk Art Center, Williamsburg, Virginia.*

The Quilting Party, Third quarter 19th Century, artist unknown

Pioneer families would often turn tiresome tasks into social events. Here several families gather while the women, young and old, piece together a patchwork quilt. The men serve the food and help mind the baby. The couple in the right-hand corner has taken advantage of the occasion to engage in a little discreet hand-holding. *Abby Aldrich Rockefeller Folk Art Center, Williamsburg, Virginia.*

Joseph Moore and His Family, 1839 by Erastus Salisbury Field (1805–1900)

New England small-town life had a certain austere elegance and sober dignity in the age of Jackson. Here Joseph Moore of Ware, Massachusetts, proudly poses with his family in their simple but properly appointed parlor. Note the formal attire on the children, who are portrayed as "little adults." *Courtesy Museum of Fine Arts, Boston (M & M Karolik Collection).*

Blacksmith Shop, Last third 19th Century, attributed to Francis A. Beckett.

This blacksmith shop in gold-rush California was exceptionally well outfitted. The leather-aproned owner sports a stovepipe hat, while his assistants wear mere derbies. Note the massive bellows suspended from the high ceiling. It could heat the fire to blast-furnace temperatures. *National Gallery of Art, Washington* (Gift of Edgar William and Bernice Chrysler Garbisch).

A Ride for Liberty, c. 1862 by Eastman Johnson (1824–1906)

Johnson was a New Englander who traveled widely in the South so as to understand better and properly interpret the hardships of black people under slavery. In this painting before emancipation, he brilliantly evoked the anxiety of fleeing slaves. *The Brooklyn Museum* (Gift of Miss Gwendolyn O. L. Conkling).

bor was widely regarded as America's future gateway to the Pacific Ocean.

The population of California in 1845 was curiously mixed. It consisted of some 7,000 sun-blessed Spanish-Mexicans, plus more than ten times as many dispirited Indians. There were fewer than a thousand foreigners, mostly Americans, some of whom had "left their consciences" behind them as they rounded Cape Horn. Given time, these transplanted Yankees might yet bring California into the Union by "playing the Texas game."

Polk was eager to buy California from Mexico, but relations with Mexico City were dangerously embittered. Among other friction points, the United States had claims against the Mexicans for some $3 million in damages to American citizens and their property. The revolution-riddled regime in Mexico had formally agreed to assume most of this debt, but had been forced to default on its payments.

A more serious bone of contention was Texas. The Mexican government, after threatening war if the United States should acquire the Lone Star Republic, had recalled its minister from Washington following annexation. Diplomatic relations were completely severed.

Deadlock with Mexico over Texas was further tightened by a question of boundaries. During the long era of Spanish-Mexican occupation, the southwestern boundary of Texas had been the Nueces River. But the expansive Texans, on rather farfetched grounds, were claiming the more southerly Rio Grande instead. Polk, for his part, felt a strong moral obligation to defend Texas in her claim, once she was annexed.

The Mexicans were far less concerned about this boundary quibble than the United States. In their eyes all of Texas was still theirs, although temporarily in revolt, and a dispute over the two rivers seemed pointless. Yet Polk was careful to keep American troops out of virtually all of the explosive no-man's-land between the Nueces and the Rio Grande, as long as there was any real prospect of peaceful adjustment.

The golden prize of California continued to cause Polk much anxiety. Disquieting rumors (now known to have been ill-founded) were circulating that the British Lion was about to buy or seize California—a grab that Americans could not tolerate under the Monroe Doctrine. In a last desperate throw of the dice, Polk dispatched John Slidell to Mexico City as minister late in 1845. The new envoy, among other alternatives, was instructed to offer a maximum of $25 million for California and territory to the east. But the proud Mexicans would not even permit Slidell to present his "insulting" proposition.

American Blood on American(?) Soil

A frustrated Polk was now prepared to force a showdown. On January 13, 1846, he ordered 4,000 men, under General Zachary Taylor, to march from the Nueces River to the Rio Grande, provocatively near Mexican forces. Polk's presidential diary reveals that he expected at any moment to hear of a clash. When none occurred after an anxious wait, he informed his Cabinet on May 9, 1846, that he proposed to ask Congress to declare war on the basis of (1) unpaid claims and (2) Slidell's rejection. These, at best, were rather flimsy pretexts. Two Cabinet members spoke up and said that they would feel better satisfied if Mexican troops should fire first.

That very evening, as fate would have it, news of bloodshed arrived. On April 25, 1846, Mexican troops had crossed the Rio Grande and attacked General Taylor's command, with a loss of sixteen Americans killed or wounded.

Polk, further aroused, sent a vigorous war message to Congress. He declared that despite "all our efforts" to avoid a clash, hostilities had been forced upon the country by the shedding of "American blood on the American soil." A patriotic Congress overwhelmingly voted for war, and enthusiastic volunteers cried, "Ho for the Halls of the Montezumas!" and "Mexico or Death!" Inflamed by the war fever, even anti-slavery Whig centers joined with the rest of the nation, though they later condemned "Jimmy Polk's war." As

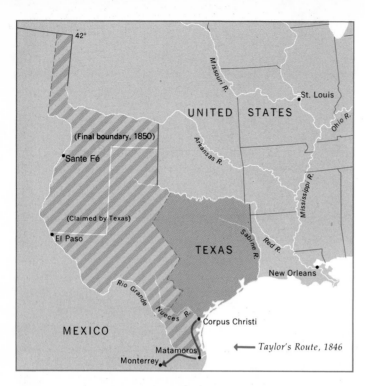

TEXAS, 1845–1846

Texas President Mirabeau Buonaparte Lamar, flushed with imperial dreams, tried to secure the Texas claim to the large striped area on this map by leading a military expedition in 1841 against the Mexicans at Santa Fe. But the weak and outgunned "army" of the Lone Star Republic, made up mostly of American drifters and adventurers, was speedily smashed. The Texans drew in their horns thereafter, and with renewed vigor sought annexation to the United States, rather than further expansion to the West of their precariously independent nation.

James Russell Lowell of Massachusetts lamented,

Massachusetts, God forgive her,
She's akneelin' with the rest.

In his message to Congress Polk was making history—not writing it. If he had been a historian, he would have explained that American blood had been shed on soil which the Mexicans had good reason to regard as their own. A gangling, rough-featured Whig congressman from Illinois, one Abraham Lincoln, introduced certain resolutions that requested information as to the precise "spot" on American soil where American blood had been shed. He pushed his "spot" resolutions with such persistence that he came to be known as the "spotty Lincoln," who could die of "spotted fever." The more extreme anti-slavery agitators of the North, many of them Whigs, branded the President a liar—"Polk the Mendacious."

Did Polk provoke war? California was an imperative point in his program, and Mexico would not sell it at any price. The only way to get it was to use force, or wait for an internal American revolt. Yet delay seemed dangerous, for the claws of the British Lion might snatch the ripening California fruit from the talons of the American Eagle. Grievances against Mexico were annoying yet tolerable; in later years America endured even worse ones. But in 1846 patience had ceased to be a virtue, as far as Polk was concerned. So he pushed the quarrel to a bloody showdown.

Both sides, in fact, were spoiling for a fight. Hotheaded Americans, especially Southwestern expansionists, were eager to teach the Mexicans a lesson. The Mexicans, in turn, were burning to humiliate the "Bullies of the North." Possessing a

Less than a year before he became President, Lincoln wrote that "the act of sending an armed force among the Mexicans was unnecessary, inasmuch as Mexico was in no way molesting or menacing the United States or the people thereof; and that it was unconstitutional, because the power of levying war is vested in Congress, and not in the President" (June 1, 1860).

considerable standing army, heavily overstaffed with generals, they boasted of invading the United States, freeing the black slaves, and lassoing whole regiments of Americans. They were hoping that the quarrel with Britain over Oregon would blossom into a full-dress war, as it came near doing, and further pin down the hated *Yanquis*. A conquest of Mexico's vast and arid expanses seemed fantastic, especially in view of the bungling American invasion of Canada in 1812.

Both sides were fired by moral indignation. The Mexicans could fight with the flaming sword of righteousness, for had not the "insolent" Yankee picked a fight by polluting their soil? Many earnest Americans, on the other hand, sincerely believed that Mexico was the aggressor.

The Mastering of Mexico

Polk wanted California—not war. But when war came he hoped to fight it on a limited scale, and then pull out when he had won the prize. The dethroned Mexican dictator Santa Anna, then exiled with his teenage bride in Cuba, let it be known that if the American blockading squadron would permit him to slip into Mexico, he would sell out his country. This discreditable intrigue was finally carried through. But the double-crossing Santa Anna, self-styled "Napoleon of the West," rallied the Mexicans to a desperate defense of their soil.

American operations in the Southwest and in California were completely successful. In 1846 General Stephen W. Kearny led a detachment of about 1,700 troops over the famous Santa Fe trail, from Fort Leavenworth to Santa Fe. This sun-baked outpost, with its drowsy plazas, was easily captured. But before Kearny could reach California, the fertile province was won. When war broke out, Captain John C. Frémont, the dashing explorer, just "happened" to be there with several dozen well-armed men. In helping to overthrow Mexican rule in 1846, he collaborated with American naval officers and with the local Americans, who had hoisted the banner of the short-lived California Bear Flag Republic.

The Bear Flag of California. (California Historical Society Library and California State Library, Sacramento)

General Zachary Taylor meanwhile had been spearheading the main thrust. Known as "Old Rough and Ready" because of his iron constitution and incredibly unsoldierly appearance—he sometimes wore a Mexican straw hat—he fought his way across the Rio Grande into Mexico. After several gratifying victories, he reached Buena Vista. There, on February 22–23, 1847, his weakened force of 5,000 men was attacked by some 20,000 march-weary troops under Santa Anna. The Mexicans were finally repulsed with extreme difficulty, and overnight Zachary Taylor became the "Hero of Buena Vista." One Kentuckian was heard to say that "Old Zack" would be elected President in 1848 by "spontaneous combustion."

Sound American strategy now called for a crushing blow at the enemy's vitals—Mexico City. General Taylor, though a good leader of modest-sized forces, could not win decisively in the semideserts of northern Mexico. The command of the main expedition, which pushed inland from the coastal city of Vera Cruz early in 1847, was entrusted to General Winfield Scott. A handsome giant of a man, Scott had emerged as a hero from the War of 1812 and had later earned the nickname of "Old Fuss and Feathers" because of his resplendent uniforms and strict discipline. He was severely handicapped in the Mexican campaign by inadequate numbers of troops, by expiring enlistments, by a more numerous enemy, by mountainous terrain, by disease, and by political backbiting at home. Yet he succeeded in battling his way up to Mexico City by September 1847 in one of the most brilliant campaigns in American mili-

tary annals. He proved to be the most distinguished general produced by his country between 1783 and 1861.

Fighting Mexico for Peace

Polk was anxious to end the shooting as soon as he could secure his territorial goals. Accordingly, he sent along with Scott's invading army the chief clerk of the State Department, Nicholas P. Trist, who among other weaknesses was afflicted with an overfluid pen. Trist and Scott arranged for an armistice with Santa Anna, at a cost of $10,000. The wily dictator pocketed the bribe, and then used the time to bolster his defenses.

Negotiating a treaty with a sword in one hand and a pen in the other was ticklish business. Polk, disgusted with his blundering envoy, abruptly recalled Trist. The wordy diplomat then dashed off a sixty-five-page letter explaining why he was not coming home. The President was furious. But Trist, grasping a fleeting opportunity to negotiate, signed the Treaty of Guadalupe-Hidalgo on February 2, 1848, and forwarded it to Washington.

The terms of the treaty were breathtaking. They confirmed the American title to Texas, and yielded the enormous area stretching westward to Oregon and the ocean and embracing coveted California. This total expanse, including Texas, was about one-half of Mexico. The United States agreed to pay $15 million for the land, and to assume the claims of its citizens against Mexico in the amount of $3,250,000.

Polk submitted the treaty to the Senate. Although Trist had proved highly annoying, he had generally followed his original instructions. And speed was imperative. The anti-slavery Whigs in Congress—dubbed "Mexican Whigs"—were condemning this "damnable war" with increasing heat. Having secured control of the House in 1847, they were even threatening to vote down supplies for the armies in the field. If they had done so, Scott probably would have been forced to retreat, and the fruits of victory might have been tossed away.

Another peril impended. A swelling group of expansionists, intoxicated by Manifest Destiny, was clamoring for all of Mexico. If America had

IOIIOIIOIIOIIOIIOIIOIIOIIOIIOIIOIIOIIOIIOIIOIIOIIOIIOIIOI

Early in 1848 the New York *Evening Post* demanded: ''Now we ask, whether any man can coolly contemplate the idea of recalling our troops from the [Mexican] territory we at present occupy . . . and . . . resign this beautiful country to the custody of the ignorant cowards and profligate ruffians who have ruled it for the last twenty-five years? Why, humanity cries out against it. Civilization and Christianity protest against this reflux of the tide of barbarism and anarchy.'' Such was one phase of Manifest Destiny.

IOIIOIIOIIOIIOIIOIIOIIOIIOIIOIIOIIOIIOIIOIIOIIOIIOIIOIIOI

seized it, the nation would have been saddled with an expensive and vexatious policing problem. Far-seeing Southerners like Calhoun, alarmed by the mounting anger of anti-slavery agitators, realized that the South would do well not to be too greedy. The treaty was finally approved by the Senate, 38 to 14. Oddly enough, it was condemned both by opponents who wanted all of Mexico and by opponents who wanted none of it.

Victors rarely pay an indemnity, especially after a costly conflict has been "forced" on them. Yet Polk, who had planned to offer $25 million before the war, arranged to pay $18,250,000 after winning the war. Cynics have charged that the Americans were pricked by guilty consciences; apologists have pointed proudly to the "Anglo-Saxon spirit of fair play." A decisive factor was the need for haste, while there was still a responsible Mexican government to carry out the treaty, and before political foes in the United States, notably the anti-slavery zealots, sabotaged Polk's expansionist program.

Profit and Loss in Mexico

As wars go, the Mexican War was a small one. It cost some 13,000 American lives, most of them taken by disease. But the fruits of the fighting were enormous.

America's total expanse, already vast, was increased by about one-third (counting Texas)—an addition even greater than that of the Louisiana Purchase. A sharp stimulus was given to the spirit of Manifest Destiny for, as the proverb has it, the appetite comes with eating.

As fate ordained, the Mexican War was the blood-spattered schoolroom of the Civil War. The campaigns provided priceless field experience for most of the officers destined to become leading generals in the forthcoming conflict, including Captain Robert E. Lee and Lieutenant U. S. Grant. The Military Academy at West Point, founded in 1802, fully justified its existence through the well-trained officers. Useful also was the navy, which did valuable work in throwing a crippling blockade around Mexican ports. The Marine Corps, in existence since 1798, won new laurels, and to this day sings in its stirring hymn about the Halls of Montezuma.

The army waged war without defeat and without a major blunder, despite formidable obstacles and a half dozen or so incredibly long marches. Chagrined British critics, as well as other foreign skeptics, reluctantly revised upward their estimate of Yankee military prowess. Opposing armies,

PLUCKED:

THE MEXICAN EAGLE BEFORE THE WAR!   THE MEXICAN EAGLE AFTER THE WAR!

A Cartoon from *Yankee Doodle*, 1847. This satiric drawing was symbolic of the "lick all creation" spirit of the times.

moreover, emerged with increased respect for each other. The Mexicans, though poorly led, fought heroically. At Chapultepec, near Mexico City, the teenage lads of the military academy there (*los niños*) perished to a boy.

Long-memoried Mexicans have never forgotten that their northern enemy tore away about half of their country. The argument that they were lucky not to lose all of it, and that they had been paid something for their land, did not lessen their bitterness. The war also marked an ugly turning point in the relations between the United States and Latin America as a whole. Hitherto, Uncle Sam had been regarded with some complacency, even friendliness. Henceforth, he was increasingly feared as the "Colossus of the North." Suspicious neighbors to the south condemned him as a greedy and untrustworthy bully, who might next despoil them of their soil.

Most ominous of all, the war rearoused the snarling dog of the slavery issue, and the beast did not stop yelping until drowned in the blood of the Civil War. Abolitionists assailed the Mexican conflict as one provoked by the Southern "slavocracy" for its own evil purposes. As James Russell Lowell had Hosea Biglow drawl in his Yankee dialect:

> They jest want this Californy
>   So's to lug new slave-states in
> To abuse ye, an' to scorn ye,
>   An' to plunder ye like sin.

In line with Lowell's charge, the bulk of the American volunteers were admittedly from the South and Southwest. But, as in the case of the Texan revolution, the basic explanation was proximity rather than conspiracy.

Quarreling over slavery extension also erupted on the floors of Congress. In 1846, shortly after the shooting started, Polk requested an appropriation of $2 million with which to buy a peace. Representative David Wilmot of Pennsylvania, fearful of the Southern "slavocracy," introduced a fateful amendment. It stipulated that slavery should never exist in any of the territory to be wrested from Mexico.

The disruptive Wilmot amendment twice passed the House, but not the Senate. Southern members, unwilling to be robbed of prospective slave states, fought the restriction tooth and nail. Anti-slavery men, in Congress and out, battled no less bitterly for the exclusion of slaves. The "Wilmot Proviso" soon came to symbolize the burning issue of slavery in the territories.

In a broad sense, the opening shots of the Mexican War were the opening shots of the Civil War. President Polk left the nation the splendid physical heritage of California and the Southwest, but also the ugly moral heritage of an embittered slavery dispute. Mexicans could later take some satisfaction in knowing that the territory wrenched from them had proved to be a frightful apple of discord that could well be called Santa Anna's revenge.

VARYING VIEWPOINTS

Historians have long probed for the real meaning behind the pulse-stirring phrase "Manifest Destiny." Some have emphasized the idealistic impulses behind continental expansion. Others have stressed the supposed "superiority" of Anglo-Saxon culture over Indian and Spanish civilizations. Still other writers have seen American expansion as simply another chapter in the familiar story of territorial conquest. In recent years many historians, no doubt influenced by the general reappraisal of America's relations with the rest of the world, have stressed the "hard"—even "imperialistic"—forces behind America's territorial growth. Scholars have also begun to show more interest in, and sympathy for, the peoples displaced or absorbed in America's sweep to the Western sea.

SELECT READINGS

A good introduction is G. G. Van Deusen, *The Jacksonian Era* (1959). R. A. Billington, *Westward Expansion* (rev. ed., 1974), is comprehensive. On Tyler, see R. Seager II, *And Tyler Too* (1963). Still useful is A. Weinberg, *Manifest Destiny* (1935), though it should be supplemented by Edward M. Burns, *The American Idea of Mission: Concepts of National Purpose and Destiny* (1957), and F. Merk, *Manifest Destiny and Mission in American History* (1963). See also F. Merk, *Monroe Doctrine and American Expansionism, 1843–1849* (1966). Paul Horgan, *Great River* (1954), is a magnificent history of the Southwest and the Rio Grande. *The Texas Revolution* is the subject of W. C. Binkley's 1952 study. It should be supplemented by F. Merk, *Slavery and the Annexation of Texas* (1972). For the Pacific region, see Francis Parkman's classic *The California and Oregon Trail* (1849), and N. A. Graebner's general account, *Empire on the Pacific* (1955). F. Merk is definitive on *The Oregon Question* (1967), and J. Caughey provides an excellent introduction to *California* (1970). C. G. Sellers analyzes *James K. Polk, Continentalist: 1843–1846* (1966). Recent studies of the conflict with Mexico are O. A. Singletary, *The Mexican War* (1960), and K. J. Bauer, *The Mexican-American War, 1846–1848* (1974). The other side's perspective is given in Gene M. Brack, *Mexico Views Manifest Destiny, 1821–1846* (1976). J. H. Schroeder analyzes an important aspect of the conflict in *Mr. Polk's War: American Opposition and Dissent, 1846–1848* (1973). D. Pletcher gives an overall view in *The Diplomacy of the Annexation of Texas, Oregon, and the Mexican War* (1973). See also B. DeVoto's popular *Year of Decision, 1846* (1943). W. H. Goetzmann brings to life *Army Exploration in the American West, 1803–1863* (1959). Unusually colorful social history of the Westward movement is provided in John Mark Faragher, *Women and Men on the Overland Trail* (1979), and John D. Unruh, Jr., *The Plains Across: The Overland Emigrants and the Trans-Mississippi West, 1840–1860* (1979).

16

Shaping the National Economy, 1790-1860

The progress of invention is really a threat [to monarchy]. Whenever I see a railroad I look for a republic.

RALPH WALDO EMERSON, 1866

The March of Mechanization

A gifted group of British inventors, beginning about 1750, perfected a series of machines for the mass production of textiles. This enslavement of steam multiplied the power of man's muscles some ten thousandfold, and ushered in the modern factory system.

The so-called Industrial Revolution has been misnamed. It was not a revolution in the sense of an overnight change or upheaval. The machines developed in England were gradually improved over several decades, and the people there were scarcely aware that a significant shift was taking place. Nor was the Industrial Revolution solely industrial. It was accompanied by a no less spectacular transformation in the methods of transportation and communication.

274

The factory system gradually spread from England—"the world's workshop"—to other lands. It took a generation or so to reach western Europe, and then the United States. Why was the youthful American Republic, destined to be an industrial giant, so slow to embrace the machine?

For one thing, virgin soil in America was cheap. Land-starved descendants of land-starved peasants were not going to coop themselves up in smelly factories when they might till their own acres in God's fresh air and sunlight. Labor was therefore generally scarce, and enough nimble hands to operate the machines were hard to find. Money for capital investment, moreover, was not plentiful in pioneering America. Raw materials lay undeveloped, undiscovered, or unsuspected. The Republic was one day to become the world's leading coal producer, but much of the coal burned in colonial times was imported all the way from England.

Just as labor was scarce, so were consumers. The young country at first lacked a domestic market large enough to make factory-scale manufacturing profitable.

Long-established British factories, which provided cutthroat competition, posed another problem. Their superiority was attested by the fact that a few unscrupulous Yankee manufacturers, out to

Early Waterwheel Powers New England Factory

make a dishonest dollar, learned to stamp their own products with faked English trademarks.

The British also enjoyed a monopoly of the textile machinery, whose secrets they were anxious to hide from foreign competitors. Parliament enacted laws, in harmony with the mercantilistic system, forbidding the export of the machines, or the emigration of mechanics able to reproduce them.

Despite all these drawbacks, a surprising amount of small-scale manufacturing existed when the Republic was launched. As early as 1791, Alexander Hamilton reported that the wheels of seventeen different kinds of enterprises were humming. Yet the future industrial colossus was still snoring. Not until well past the middle of the next century did the value of the output of the factories exceed that of the farms.

Whitney Ends the Fiber Famine

Samuel Slater has been acclaimed the "Father of the Factory System" in America, and seldom can the paternity of a movement more properly be ascribed to one person. A skilled British mechanic of twenty-one, he was attracted by bounties being offered to English workmen familiar with the textile machines. After memorizing the plans for the machinery, he escaped in disguise to America, where he won the backing of Moses Brown, a Quaker capitalist in Rhode Island. Laboriously reconstructing the essential apparatus with the aid of a blacksmith and a carpenter, he put into operation in 1791 the first efficient American machinery for the spinning of cotton thread.

The ravenous mechanism was now ready, but where was the cotton fiber? Handpicking 1 pound

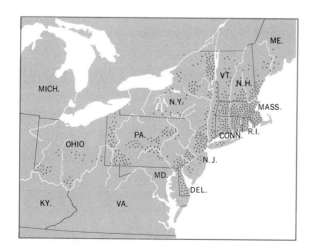

INDUSTRIAL PLANTS IN THE EARLY 1840s

(0.45 kilogram) of lint from 3 pounds (1.36 kilograms) of seed was a full day's work for one slave, and this process was so expensive that cotton cloth was relatively rare. In 1785 eight bales of cotton were seized for fraudulent entry at Liverpool, England. The officials charged that so much cotton could not have been produced in America.

Another mechanical genius, Massachusetts-born Eli Whitney, now made his mark. After graduating from Yale College, he journeyed to Georgia to serve as a private tutor while preparing for the law. There he was told that the poverty of the South would be relieved if someone could only invent a workable device for separating the seed from the short-staple cotton fiber. Within ten days, in 1793, he constructed a crude machine which was fifty times more effective than the handpicking process. The cotton gin (short for en*gine*) was so simple that rivals infringed on his patent, and

McCormick Reaper Works, 1850s. Contrast this scene of "Mass Production" with the workplace depicted in "Blacksmith Shop," in the color portfolio. (McCormick Collection, State Historical Society of Wisconsin.)

he was to net only relatively small profits from this particular brainchild.

Few machines have ever wrought so wondrous a change. The gin affected not only the history of America but that of the world. Almost overnight the raising of cotton became highly profitable, and the South was tied hand and foot to the throne of King Cotton. Human bondage had been dying out, but the insatiable demand for cotton reriveted the chains on the limbs of the luckless Southern blacks.

South and North both prospered. Slave-driving planters cleared more acres for cotton, pushing the Cotton Kingdom westward off the depleted tidewater plains, over the Piedmont, and onto the black loam bottomlands of Alabama and Mississippi. Humming gins poured out avalanches of snowy fiber for the spindles of the Yankee machines. The American phase of the Industrial Revolution, which first blossomed in cotton textiles, was well on its way. Yet many decades were to pass before the old-fashioned spinning wheel was driven into the attic, and from there into the antique shops.

Early textile factories merely spun the fiber into cotton thread. The actual weaving into cloth was done laboriously by hand in the home or by contract weavers. Not until 1814, at Waltham, Massachusetts, was the first dual-purpose plant established: it spun the fiber and wove the finished cloth under the same roof. Water power and steam power were gradually supplanting mother-and-daughter power.

Factories at first flourished most actively in New England, though branching out into the more populous areas of New York, New Jersey, and Pennsylvania. The South, increasingly wedded to the production of cotton, could boast of comparatively little manufacturing. Its capital was bound up in slaves; its local consumers for the most part were desperately poor.

New England was singularly favored as an industrial center for several reasons. Her narrow belt of stony soil discouraged farming and hence made manufacturing more attractive than else-

IOI

One observer in 1836 published a newspaper account of conditions in some of the New England factories: "The operatives work thirteen hours a day in the summer time, and from daylight to dark in the winter. At half past four in the morning the factory bell rings, and at five the girls must be in the mills. . . . So fatigued . . . are numbers of girls that they go to bed soon after their evening meal, and endeavor by a comparatively long sleep to resuscitate their weakened frames for the toil of the coming day."

IOIOIOIOIOIOIOIOIOIOIOIOIOIOIOIOIOIOIOIOIOIOIOI

where. A relatively dense population provided labor; shipping brought in capital; and snug seaports made easy the import of raw materials and the export of the finished products. Finally, the rapid rivers—notably the Merrimack in Massachusetts—provided abundant water power to turn the cogs of the machines. By 1860, more than 400 million pounds (182,000 metric tons) of Southern cotton poured annually into the gaping maws of over 1,000 mills, mostly in New England.

Marvels in Manufacturing

America's factories spread slowly until about 1807, when there began the fateful sequence of the embargo, non-intercourse, and the War of 1812. Stern necessity dictated the manufacture of substitutes for normal imports, while the stoppage of European commerce was temporarily ruinous to Yankee shipping. Both capital and labor were driven from the waves onto the factory floor, as New England, in the striking phrase of John Randolph, exchanged the trident for the distaff. Generous bounties were offered by local authorities for homegrown goods; "Buy American" and "Wear American" became popular slogans; and patriotism prompted the wearing of baggy homespun garments. President Madison donned some at his inauguration, where he was said to have been a walking argument for the better processing of native wool.

But the manufacturing boomlet broke abruptly with the Peace of Ghent in 1815. British competitors unloaded their dammed-up surpluses at ruinously low prices, and American newspapers were so full of British advertisements for goods on credit that little space was left for news. In one Rhode Island district, all 150 mills were forced to close their doors, except the original Slater plant. Responding to pained outcries, Congress provided some relief when it passed the mildly protective Tariff of 1816.

As the factory system flourished, it embraced numerous other industries in addition to textiles. Prominent among them was the manufacturing of firearms, and here the wizardly Eli Whitney again appeared with an epochal contribution. Frustrated in his earlier efforts to monopolize the cotton gin, he turned to the mass production of muskets for the United States army. Up to this time each part of a firearm had been hand-tooled, and if the trigger of one broke, the trigger of another might or might not fit. About 1798 Whitney seized upon the idea of having machines make each part, so that all the triggers, for example, would be as much alike as the successive imprints of a copperplate engraving. Journeying to Washington, he reportedly dismantled ten of his new muskets in the presence of skeptical officials, scrambled the parts together, and then quickly reassembled ten different muskets.

The principle of interchangeable parts was widely adopted by 1850, and it ultimately became the basis of modern mass-production, assembly-line methods. It gave to the North the vast industrial plant which insured military preponderance over the South. The Yankee Eli Whitney, by perfecting the cotton gin, gave slavery a renewed lease on life, and perhaps made inevitable the Civil War. The same Whitney, by popularizing the principle of interchangeable parts, caused factories to flourish in the North, and contributed heavily to the winning of that war by the Union.

Industrialization in the North received another

IOIIOIIOIIOIIOIIOIIOIIOIIOIIOIIOIIOIIOIIOIIOIIOIIOIIOI

"The patent system," said Abraham Lincoln in a lecture in 1859, ". . . secured to the inventor for a limited time exclusive use of his invention, and thereby added the fuel of interest to the fire of genius in the discovery and production of new and useful things." Ten years earlier Lincoln had received patent No. 6469 for a scheme to buoy steamboats over shoals. It was never practically applied, but he remains the only President ever to have secured a patent.

IOIIOIIOIIOIIOIIOIIOIIOIIOIIOIIOIIOIIOIIOIIOIIOIIOIIOI

strong boost about 1850, with the perfection of the sewing machine for making clothing, both in the home and in the factory. Here emerged the figure of Elias Howe, who suffered such extreme poverty that when his wife died he had to wear borrowed "Sunday" clothes to her funeral. He finally succeeded commercially where others had failed; and the royalties from his invention, patented in 1846, rapidly mounted to $4,000 a week. Even more successful in improving and promoting the machine was the versatile inventor Isaac Singer, whose name is still a household word. A new stitching device was also adapted before the Civil War for the mass production of boots and shoes.

The sewing machine was of incalculable significance. It was the foundation of the ready-made clothing industry, which took root about the time of the Civil War. It drove many a seamstress from the shelter of the private home to the factory where, like a human robot, she tended the clattering mechanisms.

Momentous inventions seem to unchain the human imagination and stimulate other inventions. American ingenuity before the Civil War is best revealed by the number of patents registered in Washington. The decade ending in 1800 saw only 306; the decade ending in 1860 saw the amazing total of 28,000. America was truly the land of the fertile-minded and the home of the ingenious. Yet in 1838 the clerk of the Patent Office had resigned in despair, complaining that all worthwhile inventions had been discovered.

Building the Business World

All these advances spurred changes in the form and legal status of business organizations. To take proper advantage of the new machine gadgetry, men needed to command great concentrations of capital and to find means to organize efficiently their far-flung affairs. Capital began to accumulate more rapidly as the principle of limited liability gained acceptance—permitting the individual investor, in cases of legal claims or bankruptcy, to risk no more than his own share of the corporation's stock. Fifteen Boston families formed one of the earliest and most powerful joint-capital ventures, the Boston Associates. They came to dominate not only the textile industry, but also the railroad, insurance, and banking business in all of Massachusetts.

The state of New York gave a powerful boost to budding capitalism in 1848, when it passed a General Incorporation Law. Businessmen no longer needed to apply for charters from the legislature; they could simply create a corporation if they complied with the terms of the law. "Free incorporation" statutes reflected the Jacksonian climate and were widely adopted in other states. They poured economic adrenalin into the veins of enterprising capitalists.

Other inventions tightened the sinews of an

Elias Howe's First Sewing Machine. The young republic often lacked the money to match the genius of its inventors, and Howe had to travel to England to secure the financial backing necessary to turn his revolutionary invention to practical use. (National Museum of History and Technology, Smithsonian Institution, Washington, D.C.)

Samuel Morse (1791–1872). Morse was the perfecter if not inventor of the electric telegraph and the Morse code.

ment of the usual jeers, an appropriation of $30,000 to support his experiment with "talking wires."

In 1844 Morse strung a wire 40 miles (64 kilometers) from Washington to Baltimore, and clicked out the historic message, "What hath God wrought?" The government might have controlled the telegraph, as it did the post office, but declined on the ground that the new device would not pay. But the invention brought fame and fortune to Morse, as he put distantly separated men of affairs in almost instant communication with one another.

Northern "Wage Slaves"

One ugly offspring of the factory system was an increasingly acute labor problem. Hitherto manufacturing had been done in the home, or in the small shop, where the master craftsman and his apprentice, rubbing elbows at the same bench, could maintain an intimate and friendly relationship. The Industrial Revolution submerged this personal association in the impersonal ownership of stuffy factories in "spindle cities." Around these,

increasingly complex business world. Prominent among them was the telegraph, developed by patriarch-bearded Samuel F. B. Morse, whose name is immortalized by the Morse code. A distinguished portrait painter, he was compelled by poverty to forsake his brush for the telegraph key. After prolonged disappointments and hunger, he finally secured from Congress, to the accompani-

Textile Workers of Lawrence (Mass.). Engraving by Winslow Homer, a famous painter. (*Harper's Weekly*, 1868.)

like tumors, the slum-like hovels of the "wage slaves" tended to cluster.

Clearly the early factory system did not shower its benefits evenly on all. While many owners waxed fat, workingpeople often wasted away at their workbenches. Hours were long, wages were low, and meals were skimpy and hastily gulped. Workers were forced to toil in unsanitary buildings that were poorly ventilated, lighted, and heated. They were forbidden by law to form labor unions to raise wages, for such cooperative activity was regarded as a criminal conspiracy. Not surprisingly, only twenty-four recorded strikes occurred before 1835.

Women and children were also sucked into the clanging mechanism of factory production. They typically toiled six days a week, earning a pittance for dreary stints of twelve or thirteen hours—"from dark to dark." The Boston Associates pridefully pointed to their textile mill at Lowell, Massachusetts, as a showplace factory. The workers were virtually all New England farm girls, carefully supervised on and off the job by watchful matrons. Escorted regularly to church from their company boardinghouses, forbidden to form unions, they were as disciplined and docile a labor force as any employer could wish. To the surprise of visitors, including Charles Dickens, they published their own newspaper. But the "Song of the Manchester Factory Girl" was no doubt overdrawn:

> She tends her loom, she watches the spindle,
>   And cheerfully talketh away;
> Mid the din of wheels, how her bright eyes kindle!
>   And her bosom is ever gay.

Few observers harbored such happy illusions about child workers. In 1820, half the nation's industrial toilers were children under ten years of age. Victims of factory labor, many children were mentally blighted, emotionally starved, physically stunted, and even brutally whipped in special "whipping rooms." In Samuel Slater's mill of 1791, the first machine tenders were seven boys and two girls, all under twelve.

Triumphs for American Toilers

The lot of the wage worker improved markedly in the 1820s and 1830s. In the full flush of Jacksonian democracy, many of the states granted the laboring man the vote. Brandishing the ballot, he first strove to lighten his burden through workingmen's parties. Aside from such goals as the ten-hour day, higher wages, and tolerable working conditions, he demanded public education for his children and an end to the inhuman practice of imprisonment for debt.

Employers, abhorring the rise of the "rabble" in politics, fought the ten-hour day to the last ditch. They argued that reduced hours would lessen production, increase costs, and demoralize the worker. He would have so much leisure time that the Devil would lead him into mischief. A red-letter gain was at length registered for labor in 1840, when President Van Buren established the ten-hour day for federal employees on public works. In ensuing years, a number of states gradually fell into line by reducing the hours of workingpeople.

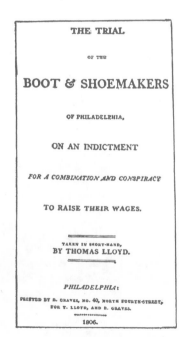

Early Pamphlet on the Trial of Strikers for Striking

Day laborers at last learned that their strongest weapon was to lay down their tools, even at the risk of prosecution under the law. Dozens of strikes erupted in the 1830s and 1840s, most of them for higher wages, some for the ten-hour day, and a few for such unusual goals as the right to smoke on the job. The workers usually lost more strikes than they won, for the employer could resort to such tactics as the importing of strike-breakers—often derisively called "scabs" or "rats," and often fresh off the boat from the Old World. Labor long raised its voice against the unrestricted inpouring of wage-depressing and union-busting immigrant workers.

Labor's early and painful efforts at organization had netted some 300,000 trade unionists by 1830. But such encouraging gains were dashed on the rocks of hard times following the severe depression of 1837. As unemployment spread, union membership shriveled. Yet toilers won a hope-giving legal victory in 1842. The supreme court of Massachusetts ruled in the case of *Commonwealth v. Hunt* that labor unions were not illegal conspiracies, provided that their methods were "honorable and peaceful." This enlightened decision did not legalize the strike overnight throughout the

country, but it was a significant signpost of the times. Trade unions still had a rocky row to hoe, stretching ahead for about a century, before they could meet management on relatively even terms.

Western Farmers Reap a Revolution in the Fields

As smoke-belching factories altered the Eastern skyline, flourishing farms were changing the face of the West. The trans-Allegheny region—especially the Ohio-Indiana-Illinois tier—was fast becoming the nation's breadbasket. Before long, it would become a granary to the world.

Pioneer farmers first hacked a clearing out of the forest, and then planted their painfully furrowed fields to corn. The yellow grain was amazingly versatile. It could be fed to hogs ("corn on the hoof") or distilled into liquor ("corn in the bottle"). Both these products could be more easily transported than the bulky grain itself, and they became the early Western farmer's staple market items. So many hogs were butchered, traded, or shipped at Cincinnati that the city was known as the "Porkopolis" of the West.

Most Western produce was at first floated down the Ohio-Mississippi River system, to feed the lusty appetite of the booming Cotton Kingdom. But Western farmers were as hungry for profits as Southern slaves and planters were for food. These soil tillers, spurred on by the easy availability of seemingly boundless acres, sought ways to bring more and more land into cultivation.

Ingenious inventors came to their aid. One of the first obstacles that frustrated the farmers was the thickly matted soil of the West, which snagged and snapped fragile wooden plows. John Deere of Illinois in 1837 finally produced a steel plow that broke the virgin soil. Sharp and effective, it was also light enough to be pulled by horses, rather than oxen.

Virginia-born Cyrus McCormick contributed the most wondrous contraption of all: a mechanical mower-reaper. The clattering cogs of McCormick's

Violence broke out along the New York waterfront in 1836 when laborers striking for higher wages attacked "scabs." "The Mayor," Philip Hone's diary records, "who acts with vigour and firmness, ordered out the troops, who are now on duty with loaded arms. . . . These measures have restored order for the present, but I fear the elements of disorder are at work; the bands of Irish and other foreigners, instigated by the mischievous councils of the trades-union and other combinations of discontented men, are acquiring strength and importance which will ere long be difficult to quell."

Harvesting Grain by Hand and by McCormick Reaper. (*Above*, Prints Division, New York Public Library; *below*, from a company advertisement.)

horse-drawn machine were to the Western farmers what the cotton gin was to the Southern planters. Seated on his red-chariot reaper, a single husbandman could do the work of five men with sickles and scythes.

No other American invention cut so wide a swath. It made ambitious capitalists out of humble plowmen, who now scrambled for more acres on which to plant more fields of billowing wheat. Large-scale ("extensive"), specialized, cash-crop agriculture came to dominate the trans-Allegheny West. With it followed mounting indebtedness, as farmers bought more land and more machinery to work it. Soon hustling farmer-businessmen were annually harvesting a larger crop than even the South could devour. They began to dream of

markets elsewhere—in the mushrooming factory towns of the East, or across the faraway Atlantic. But they were still largely landlocked. Commerce moved north and south on the river systems. Before it could begin to move east-west in bulk, a transportation revolution would have to occur.

Highways and Byways

In 1789, when the Constitution was launched, primitive methods of travel were still in use. Waterborne commerce, whether along the coast or on the rivers, was slow, uncertain, and often dangerous. Stagecoaches and wagons lurched over boneshaking roads. Passengers would be routed out to lay nearby fence rails across muddy stretches, and occasionally horses would drown in muddy pits while wagons sank slowly out of sight.

Cheap and efficient carriers were imperative if raw materials were to be transported to the factories, and if the finished product was to be delivered to the consumer. On December 3, 1803, a firm in Providence, Rhode Island, sent a shipment of yarn to a point 60 miles (97 kilometers) away, notifying the purchaser that the consignment could be expected to arrive in "the course of the winter."

A promising change for the better came in the 1790s, when a private company completed the Lancaster turnpike in Pennsylvania. It was a broad, hard-surfaced highway that thrust 62 miles (100 kilometers) westward, from Philadelphia to Lancaster. As the driver approached the toll gate, he was confronted with a barrier of sharp pikes, which were turned aside when he paid his toll. Hence the term "turnpike."

The Lancaster Pike proved to be a highly successful venture, returning as high as 15 percent annual dividends to its stockholders. It attracted a rich trade to Philadelphia, and touched off a turnpike-building boom that lasted about twenty years. It also stimulated Western development. The turnpikes beckoned to the canvas-covered Conestoga wagons, whose creakings heralded an advance that would know no real retreat.

CUMBERLAND (NATIONAL) ROAD AND MAIN CONNECTIONS

Western road building, always expensive, encountered many obstacles. Looming large among them were the noisy states'-righters, who opposed federal aid to local projects. Eastern states also protested against being bled of their populations by the westward-reaching arteries.

Westerners scored a notable triumph in 1811 when the federal government began to construct the elongated National Road, or Cumberland Road. This highway ultimately stretched from Cumberland, in western Maryland, to Vandalia, in Illinois, a distance of 591 miles (952 kilometers). The War of 1812 interrupted construction, and states'-rights shackles on internal improvements hampered federal grants. But the thoroughfare was belatedly brought to its destination, in 1852, by a combination of aid from the states and the federal government.

The famed Cumberland Road, with numerous branches, was a marvelous stimulant to American prosperity. As the vital highway to the West, it made freight carrying cheaper and faster. It hastened the flow of European immigrants over the mountains; it swelled population centers; it enhanced land values. It also wrote a colorful chapter in the history of transportation. Brightly painted stagecoaches, named after prominent statesmen and pulled by four to six foam-flecked horses, careened down the dusty highroad at breakneck speed, often better than 20 miles (32 kilometers) an hour. The age of rapid land transportation was dawning.

THE PATTERN OF AMERICAN AGRICULTURAL PRODUCTION IN 1860

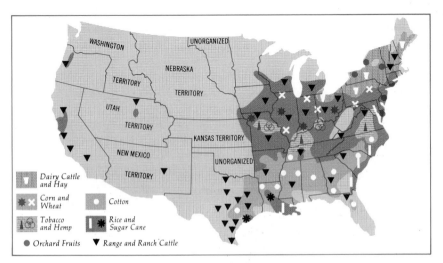

Fulton's First Steamboat.   The presence of the two sails indicates that the inventor anticipated engine trouble.

Fulton Reverses the Rivers

The steamboat craze, which overlapped the turnpike craze, was touched off by an ambitious painter-engineer named Robert Fulton. Several other men had earlier built steamboats, but these craft had all proved unprofitable, largely because of weak engines and even weaker financing.

Fulton, shrewder and luckier than the others, won financial backing from a wealthy New Yorker. He installed a powerful steam engine in a vessel which posterity came to know as the *Clermont* but which a dubious public dubbed "Fulton's Folly." On a historic day in 1807, the quaint little ship, belching sparks from its single smokestack, churned steadily from New York City up the Hudson River toward Albany. It made the run of 150 miles (242 kilometers) in 32 hours.

The success of the steamboat was sensational. Man could now in large degree defy wind, wave, tide, and downstream current. Within a few years Fulton had changed all of America's navigable streams into two-way arteries, thereby doubling their carrying capacity. Hitherto keelboats had been pushed up the Mississippi, with quivering poles and raucous profanity, at less than one mile an hour—a process that was prohibitively costly. Now the steamboats could churn rapidly against the current, ultimately attaining speeds in excess

of 10 miles (16 kilometers) an hour. The mighty Mississippi had now met her master.

By 1820 there were some sixty steamboats on the Mississippi and its tributaries; by 1860, about one thousand, some of them luxurious river palaces. Keen rivalry among the swift and gaudy steamers led to memorable races. Excited passengers would urge the captain to pile on wood at the risk of bursting the boilers, which all too often exploded with tragic results for the floating firetraps.

Chugging steamboats played a vital role in the opening of the West and South, both of which were richly endowed with navigable rivers. Like bunches of grapes on a vine, population clustered along the banks of the broad-flowing streams. Cotton growers and other farmers made haste to take up the now-profitable virgin soil. Not only could they float their produce out to market but, hardly less important, they could ship in at low cost their shoes, hardware, and other manufactured necessities.

"Clinton's Big Ditch" in New York

A canal-cutting craze paralleled the boom in turnpikes and steamboats. A few canals had been built around falls and elsewhere in colonial days, but ambitious projects lay in the future. Resourceful New Yorkers, cut off from federal aid by states'-righters, themselves dug the Erie Canal, linking the Great Lakes with the Hudson River. They were blessed with the driving leadership of Governor DeWitt Clinton, whose grandiose project was scoffingly called "Clinton's Big Ditch" or "the Governor's Gutter."

Begun in 1817, the canal eventually ribboned 363 miles (585 kilometers). On its completion in 1825, a garland-bedecked canal boat glided from Buffalo, on Lake Erie, to the Hudson River and on to New York harbor. There, with colorful ceremony, Governor Clinton emptied a cask of water from the lake to symbolize "the marriage of the waters."

The water from Clinton's cask baptized an Em-

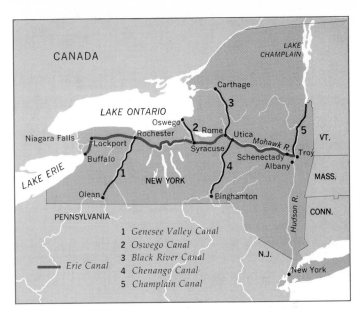

ERIE CANAL AND MAIN BRANCHES

The Erie Canal system, and others like it, tapped the fabulous agricultural potential of the Midwest, while canal construction and maintenance provided employment for displaced Eastern farmers squeezed off the land by competition from their more productive Midwestern cousins. The transportation revolution thus simultaneously expanded the nation's acreage under cultivation and speeded the shift of the work force from agricultural to manufacturing and "service" occupations. In 1820 more than three-quarters of American workers labored on farms; by 1850 only a little more than half of them were so employed.

1 *Genesee Valley Canal*
2 *Oswego Canal*
3 *Black River Canal*
4 *Chenango Canal*
5 *Champlain Canal*

— Erie Canal

pire State. Mule-drawn passengers and bulky freight could now be handled with cheapness and dispatch, at the dizzy speed of 5 miles (8 kilometers) an hour. The cost of shipping a ton of grain from Buffalo to New York City fell from $100 to $5, and the time of transit from about twenty days to six.

Ever-widening economic ripples followed the completion of the Erie Canal. The value of land along the route skyrocketed, and new cities—like Rochester and Syracuse—sprouted up. Industry in the state boomed. The new profitableness of farming in the Old Northwest—notably in Ohio,

Michigan, Indiana, Illinois—attracted thousands of European immigrants to the unaxed and untaxed lands now available. Flotillas of steamships soon plied the Great Lakes, connecting with waiting canal barges at Buffalo. Interior waterside villages like Cleveland, Detroit, and Chicago exploded into mighty cities.

Other profound economic and political changes followed the completion of the canal. The price of potatoes in New York City was cut in half, and many dispirited New England farmers, no longer able to face this ruinous competition, abandoned their rocky holdings and went elsewhere. Some

A Set of Locks on the Erie Canal.
An engineering marvel, it had to raise boats 571 feet (174 meters) from the Hudson to Lake Erie. Thousands of laborers died of afflictions ranging from malaria to snake bite—conspicuously Irish immigrant laborers, some of whom worked for 37½ cents an hour plus whiskey. (Courtesy of The New-York Historical Society, New York City.)

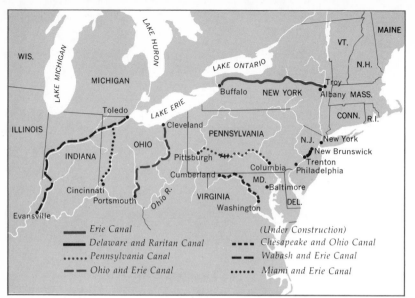

PRINCIPAL CANALS IN 1840

Note that the canals mainly facilitated east-west traffic, especially along the great Lake Erie artery. No comparable network of canals existed in the South—a disparity that helps to explain Northern superiority in the Civil War that came two decades later.

became mill hands, thus speeding the industrialization of America. Others, finding it easy to go west over the Erie Canal, took up new farmlands south of the Great Lakes, where they were joined by countless thousands of New Yorkers and other Northerners. Still others shifted to fruit, vegetable, and dairy farming. These transformations in the Northeast showed how long-established local market structures could be swamped by the emerging behemoth of a continental economy.

The astonishing success of the Erie Canal stimulated competition, especially from the urban rivals of New York City. Ingenious Philadelphians, defying both geography and gravity, constructed a temporarily profitable canal over the Allegheny Mountains. At a unique portage, a special railroad lifted barges to an elevation of nearly 2,300 feet (700 meters), from which they were lowered on the other side.

A web of canals was likewise dug in the Old Northwest to connect with the Great Lakes and the Mississippi River. On one of the Ohio waterways, the youthful James A. Garfield, later to become President, drove balky mules down the towpath.

When the Iron Horse Was a Colt

The railroad proved to be the most significant contribution to a solution of the great American problem of distance. It was fast, reliable, cheaper than canals to construct, and not frozen over in winter. Able to go almost anywhere, even through the Allegheny barrier, it defied terrain and weather.

Early experiments with railroads involved the use of various kinds of power, including wind, dogs, horses, and finally steam. The first important line was begun by the Baltimore and Ohio Company, significantly on Independence Day, 1828. At the colorful dedication ceremony, the first stone was laid at Baltimore by Charles Carroll, then aged ninety, the only surviving signer of the Declaration of Independence. But the steam locomotive for railroads—truly a declaration of independence from primitive transportation—was not, as commonly supposed, a Yankee invention. It had already been used to a limited extent in England.

American locomotives, though soon to make the grade, encountered initial setbacks. A famous nine-mile race was staged in 1830 between a horse-drawn car and the "Tom Thumb," the crack locomotive of the Baltimore and Ohio. The noisy iron horse was winning when it broke down. The gray quadruped then clattered on to victory, amid wild cheers from the foes of mechanical progress. But dumb animals rapidly lost out, as numerous railroads began to radiate from the main cities like spokes from the hub of a wheel. By 1860, only thirty-two years after the Baltimore and Ohio ceremony, the United States boasted 30,000 miles (48,000 kilometers) of railroad track, three-fourths of it in the rapidly industrializing North.

Pioneer Railroad Promoters

Inevitably the hoarse screech of the locomotive sounded the doom of various vested interests. They railed against progress and in defense of their pocketbooks, as people so often do. Turnpike investors and tavern keepers did not relish the loss of business, and farmers feared for their hay-and-horse market. The canal backers were especially violent. Mass meetings were held along the Erie Canal, and in 1833 the legislature of New York, anxious to protect its canal investment, prohibited the railroads from carrying freight—at least temporarily.

Objections to the Iron Monster did not end there. It was branded as undemocratic, for no ordinary citizen could own one. It was sacrilegious, for God had given men and animals legs. Finally, it was a public menace. Sparks set fire to haystacks and houses, and supposedly frightened chickens into not laying eggs. Good old four-legged Dobbin was preferred. He sent out no sparks, carried his own fuel, made little noise, and would not explode.

Early railway coaches were torture chambers on wheels, and no places for weaklings or cowards. Live cinders burned holes in clothes—one woman found thirteen in her gown. The brakes were so feeble that the engineer might miss the station twice, both coming and backing up. The rails were flimsy iron strips fastened on wood; and appalling accidents turned the wooden "miniature hells" into flaming funeral pyres.

Railroad pioneers ran into additional obstacles. Arrivals and departures were conjectural; timetables were little better than ill-kept promissory notes. Further complications were caused by the variance in gauge (or space between the rails). When a passenger came to a different line, he would often have to change cars, after wiping cinders from his eyes. In 1840 there were seven transfers between Philadelphia and Charleston. Violence flared up in Erie, Pennsylvania, in 1853, when the hotel and trucking men rebelled. Fearing that the trains would go through without stopping,

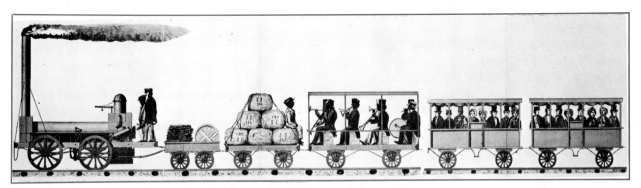

The "West Point." Second locomotive built for a railroad. (Library of Congress.)

RAILROADS IN OPERATION IN 1850

RAILROADS IN OPERATION IN 1860.
Note concentration in North.

they unsuccessfully attempted to prevent standardization of the gauge.

But needed railway improvements were gradually installed. Gauges became standardized, safety devices were adopted, solid iron rails were laid, and the Pullman sleeping "palace" was introduced in 1859. America at long last was being bound together with ribs of iron—later steel.

The Transport Web Binds the Union

More than anything else, the desire of the East to tap the West stimulated the "transportation revolution." Until about 1830, the produce of the Western region drained southward to the cotton belt or to the heaped-up wharves of New Orleans. The steamboat vastly aided the reverse flow of finished goods up the watery Western arteries, and helped bind West and South together. But the truly revolutionary changes in commerce and communication came in the three decades before the Civil War, as canals and railroad tracks radiated out from the East, across the Alleghenies and into the blossoming heartland. The ditchdiggers and tie-layers were attempting nothing less than a conquest of nature itself. They would offset the "natural" flow of trade on the interior rivers by

laying down an impressive grid of "internal improvements."

The builders succeeded beyond their wildest dreams. The Mississippi was increasingly robbed of its traffic, as goods moved eastward on chugging trains, puffing lake boats, and mule-tugged canal barges. Governor Clinton had in effect picked up the mighty Father of Waters and flung it over the Alleghenies, forcing it to empty into the sea at New York City. By the 1840s Buffalo handled more Western produce than New Orleans. Between 1836 and 1860, grain shipments through Buffalo increased a staggering sixtyfold. New York City became the seaboard queen of the nation, a gigantic port through which a vast hinterland poured its wealth, and to which it daily paid economic tribute.

By the eve of the Civil War, a truly continental economy had emerged. The principle of division of labor, which spelled productivity and profits in the factory, applied on a national scale as well. Each region now specialized in a particular type of economic activity. The South raised cotton for export to New England and Europe; the West grew grain and livestock to feed Southern slaves and Eastern factory workers; the East made machines and textiles for the other two regions.

The economic pattern thus woven had fateful political and military implications. Many Southerners regarded the Mississippi as a silver chain that naturally linked together the upper valley states and the Cotton Kingdom. They were convinced, as secession approached, that some or all of these states would have to secede with them or be strangled. But they overlooked the man-made links that now bound the upper Mississippi Valley to the East in intimate commercial union. Southern rebels would have to fight not only Northern armies, but the tight bonds of an interdependent continental economy. Economically, the two northerly sections were Siamese twins.

Wealth and Poverty

Revolutionary advances in manufacturing and transportation brought increased prosperity to all Americans, but they also widened the gulf between the rich and the poor. Millionaires had been rare in the early days of the Republic, but by the eve of the Civil War several specimens of colossal financial success were strutting across the national stage. Spectacular was the case of fur trader and real-estate speculator John Jacob Astor, who left an estate of $30 million on his death in 1848.

Cities bred the greatest extremes of economic inequality. Unskilled workers, then as always, fared worst. Many of them came to make up a floating mass of "drifters," buffeted from town to town by the shifting prospects for menial jobs. These wandering workers accounted at various times for up to half the population of the brawling industrial centers. Though their numbers were large, they left little behind them but the homely fruits of their transient labor. Largely unstoried and unsung, they are among the forgotten men and women of American history.

Many myths about "social mobility" grew up over the buried memories of these luckless day laborers. Mobility did exist in industrializing America—but not in the proportions that legend often portrays. Rags-to-riches success stories were relatively few.

Yet America, with its dynamic society and wide open spaces, undoubtedly provided more "opportunity" than did the contemporary countries of the Old World—which is why millions of immigrants packed their bags and headed for New World shores. Moreover, a rising tide lifts all boats, and the improvement in overall standards of living was real. Wages for unskilled workers in labor-hungry America rose about 1 percent a year from 1820 to 1860. This general prosperity helped to defuse the potential class conflict that might otherwise have exploded—and that did explode in several European countries.

Commerce and Cables

A new pattern of American foreign trade also emerged in the antebellum years, though businessmen concentrated on developing the wondrously rewarding domestic market. (Foreign commerce seldom added up to more than 7 percent of the national product.) Abroad as at home, cotton was king and regularly accounted for more than half the value of all American exports. After the repeal of the British exclusionary Corn Laws in 1846, the wheat gathered by McCormick's reapers began to play an increasingly important role in trade with Great Britain. Americans generally exported agricultural products and imported manufactured goods—and they generally imported more than they exported.

Most American foreign trade involved Great Britain. As time went on, a bustling Anglo-American transatlantic economy took shape. In 1818 New York's Black Ball Line inaugurated a regularly scheduled passenger and shipping service to England.

In 1858 Cyrus Field, a wealthy New York paper manufacturer, finally succeeded in stretching a cable between Newfoundland and Ireland. As "the greatest wire-puller of modern times," he had tried and failed in four previous attempts, amid much ridicule, to lay the cable through the 2 miles (3.2 kilometers) deep North Atlantic waters. When he achieved his goal, wild rejoicing rocked the nation. New York City reveled in a two-day cable carnival, and Queen Victoria exchanged congratulatory messages with President Buchanan. After three weeks and several hundred cablegrams, the cable went dead and remained useless for eight years. Heroes became villains overnight, and skeptics falsely accused the promoter of having sent faked messages so as to sell his stock at a high figure. But Field did not despair. In 1866, after the Civil War and another aborted try, he laid a heavier cable with gratifying success. The derided dreamer once more became an honored hero.

Clipper Captains and Pony Riders

The United States merchant marine encountered rough sailing during much of the early 19th Century. American vessels had been repeatedly laid up by the embargo, the War of 1812, and the panics of 1819 and 1837. American naval designers made few contributions to maritime progress. A pioneer American steamer, the *Savannah*, had crept across the Atlantic in 1819, but she used sail most of the time and was pursued for a day by a British captain who thought her afire.

In the 1840s and 1850s a golden age dawned for American shipping. Yankee naval yards, notably Donald McKay's at Boston, began to send down the ways sleek new craft called clipper ships. Long, narrow, and majestic, they glided across the sea under towering masts and clouds of canvas. In a fair breeze they could outrun any steamer.

> Stately as churches, swift as gulls,
> They trod the oceans, then—
> No man had seen such ships before
> And none will see again.*

The stately clippers sacrificed cargo space for speed, and their captains made killings by hauling high-value cargoes in record times. They wrested much of the tea-carrying trade between the Far East and England from their slower-moving British competitors, and they sped thousands of impatient adventurers to the gold fields of California and Australia.

But the hour of glory for the clipper was relatively brief. On the eve of the Civil War the British

---

*"Clipper Ships and Captains" from *A Book of Americans* by Rosemary & Stephen Vincent Benét. Copyright, 1933, by Rosemary & Stephen Vincent Benét. Copyright renewed ©, 1961, by Rosemary Carr Benét. Reprinted by permission of Brandt & Brandt Literary Agency, Inc.

A Clipper Ship. (The Peabody Museum of Salem, Massachusetts.)

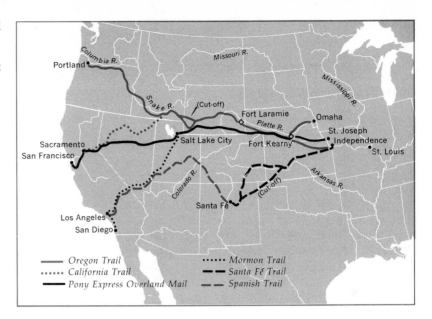

MAIN ROUTES WEST BEFORE THE CIVIL WAR
Mark Twain described his stagecoach trip to California in the 1860s:

We began to get into country, now, threaded here and there with little streams. These had high, steep banks on each side, and every time we flew down one bank and scrambled up the other, our party inside got mixed somewhat. First we would all be down in a pile at the forward end of the stage, . . . and in a second we would shoot to the other end, and stand on our heads. And . . . as the dust rose from the tumult, we would all sneeze in chorus, and the majority of us would grumble, and probably say some hasty thing, like: "Take your elbow out of my ribs!—can't you quit crowding?"

Oregon Trail
California Trail
Pony Express Overland Mail
Mormon Trail
Santa Fé Trail
Spanish Trail

had clearly won the world race for maritime ascendancy with their iron tramp steamers ("tea-kettles"). Though slower and less romantic than the clipper, these vessels were steadier, more capacious, more reliable, and hence more profitable.

No story of rapid American communication would be complete without including the Far West. By 1858 horse-drawn overland stages, immortalized by Mark Twain's *Roughing It*, were a familiar sight. Their dusty tracks stretched into California from the right bank of the muddy Missouri River.

Even more dramatic was the Pony Express, established in 1860 to carry mail speedily the 2,000 lonely miles (3,220 kilometers) from St. Joseph, Missouri, to Sacramento, California. Daring, light-weight riders, leaping onto wiry ponies saddled at stations approximately 10 miles (16 kilometers) apart, could make the trip in an amazing ten days. These unarmed horsemen galloped on, summer or winter, day or night, through dust or snow, past red Indians and white bandits. The speeding postmen missed only one trip, though the whole enterprise lost money heavily and folded after only eighteen legend-leaving months.

Just as the clippers had succumbed to steam, so were the express riders unhorsed by Morse's clacking keys, which began tapping messages to California in 1861. The swift ships and the fleet ponies ushered out a dying technology of wind and muscle. In the future, machines would be in the saddle.

|◘||◘||◘||◘||◘||◘||◘||◘||◘||◘||◘||◘||◘||◘||◘||◘||◘||◘||◘||◘||◘||◘|

As late as 1877 stagecoach passengers were advised in print: "Never shoot on the road as the noise might frighten the horses. . . . Don't point out where murders have been committed, especially if there are women passengers. . . . Expect annoyances, discomfort, and some hardships."

|◘||◘||◘||◘||◘||◘||◘||◘||◘||◘||◘||◘||◘||◘||◘||◘||◘||◘||◘||◘||◘||◘|

Pony Express. A short-lived epoch of speed. (Ernst Lehner, *American Symbols,* New York: Amiel Book Distributors.)

VARYING VIEWPOINTS

Economic history was once simply a tale of industrious inventors and inventive industrialists. But economics has become a sophisticated science, and so has the story of the material past. Historians now seek to know just *why* economic growth occurred. Was it because of the spirit or genius of the people? Their sheer numbers? The exploitation of those on the bottom? The abundance of natural resources? The quickening pace of mechanization? No doubt all of these factors were at work. But in recent years attention has focused on regional specialization of function—a kind of large-scale equivalent of the classic principle of division of labor. Thus a key to growth is seen in the national parceling-out of economic tasks: agriculture in the Midwest, cotton exports in the South, and manufacturing and services in the Northeast. This shaping of the national economic pattern, in turn, depended on the development of an efficient transportation system—hence the crucial importance of the canal and railroad network. Historians are also increasingly interested in the question: What people benefited most from economic growth? This is known as the "welfare" question, as distinct from the fact of growth alone.

SELECT READINGS

Solid introductions are P. W. Gates, *The Farmer's Age: Agriculture, 1815–1860* (1960), G. R. Taylor, *The Transportation Revolution, 1815–1860* (1951), and T. C. Cochran and W. Miller, *The Age of Enterprise* (1942). The events of the period are placed in a larger context of economic history in S. Bruchey, *The Roots of American Economic Growth, 1607–1861* (1965), and in W. W. Rostow, *The Stages of Economic Growth* (rev. ed., 1971). See also Lance Davis, *American Economic Growth: An Economist's History of the United States* (1972), and P. d'A. Jones, *The Consumer Society: A History of American Capitalism* (1969). C. M. Green treats the father of the factory system in *Eli Whitney and the Birth of American Technology* (1956). T. C. Cochran gives an overall view in *Business in American Life: A History* (1972). The laboring classes are chronicled in Norman Ware, *The Industrial Worker, 1840–1860* (1924), and in J. Rayback, *History of American Labor* (1966). Consult also Herbert Gutman's path-breaking *Work, Culture and Society in Industrializing America* (1976). Two fascinating case studies of the coming of industrialism are Alan Dawley, *Class and Community: The Industrial Revolution in Lynn* (1977), and Anthony F. C. Wallace, *Rockdale: The Growth of an American Village in the Early Industrial Revolution* (1978). Ideological aspects of this process are described in John F. Kasson, *Civilizing the Machine: Technology and Republican Values in America, 1776–1900* (1976). Highly informative is C. H. Danhof, *Change in Agriculture: The Northern United States, 1820–1870* (1969). The canal era is comprehensively described in C. Goodrich, *Government Promotion of American Canals and Railroads, 1800–1890* (1960). See also R. E. Shaw, *Erie Water West, A History of the Erie Canal, 1792–1854* (1966), and H. N. Scheiber, *The Ohio Canal Era* (1968). On railroads, consult Robert Fogel, *Railroads and American Economic Growth* (1964), which presents the startling thesis that the iron horse in fact did little to promote growth. For a different view, see A. Fishlow, *American Railroads and the Transformation of the Ante-Bellum Economy* (1965). An important aspect of the subject is studied in A. M. Johnston and B. E. Supple, *Boston Capitalists and Western Railroads* (1967). Douglas C. North has contributed a fascinating study of *Economic Growth in the United States, 1790–1860* (1961), which should be supplemented by his equally stimulating *Growth and Welfare in the American Past* (rev. ed., 1974). The clipper ships are lovingly described in C. C. Cutler, *Greyhounds of the Sea* (1930), and S. E. Morison, *By Land and By Sea* (1953). An excellent introduction to the romance of the tall ships is R. H. Dana's personal narrative, *Two Years before the Mast* (1840).

17

Creating an American Character, 1790–1860

America was bred in a cabin.

Morris Birkbeck, 1817

American Children of Environment

"In the United States," wrote Gertrude Stein, "there is more space where nobody is than where anybody is. This is what makes America what it is." Even today, as a highly industrialized and technologically sophisticated people, Americans have not fully shaken off the effects of their centuries-long battle with the wilderness.

The West, with its raw frontier, was the most typically American part of America. George Washington, a product of tidewater Virginia, was outwardly an English aristocrat, who lived most of his life under the British flag; Andrew Jackson, a product of frontier Tennessee, was clearly an American. As Ralph Waldo Emerson wrote in 1844, "Europe stretches to the Alleghenies; America lies beyond."

The "go-aheaditive" Americans sprang from a restless breed of people. Thanks to an invigorating climate and the challenge of tremendous tasks,

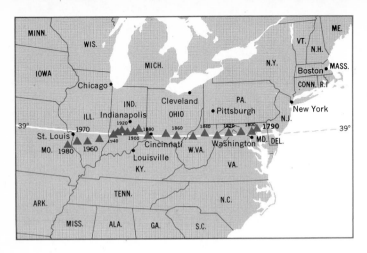

WESTWARD MOVEMENT OF CENTER OF POPULATION, 1790–1980
Note the remarkable equilibrium of the north-south pull from 1790 onward, and the strong spurt west and south after 1940. The 1980 census revealed that the nation's center of population had at last moved west of the Mississippi River.

they were nervous and energetic. Born hustlers—always "a-doin'"—they were footloose and frequently on the move. One "tall tale" of the frontier described chickens that voluntarily crossed their legs every spring, waiting to be tied for the annual move west. Even in repose, Americans were often whittling, sewing, chewing, jiggling, or rocking. The rocking chair—"the chair that travels but stays at home"—was a typically American device. At the dinner table, the rule seemed to be "gobble, gulp, and go." Americans had no time for four o'clock tea, as the English did. There was too much cream to be skimmed off the continent—furs, timber, wildlife—with a consequent wasting of soil and natural resources in some areas. All this restlessness came partly from youth; as late as 1850 the majority of Americans were under thirty.

The West attracted these nervous particles of human energy like a magnet. By 1840 the "demographic center" of the American population map had crossed the Alleghenies. On the eve of the Civil War, it had marched beyond the Ohio River. Legend portrays an army of muscular axmen triumphantly carving civilization out of the Western woods. But in reality life was downright grim for most pioneer families. Poorly fed, ill-clad, housed in hastily erected shanties, they were perpetual victims of disease, depression, and premature death. Above all, there was the awful loneliness, especially for women, who sometimes cracked under the strain. They were often cut off from human contact, especially neighbors, for whole days or even weeks, while confined to the cramped orbit of a dark cabin erected in a crude and secluded clearing. Breakdowns and even madness were all too frequently the "opportunities" that the frontier offered to pioneer women.

Rugged Pioneers

A mad scramble for riches led not only to waste but to superficiality. Wooden bridges were flung across streams, until time permitted the hurry-up American to build stone spans. The breathless pursuit of treasure inevitably led to accusations of money-chasing and crass materialism. John Stuart Mill, the noted English writer, remarked in the 1840s that in America the life of one sex was "devoted to dollar hunting, and of the other to the breeding of dollar hunters." Dollar grabbing was undeniably important, but the thrill of the chase was hardly less so. Wealth was everywhere recognized as the badge of success and the symbol of power.

The rough-and-tough American—especially the Westerner—was often crude, ruthless, brutal. Tobacco chewing and indelicate spitting—"the salivary propensity"—became a national scandal in the decades before the Civil War. One visiting Briton suggested that the spittoon, not the eagle, should be America's national emblem; and a group of Japanese visitors in 1860 noted that the white man had brown saliva. Frontier wrestling, often of the no-holds-barred type, sanctioned such niceties as the biting off of noses or the gouging out of eyes. "Look out, or I'll measure the length of your eyestrings [eye muscles]" was an expressive frontier warning. Nor was brutality directed solely at fellow white men. The Indians stood in the way of expansion, and when they fought back they were brushed aside or killed off, like the wild animals.

Americans were ingenious, inventive, adaptable, self-sufficient—jacks-of-all-trades. They had to be, especially on the frontier, where there was no place for specialists. "Root, hog, or die"—the Western saying directed at hogs left to root up their own food—might well have been the national motto.

Average Americans were strenuous, courageous, aggressive—overendowed with the "lick all creation" spirit. They had unshakeable faith in their military prowess, untrained though they might be. They were tough and tenacious. Learning to laugh at adversity, they fought the elements, the wild animals ("varmints"), their Canadian and Mexican

"The Spitter."   The famed English author, Charles Dickens, laid out his clothes one night on an American canal boat. The next morning he found them liberally bedewed with tobacco juice, the result of "a perfect storm and tempest of spitting." (*Vanity Fair.*)

neighbors, and, above all, the Indians. The Englishman Rudyard Kipling later wrote in grudging admiration:

> He greets the embarrassed Gods, nor fears
> To shake the iron hand of Fate
> Or match with Destiny for beers.

Gamblers All

Marooned by geography, Americans were self-centered, provincial, and isolationist, whether in their hometowns or in the world community. First and foremost they were individualists. The men depended on their own trusty axes and especially their rifles, which, in the Western phrase, made them all "equally tall." Their political and social beliefs might not bear a radical stamp, for many observers noted the remarkable conformity of American opinion. But they were convinced that their way in the world was for them alone to make. Emerson's popular lecture-essay, "Self-Reliance," struck a deeply responsive chord. Popular literature of the period abounded in portraits of heroically unique, even isolated, figures like Cooper's Natty Bumppo and Melville's Captain Ahab—just as Jacksonian politics aimed to emancipate the lone-wolf, enterprising businessman. Vast space and fabulous economic abundance fostered this fond self-image, and gave it a certain reality. Yet even in this heyday of "rugged individualism" there were exceptions. Pioneers, in tasks clearly beyond their own individual resources, would call upon their neighbors for logrolling and barn-raising, and upon their federal government for help in building internal improvements.

Americans in general were confident, buoyant, optimistic—born boosters, tellers of "tall tales," admirers of the giant lumberjack, the fabled Paul Bunyan. Pessimism was a kind of treason; "knockers" were not wanted. The ancestors of the Americans, as well as the immigrants themselves, had to be courageously optimistic to undertake the stormy Atlantic crossing. "The cowards never started; the weak died on the way," ran the saying.

IOI

A British magazine thus satirized American boastfulness in 1870: "If an Arkansaw man cannot boast of the education of a Boston man, at any rate he can chew more tobacco and spit more, farther and straighter than any other man. If the Mississippi steamers are not so magnificent as some on the Hudson River, they sail faster and blow up oftener and shoot men higher than any other steamers in the country."

IOIIOIIOIIOIIOIIOIIOIIOIIOIIOIIOIIOIIOIIOIIOIIOIIOIIOIIOIIOI

Those who reached the New World were all gamblers. They gambled their lives against disease and Indians, and their crops and fortunes against the elements. The American people are distilled not only from a select group of brave men and women but also from a long line of risk-takers. Even those who failed had at least one satisfaction: someone had to take the first steps if the Republic was to achieve its ultimate destiny. "It's better to be a has-been," one heard, "than a never-was."

Americans were boastful—a trait growing out of their easy optimism. The game of poker ("brag"), with its premium on successful bluffing, attained great popularity in the West, especially with Henry Clay. Americans were painfully aware of their nation's many physical and cultural shortcomings and, while smarting under the sneers of monocled foreigners, they would brag loudly and defensively about the splendid cities that would one day spring from their malarial swamps. Significantly, they boasted of the future, while Europeans boasted of their past. They also learned to worship bigness, partly because America excelled in size. Above all, they had unbounded faith in the future, in progress, in the "American dream."

The Torch of Democracy

The American people were essentially democratic except, conspicuously, for the blight of slavery. In their social democracy, especially beyond the mountains, they set little store by caste, tradition, or family trees. The first question was not "Who are you?" but "What can you do?" On the frontier, where all people were "equally better," a common expression was "I'm as good as you be." Or as a Hungarian immigrant later remarked, "The President is Mister and I am Mister too." The very first sentence of Alexis de Tocqueville's great treatise on *Democracy in America* (1835) proclaimed: "Nothing struck me more forcibly than the general equality of conditions among the people." One rousing song sung at religious camp meetings ran:

Come hungry, come thirsty, come ragged, come bare,
Come filthy, come lousy, come just as you are.

Political democracy was one of the nation's proudest boasts. White manhood suffrage came to be the rule. The people realized that the world was skeptically watching their vast experiment in political democracy, and this awareness contributed further to self-conscious boastfulness. Emerson once observed that the American eagle was something of a peacock.

Americans, moreover, were lovers of freedom. Not to be pushed about, they had forcibly overthrown George III and set up a republic. They cherished states' rights and localism, largely because these ideals enabled them to keep a more watchful eye on their public servants. They hailed freedom abroad, as well as in America. Responding to the flattery of imitation, they applauded democratic revolutions whenever they occurred, and often assisted them with money and volunteers. They cheered as thrones crashed, and they openly pitied people who did not have the "gumption" to rise up and break their autocratic chains. Mark Twain caught the spirit of anti-monarchical America when he had Huck Finn remark, "Sometimes I wish we could hear of a country that's out of kings."

Americans were intensely patriotic and nationalistic—America lovers, who annually cheered flag-flapping Fourth of July oratory. Instead of inheriting the land, they had subdued it them-

YEAR	WHITE	NON-WHITE	TOTAL POPULATION
1790	3,172,000	757,000	3,929,000
1800	4,306,000	1,002,000	5,308,000
1810	5,862,000	1,378,000	7,240,000
1820	7,867,000	1,772,000	9,639,000
1830	10,537,000	2,329,000	12,866,000
1840	14,196,000	2,874,000	17,070,000
1850	19,553,000	3,639,000	23,192,000
1860	26,922,000	4,521,000	31,443,000

POPULATION INCREASE, INCLUDING SLAVES AND INDIANS, 1790–1860

selves, battling both the elements and the Indians. And one especially cherishes the possessions one has to fight for.

The March of the Millions

An amazing multiplication of people continued decade after decade, without serious slackening. By mid-century the population was still doubling approximately every twenty-three years, as in fertile colonial days.

By 1860 the original thirteen states had more than doubled in number: thirty-three stars graced the American flag. The United States was the fourth most populous nation in the Western world, exceeded by only three European countries— Russia, France, and Austria.

Urban growth continued explosively. In 1790 there had been only two cities that could boast 20,000 or more souls: Philadelphia and New York. By 1860 there were forty-three; and about 300 other places claimed over 5,000 inhabitants apiece. New York was the metropolis; New Orleans, the "Queen of the South;" and Chicago, the swaggering lord of the Midwest, destined to be "Hog Butcher for the World."

Cincinnati in 1843. Famous as a processor of hogs, this "Queen City of the West" was a town of 2,540 people in 1800, and 161,044 in 1860, 45 percent of them foreign born. Though tied to the South by down-river commerce on the Ohio and Mississippi rivers, it remained loyal to the North during the Civil War. (Cincinnati Public Library.)

Irish and German Immigration by Decade

Years	Irish	German	All Others	Grand Total
1820–1830	Unknown	Unknown	Unknown	151,824
1831–1840	207,381	152,454	239,290	599,125
1841–1850	780,719	434,626	497,906	1,713,251
1851–1860	914,119	951,667	732,428	2,598,214
1861–1870	435,778	787,468	1,091,578	2,314,824
1871–1880	436,871	718,182	1,657,138	2,812,191
1881–1890	655,482	1,452,970	3,138,161	5,246,613
1891–1900	388,416	505,152	2,793,996	3,687,564

Such overrapid urbanization unfortunately brought undesirable by-products. It intensified the problems of smelly slums, feeble street lighting, inadequate policing, impure water, foul sewage, ravenous rats, and improper garbage disposal. Hogs poked their scavenging snouts about many city streets as late as the 1840s. Boston in 1823 pioneered with a sewage system; and New York in 1842 abandoned wells and cisterns for a piped-in water supply. The city thus unknowingly eliminated the breeding places of many disease-carrying mosquitoes.

A continuing high birthrate accounted for most of the increase in population, but by the 1840s the tides of immigration were adding hundreds of thousands more. Before this decade, immigrants had been flowing in at the rate of about 60,000 a year, but suddenly the influx was tripled in the 1840s, and then quadrupled in the 1850s. During these two feverish decades, over a million and a half Irish, and nearly as many Germans, swarmed down the gangplanks. Why did they come?

The immigrants came partly because Europe seemed to be running out of room. The population of the Old World more than doubled in the 19th Century, and Europe began to generate a great seething pool of apparently "surplus" people. They were displaced and footloose in their homelands before they felt the tug of the American magnet. Indeed, at least as many people moved about *within* Europe as crossed the Atlantic.

America benefited from these people-churning changes but did not set them all in motion. Nor was the United States the sole beneficiary of the process: of the nearly 60 million persons who abandoned Europe in the century after 1840, about 25 million went somewhere other than the United States.

Yet America still beckoned most strongly to the struggling masses of Europe, and the majority of migrants headed for the "land of freedom and opportunity." There was freedom from aristocratic caste and state church; there was abundant opportunity to secure broad acres and better one's condition. Much-read letters sent home by immigrants—"America letters"—often described in glowing terms the richer life: low taxes, no compulsory military service, and "three meat meals a day." The introduction of transoceanic steamships also meant that the immigrants could come speedily, in a matter of ten or twelve days instead of ten or twelve weeks. They were still jammed into unsanitary quarters, thus suffering an appalling death rate, but the nightmare was more endurable because it was shorter.

The Emerald Isle Moves West

Ireland, already groaning under the heavy hand of British overlords, was prostrated in the mid-1840s. A terrible rot attacked the potato crop, on which the people had become dangerously de-

Ragged Irish Immigrant Arriving in America. Bewildered newcomers were often whisked to "boardinghouses"— filthy hovels above a "grog shop" where whiskey flowed and a saucer of free tobacco sat on the bar. The hard-drinking Irish scandalized old-stock Americans, but Boston's Orestes Brownson predicted in 1852: "Out from these . . . dirty streets will come forth some of the noblest sons of our country, whom she will delight to own and honor."

maids. Broad-shouldered "Paddies" (Patricks), were pushed into pick-and-shovel drudgery on canals and railroads, where thousands left their bones as victims of disease and accidental explosions. It was said that an Irishman lay buried under every railroad tie. Even so, the Irish were hated by native workers. "No Irish Need Apply" was a sign commonly posted at factory gates, and was often abbreviated to NINA. The Irish, in turn, fiercely resented the blacks, with whom they shared society's basement. Race riots between black and Irish dockworkers flared up in several port cities, and the Irish were always cool to the abolitionist cause.

The friendless Irish were forced to fend for themselves. The Ancient Order of Hibernians, a semisecret society founded in Ireland to fight rapacious landlords, served in America as a benevolent society, aiding the downtrodden. It also helped to spawn the "Molly Maguires," a shadowy Irish miners' union that rocked the Pennsylvania coal districts in the 1860s and 1870s.

The Irish tended to remain in low-skill occupations, but gradually improved their lot, usually by acquiring modest amounts of property. The education of children was cut short as families struggled to save money to purchase a home. But for humble Irish peasants, cruelly cast out of their homeland, property ownership counted as a grand "success."

Politics quickly attracted these gregarious Gaelic newcomers. A poet urged them in 1852:

> Fellow exiles! claim your station
>   In the councils of the nation;
> Be not aliens in the soil
>   Which exacts your sweat and toil.

They soon began to gain control of powerful city machines, notably New York's Tammany Hall, and reaped the patronage rewards. Before long, beguilingly brogued Irishmen dominated police departments in many big cities, where they now drove the "Paddy wagons" that had once carted their brawling forebears to jail.

American politicians made haste to cultivate the

pendent, and about one-fourth of them were swept away by disease and hunger. Starved bodies were found dead by the roadsides with grass in their mouths. All told, about 2 million perished.

Tens of thousands of destitute souls, fleeing the Land of Famine for the Land of Plenty, flocked to America in the "Black Forties." Ireland's great export has been population; and the Irish take their place beside the Jews as a dispersed people.

These uprooted newcomers, too poor to move west and buy the necessary land, livestock, and equipment, swarmed into the larger seaboard cities. Noteworthy were Boston and particularly New York, which rapidly became the largest Irish city in the world. Before many decades had passed, more people of Hibernian blood lived in America than on the "ould sod" of Erin's Isle.

The luckless Irish received no red-carpet treatment. Forced to live in squalor, they worsened already vile slum conditions. They were scorned by the older American stock, especially "proper" Protestant Bostonians, who regarded the scruffy Catholic newcomers as a social menace. Barely literate "Biddies" (Bridgets) took jobs as kitchen

Irish vote, especially in the politically potent state of New York. Irish hatred of the British lost nothing in the transatlantic transplanting. As the Irish-Americans increased in number—nearly 2 million arrived between 1830 and 1860—officials in Washington glimpsed political gold in those Hibernian hills. Politicians often found it politically profitable to fire verbal volleys at London—a process vulgarly known as "twisting the British Lion's tail."

The German Forty-Eighters

The influx of refugees from Germany between 1830 and 1860 was hardly less spectacular than that from Ireland. During these troubled years, over a million and a half thrifty Germans stepped onto American soil. The bulk of them were poor people, displaced by crop failures and by other hardships. But a strong sprinkling were liberal political refugees. Saddened by the collapse of the democratic revolutions of 1848, they had decided to leave the autocratic Fatherland and flee to America—the one brightest hope of democracy.

The liberal German "Forty-Eighters," who came to America for free government, are not to be confused with the "Forty-Niners," who came to California for free gold. The future history of Germany—and indeed of the world—might well have been less war-torn if these rare spirits had remained at home as a seedbed for genuine democracy. But Germany's loss was America's gain. Zealous German liberals like the lanky and public-spirited Carl Schurz, a relentless foe of slavery and public corruption, contributed richly to the elevation of American political life.

Many of the Germanic newcomers, unlike the Irish, possessed a modest amount of this world's goods. Most of them pushed out to the lush lands of the Middle West, notably Wisconsin, where they settled and established model farms. Like the Irish, they formed an influential body of voters whom American politicians shamelessly wooed. But the Germans were less potent politically because their strength was more widely scattered.

The hand of Germans in shaping American life was widely felt in still other ways. They had fled from the militarism and wars of Europe, and consequently came to be a bulwark of isolationist sentiment in the upper Mississippi Valley. Better educated on the whole than the stump-grubbing Americans, they warmly supported public schools, including their *Kindergarten* (children's garden). They likewise did much to stimulate art and music. As outspoken champions of freedom, they became relentless enemies of slavery during the fevered years before the Civil War.

Yet the Germans—often dubbed "damned Dutchmen"—were occasionally regarded with suspicion by their old-stock American neighbors. Seeking to preserve their language and culture, they sometimes settled in compact "colonies" and kept aloof from the surrounding community. Accustomed to the "Continental Sunday" and uncurbed by Puritan tradition, they made merry on the Sabbath and drank huge quantities of an amber beverage called *Bier* (beer), which dates its real popularity in America to their coming.* Their Old World drinking habits, like those of the Irish newcomers, gave a severe setback to the movement for greater temperance in the use of alcohol.

Flare-Ups of Anti-Foreignism

The invasion by this so-called immigrant "rabble" in the 1840s and 1850s inflamed the hates of American "nativists." They feared that these foreign hordes would outbreed, outvote, and overwhelm the old "native" stock. Not only did the newcomers take jobs from "native" Americans, but the bulk of displaced Irishmen were Roman Catholics, as were a substantial minority of the Germans. The Church of Rome was still widely regarded by many old-line Americans as a "foreign" church; convents were commonly referred to as "Popish brothels."

Roman Catholics were now on the move. They had formed a negligible minority during colonial

---

*Frederick Pabst and Joseph Schlitz were among the German immigrant brewers who "made Milwaukee famous."

IOIIOIIOIIOIIOIIOIIOIIOIIOIIOIIOIIOIIOIIOIIOIIOIIOIIOI

> Strong anti-foreignism was reflected in the plat-
> form of the American (Know-Nothing) party in
> 1856: *"Americans must rule America;* and to
> this end, *native*-born citizens should be se-
> lected for all state, federal, or municipal offices
> of government employment, in preference to
> naturalized citizens."

IOIIOIIOIIOIIOIIOIIOIIOIIOIIOIIOIIOIIOIIOIIOIIOIIOIIOI

days, and their numbers had increased gradually.
But with the enormous influx of the Irish and
Germans in the 1840s and 1850s, the Catholics
became a powerful religious group. In 1840 they
had ranked fifth, behind the Baptists, Methodists,
Presbyterians, and Congregationalists. By 1850,
with some 1.8 million communicants, they had
bounded into first place—a position they have
never lost.

"Native" Americans were alarmed by these
mounting figures. They professed to believe that
in due time the "alien riffraff" would "establish"
the Catholic Church at the expense of Protestantism and would introduce "Popish idols." The
noisier American "nativists" rallied for political
action. In 1849 they formed the Order of the Star-

Spangled Banner, which soon developed into the
formidable American or "Know-Nothing" party—a
name derived from its secretiveness. "Nativists"
agitated for rigid restrictions on immigration and
naturalization, and for laws authorizing the de-
portation of alien paupers. They also promoted a
lurid literature of exposure, much of it pure fiction. The authors, sometimes posing as escaped
nuns, described sin as they imagined it behind
brick convent walls, including the secret burial
of babies. One of these books—Maria Monk's
Awful Disclosures (1836)—sold over 300,000 copies.

Even uglier was occasional mass violence. As
early as 1834 a Catholic convent near Boston was
burned by a howling mob, and in ensuing years
there were a few scattered attacks on Catholic
schools and churches. The most frightful flare-up
occurred during 1844 in Philadelphia, where the
Irish Catholics fought back against the threats of
the "nativists." The City of Brotherly Love did not
quiet down until two Catholic churches had been
burned and some thirteen citizens had been killed
and fifty wounded in several days of fighting.
These outbursts of intolerance, though infrequent
and generally localized in the larger cities, remain
an unfortunate blot on the record of America's
treatment of minority groups.

Reviving Religion

Church attendance was still a fairly regular ritual
for about three-fourths of the 23 million Americans in 1850. Yet the old Calvinist rigor was seep-
ing out of American religion. The rationalist ideas
of the French Revolutionary era had done much
to undermine the older orthodoxy. Thomas Paine's
widely circulated book, *The Age of Reason* (1794),
had shockingly declared that all churches were
"set up to terrify and enslave mankind, and monopolize power and profit." Free-thinking Paine
penned his own religious declaration of independence: "My own mind is my own church."

Sheer distance also broke the grip of formal
doctrine and centralized church control on American religious life. Scattered frontier communities

Crooked Voting. A bitter "nativist" cartoon charging
Irish and German immigrants with "stealing" elections.
(New York Public Library.)

A Camp Meeting at Sing Sing, New York. Note the preacher with uplifted hands under the canopy at the left. A British visitor wrote in 1839 of a revival meeting: "In front of the pulpit there was a space railed off and strewn with straw, which I was told was the anxious seat, and on which sat those who were touched by their consciences." (Library of Congress.)

bred maverick congregations, unresponsive to the voice of "higher" authority in the East.

As doctrines softened, sects multiplied. One of the most important spin-offs from the dour Puritanism of the past was the Unitarian faith, which began to gather momentum about 1800, particularly in New England. It held that God existed only in *one* person (hence *uni*tarian), and not in the orthodox Trinity—the Father, the Son, and the Holy Spirit. This disturbing new sect found its inspiration in the liberal ideas set in motion by the American Revolution and other vitalizing forces. It was primarily a protest against the hell-fire doctrines of Calvinism, especially predestined damnation and total depravity. Although denying that Jesus was divine, the Unitarians stressed the essential goodness of human nature rather than its vileness; they proclaimed salvation through integrity and good works. Embraced by many leading thinkers (including Ralph Waldo Emerson), the Unitarian movement continued to be highly intellectual—and, thought some, *too* rational and optimistic.

A sharp reaction against the growing liberalism in religion set in about 1800. A fresh wave of roaring revivals sent a Second Great Awakening surging across the land. Huge "camp meetings" were held along the frontier, with as many as 25,000 persons gathering for an encampment of several days to drink the hell-fire gospel. As one of their hymns recounted:

> My thoughts on awful subjects roll,
> Damnation and the dead;
> What horrors seize a guilty soul
> Upon a dying bed!

Thousands of emotionally starved souls "got religion," and in their ecstasy engaged in orgies of rolling, dancing, barking, and jerking. Many of the "saved" soon backslid into their former sinful ways, but the revivals stimulated church membership and humanitarian reform. Easterners were moved to engage in missionary work in the Indian backwoods, in Hawaii, and in faraway Asia.

Methodists and Baptists reaped the biggest harvests of souls from the fields fertilized by revivalism. Both sects stressed personal conversion (contrary to predestination), a relatively democratic control of church affairs, and a rousing emotionalism. As a frontier jingle ran:

> The Devil hates the Methodist
> Because they sing and shout the best.

Bishop Francis Asbury (1745–1816), English-born and somewhat domineering, was the outstanding figure in early American Methodism. A tall, frail bachelor, he traveled an estimated 300,000 miles (483,000 kilometers) over wretched roads, praying, preaching, and organizing. He rode one horse about 25,000 miles (40,250 kilometers) in five years.

Powerful Peter Cartwright (1785–1872) was the best known of the later Methodist "circuit riders" or traveling frontier preachers. This ill-educated but sinewy servant of the Lord ranged for a half-century from Tennessee to Illinois, calling upon sinners to repent. With bellowing voice and flailing arms, he converted thousands of souls to the Lord. Not only did he lash the Devil with his tongue, but with his fists he knocked out rowdies who at-

The Circuit Preacher. (From the drawing by A. R. Waud in *Harper's Weekly*, Oct. 12, 1867.)

tempted to break up his meetings. His Christianity was definitely muscular.

Denominational Diversity

Revivals also furthered the fragmentation of religious faiths. Western New York, where many descendants of New England Puritans had settled, was so blistered by sermonizers preaching "hell-fire and damnation" that it came to be known as the "Burned-Over District."

Millerites or Adventists, who mustered several hundred thousand adherents, rose from the super-heated soil of the Burned-Over region in the 1830s. Named after the eloquent and commanding William Miller, they interpreted the Bible to mean that Christ would return to earth on October 22, 1844. Donning their go-to-meeting clothes, they gathered in prayerful assemblies to greet their Redeemer. The failure of Jesus to descend on schedule dampened but did not destroy the movement.

Like the First Great Awakening, the Second Great Awakening tended to widen the lines between classes and regions. The more prosperous and conservative denominations in the East were little touched by revivalism, while Episcopalians, Presbyterians, Congregationalists, and Unitarians continued to rise mostly from the wealthier, better-educated levels of society. Methodists, Baptists, and the members of the other new sects spawned by the swelling evangelistic fervor tended to come from less prosperous, less "learned" communities in the rural South and West.

Religious diversity further reflected social cleavages when the churches faced up to the slavery issue. By 1844–1845 both the Southern Baptists and the Southern Methodists had split with their Northern brethren over human bondage. The Methodists came to grief over the case of a slave-owning bishop in Georgia, whose second wife added several household slaves to his estate. In 1857 the Presbyterians, North and South, parted company. The secession of the Southern churches foreshadowed the secession of the Southern states. First the churches split, then the political parties split, and then the Union split.

A Desert Zion in Utah

The smoldering spiritual embers of the Burned-Over District kindled one especially ardent flame in 1830. In that year Joseph Smith—a tall, blue-eyed, and visionary spirit—reported that he had received some golden plates from an angel. When deciphered, they constituted the Book of Mormon, and the Church of Jesus Christ of Latter-Day Saints (Mormons) was launched. It was a native American product, one of the few American-born denominations to spread its influence worldwide.

After establishing a religious oligarchy, Smith ran into serious opposition from his non-Mormon neighbors, first in Missouri and then in Illinois. His cooperative sect rasped rank-and-file Americans, who were individualistic and dedicated to free enterprise. The Mormons aroused further antagonism by voting as a unit and by openly but understandably drilling their militia for defensive purposes. Accusations of polygamy likewise arose and increased in intensity, for Joseph Smith was reputed to have several wives.

Continuing hostility finally drove the Mormons to desperate measures. In 1844 Joseph Smith and his brother were murdered and mangled by a mob in Carthage, Illinois, and the movement seemed near collapse. But the falling torch was seized by a remarkable Mormon Moses named Brigham Young, an aggressive leader, an eloquent preacher, and a gifted administrator. Determined to escape further persecution, Young in 1847–1848 led his oppressed and despoiled Latter-Day Saints over vast rolling plains to Utah as they sang "Come, Come, Ye Saints."

Overcoming pioneer hardships, the Mormons soon made the desert bloom like a new Eden by means of ingenious and cooperative methods of irrigation. The crops of 1848, threatened by hordes of crickets, were saved when flocks of gulls appeared, as if by a miracle, to gulp down the invaders. (A monument to the sea gulls stands in Salt Lake City today.)

Semi-arid Utah grew remarkably. By the end of 1848 some 5,000 settlers had arrived, and other

The Mormon Trail. Utah-bound Mormons with hand carts. (The Church of Jesus Christ of Latter-Day Saints.)

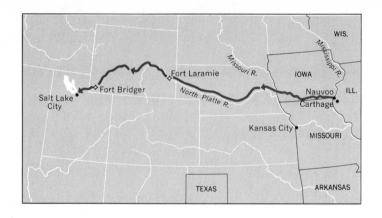

THE MORMON TREK, 1846–1847.
Accompanied by livestock, the first pioneer band, led by Brigham Young, set out for Utah in 1846. The party consisted of 146 young men and women driving 73 wagons.

large bands were to follow. Many dedicated Mormons in the 1850s actually made the 1,300-mile (2,090-kilometer) trek across the plains pulling two-wheeled carts.

Under the rigidly disciplined management of Brigham Young, the community became a prosperous frontier theocracy and a cooperative commonwealth. Young married as many as twenty-seven women—some of them wives in name only—and begot fifty-six children. The population was further swelled by thousands of immigrants from Europe, where the Mormons had established a flourishing missionary movement.

A crisis developed when the Washington government was unable to control the hierarchy of Brigham Young, who had been made territorial governor in 1850. A federal army marched in 1857 against the Mormons, who harassed its lines of supply and rallied to die in their last dusty ditch. Fortunately, the quarrel was finally adjusted without serious bloodshed. The Mormons later ran afoul of the anti-polygamy laws passed by Congress in 1862 and 1882, and their peculiar practice delayed statehood for Utah until 1896.

Polygamy was an issue of such consequence that it was bracketed with slavery in the Republican national platform of 1856: "It is both the right and the imperative duty of Congress to prohibit in the Territories those twin relics of barbarism—Polygamy and Slavery."

Daily Diversions

As the log-clearing phase passed, the masses were left with more leisure to enjoy the good things of life. The simple amusements of colonial days were continued, such as country dances, and the people still derived much satisfaction from religious and political meetings, which were primly attended in "Sunday best" clothes. But a wider range of diversions gradually beckoned.

The stage took on greater respectability as the 19th Century unfolded, even in Boston, where the Puritans had frowned upon the theater as "the Devil's chapel." Resourceful promoters attempted to quiet prejudices by stressing the moral value of their productions: one of Shakespeare's famous plays was advertised as: "Hamlet: Filial Piety." Classical English dramas continued their popularity, while in the 1850s *Uncle Tom's Cabin* and *Ten Nights in a Barroom* were also playing to packed houses.

Early in the century many of the leading actors were visitors from England, but eventually local stars began to flash across the American stage. Handsome and arrogant Edwin Forrest (1806–1872) was the first top-flight American performer, and his rivalry with a visiting English artist inflamed his New York devotees to riot in 1849. This frightful affair ended with twenty-two persons killed and thirty-six wounded.

Other headliners had their day. English-born Junius Brutus Booth (1796–1852), a marvelously gifted though alcoholic tragedian, often broke engagements and even upbraided audiences. Two of his sons trod the boards as tragedians: Edwin T. Booth (1833–1893), who gained fame as an actor; John Wilkes Booth (1838–1865), who gained infamy as the assassin of Lincoln. The most talented American actress of the century was contralto-voiced Charlotte Cushman (1816–1876), who proved to be a smash hit in male and female roles, including both Romeo and Juliet.

Sports continued to relieve the monotony of everyday drudgery. Horse racing still attracted an enthusiastic and open-pursed following. Embryonic baseball had attained so much popularity by 1845 that a uniform set of rules was adopted. Flashy and flammable showboats were churning the main rivers, bringing their variety shows to a gaping public. The traveling circus was drawing appreciative crowds, although the huge three-ring spectacles were not introduced until after the Civil War.

The most famous showman of the era was Phineas T. Barnum (1810–1891), a shrewd and cynical Connecticut Yankee, "the Prince of Humbug." He got his start during the 1830s and 1840s in New York City, where he displayed bearded ladies and other freaks. Realizing that the American public loved to be "humbugged," he operated on the golden assumption that a "sucker" was born every minute. One of his prize hoaxes was the wizened black "nurse" of George Washington, alleged to be 161 years old. (An autopsy indicated that she was about 80.)

Other activities were less amusing. Light-fingered gamblers were ever present to fleece the greedy and unwary, especially on the palatial river steamers. Dueling died hard in the honor-conscious South, its last stronghold. Crimes of violence still persisted in alarming numbers, partly as a result of the brutalizing influence of the frontier. Rough Western justice—often hempen injustice—still manifested itself to an alarming degree in lynching bees, popularly known as "necktie parties."

For the upper crust, fashionable "watering places" were established at Saratoga Springs (New York) and Newport (Rhode Island). These resorts were frequented by the gaudily dressed elite, including many cotton-rich Southerners. Growing numbers of wealthier Americans were also making the "Grand Tour" of Europe.

Culturally, by 1860 America had traveled a long and uphill road since crude pioneering days. But a high degree of polish and sophistication, at least by European standards, lay in the lap of the future.

Free Schools for a Free People

Tax-supported primary schools were scarce in the early years of the Republic. They had the odor of pauperism about them, since they existed chiefly to educate the children of the poor—the so-called ragged schools. Advocates of "free" public education met stiff opposition. A middlewestern legislator cried that he wanted only this simple epitaph when he died: "Here lies an enemy of public education."

Well-do-do, conservative Americans gradually saw the light. If they did not pay to educate "other folkses brats," the brats might grow up into a dangerous, ignorant rabble—armed with the vote. Taxation for education was an insurance premium that the wealthy paid for stability and democracy.

Tax-supported public education, though lagging in the slavery-cursed South, triumphed between 1825 and 1850. Grimy-handed laborers wielded in-

Lincoln wrote of his education (1859): "There were some schools so-called [in Indiana], but no qualification was ever required of a teacher beyond 'readin', writin' and cipherin' ' to the rule of three. . . . There was absolutely nothing to excite ambition for education. Of course, when I came of age I did not know much. Still, somehow, I could read, write and cipher to the rule of three, but that was all. I have not been to school since. The little advance I now have upon this store of education, I have picked up from time to time under the pressure of necessity. I was raised to work, which I continued till I was twenty-two."

The Dunce. Idle, stupid, or misbehaving school children were forced to wear the dunce cap. (McGuffey's *First Eclectic Reader.*)

Horace Mann deplored indolence when he said, ''Lost, yesterday, somewhere between sunrise and sunset, two golden hours, each set with sixty diamond minutes. No reward is offered, for they are gone forever.''

creased influence and demanded instruction for their children. Most important was the gaining of manhood suffrage for whites in Jackson's day. A free vote cried aloud for free education. A civilized nation that was both ignorant and free, declared Thomas Jefferson, "never was and never will be."

The famed little red schoolhouse—with one room, one stove, one teacher, and often eight grades—became the shrine of American democracy. Regrettably, it was an imperfect shrine. Early free schools stayed open only a few months of the year. Schoolmasters were too often ill trained, ill tempered, and ill paid. They frequently put more stress on "lickin'" (with a hickory stick) than on "larnin'." These knights of the blackboard often "boarded around" in the community, and some knew scarcely more than their older pupils. They usually taught only the "Three Rs"—"readin', 'ritin', and 'rithmetic." To many rugged Americans, suspicious of "book larnin'," this was enough.

Reform was urgently needed. Into the breach stepped Horace Mann (1796–1859), a brilliant and idealistic graduate of Brown University. As secretary of the Massachusetts Board of Education, he campaigned effectively for more and better schoolhouses, longer school terms, higher pay for teachers, and an expanded curriculum. His influence radiated out to other states, and impressive improvements were chalked up. Yet education remained an expensive luxury for many communities. As late as 1860 the nation counted only a few hundred public secondary schools—and nearly a million white adult illiterates.

Educational advances were aided by improved textbooks, notably those of Noah Webster (1758–1843), a Yale-educated Connecticut Yankee who was known as the "Schoolmaster of the Republic." His "reading lessons," used by millions of children in the 19th Century, were partly designed to promote patriotism. He devoted twenty years to his famous dictionary, published in 1828, which helped to standardize the American language.

Equally influential was Ohioan William H. McGuffey (1800–1873), a teacher-preacher of rare

The Wages of Sin. The sad fate of a boy who stopped to play in a pond on his way to school and was drowned. (McGuffey's *First Eclectic Reader.*)

power. His grade-school readers, first published in the 1830s, sold 122 million copies in the following decades. *McGuffey's Readers* hammered home lasting lessons in morality, patriotism, and idealism. One copy-exercise ran:

> Beautiful hands are they that do
> Deeds that are noble good and true;
> Beautiful feet are they that go
> Swiftly to lighten another's woe.

Higher Goals for Higher Learning

Higher education was likewise stirring. The religious zeal of the Second Great Awakening, beginning about 1800, led to the planting of many small, denominational, liberal arts colleges, chiefly in the South and West. Too often they were educationally anemic, established more to satisfy local pride than genuinely to advance the cause of learning. Like their more venerable, ivy-draped brethren, the new colleges offered a narrow, tradition-bound curriculum of Latin, Greek, mathematics, and moral philosophy. On new and old campuses alike there was little intellectual vitality and much boredom.

The first state-supported universities sprang up in the South, beginning with North Carolina in 1795. Federal land grants nourished the growth of state institutions of higher learning. Conspicuous among the early group was the University of Virginia, founded in 1819. It was largely the brain child of Thomas Jefferson, who designed its beautiful architecture, and who at times watched its construction through a telescope from his hilltop home. He dedicated the university to freedom from religious or political shackles, and modern languages and the sciences received unusual emphasis.

Women's higher education was frowned upon in the early decades of the 19th Century. A woman's place was in the home, and training in needlecraft seemed more important than training in algebra. In an era when the clinging-vine bride was the ideal, co-education was regarded as frivolous. Prejudices also prevailed that too much learning

Mary Lyon (1797–1849). An intrepid pioneer in the field of higher education for women, Mary Lyon was a gifted teacher who achieved an important breakthrough when, in the face of much antagonism, she managed to raise enough money to launch her "Female Seminary," now Mount Holyoke College. The year after it opened in 1837, she had to turn away some 400 applicants. She served as principal for twelve years.

injured the feminine brain, undermined health, and rendered a young lady unfit for marriage. The teachers of Susan B. Anthony, the future feminist, refused to instruct her in long division.

Women's schools at the secondary level began to attain some respectability in the 1820s, thanks in part to the dedicated work of Emma Willard (1787–1870). In 1821 she established the Troy (New York) Female Seminary. Oberlin College, in Ohio, shocked traditionalists in 1833 when it opened its doors to women as well as men. In 1837, Mary Lyon established an outstanding women's school, Mount Holyoke Seminary (later College), in South Hadley, Massachusetts. Mossback critics scoffed that "they'll be educatin' cows next."

Adults who craved more learning satisfied their thirst for knowledge at private subscription libraries, or, increasingly, at tax-supported libraries. House-to-house peddlers also did a lush business in feeding the public appetite for culture. Traveling lecturers helped to carry learning to the masses through the lyceum lecture associations, which numbered about 3,000 by 1835. The lyceums provided platforms for speakers on science, literature, and moral philosophy. Talented talkers like Ralph Waldo Emerson journeyed thousands of miles on the lyceum circuits, casting their pearls of civilization before appreciative audiences.

Magazines flourished in the pre-Civil War years, but most of them withered after a short life. The *North American Review*, founded in 1815, was the long-lived leader of the intellectuals. *Godey's Lady's Book*, founded in 1830, survived until 1898, and attained the enormous circulation (for those days) of 150,000. It was devoured devotedly by countless millions of women.

The Changing American Family

The rustling pages of publications like *Godey's Lady's Book*, perused in parlors all over America, quietly heralded a subtle, slow-moving, but eventually sweeping revolution in American society. Women were growing more conscious of themselves as individuals, and as one another's "sisters" in a world where male and female sexual roles were becoming more sharply divided. Prompted in part by the wide circulation of women's magazines like *Godey's*, this dawning self-consciousness was beginning to change women's lives—and to transform society's most fundamental institution, the family.

It was still a man's world, in America and Europe, when the 19th Century opened. A wife was supposed to immerse herself in her home, and subordinate herself to her lord and master. Like black slaves, she could not vote; like black slaves, she could be legally beaten by her overlord "with a reasonable instrument." When she married, she could not retain title to her property; it passed to her husband.

Yet American women, though legally regarded as perpetual minors, fared better than their European cousins, partly because of their scarcity in frontier communities. A western woman could warn her spouse to be respectful, for "if you don't

there's plenty will." Few American husbands were brutes; and women always had quiet ways of protecting themselves, regardless of law.

Despite these relative advantages, women were still "the submerged sex" in America in the early part of the century. But as the decades unfolded, women increasingly emerged to breathe the air of freedom and self-determination. In contrast to colonial times, many women avoided marriage altogether—about 10 percent of adult women remained "spinsters" at the time of the Civil War.

Opportunities for women to be economically self-supporting were still scarce, and consisted mainly of low-paying factory jobs, teaching, and domestic service. Perhaps one white family in ten employed servants at midcentury, most of whom

Godey's Lady's Book. The most popular women's magazine of the era. (Schlesinger Library, Radcliffe College; photo by Barry Donahue.)

were poor white, immigrant, or black women. About 10 percent of white women were working for pay outside their own homes in 1850, and estimates are that about 20 percent of all women had worked at some time prior to marriage.

The vast majority of working women were single. Upon marriage, they left their paying jobs and took up their new work (without wages) as wives and mothers. In the home they were enshrined in a "cult of domesticity," a widespread cultural creed that glorified the traditional functions of the homemaker. From their pedestal, married women commanded immense moral power, and they increasingly made decisions that altered the character of the family itself.

Families are like air—they surround most people so completely and so constantly that they have tended to be invisible, historically speaking.* But though they long went unrecorded, important changes were overtaking the life of the 19th-Century home—the traditional "women's sphere." Love, not parental "arrangement," more and more frequently determined the choice of a spouse—yet parents often retained the power of veto. Families thus became more closely knit and affectionate, providing the emotional refuge that made the threatening impersonality of big-city industrialism tolerable to many people.

Most striking, families grew smaller. The average household had nearly six members at the end of the 18th Century, but fewer than five members a century later. The "fertility rate," or number of births among women aged 14 to 45, dropped sharply among white women after the Revolution, and in the course of the 19th Century as a whole, fell by half. Birth control was still a taboo topic for polite conversation, and contraceptive technology was primitive, but clearly some form of family limitation was being practiced quietly and effectively in countless families, rural and urban alike. Women undoubtedly played a large part—perhaps the leading part—in decisions to have fewer children. This newly assertive role for women has been called "domestic feminism," because it signified the growing power and independence of women, even while they remained trapped in the "cult of domesticity."

Smaller families, in turn, meant child-centered families, since where children are fewer parents can lavish more care on them individually. European visitors to the United States in the 19th Century often complained about the unruly behavior of American "brats." But though American parents may have increasingly spared the rod, they did not spoil their children. Lessons were enforced by punishments other than the hickory stick. When the daughter of novelist Harriet Beecher Stowe neglected to do her homework, her mother sent her from the dinner table, and gave her "only bread and water in her own apartment." What Europeans saw as permissiveness was in reality the consequence of an emerging new idea of child rearing, in which the child's will was not to be simply broken, but shaped. In the little republic of the family, as in the Republic at large, good citizens were raised not to be meekly obedient to authority, but to be independent individuals who could make their own decisions on the basis of internalized moral standards. Thus the outlines of the "modern" family were clear by midcentury: it was small, affectionate, child-centered, and provided a special arena for the talents of women. Feminists of a later day might decry the stifling atmosphere of the Victorian home, but to many women of the time it seemed a big step upward from the conditions in which their mothers had lived.

Journalistic Giants

The newspaper—"the university of the public"—was further popularized by free, compulsory education and a consequent increase of literacy. Before 1830 a daily journal cost about six cents, a sum which the dollar-a-day manual laborer could ill afford to pay. The New York *Sun*, seeking the economies of mass production, reduced its price in 1833 to one cent. It thus inaugurated the era of the "penny dreadful"—dreadful because it

---

*See "The Quilting Party" and "Joseph Moore and His Family," color portfolio, for two artistic views of 19th-Century family life.

featured murders, scandals, and other human-interest stories in the manner of the modern tabloid.

A leader in the new "gutter journalism" was erratic James Gordon Bennett, who in 1835 founded the New York *Herald*. His office desk consisted of two flour barrels with a plank laid across them; and he was editor, reporter, proofreader, folder, and cashier. He believed that the function of newspapers was not only to instruct but to startle, and he and other editors lowered the public taste while lowering the price of their sheets. At all events, more Americans were now reading than ever before.

The influence of journalism was vastly increased by the march of mechanization. Telegraphy instantly updated the news, and "scoops" became the newspaperman's driving demon. Quick contact with events only hours old whetted the public's appetite for more newsprint, and publishers sought to multiply the output of their clanking presses. In 1846 Richard Hoe came to their aid with a cylindrical press that could spew forth 8,000 papers in an hour.

The decades just before the Civil War marked the dawn of the golden age of personal journalism. Newspaper publishing had not yet become a big business, and editors like Horace Greeley of the New York *Tribune* owned and published their own newspapers. His weekly edition enjoyed a wide circulation outside New York State, and

Horace Greeley, Outspoken Editor. He ran for the presidency in 1872 and was badly defeated.

since the idealistic Greeley was a merciless foe of slavery, his word was law among a host of followers. "Wait until the *Weekly Tribune* arrives," remarked a New York farmer when asked his opinion, "and then I can tell you what I think about it."

Passions ran incredibly high during this era of personalized, hit-below-the-belt journalism. The writing-fighting editors were frequently caned, stabbed, or shot by those whom they verbally abused. "You lie, you villain," wrote Greeley of a rival editor, "you sinfully, wickedly, basely lie."

Despite this violence and vulgarity, America was making praiseworthy progress in lifting the mental horizons of the masses. More people than ever were now able to inform themselves on current issues; and with increased knowledge went an increased ability to make democracy work.

VARYING VIEWPOINTS

Ever since the publication of Alexis de Tocqueville's *Democracy in America* (1835, 1840), the period from the Revolution to the Civil War has been regarded as a crucially formative phase in the shaping of American society. This was the time when new institutions were being tested, new peoples absorbed, and new values sorted out. All of these processes have traditionally been seen as adding up to a tremendous success story, in which Americans energetically forged a distinctive national culture. But recently some historians have questioned this rather upbeat view and have asked what elements were *lost* as the American people plunged so breathlessly toward the future. Did the rise of individualism corrode the cohesion of the community? What cultural baggage did the immigrants leave behind them? Were there severe social costs in the sudden flowering of numerous religious sects? Did the spread of formal education preserve or undermine traditional cultural forms?

SELECT READINGS

Satisfying detail may be found in R. B. Nye, *The Cultural Life of the New Nation, 1776–1830* (1960), and the same author's *Society and Culture in America, 1830–1860* (1974). Alexis de Tocqueville's classic account of life in the young republic is brilliantly analyzed by James R. Schlieffer in *The Making of Tocqueville's "Democracy in America"* (1980). R. A. Easterlin analyzes *Population, Labor Force, and Long Swings in Economic Growth: The American Experience* (1968). Brinley Thomas has written a landmark study of *Migration and Economic Growth: A Study of Great Britain and the Atlantic Economy* (1954). Also concentrating on the European side is Philip Taylor, *The Distant Magnet* (1971). Maldwyn Jones, *American Immigration* (1960), is a standard work. Consult also Marcus Hansen, *Atlantic Migration* (1940), and C. F. Wittke's pro-immigrant *We Who Built America* (rev. ed., 1964). Wittke has also examined *The Irish in America* (1956). Anti-Catholic bigotry is analyzed in R. A. Billington, *The Protestant Crusade* (1938), and in Carleton Beals's lurid *Brass-Knuckle Crusade: The Know-Nothing Conspiracy, 1820–1860* (1960). S. Ahlstrom, *Religious History of the American People* (1972), is sweeping. W. Sweet, *Religion in the Development of American Culture, 1765–1840* (1952), concentrates on the early national period. On revivalism, see W. G. McLoughlin, *Modern Revivalism: Charles Grandison Finney to Billy Graham* (1959), and Whitney Cross's absorbing *The Burned-Over District* (1950). Consult also B. Weisberger, *They Gathered at the River* (1958), C. A. Johnson, *The Frontier Camp Meeting* (1955), and Paul E. Johnson, *A Shopkeeper's Millenium: Society and Revivals in Rochester, New York, 1815–1837* (1978). On the Latter-Day Saints, consult T. F. O'Dea, *The Mormons* (1957), and Fawn Brodie's fascinating biography of Joseph Smith, *No Man Knows My History* (1945). Wallace Stegner writes interestingly about the Mormon Trail in *The Gathering of Zion* (1964). On education see Merle Curti, *Social Ideas of American Educators* (rev. ed., 1959), and R. M. Elson, *Guardians of Tradition: American Schoolbooks of the Nineteenth Century* (1964). Michael Katz is most provocative in *The Irony of Early School Reform* (1968), as is S. K. Schultz, *The Culture Factory: Boston Public Schools, 1789–1860* (1973). See also J. Messerli, *Horace Mann* (1972). Lawrence A. Cremin, *American Education: the National Experience, 1783–1876* (1980), is masterful, and can be usefully supplemented by David Nasaw, *Schooled to Order: A Social History of Public Schooling in the United States* (1979), and especially by Carl F. Kaestle and Maris A. Vinovskis, *Education and Social Change in Nineteenth-Century Massachusetts* (1980). Higher education is handled in F. Rudolph, *The American College and University* (1962), and in R. Hofstadter and W. P. Metzger, *The Development of Academic Freedom in the United States* (1955). A pathbreaking study is B. Wishy, *The Child and the Republic: The Dawn of Modern American Nurture* (1968). Indispensable on the same subject is R. H. Bremner, ed., *Children and Youth in America: A Documentary History* (1970–1971). Recent work of note on children and the family includes Joseph F. Kett, *Rites of Passage: Adolescence in America, 1790 to the Present* (1977), Lewis Perry, *Childhood, Marriage, and Reform: Henry Clarke Wright, 1797–1870* (1980), Carl N. Degler, *At Odds: Women and The Family in America from the Revolution to the Present* (1980), and Nancy's Cott's particularly sensitive *The Bonds of Womanhood: "Woman's Sphere" in New England, 1780–1835* (1977). Special topics are treated in Lewis O. Saum, *The Popular Mood of Pre–Civil War America* (1980), W. J. Rorabaugh, *The Alcoholic Republic* (1979), Morton J. Horowitz, *The Transformation of American Law, 1780–1860* (1977), James W. Hurst, *Law and Social Order in the United States* (1977), and James H. Kettner, *The Development of American Citizenship, 1608–1870* (1978). Also valuable are Ian R. Tyrrell, *Sobering Up: From Temperance to Prohibition in Antebellum America* (1979), and Ruth Bordin, *Woman and Temperance* (1981).

18

The Ferment of Reform and Culture, 1790-1860

We [Americans] will walk on our own feet;
we will work with our own hands; we will
speak our own minds.

RALPH WALDO EMERSON, "The American Scholar," 1837

The Dawn of Scientific Achievement

Early Americans, confronted with pioneering problems, were more interested in practical gadgets than in pure science. Thomas Jefferson, for example, was a gifted amateur who won a gold medal for a new type of plow. Noteworthy were the writings of the mathematician Nathaniel Bowditch (1773–1838) on practical navigation, and of the oceanographer Matthew F. Maury (1806–1873) on ocean winds and currents. All these writers promoted safety, speed, and economy. But as far as basic science was concerned, Americans were best known for borrowing and adapting the findings of Europeans.

Yet the Republic was not without scientific talent. The most influential American scientist of the first half of the 19th Century was Professor

Benjamin Silliman (1779–1864), a pioneer chemist and geologist who taught and wrote brilliantly at Yale College for more than fifty years. Professor Louis Agassiz (1807–1873), a distinguished French-Swiss immigrant, served for a quarter of a century at Harvard College. As a pathbreaking student of biology who sometimes carried snakes in his pockets, he insisted on original research and deplored the overemphasis on memory work. Professor Asa Gray (1810–1888) of Harvard College, the Columbus of American botany, published over 350 books, monographs, and papers. His textbooks set new standards for clarity and interest.

Lovers of American bird lore owed much to the French-descended John J. Audubon (1785–1851), who painted wild fowl in their natural habitat. His magnificently illustrated *Birds of America* attained considerable popularity. The Audubon Society for the protection of birds was named after him, although as a young man he shot much feathered game for sport.

Medicine in America, despite a steady growth of medical schools, was still primitive by modern standards. Bleeding remained a common remedy. Plagues of smallpox were still dreaded, and the terrible yellow fever epidemic of 1793 in Philadelphia took several thousand lives. "Bring out your dead!" was the daily cry of the drivers of the death wagons.

People everywhere complained of ill health—malaria, the "rheumatics," the "miseries," and the

> An outbreak of cholera occurred in New York City in 1832, and a wealthy businessman, Philip Hone, wrote in his diary for the Fourth of July: "The alarm about the cholera has prevented all the usual jollification under the public authority. . . . The Board of Health reports to-day twenty new cases and eleven deaths since noon yesterday. The disease is here in all its violence and will increase. God grant that its ravages may be confined, and its visit short."

chills. Illness often resulted from improper diet, hurried eating, perspiring and cooling off too rapidly, and ignorance of germs and sanitation. "We was sick every fall, regular," wrote the mother of the future President Garfield. Life expectancy was still dismayingly short—about forty years for a white person born in 1850, and less for blacks. The suffering from decayed or ulcerated teeth was enormous; tooth extraction was often practiced by the muscular village blacksmith.

Self-prescribed patent medicines were common (one for man, two for horse), and included Robertson's Infallible Worm Destroying Lozenges. Among home remedies was the rubbing of tumors with dead toads. The use of medicine by the regular doctors was often harmful, and Dr. Oliver Wendell Holmes declared in 1860 that if the medicines, as then employed, were thrown into the sea, humans would be better off and the fish worse off.

Victims of surgical operations were ordinarily tied down, often after a stiff drink of whiskey. The surgeon then sawed or cut with breakneck speed, undeterred by the shrieks of the patient. A priceless boon came in the early 1840s when several American doctors and dentists, working independently, successfully used laughing gas and ether as anesthetics.

Humanitarian Stirrings

As the 19th Century slowly advanced, a strong reaction began to develop against the brutalities of earlier days. The crusade against slavery came to overshadow all other reforms; to some extent it hampered them by attracting so much energy to itself.

Reform campaigns of all types flourished in bewildering abundance. Zealots hawked "health" diets, fashion fads, and folk medicine. Many faddists were simply crackbrained cranks. But most reformers were intelligent, level-headed idealists. They tended to come from the old Puritan stronghold of New England, or from those Western regions to which the sons and daughters of the

Puritans had migrated. The religious reawakening of the age had stirred their Calvinist consciences from slumber.

Idealists dreamed anew the old Puritan vision of a perfected society: free from cruelty, war, intoxicating drink, discrimination, and—ultimately—slavery. Mainly middle-class descendants of pioneer farmers, most reformers were blissfully unaware that they were witnessing the dawn of the industrial era, which posed unprecedented problems and called for novel ideas. They either ignored the factory workers, for example, or blamed their problems on bad habits. With naive single-mindedness reformers applied conventional virtue to refurbishing an older order—while events hurtled them headlong into the new.

Imprisonment for debt continued to be a nightmare, though its extent has been exaggerated. As late as 1830 hundreds of penniless persons were languishing in filthy holes, sometimes for owing less than one dollar. The poorer working classes were especially hard hit by this merciless practice. But as the embattled laborer won the ballot and asserted himself, state legislatures gradually abolished debtors' prisons.

Criminal codes in the states were likewise being softened, in accord with more enlightened European practices. The number of capital offenses was being reduced, and brutal punishments, such as whipping and branding, were being slowly eliminated. A refreshing idea was taking hold that prisons should reform as well as punish—hence "reformatories," "houses of correction," and "penitentiaries" (for penance).

Sufferers from so-called insanity were still being treated with incredible cruelty. The medieval concept had been that the mentally deranged were cursed with unclean spirits; the 19th-Century idea was that they were willfully perverse and depraved—to be treated only as beasts. Many crazed persons were chained in jails or poorhouses with sane people.

Into this dismal picture stepped a quiet New England teacher-authoress, Dorothea Dix (1802–1887). A frail spinster afflicted with persistent lung

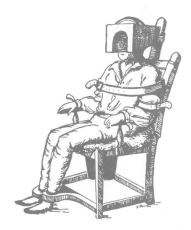

An Early Restraining Chair for the Insane

trouble, she possessed infinite compassion and will power. Never raising her voice to a screech, she traveled some 60,000 miles (97,000 kilometers) in eight years and assembled her damning reports on insanity from firsthand observations. Her classic petition of 1843 to the Massachusetts legislature, describing cells so foul that visitors were driven back by the stench, turned legislative stomachs and hearts. Her persistent prodding resulted in improved conditions and in a gain for the concept that the demented were not willfully perverse but mentally ill.

Agitation for peace also gained some momentum in the pre–Civil War years. In 1828 the American Peace Society was formed, with a ringing declaration of war on war. A leading spirit was William Ladd, who orated when his legs were so badly ulcerated that he had to sit on a stool. His ideas were finally to bear some fruit in the international organizations for collective security of the 20th Century. The American peace crusade, linked with the European crusade, was making promising progress by mid-century, when it was set back by the bloodshed of the Crimean War in Europe and the Civil War in America.

Demon Rum—The "Old Deluder"

The ever-present drink problem attracted dedicated reformers. Custom, combined with a hard and monotonous life, led to the excessive drinking

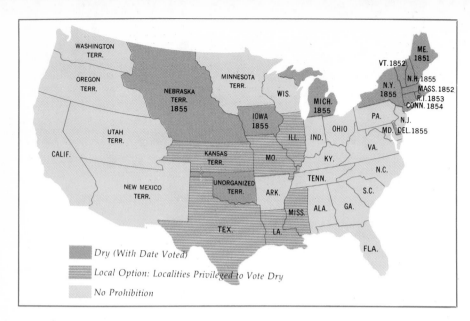

THE EXTENT OF PROHIBITION, 1855. Lax enforcement led a legendary tippler to comment that prohibition was far better than no liquor at all.

Map labels: WASHINGTON TERR.; OREGON TERR.; MINNESOTA TERR.; ME. 1851; VT. 1852; N.H. 1855; N.Y. 1855; MASS. 1852; R.I. 1853; CONN. 1854; NEBRASKA TERR. 1855; WIS.; MICH. 1855; PA.; N.J.; UTAH TERR.; IOWA 1855; ILL.; IND.; OHIO; MD.; DEL. 1855; CALIF.; KANSAS TERR.; MO.; KY.; VA.; NEW MEXICO TERR.; UNORGANIZED TERR.; ARK.; TENN.; N.C.; S.C.; MISS.; ALA.; GA.; TEX; LA.; FLA.

Legend: Dry (With Date Voted); Local Option: Localities Privileged to Vote Dry; No Prohibition

of hard liquor, even among women, clergymen, and members of Congress. Weddings and funerals all too often became disgraceful brawls, and occasionally a drunken man would fall into the open grave with the corpse. Heavy drinking decreased the efficiency of labor, while the introduction of poorly safeguarded machinery increased the danger of accident.

After earlier and feebler efforts, the American Temperance Society was formed at Boston in 1826. Within a few years about a thousand local groups sprang into existence. They implored drinkers to sign the temperance pledge and organized children's clubs, known as the "Cold

Demon Rum Plagues His Victim. One popular lecturer told of a tipsy man who fell into a pig sty. As the animals grunted in alarm, he muttered, "Hold your tongues; I'm as good as any of you." A contemporary cartoon.

Water Army." Temperance crusaders also made effective use of pictures, pamphlets, and lurid lecturers, some of whom were reformed drunkards. A popular temperance song ran:

> We've done with our days of carousing,
> Our nights, too, of frolicsome glee;
> For now with our sober minds choosing,
> We've pledged ourselves never to spree.

The most popular anti-alcohol tract of the era was T. S. Arthur's melodramatic novel, *Ten Nights in a Barroom and What I Saw There* (1854). It described in shocking detail how a once-happy village was ruined by Sam Slade's tavern. The book was second only to Mrs. Stowe's *Uncle Tom's Cabin* as a best seller in the 1850s, and it enjoyed a highly successful run on the stage. Its touching theme song began with the words of a little girl:

> Father, dear father, come home with me now,
> The clock in the belfry strikes one.

Early foes of Demon Drink adopted two major lines of attack. One was to stiffen the individual's will to resist the wiles of the little brown jug. Moderate reformers thus stressed "temperance" rather than "teetotalism," or the total elimination of intoxicants. But less patient zealots gradually came to believe that temptation should be removed by legislation. Prominent among this group was Neal S. Dow of Maine, a blue-nosed reformer who, as a mayor of Portland and an employer of labor, had often witnessed the debauching effect of alcohol.

Dow—the "Father of Prohibition"—sponsored the so-called Maine Law of 1851, which supplanted an earlier effort in 1846. This drastic new statute, hailed as "the law of Heaven Americanized," prohibited the manufacture and sale of intoxicating liquor. Other states in the North followed Maine's example, and by 1857 about a dozen had passed various prohibitory laws. But these figures are deceptive, for within a decade some of the statutes were repealed or declared unconstitutional, if not openly flouted.

It was clearly impossible to legislate thirst out of existence, especially in localities where public sentiment was hostile. Yet on the eve of the Civil War the prohibitionists had registered inspiriting gains. There was much less drinking among women than earlier in the century, and probably much less per capita consumption of hard liquor.

Women in Revolt

Sexual differences were strongly emphasized in 19th-Century America. Women were thought to be physically and emotionally weak, but also artistic, refined, and endowed with finely tuned consciences. Men were considered strong but crude, always in danger of slipping into some savage or beastly way of life if not guided by the gentle hands of their loving ladies. But if sexual roles were sharply separated, men and women could still be regarded as equals. As a sign of the prestigious position of American women, French visitor Alexis de Tocqueville noted that in his native France rape was punished only lightly, while in America it was one of the few crimes punishable by death.

The home was woman's special sphere. But some women increasingly felt that the glorified sanctuary of the home was in fact a gilded cage. They yearned to tear down the bars that separated the woman's world from the man's.

A covey of clamorous female agitators emerged as the century neared its halfway point. Most of them were broad-gauge battlers; while demanding rights for women, they were simultaneously fighting for temperance and anti-slavery reform. Homegrown feminists received much encouragement from their sisters in Europe, where a parallel movement was gaining ground. Neither foul eggs nor foul words, when hurled by disapproving males, could halt America's fiery females.

The woman's rights movement was mothered by some arresting characters. Prominent among them was Lucretia Mott, a sprightly Quaker whose ire had been aroused when she and her fellow female delegates to the London anti-slavery convention of 1840 were not recognized. Elizabeth Cady Stanton, a mother of seven who had insisted on leaving "obey" out of her marriage ceremony, shocked fellow feminists by going so far as to advocate suffrage for women. Quaker-reared Susan B. Anthony, a militant lecturer for woman's rights, exposed herself to rotten garbage and vulgar epithets. She became such a conspicuous ad-

Susan B. Anthony (1820–1906). A woman of great militancy and singleness of purpose, she was a foremost fighter in the woman's rights movement, as well as in that for temperance and abolition. Arrested in 1872 in Rochester, New York, for having voted, she was found guilty and fined $100. She vowed that she would never pay and she never did. She lived to see four states grant equal suffrage to women.

What It Would Be If Some Ladies Had Their Own Way. The men are sewing, tending the baby, and washing clothes. This scene seemed absurd then but not a century later. (Historical Pictures Service, Chicago.)

vocate of female rights that progressive women everywhere were called "Suzy Bs."

Other feminists challenged the man's world. Dr. Elizabeth Blackwell, a pioneer in a previously forbidden profession for women, was the first female graduate of a medical college. Precocious Margaret Fuller edited a Transcendentalist journal, *The Dial*, and is remembered for having said, "I accept the universe." The talented Grimké sisters, Sarah and Angelina, spoke at anti-slavery gatherings and aroused the ire of conservatives. Lucy Stone retained her maiden name after marriage—hence the latter-day "Lucy Stoners," who follow her example. Amelia Bloomer revolted against the current "street sweeping" female attire by donning a semi-masculine short skirt with Turkish trousers—"bloomers," they were called—amid much bawdy ridicule about "Bloomerism" and "loose habits." A jeering male rhyme of the times jabbed:

> Gibbey, gibbey gab
> The women had a confab
> And demanded the rights
> To wear the tights
> Gibbey, gibbey gab.

Fighting feminists met at Seneca Falls, New York, in a memorable Woman's Rights Convention (1848). The defiant Mrs. Stanton read a "Declaration of Sentiments," which in the spirit of the Declaration of Independence declared that "all men *and women* are created equal." One resolution formally demanded the ballot for females. The Seneca Falls meeting, which launched the modern woman's rights movement, not surprisingly became the object of scorn and denunciation from press and pulpit.

The crusade for woman's rights was eclipsed by that against slavery in the decade before the Civil War. Male idiots could still vote; women could not. Yet women were being gradually admitted to colleges, and some states, beginning with Mississippi in 1839, were even permitting wives to own property after marriage.

Wilderness Utopias

Leaders of the woman's rights movement often marched arm in arm with other reformers. Professional "do-gooders" popped up at every hand, giving the 1840s the distinction of being the "hot air period" of American history. About everything was tried, from communism to socialism, through polygamy and celibacy, to rule by a prophet and guidance by spirits. Societies were formed against tobacco, profanity, and the transit of mail on the Sabbath. Various faddist diets were promoted, including the whole-wheat graham bread and crackers of Sylvester Graham.

There was not "a reading man," observed Ralph Waldo Emerson, who was without some scheme for a new utopia in his "waistcoat pocket." Various reformers, ranging from the high-minded to the "lunatic fringe," set up more than forty communities of a cooperative, communistic, or "communitarian" nature. Seeking human betterment, a wealthy and idealistic Scottish textile manufacturer, Robert Owen, established in 1825 a communal society of about a thousand persons at New Harmony, Indiana. Little harmony prevailed in the colony, which, in addition to hardworking visionaries, attracted a sprinkling of radicals, lazy theorists, and outright scoundrels. The enterprise sank in a morass of contradiction and confusion.

Brook Farm in Massachusetts, comprising 200 acres of grudging soil, was started in 1841 with the brotherly cooperation of about twenty intellectuals. They prospered reasonably well until 1846, when they lost by fire a large new communal building shortly before its completion. The whole experiment in "plain living and high thinking" then collapsed in debt. Although a financial failure, Brook Farm was in some ways a social and educational success.

A more radical experiment was the Oneida Colony, founded in New York in 1848. It practiced free love ("complex marriage"), birth control, and the eugenic selection of parents to produce superior offspring. The leader finally fled to Canada to escape prosecution for adultery. This curious enterprise flourished for more than thirty years, largely because its craftsmen made superior steel traps and Oneida Community (silver) Plate. In 1879–1880 the group embraced monogamy and abandoned communism.

Various communistic experiments, mostly small-scale, have been attempted since Jamestown. But in competition with democratic free enterprise and free land, virtually all of them sooner or later failed or changed their methods. Perhaps the longest-lived sect has been the Shakers who, beginning in 1776, set up the first of a score or so of religious communities. They attained a membership of about 6,000 in 1840, but since they opposed both marriage and free love, they were virtually extinct by 1940.

Shakers in Dancing Ceremony

Artistic Endeavors and Achievements

Architecturally, America contributed little of note in the first half of the century. The rustic Republic, still under pressure to erect shelters in haste, was continuing to imitate European models. Public buildings and other important structures followed Greek and Roman lines, which seemed curiously out of place in a wilderness setting. A remarkable Greek revival came between 1820 and 1850, partly stimulated by the heroic efforts of the Greeks in the 1820s to wrest independence from the "terrible Turk." About mid-century strong interest developed in a revival of Gothic forms, with their emphasis on pointed arches and large windows.

Talented Thomas Jefferson, architect of revolution, was probably the ablest American architect of his generation. He brought a classical design to his Virginia hilltop home, Monticello—perhaps the most stately mansion in the nation (see p. 150). The quadrangle of the University of Virginia at Charlottesville, another creation of Jefferson, remains one of the finest examples of classical architecture in America.

The art of painting continued to be handicapped. It suffered from the dollar grabbing of a raw civilization; from the hustle, bustle, and absence of leisure; from the lack of a wealthy class to sit for portraits—and then pay for them. Some of the earliest painters were forced to go to England, where they found both training and patrons. America exported artists and imported art.

Painting, like the theater, also suffered from the Puritan prejudice that art was a sinful waste of time—and often obscene. John Adams boasted that "he would not give a sixpence for a bust of Phidias or a painting by Raphael." When Edward Everett, the eminent Boston scholar and orator, placed a statue of Apollo in his home, he had its naked limbs draped.

Competent painters nevertheless emerged. Gilbert Stuart (1755–1828), a spendthrift Rhode Islander and one of the most gifted of the early group, wielded his brush in England in competition with the best artists. He produced several portraits of Washington, all of them somewhat idealized and dehumanized. Truth to tell, the famous general had by then lost his natural teeth and some of the original shape of his face. Charles Willson Peale (1741–1827), a Marylander, painted some sixty portraits of Washington, who patiently sat for about fourteen of them. John Trumbull (1756–1843), who had fought in the Revolutionary War, recaptured its scenes and spirit on scores of striking canvases.

During the nationalistic upsurge after the War of 1812, American painters of portraits turned increasingly from human landscapes to romantic mirrorings of local landscapes. The Hudson River School excelled in this type of art. At the same time, portrait painters gradually encountered some unwelcome competition from the invention of a crude photograph known as the daguerreotype, perfected about 1839 by a Frenchman, Louis Daguerre.

America Bursts into Song

Music was slowly shaking off the restraints of colonial days, when the prim Puritans had frowned upon non-religious singing. Melody-minded Americans received much inspiration from the emergence of European musicians—Schubert, Mendelssohn, Chopin, Wagner. Growing numbers of citizens were studying music, and the song-loving German immigrants of the 1840s and 1850s added richly to American culture. A mid-century boom in the manufacture of pianos reflected improving tastes.

An appreciation of good music was increased by some noteworthy public performances. The New York Philharmonic Orchestra, one of the first, was organized in 1842. Ole Bull, the famous Norwegian violin virtuoso, held audiences spellbound during his five tours of the country, from 1843 to 1880. Golden-voiced Jenny Lind, the "Swedish Nightingale," who was also a talented actress and a rare Christian spirit, created a sensation in 1850–

A Satirical By-Product of Jenny Lind's Tour. (*Yankee Notions*, 1852.)

1852 ("Lindomania"). She received an unprecedented $1,000 for each of 150 concerts managed by showman Phineas T. Barnum, who for once did not "humbug" the public.

These visiting artists helped to elevate the nation's musical taste, but Americans themselves were making solid contributions. Gifted writers of hymns were adding to American hymnology. Notable in this group was Lowell Mason (1792–1872), who is perhaps best known for "Nearer, My God, to Thee" and "From Greenland's Icy Mountains."

Rhythmic and nostalgic "darky" tunes, popularized by white men, were becoming immensely popular by mid-century. Special favorites were the uniquely American minstrel shows, featuring white actors with blackened faces. "Dixie," later adopted by the Confederates as their battle hymn, was written in 1859, ironically in New York City by an Ohioan. The most famous black songs, also ironically, came from a white Pennsylvanian, Stephen C. Foster (1826–1864). His one excursion into the South occurred in 1852, after he had published "Old Folks at Home." Foster made a valuable contribution to American folk music by capturing the plaintive spirit of the slaves. An odd and pathetic figure, he finally lost both his art and his popularity, and died in a charity ward after drowning his sorrows in drink.

Sturdy yeomen were still too busy felling trees to write symphonies about their crashing. An eccentric Bohemian musician, A. P. Heinrich, undertook to play one of his own compositions about America at the White House. He was deeply affronted when President Tyler interrupted his piano-pounding to say, "That may all be very fine, sir, but can't you play us a good old Virginia reel?"

The Blossoming of a National Literature

"Who reads an American book?" sneered the British critic Sydney Smith in 1820. The painful truth was that the nation's rough-hewn, pioneering civilization gave little encouragement to "polite" literature. Much of the reading matter was imported or plagiarized from England.

Busy conquering a continent, the Americans poured most of their creative efforts into practical outlets. Praiseworthy were political essays, like *The Federalist* of Hamilton, Jay, and Madison; pamphlets, like Tom Paine's *Common Sense;* and political orations, like the masterpieces of Daniel Webster. In the category of non-religious books published before 1820, Benjamin Franklin's *Autobiography* (1818) is one of the few that achieved genuine distinction. His narrative is a classic in its simplicity, clarity, and inspirational quality. Even so, it records only a fragment of "Old Ben's" long, fruitful, and amorous life.

A genuinely American literature received a strong boost from the wave of nationalism that followed the War of Independence and especially the War of 1812. By 1820 the older seaboard areas were sufficiently removed from tree-chopping so that literature could be supported as a profession. The Knickerbocker Group in New York blazed brilliantly across the literary heavens, thus enabling America for the first time to boast of a literature to match her magnificent landscapes.

Washington Irving (1783–1859), born in New York City, was the first American to win international recognition as a literary figure. Steeped in the traditions of New Netherland, he published in 1809 his *Knickerbocker's History of New York*, with its amusing caricatures of the Dutch. When the family business failed, Irving was forced to turn to the goose-feather pen. In 1819–1820 he published *The Sketch Book*, which brought him immediate fame at home and abroad. Combining a pleasing style with delicate charm and quiet humor, he used English as well as American themes, and included such immortal Dutch-American tales as "Rip Van Winkle" and "The Legend of Sleepy Hollow." Europe was amazed to find at last an American with a feather in his hand, not in his hair. Later turning to Spanish locales and biography, Irving did much to interpret America to Europe and Europe to America. He was, said the Englishman William Thackeray,

Washington Irving's Character, Father Knickerbocker. (*The Knickerbocker*, 1834.)

"the first ambassador whom the New World of letters sent to the Old."

James Fenimore Cooper (1789–1851) was the first American novelist, as Irving was the first general writer, to gain world fame and make New World themes respectable. Marrying into a wealthy family, he settled down on the frontier of New York. Reading one day to his wife from an insipid English novel, he remarked in disgust that he could write a better one himself. She challenged him to do so—and he did.

After an initial failure, Cooper launched out upon an illustrious career in 1821 with his second novel, *The Spy*—an absorbing tale of the American Revolution. His stories of the sea were meritorious and popular, but his fame rests most enduringly on the *Leather Stocking Tales*. A deadeye rifleman named Natty Bumppo, one of nature's noblemen, meets with Indians in stirring adventures like *The Last of the Mohicans*. Cooper's novels had a wide sale among Europeans, some of whom came to think of all Americans as born with tomahawk in hand. Actually the author was seeking the good society somewhere between the anarchy of wilderness and the artificiality of modern civilization.

A third member of the Knickerbocker group in New York was the belated Puritan William Cullen Bryant (1794–1878), transplanted from Massachusetts. At age sixteen he wrote the meditative and melancholy "Thanatopsis" (published in 1817), which was one of the first high-quality poems produced in the United States. Critics could hardly believe that it had been written on "this side of the water." Although Bryant continued with poetry, he was forced to make his living by editing the influential New York *Evening Post*. For over fifty years he set a model for journalism that was dignified, liberal, and high-minded.

Trumpeters of Transcendentalism

A golden age in American literature dawned in the second quarter of the 19th Century, when an amazing outburst shook New England. One of the mainsprings of this literary flowering was Transcendentalism, especially in the Boston area, which preened itself as "the Athens of America."

The Transcendentalist movement of the 1830s resulted in part from a liberalizing of the strait-jacket Puritan theology. It also owed much to foreign thinkers, including the German romantic philosophers. The Transcendentalists rejected the prevailing theory, derived from John Locke, that all knowledge comes to the mind through the senses. Truth, rather, "transcends" the senses: it cannot be found by observation alone. Every man possesses an inner light that can illuminate the highest truth and put him in direct touch with God, or the "Oversoul."

These mystical doctrines of Transcendentalism defied precise definition, but they underlay concrete beliefs. Foremost was a stiff-backed individualism in matters religious as well as social. Closely associated was a commitment to self-reliance, self-culture, and self-discipline. These traits naturally bred hostility to authority and to formal institutions of any kind, as well as to all conventional wisdom. Finally came exaltation of the dignity of the individual, whether black or white—the mainspring of a whole array of humanitarian reforms.

Best known of the Transcendentalists was Boston-born Ralph Waldo Emerson (1803–1882).

Tall, slender, and intensely blue-eyed, he mirrored serenity in his noble features. Trained as a Unitarian minister, he early forsook his pulpit and ultimately reached a wider audience by pen and platform. He was a never-failing favorite as a lyceum lecturer, and for twenty years took a Western tour every winter. Perhaps his most thrilling public effort was a Phi Beta Kappa address, "The American Scholar," delivered at Harvard College in 1837. This brilliant appeal was an intellectual Declaration of Independence, for it urged American writers to throw off European traditions and delve into the riches of their own backyards.

Hailed as both a poet and a philosopher, Emerson was not of the highest rank as either. He was more influential as a practical philosopher, and through his fresh and vibrant essays enriched countless thousands of humdrum lives. Catching the individualistic mood of the Republic, he

In 1849 Thoreau published *On the Duty of Civil Disobedience*, asserting, "I heartily accept the motto, 'That government is best which governs least'; and I should like to see it acted up to more rapidly and systematically. Carried out, it finally amounts to this, which also I believe— 'That government is best which governs not at all'; and when men are prepared for it, that will be the kind of government which they will have. Government is at best an expedient; but most governments are sometimes, inexpedient."

stressed self-reliance, self-improvement, self-confidence, optimism, and freedom. The secret of Emerson's popularity lay largely in the fact that his ideals reflected those of an expanding America. Among his most-quoted observations are: "Whoso would be a man, must be a non-conformist"; "A foolish consistency is the hobgoblin of little minds"; "God offers to every mind its choice between truth and repose."

Henry David Thoreau (1817–1862) was Emerson's close associate—a poet, a mystic, a Transcendentalist, and a non-conformist. Condemning a government that supported slavery, he refused to pay his Massachusetts poll tax, and was jailed for a night.* A gifted prose writer, he is well known for *Walden: Or Life in the Woods* (1854). The book is a record of Thoreau's two years of simple existence in a hut which he built on the edge of Walden Pond, near Concord, Massachusetts. A stiff-necked individualist, he believed that he should reduce his bodily wants so as to gain time for a pursuit of truth through study and meditation. Thoreau's *Walden* and his essay on *Civil Disobedience* exercised a strong influence in furthering idealistic thought, both in America and abroad. His writings later encouraged Mahatma Gandhi to resist British rule in India.

Ralph Waldo Emerson (1803–1882). Emerson's philosophical observations include such statements as: "The less government we have, the better—the fewer laws, and the less confided power"; "To be great is to be misunderstood"; "Every hero becomes a bore at last"; "Shallow men believe in luck"; "When you strike a king, you must kill him." (Courtesy, Concord Free Public Library, Gift of Mrs. Arthur Holland)

*The story (probably apocryphal) is that Emerson visited Thoreau at the jail and asked, "Why are you here?" The reply came, "Why are you not here?"

Bold, brassy, and swaggering was the open-collared figure of Brooklyn's Walt Whitman (1819–1892). In his famous collection of poems, *Leaves of Grass* (1855), he gave free rein to his gushing genius with what he called a "barbaric yawp." Highly romantic, emotional, and unconventional, he dispensed with titles, stanzas, rhymes, and at times even regular meter. He handled sex with shocking frankness, although he laundered his verses in later editions, and his book was banned in Boston.

Whitman's *Leaves of Grass* was at first a financial failure. The only three enthusiastic reviews that it received were written by the author himself—anonymously. But in time the once-withered *Leaves of Grass*, revived and honored, won for Whitman an enormous following in both America and Europe. His fame increased immensely among "Whitmaniacs" after his death.

Leaves of Grass gained for Whitman the in-

In 1876 the London *Saturday Review* referred to Whitman as the author of a volume of "so-called poems which were chiefly remarkable for their absurd extravagances and shameless obscenity, and who has since, we are glad to say, been little heard of among decent people." In 1888 Whitman wrote, "I had my choice when I commenced. I bid neither for soft eulogies, big money returns, nor the approbation of existing schools and conventions. . . . I have had my say entirely my own way, and put it unerringly on record— the value thereof to be decided by time."

formal title "Poet Laureate of Democracy." Singing with Transcendental abandon of his love for the masses, he caught the exuberant enthusiasm of an expanding America that had turned her back on the Old World:

> All the Past we leave behind;
> We debouch upon a newer, mightier world, varied world;
> Fresh and strong the world we seize—world of labor and the march—
> Pioneers! O Pioneers!

Here at last was the native art for which critics had been crying.

Glowing Literary Lights

Certain other literary giants were not actively associated with the Transcendentalist movement, though not completely immune to its influences. Professor Henry Wadsworth Longfellow (1807–1882), who for many years taught modern languages at Harvard College, was one of the most popular poets ever produced in America. Handsome and urbane, he lived a generally serene life, except for the tragic deaths of two wives, the second of whom perished before his eyes when her dress caught fire. Writing for the genteel classes,

Walt Whitman. This portrait of the young poet appeared in the first edition of *Leaves of Grass* (1855). (Rare Book Division, New York Public Library, Astor, Lenox and Tilden Foundations.)

he was adopted by the less cultured masses. His wide knowledge of European literature supplied him with many themes, but some of his most admired poems were based on American traditions—*Evangeline, Hiawatha,* and *The Courtship of Miles Standish.* Immensely popular in Europe, Longfellow was the only American ever to be honored with a bust in the Poets' Corner of Westminster Abbey.

A fighting Quaker, John Greenleaf Whittier (1807–1892), with piercing dark eyes and swarthy complexion, was the uncrowned poet laureate of the anti-slavery crusade. Less talented as a craftsman than Longfellow, he was vastly more important in influencing social action. His poems cried aloud against inhumanity, injustice, and intolerance, against

> The outworn rite, the old abuse,
> The pious fraud transparent grown.

Undeterred by insults and the stonings of mobs, Whittier helped arouse a calloused America on the slavery issue. A great conscience rather than a great poet or intellect, Whittier was one of the moving forces of his generation, whether moral, humanitarian, or spiritual. Gentle and lovable, he was pre-eminently the poet of human freedom.

Many-sided James Russell Lowell (1819–1891), who succeeded Professor Longfellow at Harvard, ranks as one of America's better poets. He was also a distinguished essayist, literary critic, editor, and diplomat—a diffusion of talents that hampered his poetical output. He is remembered as a political satirist in his *Biglow Papers,* especially those of 1846 dealing with the Mexican War. Written partly as poetry in the Yankee dialect, the *Papers* condemned in blistering terms the alleged slavery-expansion designs of the Polk administration.

Slender Dr. Oliver Wendell Holmes (1809–1894), who taught anatomy with a sparkle at Harvard Medical School, was a prominent poet, essayist, novelist, lecturer, and wit. A non-conformist and a fascinating conversationalist, he shone among a group of literary lights who regarded Boston as "the hub of the universe." His poem "The Last Leaf," in honor of the last "white Indian" of the Boston Tea Party, came to apply to himself. Dying at age eighty-five, he was the "last leaf" among his distinguished contemporaries.*

The most noteworthy literary figure produced by the South before the Civil War, unless Edgar Allan Poe is regarded as a Southerner, was novelist William Gilmore Simms (1806–1870). Quantitatively, at least, he was great: eighty-two books flowed from his ever-moist pen, winning for him the title "the Cooper of the South." His themes dealt with the Southern frontier in colonial days and with the South during the Revolutionary War. But he was neglected by his own section, even though he married into the socially elite and became a slaveowner. The high-toned planter aristocracy would never accept the son of a poor Charleston storekeeper.

Literary Individualists and Dissenters

Not all writers in these years believed so keenly in human goodness and social progress. Edgar Allan Poe (1809–1849), who spent much of his youth in Virginia, was an eccentric genius. Orphaned at an early age, cursed with ill health, and married to a child-wife of fourteen who fell fatally ill of tuberculosis, he suffered hunger, cold, poverty, and debt. Failing at suicide, he took refuge in the bottle and dissipated his talent early. Poe was a gifted lyric poet, as "The Raven" attests. A master stylist, he also excelled in the short story, especially of the horror type, in which he shared his alcoholic nightmares with fascinated readers. If he did not invent the modern detective novel, he at least set new high standards in tales like "The Gold Bug."

Poe was fascinated by the ghostly and ghastly, as in "The Fall of the House of Usher" and other stories. He reflected a morbid sensibility distinctly at odds with the usually optimistic tone of American culture. Partly for this reason, Poe has per-

---

*Oliver Wendell Holmes had a son with the same name who became a distinguished justice of the Supreme Court (1902–1932) and who lived to be ninety-four, less two days.

haps been even more prized by Europeans than by his own countrymen. His brilliant career was cut short when he was found drunk in a Baltimore gutter and shortly thereafter died.

Two other writers reflected the continuing Calvinist obsession with original sin and with the never-ending struggle between good and evil. In somber Salem, Massachusetts, Nathaniel Hawthorne grew up in an atmosphere heavy with the memories of his Puritan forebears and the tragedy of his father's premature death on an ocean voyage. His masterpiece was *The Scarlet Letter* (1850), which described the Puritan practice of forcing an adultress to wear a scarlet A on her clothing.* The tragic tale chronicles the psychological effects of sin on the guilty heroine and her secret lover (the father of her baby), a minister of the gospel in Puritan Boston. In *The Marble Faun* (1860), Hawthorne dealt with a group of young American artists who witness a mysterious murder in Rome. He thus explored the concepts of the omnipresence of evil and the dead hand of the past weighing upon the present.

Herman Melville (1819–1891), an orphaned and ill-educated New Yorker, went to sea as a youth

---

*This was how Hester Prynne got her A in *The Scarlet Letter.* An H stood for heresy and an I for incest.

and served eighteen adventuresome months on a whaler. "A whale ship was my Yale College and my Harvard," he wrote. Jumping ship in the South Seas, he lived among cannibals, from whom he providentially escaped uneaten. His fresh and charming tales of the South Seas were immediately popular, but his masterpiece, *Moby Dick* (1851), was not. This epic novel was a complex allegory of good and evil, told in terms of the conflict between a whaling captain, Ahab, and a giant white whale, Moby Dick. Captain Ahab, who lost a leg to the marine monster, swore revenge. His pursuit finally ended when Moby Dick rammed and sank Ahab's ship, leaving only one survivor. The whale's exact identity and Ahab's motives remained obscure. In the end the sea, like the terrifyingly impersonal and unknowable universe of Melville's imagination, simply rolled on.

Moby Dick was widely ignored at the time of its publication; people were accustomed to more straightforward and upbeat prose. A disheartened Melville continued to write unprofitably for some years, part of the time eking out a living as a customs inspector, and then died in relative obscurity and poverty. Ironically, his brooding masterpiece about the mysterious white whale had to wait until the more jaded 20th Century for readers and proper recognition.

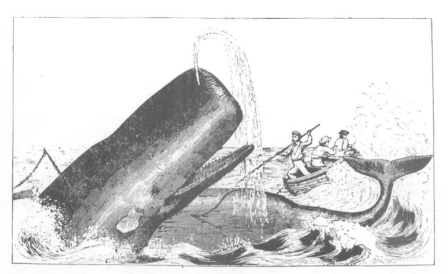

Hazardous Whaling. *Moby Dick* gives a vivid first-hand picture of whaling, which proved to be an important industry from colonial times to the end of the 19th Century. (From *Etchings of a Whaling Cruise* by John Ross Browne, 1846. Stanford University Libraries.)

Portrayers of the Past

A distinguished group of American historians was emerging at the same time that other writers were winning distinction. Energetic George Bancroft (1800–1891), who as secretary of the navy helped found the Naval Academy at Annapolis in 1845, has deservedly received the title "Father of American History." He published a spirited, super-patriotic history of the United States to 1789 in six (originally ten) volumes (1834–1876), a work that grew out of his vast researches in dusty archives in Europe and America.

Two other historians are read with greater pleasure and profit today. William H. Prescott (1796–1859), who accidently lost the sight of an eye while in college, conserved his remaining weak vision, and published classic accounts of the conquest of Mexico (1843) and Peru (1847). Francis Parkman (1823–1893), whose eyes were so defective that he wrote in darkness with the aid of a guiding machine, penned a brilliant series of volumes, beginning in 1851. In epic style he chronicled the struggle between France and England in colonial times for the mastery of North America.

Early American historians of prominence were almost without exception New Englanders, largely because the Boston area provided well-stocked libraries and a stimulating literary tradition. These writers numbered abolitionists among their relatives and friends, and hence were disposed to view

George Bancroft, Historian. With unscholarly exaggeration, he wrote of the outbreak of the American Revolution: "With one impulse, the colonies sprung to arms; with one spirit, they pledged themselves to each other 'to be ready for the supreme event.' With one heart, the continent cried: 'Liberty or Death!' "

unsympathetically the slave-cursed South. The writing of American history for generations to come was to suffer from an anti-Southern bias perpetuated by this early "made in New England" interpretation.

VARYING VIEWPOINTS

The reformist and intellectual ferment of the antebellum era was extraordinary, and historians are still seeking a satisfying explanation of this many-sided activity. Was there some single origin of the multiple impulses that animated the movements for temperance, woman's rights, communalism, and eventually abolition? Some writers have suggested the Puritan spirit, as it was transformed and rejuvenated by the religious revivals of the early 19th Century. Others have pointed to a pervasive utopianism, seen both in social movements and in the unprecedented literary outpouring of the age. Utopianism is common in revolutionary societies (which the United States in many ways still was), and it was strengthened in America by the stimulating presence of a vast, near-virgin wilderness.

SELECT READINGS

General intellectual histories are M. Curti, *The Growth of American Thought* (3rd ed., 1964), and R. H. Gabriel, *The Course of American Democratic Thought* (2nd ed., 1956). See also Perry Miller's *Life of the Mind in America: From the Revolution to the Civil War* (1965). Also of general interest are Daniel Boorstin, *The Americans: The National Experience* (1965), and Rowland Berthoff, *An Unsettled People* (1971). Y. Arieli has an intriguing essay on *Individualism and Nationalism in American Ideology* (1964), and Carl Bode dissects *The Anatomy of American Popular Culture, 1840–1861* (1959). See also G. Daniels, *American Science in the Age of Jackson* (1968), to be supplemented by R. H. Shryock, *Medicine and Science in America* (1960). A solid biography is E. Lurie's study of *Louis Agassiz* (1960). An older but still standard discussion of reform is Alice F. Tyler, *Freedom's Ferment* (1944). For particular subjects, consult David Rothman, *The Discovery of the Asylum* (1971), and G. Grob, *Mental Institutions in America: Social Policy to 1875* (1973); on juvenile delinquency, Joseph Hawes, *Children in Urban Society* (1971); and on prohibition, J. Gusfield, *Symbolic Crusade* (1963). Large-scale histories of the woman's movement are Andrew Sinclair, *The Better Half* (1965), W. O'Neill, *Everyone Was Brave* (1970), and Page Smith, *Daughters of the Promised Land* (1970). Consult also E. Flexner, *Century of Struggle* (1959), and R. Riegel, *American Feminists* (1963). Women's history for this period has recently blossomed in a number of fine studies, including Ellen Carol Dubois, *Feminism and Suffrage* (1978), Barbara J. Berg, *The Remembered Gate: Origins of American Feminism—the Woman and the City, 1800–1860* (1977), Estelle B. Freedman, *Their Sisters' Keepers: Women's Prison Reform in America, 1830–1930* (1981), Keith E. Melder, *The Beginnings of Sisterhood* (1977), and, emphasizing intellectual and literary history, Ann Douglas, *The Feminization of American Culture* (1977). Communal experiments are treated in A. Bestor, *Backwoods Utopias* (1950), M. Holloway, *Heavens on Earth* (1951), and J. F. C. Harrison's analysis of the Owenites, *Quest for the New Moral World* (1969). K. Silverman provides an excellent *Cultural History of the American Revolution* (1976). F. O. Mathiessen's masterful *American Renaissance* (1941) is indispensable on the writers of the 1840s and 1850s. D. H. Lawrence, *Studies in Classic American Literature* (1923), is a classic in its own right. For provocative overviews of the literature of the period, consult A. N. Kaul, *American Vision: Actual and Ideal Society in Nineteenth-Century Fiction* (1963), F. Somkin, *Unquiet Eagle: Memory and Desire in the Idea of American Freedom, 1815–1860* (1967), and Joel Porte, *Representative Man: Ralph Waldo Emerson in His Time* (1979). See also O. W. Larkin, *Art and Life in America* (1949), to be supplemented by J. T. Flexner, *That Wilder Image* (1962), and by Neil Harris's imaginative *Artist in American Society: The Formative Years, 1790–1860* (1968), and especially by Barbara Novak's stimulating *Nature and Culture: American Landscape and Painting, 1825–1875* (1980). On history, see John Higham et al., *History* (1965), and David Levin, *History as Romantic Art* (1959). Particularly intriguing is Anne C. Rose, *Transcendentalism as a Social Movement* (1981).

19

The South and the Slavery Controversy

If you put a chain around the neck of a slave,
the other end fastens itself around your own.

RALPH WALDO EMERSON, 1841

"Cotton Is King!"

When George Washington first took the presidential oath, the economic wheels of the South were creaking badly. They were burdened with depressed prices, unmarketable products, overcropped lands, and the dead weight of an unprofitable slave system. Some Southern statesmen, including Thomas Jefferson, were talking openly of freeing their slaves, and confidently predicting that slavery would gradually die of economic anemia.

But the introduction of Whitney's cotton gin in 1793 changed the scene. The newly popularized short-staple cotton, which brought a premium price, gradually became the dominant Southern crop, eclipsing tobacco, rice, and sugar. Slavery was reinvigorated, with the slave being chained to the gin, and the planter to the slave.

Cotton as King. In this Northern Civil War cartoon, the Confederacy appears as a lighted bomb.

As time passed, the Cotton Kingdom developed into a huge agricultural factory, pouring out avalanches of the fluffy fiber. Quick profits drew planters to the virgin bottom lands of the Gulf states. As long as the soil was still vigorous, the yield was bountiful and the rewards were high. Caught up in an economic spiral, the planters bought more slaves and land to grow more cotton, so as to buy still more slaves and land.

Northern shippers reaped a large part of the profits from the cotton trade. They would load bulging bales of cotton at Southern ports, transport them to England, sell them for pounds sterling, and buy needed manufactured goods for sale in the United States. To a large degree the prosperity of both North and South rested on the bent backs of Southern slaves.

Cotton thus came to be by far the largest and most important American export. Not only was it valuable in establishing a balance between imports and exports, but it held foreign nations in partial bondage. Britain was then the leading industrial power. Her most important single manufacture in the 1850s was cotton cloth, from which about one-fifth of her population, directly or indirectly, drew its livelihood. About 80 percent of this precious supply of fiber came from the white-carpeted acres of the South.

Southern statesmen were fully aware that England was tied to them by cotton threads, and this dependence gave them a heady sense of power. In their eyes "Cotton was King," the gin was his throne, and the black bondsmen were his henchmen. If war should ever break out between North and South, Northern warships would presumably cut off the outflow of cotton. Fiber-famished British factories would then close their gates, starving mobs would force the London government to break the blockade, and the South would triumph. Cotton was a powerful monarch indeed.

Cavaliers All

Before the Civil War the South was in some respects not so much a democracy as an oligarchy— or a government by the few, in this case heavily influenced by a planter aristocracy. In 1850 only 1,733 families owned more than 100 slaves each, and this select group provided the cream of the political and social leadership of the section and nation. Here was the mint-julep South of the tall-columned and white-painted plantation mansion— the "big house," where dwelt the "cottonocracy."

Thomas Jefferson wrote in 1782: "The whole commerce between master and slave is a perpetual exercise of the . . . most unremitting despotism on the one part, and degrading submissions on the other. . . . Indeed I tremble for my country when I reflect that God is just; that his justice cannot sleep forever." Unlike Washington, Jefferson did not free his slaves in his will; he had fallen upon distressful times.

Cotton Exports Compared with Total Exports, 1800–1860*

Year	Pounds of Cotton Exported	Value of Cotton Exported	Value of Total U.S. Exports	Percentage of Cotton in Relation to Total Exports
1800	17,789,803	$ 5,000,000	$ 70,971,780	7%
1810	93,261,462	15,108,000	66,757,970	22
1820	127,860,152	22,308,667	69,691,669	32
1830	298,459,102	29,674,883	71,670,735	41
1840	743,941,061	63,870,307	123,668,932	51
1850	635,381,604	71,984,616	144,375,726	49
1860	1,767,686,338	191,806,555	333,576,057	57

*Note that the above figures show exports alone. Hinton R. Helper pointed out that in 1850 the value of the Northern hay crop, consumed locally, exceeded that of all leading Southern agricultural products combined.

The planter aristocrat, with his blooded horses and Chippendale chairs, enjoyed a lion's share of Southern wealth. He could educate his children in the finest schools, often in the North or abroad. His money provided the leisure for study, reflection, and statecraft, as was notably true of men like John C. Calhoun (a Yale graduate) and Jefferson Davis (a West Point graduate). He felt a keen sense of obligation to serve the public. It was no accident that Virginia and her Southern sisters produced a higher proportion of front-rank statesmen before 1860 than the "dollar-grubbing" North.

But even in its best light, dominance by a favored aristocracy was basically undemocratic. It widened the gap between rich and poor. It hampered tax-supported public education, because the rich planter could and did send his children to private institutions. Yet although inequities existed, schools of the South, especially at the secondary level, were more numerous and efficient than is commonly supposed.

Southern gentry were high-strung, though generally soft-spoken, courteous, hospitable, and chivalrous. Jealous of their honor, they clung to dueling long after it had died out in the North. They carried on the somewhat spurious "Cavalier" tradition of early Virginia, and developed a martial spirit that is still reflected in high-quality Southern military academies like The Citadel (Charleston) and the Virginia Military Institute (Lexington).

A favorite author of Southerners was Sir Walter Scott, whose manors and castles, graced by brave Ivanhoes and fair Rowenas, roughly mirrored their own semi-feudal society. Southern aristocrats, who would sometimes stage jousting tournaments, strove to perpetuate a type of medievalism that had died out in Europe—or was rapidly dying out.* Mark Twain later accused Sir Walter Scott of having had a hand in starting the Civil War. The British novelist, Twain said, aroused the Southerners to fight for a decaying social structure—"a sham civilization."

Slaves of the Slave System

Unhappily the moonlight-and-magnolia tradition concealed much that was worrisome, distasteful, and sordid. Plantation agriculture was wasteful, largely because King Cotton and his money-hungry subjects despoiled the good earth. Quick profits led to excessive cultivation or "land butchery," which in turn caused a heavy leakage of population to the West and Northwest. Soil exhaustion also forced attention to scientific agriculture, and the pre-war South excelled in farm journals and agricultural societies. Edmund Ruffin of Virginia, who later fired one of the first shots of the Civil

---

*Oddly enough, by legislative enactment jousting became the official state sport of Maryland in 1962.

Harvesting Cotton. Slaves of both sexes picked cotton on the great plantations. (Boston Public Library.)

War at Fort Sumter, did notable pioneering work in soil restoration. Yet his best efforts were inadequate to cope with the problem.

The economic structure of the South became increasingly monopolistic. As the land wore thin, many small farmers sold their holdings to more prosperous neighbors, and went north or west. The big got bigger and the small smaller. When the Civil War finally broke, a large percentage of Southern farms had passed from the hands of the families that had originally cleared them.

Another cancer in the bosom of the South was the financial instability of the plantation system. The temptation to overspeculate in land and slaves caused many a planter, including Andrew Jackson in his later years, to plunge in beyond his depth. Although the black bondsmen might in extreme cases be fed for as little as ten cents a day, there were other expenses. The slaves represented a heavy investment of capital, perhaps $1,200 each in the case of prime field hands; and they might deliberately injure themselves or run away. An entire slave quarter might be wiped out by disease or even by lightning, as happened in one instance to twenty luckless blacks.

Dominance by King Cotton likewise led to a dangerous dependence on a one-crop economy, whose price level was at the mercy of world conditions. The whole system discouraged a healthy diversification of agriculture and particularly of manufacturing, for which the South was almost ideally fitted. While concentrating on cotton, the plantations had to import huge quantities of pork and grain from the upper Mississippi Valley.

Southern planters resented watching the North grow fat at their expense. They were pained by the heavy outward flow of commissions and interest to Northern middlemen, bankers, agents, and shippers. True sons of the South, especially by the 1850s, deplored the fact that when born they were wrapped in Yankee-made swaddling clothes, and that they spent the rest of their lives in servitude to Yankee manufacturing. When they died, they were laid in coffins held together with Yankee nails, and were buried in graves dug with Yankee shovels. The South furnished the corpse and the hole in the ground.

The Cotton Kingdom also repelled large-scale European immigration, which added so richly to the manpower and wealth of the North. In 1860

Basil Hall, an Englishman, visited part of the cotton belt on a river steamer (1827–1828). Noting the preoccupation with cotton, he wrote: "All day and almost all night long, the captain, pilot, crew, and passengers were talking of nothing else; and sometimes our ears were so wearied with the sound of cotton! cotton! cotton! that we gladly hailed a fresh inundation of company in hopes of some change—but alas! . . . 'What's cotton at?' was the first eager inquiry. 'Ten cents [a pound].' 'Oh, that will never do!' From the cotton in the market they went to the crops in the fields—the frost which had nipped their shoots—the hard times—the overtrading—and so round to the prices and prospects again and again."

only 4.4 percent of the Southern population was foreign-born, as compared with 18.7 percent for the North. German and Irish immigration to the South was generally discouraged by the competition of slave labor, by the high cost of fertile land, and by European ignorance of cotton growing. The diverting of non-English immigration to the North caused the white South to become the most Anglo-Saxon section of the nation.

Rich Whites and Poor Whites

Only a handful of Southern aristocrats lived in Grecian-pillared mansions. Below the 1,733 families in 1850 who owned 100 or more slaves were the less wealthy slaveowners. They totaled in 1850 some 345,000 families, representing about 1,725,000 white persons. Over two-thirds of these families— 255,268 in all—owned fewer than ten slaves each.

Beneath the slaveowners was the great body of non-slaveowning whites who, by 1860, had swelled their numbers to 6,120,825. These rank-and-file citizens, comprising about three-fourths of the free population of the South, had no direct stake in slavery. They fell roughly into three groups: (1) the lowland whites, who were by far the most numerous; (2) the poor whites, who were generally disease-ridden; and (3) the semi-isolated mountain whites, who were the most independent-minded.

The hundreds of thousands of energetic lowland whites included such folks as mechanics, lesser tradesmen, and above all, small cotton farmers.

Though owning no slaves themselves, they were among the stoutest defenders of the slave system. The carrot-on-the-stick ever dangling before their noses was the hope of buying a slave or two, and of parlaying their holdings into riches—all in accord with the "American dream." They also took fierce pride in their presumed racial superiority, which would be watered down if the slaves were freed. Many of the poorer lowland whites were hardly better off economically than the Afro-American; some, indeed, were not so well off. But they clung desperately to their one visible badge of presumed superiority.

Conspicuous among the millions of non-slaveholders was a considerable sprinkling of poor whites, whom even the slaves despised as the "poor white trash." Known also as "hillbillies," "crackers," or "clay eaters," they were often listless, pallid, shiftless, and misshapen. Later investigations have revealed that many of them were not so much lazy as sickly, suffering from malnutrition and disease, including hookworm.

Mountain whites of the South are not to be confused with the poor whites of the lowland cotton belt. They were more or less marooned in the valleys of the Appalachian range, stretching from western Virginia to northern Georgia and Alabama. Civilization had largely passed them by. They were a kind of living ancestry, for some of them retained Elizabethan speech forms and habits that had long since died out in England.

As independent small farmers, the mountain

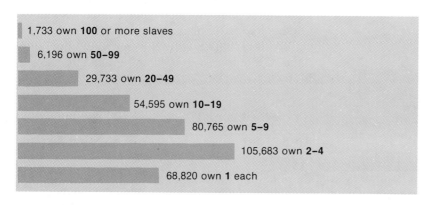

1,733 own **100** or more slaves

6,196 own **50–99**

29,733 own **20–49**

54,595 own **10–19**

80,765 own **5–9**

105,683 own **2–4**

68,820 own **1** each

SLAVEOWNING FAMILIES, 1850
The philosopher Ralph Waldo Emerson, a New Englander, declared in 1856: "I do not see how a barbarous community and a civilized community can constitute a state. I think we must get rid of slavery or we must get rid of freedom."

whites had little in common with the aristocracy of the broad cotton lands. Many of them, including the future President Andrew Johnson of Tennessee, hated both the lordly planter and his gangs of blacks. They looked upon the impending strife between North and South as "a rich man's war but a poor man's fight."

The tough-fibered mountain whites constituted a vitally important peninsula of unionism jutting down into the secessionist Southern sea. They ultimately played a significant role in crippling the Confederacy. Their attachment to the Union party of Abraham Lincoln was such that, for generations after the Civil War, the only concentrated Republican strength in the Solid South was to be found in the Southern highlands.

The Unfree Freedmen

Below the most wretched whites in the social scale of 1860 were about 250,000 free blacks, several thousand of whom owned a slave or two themselves.* They usually had been freed by kind masters, or had purchased their freedom with earnings from labor after hours. They were a kind of "third race." Their lot was unpleasant and their "fettered freedom" was precarious, because they might be highjacked back into slavery by unscrupulous white dealers. Yet as free men and women they were walking examples of what might be achieved by emancipation, and hence were frowned upon by defenders of the slave system.

Free blacks were also unpopular in the North, where several states forbade their entrance. In 1835 New Hampshire farmers, using oxen, dragged into a swamp a small schoolhouse that had enrolled fourteen black children. Northern ex-slaves were especially hated by the pick-and-shovel Irish immigrants, who feared wage-lowering competition. Much of the agitation in the North against the spread of slavery into the new territories in the

Ex-Slave Douglass Resists Indiana Mob. At times he preached extremism. In 1852, he shocked a Pennsylvania audience by declaring: "My motto is extermination. The slaveholders not only forfeit their right to liberty but to life itself."

1840s and 1850s grew out of race prejudice, not humanitarianism.

Feeling against the blacks was in fact frequently stronger in the North than in the South. The gifted and eloquent ex-slave Frederick Douglass, an abolitionist and self-educated orator of rare power, was subjected to numerous mobbings and beatings by Northern rowdies. It was frequently observed that white Southerners, who were sometimes suckled and reared by black nurses, liked the black as an individual but despised his race. The white Northerner, on the other hand, often professed to like the race but disliked individual blacks.

Black Bondsmen

At the bottom of the social pyramid in the South of 1860 were nearly 4 million black human chattels. Black slaves had existed in all of the thirteen colonies before independence. Even preachers of the

---

*William T. Johnson, a free black and "the barber of Natchez," owned fifteen slaves. His diary records that in June 1848 he flogged two slaves and a mule.

gospel in the North owned them, including the godly Jonathan Edwards, who kept two. American slaves had been originally captured in Africa during raids or wars by fellow blacks, who sold them to white slave traders. The unfortunate victims were then crammed into slavers sailing to the New World. Many coffins had more room. As a contemporary ballad ran:

> We crowded them upon the deck
> and stored them all below
> With eighteen inches to the man,
> was all they had to go.

Some of the slave ships became so filthy that, with the wind in the right direction, they could be smelled before they were sighted. Death rates on the horrible "middle passage" were incredibly high, but so were the profits, which sometimes ran to 500 percent.

The transplanting of African slaves to English America was mostly done by Englishmen and New Englanders. Some Yankee traders were descendants of early Puritans and, ironically, ancestors of later abolitionists.

Black slavery gradually died out in the North during and after the Revolutionary War. Human bondage clashed with the philosophy of the Declaration of Independence, which proclaimed

Slave Deck of the Slaver *Wildfire*.   Captured by the U.S. navy, this slave ship was brought into Key West, Florida, in April 1860. The blacks were freed. (From a daguerreotype [photograph] published in *Harper's Weekly,* June 2, 1860.)

that "all men are created equal." But perhaps as important, slavery in the North had become unprofitable. Black babies, when weaned, were sometimes given away by their owners. Financial loss helps to create a tender conscience.

Legal importations of African slaves into America ended in 1808, when Congress nailed up the bars. This action was taken precisely at the end of the twenty-year period of grace prescribed in the Constitution (see Art. I, Sec. IX, para. 1). But the price of "Black Ivory" was so high before the Civil War that uncounted thousands of blacks were smuggled into the South, despite the death penalty for slavers. Though several were captured, only one slave trader was ever executed, N. P. Gordon, and that was in New York in 1862, the second year of the Civil War.

After the cotton gin had made slavery profitable, the planters had the wolf by the ears. It was dangerous to hold on, death to let go. To ask slavemasters to free their blacks was to invite them to

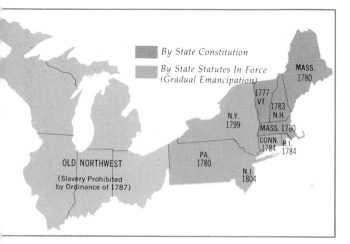

EARLY EMANCIPATION IN THE NORTH

By State Constitution

By State Statutes In Force
(Gradual Emancipation)

MASS. 1780
1777 VT
1783 N.H.
N.Y. 1799
MASS. 1780
CONN. 1784
R.I. 1784
PA. 1780
N.J. 1804
OLD NORTHWEST
(Slavery Prohibited by Ordinance of 1787)

The Slave Quarters. This Civil War—era photograph shows the stark simplicity of black family life in the South. South Carolina Senator Hammond declared in 1858: "In all social systems there must be a class to do the mean duties. . . . It constitutes the very mudsills of society. . . . Fortunately for the South, she found a race adapted to that purpose. . . . We use them for that purpose and call them slaves." (Library of Congress.)

throw away about $2 billion in human livestock and plunge into financial ruin. Even if the planters were paid for their slaves, they still feared that they would go bankrupt because they could not raise cotton profitably without a dependable labor supply. The masters believed that the blacks, unless threatened with the lash, would not toil in the blazing sun. Slaveowners also clung to the convenient fiction that white men could not labor in the fields without ruining their health. Actually, hundreds of thousands of red-necked whites hoed cotton and picked the bursting bolls without suffering ill effects.

It is true that after emancipation the ex-slaves adjusted themselves with much jarring to the wage-incentive system. But the masters doubted that this could be done—and they were unwilling to take the chance. Above all, the issue was not simply an economic one. Slavery was as much a system of racial dominance and subordination as it was a labor system. Even if the freed slaves should prove to be docile and efficient wage laborers, their freedom would weaken the notion of "white supremacy" and complicate the task of "keeping the Negroes in their place."

In theory, the race problem could have been solved—though not the labor problem—by transporting the blacks bodily back to Africa. But most of them did not want to return to a strange civilization after becoming partially Americanized. By 1860 the great majority of Southern slaves were native-born Afro-Americans, not Africans. The Republic of Liberia, on the fever-stricken West African coast, was established for ex-slaves in 1822, with its capital, Monrovia, named after President Monroe. (Ironically, Liberia itself continued to be a flourishing center for slave trade.) After much expense and effort on the part of both Southerners and Northerners, some 15,000 blacks were transplanted during the next thirty-eight years. About that many black babies were born in the South during a single month.

Human Livestock

White Southerners might romanticize about the singing, dancing, and banjo-strumming of their joyful "darkies," but how did the slaves actually live? There is no simple answer to this question. Conditions varied greatly from region to region, from large plantation to small farm, and from master to master. By the eve of the Civil War, more than half the slaves were concentrated in the "black belt" of the Deep South that stretched from South Carolina and Georgia through the new Southwest states of Mississippi, Alabama, and Louisiana. This was the region of the Southern frontier, into which the Cotton Kingdom had burst in a few short decades. As on all frontiers, life was often rough and raw, and in general the lot of the slave was harder here than in the more settled areas of the Old South.

A majority of the blacks lived on larger plantations that harbored communities of twenty or more slaves. In some counties of the Deep South, especially those along the lower Mississippi River, blacks accounted for more than 75 percent of the population. There the family life of the slaves tended to be relatively stable. Forced separations of husbands from wives and children from parents were evidently more common on smaller plantations. Marriage vows sometimes read, "Until death or *distance* do you part."

Slave auctions were brutal sights. The open selling of human flesh under the hammer, sometimes with cattle and horses, was a revolting practice. Families were separated with distressing frequency, usually for economic reasons, such as the division of "property" among heirs. Broken-hearted slaves were poor workers and potential runaways. As one black spiritual lamented:

> Nobody knows de trouble I've had,
> Nobody knows but Jesus.

Breeding slaves, as cattle are bred, was not openly encouraged. But thousands of blacks from the soil-exhausted slave states of the Old South, notably Virginia, were "sold down the river" to toil as field-gang laborers in the lower Mississippi Valley, where the lunch "hour" was often fifteen minutes and work sometimes continued in the moonlight. Women who bore thirteen or fourteen babies were regarded as "rattlin' good breeders," and some of these fecund females were promised their freedom when they had produced ten. All too frequently white males would force their attentions on female blacks, whether their own slaves or not.

Floggings were common, for the whip was the substitute for the wage-incentive system. As an abolitionist song of the 1850s lamented:

> To-night the bond man, Lord,
> Is bleeding in his chains;
> And loud the falling lash is heard
> On Carolina's plains!

A Slave Auction. A family being sold. In an address given in 1865, President Lincoln said: "Whenever I hear anyone arguing for slavery, I feel a strong impulse to see it tried on him personally."

ıoıoıoıoıoıoıoıoıoıoıoıoıoıoıoıoıoıoıoı

> Frederick Douglass, the remarkable ex-slave, told of Mr. Covey, a white owner who bought a single female slave "as a breeder." She gave birth to twins at the end of the year. "At this addition to the human stock Covey and his wife were ecstatic with joy. No one dreamed of reproaching the woman or finding fault with the hired man, Bill Smith, the father of the children, for Mr. Covey himself had locked the two up together every night, thus inviting the result."

ıoıoıoıoıoıoıoıoıoıoıoıoıoıoıoıoıoıoıoı

But savage beatings were normally not administered without some reason or provocation, because whipping made sullen laborers, and lash marks hurt resale values. There are, to be sure, always some sadistic monsters in any population. But for financial as well as humane reasons, the planter did not customarily go out and beat to death a valuable field hand before breakfast.

Slavery was undeniably degrading to the victims. They were deprived of the dignity and sense of responsibility that come from owning a home, caring for oneself, and finding labor of one's choice. They were normally denied an education, partly because reading brought ideas, and ideas brought discontent. Many states passed laws forbidding their instruction. Perhaps nine-tenths of the adult slaves at the beginning of the Civil War were totally illiterate.

Flogging Slaves. An example of anti-slavery propaganda, 1838. (Courtesy, American Antiquarian Society.)

The Burdens of Bondage

Victims of the "peculiar institution" universally pined for freedom. Many took to their heels as runaways. A black girl, asked if her mother was dead, replied, "Yassah, massah, she is daid, but she's free." Others rebelled, never successfully. In 1800 an armed insurrection led by a slave named Gabriel in Richmond, Virginia, was foiled by informers, and its leaders were hanged. Denmark Vesey, a free black, led another ill-fated rebellion in Charleston in 1822. Also betrayed by informers, Vesey and more than thirty followers were publicly strung from the gallows. In 1831 the semi-literate Nat Turner, a visionary black preacher, led an uprising that butchered about sixty white Virginians, mostly women and children. Reprisals were swift and bloody.

The dark taint of slavery also left its mark on the whites. It fostered the brutality of the whip, the bloodhound, and the branding iron. White Southerners increasingly lived in a state of imagined siege, surrounded by potentially rebellious blacks inflamed by abolitionist propaganda from the North. Their fears bolstered an intoxicating theory of biological racial superiority and turned the South into a reactionary backwater in an era of progress. The defenders of slavery were forced to degrade themselves, along with their victims. As Booker T. Washington, a distinguished black leader and ex-slave, later observed, a white man cannot hold a black man in a ditch without getting down there with him.

Reasonable Abolitionism

The inhumanity of the "peculiar institution" gradually caused anti-slavery societies to sprout forth. In the 1820s, in fact, they were far more numerous in the South than in the North, as many white Southerners felt shame and guilt about slavery. But in the 1830s and 1840s Northern crusaders intensified their efforts, partly caught up by the general reform movement sweeping the country. Additional support was given their cause by the unchaining of slaves in the British Empire in the 1830s, including the nearby British West Indies.

A leading abolitionist in these early decades was Theodore Dwight Weld, a passionate soul whose conscience had been deeply aroused by the revivalism of the Second Great Awakening. After studying for the ministry at Lane Theological Seminary in Cincinnati, Weld devoted himself to organizing and preaching against slavery. His potent propaganda pamphlet, *American Slavery As It Is* (1839), was among the most effective abolitionist tracts, and greatly influenced Harriet Beecher Stowe's *Uncle Tom's Cabin* (1852).

Weld was unflinching in his hatred of the "sin" of slavery, but he and his followers were "gradualists." They favored a gradual erasure of the black blot of slavery by action of the Southern legislatures. Serious economic and social maladjustments, they believed, would thus be avoided. Some moderate abolitionists even suggested at least partial financial compensation to the owners.

Garrisonian Militants

The atmosphere of moderation was shattered in 1831, when a new and ominous blast came from the trumpet of William Lloyd Garrison, a mild-looking reformer of twenty-six. As James Russell Lowell put it:

> There's Garrison, his features very
> Benign for an incendiary;
> Beaming forth sunshine through his glasses
> On the surrounding lads and lasses.

The emotionally high-strung son of a drunken father, Garrison published in Boston the first issue of his militant abolitionist newspaper, *The Liberator*. This was perhaps the first paper broadside of a thirty years' verbal war, and in a sense one of the opening guns of the Civil War.

At the outset, Garrison nailed his colors to the masthead of his weekly. He proclaimed in violent tones that he would never compromise with the poisonous growth of slavery, but would stamp it

William Lloyd Garrison (1805–1879). The most conspicuous and most hated of the abolitionists, Garrison was a nonresistant pacifist and a poor organizer. He favored Northern secession from the South, and antagonized both sections with his intemperate language.

out at once, root and branch. "I am in earnest—I will not equivocate—I will not excuse—I will not retreat a single inch—and I WILL BE HEARD!" A close associate of Garrison was Wendell Phillips, a Boston patrician and renowned orator who came to be known as "abolition's golden trumpet." He would eat no cane sugar and wear no cotton cloth: both were produced by Southern slaves.

Many free blacks rallied to Garrison's standard. Their ranks included David Walker, whose incendiary *Appeal to the Colored Citizens of the World* (1829) advocated a bloody end to white supremacy. Also noteworthy was Sojourner Truth, a freed black woman in New York, who reported hearing heavenly voices. Eloquent, though illiterate, she fought tirelessly for black emancipation and woman's rights.

The extreme Garrison wing of the abolition movement did not understand the complex problems of the South—and evidently had no real desire to do so. Few, if any, of the abolitionist leaders had ever been near a Southern plantation. Yet, "angry for the right," they demanded immediate abolition—without compensation. Why compensate the "sinful" slaveowners who, themselves, should compensate their own exploited slaves? As for "gradualism," should a mother, as Garrison proclaimed, "gradually extricate her babe from the fire into which it has fallen?"

The Garrisonians adopted an extreme approach to a dilemma that plagued all the abolitionists. The

Constitution upheld slavery, and the federal government had no legal authority to interfere with the "peculiar institution" in the existing states. Just what *political* means could be taken to topple the slave power?

The moderate abolitionists hoped to prod the conscience of the white South and meanwhile take what piecemeal political steps they could. These might include legislation prohibiting the interstate slave trade, ending slavery in the federal District of Columbia, and banning slavery from new territories brought into the Union.

But the Garrisonians appeared to be more interested in their own righteousness than in the substance of the slavery evil itself. They flayed the "slavocrats" as brothel keepers and criminals. Garrison himself repeatedly demanded that the "virtuous" North secede from the "wicked" South. Yet he did not explain how the creation of an independent slave republic would bring a speedy end to the "damning crime" of slavery. "All Hail Disunion" and "No Union with Slaveholders" became his slogans. As a deep-dyed "non-resistant" pacifist, he publicly burned a copy of the Constitution as "a covenant with death and an agreement with hell." He refused to commit the sin of voting under such a government. Renouncing

politics, Garrison cruelly probed the moral wound in America's underbelly, but offered no acceptable balm to ease the pain.

The error persists that Garrison was the "voice" of the abolitionists. Actually he and his colleagues were only a small minority—the "lunatic fringe"—of the whole abolitionist movement. But his voice was so shrill, and his antics were so spectacular, that he overshadowed and obstructed the efforts of the more sober anti-slave majority. His weekly *Liberator* was never self-supporting, and though widely known, attained a circulation of only 5,000 or so. This figure contrasts with the 28,000 in 1853 for the *National Era*, a weekly newspaper of the moderate abolitionists, and only one of the many anti-slavery papers. Most moderates, who favored the Union and the ballot box, disliked Garrison—the "Massachusetts Madman." Some of them came to hate the Garrisonians even more than they hated slavery itself.

Violence Begets Violence

Abolitionists—especially the extreme Garrisonians—were unpopular in many parts of the North. Northerners had been brought up to revere the Constitution, and to regard the clauses on slavery as a lasting bargain. The ideal of Union, hammered home by the thundering eloquence of Daniel Webster and others, had taken deep root; and Garrison's wild talk of secession grated harshly on Northern ears.

The North also had a heavy economic stake in Dixieland. By the late 1850s the Southern planters owed Northern bankers and other creditors about $300 million and much of this immense sum would be lost—as, in fact, it later was—should the Union dissolve. New England textile mills were fed with cotton raised by the slaves, and a disrupted labor system might cut off this vital supply and bring unemployment. The Union during these critical years was partly bound together with cotton threads, tied by Lords of the Loom in collaboration with the so-called Lords of the Lash. Not surprisingly, strong hostility developed in the

"Am I Not a Woman and a Sister?" A popular appeal. (Garrison's *Liberator.*)

Lovejoy's Press Destroyed

North against the boat-rocking tactics of the radical anti-slaveryites.

Repeated tongue-lashings by the extreme abolitionists ultimately provoked scores of mob outbursts in the North, some of them led by respectable gentlemen. In 1835 Garrison, with a rope tied around him, was dragged through the streets of Boston by the so-called Broadcloth Mob, but escaped almost miraculously. The Reverend Elijah P. Lovejoy, of Alton, Illinois, not content to assail slavery, impugned the chastity of Catholic women. His printing press was destroyed four times, and in 1837 he was killed by a mob, thus becoming "the martyr abolitionist." So unpopular were the anti-slavery zealots that ambitious politicians, like Lincoln, usually avoided the taint of Garrisonian abolition like the plague.

Yet by the 1850s the abolitionist outcry had made a deep dent in the Northern mind. Many citizens had come to see the South as the land of the unfree and the home of a hateful institution. Few Northerners were prepared to abolish slavery outright, but a growing number, including Abraham Lincoln, opposed extending it to the territories in the West. Men of this stamp, commonly called "free-soilers," swelled their ranks as the Civil War approached.

The South Lashes Back

Anti-slavery sentiment was not unknown in the South, but after about 1830 the voice of white Southern abolitionism was silenced. Nat Turner's rebellion sent a wave of hysteria sweeping over the white cotton fields, and planters in increasing numbers slept with pistols by their pillows. Although Garrison had no demonstrable connection with the Turner conspiracy, his *Liberator* appeared at about the same time, and he was bitterly condemned as a terrorist and an inciter of murder. The state of Georgia offered $5,000 for his arrest and conviction.

The Nullification Crisis in 1832 further implanted haunting fears in Southern minds, which conjured up nightmares of black incendiaries and abolitionist devils. Jailings, whippings, and lynchings now greeted rational efforts to discuss the slavery problem in the South.

Pro-slavery whites responded by launching a massive defense of slavery as a positive good. In doing so, they forgot their own section's previous doubts about the morality of the "peculiar institution." Slavery, they claimed, was supported by the authority of the Bible and the wisdom of Aristotle. It was good for the Africans, who were lifted from the barbarism of the jungle and clothed with the blessings of Christian civilization. Slavemasters did indeed encourage religion in the slave quarters. A catechism for blacks contained such passages as:

Q. Who gave you a master and a mistress?
A. God gave them to me.
Q. Who says that you must obey them?
A. God says that I must.

White apologists also pointed out that master-slave relationships really resembled those of a family. On many plantations, especially those in the Old South of Virginia and Maryland, this argument had a certain plausibility. A slave's tombstone bore this touching inscription:

> JOHN:
> A faithful servant
> and true friend:
> Kindly, and considerate:
> Loyal, and affectionate:
> The family he served
> Honours him in death:
> But, in life they gave him love:
> For he was one of them

A Two-Way Pro-Slavery Cartoon. Published in New York, the cartoon shows a chilled and rejected free black in the North (left) disconsolately passing a grogshop, while (*right*) a happy Southern slave enjoys life with a fishing rod in the company of a white youth.

Southern whites were quick to contrast the "happy" lot of their "servants" with that of the overworked Northern wage slaves, including sweated women and stunted children. The blacks mostly toiled in the fresh air and sunlight, not in dark and stuffy factories. They did not have to worry about slack times or unemployment, as did the "hired hands" of the North. Provided with a jail-like form of Social Security, they were cared for in sickness and old age, unlike the Northern workers, who were turned adrift. And they were sometimes, though by no means always, spared dangerous work, like putting a roof on a house. If a neck was going to be broken, the master preferred it to be that of a wage-earning Irishman, rather than that of a field hand worth $1,200.

These curious pro-slavery arguments only widened the chasm between a backward-looking South and a forward-looking North—and indeed much of the rest of the Western world. The Southerners reacted to the pressure of their own fears and the merciless nagging of the Northern abolitionists. Increasingly the white South turned in upon itself and grew hotly intolerant of any embarrassing questions about the status of slavery.

Regrettably, also, the controversy over free men endangered free speech in the entire country. Piles of petitions poured in upon Congress from the anti-slavery reformers; and in 1836 sensitive Southerners drove through the House the so-called gag resolution. It required all such anti-slavery appeals to be tabled without debate. This attack on the right of petition aroused the sleeping lion in an aged ex-President, Representative John Quincy Adams, and he waged a successful eight-year fight for its repeal.

Southern whites likewise resented the flooding of their mails with incendiary abolitionist literature. Even if the blacks could not read, they could interpret the inflammatory drawings, such as those that showed masters knocking the teeth out of their slaves with clubs. In 1835 a mob in Charleston, South Carolina, looted the local post office and burned a pile of abolitionist propaganda. The authorities in Washington were unable to force the local postmasters to deliver such mail. Such was "freedom of the press" as guaranteed by the Constitution.

The Fruits of Extremism

The South no doubt took extremists like the Garrisonians much too seriously, and made the mistake of regarding them as the mouthpiece of the entire North. Southerners would have been well advised to hit the abolitionists with "a chunk of silence." But this was asking too much of human nature. The more violently the winds of abolitionism blew down from the North, the more tightly the South wrapped the black cloak of slavery about itself, and the more savagely it struck back at its tormentors. After thirty years of abolitionist agitation, the "peculiar institution" was more firmly rooted than ever before.

All this uproar produced a bitter harvest. For over a generation, it partially eclipsed other worthy reforms, including woman's rights. It blasted hope for gradual emancipation in the northernmost slave states, where the movement had been making encouraging progress. It contributed to a splitting of parties and churches into sectional groupings. It resulted in jeopardy to fundamental American rights, of both North and South, including the right to petition, freedom of speech, freedom of the press, freedom of inquiry, freedom of travel, and freedom of teaching—almost everything "free." These priceless freedoms were most severely restricted in the South, but occasionally there were disagreeable incidents in the North, as, for example, when a professor at Harvard College was dismissed for his anti-slavery views. Finally, mobbings and lynchings shook the foundations of law and order, while making more abolitionists by making more martyrs.

Radical abolitionists also helped destroy mutual respect between the sections—the goodwill that was the cement of union. Delicate social problems cannot be solved by name-calling, and the Garrisonians injected emotion into a situation that called for light—not heat. Shouting led inexorably to shooting.

The South, angered by the holier-than-thou abuse of the extreme abolitionists, responded in kind. Fiery South Carolina orators like Senator Rhett and Congressman Keitt could fully hold their own. This exchange of epithets, in an ever-widening circle, elicited even more violent epithets. Men spoke the same language, but no longer understood one another. Bonfires of hatred were lighted that in the end were only partially extin-

Abraham Lincoln, in a speech at Springfield, Illinois (July 16, 1852), expressed little sympathy for the more fanatical abolitionists: "Those who would shiver into fragments the Union of these states, tear to tatters its now venerated Constitution, and even burn the last copy of the Bible, rather than slavery continue a single hour, together with all their more halting sympathizers, have received, and are receiving their just execration."

guished by buckets of blood. When secession finally came, many Southerners felt a sense of relief in getting away from "abolitionist nagging."

Was Bloodshed Necessary?

The heat generated by the extremists on both sides helped destroy all hope of compromise. The South finally worked itself into a state of mind that would not accept compensated emancipation, and the North into a state of mind that would not offer it.

"Like Meets Like."   Garrison (*right*) is here pilloried as a foe of the Union no less dangerous than the South Carolina secessionist Keitt. (*Vanity Fair*, 1861.)

If the South had been approached more diplomatically, it might ultimately have accepted such a reasonable arrangement. Yet even this assumption is questionable because of the issue of presumed racial superiority.

Abolitionists, so their defenders say, helped prick the moral conscience of the North, at a time when there was widespread apathy and callousness. When someone assured the Massachusetts clergyman Theodore Parker that God in his own good time would end slavery, Parker shot back, "The trouble is God isn't in any hurry and I am." The abolitionists were generally men and women of goodwill and various colors who faced the cruel choice that people in many ages have had thrust upon them. When is evil so enormous that it must be denounced, even at the cost of bloodshed and butchery?

Abolitionist extremists no doubt hastened the freeing of the slave by a number of years. But emancipation came at the price of a civil conflict that tore apart the social and economic fabric of the South. About a million whites were to be killed or disabled before some 4 million slaves could be freed, under conditions that took the lives of tens of thousands of black soldiers and ex-slaves. The war itself cost some $20 billion, including interest and long-term pensions—for Union veterans only. Compensated emancipation at full value—about $2 billion—would have been far cheaper in dollars and cents.

The bewildered blacks were caught in the middle. Sudden, overnight liberation, though a giant step in the right direction, was in many ways a disillusionment. And freedom by no means solved the race problem or brought complete liberty.

Emotionalism on both sides thus slammed the door on any fair adjustment. Statesmen like Daniel Webster and Abraham Lincoln came to believe, not unreasonably, that the extreme abolitionists were doing more harm than good. All other Western nations, including Brazil, ultimately rid themselves of the tumor of slavery without the surgery of the sword, although admittedly their problems were different. Solution by civil war, even though it called forth much self-sacrifice and devotion to ideals, tragically scarred the body and soul of America. Its effects are visible even today.

VARYING VIEWPOINTS

Ulrich B. Phillips made two key points in his memorable study, *American Negro Slavery* (1918). One was that slavery was a relatively benign social system; the other was that slavery was a dying economic institution, unprofitable to the slaveowner and an obstacle to the economic development of the South as a whole. From these conclusions there followed two disturbing implications. First, the abolitionists had fundamentally misconstrued the nature of the "peculiar institution." Second, the Civil War was probably unnecessary, because slavery might eventually have expired from "natural" economic causes.

For more than half a century, historians have debated these issues, sometimes heatedly. Despite increasing sophistication of economic analysis, there is still no consensus on the degree of slavery's profitability. With regard to the social character of the system, a large number of modern scholars refuse to concede that slavery was a benign institution. On the other hand, much evidence confirms the health and vitality of black culture in slavery—the strength of family ties, religious institutions, and cultural forms of all kinds.

The reputation of the abolitionists, both moderate and extreme, has greatly improved, reflecting the changed pro-black atmosphere generated by the civil rights struggles of the 1960s and 1970s. Once vilified as irresponsible provokers of a needless war, they are now commonly hailed as champions of human rights.

SELECT READINGS

A good introduction to Southern history is Clement Eaton, *A History of the Old South: The Emergence of a Reluctant Nation* (1975). W. J. Cash, *The Mind of the South* (1941), is an engagingly written classic. Always incisive is C. Vann Woodward, *The Burden of Southern History* (1960) and *American Counterpoint* (1971). F. Owsley, *Plain Folk of the Old South* (1949), illuminates the lives of non-slaveholding whites. Eugene Genovese analyzes *The Political Economy of Slavery* (1965) and *The World the Slaveholders Made* (1970). J. H. Franklin, *The Militant South* (1956), stresses the tradition of violence. H. D. Woodman reviews an important controversy in *Slavery and the Southern Economy* (1966), which should be supplemented by Gavin Wright, *The Political Economy of the Cotton South* (1978). The literature on slavery and Afro-Americans is enormous; the best place to start is J. H. Franklin, *From Slavery to Freedom* (1974), and consult also Nathan Irving Huggins' sometimes lyrical *Black Odyssey* (1977). The modern debate on slavery began with Ulrich B. Phillips' classic *American Negro Slavery* (1918); a darker view of the same subject is found in K. M. Stampp, *The Peculiar Institution* (1956). Consult also Stanley Elkins' stimulating essay, *Slavery* (2nd ed., 1968). More recently, considerable furor has surrounded the publication of R. Fogel and S. Engerman, *Time on the Cross: The Economics of American Slavery* (2 vols., 1974). For contrasting views and rebuttals, see J. W. Blassingame, *The Slave Community* (rev. ed., 1979), H. Gutman, *Slavery and the Numbers Game* (1975), the same author's *The Black Family in Slavery and Freedom, 1750–1925* (1976), Paul David, *Reckoning with Slavery* (1976), E. Genovese, *Roll, Jordan, Roll* (1974), and Carl N. Degler's comparison of slavery and race relations in Brazil and the United States, *Neither Black nor White* (1971). Albert J. Raboteau describes *Slave Religion* (1978), and Lawrence W. Levine imaginatively recreates Afro-American folk-life in *Black Culture and Black Consciousness* (1977). R. Starobin examines *Industrial Slavery in the Old South* (1970), and Ira Berlin tells the story of free blacks in *Slaves without Masters* (1975). See also L. Litwack, *North of Slavery* (1961), for the situation of blacks outside the South. D. B. Davis provides indispensable background to the history of abolitionism in *The Problem of Slavery in Western Culture* (1966) and *The Problem of Slavery in the Age of Revolution* (1975). The best brief history of the abolitionists is James B. Stewart, *Holy Warriors* (1976). Lively and pro-abolitionist are G. H. Barnes, *The Anti-Slavery Impulse* (1933), and Louis Filler, *The Crusade against Slavery* (1960). Markedly unsympathetic to the white South is D. L. Dumond, *Antislavery* (1961). J. L. Thomas is critical of William Lloyd Garrison in *The Liberator* (1963), while Aileen Kraditor is much more favorably disposed in *Means and Ends in American Abolitionism: Garrison and His Critics* (1967). Consult also Lewis Perry, *Radical Abolitionists* (1973). Stanley Elkins' *Slavery* has interesting observations on abolitionist intellectuals. Benjamin Quarles examines *Black Abolitionists* (1969), as do J. H. and W. H. Pease in *They Who Would Be Free: Blacks Search for Freedom, 1830–1861* (1974). Arna Bontemps presents the life of Frederick Douglass, the most prominent black abolitionist, in *Free at Last* (1971). White attitudes can be studied in Winthrop Jordan's masterful *White over Black* (1968) and George Frederickson's incisive *The Black Image in the White Mind* (1971), as well as in Leonard Richard's illuminating *"Gentlemen of Property and Standing": Anti-Abolitionist Mobs in Jacksonian America* (1970). R. B. Nye looks at the effects of the slavery controversy on civil liberties in *Fettered Freedom* (1963). Carl Degler portrays the dilemma of some Southern abolitionists in *The Other South* (1974). William J. Cooper, Jr., probes his subject with keen intelligence in *The South and the Politics of Slavery, 1828–1856* (1978). J. Mills Thornton III, *Politics and Power in a Slave Society: Alabama, 1800–1860* (1981), is an intriguing, inventive study with implications that reach well beyond Alabama. The semi-mythical Underground Railway is treated in W. Breyfogle, *Make Free* (1958), Larry Gara, *The Liberty Line* (1961), and Henrietta Buckmaster, *Let My People Go* (1959). Willie Lee Rose offers her customarily sensitive insights on several aspects of the subject in *Slavery and Freedom* (1982).

20

Renewing the Sectional Struggle, 1848-1854

*Secession! Peaceable secession! Sir, your eyes
and mine are never destined to see that miracle.*

DANIEL WEBSTER, Seventh of March speech, 1850

The Popular Sovereignty Panacea

The year 1848, highlighted by a rash of revolutions
in Europe, was filled with unrest in America. Land
recently wrested from Mexico proved to be a bone
of contention, for it raised anew the issue of extending slavery into the territories. The danger was
ever present that the explosive question might
disrupt the ranks of both Whigs and Democrats.

Each of the two great political parties was a vital
bond of national unity, for each enjoyed powerful
support in both North and South. If they should be
replaced by two purely sectional groupings, the
Union would be in peril. To politicians, the wisest
strategy seemed to be to sit on the lid of the slavery
issue and ignore the boiling beneath. Even so, the
cover bobbed up and down ominously in response
to the agitation of zealous Northern abolitionists
and hotheaded Southern "fire-eaters."

Anxious Democrats were forced to seek a new

standard-bearer in 1848. President Polk, broken in health by overwork and chronic diarrhea, had pledged himself to a single term. The Democratic national convention at Baltimore turned to an aging leader, General Lewis Cass, a veteran of the War of 1812. Though a senator and diplomat of wide experience and considerable ability, he was sour-visaged and somewhat pompous. His enemies dubbed him General "Gass," and quickly noted that Cass rhymed with jackass. The Democratic platform, in line with the lid-sitting strategy, was silent on the burning issue of slavery in the territories.

But Cass himself had not been silent. His views on the extension of slavery were well known, because he was the reputed father of "popular sovereignty." This was the doctrine that the sovereign people of a territory, under the general principles of the Constitution, should themselves determine the status of slavery.

Popular sovereignty had a persuasive appeal. The public liked it because it accorded with the democratic tradition of self-determination. Politicians liked it because it seemed a comfortable compromise between a ban on slavery in the territories and Southern demands that Congress protect slavery in the territories. Popular sovereignty tossed the slavery problem into the laps of the people in the various territories. Advocates of the doctrine thus hoped to dissolve the most stubborn national issue of the day into a series of local issues. Yet popular sovereignty had one fatal defect: it might serve to spread the blight of slavery.

Political Triumphs for General Taylor

The Whigs, meeting in Philadelphia, cashed in on the "Taylor fever." They nominated frank and honest Zachary Taylor, the "Hero of Buena Vista," who had never held civil office or even voted for President. Henry Clay, the living embodiment of Whiggism, should logically have been nominated. But he had made too many speeches—and too many enemies.

As usual, the Whigs pussyfooted in their platform. Eager to win at any cost, they dodged all troublesome issues and merely extolled the home-spun virtues of their candidate. The self-reliant old frontier fighter, actually a babe in the woods politically, had not committed himself on the issue of slavery extension. But as a wealthy resident of Louisiana, living on a sugar plantation, he owned scores of slaves.

Ardent anti-slavery men in the North, distrusting both Cass and Taylor, organized the Free-Soil party. Aroused by the conspiracy of silence in the Democratic and Whig platforms, they made no bones about their own stand. They came out four-square for the Wilmot Proviso and against slavery in the territories. Going beyond other anti-slavery groups, they broadened their appeal by advocating federal aid for internal improvements and by urging free government homesteads for settlers.

General Zachary Taylor. This Democratic campaign cartoon of 1848 charges that Taylor's reputation rested on Mexican skulls. (Courtesy of The New-York Historical Society, New York City.)

The new party trotted out wizened ex-President Van Buren, and marched into the fray shouting, "Free soil, free speech, free labor, and free men."

With the slavery issue officially shoved under the rug by the two major parties, the politicians on both sides opened fire on personalities. The amateurish Taylor had to be carefully watched, lest his indiscreet pen puncture the reputation won by his sword. His admirers puffed him up as a gallant knight and a Napoleon, and sloganized his remark, allegedly uttered during the Battle of Buena Vista, "General Taylor never surrenders."

Taylor's wartime popularity pulled him through. He harvested 1,360,099 popular and 163 electoral votes, as compared with Cass's 1,220,544 popular and 127 electoral votes. Free-Soiler Van Buren, although winning no state, polled 291,263 ballots, and apparently diverted enough Democratic strength from Cass in the crucial state of New York to throw the election to Taylor.

"Californy Gold"

Tobacco-chewing President Taylor—with his stumpy legs, rough features, heavy jaw, black hair, ruddy complexion, and squinty gray eyes—was a military square peg in a political round hole. He would have been spared much turmoil if he could have continued to sit on the slavery lid. But the discovery of gold in California, early in 1848, blew the cover off.

A horde of adventurers poured into the valleys of California. Singing "O Susannah!" and shouting "Gold! Gold! Gold!" they began tearing frantically at the yellow-graveled streams and hills. A fortunate few of the bearded miners "struck it rich" at the "diggings." But the luckless many, who netted blisters instead of nuggets, probably would have been money well ahead if they had stayed at home unaffected by the "gold fever," which was often followed by more deadly fevers. The most reliable profits were made by those who mined the miners, notably by charging outrageous rates for laundry and other personal services. Some soiled clothing was even sent as far away as the Hawaiian Islands for washing.

The overnight inpouring of tens of thousands of people into the future Golden State completely overwhelmed the one-horse government of California. A distressingly high proportion of the newcomers were lawless men, accompanied or followed by virtueless women. A contemporary song ran:

> Oh what was your name in the States?
> Was it Thompson or Johnson or Bates?
> Did you murder your wife,
> And fly for your life?
> Say, what was your name in the States?

An outburst of crime inevitably resulted from the presence of so many outcasts. Robbery, claim

The Washing-Bowl. One method of panning for gold. (*Harper's New Monthly Magazine.*)

The idea that many ne'er-do-wells went west is found in Ralph Waldo Emerson's *Journals* (January 1849): "If a man is going to California, he announces it with some hesitation; because it is a confession that he has failed at home."

jumping, and murder were commonplace; and such violence was only partly discouraged by rough vigilante justice. In San Francisco, from 1848 to 1856, there were scores of lawless killings but only three semilegal hangings.

A majority of the Californians, as decent and law-abiding citizens needing protection, grappled earnestly with the problem of erecting an adequate state government. Privately encouraged by President Taylor, they drafted a constitution in 1849 which excluded slavery, and then boldly applied to Congress for admission. California would thus bypass the usual territorial stage, thwarting Southern congressmen seeking to block free soil. Southern politicians, alarmed by this "impertinent" stroke for freedom, arose in violent opposition. Would California prove to be the golden straw that broke the back of the Union?

Sectional Balance and the Underground Railroad

The South of 1850 was relatively well off. It then enjoyed, as it had from the beginning, more than its share of the nation's leadership. It had seated in the White House the war hero Zachary Taylor, a Virginia-born, slave-owning planter from Louisiana. It had a majority in the Cabinet and on the Supreme Bench. If outnumbered in the House, the South had equality in the Senate, where it could hope to exercise a veto voice. Its cotton fields were expanding, and the price of the snowy fiber was profitably high. Few sane people, North or South, believed that slavery was seriously threatened where it already existed below the Mason-Dixon line.* The fifteen slave states could easily veto any proposed constitutional amendment.

Yet the South was deeply worried, as it had been for several decades, by the ever-tipping political balance. There were then fifteen slave states and fifteen free states. The admission of California would destroy the delicate equilib-

---
*Originally the southern boundary of colonial Pennsylvania.

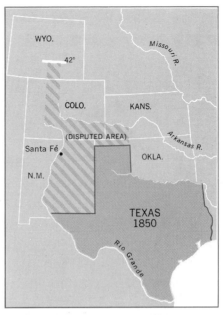

TEXAS AND THE COMPROMISE OF 1850

rium in the Senate, perhaps forever. Potential slave territory under the American flag was running short, if it had not already disappeared. Agitation had already developed in the territories of New Mexico and Utah for admission as non-slave states. The fate of California might well establish a precedent for the rest of the Mexican Cession territory—an area purchased largely with Southern blood.

Texas nursed an additional grievance of her own. She claimed a huge area east of the Rio Grande and north to the 42nd parallel, embracing in part about half the territory of present New Mexico. The federal government was proposing to detach this prize, while hot-blooded Texans were threatening to descend upon Santa Fe and seize what they regarded as rightfully theirs. The explosive quarrel foreshadowed shooting.

Many Southerners were also angered by the nagging agitation in the North for the abolition of slavery in the District of Columbia. They looked with alarm on the prospect of a ten-mile-square

Resurrection of Henry Box Brown. Brown, a slave, was shipped to Philadelphia abolitionists from Virginia in a box. (Library of Congress.)

oasis of free soil, thrust between slaveholding Maryland and slaveholding Virginia.

Even more disagreeable to the South was the loss of runaway slaves, many of whom were assisted north by the Underground Railroad. It consisted of an informal chain of "stations" (antislavery homes), through which scores of "passengers" (runaway slaves) were spirited by "conductors" (usually white and black abolitionists) from the slave states to the free-soil sanctuary of Canada.

The most amazing of these "conductors" was an illiterate runaway slave from Maryland, fearless Harriet Tubman. During nineteen forays into the South, she rescued more than 300 slaves, including her aged parents, and deservedly earned the title "Moses." Lively imaginations later exaggerated the role of the Underground Railroad and its "station masters," but its existence was a fact. Another significant fact is that the most difficult part of the escape was to get to the Ohio River, for up to that point runaway slaves were generally on their own.

By 1850 Southerners were demanding a new and more stringent fugitive slave law. The old one, passed by Congress in 1793, had proved inade-

quate to cope with runaways, especially since unfriendly state authorities failed to provide needed cooperation. Unlike cattle thieves, the abolitionists who ran the Underground Railroad did not gain personally from their lawlessness. But to the slaveowners the loss was infuriating, whatever the motives. The moral judgments of the abolitionists seemed, in some ways, more galling than outright

Harriet Tubman, Premier Assistant of Runaway Slaves. John Brown called her "General Tubman" for her effective work in helping slaves escape to Canada. During the Civil War she served as a Union spy behind Confederate lines. Herself illiterate, she worked after the war to bring education to the freed slaves in North Carolina. (The New York Public Library, Astor, Lenox, and Tilden Foundations.) (Library of Congress)

theft. They reflected not only a holier-than-thou attitude but a refusal to obey the laws solemnly passed by Congress.

Estimates indicate that the South in 1850 was losing perhaps 1,000 runaways a year, out of its total of some 4 million slaves. In fact, the owners probably freed more blacks voluntarily than ever escaped. But the principle weighed heavily with the slavemasters. They rested their argument on the Constitution, which protected slavery, and on the laws of Congress, which provided for slavecatching.

Twilight of the Senatorial Giants

Southern fears were such that Congress was confronted with catastrophe in 1850. Free-soil California was banging on the door for admission, and "fire-eaters" in the South were voicing ominous threats of secession. The crisis brought into the congressional forum the most distinguished assemblage of statesmen since the Constitutional Convention of 1787—the Old Guard of the dying generation and the young gladiators of the new. That "immortal trio"—Clay, Calhoun, and Webster—appeared together for the last time on the public stage.

Henry Clay, now seventy-three years of age, played a crucial role. The "Great Pacificator" had come to the Senate from Kentucky to engineer his third great compromise. The once-glamorous statesman—though disillusioned, enfeebled, and racked by a cruel cough—was still eloquent, conciliatory, captivating. He proposed and skillfully defended a series of compromises. He was ably seconded by thirty-seven-year-old Senator Stephen A. Douglas of Illinois, the "Little Giant" (5 feet 4 inches; 1.62 meters), whose role was less spectacular but even more important. Clay urged with all his persuasiveness that the North and South both make concessions, and that the North partially yield by enacting a more effective fugitive slave law.

Senator John C. Calhoun, then sixty-eight and dying of tuberculosis, championed the South in his last formal speech. Too weak to deliver it himself, he sat bundled up in the Senate chamber, his eyes glowing within a stern face, while a younger colleague read his fateful words. Although approving the purpose of Clay's proposed concessions, Calhoun rejected them as not providing adequate safeguards. His impassioned plea was to leave slavery alone, return runaway slaves, give the South its rights as a minority, and restore the political balance. He had in view, as was later revealed, an utterly unworkable scheme of electing two Presidents, one from the North and one from the South, each wielding a veto.

Calhoun died in 1850, before the debate was over, uttering the sad words, "The South! The South! God knows what will become of her!" Appreciative fellow citizens in Charleston erected to his memory an imposing monument, which bore the inscription "Truth, Justice, and the Constitution." Calhoun had labored to preserve the Union, and had taken his stand on the Constitution, but his proposals in their behalf almost undid both.

Daniel Webster next took the Senate spotlight to uphold Clay's compromise measures in his last great speech, a three-hour effort. Now sixty-eight years old, and suffering from a liver complaint aggravated by high living, he had lost some of the fire in his magnificent voice. Speaking deliberately and before overflowing galleries, he urged all reasonable concessions to the South, including a new fugitive slave law with teeth.

As for slavery in the territories, asked Webster, why legislate on the subject? To do so was an act of sacrilege, for Almighty God had already passed the Wilmot Proviso. The good Lord had decreed—through climate, topography, and geography—that a plantation economy, and hence a slave economy, could not profitably exist in the Mexican Cession territory.* Webster sanely concluded that compromise, concession, and sweet reasonableness would provide the only solutions. "Let

---

*Webster was wrong here; within 100 years California had become one of the great cotton-producing states of the Union.

us not be pygmies," he pleaded, "in a case that calls for men."

Webster's famed Seventh of March speech, 1850, was his finest, if measured by its immediate effects. It helped turn the tide in the North toward compromise. The clamor for printed copies became so great that Webster mailed out more than 100,000, remarking that 200,000 would not satisfy the demand. His tremendous effort visibly strengthened Union sentiment. It was especially pleasing to the banking and commercial centers of the North, which stood to lose millions of dollars by secession. One prominent Washington banker canceled two notes of Webster's, totaling $5,000, and sent him a personal check for $1,000 and a message of congratulations.

But the abolitionists, who had regarded Webster as one of themselves, upbraided him as a traitor, worthy of bracketing with Benedict Arnold. The poet Whittier lamented:

> So fallen! so lost! the light withdrawn
>   Which once he wore!
> The glory from his gray hairs gone
>   For evermore!

These reproaches were most unfair. Webster, who had long regarded slavery as evil but disunion as worse, despised the abolitionists and never joined their ranks.

Ralph Waldo Emerson, the philosopher and moderate abolitionist, was outraged by Webster's support of concessions to the South in the Fugitive Slave Act. In February 1851 he wrote in his *Journal:* "I opened a paper to-day in which he [Webster] pounds on the old strings [of liberty] in a letter to the Washington Birthday feasters at New York. 'Liberty! liberty!' Pho! Let Mr. Webster, for decency's sake, shut his lips once and forever on this word. The word *liberty* in the mouth of Mr. Webster sounds like the word *love* in the mouth of a courtesan."

Deadlock and Danger on Capitol Hill

The stormy congressional debate of 1850 was not finished, for the Young Guard from the North were yet to have their say. This was the group of newer statesmen who, unlike the aging Old Guard, had not grown up with the Union. They were more interested in purging and purifying it than in patching and preserving it.

William H. Seward, the wiry and husky-throated freshman senator from New York, was the able spokesman for many of the younger Northern radicals. A strong anti-slaveryite, he came out flat-footedly against concession. He seemed not to realize that compromise had brought the Union together, and that when the sections could no longer compromise, they would have to part company.

Seward argued earnestly that Christian legisla-

A Seward Caricature. He later became Lincoln's foremost rival for the presidency, and still later his secretary of state.

Compromise of 1850

Concessions to the North	*Concessions to the South*
California admitted as a free state	The remainder of the Mexican Cession area to be formed into the territories of New Mexico and Utah, without restriction on slavery, hence open to popular sovereignty
Territory disputed by Texas and New Mexico to be surrendered to New Mexico	Texas to receive $10 million from the federal government as compensation
Abolition of the slave trade (but not slavery) in the District of Columbia	A more stringent Fugitive Slave Law, going beyond that of 1793

tors must obey God's moral law as well as man's mundane law. He therefore appealed, with reference to excluding slavery in the territories, to an even "higher law" than the Constitution. This alarming phrase, wrenched from its context, may have cost him the presidential nomination and the presidency in 1860.

As the great debate in Congress ran its heated course, deadlock seemed certain. Blunt old President Taylor, who had allegedly fallen under the influence of men like "Higher Law" Seward, seemed bent on vetoing any compromise passed by Congress. His military ire was aroused by the threats of Texas to seize Santa Fe. He appeared to be doggedly determined to "Jacksonize" the dissenters, if need be, by leading an army against the Texans in person and hanging all "damned traitors." If troops had begun to march, the South probably would have rallied to the defense of her sister state, and the Civil War might have erupted in 1850.

Breaking the Congressional Logjam

At the height of the controversy in 1850, President Taylor unknowingly helped the cause of concession by dying suddenly, probably of an acute intestinal disorder. Portly, round-faced Vice-President Millard Fillmore, a colorless and conciliatory New York lawyer-politician, took over the reins. As presiding officer of the Senate, he had been impressed with the arguments for conciliation,

and he gladly signed the series of compromise measures that passed Congress after seven long months of stormy debate. The balancing of interests in the Compromise of 1850 was delicate in the extreme.

The struggle to get these measures accepted by the country was hardly less heated than in Congress. In the Northern states, "Union savers" like Senators Clay, Webster, and Douglas orated on behalf of the compromise. The ailing Clay himself delivered more than seventy speeches, as a powerful sentiment for acceptance gradually crystallized in the North. It was strengthened by a growing spirit of goodwill, which sprang partly from a feeling of relief, and partly from an upsurge of prosperity enriched by California gold.

But the "fire-eaters" of the South were still violently opposed to concessions. One extreme South Carolina newspaper avowed that it loathed the Union and hated the North as much as it did Hell itself. A movement in the South to boycott Northern goods gained some headway, but in the end the Southern Unionists, assisted by the warm glow of prosperity, prevailed.

In mid-1850, an assemblage of Southern extremists had met in Nashville, Tennessee, ironically near the burial place of Andrew Jackson. The delegates not only took a strong position in favor of slavery, but condemned the compromise measures then being hammered out in Congress. Meeting again later in the year after the bills had passed, the convention proved to be a dud. By that

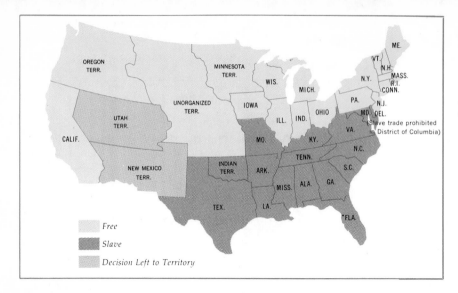

SLAVERY AFTER THE
COMPROMISE OF 1850

Map legend:
Free
Slave
Decision Left to Territory

time Southern opinion had reluctantly accepted the verdict of Congress.

Like the calm after a storm, a second Era of Good Feelings dawned. Disquieting talk of secession subsided. Reasonable men, both North and South, were determined that the compromises should be a "finality," and that the explosive issue of slavery should be buried. But this reign of reason proved all too brief.

Balancing the Compromise Scales

Who got the better of the Compromise of 1850?

The answer is clearly the North. California, as a free state, tipped the Senate balance permanently against the South. The territories of New Mexico and Utah were open to slavery on the basis of popular sovereignty. But the iron law of nature—the "highest law" of all—had loaded the dice in favor of free soil. The Southerners urgently needed more slave territory to restore the "sacred balance." If they could not carve new states out of the recent conquests from Mexico, where else would they get them?

Even the apparent gains of the South rang hollow. Disgruntled Texas was to be paid $10 million toward discharging her indebtedness, but in the long run this was a modest sum. The immense area in dispute had been torn from the side of slaveholding Texas, and was almost certain to be free. The South had halted the drive toward abolition in the District of Columbia, at least temporarily, by permitting the outlawing of the slave traffic. But even this move was an entering wedge toward complete emancipation in the nation's capital.

Most alarming of all, the drastic new Fugitive Slave Law—"the Bloodhound Bill"—stirred up a storm of opposition in the North. The fleeing slave could not testify in his own behalf, and he was denied a jury trial. These harsh practices threatened to create dangerous precedents for the whites. The federal commissioner who handled

Regarding the Fugitive Slave Act of 1850, Ralph Waldo Emerson, the abolitionist, declared (May 1851) at Concord, Massachusetts: "The act of Congress . . . is a law which every one of you will break on the earliest occasion— a law which no man can obey, or abet the obeying, without loss of self-respect and forfeiture of the name of gentleman." Privately he wrote in his *Journal:* "This filthy enactment was made in the nineteenth century, by people who could read and write. I will not obey it, by God" (July 1851).

the case would receive five dollars if the runaway was freed, and ten dollars if not—an arrangement that strongly resembled a bribe. Freedom-loving Northerners who aided the slave to escape were liable to heavy fines and jail sentences. They might even be ordered to join the slavecatchers, and this possibility rubbed salt into old sores.

So savage was this "Man-Stealing Law" that it touched off an explosive chain reaction in the North. Many shocked moderates, hitherto passive, were driven into the swelling ranks of the abolitionists. Cried John Pierpont:

> Lashed with her hounds, must we
> Run down the poor who flee
> From Slavery's hell?

The Underground Railroad stepped up its timetable, while infuriated Northern mobs rescued slaves from their pursuers. Massachusetts, in a move toward nullification suggestive of South Carolina in 1832, made it a penal offense for any state official to enforce the new federal statute. Other states passed "personal liberty laws," which denied local jails to federal officials and otherwise hampered enforcement. The abolitionists rent the heavens with their protests against the man-stealing statute. A meeting presided over by Garrison in 1851 declared, "We execrate it, we spit upon it, we trample it under our feet."

Beyond question, the Fugitive Slave Law was an appalling blunder on the part of the South. No single irritant of the 1850s was more persistently galling to both sides, and none did more to awaken in the North a spirit of antagonism against the South. The Southerners in turn were embittered because the Northerners would not in good faith execute the law—the one real and immediate "gain" from the Great Compromise. Slavecatchers, with some success, redoubled their efforts.

Should the shooting showdown have come in 1850? From the standpoint of the secessionists, yes; from the standpoint of the Unionists, no. Time was fighting for the North. With every passing decade this huge section was forging farther ahead in population and wealth—in crops, factories, foundries, ships, and railroads.

Delay also added immensely to the moral strength of the North— to its will to fight for the Union. In 1850 countless thousands of Northern moderates were unwilling to pin the South to the rest of the nation with bayonets. But the inflammatory events of the 1850s did much to bolster the Yankee will to resist secession, whatever the cost. This one feverish decade gave the North time to accumulate the physical and moral strength that provided the margin of victory. Thus the Compromise of 1850, from one point of view, won the Civil War for the Union.

Defeat and Doom for the Whigs

Meeting in Baltimore, the Democratic nominating convention of 1852 startled the nation. Hopelessly deadlocked, it finally stampeded to the second "dark horse" candidate in American history, an unrenowned lawyer-politician, Franklin Pierce, from the hills of New Hampshire. The Whigs tried to jeer him back into obscurity with the cry, "Who is Frank Pierce?" Democrats replied, "The Young Hickory of the Granite Hills."

Pierce, though handsome, was a weak and indecisive figure. Youngish, militarily erect, smiling, and convivial, he had served without real distinction in the Mexican War. As a result of a painful

Runaway Slaves Rout Slave Catchers.   Christiana, Pa., 1851.

President Franklin Pierce (1804–1869). Pierce was never a strong President. On the eve of his inauguration, he and his wife saw their one surviving son being mangled to death in a railroad wreck. In the White House the distraught First Lady wore only black and spent much time writing letters to one of her three dead sons.

groin injury that caused him to fall off a horse, he was known as the "Fainting General," though scandalmongers pointed to a fondness for alcohol. But he was enemyless because he had been inconspicuous, and as a pro-Southern Northerner he was acceptable to the slavery wing of the Democratic party. His platform came out emphatically for the finality of the Compromise of 1850, Fugitive Slave Law and all.

The Whigs, also convening in Baltimore, missed a splendid opportunity to capitalize on their record in statecraft. Able to boast of a praiseworthy achievement in the Compromise of 1850, they might logically have nominated President Fillmore or Senator Webster, both of whom were associated with it. But having won in the past only with military heroes, they turned to another, "Old Fuss and Feathers" Winfield Scott, perhaps the ablest American general of his generation. Although he was a huge and impressive figure, his manner bordered on haughtiness. His personality not only repelled the masses but eclipsed his genuinely

statesmanlike achievements. The Whig platform praised the Compromise of 1850 as a lasting arrangement, though less enthusiastically than the Democrats.

With slavery and sectionalism to some extent soft-pedaled, the campaign again degenerated into a dull and childish attack on personalities. Democrats ridiculed Scott's pomposity; Whigs charged that Pierce was the hero of "many a well-fought *bottle.*" Democrats cried exultantly, "We Polked 'em in '44; we'll Pierce 'em in '52."

Luckily for the Democrats, the Whig party was hopelessly split. Anti-slavery Whigs of the North swallowed Scott as their standard-bearer but deplored his platform, which endorsed the hated Fugitive Slave Law. The current phrase ran, "We accept the candidate but spit on the platform." Southern Whigs, who doubted Scott's loyalty to the Compromise of 1850 and especially to the Fugitive Slave Law, accepted the platform but spat on the candidate. More than 5,000 Georgia Whigs—"finality men"—futilely voted for Webster, although he had died nearly two weeks before the election.

General Scott, victorious on the battlefield, met defeat at the ballot box. His friends remarked whimsically that he was not used to "running." Actually, he was stabbed in the back by his fellow Whigs, notably in the South. The pliant Pierce won in a landslide, 254 electoral votes to 42, though the

In assailing the candidacy of "Fuss and Feathers" Scott, James Buchanan, himself elected President some four years later, declared that to elevate generals would cause "aspiring officers" to favor "foreign wars, as the best means of acquiring military glory. . . . Napoleon was endeared to his army by his designation of 'the little Corporal'; General Jackson, by that of 'Old Hickory'; and General Taylor was 'Rough and Ready'; but what shall we say to 'Fuss and Feathers'?"

GULF OF MEXICO

MEXICO

BELIZE
(BRITISH
HONDURAS)

GUATEMALA

HONDURAS

(British agents and traders
influence natives)

SALVADOR

NICARAGUA

CUBA
(Spanish)

JAMAICA
(British)

CARIBBEAN SEA

(Proposed canal route,
then a land-and-water route)

Greytown

(Future
Panama
Canal)

PACIFIC OCEAN

COSTA RICA

COLOMBIA
(NEW GRANADA)

CENTRAL AMERICA, c. 1850,
SHOWING BRITISH POSSESSIONS
AND PROPOSED CANAL ROUTES
Until President Theodore Roosevelt
swung into action with his Big Stick in
1903, a Nicaraguan canal, closer to the
United States, was generally judged more
desirable than a canal across Panama.

popular count was closer, 1,601,274 to 1,386,580.

The election of 1852 was fraught with frightening significance, though it may have seemed tame at the time. It marked the effective end of the disorganized Whig party, and within a few years its complete death. The Whigs were governed at times by the crassest opportunism, and they won only two presidential elections (1840, 1848) in their colorful career, both with war heroes. They finally choked to death trying to gag down the Fugitive Slave Law. But their great contribution—and a noteworthy one indeed—was to help implant and uphold the ideal of Union through leaders like Clay and Webster. Both of these statesmen, by unhappy coincidence, died during the campaign. But the good that they had done lived after them, and contributed powerfully to the preservation of a united United States.

President Pierce the Expansionist

At the outset the Pierce administration displayed vigor. The new President, standing confidently before some 15,000 people on inauguration day, delivered from memory a clear-voiced inaugural address. His Cabinet contained aggressive South-erners, including as secretary of war one Jefferson Davis, future president of the Confederacy. The men of Dixie were determined to acquire more slave territory, and the compliant Pierce was prepared to be their willing tool.

The intoxicating victories of the Mexican War stimulated the spirit of Manifest Destiny, especially among "slaveocrats" lusting for new slave territory. The conquest of a Pacific frontage, and the discovery of gold on it, aroused lively interest in the trans-Isthmian land routes of Central America, chiefly in Panama and Nicaragua. Many Americans were looking even farther ahead to potential canal routes, and to the islands flanking them, notably Spain's Cuba.

Nicaragua was of vital concern to Great Britain, the world's leading maritime and commercial power. Fearing that the grasping Yankees would monopolize the trade arteries there, the British made haste to secure a solid foothold at Greytown, the eastern end of the proposed Nicaraguan canal route. This challenge to the Monroe Doctrine forthwith raised the ugly possibility of an armed clash. The crisis was surmounted in 1850 by the Clayton-Bulwer Treaty, which stipulated that neither America nor Britain would fortify or secure exclusive control over any future Isthmian waterway. This agreement, at the time, seemed necessary to halt the British, but to American canal promoters in later years it proved to be a ball and chain.

America had become a Pacific power with the acquisition of California and Oregon, both of which faced the Orient. The prospects of a rich trade with the Far East now seemed rosier. Americans had already established contacts with China, and shippers were urging Washington to push for commercial intercourse with Japan. The Mikado's empire, after some disagreeable experiences with the European world, had withdrawn into a cocoon of isolationism and had remained there for over 200 years. But by 1853, as events proved, Nippon was ready to emerge, partly because of the Russian menace.

The Washington government was now eager to pry open the bamboo gates of Japan. It dispatched a fleet of awesome, smoke-belching warships, commanded by Commodore Matthew C. Perry, brother of the hero of the Battle of Lake Erie in 1813. By a judicious display of force and tact, he persuaded the Japanese in 1854 to sign a memorable treaty. It provided for only a commercial foot in the door, but it was the beginning of an epochal relationship between the Land of the Rising Sun and the Western world. Ironically, this achievement attracted little notice at the time, partly because Perry devised no memorable slogan.

Coveted Cuba: Pearl of the Antilles

Sugar-rich Cuba, lying off the nation's southern doorstep, was the prime objective of Manifest Destiny in the 1850s. Supporting a large population of enslaved blacks, it was coveted by the South as the most desirable slave territory available. Carved into several states, it would once more restore the political balance in the Senate.

Cuba was a kind of heirloom—the most important remnant of Spain's once-mighty New World empire. Polk, the expansionist, had taken steps to offer $100 million for it, but the sensitive Spaniards had replied that they would see it sunk into the ocean before they would sell it to the Americans at any price. With purchase completely out of the question, seizure was apparently the only way to pluck the ripening fruit.

Private adventurers from the South now undertook to shake the tree of Manifest Destiny. During 1850–1851 two filibustering expeditions, each numbering several hundred armed men, descended upon Cuba. Both feeble efforts were repelled, and the last one ended in tragedy when the leader and fifty followers—some of them from the "best families" of the South—were summarily shot or strangled. So outraged were the Southerners that an angry mob sacked Spain's consulate in New Orleans.

Spanish officials in Cuba rashly forced a showdown in 1854, when they seized an American

A Japanese Portrait of Commodore Perry. A blunt officer, known as "Old Bruin" by his men, he was held in high regard by the Japanese until World War II. Early in 1944, in the wake of American bombings, a monument to him in Yokohama was torn down.

Cuban Discomfort. "Master Jonathan tries to smoke a Cuba, but it doesn't agree with him!" English chortle over America's Cuban blunder. (*Punch*, 1850.)

The first platform of the newly born (anti-slavery) Republican party in 1856 lashed out at the Ostend Manifesto, with its transparent suggestion that Cuba be seized. The plank read: "*Resolved,* That the highwayman's plea, that 'might makes right,' embodied in the Ostend Circular, was in every respect unworthy of American diplomacy, and would bring shame and dishonor upon any Government or people that gave it their sanction."

steamer, *Black Warrior*, on a technicality. Now was the time for President Pierce, dominated as he was by the South, to provoke a war with Spain and seize Cuba. The major powers of Europe—England, France, and Russia—were about to become bogged down in the Crimean War, and hence were unable to aid Spain.

An incredible cloak-and-dagger episode followed. The secretary of state instructed the American ministers in Spain, England, and France to prepare confidential recommendations for the acquisition of Cuba. Meeting initially at Ostend, Belgium, the three envoys drew up a top-secret dispatch, soon known as the Ostend Manifesto. This startling document urged that the administration offer $120 million for Cuba. If Spain refused, and if her continued ownership endangered American interests, the United States would "be justified in wresting" the island from her.

The secret Ostend Manifesto quickly leaked out. Northern free-soilers, already angered by the Fugitive Slave Law and other gains for slavery, rose in an outburst of wrath against the "manifesto of brigands." Confronted with disruption at home, the red-faced Pierce administration was forced to drop its brazen schemes for Cuba.

Clearly the slavery issue, like a two-headed snake with the heads at cross purposes, dead-locked territorial expansion in the 1850s. The North, flushed with Manifest Destiny, was developing a renewed appetite for Canada. The South coveted Cuba. Neither section would permit the other to get the apple of its eye, so neither got either. The shackled black hands of Harriet Beecher Stowe's Uncle Tom, who had already aroused the North, held the South back from Cuba. The internal distresses of the United States were such that, for once, it could not take advantage of Europe's distresses—in this case the Crimean War.

Pacific Railroad Promoters and the Gadsden Purchase

Acute transportation problems were another legacy of the Mexican War. The newly acquired prizes of California and Oregon might just as well have been islands some 8,000 miles (13,000 kilometers) west of the nation's capital. The sea routes to and from the Isthmus, to say nothing of those around South America, were too long. Covered-wagon travel past bleaching animal bones was possible, but it was slow and dangerous. A popular song recalled:

They swam the wide rivers and crossed the tall peaks,
And camped on the prairie for weeks upon weeks.
Starvation and cholera and hard work and slaughter,
They reached California spite of hell and high water.

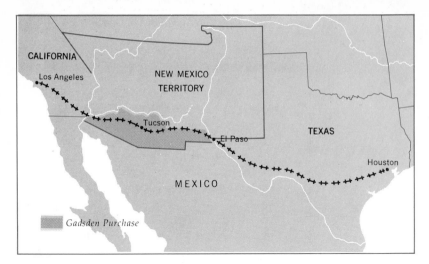

GADSDEN PURCHASE, 1853
Future Southern Pacific Railroad
(completed 1882) is shown.

Feasible land transportation was imperative—or the newly won possessions on the Pacific Coast might break away. Camels were even proposed as the answer. Several score of these temperamental beasts—"ships of the desert"—were imported from the Near East, but mule-driving Americans did not adjust to them. A transcontinental railroad was clearly the only real solution to the problem.

Railway promoters, both North and South, had projected many drawing-board routes to the Pacific Coast. But the estimated cost in all cases was so great that for many years there could obviously be only one line. Should its terminus be in the North or in the South? The favored section would reap rich rewards in wealth, population, and influence. The South, losing the economic race with the North, was eager to extend a railroad through adjacent Southwestern territory all the way to California.

Another chunk of Mexico now seemed desirable, because the campaigns of the recent war had shown that the best railway route ran slightly south of the Mexican border. Secretary of War Jefferson Davis, a Mississippian, arranged to have James Gadsden, a prominent South Carolina railroad man, appointed minister to Mexico. Finding Santa Anna in power for the sixth and last time, and as usual in need of money, Gadsden made gratifying headway. He negotiated a treaty in 1853, which ceded to the United States the Gadsden Purchase area for $10 million. The transaction aroused much criticism among Northerners, who objected to paying a huge sum for a cactus-strewn desert nearly the size of Gadsden's South Carolina. Undeterred, the Senate approved the pact after shortsightedly eliminating a window on the Gulf of California.

No doubt the Gadsden Purchase enabled the South to claim the coveted railroad with even greater insistence. A southern track would be easier to build, because the mountains were less high and because the route, unlike the proposed northern lines, would not pass through unorganized territory. Texas was already a state, and New Mexico (with the Gadsden Purchase added) was a formally organized territory, with federal troops available to provide protection against marauding red men. Any northern or central line would have to be thrust through the unorganized territory of Nebraska, where the buffalo and Indians roamed.

Northern railroad boosters quickly replied that if organized territory was the test, then Nebraska should be organized. Such a move was not premature, because thousands of land-hungry pioneers were already poised on the Nebraska border. But all schemes proposed in Congress for organizing the territory were greeted with apathy or hostility by many Southerners. Why should the South help create new free-soil states, and thus cut its own throat by facilitating a northern railroad?

Douglas's Kansas-Nebraska Scheme

At this point in 1854 Senator Stephen A. Douglas of Illinois delivered a counterstroke to offset the Gadsden thrust for Southern expansion westward. A squat, bull-necked, and heavy-chested figure, the "Little Giant" radiated the energy and breezy optimism of the self-made man. An ardent booster for the West, he longed to break the North-South deadlock over westward expansion and stretch a line of settlements across the continent. He had also invested heavily in Chicago real estate and in railway stock, and was eager to have the Windy City become the eastern terminus of the proposed Pacific railroad. He would thus endear himself to the voters of Illinois, benefit his own section, and enrich his own purse.

Stephen A. Douglas (1813–1861). Despite having stirred up sectional bitterness, Douglas was so devoted to the Union that he warmly supported his rival, Lincoln, when war broke out. He attended the inauguration and reportedly held Lincoln's stovepipe hat while the President spoke. (National Portrait Gallery, Smithsonian Institution, Washington, D.C.)

A veritable "steam engine in breeches," Douglas threw himself behind a legislative scheme that would enlist the support of a reluctant South. The proposed Territory of Nebraska would be carved into two territories, Kansas and Nebraska. Their status regarding slavery would be settled by popular sovereignty—a democratic concept to which Douglas and his Western constituents were deeply attached. Kansas, which lay due west of slaveholding Missouri, would presumably choose to become a slave state. But Nebraska, lying west of free-soil Iowa, would presumably become a free state.

Douglas's Kansas-Nebraska scheme ran headlong into a formidable political obstacle. The Missouri Compromise of 1820 had forbidden slavery in the Nebraska Territory, which lay north of the sacred 36°30′ line; and the only way to open the region to popular sovereignty was to repeal the ancient compact outright. This bold step Douglas was prepared to take, even at the risk of shattering the uneasy truce patched up by the Great Compromise of 1850.

Many Southerners, who had not conceived of Kansas as slave soil, rose to the bait. Here was a chance to gain one more slave state. The pliable President Pierce, under the thumb of Southern advisers, threw his full weight behind the Kansas-Nebraska Bill.

But the Missouri Compromise, now thirty-four years old, could not be brushed aside lightly. Whatever Congress passes it can repeal, but by this time the North had come to regard the sectional pact as almost as sacred as the Constitution itself. Free-soil members of Congress struck back furiously. They met their match in the violently gesticulating Douglas, who was the ablest rough-and-tumble debater of his generation. Employing twisted logic and oratorical fireworks, he rammed the bill through Congress, with strong support from many Southerners. So heated were political passions that bloodshed was barely averted. Some members carried a concealed revolver or a bowie knife—or both.

Douglas's motives in prodding anew the snarling dog of slavery have long puzzled historians. His

Douglas Hatches a Slavery Problem. Note the already hatched Missouri Compromise, Squatter Sovereignty, and Filibustering (in Cuba), and the about-to-hatch Free Kansas and Dred Scott decision. So bitter was the outcry against Douglas at the time of the Kansas-Nebraska controversy that he claimed with exaggeration that he could have traveled from Boston to Chicago at night by the light from his burning effigies. Republican cartoon.

personal interests have already been mentioned. In addition, his foes accused him of angling for the presidency in 1856. Yet his admirers have argued plausibly in his defense that if he had not championed the ill-omened bill, someone else would have.

The truth seems to be that Douglas acted somewhat impulsively and recklessly. His heart did not bleed over the issue of slavery, and he declared repeatedly that he did not care whether it was voted up or down in the territories. What he failed to perceive was that hundreds of thousands of his fellow countrymen in the North *did* feel deeply on this moral issue. They regarded the repeal of the Missouri Compromise as an intolerable breach of faith, and they would henceforth resist to the last trench all future demands of the South for slave territory.

A genuine statesman, like a skillful chess player, must foresee the possible effects of his moves.

Douglas predicted a "hell of a storm," but he grossly underestimated its proportions. His critics in the North, branding him a "Judas" and a "traitor," greeted his name with frenzied boos, hisses, and "three groans for Doug." But he still enjoyed a high degree of popularity among his own loyal following in the Democratic party, especially in Illinois, a stronghold of popular sovereignty.

Congress Legislates a Civil War

The Kansas-Nebraska Act—a curtain raiser to a terrible drama—was one of the most momentous measures ever to pass Congress. By one way of reckoning, it led directly down the slippery slope to Civil War.

Anti-slavery Northerners were angered by what they condemned as an act of bad faith by the "Neb-rascals" and their "Nebrascality." All future compromise with the South would be immeasurably more difficult, and without compromise there was bound to be conflict.

Henceforth the Fugitive Slave Law of 1850, previously enforced in the North only halfheartedly, was a dead letter. The Kansas-Nebraska Act wrecked two compromises: that of 1820, which it repealed specifically, and that of 1850, which Northern opinion repealed indirectly. Emerson wrote, "The Fugitive [Slave] Law did much to unglue the eyes of men, and now the Nebraska Bill leaves us staring."

Northern abolitionists and Southern "fire-eaters" alike were stirred to new outbursts. The growing legion of anti-slaveryites gained numerous recruits, who resented the grasping move by the "slavocracy" for Kansas. The Southerners, in turn, became inflamed when the free-soilers attempted to control Kansas, contrary to the presumed "deal."

The proud Democrats—a party now over half a century old—were shattered by the Kansas-Nebraska Act. They managed to elect a President two years later, but he was the last one they were

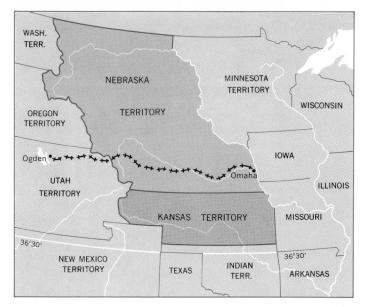

KANSAS AND NEBRASKA, 1854
Future Union Pacific Railroad (completed 1869) is shown. Note the Missouri Compromise line of 36°30' (1820).

to boost into the White House for twenty-eight long years.

Undoubtedly the most durable offspring of the Kansas-Nebraska blunder was the new Republican party. It sprang up spontaneously in the Middle West, notably in Wisconsin and Michigan, as a mighty moral protest against the gains of slavery. Gathering together dissatisfied elements, it soon included disgruntled Whigs (including Abraham Lincoln), Democrats, Free-Soilers, Know-Nothings, and other foes of the Kansas-Nebraska Act. The hodgepodge party spread eastward with the rapidity of a prairie fire and with the zeal of a religious crusade. Unheard of and unheralded at the beginning of 1854, it elected a Republican speaker of the House of Representatives within two years. Never really a third-party movement, it erupted with such force as to become almost overnight the second major political party—and a purely sectional one at that.

At long last the dreaded sectional rift had appeared. The new Republican party would not be allowed south of the Mason-Dixon line. Countless Southerners subscribed wholeheartedly to the sentiment that it was "a nigger stealing, stinking, putrid, abolition party." The Union was in dire peril.

VARYING VIEWPOINTS

Historical treatments of the 1850s have long reflected the major controversy of that decade: whether the principal issue was slavery itself or simply the *expansion* of slavery into the Western territories. In short, did slavery need to be abolished or merely contained? Historians have generally emphasized the geographical factor, describing a contest for control of the territories, and for control of the central government that disposed of those territories. But recently some analysts, probably reflecting the pro–civil rights agitation of the times, have stressed broader issues, including morality. In this view the territorial question was real enough, but it also symbolized a pervasive threat by the slave-power to the "free" Northern way of life. In the end, the problems of Southern slavery and Western "free soil" proved inseparable and insoluble, except by war.

SELECT READINGS

The best account of the events of the 1850s is David Potter's masterful *The Impending Crisis, 1848–1861* (1976). Sketchy but penetrating is Roy F. Nichols, *The Stakes of Power, 1845–1877* (1961); see also his more detailed *The Disruption of American Democracy* (1948). Comprehensive treatments may be found in J. G. Randall and David Donald, *The Civil War and Reconstruction* (rev. ed., 1969), and Allan Nevins, *Ordeal of the Union* (2 vols., 1947). See also A. O. Craven, *The Coming of the Civil War* (2nd ed., 1957), his *Civil War in the Making* (1959), and his *Growth of Southern Nationalism* (1953). David Potter also offers illuminating insights in *The South and the Sectional Conflict* (1968). The standard work is Holman Hamilton, *Prologue to Conflict: The Crisis and Compromise of 1850* (1964). The emergence of the Republican party can be studied in Eric Foner's brilliant discussion of ideology, *Free Soil, Free Labor, Free Men* (1970), in J. G. Rayback's analysis of the election of 1848, *Free Soil* (1970), and in Michael Holt's perceptive *Forging a Majority: The Formation of the Republican Party in Pittsburgh* (1969). Foner's ideas can be pursued further in his *Politics and Ideology in the Age of the Civil War* (1980), while Holt has developed his views in *The Political Crisis of the 1850s* (1978), an unusually provocative book. Robert W. Johannsen, *Stephen Douglas* (1973), analyzes with perception the "Little Giant's" motives. Other useful biographies are M. L. Coit, *John C. Calhoun* (1950), C. M. Wiltse, *John C. Calhoun: Sectionalist* (1951), R. J. Rayback, *Millard Fillmore* (1959), R. F. Nichols, *Franklin Pierce* (1958), and G. G. Van Deusen, *William Henry Seward* (1967).

21

Drifting Toward Disunion, 1854-1861

*A house divided against itself cannot stand.
I believe this government cannot endure permanently half slave and half free.*

ABRAHAM LINCOLN, 1858

Stowe and Helper: Literary Incendiaries

Sectional tensions were further strained in 1852, and later, by an inky phenomenon. Harriet Beecher Stowe, a wisp of a woman and the mother of a half-dozen children, published her heart-rending novel, *Uncle Tom's Cabin*. Dismayed by the passage of the Fugitive Slave Law, she was determined to awaken the North to the wickedness of slavery by laying bare its terrible inhumanity. Her book, though lacking high literary quality, was distinguished by powerful imagery and touching pathos. "God wrote it," she explained in later years.

The success of the novel at home and abroad was sensational. Several hundred thousand copies were published in the first year, and the totals soon ran into the millions as the tale was translated into more than a score of languages. It was also put on the stage in "Tom shows" for lengthy runs. No other novel in American history—perhaps in all history—can be compared with it as a political force. To millions of people it made slavery appear almost as evil as it really was.

When Mrs. Stowe was introduced to President Lincoln in 1862, he reportedly remarked with twinkling eyes, "So you're the little woman who wrote the book that made this great war." The truth is that *Uncle Tom's Cabin* helped start the Civil War—and win it. The South condemned that "vile wretch in petticoats" when it learned that hundreds of thousands of fellow Americans were reading and believing her "unfair" indictment. Mrs. Stowe had never witnessed slavery at first hand in the Deep South, but she had seen it briefly during a visit to Kentucky, and she had lived for many years in Ohio, a center of Underground Railway activity.

Harriet Beecher Stowe (1811–1896). She was a remarkable woman whose pen helped to change the course of history. (The Metropolitan Museum of Art, Gift of I. N. Phelps Stokes, Edward S. Hawes, Alice Mary Hawes, and Marion Augusta Hawes, 1937)

In the closing scenes of Mrs. Stowe's novel, Uncle Tom's brutal master, Simon Legree, orders the $1,200 slave savagely beaten (to death) by two fellow slaves. Through tears and blood Tom exclaims, "No! no! no! my soul an't yours, Mas'r! You haven't bought it—ye can't buy it! It's been bought and paid for by One that is able to keep it. No matter, no matter, you can't harm me!" "I can't!" said Legree, with a sneer; "we'll see—we'll see! Here, Sambo, Quimbo, give this dog such a breakin' in as he won't get over this month!"

Uncle Tom, endearing and enduring, left a profound impression on the North. Uncounted thousands of readers swore that henceforth they would have nothing to do with the enforcement of the Fugitive Slave Law. The tale was devoured by millions of impressionable youths in the 1850s—the later Boys in Blue who volunteered to fight the Civil War through to its grim finale. The memory of a beaten and dying Uncle Tom helped sustain them in their determination to wipe out the plague of slavery.

The novel was immensely popular abroad, especially in England and France. Countless readers wept over the kindly Tom and the angelic Eva, while deploring the brutal Simon Legree. When the guns in America finally began to boom, the common people of England sensed that the triumph of the North would spell the end of the black curse. The governments in London and Paris seriously considered intervening in behalf of the South, but they were sobered by the realization that many of their own people, aroused by the "Tom-mania," might not support them.

Another trouble-brewing book appeared in 1857, five years after the debut of Uncle Tom. Entitled *The Impending Crisis of the South*, it was written by Hinton R. Helper, a non-aristocratic white from North Carolina. Hating both slavery and blacks, he attempted to prove by an array of statistics that indirectly the non-slaveholding

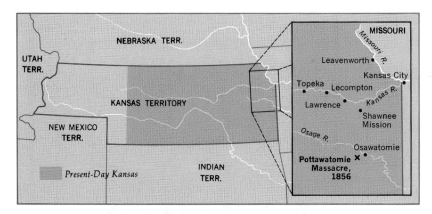

whites were the ones who suffered most from the millstone of slavery. Unable to secure a publisher in the South, he finally managed to find one in the North.

Helper's influence was negligible among the poorer whites to whom he addressed his message. His book, with its "dirty allusions," was banned in the South, where book-burning parties were held. But in the North countless thousands of copies, many in condensed form, were distributed as campaign literature by the Republicans. Southerners were further embittered when they learned that their Northern brethren were spreading these wicked "lies." Thus the sons of the South, reacting much as they did to *Uncle Tom's Cabin,* became increasingly unwilling to sleep under the same federal roof with their hostile Yankee bedfellows.

The North-South Contest for Kansas

The rolling plains of Kansas had meanwhile been providing a horrible example of the workings of popular sovereignty, although admittedly under abnormal conditions.

Newcomers who ventured into Kansas were a motley lot. Most of the Northerners were just ordinary westward-moving pioneers in search of richer lands beyond the sunset. But a small part of the inflow was financed by groups of Northern abolitionists or free-soilers. The most famous of these anti-slavery organizations was the New England Emigrant Aid Company, which sent about

2,000 persons to the troubled area to forestall the South—and also to make a profit. Shouting "Ho for Kansas," many of them carried the deadly new breech-loading Sharps rifles, nicknamed "Beecher's Bibles" after the prominent clergyman who had helped raise money for their purchase. Many of the Kansas-bound pioneers sang Whittier's marching song (1854):

> We cross the prairie as of old
>   The pilgrims crossed the sea,
> To make the West, as they the East,
>   The homestead of the free!

Southern spokesmen, now more than ordinarily touchy, raised furious cries of betrayal. They had supported the Kansas-Nebraska scheme of Douglas with the informal understanding that Kansas would become slave and Nebraska free. The Northern "Nebrascals," allegedly by foul means, were now apparently out to "abolitionize" *both* Kansas and Nebraska.

A few Southern hotheads, quick to respond in kind, attempted to "assist" small groups of well-armed slaveowners to Kansas. Some carried banners proclaiming:

> Let Yankees tremble, abolitionists fall,
> Our motto is, "Give Southern Rights to All."

But planting blacks on Kansas soil was a losing game. The slave was valuable and volatile property, and foolish indeed were owners who would take him where bullets were flying, and where the soil might be voted free under popular sovereignty. The census of 1860 found only two slaves among 107,000 souls in all the territory, and only fifteen in Nebraska. There was much force in the charge that the whole quarrel over slavery in the territories revolved around "an imaginary Negro in an impossible place."

Crisis conditions in Kansas rapidly worsened. When the day came in 1855 to elect members of the first territorial legislature, pro-slavery "border ruffians" poured in from Missouri to vote early and often. The slavery men triumphed, and then set up their own puppet government at Shawnee Mission. The free-soilers, unable to stomach this fraudulent conspiracy, established an extra-legal regime of their own in Topeka. The confused Kansan thus had his choice between two governments —one based on fraud, the other on illegality.

Tension mounted as men also feuded over conflicting land claims. The breaking point came in 1856 when a gang of pro-slavery raiders, alleging provocation, shot up and burned a part of the free-soil town of Lawrence. This outrage was but the prelude to a bloodier tragedy.

Kansas in Convulsion

The fanatical figure of John Brown now stalked upon the Kansas battlefield. Spare, gray-bearded, iron-willed, and narrowly ignorant, he was dedicated to the abolitionist cause. The power of his glittering gray eyes was such, so he claimed, that his stare could force a dog or cat to slink out of a room. Becoming involved in dubious dealings, including horse stealing, he moved to Kansas from Ohio with a part of his large family. Brooding over the recent attack on Lawrence, "Old Brown" of Osawatomie led a band of his followers to Pottawatomie Creek, in May 1856. There they literally hacked to pieces five surprised men, allegedly pro-slaveryites. This fiendish butchery, clearly the product of a deranged mind, besmirched the free-soil cause and brought vicious retaliation from the pro-slavery men.

Civil war in Kansas, which thus flared forth in 1856, continued intermittently until it merged with the large-scale Civil War of 1861–1865. Alto-

John Brown (1800–1859). A militant abolitionist, Brown became perhaps the most sung-about man up to that time, except Jesus. From a primitive photograph (daguerreotype) taken in 1856. (Courtesy Kansas Historical Society.)

gether, the Kansas conflict destroyed millions of dollars' worth of property, paralyzed agriculture in certain areas, and cost scores of lives.

Yet by 1857 Kansas had enough people, chiefly

John Brown, an avid reader of the Old Testament, evidently believed in the principle of an eye for an eye, and a hand for a hand. A surviving son of one of his victims later testified under oath that "I found my father and one brother, William, lying dead in the road . . . I saw my other brother lying dead on the ground . . . in the grass, near a ravine; his fingers were cut off and his arms were cut off; his head was cut open; there was a hole in his breast. William's head was cut open, and a hole was in his jaw . . . and a hole was also in his side. My father was shot in the forehead and stabbed in the breast."

free-soilers, to apply for statehood on a popular-sovereignty basis. The pro-slavery men, then in the saddle, devised a tricky document known as the Lecompton Constitution. The people were not allowed to vote for or against the constitution as a whole, but for the constitution either "with slavery" or "with no slavery." If they voted against slavery, one of the remaining provisions of the constitution would protect the owners of slaves already in Kansas. So whatever the outcome, there would still be black bondage in Kansas. Many free-soilers, infuriated by this trick, boycotted the polls. Left to themselves, the slaveryites approved the constitution with slavery late in 1857.

The scene next shifted to Washington. President Pierce had been succeeded by the no-less-pliable James Buchanan, who was also strongly under Southern influence. Blind to sharp divisions within his own Democratic party, Buchanan threw the weight of his administration behind the notorious Lecompton Constitution. But Senator Douglas, who had championed true popular sovereignty, would have none of this semi-popular fraudulency. Deliberately tossing away his strong support in the South for the presidency, he fought courageously for fair play and democratic principles. The outcome was a compromise which, in effect, submitted the *entire* Lecompton Constitution to a popular vote. The free-soil men thereupon thronged to the polls and snowed it under. But Kansas was denied statehood until 1861, when the Southern secessionists left Congress.

President Buchanan, by antagonizing the numerous Douglas Democrats in the North, hopelessly divided the once-powerful Democratic party. Until then, it had been the only remaining *national* party, for the Whigs were dead and the Republicans were sectional. With the disruption of the Democrats came the snapping of one of the last important strands in the rope that was barely binding the Union together.

"Bully" Brooks and His Bludgeon

"Bleeding Kansas" also splattered blood on the floor of the United States Senate in 1856. Senator Charles Sumner of Massachusetts, a tall and imposing figure, was a leading abolitionist—one of the few prominent in political life. Highly edu-

Sumner Beaten by Brooks. Note that the cartoonist has two of the senators smiling or laughing, and one of them preventing interference with his cane. Note also that Sumner is defending himself with a quill pen while Brooks is wielding a club. (Courtesy the New York Public Library, Astor, Lenox, and Tilden Foundations.)

SOUTHERN CHIVALRY — ARGUMENT versus CLUB'S.

cated but cold, humorless, intolerant, and ego-tistical, he had made himself one of the most disliked men in the Senate. Brooding over the turbulent miscarriage of popular sovereignty, he delivered a blistering speech entitled "The Crime against Kansas." Sparing few epithets, he condemned the pro-slavery men as "hirelings picked from the drunken spew and vomit of an uneasy civilization." He also referred insultingly to South Carolina, and to her white-haired Senator Butler, one of the best-liked members of the Senate.

Hot-tempered Congressman Brooks, of South Carolina, now took vengeance into his own hands. Ordinarily gracious and gallant, he resented the insults to his state and to her senator, a distant cousin. His code of honor called for a duel, but in the South one fought only with one's social equals. And had not the coarse language of the Yankee, who probably would reject a challenge, dropped him to a lower order? To Brooks, the only alternative was to chastise the senator as one would beat an unruly dog. On May 22, 1856, he approached Sumner, then sitting at his Senate desk, and pounded the orator with a heavy cane until it broke. The victim fell bleeding and un-conscious to the floor, while several nearby sena-tors refrained from interfering.

Sumner had been provocatively insulting, but this counter-outrage put Brooks in the wrong. The House of Representatives could not muster enough votes to expel the Carolinian, but he re-signed and was triumphantly re-elected. Southern admirers deluged Brooks with canes, some of them gold-headed, to replace the one that had been broken. The injuries to Sumner's head and nervous system were serious. He was forced to leave his seat for three and a half years and go to Europe for treatment that was both painful and costly. Meanwhile Massachusetts defiantly re-elected him, leaving his seat eloquently empty. Bleeding Sumner was thus joined with Bleeding Kansas as a political issue.

The free-soil North was mightily aroused against the "uncouth" and "cowardly" "Bully" Brooks. Copies of Sumner's abusive speech, otherwise

Regarding the Brooks assault on Sumner, one of the more moderate anti-slavery journals (*Illinois State Journal*) declared, "Brooks and his Southern allies have deliberately adopted the monstrous creed than any man who dares to utter sentiments which they deem wrong or unjust, shall be brutally assailed. . . ." One of the milder Southern responses came from the *Petersburg* (Virginia) *Intelligencer*: "Although Mr. Brooks ought to have selected some other spot for the altercation than the Senate chamber, if he had broken every bone in Sumner's carcass it would have been a just retribution upon this slanderer of the South and her individual citizens."

doomed to obscurity, were sold by the tens of thousands. Every blow that struck the senator doubtless made thousands of Republican votes. The South, although not unanimous in approving Brooks, was angered not only because Sumner had made such an intemperate speech but be-cause it had been so extravagantly applauded in the North.

The Sumner-Brooks clash and the ensuing re-actions revealed how dangerously inflamed pas-sions were becoming, North and South. It was ominous that the cultured Sumner should have used the language of a barroom bully, and that the gentlemanly Brooks should have employed the tactics and tools of a thug. Emotion was dis-placing thought. The blows rained on Sumner's head were, broadly speaking, among the first blows of the Civil War.

"Old Buck" versus "The Pathfinder"

With bullets whining in Kansas, the Democrats met in Cincinnati to nominate their presidential standard-bearer of 1856. They shied away from both the weak-kneed President Pierce and the dynamic Douglas. Each was too heavily blackened

Frémont, the Explorer, in Heroic Pose. It was said with exaggeration that from the ashes of his campfires have sprung cities. Actually he was a pathmarker as much as a pathfinder; a great deal of the land he explored had already been traversed by fur-seeking "mountain men." (Library of Congress.)

by the Kansas-Nebraska Act. The delegates finally chose James Buchanan (pronounced by many *Buck*-anan), who was muscular, white-haired, and tall (6 feet; 1.83 meters), with a short neck and a protruding chin. Because of an eye defect, he carried his head cocked to one side. As a well-to-do Pennsylvania lawyer, he had been serving as minister to London during the recent Kansas-Nebraska uproar. He was therefore "Kansasless," and hence relatively enemyless. But in a crisis that called for giants, "Old Buck" Buchanan was mediocre, irresolute, confused.

Delegates of the fast-growing Republican party met in Philadelphia with bubbling enthusiasm. "Higher Law" Seward was their most conspicuous leader, and he probably would have arranged to win the nomination had he been confident that

this was a "Republican year." The final choice was Captain John C. Frémont, the so-called Pathfinder of the West—a dashing but erratic explorer-soldier-surveyor who was supposed to find the path to the White House. The black-bearded and flashy young adventurer was virtually without political experience, but like Buchanan he was not tarred with the Kansas brush. The Republican platform came out vigorously against the extension of slavery into the territories, while the Democrats declared no less emphatically for popular sovereignty.

An ugly dose of anti-foreignism was injected into the campaign, even though slavery extension loomed largest. The recent horde of immigrants from Ireland and Germany had alarmed "nativists," as many old-stock Protestants were called. They organized the American party, known also as the Know-Nothing party because of its secretiveness, and in 1856 nominated the lackluster ex-President Fillmore. Anti-foreign and anti-Catholic, these superpatriots adopted the slogan "Americans Must Rule America." Remnants of the dying Whig party likewise endorsed Fillmore, and they and the Know-Nothings threatened to cut into Republican strength.

Republicans fell in behind Frémont with the zeal of crusaders. Shouting "We Follow the Pathfinder" and "We Are Buck Hunting," they organized glee clubs which sang (to the tune of the "Marseillaise"):

> Arise, arise ye brave!
>   And let our war-cry be,
> Free speech, free press, free soil, free men,
>   Fre-mont and victory!

"And free love," sneered the Buchanan men ("Buchaneers").

Mudslinging bespattered both candidates. "Old Fogy" Buchanan was assailed because he was a bachelor: the fiancée of his youth had died after a lovers' quarrel. Frémont was reviled because of his illegitimate birth, for his young mother had left her elderly husband, a Virginia planter, to run away with a French adventurer. In due season she gave birth to John in Savannah, Georgia—

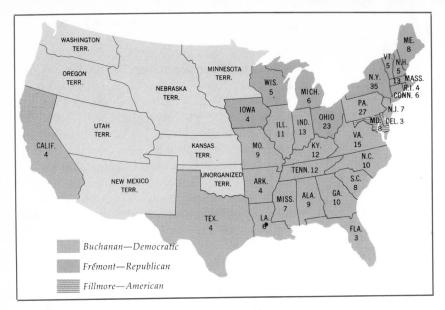

PRESIDENTIAL ELECTION OF 1856 (with electoral vote by state) The fateful split of 1860 was here foreshadowed. The regional polarization in 1856, shown here, was to be even sharper four years later, as illustrated by the maps on p. 381.

Buchanan—Democratic

Frémont—Republican

Fillmore—American

further to shame the South. More harmful to Frémont was the allegation, which alienated many bigoted Know-Nothings and other "nativists," that he was a Roman Catholic.

The Electoral Fruits of 1856

A bland Buchanan, although polling less than a majority of the popular vote, won handily. His tally in the Electoral College was 174 to 114 for Frémont, with Fillmore garnering 8. The popular vote was 1,838,169 for Buchanan to 1,341,264 for Frémont, with 874,534 for Fillmore.

Why did the aroused Republicans go down to defeat? Frémont lost much ground because of grave doubts as to his honesty, capacity, and

Spiritual overtones developed in the Frémont campaign, especially over slavery. The *Independent*, a foremost religious journal, saw in Frémont's nomination "the good hand of God." As election day neared it declared, "Fellow-Christians! Remember it is for Christ, for the nation, and for the world that you vote at this election! Vote as you pray! Pray as you vote!"

sound judgment. Perhaps more damaging were the violent threats of the Southern "fire-eaters" that the election of a sectional "Black Republican" would be a declaration of war on them, forcing them to secede. Many Northerners, anxious to save both the Union and their profitable business connections with the South, were thus intimidated into voting for Buchanan. Innate conservatism triumphed, assisted by so-called Southern bullyism.

It was probably fortunate for the Union that secession and civil war did not come in 1856, following a Republican victory. Frémont, an ill-balanced and second-rate figure, was no Abraham Lincoln. And in 1856 the North was more willing to let the South depart in peace than in 1860. Dramatic events from 1856 to 1860 were to arouse hundreds of thousands of still-apathetic Northerners to a fighting pitch.

Yet the Republicans in 1856 could rightfully claim a "victorious defeat." The new party—a mere two-year-old infant—had made an astonishing showing against the well-oiled Democratic machine. Whittier exulted:

Then sound again the bugles,
  Call the muster-roll anew;
If months have well-nigh won the field,
  What may not four years do?

The election of 1856 cast a long shadow forward, and politicians, North and South, peered anxiously toward 1860.

The Dred Scott Bombshell

The Dred Scott decision, handed down by the Supreme Court on March 6, 1857, abruptly ended the two-day presidential honeymoon of the unlucky bachelor, James Buchanan. This pronouncement was one of the opening paper-gun blasts of the Civil War.

Basically, the case was simple. Dred Scott, a black slave, had lived with his master for five years in Illinois and Wisconsin Territory. Backed by interested abolitionists, he sued for freedom on the basis of his long residence on free soil.

The Supreme Court proceeded to turn a simple legal case into a complex political issue. It ruled, not surprisingly, that Dred Scott was a black slave and not a citizen, and hence could not sue in federal courts.* The tribunal could then have thrown out the case on these technical grounds alone. But a majority decided to go further, under the leadership of emaciated Chief Justice Taney from the slave state of Maryland. A sweeping judgment on the larger issue of slavery in the territories seemed desirable, particularly to forestall arguments by two free-soil members who were preparing dissenting opinions. The pro-Southern majority evidently hoped in this way to lay the vexed question to rest.

Taney's thunderclap rocked the free-soilers back on their heels. A majority of the Court had decreed that because a slave was private property, he could be taken into *any* territory and held there. The reasoning was that the 5th Amendment clearly forbade Congress to deprive persons of their property without due process of law. The Court, to be consistent, went further. The Missouri Compromise, banning slavery north of 36°30′, had been repealed three years earlier by the Kansas-

---

*This part of the ruling, denying blacks their citizenship, seriously menaced the precarious position of the South's quarter-million "free" blacks.

Taney's decision, in the case of Dred Scott, referred to the status of slaves when the Constitution was adopted: "They had for more than a century before been regarded as beings of an inferior order; and altogether unfit to associate with the white race, either in social or political relations; and so far inferior that they had no rights which the white man was bound to respect. . . . This opinion was at that time fixed and universal in the civilized portion of the white race." Taney's statement was historically sound as it related to the United States, but highly offensive to anti-slaveryites when applied to conditions in 1857.

Nebraska Act. But its spirit was still venerated in the North. Now the Court had ruled that the Compromise of 1820 had been unconstitutional all along: Congress had no power to ban slavery from the territories, regardless even of what the territorial legislatures themselves might want.

A cry of delight broke from Southern throats over this unexpected victory. Champions of popular sovereignty were aghast, including Senator Douglas and a host of Northern Democrats. Another lethal wedge was thus driven between the Northern and Southern wings of the once-united Democratic party.

Foes of slavery extension, especially the Republicans, were infuriated by the Dred Scott setback. Their chief rallying cry had been the banishing of bondage from the territories. They now insisted that the ruling of the Court was merely an opinion, not a decision, and just as binding as the views of a "Southern debating society." Republican defiance of the exalted tribunal was intensified by an awareness that a majority of its members were Southerners, and by the conviction that it had debased itself—"sullied the ermine"—by wallowing in the gutter of politics.

Southerners in turn were inflamed by all this defiance. They began to wonder anew how much longer they could remain married to a section that refused to honor the Supreme Court, to say nothing of the constitutional compact which had established it.

The Financial Crash of 1857

Bitterness caused by the Dred Scott decision was deepened by hard times, which dampened a period of feverish prosperity. Late in 1857 a panic burst about Buchanan's harassed head. The storm was not so bad economically as the Panic of 1837, but psychologically it was probably the worst of the 19th Century.

What caused the crash? Inpouring California gold played its part by helping to inflate the currency. The demands of the Crimean War had overstimulated the growing of grain, while frenzied speculation in land and railroads had further ripped the economic fabric. When the collapse came, over 5,000 businesses failed within a year. Unemployment, accompanied by hunger meetings in urban areas, was widespread. "Bread or Death" was one desperate slogan.

The North, including the grain growers, was hardest hit. The South, enjoying favorable cotton prices abroad, rode out the storm with flying colors. Panic conditions seemed further proof that

A New York Panic Scene, 1857

cotton *was* king, and that his economic kingdom was stronger than that of the North. This fatal delusion helped drive the overconfident Southerners closer to a shooting showdown.

Financial distress in the North, especially in agriculture, gave a new vigor to the demand for free farms of 160 acres from the public domain. For several decades interested groups had been urging the federal government to abandon its ancient policy of selling the land for revenue. Instead, the argument ran, acreage should be given outright to the sturdy pioneers as a reward for risking health and life to develop it.

A scheme to make outright gifts of homesteads encountered two-pronged opposition. Eastern industrialists had long been unfriendly to free land; some of them feared that their underpaid workmen would be drained off to the West. The South was even more bitterly opposed, partly because gang-labor slavery could not flourish on a mere 160 acres. Free farms would merely fill up the territories more rapidly with free-soilers, and further tip the political balance against the South. In 1860, after years of debate, Congress finally passed a homestead act—one that made public lands available at a nominal sum of twenty-five cents an acre. But it was stabbed to death by the veto pen of Buchanan, near whose elbow sat leading Southern sympathizers.

The Panic of 1857 also created a clamor for higher tariff rates. Several months before the crash, Congress, embarrassed by a large Treasury surplus, had enacted the Tariff of 1857. The new law, responding to pressures from the South, reduced duties to about 20 percent on dutiable goods—the lowest point since the War of 1812. Hardly had the revised rates been placed on the books when financial distress descended like a black pall. Northern manufacturers, many of them Republicans, noisily blamed their misfortunes on the low tariff. As the surplus melted away in the Treasury, industrialists in the North pointed to the need for higher duties. But what really concerned them was their desire for increased protection. Thus the Panic of 1857 gave the Republicans two sure-fire issues for the election of 1860: protection for the unprotected and farms for the farmless.

An Illinois Rail Splitter Emerges

The Illinois senatorial election of 1858 now claimed the national spotlight. Senator Douglas's term was about to expire, and the Republicans decided to run against him a rustic Springfield lawyer, one Abraham Lincoln. The candidate—6 feet 4 inches (1.93 meters) in height and 180 pounds (81.7 kilograms) in weight—presented an awkward but arresting figure. His legs, arms, and neck were grotesquely long; his head was crowned by coarse, black, and unruly hair; and his face was sad, sunken, and weather-beaten.

Lincoln was no silver-spoon child of destiny. Born in a Kentucky log cabin to impoverished parents, he attended a frontier school for not more than a year; being an avid reader, he was mainly self-educated. All his life he said "git," "thar," "heered." Though narrow-chested and somewhat stoop-shouldered, he shone in his frontier community as a wrestler and weight-lifter, and spent some time, among other pioneering pursuits, as a splitter of logs for fence rails. A superb teller

In 1832, when Lincoln became a candidate for the Illinois legislature, he delivered a speech at a political gathering: "I presume you all know who I am. I am humble Abraham Lincoln. I have been solicited by many friends to become a candidate for the Legislature. My [Whiggish] politics are short and sweet, like the old woman's dance. I am in favor of a national bank. I am in favor of the internal-improvement system, and a high protective tariff. These are my sentiments and political principles. If elected, I shall be thankful; if not, it will be all the same." He was elected two years later.

of earthy and amusing stories, he would oddly enough plunge into protracted periods of melancholy.

Lincoln's private and professional life was not especially noteworthy. He married "above himself" socially, into the influential Todd family of Kentucky; and the temperamental outbursts of his high-strung wife, known by her enemies as the "she wolf," helped to school him in patience and forbearance. After reading a little law, he gradually emerged as one of the dozen or so better-known trial lawyers in Illinois, although still accustomed to carrying important papers in his stovepipe hat. He was widely referred to as "Honest Abe," partly because he would refuse cases that he could not conscientiously defend.

The rise of Lincoln as a political figure was less than rocket-like. After making his mark in the Illinois legislature as a Whig politician of the log-rolling variety, he served one undistinguished term in Congress, 1847–1849. Until 1854, when he was forty-five years of age, he had done nothing to establish a claim to statesmanship. But the passage of the Kansas-Nebraska Act in that year lighted within him unexpected fires. After mounting the Republican bandwagon, he emerged as one of the foremost politicians and orators of the Northwest. At the Philadelphia convention of 1856, where Frémont was nominated, Lincoln actually received 110 votes for the vice-presidential nomination.

The Great Debate: Lincoln versus Douglas

Lincoln, as Republican nominee for the Senate seat, boldly challenged Douglas to a series of joint debates. This was a rash act, because the stumpy senator was probably the nation's most devastating debater. Douglas promptly accepted the challenge, and seven meetings were arranged from August to October 1858.

At first glance, the two contestants seemed ill-matched. The well-groomed and polished Douglas, with stocky figure and bullish voice, presented a striking contrast to the lanky Lincoln, with his

A Lincoln-Douglas Debate. On one occasion, Lincoln charged that Douglas's logic would prove that a horse chestnut was a chestnut horse.

Abraham Lincoln, A Most Uncommon Common Man. Early photograph (daguerreotype) by Mathew B. Brady, distinguished photographer of the era.

baggy clothes and unshined shoes. Moreover, "Old Abe," as he was called in both affection and derision, had a piercing, high-pitched voice, and was often ill at ease when he began to speak. But as he threw himself into an argument, he seemed to grow in height, while his glowing eyes lighted up a rugged face. He relied on logic rather than on table-thumping.

The most famous of the forensic clashes came at Freeport, Illinois, where Lincoln neatly impaled his opponent on the horns of a dilemma. Suppose, he queried, the people of a territory should vote slavery down? The Supreme Court in the Dred Scott decision had decreed that they could not. Who would prevail, the Court or the people?

Legend to the contrary, Douglas and some Southerners had already publicly answered the Freeport question. The "Little Giant" therefore did not hesitate to meet the issue head on, honestly and consistently. He replied that no matter how the Supreme Court ruled, slavery would stay down if the people voted it down. Laws to protect slavery would have to be passed by the territorial legislatures. These would not be forthcoming in the absence of popular approval, and black bondage would soon disappear. Douglas, in truth, had American history on his side. Where public opinion does not support the federal government, as in the case of Jefferson's embargo, the law is almost impossible to enforce.

The upshot was that Douglas defeated Lincoln for the Senate seat. The "Little Giant's" loyalty to popular sovereignty, which still had a powerful appeal in Illinois, probably was decisive. Senators were then chosen by state legislatures; and in the general election that followed the debates, more pro-Douglas members were elected than pro-Lincoln members. Yet thanks to inequitable apportionment, the districts carried by Douglas men represented a smaller population than those carried by the Lincoln men. "Honest Abe" thus won a clear moral victory.

Lincoln possibly was playing for larger stakes than just the senatorship. Although defeated, he had shambled into the national limelight in company with the most prominent Northern politicians. Newspapers in the East published detailed accounts of the debates, and Lincoln began to emerge as a potential Republican nominee for President. But Douglas, in winning Illinois, hurt his chances of winning the presidency, while further splitting his splintering party. After his opposition to the Lecompton Constitution for Kansas and his further defiance of the Supreme Court at Freeport, Southern Democrats were determined to break up the party (and the Union) rather than accept him. The Lincoln-Douglas debate platform thus proved to be one of the preliminary battlefields of the Civil War.

The efforts of the Douglasites to represent Lincoln as a lover of the blacks were sharply rebutted by "Old Abe" in the opening of his debate at Charleston, Illinois: "While I was at the hotel to-day an elderly gentleman called upon me to know whether I was really in favor of producing a perfect equality between the negroes and white people. [Great laughter.] . . . I will say, then, that I am not, nor ever have been, in favor of bringing about in any way the social and political equality of the white and black races; [applause] that I am not, nor ever have been, in favor of making voters or jurors of negroes, nor of qualifying them to hold office, nor to intermarry with white people. . . . I as much as any other man am in favor of having the superior position assigned to the white race."

John Brown: Murderer or Martyr?

The gaunt, grim figure of John Brown of Kansas fame now appeared again in a more terrible way. His crackbrained scheme was to invade the South secretly with a handful of followers, call upon the slaves to rise, furnish them with arms, and establish a kind of black free state as a sanctuary. Brown secured several thousand dollars for firearms from Northern abolitionists, and finally arrived in hilly western Virginia with some twenty men. At scenic Harpers Ferry he seized the federal arsenal in October 1859, incidentally killing seven innocent people, including a free black, and injuring ten or so more. But the slaves refused to rise, and the wounded Brown and the remnants of his tiny band were quickly captured.

"Old Brown" was convicted of murder and treason, after a hasty but legal trial. His presumed insanity was supported by affidavits from seventeen friends and relatives, who were trying to save his neck. Actually thirteen of his near relations were regarded as insane, including his mother and grandmother. Governor Wise of

"A Premature Movement."   John Brown hands the pike to the slave and says "Follow me!" but the startled black protests that they have not finished seeding "at our house." Brown had made the fatal error of not earlier asking the slaves in question if they were willing to rise. (*Harper's Weekly,* 1859.)

Virginia would have been most wise, so his critics say, if he had only clapped the culprit into a lunatic asylum.

But Brown—"God's angry man"—was given every opportunity to pose and to enjoy martyrdom. Though probably of unsound mind, he was clever enough to see that he was worth much more to the abolitionist cause dangling from a rope than in any other way. His demeanor during the trial was dignified and courageous, his last words were to become a classic, and he marched up the scaffold steps without flinching. His conduct was so exemplary, his devotion to freedom so inflexible, that he took on an exalted character, however deplorable his previous record may have been. So the hangman's trap was sprung, and Brown plunged not into oblivion but into world fame. A memorable marching song of the impending Civil War ran:

> John Brown's body lies a-mould'ring in the grave,
> His soul is marching on.

The effects of Harpers Ferry were calamitous. In the eyes of the South, already embittered, "Osawatomie Brown" was a wholesale murderer and an apostle of treason. Many Southerners asked how they could possibly remain in the Union while a "murderous gang of abolitionists" were financing armed bands to "Brown" them. Moderate Northerners, including Republican leaders, openly deplored this mad exploit. But the South naturally concluded that the violent

abolitionist view was shared by the entire North, dominated by "Brown-loving" Republicans.

Abolitionists and other ardent free-soilers were infuriated by Brown's execution. Many of them were ignorant of his bloody past and his even more bloody purposes, and they were outraged because the Virginians had hanged so earnest a reformer who was working for so righteous a cause. On the day of his execution, free-soil centers in the North tolled bells, fired guns, half-masted flags, and held mass meetings. Some spoke of "Saint John" Brown, while the serene Ralph Waldo Emerson compared the new martyr-hero with Jesus. The gallows became a cross. E. C. Stedman wrote:

> And Old Brown,
> Osawatomie Brown,
> May trouble you more than ever,
>   when you've nailed his coffin down!

The ghost of the martyred Brown would not be laid to rest.

The Disruption of the Democrats

Beyond question the presidential election of 1860 was the most fateful in American history. On it hung the issue of peace or civil war.

Deeply divided, the Democrats met in Charleston, South Carolina, with Douglas the leading candidate of the Northern wing of the party. But the Southern "fire-eaters" regarded him as a traitor, as a result of his unpopular stand on the Lecompton Constitution and the Freeport Doctrine. After a bitter wrangle over the platform, the delegates from most of the cotton states walked out. When the remainder could not scrape together the necessary two-thirds vote for Douglas, the entire body dissolved in confusion. The first tragic secession was the secession of Southerners from the Democratic national convention. It became habit-forming.

The Democrats tried again in Baltimore. This time the Douglas Democrats, chiefly from the

ΙΟΙΟΙΟΙΟΙΟΙΟΙΟΙΟΙΟΙΟΙΟΙΟΙΟΙΟΙΟΙΟΙΟΙΟΙΟΙΟΙΟΙ

Sentenced to be hanged, John Brown wrote to his brother, "I am quite cheerful in view of my approaching end, being fully persuaded that I am worth inconceivably more to hang than for any other purpose. . . . I count it all joy. 'I have fought the good fight,' and have, as I trust, 'finished my course.'"

ΙΟΙΟΙΟΙΟΙΟΙΟΙΟΙΟΙΟΙΟΙΟΙΟΙΟΙΟΙΟΙΟΙΟΙΟΙΟΙΟΙΟΙ

Alexander H. Stephens, destined the next year to become vice-president of the new Confederacy, wrote privately in 1860 of the anti-Douglas Democrats who seceded from the Charleston convention: "The seceders intended from the beginning to rule or ruin; and when they find they cannot rule, they will then ruin. They have about enough power for this purpose; not much more; and I doubt not but they will use it. Envy, hate, jealousy, spite . . . will make devils of men. The secession movement was instigated by nothing but bad passions."

North, were firmly in the saddle. Many of the cotton-state delegates again took a walk, and the rest of the convention enthusiastically nominated their hero. The platform came out squarely for popular sovereignty and, as a sop to the South, against obstruction of the Fugitive Slave Law by the states.

Angered Southern Democrats promptly organized a rival convention in Baltimore, in which many of the Northern states were unrepresented. They selected as their leader the stern-jawed Vice-President, John C. Breckinridge, a man of moderate views from the border state of Kentucky. The platform favored the extension of slavery into the territories and the annexation of slave-populated Cuba.

A middle-of-the-road group, fearing for the Union, hastily organized the Constitutional Union party, sneered at as the "Do Nothing" or "Old Gentleman's" party. It consisted mainly of former Whigs and Know-Nothings, a veritable "Gathering of Graybeards." Desperately anxious to elect a compromise candidate, they met in Baltimore and nominated for the presidency John Bell of Tennessee. They went into battle ringing hand bells for Bell, and voicing the slogan, "The Union, the Constitution, and the Enforcement of the Laws."

A Rail Splitter Splits the Union

Elated Republicans were presented with a heaven-sent opportunity. Scenting victory in the breeze as their opponents split hopelessly, they gathered in Chicago in a huge, boxlike wooden structure called the Wigwam. William H. Seward was by far the best known of the contenders. But his radical utterances, including his "irrepressible conflict" speech at Rochester in 1858, had fatally injured his prospects.* His numerous enemies coined the slogan "Success Rather than Seward." Lincoln, the favorite son of Illinois, was definitely a "Mr. Second Best," but he was a stronger candidate because he had made fewer enemies. Overtaking Seward on the third ballot, he was nominated amid scenes of the wildest excitement.

The Republican platform had a seductive appeal for just about every important non-Southern group. For the free-soilers, non-extension of slavery; for the Northern manufacturers, a protective tariff; for the immigrants, no abridgment of rights; for the Northwest, a Pacific railroad; for the West, internal improvements at federal expense; and for the farmers, free homesteads from the public domain. Seductive slogans were "Vote Yourselves a Farm" and "Land for the Landless."

Southern secessionists promptly served notice that the election of the "baboon" Lincoln—the "abolitionist" rail splitter—would split the Union. "Honest Abe," though hating slavery, was no abolitionist. But he saw fit, perhaps mistakenly, to issue no statements to quiet Southern fears. He had already put himself on record; and fresh statements might stir up fresh antagonisms.

As the election campaign ground noisily forward, Lincoln enthusiasts staged roaring rallies and parades, complete with pitch-dripping torches and oilskin capes. They extolled "High Old Abe," the "Woodchopper of the West," and the "Little Giant Killer," while groaning dismally for "Poor Little Doug." Enthusiastic "Little Giants" and

*Seward had referred to an "irrepressible conflict" between slavery and freedom, though not necessarily a bloody one.

A Republican Campaign Caricature. Douglas is represented as a pious character prepared to bury Lincoln politically. (*Vanity Fair*, 1860.)

"Little Dougs" retorted with "We want a statesman, not a rail splitter, as President." Douglas himself waged a vigorous speaking campaign, even in the South, and threatened to put the hemp with his own hands around the neck of the first secessionist.

The returns, breathlessly awaited, proclaimed a sweeping victory for Lincoln (see table below).

The Electoral Upheaval of 1860

Awkward "Abe" Lincoln had run a curious race. To a greater degree than any other President (except J. Q. Adams), he was a minority President. Sixty percent of the voters preferred some other candidate. He was also a sectional President, for in ten Southern states, where he was not allowed on the ballot, he polled no popular votes. The election of 1860 was virtually two elections: one in the North, the other in the South. South Carolinians rejoiced over Lincoln's victory; they now had their excuse to secede. In winning the North the "Rail Splitter" had split off the South.

Douglas, though scraping together only 12 electoral votes, made an impressive showing. He drew important strength from all sections, and ranked a fairly close second in the popular-vote column. In fact, the Douglas Democrats and the Breckinridge Democrats together amassed 366,484 more votes than Lincoln.

A myth persists that if the Democrats had only united behind Douglas, they would have triumphed. Yet the cold figures tell a different story. Even if the "Little Giant" had received all the electoral votes cast for all three of Lincoln's opponents, the "Rail Splitter" would have won, 169 to 134, instead of 180 to 123. Lincoln still would have carried the populous states of the North and the Northwest. On the other hand, if the Democrats had not broken up, they could have entered the campaign with higher enthusiasm and better organization, and might have won.

Significantly, the verdict of the ballot box did not indicate a strong sentiment for secession. Breckinridge, while favoring the extension of slavery, was no disunionist. Although the candidate of the "fire-eaters," in the slave states he polled fewer votes than the combined strength of his opponents, Douglas and Bell. He even failed to carry his own Kentucky.

Yet the South, despite its electoral defeat, was not badly off. It still had a five-to-four majority on

Election of 1860

Candidate	Popular Vote	Percentage of Popular Vote	Electoral Vote
Lincoln	1,867,198	39.79%	180 (every vote of the free states except for 3 of New Jersey's 7 votes)
Douglas	1,379,434	29.40	12 (only Missouri and 3 of New Jersey's 7 votes)
Breckinridge	854,248	18.20	72 (all the cotton states)
Bell	591,658	12.61	39 (Virginia, Kentucky, Tennessee)

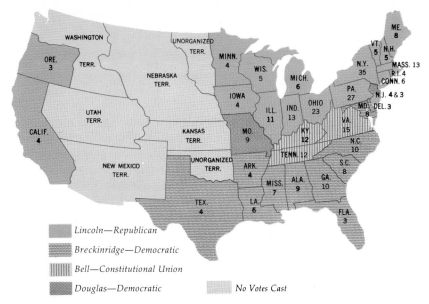

PRESIDENTIAL ELECTION OF 1860
(with electoral vote by state)
A surprising fact is that Lincoln, often rated among the greatest Presidents, ranks near the bottom in percentage of popular votes. In all the eleven states that seceded, he received only a scattering of one state's votes—about 1.5 percent in Virginia.

Lincoln—Republican
Breckinridge—Democratic
Bell—Constitutional Union
Douglas—Democratic   No Votes Cast

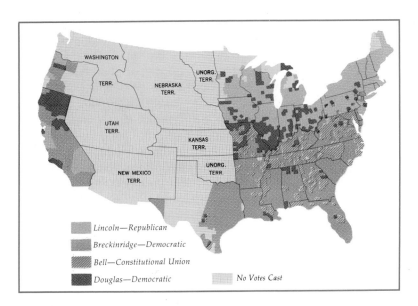

PRESIDENTIAL ELECTION OF 1860
(showing popular vote by county)
Note that the vote by counties for Lincoln was virtually all cast in the North. The Northern Democrat, Douglas, was also nearly shut out in the South, which divided its votes between Breckinridge and Bell. (Note that only citizens of states could vote; inhabitants of territories could not.)

Lincoln—Republican
Breckinridge—Democratic
Bell—Constitutional Union
Douglas—Democratic   No Votes Cast

the Supreme Bench. Although the Republicans had elected Lincoln, they controlled neither the Senate nor the House of Representatives. The federal government could not touch slavery in those states where it existed except by a constitutional amendment, and such an amendment could be defeated by one-fourth of the states. The fifteen slave states numbered nearly one-half of the total—a fact not fully appreciated by Southern hotheads.

The Secessionist Exodus

A tragic chain reaction of secession now began to explode. South Carolina, which had threatened to go out if the "sectional" Lincoln came in, was as good as her word. Four days after the election of the "Illinois Baboon" by "insulting" majorities, her legislature voted unanimously to call a special convention. Meeting at Charleston in December 1860, it unanimously voted to secede. During

President Jefferson Davis (1808–1889). Faced with grave difficulties, he was probably as able a man for the position as the Confederacy could have chosen. The Davis family had moved south from Kentucky; the Lincoln family, north. If the migrations had been reversed, the presidential roles might have been reversed, as some have speculated. (Library of Congress.)

Three days after Lincoln's election, Horace Greeley's influential New York *Tribune* (November 9, 1860) had declared: "If the cotton States shall decide that they can do better out of the Union than in it, we insist on letting them go in peace. The right to secede may be a revolutionary one, but it exists nevertheless. . . . Whenever a considerable section of our Union shall deliberately resolve to go out, we shall resist all coercive measures designed to keep it in. We hope never to live in a republic, whereof one section is pinned to the residue by bayonets." After the secession movement got well under way, Greeley's *Tribune* changed its tune.

the next six weeks, six other states of the lower South, though somewhat less united, followed South Carolina over the precipice. Four more were to join them later, bringing the total to eleven.

With the eyes of destiny upon them, the seven seceders, formally meeting at Montgomery, Alabama, created a government known as the Confederate States of America. As their president they chose Jefferson Davis, a dignified and austere recent member of the United States Senate from Mississippi. He was a West Pointer and a former Cabinet member with wide military and administrative experience; but he suffered from chronic ill-health, as well as from a frustrated ambition to be a Napoleonic strategist.

The crisis, already critical enough, was deepened by the "lame duck"* interlude. Lincoln,

---

*The "lame duck" period was shortened to ten weeks in 1933 by the 20th Amendment (See Appendix).

although elected President in November 1860, could not take office until four months later, March 4, 1861. During this period of protracted uncertainty, when he was still a private citizen in Illinois, seven of the eleven deserting states pulled out of the Union.

President Buchanan, the aging incumbent, has been blamed for not holding the seceders in the Union by sheer force—for wringing his hands instead of secessionist necks. Never a vigorous man and habitually conservative, he was now nearly seventy, and although devoted to the Union, he was surrounded by pro-Southern advisers. As an able bachelor-lawyer wedded to the Constitution, he did not believe that the Southern states could legally secede. Yet he could find no authority in the Constitution for stopping them with guns.

"Oh for one hour of Jackson!" cried the advocates of strong-arm tactics. But "Old Buck" Buchanan was not "Old Hickory," and he was faced with a far more complex and serious problem. One important reason why he did not resort to force was that the tiny standing army of some 15,000 men, then widely scattered, was urgently needed to control the Indians in the West. Public

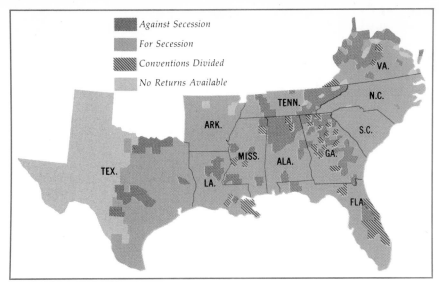

SOUTHERN OPPOSITION TO SECESSION, 1860–1861 (showing vote by county) This county vote shows the opposition of the anti-planter, anti-slavery mountain whites in the Appalachian region. There was also considerable resistance to secession in Texas, where Governor Sam Houston, who led the Unionists, was deposed by secessionist hotheads.

opinion in the North, at that time, was far from willing to unsheathe the sword. Fighting would merely shatter all prospects of adjustment, and until the guns began to boom there was still a flickering hope of reconciliation rather than a contested divorce. The weakness lay not so much in Buchanan as in the Constitution and in the Union itself. Ironically, when Lincoln became President, he continued essentially Buchanan's wait-and-see policy.

The Collapse of Compromise

Impending bloodshed spurred final and frantic attempts at compromise—in the American tradition. The most promising of these efforts was sponsored by Senator Crittenden of Kentucky, on whose shoulders had fallen the mantle of a fellow Kentuckian, Henry Clay.

The proposed Crittenden amendments to the Constitution were designed to appease the South. Slavery in the territories was to be prohibited north of 36°30′, but south of that line it was to be given federal protection in all territories existing or "hereafter to be acquired" (such as Cuba). Future states, north or south of 36°30′, could come into the Union with or without slavery, as they should choose. In short, the slavery men were

to be guaranteed full rights in the southern territories, as long as they were territories, regardless of the wishes of the majority under popular sovereignty. Federal protection in a territory south of 36°30′ might conceivably, though improbably, turn the entire area permanently to slavery.

Lincoln flatly rejected the Crittenden scheme, which offered some slight prospect of success, and all hope of compromise fled. For this refusal he must bear a heavy responsibility. Yet he had been elected on a platform that opposed the extension

One reason why the Crittenden Compromise failed in December 1860 was the prevalence of an attitude reflected in a private letter of Senator Hammond of South Carolina on April 19: "I firmly believe that the slave-holding South is now the controlling *power* of the world—that no other power would face us in hostility. Cotton, rice, tobacco, and naval stores command the world; and we have sense to know it, and are sufficiently Teutonic to carry it out successfully. The North without us would be a motherless calf, bleating about, and die of mange and starvation."

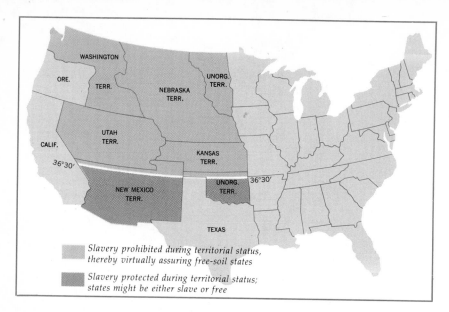

PROPOSED CRITTENDEN
COMPROMISE, 1860
Stephen A. Douglas claimed that "if
the Crittenden proposition could have
been passed early in the session [of
Congress], it would have saved all the
States, except South Carolina." But
Crittenden's proposal was doomed—
Lincoln opposed it, and Republicans
cast not a single vote in its favor.

WASHINGTON

ORE.

TERR.

UNORG.
TERR.

NEBRASKA
TERR.

UTAH
TERR.

CALIF.

36°30'

KANSAS
TERR.

36°30'

NEW MEXICO
TERR.

UNORG.
TERR.

TEXAS

*Slavery prohibited during territorial status,
thereby virtually assuring free-soil states*

*Slavery protected during territorial status;
states might be either slave or free*

of slavery, and he felt that as a matter of principle he could not afford to yield, even though gains for slavery in the territories might be only temporary. Larger gains might come later in Cuba and Mexico.

As for the supposedly spineless "Old Fogy" Buchanan, how could he have prevented the Civil War by starting a civil war? No one has yet come up with a satisfactory answer. If he had used force on South Carolina in December 1860, the fighting almost certainly would have erupted three months sooner than it did, and under less favorable circumstances for the Union. The North would have appeared as the heavy-handed aggressor. And the crucial Border States, so vital to the Union, probably would have been driven into the arms of their "wayward sisters."

"Wretched Condition of the Old Party at the White House." Buchanan is hard pressed between Southern threats of violence and Northern reminders of his obligation to uphold the Constitution. (*Harper's Weekly*, 1861.)

Farewell to Union

Secessionists who parted company with their sister states left for a number of avowed reasons, mostly relating in some way to slavery. They were alarmed by the inexorable tipping of the political balance against them—"the despotic majority of numbers." The "crime" of the North, observed James Russell Lowell, was the census returns. Southerners were also dismayed by the triumph of the new sectional Republican party, which seemed to threaten their rights as a slaveholding minority. They were weary of free-soil criticism, abolitionist nagging, and Northern interference, ranging from the Underground Railroad to John Brown's raid. "All we ask is to be let alone," declared president Jefferson Davis in an early message to his congress.

Many Southerners supported secession because they felt sure that their departure would be unopposed, despite "Yankee yawp" to the contrary. They were confident that the clodhopping and codfishing Yankee would not or could not fight. They believed that Northern manufacturers and bankers, so heavily dependent on Southern cotton and markets, would not dare to cut their own economic throats with their own swords. But should war come, the immense debt owed to Northern creditors by the South—happy thought—could be promptly repudiated, as it later was.

Southern leaders regarded secession as a golden opportunity to cast aside their generations of "vassalage" to the North. An independent Dixieland could develop its own banking and shipping, and trade directly with Europe. The low Tariff of 1857, which had been passed largely by Southern votes, was not in itself menacing. But who could tell when the "greedy" Republicans would win control of Congress and drive through an oppressive protective tariff of their own? For decades there had been this fundamental friction between the North, with its manufacturing plants, and the South, with its agrarian economy.

Worldwide impulses of nationalism—then stirring in Italy, Germany, Poland, and elsewhere—were fermenting in the South. This huge area, with its distinctive culture, was not so much a section as a sub-nation. It could not view with complacency the possibility of being lorded over, then or later, by what it regarded as a hostile nation of Northerners.

The principles of self-determination—of the Declaration of Independence—seemed to many Southerners to apply perfectly to them. Few, if any, of the seceders felt that they were doing anything wrong or immoral. The thirteen original states had voluntarily entered the Union and now seven—ultimately eleven—Southern states were voluntarily withdrawing from it.

Historical parallels ran even deeper. In 1776, thirteen American colonies, led by the rebel George Washington, had seceded from the British Empire by throwing off the yoke of King George. In 1860–1861, eleven American states, led by the rebel Jefferson Davis, were seceding from the Union by throwing off the yoke of "King" Abraham Lincoln. With that burden gone, the South was confident that it could work out its own peculiar destiny more quietly, happily, and prosperously.

IOIIOIIOIIOIIOIIOIIOIIOIIOIIOIIOIIOIIOIIOIIOIIOIIOIIOIIOIIOIIOI

James Russell Lowell, the Northern poet and essayist, wrote in the *Atlantic Monthly* shortly after the secessionist movement began: "The fault of the free States in the eyes of the South is not one that can be atoned for by any yielding of special points here and there. Their offence is that they are free, and that their habits and prepossessions are those of freedom. Their crime is the census of 1860. Their increase in numbers, wealth, and power is a standing aggression. It would not be enough to please the Southern States that we should stop asking them to abolish slavery: what they demand of us is nothing less than that we should abolish the spirit of the age. Our very thoughts are a menace."

IOIIOIIOIIOIIOIIOIIOIIOIIOIIOIIOIIOIIOIIOIIOIIOIIOIIOIIOIIOIIOI

VARYING VIEWPOINTS

Few issues have generated as much heat among American historians as the causes of the War for Southern Independence. The very names chosen to describe the conflict—notably "Civil War" or "War Between the States"—reveal much about various authors' points of view. Opinions have naturally differed according to section, but in general the appraisals of the war have gone through four phases.

The so-called nationalist school in the late 19th Century found slavery and Union to be the fundamental causes of the bloodletting, and approved the war because it ended slavery and preserved the Union. In the early 20th Century, some writers, notably Charles Beard, argued that the war was not about slavery per se, but about the basic economic conflict between an industrial North and an agricultural South. Yet if there had been no slavery there would have been no Civil War, at least not in 1861.

After the disappointing results of World War I, some historians argued that the Civil War itself had been a great mistake, traceable not to any fundamentally "irreconcilable conflict," whether racial or economic, but to the breakdown of political institutions and the ineptitude of a blundering generation of leaders. But since World War II, a "neo-nationalist" view has generally prevailed. It pictures the Civil War as an all-but-inevitable clash between two cultures and two sets of social values, ending in victory for the forces of virtue and progress.

SELECT READINGS

Refer to the previous chapter for the titles by Nichols, Randall and Donald, and Craven. Richly detailed is Allan Nevins, *The Emergence of Lincoln* (2 vols., 1950). David Donald, *Charles Sumner and the Coming of the Civil War* (1960), is an outstanding biography. See also his able *Charles Sumner and the Rights of Man* (1970). Lincoln's rise is developed in Don E. Fehrenbacher's *Prelude to Greatness* (1962), and in Carl Sandburg's *Abraham Lincoln: The Prairie Years* (2 vols., 1926). Consult also Benjamin Quarles, *Lincoln and the Negro* (1962). Stanley W. Campbell describes *The Slave Catchers: Enforcement of the Fugitive Slave Law, 1840–1860* (1968). The explosive Kansas issue is dealt with in James A. Rawley, *Race and Politics: "Bleeding Kansas" and the Coming of the Civil War* (1969), and in Paul W. Gates, *Fifty Million Acres: Conflicts over Kansas Land Policy, 1854–1890* (1954). On the Lincoln-Douglas debates see H. V. Jaffa, *Crisis of the House Divided* (1959). Don E. Fehrenbacher brilliantly and thoroughly dissects *The Dred Scott Case* (1978). P. S. Klein, in *President James Buchanan* (1962), does his subject belated justice. The final moments before the fighting began are scrutinized in David Potter, *Lincoln and His Party in the Secession Crisis* (1942), and in K. M. Stampp, *And the War Came* (1950). The Southern side of the question appears in Steven A. Channing, *Crisis of Fear: Secession of South Carolina* (1970), W. L. Barney, *The Secessionist Impulse: Alabama and Mississippi* (1974), W. J. Evitts, *A Matter of Allegiances: Maryland from 1850 to 1861* (1974), and R. A. Wooster, *The Secessionist Conventions of the South* (1962). See also Michael P. Johnson, *Toward a Patriarchal Republic: The Secession of Georgia* (1977). Stephen B. Oates paints a vivid portrait of John Brown in *To Purge This Land with Blood* (1970). Thomas J. Pressley reviews the copious literature about the war in *Americans Interpret their Civil War* (1954). George Forgie offers a psychoanalytical explanation of the coming of the war in *Patricide in the House Divided: A Psychological Interpretation of Lincoln and His Age* (1979).

22

The War for Southern Independence

My paramount object in this struggle is to save the Union, and is not either to save or to destroy slavery.

ABRAHAM LINCOLN, 1862

President of the Disunited States of America

Abraham Lincoln solemnly took the oath of office on March 4, 1861, after having slipped into Washington at night, partially disguised to thwart assassins. He thus became President, not of the *United* States of America, but of the disunited states of America. Seven had departed; eight more were teetering on the edge. The girders of the unfinished Capitol dome loomed nakedly in the background, as if to symbolize the imperfect state of the Union.

Lincoln's inaugural address was firm yet conciliatory: there would be no conflict unless the South provoked it. Secession, the President declared, was wholly impracticable, because "Physically speaking, we cannot separate."

Here Lincoln put his finger on a profound geographical truth. The North and South were Siamese twins, bound inseparably together. If they had been divided by the Pyrenees Mountains or the Danube River, a sectional divorce would have been more feasible. But the Appalachian Mountains and the mighty Mississippi River both ran the wrong way.

Uncontested secession would only create new controversies. What share of the national debt should the South be forced to take with it? What portion of the jointly held federal territories, if any, should the Confederate states be allotted—areas so largely purchased with Southern blood? How would the fugitive-slave issue be dealt with? The Underground Railroad would certainly redouble its activity, and it would have to transport its passengers only across the Ohio River, not all the way to Canada. Was it conceivable that all such problems could have been solved without ugly armed clashes?

A united United States had hitherto been the top-dog republic in the Western Hemisphere. If this powerful democracy should break into two hostile parts, the European nations would be delighted. They could gleefully transplant to America their hoary concept of the balance of power. Playing the no less hoary game of divide and conquer, they could incite one snarling fragment of the dis-United States against the other. The colonies of the European powers in the New World, notably those of Britain, would thus be made safer against the rapacious Yankees. And European imperialists, with no unified republic to stand across their path, could the more easily defy the Monroe Doctrine and seize territory in the Americas.

Lincoln's Contentious Cabinet

A greedy horde of hungry office seekers, elbowing for the patronage gravy trough, overwhelmed Lincoln at the very outset. At a time when he needed a clear mind for pressing affairs of state, he was forced to worry about the "postmastership at Podunk." There were, in his earthy phrase, "too many hogs for the tits."

Secretary William H. Seward (1801–1872). Seward was a senator, a secretary of state, and the purchaser of Alaska ("Seward's Folly"), where both a peninsula and a city were named after him. (National Archives.)

The Cabinet was dominated by Lincoln's former rivals for the presidential nomination. Headstrong and egotistical William H. Seward, the front-running contender at Chicago in 1860, was of necessity made secretary of state. He regarded himself as a kind of prime minister, but after some difficulty Lincoln tactfully put him in his place. Happily, Seward turned out to be one of the abler secretaries of state.

Other Cabinet members were likewise problem children. The secretary of the treasury was a leading abolitionist, Salmon P. Chase of Ohio. A massive, handsome man, he was self-righteous, opinionated, and constantly stung by the presidential bee buzzing in his bonnet. The original secretary of war, Simon Cameron, became involved in graft, and was succeeded by bulldog-like Edwin M. Stanton, stocky, black-haired, and asthmatic. Though tireless and decisive, he was arrogant, irascible, vindictive, and double-dealing. A Democrat and a more distinguished lawyer than Lincoln, he had savagely criticized the "imbecility" of his future chief, whom he dubbed the "original gorilla."

Unhappily the Cabinet was never completely harmonious or loyal to the President. A minor civil war within his official family was but one of

Secretary of State Seward entertained the dangerous idea that if the North picked a fight with one or more European nations, the South would once more rally around the flag. On April Fool's Day, 1861, he submitted to Lincoln a memorandum recommending:

"I would demand explanations from Spain and France, categorically, at once. I would seek explanations from Great Britain and Russia. . . . And, if satisfactory explanations are not received from Spain and France . . . would convene Congress and declare war against them."

Lincoln quietly but firmly quashed Seward's scheme.

the many crosses that Lincoln had to bear while prosecuting the larger Civil War.

The South Assails Fort Sumter

The plight of the federal forts had meanwhile partially overshadowed political squabbles. As the seceding states left, they had seized the United States arsenals, mints, and other public property within their borders. When Lincoln took office, only two significant forts in the South still flew the Stars and Stripes. The more important of the pair was square-walled Fort Sumter, in Charleston Harbor, with fewer than 100 men.

Ominously the choices presented to Lincoln by Fort Sumter were all bad. This stronghold had provisions that would last only a few weeks—until the middle of April 1861. If no supplies were forthcoming, its commander would have to surrender without firing a shot. Lincoln, quite understandably, did not feel that such a weak-kneed course squared with his obligation to protect federal property. But if he sent reinforcements, the South Carolinians would undoubtedly fight back; they could not tolerate a federal fort blocking the mouth of their most important Atlantic seaport.

After agonizing indecision, Lincoln adopted a middle-of-the-road solution. He notified the South Carolinians that an expedition would be sent to *provision* the garrison, though not to *reinforce* it. But in Southern eyes "provision" spelled "reinforcement."

A Union naval force was next started on its way to Fort Sumter—a move that the South regarded as an act of aggression. On April 12, 1861, the cannon of the Carolinians opened fire on the fort, while crowds in Charleston applauded and waved handkerchiefs. After a thirty-four-hour bombardment, which took no life, the dazed garrison surrendered.

The firing on the fort electrified the North, which at once responded with cries of "Remember Fort Sumter" and "Save the Union." Hitherto countless Northerners had been saying that if the Southern states wanted to go, they should not be pinned to the rest of the nation with bayonets.

"A House Divided Against Itself Cannot Stand."
Contemporary cartoon of Lincoln.

"Wayward sisters, depart in peace" was a common sentiment, expressed even by the commander of the army, war hero General Winfield Scott, now so old at seventy-five that he had to be boosted onto his horse.

But the assault on Fort Sumter provoked the North to a fighting pitch: the fort was lost but the Union was saved. Lincoln had contrived to win a great strategic victory. Southerners had wantonly fired upon the glorious Stars and Stripes, and honor demanded an armed response. Lincoln promptly (April 15) issued a call to the states for 75,000 militiamen; and volunteers sprang to the colors in such enthusiastic numbers that many were turned away—a mistake not often repeated. On April 19 and 27 the President proclaimed a leaky blockade of Southern seaports.

The call for troops, in turn, aroused the South much as the attack on Fort Sumter had aroused the North. Lincoln was now waging war—from the Southern view an aggressive war—on the Confederacy. Virginia, Arkansas, and Tennessee, all of which had earlier voted down secession, reluctantly joined their embattled sister states, as did North Carolina. Thus the seven became eleven as the "submissionists" and "Union shriekers" were

James L. Petigru, a South Carolinian, was one of the few prominent citizens of the state to oppose secession. When asked by a stranger in December 1860 where the insane asylum could be found, he pointed out the Baptist church, in which the secession convention had gathered. "It looks like a church," he said, "but it is now a lunatic asylum; go right there and you will find one hundred and sixty-four maniacs within." They voted unanimously for secession.

overcome. Yet Richmond in Virginia, replacing Montgomery in Alabama as the Confederate capital, was too near Washington for strategic comfort on either side.

Brothers' Blood and Border Blood

The only slave states left were the crucial Border States. This group consisted of Missouri, Kentucky, Maryland, Delaware, and later West Virginia—the "mountain white" area which somewhat

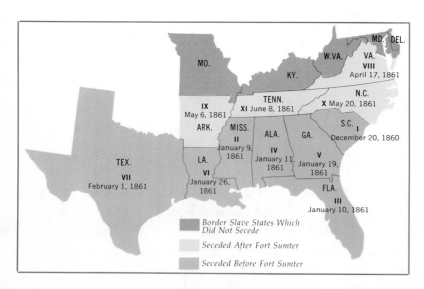

SECEDING STATES
(with dates and order of secession)
Note the long period of time between the secession of South Carolina, the first state to go, and that of Tennessee, the last state to leave the Union. These six months were a time of terrible trial for moderate Southerners. When a Georgia statesman pleaded for restraint and negotiations with Washington, he was rebuffed with the cry: "Throw the bloody spear into this den of incendiaries!"

illegally tore itself from the side of Virginia in mid-1861. If the North had fired the first shot, some or all of these doubtful states probably would have seceded, and the South might well have succeeded. The Border group actually boasted a white population more than half that of the entire Confederacy. Lincoln reportedly said that he hoped to have God on his side, but he had to have Kentucky.

In dealing with the Border States, the President did not rely solely on moral suasion but successfully used methods of dubious legality. In Maryland he declared martial law where needed and sent in troops, because this state threatened to cut off Washington from the North. He also deployed Union soldiers in western Virginia and notably in Missouri, where they fought beside Unionists in a local civil war within the larger Civil War.

Any official statement of the North's war aims was profoundly influenced by the teetering Border States. At the very outset, Lincoln was obliged to declare publicly that he was not fighting to free the blacks. An anti-slavery declaration would no doubt have driven the Border States into the welcoming arms of the South. Lincoln had to insist repeatedly—even though weakening his moral cause—that his primary purpose was to preserve the Union at all costs. Thus the war began not as one between slave soil and free soil, but one for the Union with slaveholders on both sides.

Unhappily, the conflict between "Billy Yank" and "Johnny Reb" was a brothers' war. There were many Northern volunteers from the Southern states, and many Southern volunteers from the Northern states. The "mountain whites" of the South sent north some 50,000 men, and the loyal slave states contributed some 300,000 soldiers to the Union. In many a family of the Border states, one brother rode north to fight with the Blue, another south to fight with the Gray. Senator Crittenden of Kentucky, who fathered the abortive Crittenden Compromise, fathered two sons: one became a general in the Union army, the other a general in the Confederate army.

Europe's Aristocracy Sticks Together

Confederates were inspirited by the open sympathy of Europe's ruling classes, with the conspicuous exception of Russia. The South could reasonably hope for mediation or armed intervention, which almost came. At the very least, it could expect the sale of weapons, warships, and supplies, all of which did come.

Why were the upper classes of Western Europe so favorably disposed to the Confederacy? They had from the beginning abhorred the incendiary example of the American democratic experiment, and were overjoyed to see the long-smoking chimney at last "take fire." Moreover, the semi-feudal, aristocratic elements, especially in England, had long cherished something of a fellow feeling for the semi-feudal, aristocratic society of the South. The Foreign Offices of both Britain and France, reflecting these pro-Southern sentiments, naturally welcomed the breakup of the fast-growing and ever-threatening United States.

Leaders of British industrial and commercial life likewise hailed the newly born Confederacy. For one thing, it would provide the long-coveted independent cotton supply. For another, it would increase the opportunities of British shippers and

"Oh, Ain't We Sorry!"   The cartoon shows what the tyrants of the Old World think of secession. Note that the royal group is doubled up with laughter. (*Harper's Weekly*, 1860.)

IOIIOIIOIIOIIOIIOIIOIIOIIOIIOIIOIIOIIOIIOIIOIIOIIOIIOI

> Regarding the Civil War, the London *Times* (Nov. 7, 1861) editorialized: "The contest is really for empire on the side of the North, and for independence on that of the South, and in this respect we recognize an exact analogy between the North and the Government of George III, and the South and the Thirteen Revolted Provinces."

IOIIOIIOIIOIIOIIOIIOIIOIIOIIOIIOIIOIIOIIOIIOIIOIIOIIOI

manufacturers to make profits from the South, without the hurdle of a Yankee protective tariff.

On the other hand, countless workingmen in England, and to some extent in France, were pulling or praying for the North. Many of them had read *Uncle Tom's Cabin*, and they sensed that a victory for the Union would result in freeing the slaves. The ending of human bondage anywhere would further dignify free labor everywhere.

The common folk in Britain could not yet cast the ballot, but they could cast the brick. Their certain hostility to any official intervention on behalf of the South evidently had a sobering effect on the British Cabinet. Thus the dead hands of Uncle Tom helped Uncle Sam by restraining the British and French ironclads from breaking the Union blockade.

Southern Assets

Both North and South were unready for war, as Americans are inclined to be. Each gained valuable experience from the other, and this fact partly explains why they battled so long on relatively even terms.

The South had only to fight defensively, behind interior lines, and hence needed fewer troops. The North had to invade the Confederacy, conquer it, and drag it back bodily into the Union—a prodigious task involving an area about as large as all Western Europe south of Scandinavia. Indeed the South did not have to win the war to win its independence; it had merely to repulse or dis-

courage the invader. A draw would be a victory. The Confederate states would then be left independent—and this was all they really wanted.

Until the emancipation proclamations of 1862–1863, many observers conceded to the South the superior moral cause, despite the dark stain of slavery. It was fighting for self-determination, for self-government, for its peculiar social structure, for hearth and home, for fundamental freedoms (for whites, not slaves). Favorite slogans were "Death before Dishonor" and "For Our Altars and Our Firesides."

The South not only had talented officers but had them from the beginning. Conspicuous among the dozen or so first-rate leaders was General Robert E. Lee, with his florid face, graying hair, and knightly bearing. In poise, magnanimity, and sense of honor he embodied the Southern ideal. President Lincoln had unofficially offered him the command of the armies of the North, but when Virginia seceded Lee felt honor-bound to go along with his native state. His chief lieutenant was black-bearded and unpretentious young Thomas J. ("Stonewall") Jackson, a somewhat eccentric teacher of tactics and philosophy at the Virginia Military Institute. With his "foot cavalry," he was a master of speed and deception.

The North was much less fortunate. It was forced to use costly trial-and-error methods until it uncovered a general, in the person of Ulysses Simpson Grant, who would crunch his way to victory. The Union was further handicapped by numerous political officers, including the pompously incompetent General Benjamin F. ("Beast Ben") Butler, who aroused a storm by threatening harsh measures against the defiant women of New Orleans. His famous "woman order" decreed that females insulting his soldiers were to be jailed as common prostitutes. Their misbehavior stopped quickly.

Southern men were of a fighting breed. Accustomed to manage horses and bear arms from boyhood, they made excellent cavalrymen and foot soldiers. They were supremely self-confident, and their high-pitched "rebel yell" ("Yeeeahhhh") was designed to strike terror into the hearts of fuzz-chinned Yankee recruits known as "fresh fish." Yet the Northern "shopkeepers" and "clodhoppers" adjusted themselves surprisingly well to the rugged demands of military life. They may have been short on dash but they were long on discipline and determination.

Confederate Chances

The South, as primarily an immense farm, was severely hampered by the fewness of its factories. Yet it seized the weapons stored in federal arsenals when it seceded, and managed to sneak through the Union blockade an impressive mass of munitions. Displaying remarkable resourcefulness, the Southerners developed ironworks which, though limited, turned out much artillery. "Yankee ingenuity" was not confined to Yankees.

As the war dragged on, grave shortages developed among the Southerners in such necessities as shoes, uniforms, and blankets. There were immense stores of food in the South but the civilians and soldiers often went hungry. "Forward, men! They have cheese in their haversacks," was the reported cry of one Southern officer as he attacked the Yankees. Much of the hunger was caused by a breakdown of transportation, especially where the railroads were cut or destroyed by the Northern invader.

Formidable though all these handicaps were, the chances for Southern independence were unusually favorable. This was true even though

the Confederates had to start from scratch in building a government, an army, and a navy. As one Southern general remarked, never was a major revolution undertaken with better prospects of success. Certainly the thirteen colonies in 1776 had faced more hazardous odds.

The might-have-beens are fascinating. *If* the Border States had seceded, *if* the uncertain states of the upper Mississippi Valley had turned against the Union, *if* a wave of Northern defeatism had demanded an armistice, and *if* England and/or France had broken the blockade, the South probably would have won. All of these possibilities came close to realities, but none of them happened. Successful revolutions, including the American Revolution of 1776, have generally succeeded because of foreign intervention. The South counted on it, did not get it, and lost.

Yankee Advantages

The North was not only a huge farm but a sprawling factory as well—and wars were already being fought with both smokestacks and guns. Yankees boasted about three-fourths of the nation's wealth, including overwhelming superiority in manufacturing, shipping, and banking. The Union also possessed nearly three-fourths of the 30,000 miles (48,000 kilometers) of railroads. Not only did it have longer and better trackage, but it had abundant facilities for repair and replacement, all of which the South sorely lacked.

Additionally the North controlled the sea. With

Manufacturing by Sections, 1860

Section	Number of Establishments	Capital Invested	Average Number of Laborers	Annual Value of Products	Percentage of Total Value
New England	20,671	$ 257,477,783	391,836	$ 468,599,287	24%
Middle States	53,387	435,061,964	546,243	802,338,392	42
Western States	36,785	194,212,543	209,909	384,606,530	20
Southern States	20,631	95,975,185	110,721	155,531,281	8
Pacific States	8,777	23,380,334	50,204	71,229,989	3
Territories	282	3,747,906	2,333	3,556,197	1
	140,533	$1,009,855,715	1,311,246	$1,885,861,676	

Tredegar Iron Works, Richmond, Virginia. This was by far the most important of the Confederate iron works. Using skilled slave labor, this plant equipped the army with nearly 1,200 scarce cannons. Without these works, the Confederacy probably would have collapsed. Their presence in Richmond helps to explain why the South fought so hard to keep the city.

its vastly superior navy, it established a blockade that choked off the bulk of Southern exports and imports. This stoppage not only hampered the South economically and militarily, but finally shattered its morale. While strangling the Confederacy with one hand, the North could simultaneously keep open the sea lanes to Europe. It was thus able to exchange huge quantities of grain for munitions, and in this way it used the factories of Europe to supplement its own. During the early months of the war, the North imported many more firearms from abroad than it was able to manufacture at home.

Union forces likewise enjoyed a much larger reservoir of manpower. The loyal states had a population of some 22 million; the seceding states, 9 million. This latter figure included about 3.5 million slaves. The population advantage of the North was somewhat greater than 2 to 1, and the estimated enlistments ran 1,556,000 to 1,082,000. Manpower odds against General Lee were ordinarily about 3 to 2, sometimes 3 to 1. Such superior numbers usually gave the North the advantage of choosing the point of attack.

A broad stream of European immigrants con-

Lieutenant Porter and Soldiers. Union soldiers of the 4th Michigan Infantry. (Library of Congress.)

Immigration to U.S., 1860–1866

Year	Total	Britain	Ireland	Germany	All Others
1860	153,640	29,737	48,637	54,491	20,775
1861	91,918	19,675	23,797	31,661	16,785
1862	91,985	24,639	23,351	27,529	16,466
1863	176,282	66,882	55,916	33,162	20,322
1864	193,418	53,428	63,523	57,276	19,191
1865*	248,120	82,465	29,772	83,424	52,459
1866	318,568	94,924	36,690	115,892	71,062

*Only the first three months of 1865 were war months.

tinued to pour into the North, thanks to Northern control of the seas. Though slowed down a bit by the war, especially during the first two years, the inflow totaled over 800,000 newcomers of both sexes from 1861 through 1865—or more than the total casualties in the armed services of the North. The bulk of the new arrivals were British, Irish, and German; and large numbers of them were induced to enlist in the Union armies. Tens of thousands of earlier immigrants, inspired by a love of freedom and gratitude to their adopted land, likewise joined the colors. Altogether, about one-fifth of the Union forces were foreign-born. In one division, commands were given in four different languages; and some German units even had guttural-accented officers of their own nationality. Southerners branded foreign enlistees as "Hessians" or "Yankee Hessians."

The two most prominent German-American generals, Franz Sigel and Carl Schurz, were both refugees from the German revolutions of 1848. Sigel did yeoman work in saving Missouri, with its large German population, for the Union. Both generals suffered reverses, but Schurz, through no fault of his own, was routed. German-speaking soldiers, when asked whom they were serving with, would reply, "I fights mit Sigel and I runs mit Schurz."

Black Men Battle Bondage

Altogether about 180,000 blacks served in the Union armies, most of them from the slave states but many from the free-soil North. Blacks accounted for about 10 percent of the total enlistments in Union forces, on land or sea, and included two Massachusetts regiments raised largely through the efforts of the ex-slave Frederick Douglass.

Black volunteers were at first rejected. Race prejudice, fear of arming blacks, and a feeling that white men should fight their own war raised a forbidding hand. But as manpower ran low and emancipation was proclaimed, black enlistees

Frederick Douglass (c. 1817–1895). Born a slave in Maryland, Douglass escaped to the North and became the most prominent black abolitionist. Gifted as an orator, writer, and editor, he continued to battle for the civil rights of his people after emancipation. Near the end of a distinquished career he served as U.S. Minister to Haiti. (Library of Congress.)

Proud Black Soldiers of the Union Army. (Library of Congress.)

were welcomed, although at first they were not paid as well as the whites. Strangely enough, the blacks had to fight for the privilege of fighting for freedom.

Black fighting men unquestionably had their hearts in a war against slavery. They participated in about 500 engagements, major and minor, and received 22 Congressional Medals of Honor—the highest military award. Their casualties were ex-

In August 1863, Lincoln wrote to Grant that enlisting black soldiers "works doubly, weakening the enemy and strengthening us." In December 1863, he announced that "it is difficult to say they are not as good soldiers as any." In August 1864, he said, "Abandon all the posts now garrisoned by black men, take 150,000 [black] men from our side and put them in the battle-field or cornfield against us, and we would be compelled to abandon the war in three weeks."

tremely heavy; over 38,000 died, whether from battle, sickness, or reprisals by vengeful masters. A few were put to death as slaves in revolt, for not until 1864 did the South recognize them as prisoners of war. In later years many Southerners blamed their defeat on the "unfair" use of blacks and foreigners.

For reasons of pride, prejudice, and principle, the Confederacy could not bring itself to enlist slaves until a month before the war ended and then it was too late. Meanwhile tens of thousands were impressed into labor battalions, the building of fortifications, the supplying of armies, and other war-connected activities. Slaves moreover were "the stomach of the Confederacy," for they kept the farms going while the white men fought.

Ironically, the great mass of Southern slaves did little to help their Northern liberators, white or black. A thousand scattered torches in the hands of a thousand slaves would have brought the Southern soldiers home, and the war would have ended. Through the "grapevine," the blacks learned of Lincoln's Emancipation Proclamation. Yet the bulk of them, whether because of lethargy, loyalty, lack of leadership, or strict policing, did not cast off their chains. But tens of thousands revolted "with their feet," when they abandoned their plantations upon the arrival or imminent arrival of Union armies, with or without emancipation proclamations. About 25,000 joined Sherman's march through Georgia in 1864, and their presence in such numbers created problems of supply and discipline.

Rallying to the Flag of the Union

The ideal of Union was a tremendous asset to the North. This ideal was compounded largely of pride in the flag, in the past, and in the future. America could not hope to shame its monarchical critics and achieve its Manifest Destiny if it divided. The teachings of Webster and Clay had been driven home, as indicated by such popular Northern watchwords as "Union Forever" and "What God Hath Joined Let No Man Put Asunder." A rousing Northern song, widely sung since the 1850s, proudly proclaimed:

> The union of lakes, the union of lands,
>   The union of States none can sever,
> The union of hearts, the union of hands,
>   And the flag of our union forever.*

Devotion to the Union aroused the North with unexpected fury against the "flag of disunion," and helped to hold the Border States in line. The concept infused in the North the will to fight, and retained the Southerner-infiltrated states of the upper Mississippi Valley. Finally, the ideal provided the Northerners with the inspiring war cry of Union, until such time as the moral issue of slavery could be brought out into the open, as it was late in 1862.

Dethroning King Cotton

Textile mills in Britain were fatally dependent on Southern cotton, and the Confederates were supremely confident that the British fleet would be forced to break the blockade. Why did King Cotton fail them?

English manufacturers had on hand, when the shooting started in 1861, a heavy oversupply of fiber. The real pinch did not come until about a year and a half later, when thousands of hungry operatives were thrown out of work. But by this time Lincoln had announced his slave-emancipation policy, and the "wage slaves" of England were not going to demand a war for the slaveowners of the South.

The direst effects of the "cotton famine" in England were relieved in several ways. Hunger among unemployed workers was partially eased when certain kindhearted Americans sent over several cargoes of foodstuffs. As Union armies penetrated the South, they captured or bought considerable supplies of cotton and shipped them to England; and the Confederates also ran a limited quantity through the blockade. In ad-

---

*George P. Morris, "The Flag of Our Union."

As the Civil War neared the end of its third year, the London *Times* (Jan. 7, 1864) could boast: "We are as busy, as rich, and as fortunate in our trade as if the American war had never broken out, and our trade with the States had never been disturbed. Cotton was no King, notwithstanding the prerogatives which had been loudly claimed for him."

dition, the cotton growers of Egypt and India, responding to high prices, increased their output. Finally, booming war industries in England, which supplied both North and South, relieved unemployment.

King Wheat and King Corn—of the Northern agricultural royalty—proved to be more potent potentates than King Cotton. During these war years the North, blessed with ideal weather, produced bountiful crops of grain and harvested them with McCormick's mechanical reaper. In the same period the British suffered a series of bad harvests. They were forced to import huge quantities of grain from America, which happened to have the cheapest and most abundant supply. If the British had broken the blockade to get cotton, they would have provoked the North to war and would have cut off this precious granary. Unemployment for some seemed better than hunger for all. Hence one Yankee journal could exult:

> Wave the stars and stripes high o'er us,
> Let every freeman sing . . .
> Old King Cotton's dead and buried:
>   brave young Corn is King.

President Davis versus President Lincoln

The Confederate government, like King Cotton, betrayed fatal weaknesses. Its constitution, borrowing liberally from that of the Union, had one deadly defect. Created by secession, it could not logically deny future secession to its states. Jefferson Davis, while making his bow to states' rights, had in view a well-knit central government. But determined states'-rights men fought him bitterly to the end. The Richmond regime even encountered difficulty in persuading certain state troops to serve outside their own borders. Governor Brown of Georgia, a belligerent states'-righter, at times seemed ready to secede from the secession and fight both sides. States' rights were actually more damaging to the Confederacy than Yankee sabers.

Sharp-featured President Davis—tense, humorless, legalistic, stubborn—was repeatedly in hot water. Though an eloquent orator and an able administrator, he at no time enjoyed real personal popularity, and was often at loggerheads with

President Davis, the Acrobat, on Rope of Cotton. The "Confederacy" is a fuse bomb, the flag reads, "Let Us Alone," a Davis theme. The cotton rope is unraveling.

his congress. At times there was serious talk of impeachment. Unlike Lincoln, Davis was somewhat imperious and inclined to defy rather than lead public opinion. Suffering acutely from neuralgia and other nervous disorders (including a tic) he overworked himself with the details of both civil government and military operations. No one could doubt his courage, sincerity, integrity, and devotion to the South, but the task proved beyond his powers. It was probably beyond the powers of any mortal man.

Lincoln also had his troubles, but on the whole they were less prostrating. The North enjoyed the prestige of a long-established government, financially stable and fully recognized both at home and abroad. Lincoln, the inexperienced prairie politician, proved superior to the more experienced but less flexible Jefferson Davis. Able to relax with droll stories at critical times, "Old Abe" grew as the war dragged on. Tactful, quiet, patient, yet firm, he developed a genius for interpreting and leading a fickle public opinion. Holding aloft the banner of Union with inspiring utterances, he revealed charitableness toward the South and forbearance toward backbiting colleagues. "Did [Secretary] Stanton say I was a damned fool?" he reportedly replied to a talebearer. "Then I dare say I must be one, for Stanton is generally right and he always says what he means."

Strangulation of the South by Sea

As finally developed, the general plan of Northern attack had four phases. First, slowly suffocate the South by blockading its coasts. Second, cut it in half by seizing control of the Mississippi River backbone. Third, chop it to pieces (a later idea) by sending troops through Georgia, and then north into the Carolinas. Fourth, strangle it by capturing its capital (Richmond), and by pounding its remaining armies into submission. The overall strategy called for slowly beating down the enemy rather than delivering a knockout punch.

The blockade started leakily: it was not clamped

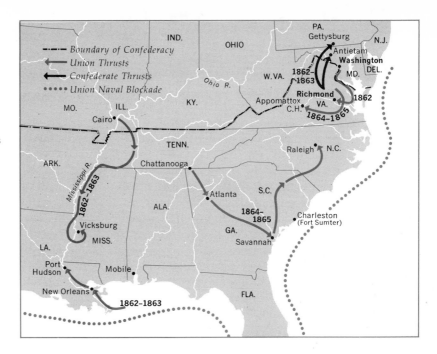

MAIN THRUSTS, 1861–1865
Northern strategists at first believed that
the rebellion could be snuffed out quickly
by a swift, crushing blow. But the stiffness
of Southern resistance to the Union's
early probes revealed that the conflict
would be a war of attrition, long and
bloody.

down all at once, but was extended by degrees.
An airtight patrol of some 3,500 miles (5,635 kilometers) of coast was impossible for the hastily improvised Northern navy, which consisted partly of
converted yachts and ferryboats. But blockading
was simplified by concentrating on the principal
ports and inlets. Only at such places were dock
facilities available for loading bulky bales of
cotton.

How was the blockade regarded by the naval
powers of the world? Ordinarily, they probably
would have defied it, for it was never completely
effective, and was especially sievelike at the outset.
But England, the greatest maritime nation, recognized it as binding, and warned her shippers that
they ignored it at their peril. An explanation is
easy. Blockade happened to be the chief offensive
weapon of Britain, which was still Mistress of
the Seas. She plainly did not want to tie her hands
in a future war by insisting that Lincoln maintain
impossibly high blockading standards.

Blockade-running soon became riskily profitable, as the growing scarcity of Southern goods
drove prices skyward. The most successful runners
were swift, gray-painted steamers, scores of which

were specially built in Scotland. A leading rendez-
vous was the West Indian port of Nassau, in the
British Bahamas, where at one time thirty-five
of the speedy ships were counted. The low-lying
craft would take on cargoes of arms brought in
by tramp steamers from England, leave with fraudulent papers for "Halifax" (Canada), and return a
few days later with a cargo of cotton. The risks
were great, but the profits would mount to 700
percent and more for lucky gamblers. Two successful voyages might well pay for capture on a

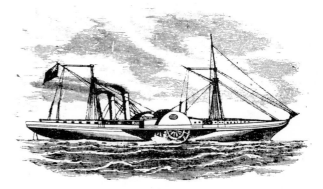

Confederate Blockade Runner. (Courtesy of The New
York Public Library, Astor, Lenox and Tilden Foundations.)

third. The lush days of blockade-running finally passed as Union squadrons gradually pinched off the leading Southern ports, from New Orleans to Charleston.

The Northern navy enforced the blockade with high-handed practices. Yankee captains, for example, would seize British freighters on the high seas, if laden with war supplies for the tiny port of Nassau and other halfway stations. The justification was that obviously these shipments were "ultimately" destined, by devious routes, for the Confederacy.

London, although not happy, acquiesced in this disagreeable doctrine of "ultimate destination" or "continuous voyage." British blockaders might find such a farfetched interpretation highly useful in a future war—as in fact they did in the World War of 1914–1918.

The most alarming Confederate threat to the blockade came in 1862. Resourceful Southerners raised and reconditioned a former wooden United States warship, the *Merrimack*, and plated its sides with old iron railroad rails. Renamed the *Virginia*, this clumsy but powerful monster easily destroyed two wooden ships of the Union navy in the Virginia waters of Chesapeake Bay; it also threatened

When news reached Washington that the *Merrimack* had sunk two wooden Yankee warships with ridiculous ease, President Lincoln, much "excited," summoned his advisers. Secretary of the Navy Welles records: "The most frightened man on that gloomy day . . . was the Secretary of War [Stanton]. He was at times almost frantic. . . . The *Merrimack*, he said, would destroy every vessel in the service, could lay every city on the coast under contribution, could take Fortress Monroe. . . . Likely the first movement of the *Merrimack* would be to come up the Potomac and disperse Congress, destroy the Capitol and public buildings."

catastrophe to the entire Yankee blockading fleet. (Actually the homemade ironclad was not a seaworthy craft.)

A tiny Union ironclad, the *Monitor*, built in about 100 days, arrived on the scene in the nick of time. For four hours, on March 9, 1862, the little "Yankee cheesebox on a raft" fought the wheezy *Merrimack* to a standstill. Britain and France had already built several powerful ironclads, but the first battle-testing of these new craft heralded the doom of wooden warships. A few months after the historic battle, the Confederates destroyed the *Merrimack* to keep her from the grasp of advancing Union troops.

The Runners of Bull Run

By the summer of 1861, a Union army of some 30,000 men was being drilled near Washington. It was ill-prepared for battle, but Northern newspaper editors, eager to end the war in a hurry, raised the cry, "On to Richmond!" Proddings by the press and public finally forced action, contrary to the better judgment of some of the generals. This was a classic example of the dangerous pressure that can be exerted by an ill-informed public.

Preliminaries of the clash at Bull Run, on July 21, 1861, seemed like those of a sporting event. The raw Yankee recruits marched or straggled from the capital, accompanied by congressmen, ladies, and others riding out with lunch baskets to see the fun. The ill-trained Union force encountered a smaller Confederate army at Bull Run (Manassas Junction), some 30 miles (48 kilometers) southwest of Washington. At first the battle went well for the Yankees. But "Stonewall" Jackson's gray-clad warriors stood like a stone wall (here he won his nickname), and Confederate reinforcements arrived unexpectedly. Panic suddenly seized the weary Union soldiers, many of whom fled in disgraceful confusion. The Confederates, too exhausted or too disorganized to pursue effectively, feasted on captured lunches.

The "military picnic" at Bull Run, though not decisive militarily, was significant psychologically.

Defeat was better than victory for the Union, because it dispelled all illusions of a one-punch war and caused the Northerners to buckle down to the staggering task at hand. Conversely, the victory was worse than a defeat for the South, because it inflated an already dangerous overconfidence. Many soldiers deserted, some boastfully to display their trophies, others sure that the war was over. Southern enlistments fell off sharply, and preparations for a protracted war slackened.

"Tardy George" McClellan

Northern hopes brightened later in 1861, when General George B. McClellan was given command of the Army of the Potomac, as the major Union force near Washington was now called. Red-haired and red-mustached, strong and stocky, McClellan was a brilliant, thirty-four-year-old West Pointer. As a serious student of warfare who was dubbed "Young Napoleon," he had seen plenty of fighting, first in the Mexican War and then as an observer of the Crimean War in Russia.

Cocky George McClellan embodied a curious mixture of virtues and defects. He was a superb organizer and drillmaster, and he injected splendid morale into the Army of the Potomac. Hating to sacrifice his troops, he was idolized by his men, who affectionately called him "Little Mac." But he was a perfectionist who seems not to have realized that an army is never ready to the last button, and that wars cannot be won without running some risks. He consistently but erroneously believed that the enemy outnumbered him, partly because his intelligence reports from the head of Pinkerton's Detective Agency were unreliable. He was overcautious—Lincoln once accused him of having "the slows"—and he addressed the President in an arrogant tone which a less forgiving person would never have tolerated. Privately the general referred to his Chief as a "baboon."

As McClellan discreetly continued to drill his army without moving it toward Richmond, the derisive Northern watchword became "All Quiet

Lincoln treated McClellan's demands for reinforcements and his excuses for inaction with infinite patience. One exception came when the general complained that his horses were tired. Lincoln wrote, "I have just read your dispatch about sore-tongued and fatigued horses. Will you pardon me for asking what the horses of your army have done since the battle of Antietam that fatigues anything?" (October 24, 1862)

along the Potomac." The song of the hour was "Tardy George" [McClellan]. After threatening to "borrow" the army if it was not going to be used, Lincoln finally issued firm orders to move.

A reluctant McClellan decided upon a waterborne flanking approach to Richmond. Choosing the route up the peninsula formed by the James and York Rivers, he warily advanced toward the city in the spring of 1862 with about 100,000 men. After taking a month to capture historic Yorktown, which bristled with imitation wooden can-

"Masterly Inactivity, or Six Months on the Potomac." McClellan and his Confederate foe view each other cautiously, while their troops engage in visiting, marrying, and sports. (*Frank Leslie's Illustrated Newspaper,* 1862.)

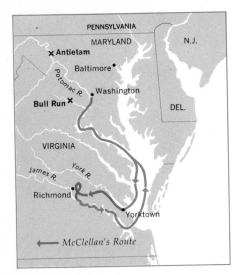

PENINSULAR CAMPAIGN, 1862

non, he finally came within sight of the spires of Richmond. Then General Lee suddenly struck with about 70,000 troops. Brilliantly assisted by "Stonewall" Jackson, he slowly drove McClellan back to his base on Chesapeake Bay. Although the Union army was still in fighting shape, the whole Peninsular Campaign was abandoned as a costly failure.

McClellan was now given a less active command, amid a storm of controversy. His enemies accused "Mac the Unready" of having moved too timorously. His defenders claimed that he would have captured Richmond if Lincoln had not withdrawn troops for the defense of Washington, which had been jeopardized by the lightning feints of General Jackson in the Shenandoah Valley. It is worth noting that McClellan was never decisively defeated, and that after the war Lee rated him the ablest of his many opponents.

A Union army near Washington, strengthened by units from McClellan's command, was now entrusted to overconfident General Pope. A handsome, dashing, soldierly figure, he boasted that in the Western theater, from which he had come, he had seen only the backs of the enemy. He quickly got a front view, for General Lee, at the

Second Battle of Bull Run (August 29–30, 1862), furiously attacked him and inflicted a crushing defeat. Gloom once more enshrouded the North.

The Antietam Pivotal Point

Lee now undertook a daring thrust into Maryland. He hoped to win a victory that would not only encourage foreign intervention, but also seduce this wavering Border State and her sisters from the Union. The Confederate troops sang lustily:

> Thou wilt not cower in the dust,
> Maryland! my Maryland!
> Thy gleaming sword shall never rust,
> Maryland! my Maryland!

But the Marylanders did not respond to the siren song. The presence among the invaders of so many blanketless, hatless, and shoeless soldiers dampened the state's ardor.

Events finally shaped up for a critical battle at Antietam Creek, Maryland. Lincoln, responding to popular pressures, hastily restored "Little Mac" to active command of the main Northern army. The soldiers tossed their caps into the air and hugged his horse as they hailed his return. At Antietam, on September 17, 1862, McClellan succeeded in halting Lee in one of the bitterest and bloodiest days of the war.

Antietam was more or less a draw militarily. But Lee, finding his thrust parried, retired across the Potomac. McClellan, from whom much more had been hoped, was removed from his field command for the second and final time. His numerous critics, condemning him for not having boldly pursued the ever-dangerous Lee, finally got his scalp.

The landmark Battle of Antietam was one of the decisive battles of world history—probably the most decisive of the Civil War. Jefferson Davis was perhaps never again so near victory as on that fateful summer day. The British and French governments were on the verge of diplomatic mediation, a species of interference sure to be

Confederate Corpses at Antietam. Unknown to Lee, who had dangerously divided his army, McClellan had somehow obtained a copy of the Confederate battle plan. The Union forces thus had a great tactical advantage, and the result was appalling slaughter. The twelve-hour fight at Antietam Creek ranks as the bloodiest day of the war, with more than ten thousand Confederate casualties, and even more on the Union side. ''At last the sun went down and the battle ended,'' one historian wrote, ''smoke heavy in the air, the twilight quivering with the anguished cries of thousands of wounded men.'' (Library of Congress.)

angrily resented by the North. An almost certain rebuff by Washington might well have spurred Paris and London into armed intervention. But both capitals cooled off when the Union displayed unexpected power at Antietam, and their chill deepened with the passing months.

Bloody Antietam was also the long-awaited ''victory'' which Lincoln needed for launching his Emancipation Proclamation. The abolitionists had long been clamoring for action: Wendell Phillips was denouncing the President as a ''first-rate second-rate man.'' By midsummer of 1862, with the Border States safely in the fold, Lincoln was ready to move. But he believed that to issue such an edict on the heels of a series of military disasters would be folly. It would seem like a confession that the North, unable to conquer the South, was forced to call upon the slaves to murder their masters. Lincoln therefore decided to await the outcome of Lee's invasion.

Antietam served as the needed emancipation springboard. The halting of Lee's offensive was just enough of a victory to justify Lincoln's issuing, on September 23, 1862, the preliminary Emancipation Proclamation. This hope-giving document announced that on January 1, 1863, the President would issue a final proclamation. On the scheduled date he fully redeemed his promise, and the Civil War became more of a moral crusade.

A Proclamation Without Emancipation

Lincoln's Emancipation Proclamation of 1863 declared ''forever free'' the slaves in those Confederate states still in rebellion. The blacks in the loyal Border States were not affected, nor were those in specific conquered areas in the South—all told, about 800,000. The tone of the document was dull and legalistic: there was no clarion call for a holy war to achieve freedom. Lincoln in fact is on record as favoring cash compensation to the owners of all slaves as late as February of 1865.

The presidential pen did not formally strike the shackles from a single slave. Where Lincoln could presumably free the slaves—that is, in the loyal Border States—he refused to do so, lest he spur disunion. Where he could not—that is, in the Confederate states—he tried to. In short, where he *could* he would not, and where he *would* he could not. Thus the Emancipation Proclamation was stronger on proclamation than emancipation.

Yet much unofficial do-it-yourself liberation did

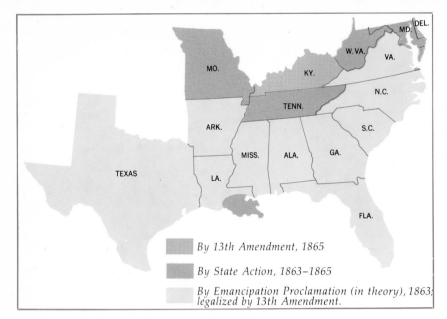

EMANCIPATION IN THE SOUTH
President Lincoln believed that compensated emancipation of the slaves would be fairest to the South. He formally proposed such an amendment to the Constitution in December, 1862. What finally emerged was the Thirteenth Amendment of 1865, which freed all slaves *without* compensation.

Map legend:
- By 13th Amendment, 1865
- By State Action, 1863–1865
- By Emancipation Proclamation (in theory), 1863; legalized by 13th Amendment.

take place. Thousands of jubilant slaves, learning of the proclamation, flocked to the invading Union armies, sometimes hindering military operations. In this sense the Emancipation Proclamation was heralded by the patter of running feet. But many fugitives would have come anyhow, as they had from the war's outset. Actually, Lincoln did not go so far as legislation already passed by Congress for freeing enemy-owned blacks. His immediate goal was not so much to liberate the slaves as to strengthen the moral cause of the Union at home and abroad. This he succeeded in doing.

Many of the British aristocrats were unfriendly to the North, and the London *Spectator* sneered at Lincoln's so-called Emancipation Proclamation: "The Government liberates the enemy's slaves as it would the enemy's cattle, simply to weaken them in the coming conflict. . . . The principle asserted is not that a human being cannot justly own another, but that he cannot own him unless he is loyal to the United States."

At the same time his proclamation, though of dubious constitutionality, clearly foreshadowed the ultimate doom of slavery. This was legally achieved by action of the individual states and by their ratification of the 13th Amendment in 1865, eight months after the war had ended. (For text, see Appendix.)

Public reactions to the long-awaited proclamation of 1863 were varied. "God bless Abraham Lincoln," exulted the anti-slavery editor Horace Greeley in his New York *Tribune*. But many ardent abolitionists complained that Lincoln had not gone far enough. On the other hand, formidable numbers of Northerners, especially in the Old Northwest and the Border States, felt that he had gone too far. A Democratic rhymester sneered:

Honest old Abe, when the war first began,
Denied abolition was part of his plan;
Honest old Abe has since made a decree,
The war must go on till the slaves are all free.
As both can't be honest, will some one tell how,
If honest Abe then, he is honest Abe now?

Opposition mounted in the North against supporting an "abolition war"; ex-President Pierce and others felt that emancipation should not be "inflicted" on the slaves. Many Boys in Blue, especially from the Border States, had volunteered to fight for the Union, not against slavery. Desertions increased sharply. The crucial congressional elections in the autumn of 1862 went heavily against the administration, particularly in New York, Pennsylvania, and Ohio. Democrats even carried Lincoln's Illinois, although they failed to secure control of Congress.

The Emancipation Proclamation caused an outcry to rise from the South that "Lincoln the fiend" was trying to stir up the "hellish passions" of a slave insurrection. Aristocrats of Europe, noting that the proclamation applied only to rebel slaveholders, were inclined to sympathize with Southern protests. But the Old World working classes, especially in England, reacted otherwise. They sensed that the proclamation spelled the ultimate doom of slavery, and many laborers were more determined than ever to oppose intervention. Gradually the diplomatic position of the Union improved.

The North now had much the stronger moral cause. In addition to preserving the Union, it had committed itself to freeing the slaves. The moral position of the South was correspondingly weakened.

Lincoln Plays His Last Card. Lincoln's last card was the Emancipation Proclamation, shown as a black spade. (London *Punch*, 1862.)

Bisecting the South

Luckily the spectacular rise of Ulysses S. Grant provided Lincoln at last with an able general—and one who did not have to be shelved after every reverse. As a mediocre student at West Point, Grant had distinguished himself only in horsemanship, although he did fairly well in mathematics. After participating with credit in the Mexican War, he was stationed at lonely frontier posts, where boredom and loneliness drove him to drink. Resigning from the army to avoid a court martial for drunkenness, he failed at various business ventures, and when war came he was working in his father's leather store in Illinois at $50 a month.

Grant did not cut much of a figure. The shy and silent shopkeeper was short, stooped, awkward, stubble-bearded, and sloppy in dress. He managed with some difficulty to secure a colonelcy in the volunteers. From then on his military experience—combined with boldness, resourcefulness, and doggedness—brought a meteoric rise.

Grant's first signal success came in the northern Tennessee theater. After heavy fighting, he succeeded in capturing Fort Henry and Fort Donelson on the Tennessee and Cumberland Rivers in

Lincoln "the Fiend." Unflattering English cartoon. Critics of Lincoln, North and South, called him "Caesar," "Buffoon," "Illinois Baboon," and "Simple Susan Tyrant." (London *Fun*.)

February 1862. When the Confederate commander at Fort Donelson asked for terms, Grant bluntly demanded "an unconditional and immediate surrender."

This triumph in Tennessee was of major significance. Kentucky was riveted more securely to the Union, and the gateway was opened to the rest of Tennessee as well as to Georgia and the heart of the South. Grant's exploit also captured the imagination of the victory-starved North, and infused badly needed life into the Union cause.

"Unconditional Surrender" Grant was caught napping several weeks later at Shiloh, in southern Tennessee, April 6–7, 1862. But he finally managed to beat off the enemy on one of the goriest fields of the war. Lincoln resisted all demands for his removal by saying, "I can't spare this man, he fights." When talebearers later told Lincoln that Grant drank too much, the President allegedly replied, "Find me the brand, and I'll send a barrel to each of my other generals." There is no evidence that Grant's drinking habits had a seriously adverse effect on his performance.

Other Union thrusts were in the making. In the spring of 1862, a flotilla commanded by David G. Farragut joined with a Northern army to strike the South a staggering blow by seizing New Orleans. With Union gunboats both ascending and descending the Mississippi, the Eastern part of the Confederacy was left with a precarious back door. Through this narrowing entrance, between Vicksburg and Port Hudson, flowed herds of vitally needed cattle and quantities of other provisions from Louisiana and Texas. The fortress of Vicksburg,.located on a hairpin turn of the Mississippi, was the South's sentinel protecting the lifeline to the Western sources of supply.

General Grant was now given command of the Union forces attacking Vicksburg, and in the teeth of grave difficulties displayed rare skill and daring. This was his best-fought campaign of the war. Vicksburg at length surrendered, on July 4, 1863, with the garrison reduced to eating mules and rats. Five days later came the fall of Port Hudson, the last Southern bastion on the Mississippi. The

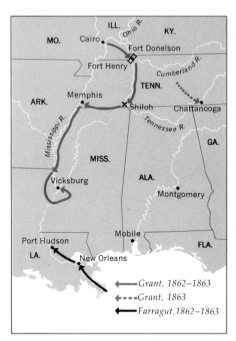

THE MISSISSIPPI RIVER AND
TENNESSEE, 1862–1863

spinal cord of the Confederacy was now severed and, in Lincoln's quaint phrase, the Father of Waters at last flowed "unvexed to the sea."

Sherman Scorches Georgia

General Grant, the victor of Vicksburg, was now transferred to the east Tennessee theater. There, in November 1863, he won a series of desperate engagements in the vicinity of Chattanooga, including Missionary Ridge and Lookout Mountain ("the Battle above the Clouds"). The state was thus cleared of Confederates, and the way was opened for an invasion of Georgia. Grant was rewarded by being made general-in-chief.

The conquest of Georgia was entrusted to General William Tecumseh Sherman. Red-haired and red-bearded, grim-faced and ruthless, he captured and burned Atlanta in September 1864. He then daringly undertook to cut loose from his base of supplies, live off the country for some 250 miles

(402 kilometers), and emerge at Savannah on the sea. As a rousing Northern song ("Marching through Georgia") put it:

"Sherman's dashing Yankee boys will never reach
   the coast!"
So the saucy rebels said—and 't was a handsome
   boast.

But Sherman's hated "Blue Bellies," 60,000 strong, cut a 60-mile (97-kilometer) swath of destruction through Georgia. They burned buildings, leaving only the blackened chimneys ("Sherman's Sentinels"). They tore up railroad rails, heated them red-hot, and twisted them into "iron doughnuts" and "Sherman's hairpins." They bayoneted family portraits and ran off with valuable "souvenirs." "War . . . is all hell," admitted Sherman later, and he proved it by his efforts to "make Georgia howl." One of his major purposes was to destroy supplies destined for the Confederate army, and to weaken the morale of the men at the front by waging war on their homes.

Sherman was a pioneer practitioner of "total war." His success in "Shermanizing" the South was attested by increasing numbers of Confederate desertions. Although his methods were brutal, he probably shortened the struggle and hence saved lives. But there can be no doubt that the

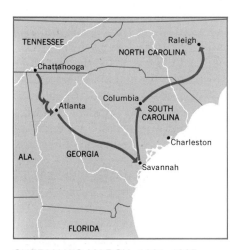

SHERMAN'S MARCH, 1864–1865

A letter picked up on a dead Confederate in North Carolina and addressed to his "deer sister" concluded that it was "dam fulishness" trying to "lick shurmin." He had been getting "nuthin but hell & lots uv it" ever since he saw the "dam yanks" and he was "tirde uv it." He would head for home now, but his old horse was "plaid out." If the "dam yankees" had not got there yet it would be a "dam wunder." They were thicker than "lise on a hen and a dam site ornerier."

discipline of his army at times broke down, as roving riffraff (Sherman's "bummers") engaged in an orgy of pillaging. "Sherman the Brute" was universally damned in the South.

After seizing Savannah as a Christmas present for Lincoln, Sherman's army veered north into South Carolina, where the destruction was even more vicious. Many Union soldiers believed that this state, the "hell-hole of secession," had wantonly provoked the war. The capital city, Columbia, burst into flames, in all probability the handiwork of the Yankee invader. Crunching northward, Sherman's conquering army had rolled deep into North Carolina by the time the war ended.

Lee's Last Lunge

After Antietam, Lincoln replaced McClellan as commander of the Army of the Potomac with General A. E. Burnside, whose ornate side-whiskers came to be known as "burnsides" or "sideburns." Protesting his unfitness for this responsibility, Burnside proved it when he launched a rash frontal attack on Lee's strong position at Fredericksburg, Virginia, on December 13, 1862. A chicken could not have lived in the line of fire, remarked one Confederate officer. More than 10,000 Northern soldiers were killed or wounded in "Burnside's Slaughter Pen."

A new slaughter pen was prepared when General Burnside yielded his command to "Fighting

Joe" Hooker, an aggressive officer but a head-strong subordinate. At Chancellorsville, Virginia, May 2–4, 1863, Lee daringly divided his numerically inferior force, and sent "Stonewall" Jackson to attack the Union flank. The strategy worked. Hooker, temporarily dazed by a near hit from a cannon ball, was badly beaten but not crushed. This victory was probably Lee's most brilliant, but it was dearly bought. Jackson was mistakenly shot by his own men in the gathering dusk, and died a few days later. "I have lost my right arm," lamented Lee. Southern folklore relates how Jackson outflanked the angels while getting into Heaven.

Lee now prepared to follow up his brilliant victory by invading the North again, this time through Pennsylvania. A decisive blow would add strength to the peace movement in the North, while encouraging foreign intervention. Three days before the battle was joined, General George G. Meade—scholarly, unspectacular, abrupt—was aroused from his sleep at 2 A.M. with the unwelcome news that he would replace Hooker. The high tide of the Confederacy was at hand.

Quite by accident Meade took his stand on the green rolling hills near quiet little Gettysburg, Pennsylvania. There his 92,000 men in blue locked in furious combat with Lee's 76,000 gray-clad warriors. The battle seesawed throughout three days, July 1–3, 1863, and the outcome was in doubt until almost the very end. The failure of General Pickett's magnificent but bloodily futile charge finally broke the back of the Confederates.

Lee's defeat was his worst to date, but he took full responsibility for it, even though some of his subordinates had failed him. From now on the Southern cause was doomed, for Vicksburg had surrendered on the day after the reverse at Gettysburg. Yet the men of Dixie fought on, through sweat, blood, and weariness of spirit. The Confederacy was like a cut flower—outwardly blooming but slowly dying.

Later in that dreary autumn of 1863, with the graves still fresh, Lincoln journeyed to Gettysburg to dedicate the cemetery. He read a two-minute address, following a two-hour speech by the orator

LEE'S CHIEF BATTLES,
DECEMBER 1862–JULY 1863

of the day. Lincoln's noble remarks were branded by the London *Times* as "ludicrous" and by Democratic editors as "dishwatery" and "silly." The address attracted relatively little attention at the time, but the President was speaking for the ages.

Grant Outlasts Lee

Grant was now brought in from the West over Meade, who was blamed for failing to pursue the defeated but always dangerous Lee. Lincoln needed a general who, employing the superior resources of the North, would have the intestinal stamina to drive straight ahead, regardless of casualties. A soldier of bulldog tenacity, Grant was the man for this meat-grinder type of warfare. His overall basic strategy was to assail the enemy's armies simultaneously, so that they could not assist one another, and hence could be destroyed piecemeal. His personal motto was "When in doubt, fight." Lincoln urged him "to chew and choke, as much as possible."

A grimly determined Grant, with more than 100,000 men, struck for Richmond. He engaged Lee in a series of furious battles in the Wilderness of Virginia, during May and June of 1864, notably

in the leaden hurricane of the "Bloody Angle" and "Hell's Half Acre." In this Wilderness Campaign Grant suffered about 50,000 casualties, or nearly as many men as Lee had at the start. But Lee lost about as heavily in proportion.

In a ghastly gamble, on June 3, 1864, Grant ordered a frontal assault on the impregnable position of Cold Harbor. The Union soldiers advanced to almost certain death with papers pinned on their backs bearing their names and addresses. In a few minutes, about 7,000 men were killed or wounded.

Public opinion in the North was appalled by this "blood and guts" type of fighting. Critics cried that "Grant the Butcher" had gone insane. But his basic strategy of hammering ahead seemed brutally necessary; he could trade two men for one and still beat the enemy to its knees. "I propose to fight it out on this line," he wrote, "if it takes all summer." It did—and all autumn, all winter, and a part of the spring.

Early in 1865 the Confederates, tasting the bitter dregs of defeat, tried desperately to negotiate for peace between the "two countries." But Lincoln could accept nothing short of Union, and the Southerners could accept nothing short of independence. So the war had to grind on—amid smoke and agony—to its terrible climax.

The end came with dramatic suddenness. Rapidly advancing Northern troops captured Richmond and cornered Lee at Appomattox Court House in Virginia, in April 1865. Grant—stubble-bearded and informally dressed—met with Lee on Palm Sunday and granted generous terms of surrender. Among other concessions, the hungry Confederates were allowed to keep their own horses for spring plowing.

General Ulysses S. Grant and General Robert E. Lee. Trained at West Point, Grant (*above*) proved to be a better general than a President. Oddly, he hated the sight of blood and recoiled from rare beef. Lee (*below*), a gentlemanly general in an ungentlemanly business, remarked when the Union troops were bloodily repulsed at Fredericksburg, "It is well that war is so terrible, or we should get too fond of it." (*Above and below*, National Archives.)

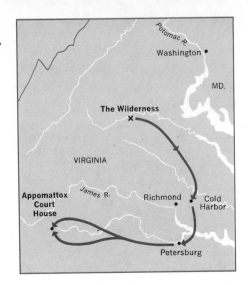

GRANT'S VIRGINIA CAMPAIGN, 1864–1865

Tattered Southern veterans—"Lee's Ragamuffins"—wept as they took leave of their beloved commander. The elated Union soldiers cheered, but they were silenced by Grant's stern admonition, "The war is over; the rebels are our countrymen again." Unfortunately, as the tragic sequel proved, this soldierly forgiveness was not shared by all Northern hearts.

VARYING VIEWPOINTS

Why did the North win the Civil War? The usual answer is that superior industry and transportation tipped the scales in the Union's favor. This line of reasoning leads to the conclusion that the Civil War was the first "modern" war, in which victory turned at least as much on home-front economic mobilization as on battlefield prowess. And yet the war contained many traditional, "pre-industrial" features as well—for how else could the smaller, agrarian South have held out for four bloody years? Debate continues over the relative importance of battlefront and behind-the-lines factors in accounting for the North's crushing triumph.

SELECT READINGS

An able survey is J. G. Randall and David Donald, *The Civil War and Reconstruction* (rev. ed., 1969); greater detail appears in J. G. Randall, *Lincoln the President* (4 vols.; 1945–1955). A good one-volume history is Peter J. Parish, *The American Civil War* (1975). Full-scale accounts are Shelby Foote, *The Civil War* (3 vols., 1958–1974), and Allan Nevins' monumental *Ordeal of the Union* (8 vols., 1947–1971). Russell T. Weigley, *The American Way of War* (1973), puts military history in a broader context. R. N. Current, *Lincoln and the First Shot* (1963), partially exculpates Lincoln. See also T. H. Williams, *Lincoln and His Generals* (1952). J. H. Franklin, *The Emancipation Proclamation* (1963), is informative; consult also Robert Durden, *The Gray and the Black: The Confederate Debate on Emancipation* (1973). Bruce Catton has a series of a dozen or so books on aspects of the Civil War, all readable and knowledgeable, including *A Stillness at Appomattox* (1953) and *This Hallowed Ground* (1956). D. S. Freeman, *R. E. Lee* (4 vols., 1934–1935) and *Lee's Lieutenants* (3 vols., 1942–1944), are detailed but absorbing. See also Jay Luvaas, *The Military Legacy of the Civil War* (1959). D. T. Cornish, *The Sable Arm: Negro Troops in the Union Army* (1956), is an illuminating study. See also B. Quarles, *The Negro in the Civil War* (1953), and J. M. McPherson's collection of documents, *The Negro's Civil War* (1965). On the Confederacy see Clement Eaton, *A History of the Southern Confederacy* (1956), and Clifford Dowdey, *The Land They Fought For* (1955). Important too are B. I. Wiley, *Southern Negroes, 1861–1865* (1938), and the same author's descriptions of common soldiers, *The Life of Johnny Reb* (1943) and *The Life of Billy Yank* (1952). See also his *Plain People of the Confederacy* (1943). Hudson Strode has completed his detailed three-volume biography with *Jefferson Davis, Tragic Hero* (1964). Recent biographies are by W. W. Hassler on McClellan (1957); Freeman Cleaves on Meade (1960); Lenoir Chambers on Jackson (2 vols., 1959); Clifford Dowdey on Lee (1965); and William McFeeley on Grant (1981).

23

Behind the Lines: North and South

Diplomatic Warriors Abroad

America's diplomatic front, ordinarily second fiddle in wartime, has seldom been so critical as during the Civil War. The attitude of the major European countries, particularly France and Britain, was crucial. Both nations had formidable ironclads in their navies, and if either power had decided to intervene, it probably could have smashed the wooden blockading fleet of the Union with terrifying ease—at least in the early years of the war. If this had happened, the South almost certainly would have won its independence. An infuriated North no doubt would have turned its bayonets against British Canada, there to seek vengeance and compensation.

Napoleon III, the slippery dictator of France, was openly unfriendly to the North. Behind the smoke screen of the Civil War he was attempting to prop up his puppet, the Austrian noble-man Maximilian, on the throne of Mexico. The success of this hazardous venture depended on the collapse of the Union. Napoleon had the naval strength to break the Northern blockade, but because he did not have the nerve to go it alone, he sought the support of Britain. The London government saw fit to restrain him, so intervention never came.

British officialdom, heavily tinged with aris-tocracy, was personally more friendly to the aris-tocratic South than to the "shopkeeping" North. But London proclaimed an official neutrality, and observed it rather well—at least as well as it could with its leaky neutrality laws. The North had ex-pected the British, who were anti-slavery, to sym-pathize with its cause, which initially was officially concerned only with preserving the Union, not freeing the slaves. In these circumstances the cold neutrality of Britain should not have been surprising, but it seemed like veiled hostility. James Russell Lowell sorrowfully addressed John Bull:

> We know we've gut a cause, John,
>   Thet's honest, just, an' true;
> We thought 't would win applause, John,
>   Ef nowheres else, from you.

The first real crisis with Britain came over the *Trent* affair, late in 1861. A Union warship cruising on the high seas north of Cuba stopped a British mail steamer, the *Trent*, and forcibly removed from it two Confederate diplomats who were on their way to England. The American captain was guilty of a serious error: he should have brought the entire ship to port for proper judicial judg-ment.

An outburst of rejoicing arose from the North-erners. They had as yet won no important military victory, and they regarded the seizure of these two eminent envoys as a brilliant stroke. Many a loyal Union man feared that if they had continued on their journey, they might have persuaded Britain and France to break the blockade. Besides, patri-otic citizens, remembering the impressment days of 1812, thought it great sport to give John Bull a dose of his own medicine. Americans were now dragging men from the decks of British ships for a change.

Britons were outraged: upstart Yankees could not do this sort of thing to the Mistress of the Seas. War preparations buzzed, and red-coated troops embarked for Canada, with bands blaring, "I Wish I Was in Dixie." The London Foreign Office forth-with prepared an ultimatum, demanding a sur-render of the prisoners and a proper apology.

Luckily the *Trent* crisis was surmounted, but only with grave difficulty. The recently laid Atlantic cable had gone dead, and the delays caused by slow steamship communication gave passions on both sides a chance to cool. Lincoln gradually perceived that the North had on its hands two "white elephants," and despite the popularity of their seizure, he reluctantly decided to release them. Secretary of State Seward was at pains to sweeten the pill for the American public. In a clever note he in effect congratulated the British on having accepted, at long last, the views for which the Republic had futilely fought them in the War of 1812.

Outraged by the outcome of the *Trent* affair, Representative Lovejoy of Illinois, who "literally wept tears of vexation," proclaimed on the floor of Congress: "I hate the British govern-ment. . . . I now here publicly avow and re-cord my inextinguishable hatred. . . . I mean to cherish it while I live, and to bequeath it as a legacy to my children when I die. And if I am alive when war with England comes, as sooner or later it must, for we shall never for-get this humiliation, and if I can carry a musket in that war I will carry it."

Destructive Confederate "Pirates"

A dangerous development for the United States came in the autumn of 1862. The British Cabinet, yielding to the urgings of Napoleon III, seemed about to join France in mediating between North and South, with consequent dangers of shooting. The Union "victory" at Antietam came as a bucket of cold water to such schemes, for Canada was vulnerable to Union bayonets and British shipping was exposed to Yankee privateers. Prime Minister Palmerston was reminded of the ancient couplet:

> Those who in quarrels interpose,
> Must often wipe a bloody nose.

A new major crisis in Anglo-American relations arose over the unneutral building in England of Confederate commerce-raiders, notably the *Alabama*. These vessels were not warships within the meaning of loopholed British law, because they left their shipyards unarmed and picked up their guns elsewhere. The *Alabama* escaped in 1862 to the Portuguese Azores, and there took on weapons

The *Alabama* Sunk, 1864

and a crew from two English ships that followed her. Although flying the Confederate flag and officered by Confederates, she was manned by Britons and never entered a Confederate port. England was thus the chief naval base of the Confederacy.

The *Alabama* lighted the skies from Europe to the Far East with the burning hulks of Yankee merchantmen. All told, this "British pirate" captured over sixty vessels. Competing British shippers were delighted, while an angered North had to divert naval strength from its blockade for wild-goose chases. The barnacled *Alabama* finally accepted a challenge from a stronger Union cruiser off the coast of France in 1864, and was quickly destroyed. A picture of the battle, widely sold in the North, bore the words: "Built of English oak in an English yard, armed with English guns, manned by an English crew, and sunk in the English Channel."

As time passed, the shortsighted officials in London began to develop twinges of conscience. They were given no peace by the American minister, Charles Francis Adams, who persistently presented lists of sinkings and bills for damages by the British-built raider. The Foreign Office gradually perceived that it was sanctioning a dangerous precedent that might one day be used against Britain by a future foe—perhaps one without a navy (Ireland?) or even one without a seacoast. Fearing that provocation might push the Americans too far, London took drastic action in 1863. It openly violated its own leaky laws when it seized another raider being built for the South. In the subsequent trial the British government was assessed costs and damages, but its action was clear evidence of a determination to be truly neutral.

Confederate commerce-destroyers, chiefly British-built, captured in all more than 250 Yankee ships, including many whalers. The owners of several hundred others, fearing destruction, transferred them to foreign flags. Under existing federal laws, these could not be transferred back to American registry. Fortunately for the North,

Charles Francis Adams (1807–1886). Son of President John Quincy Adams, grandson of President John Adams, and father of author Henry Adams, he was himself widely regarded as of presidential timber, especially in 1872. His chief claim to distinction was his bold and dignified diplomacy in London during the Civil War. (Courtesy of the Harvard University Portrait collection)

the *Alabama*s did not cripple the war effort, because British and other neutral shipping was available. But the American merchant marine, only recently the proud challenger of England, was riddled. Earnest citizens, deeply angered, talked openly of securing both revenge and recompense by seizing Canada when the war was over.

Foreign Flare-Ups

A final Anglo-American crisis was touched off in 1863 by the Laird rams—two Confederate warships being constructed in Great Britain. Designed to destroy the wooden ships of the Union navy with their iron rams and large-caliber guns, they were far more dangerous than the swift and lightly armed *Alabama*. If delivered to the South, they probably would have sunk the blockading squadrons, and then brought Northern cities under their fire. In angry retaliation, the North doubtless

would have invaded Canada, and a full-dress war with Britain would have erupted.

There were no legal grounds for detaining the rams, for their fraudulent papers indicated a non-Confederate purchaser. But Minister Adams took a hard line, warning that "this is war" if the rams were released. At the last minute the London government relented, and bought the two ships for the Royal Navy. Everyone seemed satisfied—except the disappointed Confederates. Britain also eventually repented her sorry role in the *Alabama* business. She agreed in 1871 to submit the *Alabama* dispute to arbitration, and in 1872 paid American claimants $15.5 million for damages caused by wartime commerce raiders. On the London Foreign Office wall was hung the cancelled draft for $15.5 million, as a warning to future ministries to be more careful.

American anger was also directed at Canada, where despite the vigilance of British authorities, Southern agents plotted to burn Northern cities. One Confederate raid into Vermont left three banks plundered and one American citizen dead. Hatred of England burned especially fiercely among Irish-Americans, and they unleashed their fury on Canada. They raised several tiny "armies" of a few hundred green-shirted men, and launched invasions of Canada, notably in 1866 and 1870. The Canadians condemned the Washington government for permitting such violations of neutrality, but the administration was hampered by the presence of so many Irish-American voters.

As fate would have it, two great nations emerged from the fiery furnace of the American Civil War. One was a reunited United States, the other was a united Canada. The British Parliament established the Dominion of Canada in 1867. It was partly designed to bolster the Canadians, both politically and spiritually, against the possible vengeance of the United States.

The Czar of Russia watched with interest as Anglo-American tensions mounted. He was himself on the verge of war with both Britain and France over Poland. In that event, he needed to make sure that his navy was not icebound or bottled up in the Baltic or Black Seas. Accordingly, he sent two fleets in the war-weary autumn of 1863 to visit New York and San Francisco. From those ports they might roam as *Alabama*s to ravage vulnerable British and French shipping. The Czar thus acted in his own self-interest—though many Americans leaped to the conclusion that his fleets were meant to forestall British and French intervention in the American Civil War. Several years later Oliver Wendell Holmes declared:

> Bleak are our shores with the blasts of December,
>   Fettered and chill is the rivulet's flow;
> Throbbing and warm are the hearts that remember
>   Who was our friend when the world was our foe.

The outpouring of friendship for Russia was based on mistaken assumptions, but in any case helped pave the way for the later purchase of Alaska.

The haughty Emperor Napoleon III of France dispatched a French army to occupy Mexico City in 1863. On the ruins of a crushed republic the following year he enthroned an Austrian tool, the Archduke Maximilian, as Emperor of Mexico. Both sending the army and installing Maximilian were done in flagrant violation of the Monroe Doctrine.

The North, as long as it was convulsed by war, pursued a walk-on-eggs policy toward France. But when the shooting stopped, Secretary of State Seward, speaking with the authority of nearly a million bayonets, prepared to march south. Napo-leon realized that his costly gamble was doomed. He reluctantly took "French leave" of his ill-starred puppet in 1867, and Maximilian soon crumpled ingloriously before a Mexican firing squad. With his death the Monroe Doctrine took on new life.

Volunteers and Draftees: North and South

Ravenous, the gods of war demanded men—lots of men. Northern armies were at first manned solely by volunteers, with each state assigned a quota based on population. But in 1863, after volunteering had slackened off, Congress passed a federal conscription law for the first time on a nationwide scale in the United States. The provisions were grossly unfair to the poor. Rich boys, including young John D. Rockefeller, could hire substitutes to go in their places, or purchase exemption outright by paying $300. "Three-hundred-dollar men" was the scornful epithet applied to these slackers. Draftees who did not have the necessary cash complained that their bandit-like government demanded "three hundred dollars or your life."

The draft was especially damned in the Democratic strongholds of the North, notably in New York City. A frightful riot broke out in 1863, touched off largely by underprivileged and anti-black Irish-Americans who shouted, "Down with Lincoln!" and "Down with the Draft!" For several

The New York Draft Riot, 1863. Irish workmen resented competition for jobs by "nagurs." The free blacks in turn called the Irish "white niggers." (Museum of the City of New York.)

days the city was at the mercy of a burning, drunken, pillaging mob, and scores of lives were lost, including many lynched blacks. Elsewhere in the North conscription met with resentment and an occasional minor riot.

More than 90 percent of the Union armies were volunteers, since social and patriotic pressures to enlist were strong. As ablebodied men became scarcer, generous bounties for enlistment were offered by federal, state, and local authorities. An enterprising and money-wise volunteer might legitimately pocket more than $1,000.

With money flowing so freely, an unsavory crew of "bounty brokers" and "substitute brokers" sprang up, at home and abroad. They combed the poorhouses of the British Isles and Western Europe; and many an Irishman or German was befuddled with whiskey and induced to enlist. A number of the slippery "bounty boys" deserted, volunteered elsewhere, and netted another handsome haul. The records reveal that one "bounty jumper" repeated his profitable operation thirty-two times. But desertion was by no means confined to "bounty jumpers." The rolls of the Union army recorded about 200,000 deserters of all classes, and the Confederate authorities were plagued with a problem of similar dimensions.

Like the North, the South relied mainly on volunteers. But since the Confederacy was much less populous, it scraped the bottom of its manpower barrel much more quickly. The Richmond regime,

Enlistees North and South
(NUMBER OF MEN IN UNIFORM AT DATE GIVEN)

Date	Union	Confederate
July 1861	186,751	112,040
January 1862	575,917	351,418
March 1862	637,126	401,395
January 1863	918,121	446,622
January 1864	860,737	481,180
January 1865	959,460	445,203

robbing both "cradle and grave" (ages 17 to 50) was forced to resort to conscription as early as April 1862, nearly a year earlier than the Union.

Confederate draft regulations also worked serious injustices. As in the North, a rich man could hire a substitute or purchase exemption. Slave-owners or overseers with twenty slaves might also claim exemption. These special privileges, later modified, made for bad feeling among the less prosperous, many of whom complained that this was "a rich man's war but a poor man's fight." Why sacrifice one's life to save slavery? No large-scale draft riots broke out in the South, as in New York City. But the Confederate conscription agents often found it prudent to avoid those areas inhabited by sharp-shooting mountain whites, who were branded "Tories," "traitors," and "Yankee-lovers."

The Dollar Goes to War

Blessed with a lion's share of the wealth, the North rode through the financial breakers much more smoothly than the South. Excise taxes on tobacco and alcohol were substantially increased by Congress. An income tax was levied for the first time in the nation's experience; and although the rates were painlessly low by later standards, they netted millions of dollars.

Customs receipts likewise proved to be important revenue-raisers. Early in 1861, after enough anti-protection Southern members had seceded, Congress passed the Morrill Tariff Act, superseding the low Tariff of 1857. It increased the existing duties some 5 to 10 percent, boosting them to

A Northern Draft Drawing

about the moderate level of the Walker Tariff of 1846. But these modest rates were soon pushed sharply upward by the war. The increases were designed partly to raise additional revenue, and partly to provide more protection for the prosperous manufacturers who were being plucked by the new internal taxes. A protective tariff thus became identified with the Republican party, as American industrialists, predominantly Republicans, waxed fat on these welcome benefits.

The Washington Treasury also issued greenbacked paper money, totaling nearly $450 million at face value. This printing-press currency was inadequately supported by gold, and hence its value was determined by the nation's credit. Greenbacks thus fluctuated with the fortunes of Union arms, and at one low point were worth only 39 cents on the gold dollar. The holders of the notes, victims of creeping inflation, were indirectly taxed as the value of the currency slowly withered in their hands.

Yet borrowing far outstripped both greenbacks and taxes as a money-raiser. The Federal Treasury netted $2,621,916,786 through the sale of bonds, which bore interest and which were payable at a later date. The modern technique of selling these issues to the people directly through "drives" and payroll deductions had not yet been devised. Accordingly, the Treasury was forced to market its bonds through the private banking house of Jay Cooke and Company, which received a commission of three-eighths of 1 percent on all sales. With both profits and patriotism at stake, the bankers succeeded in making effective appeals to citizen purchasers.

A financial landmark of the war was the National Banking System, authorized by Congress in 1863. Launched partly as a stimulant to the sale of government bonds, it was also designed to establish a standard banknote currency. (The country was then flooded with depreciated "rag money" issued by unreliable bankers.) Banks that joined the National Banking System could buy government bonds and issue sound paper money backed by them. The war-born National Banking Act thus turned out to be the first significant step taken toward a unified banking network since 1836, when the "monster" Bank of the United States was killed by Andrew Jackson. Spawned by the war, this new system continued to function for fifty years.

Taxation by Inflation

An impoverished South was beset by different financial problems. Customs duties were choked off as the coils of the Union blockade tightened. Large issues of Confederate bonds were sold at home and abroad, amounting to nearly $400 million. The Richmond regime also increased taxes sharply, and imposed a 10 percent levy on farm produce. But in general the states'-rights Southerners were vigorously opposed to heavy direct taxation by the central authority: only about 1 percent of the total income was raised in this way.

As revenue began to dry up, the Confederate government was forced to print blue-backed paper money with complete abandon. "Runaway inflation" occurred as Southern presses continued to grind out the poorly backed treasury notes, total-

Civil War Financing in the North

Fiscal Year	Customs	Internal Revenue and Income Tax	Total Taxes	Loans, Including Treasury Notes
1861–1862	$ 49,056,397		$ 50,851,729	$ 433,663,538
1862–1863	69,059,642	$ 37,640,787	108,185,534	596,203,071
1863–1864	102,316,152	109,741,134	212,532,936	719,476,032
1864–1865	84,928,260	209,464,215	295,593,048	872,574,145
TOTAL	$305,360,451	$356,846,136	$667,163,247	$2,621,916,786

ı◻

> A contemporary (Oct. 22, 1863) Richmond
> diary portrays the ruinous effects of inflation:
> "A poor woman yesterday applied to a mer-
> chant in Carey Street to purchase a barrel
> of flour. The price he demanded was $70.
>
>   'My God!' exclaimed she, 'how can I pay
> such prices? I have seven children; what shall
> I do?'
>
>   'I don't know, madam,' said he coolly,
> 'unless you eat your children.'"

◻ı

ing in all more than $1 billion. One breakfast for three in Richmond in 1864 cost $141. The Confederate paper dollar finally sank to the point where it was worth only 1.6 cents when Lee surrendered. The extent to which the Southern currency melted away in the pockets of its holder was the extent to which that citizen was taxed in a roundabout way by his government. Tens of millions of dollars were thus quietly filched from Confederate wallets. Yet inflation did not ruin the South, as was commonly believed. Rather, an inflation of the currency, together with the levy on farm produce, kept the Confederacy going to the end.

"Shoddy" Millionaires in the North

Wartime prosperity in the North was little short of miraculous. The marvel is that a divided nation could fight a costly conflict for four long years and then emerge seemingly more prosperous than ever before. It is true that the early months after secession, with the stoppage of cotton imports and other dislocations, brought temporary depression. But the clouds soon gave way to the sunshine of military orders and war-born civilian prosperity.

New factories, sheltered by the friendly umbrella of the new protective tariffs, mushroomed forth. Soaring prices, resulting from inflation, unfortunately pinched the day laborer and the white-collar worker to some extent. But the manufacturers and businessmen raked in "the fortunes of war."

The Civil War spawned a millionaire class for the first time in American history, though a few men of extreme wealth could have been found earlier. Many of these newly rich were noisy, gaudy, brassy, and given to extravagant living. Their emergence merely illustrates the truth that some gluttony and greed always mar the devotion and self-sacrifice called forth by war. The story of speculators and peculators was roughly the same in both camps. But graft was more flagrant in the North than in the South, partly because there was more to steal.

Yankee "sharpness" appeared at its worst. Dishonest agents, putting profits above patriotism, palmed off aged and blind horses on government purchasers. Unscrupulous Northern manufacturers supplied shoes with cardboard soles, and fast-disintegrating uniforms of reprocessed or "shoddy" wool, rather than virgin wool. Hence the reproachful term "shoddy millionaires." One

"Nightmare of a War Profiteer." A dead soldier forces on him the same poisonous food and drink with which he supplied the army. (*Vanity Fair,* 1861.)

profiteer reluctantly admitted that his profits were "painfully large."

Newly invented labor-saving machinery enabled the North to expand economically, even though the cream of its manpower was being drained off by the fighting front. The sewing machine wrought wonders in fabricating uniforms and military footwear. Clattering mechanical reapers, which numbered about 250,000 by 1865, proved hardly less potent than thundering guns. It not only released tens of thousands of farm boys for the army but fed them while there. It produced vast surpluses of grain which, when sent abroad, helped dethrone King Cotton. It provided profits with which the North was able to buy munitions and supplies from abroad. It contributed to the feverish prosperity of the North—a prosperity that enabled the Union to weather the war with flying colors.

Other industries were humming. The discovery of petroleum gushers in 1859 had led to a rush of "Fifty-Niners" to Pennsylvania. The result was the birth of a new industry, with its "petroleum plutocracy" and "coal oil Johnnies." Pioneers continued to push westward during the war, altogether an estimated 300,000 souls. Major magnets were free gold nuggets and free lands under the Homestead Act of 1862. Strong propellants were the federal draft agents. The only major Northern industry to suffer a crippling setback was the ocean-carrying trade, which fell prey to the *Alabama* and her sister raiders.

A Crushed Cotton Kingdom

Dismally different was the plight of the South, which had fought to exhaustion. The suffocation caused by the blockade, together with the destruction by invaders, took a terrible toll. Transportation collapsed. The South was even driven to the economic cannibalism of pulling up rails from the less-used lines to repair the main ones. Window weights were melted down into bullets; gourds replaced dishes; pins became so scarce that they were loaned with reluctance.

The blockade produced acute shortages, including morphine for the wounded. One North Carolinian recalled his boyhood: "There was a poppy bed in every garden planted for this purpose, and when I was seven years old I worked daily for the soldiers, scraping the inspissated juice of the poppy from the bulbar ovaries which had been punctured a few days before, and, like everyone else, I worked under the eternal mandate, 'Don't taste it!' On some fifty poppy heads it was a morning's work to get a mass about as big as a small peanut."

To the brutal end, the South revealed magnificent resourcefulness and spirit. Women buoyed up their menfolk, many of whom had seen enough of war at first hand to be heartily sick of it. A proposal was made by a number of women that they cut off their long hair and sell it abroad. But the project was not adopted, partly because of the blockade. The self-sacrificing women took pride in denying themselves the silks and satins of their Northern sisters. The chorus of a song, "The Southern Girl," touched a cheerful note:

So hurrah! hurrah! For Southern Rights, hurrah!
Hurrah! for the homespun dress the Southern
    ladies wear.

The Northern Captains of Industry had conquered the Southern Lords of the Manor. A crippled South left the capitalistic North free to work its own way, with high tariffs and other benefits. The industrial giants of the North, ushering in the full-fledged Industrial Revolution, were destined for increased dominance over American economic and political life. Hitherto the agrarian "slavocracy" of the South, by using sectional alliances, had partially checked the rising plutocracy of the North. Now cotton capitalism had lost out to industrial capitalism. The South of 1865 was rich in little but amputees, war heroes, ruins, and memories.

Limitations on Wartime Liberties

"Honest Abe" Lincoln, when inaugurated, laid his hand on the Bible and swore a solemn oath to uphold the Constitution. Then, driven by sheer necessity, he proceeded to tear a few holes in that hallowed document. He sagely concluded that if he did not do so, and patch the parchment later, there might not be a Constitution of a *united* United States to mend. The "Rail Splitter" was no hairsplitter.

But such infractions were not, in general, sweeping. Congress, as is often true in time of crisis, generally accepted or confirmed the President's questionable acts. Lincoln, though accused of being a "Simple Susan Tyrant," did not believe that his ironhanded authority would continue, once the Union was preserved. As he pointedly remarked in 1863, a man suffering from "tempo-

rary illness" would not persist in feeding on bitter medicines for "the remainder of his healthful life."

Congress was not in session when war erupted, so Lincoln gathered the reins into his own hands. Brushing aside legal objections, he boldly proclaimed a blockade. (His action was later upheld by the Supreme Court.) He arbitrarily increased the size of the Federal army—something that only Congress can do under the Constitution (see Art. I, Sec. VIII, para. 12). (Congress later approved.) He directed the secretary of the treasury to advance $2 million without appropriation or security to three private citizens for military purposes— a grave irregularity contrary to the Constitution (see Art. I, Sec. IX, par. 7). He suspended the precious privilege of the writ of habeas corpus, so that anti-Unionists might be summarily arrested. In taking this step, he defied a ruling by the chief justice that the safeguards of habeas corpus could be set aside only by authorization of Congress, as provided in the Constitution (see Art. I, Sec. IX, para. 2). Nearly two years later, in 1863, Congress acquiesced in the suspension.

Lincoln's regime was also guilty of many other high-handed acts. For example, it arranged for "supervised" voting in the Border States. There the intimidated citizen, holding a colored ballot indicating his party preference, had to march between two lines of armed troops. The federal officials also ordered the suspension of certain

The Yankee Guy Fawkes. Lincoln is represented as destroying American liberties by the draft, the suspension of habeas corpus, and the Emancipation Proclamation. (London *Fun*, 1863.)

Lincoln, Kentucky-born like Jefferson Davis, was aware of Kentucky's crucial importance. In September 1861 he remarked, "I think to lose Kentucky is nearly the same as to lose the whole game. Kentucky gone, we cannot hold Missouri, nor, I think, Maryland. These all against us, and the job on our hands is too large for us. We would as well consent to separation at once, including the surrender of this capital [Washington].

newspapers and the arrest of their editors on grounds of obstructing the war.

Jefferson Davis was less able than Lincoln to exercise arbitrary power, mainly because of confirmed states'-righters who revealed an intense spirit of localism. To the very end of the conflict the owners of horse-drawn vans in Petersburg, Virginia, prevented the joining of the incoming and outgoing tracks of a militarily vital railroad. The South seemed willing to lose the war before it would surrender local rights—and it did.

The Curse of Copperheadism

Hundreds of Northern citizens were arrested by the military authorities, chiefly on charges of hindering the Union cause by preaching defeatism or peace-at-any-price-ism. Many were seized without a warrant and were held for prolonged periods without trial, as in Czarist Russia. A large percentage of the persons thus abused were so-called Copperhead Democrats. The Copperheads were partisans who obstructed the war effort by disloyal talk—or worse—and they were named after the poisonous snake, which strikes without warning rattle. Dubbed members of the "White Feather Party," the Copperheads accused the Lincolnites of urging "War to the knife, and the knife to the hilt" in this uncivil Civil War.

Notorious among the victims of autocratic arrest was a prominent Copperhead, Clement L. Vallandigham. This tempestuous character was an Ohio ex-congressman who possessed brilliant oratorical gifts and unusual talents for stirring up trouble. A Southern partisan, he publicly demanded an end to the "wicked and cruel" war. The civil courts in Ohio were open, and he should have been tried in them. But he was convicted by a military tribunal in 1863 for treasonable utterances, and was then sentenced to prison. Lincoln decided that if Vallandigham liked the Confederates so much, he ought to be banished to their lines. This was done.

Vallandigham was not so easily silenced. Working his way to Canada, he ran for the governorship

The Copperhead Party. The cartoon shows the party in favor of a vigorous prosecution of peace. (*Harper's Weekly*, 1863.)

of Ohio on foreign soil, and polled a substantial but insufficient vote. He returned to his own state before the war ended, and although he defied "King Lincoln" and spat upon a military decree, he was not further prosecuted. The strange case of Vallandigham inspired Edward Everett Hale to write his moving but fictional story of Philip Nolan, *The Man without a Country* (1863), which was immensely popular in the North and which helped stimulate devotion to the Union. Nolan was a young army officer found guilty of participation in the Aaron Burr plot of 1806. He had cried out in court, "Damn the United States! I wish I may never hear of the United States again!" For this outburst he was condemned to a life of complete exile on American warships.

Considering the hatreds aroused, civil liberties and constitutional rights fared rather well. Some of the power usurped by the Chief Executive was retained, but most of it was gradually restored to the courts and Congress after the shooting stopped. Wartime penalties on the whole were mild and pardons speedy. Thousands of unterrified and unmolested Copperhead Democrats openly denounced Lincoln as "the Illinois Ape," demanded an end to the "Nigger War," discouraged enlistments, and encouraged desertions.

Politics as Usual in 1864

Political infighting in the North added greatly to Lincoln's cup of woe. Factions within his own party, distrusting his ability, sought to tie his hands. Conspicuous among these critics was the group led by the overambitious Secretary of the Treasury Chase. The master stroke of the anti-Lincoln Republicans was the creation of the meddlesome Congressional Committee on the Conduct of the War, which may have stirred up about as much trouble as it smoothed over. The extreme abolitionists, in addition, clamored for an immediate freeing of the slaves, regardless of the political and military consequences.

Most dangerous of all were the Northern Democrats. Deprived of the brains that had departed with the Southern wing, they were left with the taint of association with the seceders. A tragedy befell the Democrats—and the Union—when their gifted leader, Stephen A. Douglas, died of typhoid fever seven weeks after war began. Inflexibly devoted to the Union, he probably could have kept much of his following on the straight and narrow path of loyalty.

Lacking a leader, the Democrats became badly divided. A large group of so-called War Democrats patriotically supported the Lincoln administration, but tens of thousands of Peace Democrats and regular Democrats did not. Many of the dissenters were outright Copperheads. They ranged all the way from those who wished the enemy Godspeed to those who favored a restored Union—but one restored by negotiation, not war.

Lincoln's precarious authority depended on his retaining Republican control of Congress. His majority was menaced by the Copperheads, who were especially strong in Ohio, Indiana, and Illinois, all of which contained many Southerners. Only with difficulty did the war governors of these states manage to keep them cooperating with Washington.

Lincoln Defeats McClellan at the Polls

Presidential elections come by the calendar and not by the crisis. As fate would have it, the election of 1864 fell most inopportunely in the midst of war.

The Republican party, fearing defeat, executed a clever maneuver. Joining with the War Democrats, it proclaimed itself to be the Union party. Thus the Republican party passed temporarily out of existence.

Lincoln's renomination at first encountered surprisingly strong opposition. Hostile factions whipped up considerable agitation to shelve

Salmon P. Chase (1808–1873). Chase was so conspicuously identified with anti-slavery in Ohio that he was known as "The Attorney General for Fugitive Slaves." He served conspicuously during the Civil War as secretary of the treasury, in which capacity he inaugurated the National Banking System. (Frick Art Reference Library)

NORTHERN DEMOCRATS			REPUBLICANS
COPPER-HEADS	PEACE DEMO-CRATS	WAR DEMO-CRATS	

UNION PARTY, 1864

homely "Old Abe" in favor of handsome Secretary of the Treasury Chase. Lincoln was accused of lacking force; of being overready to compromise; of not having won the war; and of having shocked many sensitive souls by his ill-timed and earthy jokes. ("Prince of Jesters," one journal called him.) But the "ditch Lincoln" move collapsed, and the President was nominated by the Union party without serious dissent.

Lincoln's running mate was ex-tailor Andrew Johnson, a loyal War Democrat from Tennessee who had been a small slaveowner when the conflict began. He was placed on the Union party ticket to "sew up" the election by attracting War Democrats and the voters in the Border States, and not with proper regard for the possibility that Lincoln might die in office. Southerners and Copperheads alike condemned both candidates as birds of a feather: two ignorant, third-rate, boorish, backwoods politicians born in log cabins.

Embattled Democrats—regular and Copperhead—nominated the deposed and overcautious war hero, General McClellan. The Copperheads managed to force into the Democratic platform a plank denouncing the prosecution of the war as a failure. But McClellan, who could not otherwise have faced his old comrades-in-arms, repudiated this defeatist declaration.

The ensuing campaign was noisy and heated. The Democrats cried, "Old Abe removed McClellan. We'll now remove Old Abe." They also sang, "Mac Will Win the Union Back." The Union party men shouted for "Uncle Abe and Andy,"

and urged, "Vote as you shot." Their most effective slogan, growing out of a remark by Lincoln, was: "Don't swap horses in the middle of the river."

Lincoln's re-election was at first gravely in doubt. The war was going badly, as "Butcher" Grant continued to be bogged down in the Wilderness of Virginia. Lincoln himself gave way to despondency, fearing that political defeat was imminent. The anti-Lincoln Republicans, taking heart, started a new movement to "dump" Lincoln in favor of someone else.

But the atmosphere of gloom was changed electrically, as balloting day neared, by a succession of Northern victories. Admiral Farragut captured Mobile, Alabama, after defiantly shouting,

An Anti-Lincoln Cartoon. *Columbia:* "Where are my 15,000 sons—murdered at Fredericksburg?" *Lincoln:* "This reminds me of a little joke—" *Columbia:* "Go tell your joke at Springfield!" (*Harper's Weekly*, 1863.)

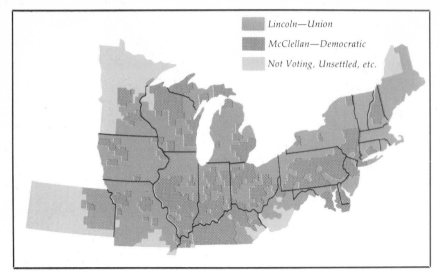

PRESIDENTIAL ELECTION OF 1864 (showing popular vote by county)
Lincoln also carried California, Oregon, and Nevada, but there was a considerable McClellan vote in each.

"Damn the torpedoes! Go ahead." General Sherman seized Atlanta. General ("Little Phil") Sheridan laid waste the verdant Shenandoah Valley of Virginia so thoroughly that in his words "a crow could not fly over it without carrying his rations with him."

The President pulled through, but nothing more than necessary was left to chance. At election time many Northern soldiers were furloughed home to support Lincoln. One Pennsylvania veteran voted forty-nine times—once for himself and once for each absent member of his company. Other soldiers were permitted to cast their ballots at the front.

Lincoln, who could have won anyhow without the "bayonet vote," vanquished McClellan by 212 electoral votes to 21, with the loss of only Kentucky, Delaware, and New Jersey. But "Little Mac" ran a much closer race than the electoral count indicates. He netted a surprising 45 percent of the popular vote, 1,805,237 to Lincoln's 2,213,665, piling up much support in the Southerner-infiltrated states of the Old Northwest, in New York, and in his native state of Pennsylvania.

One of the most crushing defeats suffered by the South was the defeat of the Northern Democrats in 1864. The removal of Lincoln was the last real hope for a Confederate victory, and the Southern soldiers would wishfully shout, "Hurrah for McClellan!" When Lincoln triumphed, desertions from the sinking Southern ship increased sharply.

The Martyrdom of Lincoln

On the night of April 14, 1865 (Good Friday), only five days after Lee's surrender, Ford's Theater in Washington witnessed its most sensational drama. A half-crazed, fanatically pro-Southern actor, John Wilkes Booth, slipped behind Lincoln as he sat in his box and shot him in the head. After lying unconscious all night, the Great Emancipator died the following morning. "Now he belongs to the ages," remarked the once-critical Secretary Stanton—probably the finest thing he ever said.

Lincoln expired in the arms of victory, at the very pinnacle of his fame. From the standpoint of his reputation, his death could not have been better timed if he had hired the assassin. A large number of his countrymen had not suspected his greatness, and many others had even doubted his ability. But his dramatic death helped to erase the memory of his shortcomings, and caused his nobler qualities to stand out in clearer relief. A contemporary, J. T. Trowbridge, lamented:

Heroic soul, in homely garb half-hid,
 Sincere, sagacious, melancholy, quaint;
What he endured, no less than what he did,
 Has reared his monument, and crowned him saint.

The full impact of Lincoln's death was not at once apparent to the South. Hundreds of bedraggled ex-Confederate soldiers cheered, as did some Southern civilians and Northern Copperheads, when they learned of the assassination. This reaction was only natural, because Lincoln had kept the war grinding on to the bitter end. If he had only been willing to stop the shooting, the South would have won.

As time wore on, increasing numbers of Southerners perceived that Lincoln's death was a calamity for them. Belatedly they recognized that his kindliness and moderation would have been the most effective shields between them and vindictive treatment by the victors. The assassination unfortunately increased the bitterness in the North, partly because of the fantastic rumor that Jefferson Davis had plotted it.

A few historians have argued that Andrew Johnson, now President-by-bullet, was crucified for Lincoln. The implication is that if the "Rail Splitter" had lived he would have run into serious trouble, perhaps impeachment, at the hands of the embittered members of his own party who demanded harsh treatment of the South.

The crucifixion thesis does not stand up under

The powerful London *Times*, spokesman of the upper classes, had generally criticized Lincoln during the war, especially after the Emancipation Proclamation of 1862. He was then condemned as "a sort of moral American Pope" destined to be "Lincoln the Last." When the President was shot, the *Times* reversed itself (April 29, 1865): "Abraham Lincoln was as little of a tyrant as any man who ever lived. He could have been a tyrant had he pleased, but he never uttered so much as an ill-natured speech. . . . In all America there was, perhaps, not one man who less deserved to be the victim of this revolution than he who has just fallen."

---

scrutiny. Lincoln no doubt would have clashed with Congress; in fact, he had already found himself in some hot water. The legislative branch normally struggles to win back the power that has been wrested from it by the executive in time of crisis. But the surefooted and experienced Lincoln could hardly have blundered into the same quicksands that engulfed Johnson. Lincoln was a victorious President; and there is no arguing with victory. Enjoying battle-tested powers of leadership, he possessed in full measure tact, sweet reasonableness, and an uncommon amount of common sense. Andrew Johnson, hot-tempered and impetuous, lacked all of these priceless qualities.

Ford's Theater, with its tragic murder of Lincoln, set the stage for the terrible ordeal of Reconstruction.

The Aftermath of the Nightmare

The Civil War took a grisly toll in gore, about as much as all of America's subsequent wars combined. Over 600,000 men died in action or of disease, and in all over a million were killed or seriously wounded. To its lasting hurt, the white South lost the cream of its young manhood and potential leadership. In addition, tens of thousands of babies went unborn because potential fathers were at the front.

Direct monetary costs of the conflict totaled about $15 billion. But this colossal figure does not include continuing expenses, such as pensions and interest on the national debt. The intangible costs—dislocations, disunities, wasted energies, lowered ethics, blasted lives, bitter memories, and burning hates—cannot be calculated.

The greatest constitutional decision of the century, in a sense, was written in blood and handed down at Appomattox Court House, near which Lee surrendered. The extreme states'-righters were crushed. The national government, rewelded in the fiery furnace of war, emerged unbroken. Nullification and secession, those twin nightmares of previous decades, were laid to rest.

Union Troops Enter Richmond.   Note the cheering blacks. (Valentine Museum, Richmond, Virginia.)

Beyond doubt the Civil War—the nightmare of the Republic—was the supreme test of American democracy. It finally answered the question, in the words of Lincoln at Gettysburg, whether a nation dedicated to such principles "can long endure." The preservation of democratic ideals, though not an officially announced war aim, was subconsciously one of the major objectives of the North.

Victory for Union arms also provided inspiration to the champions of democracy and liberalism the world over. The great English Reform Bill of 1867, under which Britain became a true political democracy, was passed two years after the Civil War ended. American democracy had proved itself, and its success was an additional argument used by the disfranchised British masses in securing similar blessings for themselves.

The "Lost Cause" of the South was lost, but few Americans today would argue that the end result was not for the best. America was again united physically, though for many years still divided spiritually by the passions of war. With the shameful cancer of slavery sliced away, free labor was further dignified by the removal of servile competition. Grave dangers were averted, including constant friction and conflict between North and South, each bristling with guns. The Monroe Doctrine, as foreigners could readily observe, took on more muscle. A strong and united nation was thus left free to fulfill its destiny as the overshadowingly powerful republic of the hemisphere—and ultimately of the world.

VARYING VIEWPOINTS

When the Civil War ended, slavery was officially defunct, secession was a dead issue, and industrial growth was surging forward. Charles Beard later hailed the war as the "Second American Revolution" because it had transformed the legal and institutional structure of government, and placed the levers of power firmly in the hands of a new business class. But did the bloody conflict neatly bisect the nation's history? In recent years many scholars have questioned the concept that the war constituted a dramatic turning point. Slavery may have formally disappeared, but blacks remained a scandalously subordinated social group. Regional differences persisted, even down to the present day. Thomas Cochran has even argued that the Civil War may have *retarded* overall industrialization. As for the rising commercial class of the post-war "Gilded Age," many historians now point to its antecedents in both the Whig and Jacksonian movements. History, it seems, is a mighty stream, which in time partially submerges even momentous events like the Civil War beneath the surface of its relentless flow.

SELECT READINGS

See the references for the previous chapter, especially those by Randall and Nevins. The best one-volume biography is B. P. Thomas, *Abraham Lincoln* (1952); see also R. H. Luthin, *The Real Abraham Lincoln* (1960). A multivolume, anecdotal work by a famed poet is Carl Sandburg, *Abraham Lincoln* (6 vols., 1926–1939). For social conditions see A. C. Cole, *The Irrepressible Conflict, 1850–1865* (1934); and E. D. Fite, *Social and Industrial Conditions in the North* (1910). A masterly synthesis is P. W. Gates, *Agriculture and the Civil War* (1965). Homefront politics are treated in J. A. Rawley, *The Politics of Union* (1974), and in Joel Silbey, *A Respectable Minority: The Democratic Party in The Civil War Era* (1977). Lincoln's problems are analyzed in W. B. Hesseltine, *Lincoln and the War Governors* (1948), J. G. Randall, *Constitutional Problems under Lincoln* (rev. ed., 1951), and T. H. Williams, *Lincoln and the Radicals* (1941). For a different view of the same subject, see H. L. Trefousse, *The Radical Republicans: Lincoln's Vanguard for Racial Justice* (1969). R. N. Current, *The Lincoln Nobody Knows* (1958), and David Donald, *Lincoln Reconsidered* (1956), offer interesting insights. On "disloyalty" see Wood Gray, *The Hidden Civil War* (1942), and especially F. L. Klement, *The Copperheads in the Middle West* (1960). Another aspect of Midwestern affairs is discussed in V. J. Voegeli, *Free but Not Equal: The Midwest and the Negro during the Civil War* (1967). Benjamin Quarles looks at *Lincoln and the Negro* (1962), and J. M. McPherson examines *The Struggle for Equality: Abolitionists and the Negro in the Civil War and Reconstruction* (1964). E. C. Murdoch analyzes the military draft in the North in *One Million Men* (1971), while Adrian Cook treats an important by-product of the draft, the New York City riots, in *Armies of the Street* (1974). Mary E. Massey presents the interesting story of women in the Civil War in *Bonnet Brigades* (1966); that topic also figures in Anne Firor Scott's *The Southern Lady* (1970). On the Confederacy, see E. M. Coulter, *The Confederate States of America* (1950), C. P. Roland, *The Confederacy* (1960), Emory M. Thomas, *The Confederate Nation, 1861–1865* (1979), and, for a fascinating first-person account, C. Vann Woodward, ed., *Mary Chestnut's Civil War* (1981). Diplomatic history is presented in F. L. Owsley's revised *King Cotton Diplomacy* (1959), and Martin Duberman's *Charles Francis Adams* (1961). See also Lynn M. Case and Warren F. Spencer, *The United States and France: Civil War Diplomacy* (1970). Economic matters are handled in R. T. Andreano, ed., *The Economic Impact of the American Civil War* (1962), and D. T. Gilchrist and W. D. Lewis, eds., *Economic Change in the Civil War Era* (1965). See David Donald, ed., *Why the North Won the Civil War* (1960). The war's literary legacy is keenly analyzed in Edmund Wilson's classic *Patriotic Gore* (1962) and in Daniel Aaron's *The Unwritten War: American Writers and the Civil War* (1973). For a fascinating discussion of Northern intellectuals and the conflict, consult George M. Frederickson, *The Inner Civil War* (1965).

24

The Ordeal of Reconstruction

With malice toward none, with charity for all, with firmness in the right as God gives us to see the right, let us strive on to finish the work we are in, to bind up the nation's wounds, to care for him who shall have borne the battle and for his widow and orphan, to do all which may achieve and cherish a just and lasting peace among ourselves and with all nations.

ABRAHAM LINCOLN, Second Inaugural, March 4, 1865

The Problems of Peace

Staggering tasks confronted the American people, North and South, when the guns grew cold. About a million and a half warriors in blue and gray had to be demobilized, readjusted to civilian life, and reabsorbed by the war-blasted economy. Civil government likewise had to be put back on a peacetime basis, and purged of encroachments by the military men.

The desperate plight of the South has eclipsed the fact that reconstruction had to be undertaken also in the North, though less spectacularly. War-inflated industries had to be deflated to a peace footing; factories had to be retooled for civilian needs.

Financial problems also loomed large in the North, now that the piper was to be paid. The national debt had shot up from a modest $65 million in 1860 to nearly $3 billion in 1865—a colossal sum for those days but one that a prudent government could pay. At the same time, war taxes had to be reduced to less burdensome levels.

Physical devastation inflicted by invading armies, chiefly in the South and Border States, had to be repaired. This herculean task was ultimately completed, but with discouraging slowness. Moral devastation in the North, most evident in greed and loose living, took longer to mend because it was deeper-rooted and harder to see.

Other weighty questions clamored for answers. What was to be done with approximately 4 million black slaves suddenly being plunged into the cold bath of freedom? Were the seceded states to be brought back into the Union on the old basis, and if so, with or without punishment?

What of the captured Confederate ringleaders, all of whom were liable to charges of treason? During the war a popular song had been "Hang Jeff Davis to a Sour Apple Tree," and even innocent children had lisped it. Davis was temporarily clapped into irons during the early days of his two-year imprisonment. But he and his fellow "conspirators" were finally released, partly

Richmond Devastated. Charleston, Atlanta, and other Southern cities looked much the same, resembling bombed-out Berlin and Munich in 1945. (Library of Congress.)

President Andrew Johnson (1808–1875). An "accidental President," Johnson was the only Chief Executive to be impeached by the House, though narrowly acquitted by the Senate. A former U.S. senator from Tennessee, he was re-elected in 1875 to the Senate that had formally tried him seven years earlier. As he said in a public speech in 1866: "I love my country. Every public act of my life testifies that is so. Where is the man who can put his finger upon one act of mine . . . to prove the contrary." (Library of Congress.)

because the odds were that no Virginia jury would convict them. All "rebel" leaders were finally pardoned by President Johnson as á Christmas present in 1868. But Congress did not remove all remaining civil disabilities until thirty years later.

The Prostrate South

Dismal indeed was the picture presented by the war-racked South when the rattle of musketry died. Not only had an age perished but a civilization had collapsed, in both its economic and its social structure. The moonlight-and-magnolia Old South of antebellum days, largely imaginary, had gone with the wind.

Handsome cities of yesteryear, like Charleston and Richmond, were gutted and weed-choked. An Atlantan returned to his once-fair home town and remarked, "Hell has laid her egg, and right here it hatched."

War had everywhere left its searing mark on social institutions. Churches were battered and dilapidated. The educational system was in chaos, with countless schools destroyed, many teachers killed in battle, and endowments wiped out. Sherman's Yankee invaders had reputedly stabled their horses in the dormitories of the University of South Carolina.

Economic life had creaked to a halt. Banks and business houses had locked their doors, ruined by runaway inflation. Factories were smokeless, silent, dismantled. The transportation system had broken down almost completely. Before the war, five different railroad lines had converged on Columbia, South Carolina; now the nearest connected track was twenty-nine miles (46.7 km) away. Efforts to untwist the rails corkscrewed by Sherman's soldiers were bumpily unsatisfactory.

Agriculture—the economic lifeblood of the South—was almost hopelessly crippled. Once-white cotton fields now yielded a lush harvest of green weeds. Seed was scarce, livestock had

A "Jeff Davis Necktie." A twisted iron rail after having been heated in a Yankee bonfire.

been driven off by plundering Yankees, and much of the black labor supply had taken off to enjoy the new freedom. Pathetic instances were reported of men hitching themselves to plows, while women and children gripped the handles. Not until 1870 did the seceded states produce as large a cotton crop as that of the fateful year 1860, and much of that came from new acreage in the Southwest.

Unfettered Freedmen

Confusion abounded in the still-smoldering South about the precise meaning of "freedom" for blacks. Emancipation took effect haltingly and unevenly in different parts of the conquered Confederacy, and in some regions planters stubbornly protested that slavery was legal until state legislatures or the Supreme Court might act. Newspapers in Mississippi earnestly discussed *gradual* emancipation. For many bondsmen, the shackles of slavery were not struck off in a single mighty blow; long-suffering blacks often had to struggle out of their chains link by link.

The variety of responses to emancipation, by whites as well as blacks, illustrated the sometimes startling complexity of the master-slave relationship. Unbending loyalty to "ole Massa" prompted many slaves to help their owners resist the liberating Union armies. Blacks blocked the door of the

---

Carl Schurz described a Fourth of July affair in Savannah, Georgia, in 1865: "The colored firemen of this city desired to parade their engine on the anniversary of our independence. . . . In the principal street of the city the procession was attacked with clubs and stones by a mob . . . and by a crowd of boys swearing at the d——d niggers. The colored firemen were knocked down, some of them severely injured, their engine was taken away from them, and the peaceable procession dispersed."

"big house" with their bodies, or stashed the plantation silverware under mattresses in their own humble huts, where it would be safe from the plundering "bluebellies." On other plantations, pent-up bitterness burst violently forth on the day of liberation. A group of Virginia slaves laid twenty lashes on the back of their former master—a painful dose of his own favorite medicine. Newly emancipated slaves sometimes eagerly accepted the invitation of Union troops to join in the pillaging of their master's possessions. One freedman said that he felt entitled to steal a chicken or two, since the whites had robbed him of his labor and his children.

Emancipation followed by re-enslavement, or worse, was the bewildering lot of many blacks, as Union armies marched in and out of various localities. A North Carolina slave estimated that he had celebrated emancipation about twelve times. As blacks in one Texas county flocked to the free soil of the liberated county next door, their owners bushwacked them with rifle fire as they swam for freedom across the river that marked the county line. The next day, trees along the riverbank were bent with swinging corpses—a grisly warning to others dreaming of liberty.

Prodded by the bayonets of Yankee armies of occupation, all masters were eventually forced to recognize their slaves' permanent freedom. The once-commanding planter would assemble his former human chattels in front of the porch of the "big house," and announce their liberty. This "Day of Jubilo" was the occasion of wild rejoicing. Tens of thousands of blacks naturally took to the roads. They sought long-separated loved ones, as formalizing a "slave marriage" was the first goal of many newly free men and women. Others travelled in search of economic opportunity in the towns or in the still-wild West. Many moved simply to test their new freedom.

Inexperienced ex-slaves unfortunately fell victims to the schemes of greedy whites. A "grapevine" rumor spread among blacks that on a given day the Washington government would present each family with "forty acres and a mule." White

Free at Last. A black family in South Carolina photographed just after Emancipation. Three generations are apparently present here, suggesting the cohesiveness and endurance of the Afro-American family, despite the harshness of slavery. (Library of Congress.)

swindlers sometimes sold for five dollars a set of red, white, and blue pegs, with which the trusting black had only to stake out his acreage. Quickly disillusioned, he was left with neither acres nor mule—nor his five dollars!

Uncertain about just how "free" they were, the former slaves were not instantly relieved of the yoke of centuries of oppression. Blacks had suffered many cruelties during slavery, but one of the cruelest strokes of all was being jerked from chains to freedom without adequate preparation or safeguards. In many ways, the war changed little. Poor, powerless, and illiterate, the majority of blacks carried on much as they had before. They worked at the same jobs for the same "massa," receiving pittance wages.

Desperately trying to bootstrap themselves up from slavery, blacks assembled in "Conventions of Freedmen" to fight for their newly gained rights. Led by ministers of God and free-born blacks from the North, these conventions expressed surpris-

ingly moderate views. But moderation could not guarantee a warm reception by embittered white Southerners. The freed blacks were going to need all the friends—and the power—they could find in Washington.

A Dethroned but Defiant Aristocracy

The planter aristocrats were virtually ruined by the war. Reduced to proud poverty, they were confronted with damaged or burned mansions, lost investments, and semi-worthless land. In addition, their slaves, once worth about $2 billion, had been freed in one of the costliest confiscations of history. Some whites were assisted by the pitiful savings of their former slaves; a few peddled pies or took in washing. Women and children, some reared in luxury, were found begging from door to door.

Several thousand of the former "cotton lords" were unable to face up to their overpowering

"The Re-United States." This English cartoon reflects sympathy for the South. (*Punch*, 1865.)

leveling took place, with the rich leveled down and the poor partially leveled up. But many dreary years were to pass before the economic health of the South equaled that of 1860.

The high-spirited Southerners, including many women, were unwilling to acknowledge defeat Having fought gallantly, they felt that they had not been beaten but had worn themselves out beating the North, like an arm-weary pugilist. Many of them, mourning the triumph of brute strength over righteousness, believed that they had won a moral victory. To them the struggle, though a "Lost Cause," was still a just war. They were conscious of no crime, and still believed that their view of secession was correct. A song sung in the South during the post-war years revealed no love for the Union:

I'm glad I fought agin her, I only wish we'd won,
And I ain't axed any pardon for anything I've done.

Continued defiance by Southerners was disquieting. It revealed itself in references to "damyankees" and to "your government" instead of "our government." A bishop in one Southern diocese even refused to pray for President Andrew Johnson, though the latter was in sore need of divine guidance. The Southerners would have avoided much misery if they had only realized that no great rebellion has ever ended with the victors sitting down to a love feast with the vanquished.

Black Codes in the Black South

Abolitionists had long preached that slavery was a degrading institution. Now the emancipators had to face the fact that the ex-slaves were in many ways actually degraded. The freedmen were largely unskilled, unlettered, without property or capital, and without even the knowledge of how to survive in free society. To cope with this problem throughout the conquered South, Congress created the Freedmen's Bureau in 1865. On paper at least, the bureau was to be a kind of primitive welfare

burdens. They departed for the Far West, or for Mexico and Brazil, where their children gradually became Mexicanized or Brazilianized. A few desperate Southerners sought escape in suicide, including the distinguished Virginia soil expert, Edmund Ruffin, who ironically had fired one of the first shots at Fort Sumter.

But most of the impoverished planters labored courageously to restore the glory that had once been the South. General Robert E. Lee, for example, accepted the presidency of Washington College in Virginia—later Washington and Lee—and became a respected educator.

In teeter-totter fashion, the loss of the aristocrats was in some degree the gain of the common folk. The poor whites, not possessing much to begin with, stood to gain from change—and some of them did. As the once-rich abandoned their broad ancestral estates, a number of small farms became available. A kind of curious economic

Primary School for Freedmen in Vicksburg, Mississippi. Note wide ranges of ages. (*Harper's Weekly*, 1866.)

agency. It was to provide food, clothing, and education both to white refugees and to freedmen. It was also authorized to distribute up to forty acres of abandoned or confiscated land to every adult male.*

In practice, the bureau met with scant success. But it did teach an estimated 200,000 black folk the elements of reading. Many ex-slaves had a passion for learning, partly because they wanted to close the gap between themselves and the whites, and partly because they longed to read the Word of God. In one elementary class in North Carolina sat four generations of the same family, ranging from a six-year-old tot to the seventy-five-year-old grandmother. But the bureau redistrib-

uted virtually no land, and its local administrators often yielded to white sentiment. Yet the white South resented the bureau as a meddlesome federal interloper that threatened to upset white racial dominance.

White Southern legislatures had their own ideas about how to handle the freedmen, and in 1865 and 1866 they enacted the iron-toothed Black Codes. These laws were designed to regulate the affairs of the emancipated blacks, much as the slave statutes had done in pre–Civil War days. The Black Codes aimed, first of all, to insure a stable labor supply. The crushed Cotton Kingdom could not rise from its weeds until the fields were once again put under the plow and hoe—and many whites feared that black plowmen and field hands would not work unless forced to do so.

Severe penalties were thus imposed by the codes on blacks who "jumped" their labor contracts. The ex-slaves could be made to forfeit their

---

*A Union general, Oliver O. Howard, was the first head of the Freedmen's Bureau. Sympathetic toward blacks, he founded and later served as president of Howard University, in Washington, D. C.

Black Huts at the Trent River Settlement, North Carolina. (*Harper's Weekly*, June 9, 1866.)

Early in 1866 one congressman quoted a Georgian: "The blacks eat, sleep, move, live, only by the tolerance of the whites, who hate them. The blacks own absolutely nothing but their bodies; their former masters own everything, and will sell them nothing. If a black man draws even a bucket of water from a well, he must first get the permission of a white man, his enemy. . . . If he asks for work to earn his living, he must ask it of a white man; and the whites are determined to give him no work, except on such terms as will make him a serf and impair his liberty."

back wages, or could be forcibly dragged back to work by a paid "Negro-catcher." In Mississippi the captured freedman could be fined and then hired out to pay off his fine—an arrangement that closely resembled slavery itself.

The codes also aimed to restore as nearly as possible the pre-emancipation system of race relations. Freedom itself was legally recognized, as were some lesser privileges, such as the right to marry. But all the codes forbade a black to serve on a jury; some even barred blacks from renting or leasing land. A black could be punished for "idleness" by being sentenced to work on the chain gang.

These oppressive laws were a terrible burden to the unfettered blacks, struggling against ignorance and poverty to make their way as free persons. Thousands of impoverished ex-slaves slipped into the status of share crop farmers, as did many of the former landowning whites. The luckless sharecroppers gradually sank into a debtor's morass of virtual peonage, and remained there for generations. Formerly slaves to masters, countless blacks became slaves to the soil and their creditors.

The Black Codes naturally left a painful impression in the North. This was notably true of former anti-slavery centers, where the Southern restrictions were painted in especially lurid hues. If the ex-slaves were being re-enslaved, people asked one another, had not the Boys in Blue spilled their blood in vain? Had the North really won the war?

Johnson: The Tailor President

Few Presidents have ever been faced with a more perplexing sea of troubles than that confronting Andrew Johnson. What manner of man was this medium-built, dark-eyed, black-haired Tennessean, now Chief Executive by virtue of the bullet that killed Lincoln?

No citizen, not even Lincoln, has ever reached the White House from humbler beginnings. Born to impoverished parents in North Carolina and

Johnson's Tailor Shop. (Library of Congress.)

early orphaned, Johnson never attended school but was apprenticed to a tailor at age ten. Ambitious to get ahead, he taught himself to read, and later his wife taught him to write and do simple arithmetic. Like many another self-made man, he was inclined to overpraise his maker.

Johnson early became identified with politics in Tennessee, to which he had moved when seventeen years old. He shone as an impassioned champion of the poor whites against the planter aristocrats, although he himself ultimately owned a few slaves. He excelled as a two-fisted stump speaker before angry and heckling crowds, among whom on occasion he could hear a pistol being cocked. Elected to Congress, he attracted much favorable attention in the North (but not the South) when he refused to secede with his own state. After Tennessee was partially "redeemed" by Union armies, he was appointed war governor, and served courageously in an atmosphere of danger.

Destiny next thrust Johnson into the vice-presidency. Lincoln's Union party in 1864 needed to attract support from the War Democrats and other pro-Southern elements, and Johnson, a Democrat, seemed to be the ideal man. Unfortunately, he appeared at the vice-presidential inaugural ceremonies the following March in a scandalous condition. He had recently been afflicted with typhoid fever, and although not known as a heavy drinker, he was urged by his friends to take a stiff bracer of whiskey. This he did—with disgraceful results.

"Old Andy" Johnson was no doubt a man of parts—unpolished parts. He was intelligent, able, forceful, and gifted with homespun honesty. Steadfastly devoted to duty and to the people, he was a dogmatic champion of states' rights and the Constitution. He would often present a copy of the document to visitors, and he was buried with one as a pillow.

Yet the man who had raised himself from the tailor's bench to the President's chair was a misfit. A Southerner who did not understand the North, a Tennessean who had earned the distrust of the South, a Democrat who had never been accepted by the Republicans, a President who had never

Johnson as a Parrot. He was constantly invoking the Constitution. (*Harper's Weekly.*)

been elected President, he was not at home in a Republican White House. Hotheaded, contentious, and stubborn, he was the wrong man in the wrong place at the wrong time. A Reconstruction policy devised by the angels might well have failed in his tactless hands.

Lenient Johnsonian Justice

Johnson got off on the right foot as far as vengeful Northerners were concerned. Upon Lincoln's death, his hatred of the "stuck-up" planter aristocrats again flared forth, and he threatened to reconstruct the South with fire and hemp.

Applause burst from Republicans, especially the Radical or dominant wing of the party. These were the extremists who had condemned Lincoln's go-slow abolition policy, and they were determined to reconstruct the South radically—that is, with a rod of iron. Many Radicals wanted to safeguard the rights of the blacks; others were also driven by an urge for power and punishment. Some of them were secretly pleased when the assassin's bullet removed Lincoln, for the martyred President had shown tenderness toward the South. Spiteful "Andy" Johnson would presumably be a pliant tool in their hands.

But time and responsibility sobered Johnson, and within a few weeks he veered toward Lincoln's "rosewater" 10-percent plan. Lincoln had decreed in 1863 that, as a first step, a group of voters equal to one-tenth of the voting population of any Southern state in 1860 must take the oath of allegiance to the United States. The next step would be the erection of a new state government under a constitution which accepted the abolition of slavery. Lincoln would then recognize the purified new regime.

Several conquered Southern states, taking advantage of Lincoln's lenient 10-percent proposal, had reorganized their governments by 1864. But Congress flatly refused to seat their duly elected representatives. The Radical Republicans, though by no means all Republicans, were determined that the South should suffer more severely for its sins.

The plan adopted by Johnson in 1865 rather resembled Lincoln's 10-percent scheme; in some respects it was even more generous. It disfranchised certain leading Confederates, including those with taxable property worth more than $20,000, but it permitted the other whites to reorganize their own state governments. Special state conventions were to be summoned. These would be required to repeal the ordinances of secession, repudiate all Confederate debts, and ratify the slave-freeing 13th Amendment.

Republican Radicals in the Saddle

In the second half of 1865, the new Southern state governments were rapidly organized under the "soft" Lincoln-Johnson plan. Among the first acts of these regimes was the passage of the Black Codes, so offensive to the North. Elections were duly held for senators and representatives in Congress. When that body convened in December 1865, scores of distinguished Southerners were on hand to claim their seats.

The appearance of these ex-rebels was a natural but costly blunder. Voters of the South, seeking able representatives, had turned instinctively to

Before President Johnson softened his Southern policy, his views were Radical. Speaking on April 21, 1865, he declared: "It is not promulgating anything that I have not heretofore said to say that traitors must be made odious, that treason must be made odious, that traitors must be punished and impoverished. They must not only be punished, but their social power must be destroyed. If not, they will still maintain an ascendancy, and may again become numerous and powerful; for, in the words of a former Senator of the United States, 'When traitors become numerous enough, treason becomes respectable.'"

their experienced statesmen. But most of the Southern leaders were "tainted" by active association with the "Lost Cause." Among the delegations elected to Congress were four former Confederate generals, five colonels, and various members of the Richmond cabinet and Congress. Worst of all, there was the 90-pound (40.8-kilogram) but brainy Alexander Stephens, former vice-president of the Confederacy, still under indictment for treason.

Inevitably, the presence of those "whitewashed rebels" infuriated the Radical Republicans in Congress. The war had been fought to restore the Union, but the Radicals wanted it restored on their own terms. They were in no hurry to embrace their former enemies, virtually all of them Democrats, in the chambers of the Capitol. While the South had been "out" from 1861 to 1865, the Republicans in Congress had enjoyed a relatively free hand. They had passed much legislation that favored the North, such as the Homestead Act and the Pacific Railroad Act. Now many Republicans balked at giving up this political advantage. On December 4, 1865, the first day of the session, they banged shut the door in the faces of the newly elected Southern delegations.

Looking to the future, the Radical Republicans were alarmed to note that a restored South would be stronger than ever in Congress. Before the war a black slave had counted as three-fifths of a person in apportioning congressional representation. Now he was five-fifths of a person. Eleven Southern states had seceded and had lost the war. But now, owing to full counting of free blacks, the rebel states were entitled to twelve more votes in Congress than they had previously enjoyed. Again the question was being raised in the North: Who won the war?

Radicals had good reason to fear that ultimately they would be elbowed aside. Southerners might join hands with ex-Copperheads and discontented farmers of the North and West, and then win control of Congress. If this happened, they could destroy the industrial and financial foundations of the Republican party, which had entrenched itself deeply behind the smoke screen of the Civil War. Specifically, the Southerners might lower the high war tariffs, restrict the new industrial monopolies, repeal the free-farm Homestead Act, and curtail the lavish grants of land to the railroads. The ex-Confederates might even go so far as to repudiate the national debt and re-enslave the blacks. These last two possibilities, though remote, alarmed Republican bondholders and ex-abolitionists alike.

Fearing such disasters, the Radical Republicans found a potent trump card—the black vote. If they could give the ballot to the ex-slave and induce him to vote Republican, they would hold a powerful hand. They probably could offset the efforts of the Southerners to unite with the numerous Northern agrarians to destroy Republican dominance in Washington.

Republican agitation for black suffrage—that is, more democracy—was prompted by both idealistic and selfish motives. Idealists like Senator Charles Sumner were striving not only for black freedom but for racial equality. They believed that the ex-bondsman should have the ballot for protection against the whites, and for the development of civic responsibility as well. But less idealistic Radical Republicans—how numerous one cannot say—were plainly more interested in the welfare of the party than in that of the black. They would "Republicanize" the South by making the freedman their tool; they would rule or ruin. For a time they did both.

Johnson Clashes with Congress

On what terms should the seceded states now be readmitted? Lincoln had argued—and Johnson agreed—that the Southern states had never legally withdrawn from the Union. Their formal restoration would therefore be relatively simple. But the Radical Republicans insisted that the seceders had forfeited all their rights—had committed "suicide"—and could be readmitted only as "conquered provinces" on such conditions as Congress should decree.

Most powerful of the Radical Republicans was crusty Congressman Thaddeus Stevens of Pennsylvania, then seventy-four years old. He was a curious figure, with a protruding lower lip, a heavy black wig on a bald head, and a deformed foot. A devoted friend of the blacks, he had defended runaway slaves without fee and, before dying, insisted on burial in a black cemetery. His hatred of the South, already violent, was intensified when Confederate cavalry raiders pillaged and burned his Pennsylvania ironworks. He even talked wildly at times of exterminating the ex-Confederates, and of handing their estates over to the ex-slaves as compensation for unpaid sweat.

When Congress convened for its fateful session

Thaddeus Stevens (1792–1868). Stevens, who regarded the seceded states as "conquered provinces," promoted much of the major Reconstruction legislation, including the 14th (civil rights) Amendment. He was among the foremost in the impeachment of President Johnson. (Library of Congress.)

An Inflexible President. This Republican cartoon shows Johnson knocking blacks out of the Freedmen's Bureau by his veto. (Thomas Nast, (*Harper's Weekly*, 1866.)

in December 1865, the Radical Republicans were prepared to call the tune. Led by the zealous Stevens, a masterly parliamentarian with a razor-sharp mind and withering sarcasm, they not only denied the Southern members seats, but promptly set up the Joint (House-Senate) Committee on Reconstruction. The domineering Stevens, as chairman of the House contingent, was the most influential member of this committee of fifteen. Cracking the whip relentlessly from his driver's seat, he became, as much as any one man, virtual ruler of the nation for more than a year.

A clash between the high-riding Radicals and the strong-willed Johnson was inevitable. It came in February 1866, when the President vetoed a bill (later repassed) to extend the life of the controversial Freedmen's Bureau. He stubbornly regarded the measure as an unconstitutional invasion of the rights of the Southern states.

Aroused, the Radicals quickly struck back. In March 1866, they passed the Civil Rights Bill, which conferred on the blacks the privilege of American citizenship and also struck at the Black Codes. Johnson resolutely vetoed this forward-looking measure on constitutional grounds, but in April the Radicals in Congress steam-rollered it over his veto—something they repeatedly did henceforth. The helpless President, dubbed "Sir Veto" and "Andy Veto," was reduced to a partial figurehead as Congress assumed the dominant role in running the government. One critic called Johnson "the dead dog of the White House."

The Radicals now undertook to rivet the principles of the Civil Rights Bill into the Constitution as the 14th Amendment. They feared that the Southerners might one day win control of Congress and repeal the hated law. The proposed amendment, as approved by Congress and sent to the states in June 1866, was sweeping. It (1) conferred civil rights (but not the vote) on the blacks; (2) reduced proportionately the representation of a state in Congress and in the Electoral College if it denied the blacks the ballot; (3) disqualified from federal and state office ex-Confederates who as federal officeholders had once taken an oath "to support the Constitution of the United States"; and (4) guaranteed the federal debt, while repudiating all Confederate debts. (See text of 14th Amendment in Appendix.)

Thus the scheme of the Radicals was roughly the broad 14th Amendment superimposed upon the lenient Lincoln-Johnson plan. These terms were not intolerably severe, though highly ob-

Principal Reconstruction Proposals and Plans

1864–1865	*1865–1866*	*1866–1867*	*1867–1877*
Lincoln's 10-percent proposal	Johnson's version of Lincoln's proposal	Congressional plan: 10-percent plan with 14th Amendment	Congressional plan of military Reconstruction: 14th Amendment plus black suffrage, later established nationwide by 15th Amendment

jectionable to the still-defiant white Southerners. Black suffrage was not yet forced on them, but they would be shorn of considerable political power if they did not adopt it voluntarily.

Swinging 'Round the Circle with Johnson

As 1866 lengthened, the battle intensified between the Radical Congress and the President. The root of the controversy went back to Johnson's "10-percent" governments that had passed the most severe Black Codes. Congress tried to temper the worst features of the codes by extending the life of the embattled Freedmen's Bureau and passing the Civil Rights Bill. Both measures Johnson had vetoed. Now the burning issue was whether Reconstruction was to be carried on with or without the drastic 14th Amendment. The Radicals would settle for nothing less; they insisted that the Southern states ratify the amendment as a condition for readmitting their representatives to Congress.

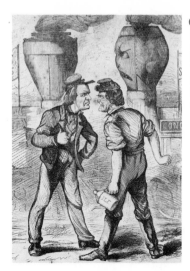

Collision Course. President Andrew Johnson and Radical Republican leader Thaddeus Stevens square off during Reconstruction. (Library of Congress)

The crucial congressional elections of 1866—more crucial than some presidential elections—were fast approaching. President Johnson was naturally eager to escape from the clutch of the Radical Congress by securing a majority favorable to his soft-on-the-South policy. Invited to dedicate a Chicago monument to Stephen A. Douglas, he undertook to speak at various cities en route in support of his views.

Johnson's famous "Swing around the Circle," beginning in the late summer of 1866, was a serio-comedy of errors. The President delivered a series of "give 'em hell" speeches, in which he accused the Radicals in Congress of having planned large-scale anti-black riots and murder in the South. As he spoke, hecklers hurled insults at him. Reverting to his stump-speaking days in Tennessee, he shouted back angry retorts, amid cries of "You be damned" and "Don't get mad, Andy." The dignity of his high office sank to a new low, as the old charges of drunkenness were revived.

As a vote-getter, Johnson was highly successful—for the opposition. His inept speechmaking heightened the cry "Stand by Congress" against the "Tailor of the Potomac." When the ballots were counted, the Radicals had rolled up more than a two-thirds majority in both Houses of Congress. Yet the outcome did not necessarily mean that

"The Reconstruction Dose."   This Republican cartoon shows Johnson as a bad boy urging the South to reject the medicine with which Dr. Congress, backed up by Mrs. Columbia, is trying to restore her health. (*Frank Leslie's Illustrated Newspaper*, 1867.)

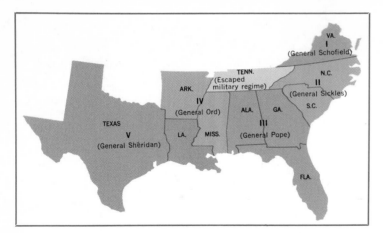

MILITARY RECONSTRUCTION, 1867
(five districts and commanding generals)
For many white Southerners, military reconstruction
amounted to turning the knife in the wound of defeat.
An often-repeated story of later years had a Southerner
remark, "I was sixteen years old before I discovered
that damnyankee was two words."

the country favored Radical Reconstruction. In many congressional districts the voters had a devil's choice between an ex-Copperhead and a Radical; they held their noses and chose the latter.

The setback at the polls merely widened the gap between the determined Radicals and the stiff-necked Southerners. If Johnson had been far-sighted, he would have urged the Southern states to accept the 14th Amendment as the best possible terms they could get. But he encouraged them to resist. They probably needed no prompting, for all of the "sinful eleven," except Tennessee, defiantly spurned the 14th Amendment. Their spirit was reflected in a Southern song:

And I don't want no pardon for what I was or am,
I won't be reconstructed and I don't give a damn.

Reconstruction by the Sword

Radicals in Congress now felt fully justified in imposing on the South the drastic Military Reconstruction Act of March 2, 1867, supplemented by three other measures. The controversial legislation swept away the lily-white Southern state governments, which had been reorganized under Johnson's auspices. It set up five military districts, each commanded by a Union general and policed by blue-clad soldiers, about 20,000 all told. More than that, the Radical restrictions, reinforced by requirements forced into the new state constitutions, disfranchised additional tens of thousands of Southern white leaders.

Congress additionally laid down stringent conditions for the readmission of the seceded states. The wayward sisters were required to ratify the 14th Amendment, thus giving the ex-slaves their rights as citizens. But the bitterest pill of all to white Southerners was the stipulation that they guarantee in their state constitutions full suffrage for their former slaves. One result was the election of more than a dozen black congressmen, including two senators, who as a group did creditable work.

The Radical Republicans were still worried. The danger loomed that once the unrepentant states were readmitted, they would amend their constitutions so as to withdraw the ballot from the blacks. The only ironclad safeguard was to incorporate black suffrage in the federal Constitution. This goal was finally achieved, three years after the Military Reconstruction Act of 1867, by the 15th Amendment. Passed by Congress in 1869, it was ratified by the required number of states in 1870. (For text, see Appendix.)

Military Reconstruction of the South was thus launched in 1867. Congress not only usurped certain functions of the President as commander-in-chief, but it set up a questionable martial regime. The Supreme Court had already ruled, in the case of *Ex parte Milligan* (1866), that military tribunals could not properly try civilians, even during wartime, in areas where the civil courts were open. Peacetime military rule, which involved an arbitrary suppression of newspapers, was obviously contrary to the spirit of the Constitution.

After shackling "Old Veto" Johnson, the Radicals even succeeded in subduing the Supreme Court. The learned justices, no doubt fearing that their own powers were in jeopardy, avoided giving serious offense to the Radical Congress. They even refused, on technicalities, to assert themselves when they might have intervened. But public sentiment in the North gradually turned against the Radicals. The Supreme Court took heart from this changing atmosphere, and beginning in 1876 it stamped the brand of unconstitutionality on a number of the congressional Reconstruction laws. But by this time—nine years after the first Military Reconstruction Act—the eggs had been scrambled.

Beginning in 1867, and under the stern eye of Union soldiers, new state governments had been set up in the South. They promptly fell under the control of the much-maligned "scalawags" and "carpetbaggers," who in turn used the blacks as political henchmen. The "scalawags" were

Senator Hiram R. Revels (1822–1901). The first black U.S. senator, Revels was elected in 1870 to the seat that had been occupied by Jefferson Davis when the South seceded. (Library of Congress.)

Southerners, sometimes able Southern Unionists and ex-Whigs. They collaborated in creating the new regimes and hence were regarded as traitors by the ex-Confederates. The "carpetbaggers" were mainly Northern adventurers and fortune seekers ("vultures"), who supposedly packed all their worldly goods into a single carpetbag. Though many of these "damn Yankees" were offensive to the South, a kinder feeling was shown toward carpetbaggers who came down with some capital, a willingness to work, and a capacity to "mind their own business"—that is, not "meddle" with the blacks.

Prodded into line by federal officials, the Southern states got on with the distasteful task of constitution making. By 1870 all of them had reorganized their governments and had been accorded full rights. The hated "Blue Bellies" were withdrawn from police work only when the new Radical regimes seemed to be firmly entrenched. Finally, in 1877, ten years after the long ordeal of military Reconstruction had begun, the last federal bayonets were removed from state politics.

Enfranchised Freedmen

The ex-slaves were now free. But should they have the full rights of citizenship, including the most important of all, the right to vote? The question was a thorny one. In justice, if blacks were to be equal, they would have to wield the ballot. But many Radical Republicans at first hesitated to bestow suffrage on the freedmen. The 14th Amendment had conferred citizenship but had stopped short of guaranteeing the right to vote. It merely imposed relatively mild penalties on those states that refused to enfranchise blacks. But the Radicals soon grew steely in their determination to gain the power of the ballot box for the emancipated slaves.

White Southerners bitterly resented the efforts of the Republican Radicals from 1867 to 1870 to elevate the uneducated blacks to full political equality. The ex-slaves themselves were often

Southern Reconstruction by State

State	Readmitted to Representation in Congress	Home Rule (Democratic Regime) Re-established	Comments
Tennessee	July 24, 1866		Ratified 14th Amendment in 1866, and hence avoided Military Reconstruction.*
Arkansas	June 22, 1868	1874	
North Carolina	June 25, 1868	1870	
Alabama	June 25, 1868	1874	
Florida	June 25, 1868	1877	
Louisiana	June 25, 1868	1877	Federal troops restationed in 1877, as result of Hayes-Tilden electoral bargain.
South Carolina	June 25, 1868	1877	Same as above.
Virginia	January 26, 1870	1869	
Mississippi	February 23, 1870	1876	
Texas	March 30, 1870	1874	
Georgia	[June 25, 1868] July 15, 1870	1872	Readmitted June 25, 1868, but returned to military control after expulsion of blacks from legislature.

*For many years Tennessee was the only state of the secession to observe Lincoln's birthday as a legal holiday. Many Southern states still observe the birthdays of Jefferson Davis and Robert E. Lee.

bewildered by such unaccustomed responsibilities. When they registered to vote many of them did not know their ages; even boys of sixteen signed the rolls. Some of these future voters could not even give their last names, if indeed they had

IOIIOIIOIIOIIOIIOIIOIIOIIOIIOIIOIIOIIOIIOIIOIIOIIOI

Representative Thaddeus Stevens, in a congressional speech on January 3, 1867, urged the ballot for blacks out of concern for them and out of bitterness against the whites: "I am for Negro suffrage in every rebel state. If it be just, it should not be denied; if it be necessary, it should be adopted; if it be a punishment to traitors, they deserve it."

IOIIOIIOIIOIIOIIOIIOIIOIIOIIOIIOIIOIIOIIOIIOIIOIIOI

any, and many took any surname that popped into their heads, often that of old "Massa."

Thousands of Southern whites were meanwhile being denied the vote, either by act of Congress or by the new state constitutions. At one dinner in South Carolina, the company consisted of a distinguished group of ex-governors, ex-congressmen, and ex-judges. The only voter in the room was the black waiter who served the meal. In some localities, about half the eligible white voters were temporarily disfranchised, and at one time the black voters in five Southern states outnumbered the white voters, many of whom were also illiterate.

By glaring contrast most of the Northern states, before the ratification of the 15th Amendment in

1870, withheld the ballot from their tiny black minorities. Southerners naturally concluded that the Radicals were hypocritical in insisting that blacks in the South be allowed to vote. One prominent North Carolinian jibed:

> To every Southern river shall Negro suffrage come,
> But not to fair New England, for that's too close
>   to hum.

Both Presidents Lincoln and Johnson had proposed to give the ballot gradually to blacks who qualified for it through education, property ownership, or soldier-service. Such a moderate program might have proved more acceptable to the ex-Confederates. But in the stormy aftermath of the war, the voices of moderation were lost in the gale. Gradualism gave way to the hard insistence by Stevens and other Radicals that the ex-slaves be enfranchised wholesale and immediately. In the end, Radical policy backfired in many ways. It conferred only fleeting benefits on the blacks, envenomed the whites, and eventually crippled the Republican party for nearly 100 years in the ex-Confederate states.

Black-and-White Legislatures in the South

In five states—Alabama, Florida, Louisiana, Mississippi, and South Carolina—the black voters enfranchised by the new state constitutions made up a majority. But only in South Carolina did they manage to dominate the lower house of the legislature. There were no state senates with a black majority, and no black governors during "black Reconstruction." Many of the newly elected black legislators were literate and able; more than a few came from the ranks of the pre-war free blacks, who had often acquired considerable education.

Yet in many Southern capitols, the ex-slaves, to the bitter resentment of their ex-masters, held offices ranging from doorkeeper to speaker. Blacks who had once raised cotton under the lash of an overseer were now raising points of order under the gavel of a parliamentarian. In many Southern states—as in many Northern states

"The First Vote." (Alfred R. Waud, *Harper's Weekly*, November 16, 1867.)

at the same time—graft and theft ran rampant. This was especially true of South Carolina and Louisiana, where promoters and other pocket-padders used politically inexperienced blacks as catspaws. The worst black-and-white legislatures purchased, under "legislative supplies," such "stationery" as hams, perfumes, suspenders, bonnets, corsets, champagne, and a coffin. One "thrifty" carpetbag governor in a single year "saved" $100,000 from a salary of $8,000.

To their credit, the black-and-white legislatures also passed much desirable legislation and introduced many overdue reforms. In some states the tax system was streamlined; charities were established; public works were launched; property rights were guaranteed to women; and free public schools were encouraged for blacks as well as whites. Many of these reforms were so welcome that they were retained even by the all-white "Redeemer" governments that later returned to power.

IOIIOIIOIIOIIOIIOIIOIIOIIOIIOIIOIIOIIOIIOIIOIIOIIOI

> A white Virginian wrote from his deathbed: "Now with what will be my lastest breath, I here repeat and would willingly proclaim my unmitigated hatred to Yankee rule . . . and all connections with Yankees, and the perfidious, malignant and vile Yankee race." A Virginia woman noted at about the same time: "I have this morning witnessed a procession of nearly a thousand children belonging to colored schools. . . . When I thought that the fetters of ignorance were broken, and that they might not be forced from their parents and sold at auction to the highest bidder, my heart went up in adoring gratitude to the great God; not only on their account, but that we white people were no longer permitted to go on in such wickedness, heaping up more and more wrath of God upon our devoted heads."

OIIOIIOIIOIIOIIOIIOIIOIIOIIOIIOIIOIIOIIOIIOIIOIIOII

Public debt in the Southern states doubled and tripled. Sometimes the expenditures were for legitimate purposes, such as rebuilding war-torn bridges or providing new educational services for the suddenly liberated blacks. Southern debts were further bloated by the unwillingness of Northern financiers to invest their capital in ravaged Dixieland. This reluctance proved so great that issues of Southern state bonds sold at deeply depressed discounts in the money markets of the North. And much of the new debt slipped down the sinkhole of fraud and corruption.

Tax rates meanwhile shot up ten- and fifteen-fold, and many propertied but disfranchised whites raised the ancient cry, "No taxation without representation." When these whites (the "Redeemers") finally regained control of their state governments, they openly repudiated over $100 million of the indebtedness they regarded as improperly incurred.

Knights of the White Sheet

Deeply embittered, some Southern whites resorted to savage measures against "Radical" rule. Many whites resented the success and ability of black legislators as much as they resented alleged "corruption." A number of secret organizations mushroomed forth, the most notorious of which was the "Invisible Empire of the South," or Ku Klux Klan, founded in Tennessee in 1866. Be-sheeted night riders, their horses' hoofs muffled, would approach the cabin of an "upstart" black and hammer on the door. In ghoulish tones one thirsty horseman would demand a bucket of water. Then, under pretense of drinking, he would pour it into a rubber attachment concealed beneath his mask and gown, smack his lips, and declare that this was the first water he had tasted since he was killed at the Battle of Shiloh. If fright did not produce the desired effect, force was employed.

Such tomfoolery and terror proved partially effective. Many ex-bondsmen and white "carpetbaggers," quick to take a hint, shunned the polls. But those stubborn souls who persisted in their "upstart" ways were flogged, mutilated, or even murdered. In one Louisiana parish in 1868, the whites in two days killed or wounded 200 victims; a pile of 25 bodies was found half-buried in the woods. By such atrocious practices was the black "kept in his place"—that is, down. The Klan be-

IOIIOIIOIIOIIOIIOIIOIIOIIOIIOIIOIIOIIOIIOIIOIIOIIOI

> In a 1900 speech Senator Tillman of South Carolina brutally boasted: "We preferred to have a United States army officer rather than a government of carpetbaggers and thieves and scallywags and scoundrels who had stolen everything in sight and mortgaged posterity . . . by issuing bonds. When that happened we took the government away. We stuffed the ballot boxes. We shot them. We are not ashamed of it."

IOIIOIIOIIOIIOIIOIIOIIOIIOIIOIIOIIOIIOIIOIIOIIOIIOI

Lynching: Aftermath of Reconstruction
(PERSONS IN U.S. LYNCHED [BY RACE], 1882–1970*)

Year	Whites	Blacks	Total
1882	64	49	113
1885	110	74	184
1890	11	85	96
1895	66	113	179
1900	9	106	115
1905	5	57	62
1910	9	67	76
1915	13	56	69
1920	8	53	61
1925	0	17	17
1930	1	20	21
1935	2	18	20
1940	1	4	5
1945	0	1	1
1950	1	1	2
1965	0	0	0

*There were no lynchings in 1965–1970. In every year from 1882 (when records were first kept) to 1964 the number of lynchings corresponded roughly to the figures here given. The worst year was 1892, when 161 blacks and 69 whites were lynched (total 230); the next worst was 1884, when 160 whites and 51 blacks were lynched (total 211).

The Ku Klux Klan. Two contemporary views of the Klan—masked and unmasked. (*Left,* from an anonymous pamphlet of 1872; *right,* Archives of Rutherford B. Hayes Library.)

came a refuge for numerous bandits and cut-throats. Any scoundrel could don a sheet.

Radicals in Congress, outraged by this night-riding lawlessness, passed the harsh Force Acts of 1870 and 1871. Federal troops were able to stamp out much of the "lash law," but by this time the "Invisible Empire" had already done its work of intimidation. Many of the outlawed groups continued their tactics in the guise of "dancing clubs," "missionary societies," and "rifle clubs," though the net effect of all the hooded terrorists has probably been exaggerated. Economic reprisals were often more effective, especially when causing the black to lose his job.

The following excerpt is part of a pathetic appeal to Congress in 1871 by a group of Kentucky blacks:

"We believe you are not familiar with the description of the Ku Klux Klans riding nightly over the country, going from county to county, and in the county towns, spreading terror wherever they go by robbing, whipping, ravishing, and killing our people without provocation, compelling colored people to break the ice and bathe in the chilly waters of the Kentucky River.

"The [state] legislature has adjourned. They refused to enact any laws to suppress Ku-Klux disorder. We regard them [the Ku-Kluxers] as now being licensed to continue their dark and bloody deeds under cover of the dark night. They refuse to allow us to testify in the state courts where a white man is concerned. We find their deeds are perpetrated only upon colored men and white Republicans. We also find that for our services to the government and our race we have become the special object of hatred and persecution at the hands of the Democratic Party. Our people are driven from their homes in great numbers, having no redress only [except] the United States court, which is in many cases unable to reach them."

A black leader protested to whites in 1868: "It is extraordinary that a race such as yours, professing gallantry, chivalry, education, and superiority, living in a land where ringing chimes call child and sire to the Gospel of God—that with all these advantages on your side, you can make war upon the poor defenseless black man."

Shortsighted attempts by the Radicals to exploit the ex-slave as a voter failed miserably. The white South, for many decades, openly flouted the 14th and 15th Amendments. Wholesale disfranchisement of the black, starting conspicuously about 1890, was achieved by intimidation, fraud, and trickery. Among various underhanded schemes were the literacy tests, unfairly administered by whites to the advantage of illiterate whites. In the eyes of otherwise honorable Southerners, the goal of White Supremacy fully justified dishonorable devices.

Johnson Walks the Impeachment Plank

Radicals meanwhile had been sharpening their hatchets for President Johnson. Annoyed by the obstruction of the "drunken tailor" in the White House, they falsely accused him of maintaining there a harem of "dissolute women." Not content with curbing his authority, they decided to remove him altogether by constitutional processes.* Under existing law the president pro tempore of the Senate, the unscrupulous and rabidly Radical "Bluff Ben" Wade of Ohio, would then become President.

As an initial step, the Radicals in 1867 passed the Tenure of Office Act—as usual over Johnson's veto. Contrary to precedent, the new law required the President to secure the consent of the Senate before he could remove his appointees, once they had been approved by that body. One purpose of the Radicals was to freeze into the Cabinet the secretary of war, Edwin M. Stanton, a holdover from the Lincoln administration. Though outwardly loyal to Johnson, he was secretly serving as a spy and informer for the Radicals. Another purpose was to goad Johnson into breaking the law, and thus establish grounds for his impeachment.

An aroused Johnson was eager to get a test case before the Supreme Court, for he believed the Tenure of Office Act to be unconstitutional. (That slow-moving tribunal finally ruled indirectly in his favor fifty-eight years later.) Expecting reason-

*For impeachment, see Art. I, Sec. II, para. 5; Art. I, Sec. III, paras. 6, 7; Art. II, Sec. IV, in Appendix.

able judicial speed, Johnson abruptly dismissed the two-faced Stanton early in 1868. The President did not believe that the law applied to Lincoln's holdovers, even though the Radicals insisted otherwise.

A Radical-influenced House of Representatives struck back swiftly. By a count of 126 to 47, it voted to impeach Johnson for "high crimes and misdemeanors," as called for by the Constitution. Most of the specific accusations grew out of the President's so-called violation of the ("unconstitutional") Tenure of Office Act. Two added articles related to Johnson's verbal assaults on Congress, involving "disgrace, ridicule, hatred, contempt, and reproach."

A Not-Guilty Verdict for Johnson

With evident zeal, the Radical-led Senate now sat as a court to try Johnson on the dubious impeachment charges. The House conducted the prosecution. The trial aroused intense public interest and, with 1,000 tickets printed, proved to be the biggest show of 1868. Johnson kept his

A Crippled Stevens Carried to the Trial. Stevens, too weak to walk, is borne into the Senate chamber for Johnson's impeachment trial. (Rare Book Division, The New York Public Library, Astor, Lenox and Tilden Foundations.)

dignity and sobriety, and maintained a discreet silence. His battery of attorneys was extremely able, while the House prosecutors, including oily-tongued Benjamin F. Butler and embittered Thaddeus Stevens, bungled their flimsy case.

On May 16, 1868, the day for the first voting in the Senate, the tension was electric, and heavy breathing could be heard in the galleries. By a margin of only one vote, the Radicals failed to muster the two-thirds majority for Johnson's removal. Seven independent-minded Republican senators, courageously putting country above party, voted "not guilty."

The Radicals were infuriated. "The country is going to the Devil!" cried the crippled Stevens as he was carried from the hall. President-to-be Wade had even chosen his Cabinet, with the unscrupulous Benjamin F. Butler as secretary of state. But the nation, though violently aroused, accepted the verdict with a good temper that did credit to its political maturity. In a less stable Republic, an armed uprising might have erupted against the President.

A bad precedent was thus narrowly avoided that would have gravely weakened one of the three branches of the federal government. Johnson was clearly guilty of bad speeches, bad judgment, and bad temper, but not of "high crimes and misdemeanors." From the standpoint of the Radicals, his greatest crime had been to stand inflexibly in their path.

The Purchase of Alaska

Johnson's administration, though largely reduced to a figurehead, achieved its most enduring success in the field of foreign relations.

The Russians by 1867 were in a mood to sell the vast and chilly expanse now known as Alaska. They had already overextended themselves in North America, and they saw that in the likely event of another war with England they probably would lose their defenseless province to the sea-dominant British. Alaska, moreover, had been ruthlessly "furred out" and was a growing economic liability. The Russians were therefore eager

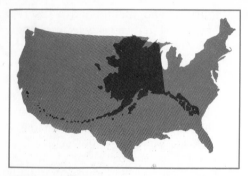

ALASKA AND THE LOWER FORTY-EIGHT STATES
(a size comparison)

to unload their "frozen asset" on the Americans, and they put out seductive feelers in Washington. They preferred the United States to any other purchaser, primarily because they wanted to strengthen further the Republic as a barrier against their ancient enemy, Britain.

In 1867 Secretary of State Seward, an ardent expansionist, signed a treaty with Russia which transferred Alaska to the United States for the bargain price of $7.2 million. But Seward's enthusiasm for these frigid wastes was not shared by

The Alaska Purchase Satirized.   It is pilloried as a scheme to get votes for the Johnson administration. Ursus, a polar bear, is hailed as the bears' candidate. (American Antiquarian Society.)

his ignorant or uninformed countrymen, who jeered at "Seward's Folly," "Seward's Icebox," "Frigidia," and "Walrussia." The American people, still preoccupied with Reconstruction and other internal vexations, were economy-minded and anti-expansionist.

Then why did Congress and the American public sanction the purchase? For one thing Russia, alone among the powers, had been conspicuously friendly to the North during the recent Civil War. Americans did not feel that they could offend their great and good friend, the Czar, by hurling his walrus-covered icebergs back into his face. Besides, the territory was rumored to be teeming with furs, fish, and gold, and it might yet "pan out" profitably—as it later did with natural resources, including oil and gas. So Congress and the country accepted "Seward's Polar Bear Garden," somewhat wry-facedly and derisively but nevertheless hopefully. The speculative nature of the transaction not only appealed to Yankee love of a bargain, but did something to dispel the gloom of the Reconstruction era.

Heritage of Reconstruction

Many historians have ranked Reconstruction as one of America's tragic failures. The Republic fumbled away the opportunity to close the bloody chasm between North and South. Yet such were the war-born hatreds that much of this unreason was perhaps inevitable.

The Civil War was fought openly—and on the whole honorably. When it was over, there were no wholesale blood purges. No one was executed for a purely political offense, though the foreign-born commander of a Confederate prison (Andersonville) was hanged for murder, as were surviving conspirators in the Lincoln assassination. Probably no large-scale and unsuccessful revolt has ever ended with so little head-rolling.

But if the Yankee victor chopped off no heads, the ex-Confederates regarded themselves as ground into the dust over the race issue. The Northern ideals of national unity and human freedom, they cried, were submerged in an orgy of

The remarkable ex-slave Frederick Douglass, wrote in 1882: "Though slavery was abolished, the wrongs of my people were not ended. Though they were not slaves, they were not yet quite free. No man can be truly free whose liberty is dependent upon the thought, feeling, and action of others, and who has himself no means in his own hands for guarding, protecting, defending, and maintaining that liberty. Yet the Negro after his emancipation was precisely in this state of destitution. . . . He was free from the individual master, but the slave of society. He had neither money, property, nor friends. He was free from the old plantation, but he had nothing but the dusty road under his feet. He was free from the old quarter that once gave him shelter, but a slave to the rains of summer and the frosts of winter. He was, in a word, literally turned loose, naked, hungry, and destitute, to the open sky."

hate and corruption. To many white Southerners, reconstructing was a more grievous wound than the fighting; it left the "Angry Scar."

The Republican party, with its luckless black recruits, was indelibly tarred by the brush of Reconstruction. Southern devotees of White Supremacy were driven into the ranks of the Democratic party, and the Solid South solidified for decades as the Democratic South. The blacks were freed but only partially free.

In the light of hindsight, the Radical Reconstruction program seems for too narrowly conceived. It might well have embraced the social and economic rehabilitation of the South, including the blacks. At a time when weed-choked Southern lands were lying idle, hundreds of thousands of acres could have been made available to the ex-slaves at low cost, or no cost, as Thaddeus Stevens and others had urged. But indifference and ingrained American resistance to drastic change, especially regarding property rights, proved too strong.

VARYING VIEWPOINTS

Few topics have triggered as much intellectual warfare as the "dark and bloody ground" of Reconstruction. The period provoked questions—sectional, racial, and constitutional—about which people felt deeply and remain deeply divided even today. Scholarly argument goes back conspicuously to a Columbia University historian, William A. Dunning, and his *Reconstruction, Political and Economic* (1907). Dunning was influenced by the turn-of-the-century spirit of sectional reconciliation and by then current theories about black racial inferiority. Sympathizing with the white South, he wrote of Reconstruction as a kind of national disgrace, foisted upon a prostrate region by vindictive, self-seeking Radical Republican politicians. If the South had wronged the North by seceding, the North had wronged the South by reconstructing. For a long time this persuasive view held sway, reinforced by a widespread suspicion in the 1920s and 1930s that the Civil War itself

had been a tragic and unnecessary blunder. Black historian W. E. B. Du Bois' *Black Reconstruction* in 1935 represented virtually the only serious attack on the "Dunning School" until World War II.

Following the Second World War, two developments in American culture encouraged a new examination of the Dunning approach. One was the spread of a more egalitarian attitude toward racial questions, especially following the black agitation of the 1960s. The other factor was the growing conviction that ideals counted for a great deal in this controversy. Consequently, many historians now showed much more interest in the real problems of the black freedmen, more admiration for the "helpful" Radical Republicans as genuine idealists rather than as self-seeking politicians, and less sympathy for the beaten and defiant white South. Kenneth Stampp's *Era of Reconstruction* (1965) probably best summarizes these newer views, which continue to spark debate.

SELECT READINGS

Overall accounts may be found in J. G. Randall and David Donald, *The Civil War and Reconstruction* (rev. ed., 1969), R. W. Patrick, *The Reconstruction of the Nation* (1967), Avery Craven, *Reconstruction* (1969), J. H. Franklin, *Reconstruction After the Civil War* (1961), and Kenneth Stampp, *The Era of Reconstruction* (1965), perhaps the best brief introduction. Howard K. Beale, *The Critical Year* (1930), is sympathetic to Johnson. More critical of the accidental President are E. L. McKitrick, *Andrew Johnson and Reconstruction* (1960), W. R. Brock, *An American Crisis* (1960), and LaWanda and J. H. Cox, *Politics, Principle, and Prejudice, 1865–1866* (1963). Sympathetic to the Radical Republicans are J. M. McPherson, *The Struggle for Equality* (1964), and H. L. Trefousse, *The Radical Republicans* (1969). See also David Montgomery, *Beyond Equality: Labor and the Radical Republicans, 1862–1872* (1967). Radiating pro-Southern indignation is E. M. Coulter, *The South during Reconstruction* (1947). Siding with the Radicals in the impeachment fight are M. L. Benedict, *The Impeachment and Trial of Andrew Johnson* (1973), and H. L. Trefousse, *Impeachment of a President* (1975).

Conditions in the South are analyzed in W. E. B. Du Bois's controversial classic, *Black Reconstruction* (1935), in Peter Kolchin, *First Freedom* (1973), and in Leon F. Litwack's brilliantly evocative *Been in the Storm So Long* (1979), a revealing study of the initial responses, by both blacks and whites, to emancipation. It can be usefully supplemented by Roger Ransom and Richard L. Sutch, *One Kind of Freedom: The Economic Consequences of Emancipation* (1977). See also James Roark, *Masters Without Slaves: Southern Planters in the Civil War and Reconstruction* (1977). Willie Lee Rose engagingly describes a *Rehearsal for Reconstruction: The Port Royal Experiment* (1964). O. A. Singletary discusses *The Negro Militia and Reconstruction* (1957). Local studies of merit are Joel Williamson, *After Slavery: The Negro in South Carolina during Reconstruction* (1965), J. W. Blassingame, *Black New Orleans, 1860–1880* (1973), and Thomas Holt, *Black Over White: Negro Political Leadership in South Carolina during Reconstruction* (1977). W. P. Vaughan examines the movement to educate the freedmen in *Schools for All* (1974). C. Vann Woodward looks for the roots of segregation in *The Strange Career of Jim Crow* (rev. ed., 1974). See also Robert Cruden, *The Negro in Reconstruction* (1969). A unique collection of documents is George P. Rawick, ed., *The American Slave: A Composite Autobiography* (19 vols., 1972), a collection of oral history interviews conducted with ex-slaves and their families by the Federal Writers Project during the Depression of the 1930s. For Southern white responses to Reconstruction, see Michael Perman, *Reunion without Compromise* (1973), and Allen W. Trelease, *White Terror* (1971).

Special studies of value are W. B. Hesseltine, *Lincoln's Plan of Reconstruction* (1960). W. S. McFeely, *Yankee Stepfather: General O. O. Howard and the Freedmen* (1968), J. B. James, *The Framing of the Fourteenth Amendment* (1956), W. Gillette, *The Right to Vote: Politics and the Passage of the 15th Amendment* (1965), S. I. Kutler, *Judicial Power and Reconstruction Politics* (1968), H. M. Hyman, *A More Perfect Union: The Impact of the Civil War and Reconstruction on the Constitution* (1973), R. P. Sharkey, *Money, Class, and Party: An Economic Study of Civil War and Reconstruction* (1959), and W. T. K. Nugent, *The Money Question during Reconstruction* (1967). Useful biographies are David Donald, *Charles Sumner and the Rights of Man* (1970), Fawn M. Brodie, *Thaddeus Stevens* (1959), and B. P. Thomas and H. M. Hyman, *Stanton* (1962). A comprehensive study of the climax of this troubled period is William Gillette, *Retreat from Reconstruction, 1869–1879* (1979).

DECLARATION OF INDEPENDENCE
In Congress, July 4, 1776

The Unanimous Declaration of the Thirteen United States of America

[Bracketed material in color has been inserted by the authors. For adoption background, see pp. 104–105.]

When, in the course of human events, it becomes necessary for one people to dissolve the political bands which have connected them with another, and to assume, among the powers of the earth, the separate and equal station to which the laws of nature and of nature's God entitle them, a decent respect to the opinions of mankind requires that they should declare the causes which impel them to the separation.

We hold these truths to be self-evident: That all men are created equal; that they are endowed by their Creator with certain unalienable rights; that among these are life, liberty, and the pursuit of happiness; that, to secure these rights, governments are instituted among men, deriving their just powers from the consent of the governed; that whenever any form of government becomes destructive of these ends, it is the right of the people to alter or to abolish it, and to institute new government, laying its foundation on such principles, and organizing its powers in such form, as to them shall seem most likely to effect their safety and happiness. Prudence, indeed, will dictate that governments long established should not be changed for light and transient causes; and accordingly all experience hath shown that mankind are more disposed to suffer, while evils are sufferable, than to right themselves by abolishing the forms to which they are accustomed. But when a long train of abuses and usurpations, pursuing invariably the same object, evinces a design to reduce them under absolute despotism, it is their right, it is their duty, to throw off such government, and to provide new guards for their future security. Such has been the patient sufferance of these colonies; and such is now the necessity which constrains them to alter their former systems of government. The history of the present King of Great Britain is a history of repeated injuries and usurpations, all having in direct object the establishment of an absolute tyranny over these states. To prove this, let facts be submitted to a candid world.

He has refused his assent to laws, the most wholesome and necessary for the public good. [See royal veto, p. 84.]

He has forbidden his governors to pass laws of immediate and pressing importance, unless suspended in their operation till his assent should be obtained; and, when so suspended, he has utterly neglected to attend to them.

He has refused to pass other laws for the accommodation of large districts of people [by establishing new counties], unless those people would relinquish the right of representation in the legislature, a right inestimable to them, and formidable to tyrants only.

He has called together legislative bodies at places unusual, uncomfortable, and distant from the depository of their public records, for the sole purpose of fatiguing them into compliance with his measures. [E.g., removal of Massachusetts Assembly to Salem, 1774.]

He has dissolved representative houses repeatedly, for opposing, with manly firmness, his invasions on the rights of the people. [E.g., Virginia Assembly, 1765.]

He has refused for a long time, after such dissolutions, to cause others to be elected; whereby the legislative powers, incapable of annihilation, have returned to the people at large for their exercise; the state remaining, in the mean time, exposed to all the dangers of invasions from without and convulsions within.

He has endeavored to prevent the population [populating] of these states; for that purpose obstructing the laws for naturalization of foreigners; refusing to pass others to encourage their migration hither, and raising the conditions of new appropriations of lands. [E.g., Proclamation of 1763, p. 57.]

He has obstructed the administration of justice, by refusing his assent to laws for establishing judiciary powers.

He has made judges dependent on his will alone, for the tenure of their offices, and the amount and payment of their salaries. [See Townshend Acts, p. 90.]

He has erected a multitude of new offices, and sent hither swarms of officers to harass our people and eat out their substance. [See enforcement of Navigation Laws, p. 90.]

He has kept among us, in times of peace, standing armies, without the consent of our legislatures. [See pp. 86, 90.]

He has affected to render the military independent of, and superior to, the civil power.

He has combined with others to subject us to a jurisdiction foreign to our constitution, and unacknowledged by our laws, giving his assent to their acts of pretended legislation:

> For quartering large bodies of armed troops among us [see Boston Massacre, pp. 86, 90];
>
> For protecting them, by a mock trial, from punishment for any murders which they should commit on the inhabitants of these states [see 1774 Act, pp. 92, 93];
>
> For cutting off our trade with all parts of the world [see Boston Port Act, p. 92];
>
> For imposing taxes on us without our consent [see Stamp Act, p. 87];
>
> For depriving us, in many cases, of the benefits of trial by jury;
>
> For transporting us beyond seas, to be tried for pretended offenses;
>
> For abolishing the free system of English laws in a neighboring province [Quebec], establishing therein an arbitrary government, and enlarging its boundaries, so as to render it at once an example and fit instrument for introducing the same absolute rule into these colonies [Quebec Act, p. 93];
>
> For taking away our charters, abolishing our most valuable laws, and altering fundamentally the forms of our governments [E.g., in Massachusetts, p. 92];
>
> For suspending our own legislatures, and declaring themselves invested with power to legislate for us in all cases whatsoever [see Stamp Act repeal, p. 89].

He has abdicated government here, by declaring us out of his protection and waging war against us. [Proclamation, p. 102.]

He has plundered our seas, ravaged our coasts, burned our towns, and destroyed the lives of our people. [E.g., the burning of Falmouth (Portland), p. 102.]

He is at this time transporting large armies of foreign mercenaries [Hessians, p. 102] to complete the works of death, desolation, and tyranny already begun with circumstances of cruelty and perfidy scarcely paralleled in the most barbarous ages, and totally unworthy the head of a civilized nation.

He has constrained our fellow-citizens, taken captive on the high seas [by impressment], to bear arms against their country, to become the executioners of their friends and brethren, or to fall themselves by their hands.

He has excited domestic insurrection among us [i.e., among slaves], and has endeavored to bring on the inhabitants of our frontiers the merciless Indian savages, whose known rule of warfare is an undistinguished destruction of all ages, sexes, and conditions.

In every stage of these oppressions we have petitioned for redress in the most humble terms; our repeated petitions have been answered only by repeated injury. [E.g., pp. 100, 102.] A prince, whose character is thus marked by every act which may define a tyrant, is unfit to be the ruler of a free people.

Nor have we been wanting in our attentions to our British brethren. We have warned them, from time to time, of attempts by their legislature to extend an unwarrantable jurisdiction over us. We have reminded them of the circumstances of our emigration and settlement here. We have appealed to their native justice and magnanimity; and we have conjured them, by the ties of our common kindred, to disavow these usurpations, which would inevitably interrupt our connections and correspondence. They, too, have been deaf to the voice of justice and of consanguinity [blood relationship]. We must, therefore, acquiesce in the necessity which denounces [announces] our separation, and hold them, as we hold the rest of mankind, enemies in war, in peace friends.

We, therefore, the representatives of the United States of America, in General Congress assembled, appealing to the Supreme Judge of the world for the rectitude of our intentions, do, in the name and by the authority of the good people of these colonies, solemnly publish and declare, That these United Colonies are, and of right ought to be, FREE AND INDE-PENDENT STATES; that they are absolved from all allegiance to the British crown, and that all political connection between them and the state of Great Britain is, and ought to be, totally dissolved; and that, as free and independent states, they have full power to levy war, conclude peace, contract alliances, establish commerce, and do all other acts and things which independent states may of right do. And for the support of this declaration, with a firm reliance on the protection of Divine Providence, we mutually pledge to each other our lives, our fortunes, and our sacred honor.

[Signed by]   JOHN HANCOCK [President]
                                                       [and fifty-five others]

CONSTITUTION OF
THE UNITED STATES OF AMERICA

[Boldface headings and bracketed explanatory matter and marginal comments (both in color) have been inserted for the reader's convenience. Passages that are no longer operative are printed in italic type.]

PREAMBLE

On "We the people," see p. 236n.

We the people of the United States, in order to form a more perfect union, establish justice, insure domestic tranquillity, provide for the common defense, promote the general welfare, and secure the blessings of liberty to ourselves and our posterity, do ordain and establish this CONSTITUTION for the United States of America.

Article I. Legislative Department

Section I. Congress

Legislative power vested in a two-House Congress. All legislative powers herein granted shall be vested in a Congress of the United States, which shall consist of a Senate and a House of Representatives.

Section II. House of Representatives

1. The people elect representatives biennially. The House of Representatives shall be composed of members chosen every second year by the people of the several States, and the electors [voters] in each State shall have the qualifications requisite for electors of the most numerous branch of the State Legislature.

2. Who may be representatives. No person shall be a Representative who shall not have attained to the age of twenty-five years, and been seven years a citizen of the United States, and who shall not, when elected, be an inhabitant of that State in which he shall be chosen.

See 1787 compromise, p. 132.

See 1787 compromise, p. 133.

3. Representation in the House based on population; census. Representatives and direct taxes[1] shall be apportioned among the several States which may be included within this Union, according to their respective numbers, *which shall be determined by adding to the whole number of free persons, including those bound to service for a term of years* [apprentices and indentured servants], *and excluding Indians not taxed, three-fifths of all other persons* [slaves].[2] The actual enumeration [census] shall be made within three years after the first meeting of the Congress of the United States, and within every subsequent term of ten years, in such manner as they shall by law direct. The number of Representatives shall not exceed one for every thirty thousand, but each State shall have at least one Representative; *and until such enumeration shall be made, the State of New Hampshire shall be entitled to choose three, Massachusetts eight, Rhode Island and Providence Plantations one, Connecticut five, New York six, New Jersey four, Pennsylvania eight, Delaware one, Maryland six, Virginia ten, North Carolina five, South Carolina five, and Georgia three.*

4. Vacancies in the House are filled by election. When vacancies happen in the representation from any State, the Executive authority [governor] thereof shall issue writs of election [call a special election] to fill such vacancies.

---

[1] Modified in 1913 by the 16th Amendment re income taxes (see p. 630).

[2] The word "slave" appears nowhere in the Constitution; "slavery" appears in the 13th Amendment. The three-fifths rule ceased to be in force when the 13th Amendment was adopted in 1865 (see p. 404 and Amendments below).

See Chase and Johnson trials, pp. 171, 448–449; Nixon trial preliminaries, pp. 895–897.

5. The House selects its Speaker; has sole power to vote impeachment charges (i.e., indictments). The House of Representatives shall choose their Speaker and other officers; and shall have the sole power of impeachment.

Section III. Senate

1. Senators represent the states. The Senate of the United States shall be composed of two Senators from each State, *chosen by the legislature thereof,*[1] for six years; and each Senator shall have one vote.

2. One-third of Senators chosen every two years; vacancies. *Immediately after they shall be assembled in consequence of the first election, they shall be divided as equally as may be into three classes. The seats of the Senators of the first class shall be vacated at the expiration of the second year, of the second class at the expiration of the fourth year, and of the third class at the expiration of the sixth year,* so that one-third may be chosen every second year; *and if vacancies happen by resignation or otherwise, during the recess of the legislature of any State, the Executive* [governor] *thereof may make temporary appointments until the next meeting of the legislature, which shall then fill such vacancies.*[2]

3. Who may be Senators. No person shall be a Senator who shall not have attained to the age of thirty years, and been nine years a citizen of the United States, and who shall not, when elected, be an inhabitant of that State for which he shall be chosen.

4. The Vice-President presides over the Senate. The Vice-President of the United States shall be President of the Senate, but shall have no vote, unless they be equally divided [tied].

5. The Senate chooses its other officers. The Senate shall choose their other officers, and also a President *pro tempore,* in the absence of the Vice-President, or when he shall exercise the office of President of the United States.

See Chase and Johnson trials, pp. 171, 448–449.

6. The Senate has sole power to try impeachments. The Senate shall have the sole power to try all impeachments. When sitting for that purpose, they shall be on oath or affirmation. When the President of the United States is tried, the Chief Justice shall preside:[3] and no person shall be convicted without the concurrence of two-thirds of the members present.

7. Penalties for impeachment conviction. Judgment in cases of impeachment shall not extend further than to removal from office, and disqualification to hold and enjoy any office of honor, trust or profit under the United States: but the party convicted shall nevertheless be liable and subject to indictment, trial, judgment and punishment, according to law.

Section IV. Election and Meetings of Congress

1. Regulation of elections. The times, places and manner of holding elections for Senators and Representatives shall be prescribed in each State by the legislature thereof; but the Congress may at any time by law make or alter such regulations, except as to the places of choosing Senators.

2. Congress must meet once a year. The Congress shall assemble at least once in every year, and such meeting *shall be on the first Monday in December, unless they shall by law appoint a different day.*[4]

---

[1] Repealed in favor of popular election in 1913 by the 17th Amendment.
[2] Changed in 1913 by the 17th Amendment.
[3] The Vice-President, as next in line, would be an interested party.
[4] Changed in 1933 to January 3 by the 20th Amendment (see p. 767 and below).

Section V.   Organization and Rules of the Houses

1. Each House may reject members; quorums. Each house shall be the judge of the elections, returns and qualifications of its own members, and a majority of each shall constitute a quorum to do business; but a smaller number may adjourn from day to day, and may be authorized to compel the attendance of absent members, in such manner, and under such penalties, as each house may provide.

See "Bully" Brooks case, p. 370.

2. Each House makes its own rules. Each house may determine the rules of its proceedings, punish its members for disorderly behavior, and with the concurrence of two-thirds, expel a member.

3. Each House must keep and publish a record of its proceedings. Each house shall keep a journal of its proceedings, and from time to time publish the same, excepting such parts as may in their judgment require secrecy; and the yeas and nays of the members of either house on any question shall, at the desire of one-fifth of those present, be entered on the journal.

4. Both Houses must agree on adjournment. Neither house, during the session of Congress, shall, without the consent of the other, adjourn for more than three days, nor to any other place than that in which the two houses shall be sitting.

Section VI.   Privileges of and Prohibitions upon Congressmen

1. Congressional salaries; immunities. The Senators and Representatives shall receive a compensation for their services, to be ascertained by law and paid out of the treasury of the United States. They shall in all cases except treason, felony and breach of the peace, be privileged from arrest during their attendance at the session of their respective houses, and in going to and returning from the same; and for any speech or debate in either house, they shall not be questioned in any other place [i.e., they shall be immune from libel suits]

2. A Congressman may not hold any other federal civil office. No Senator or Representative shall, during the time for which he was elected, be appointed to any civil office under the authority of the United States, which shall have been created, or the emoluments whereof shall have been increased, during such time; and no person holding any office under the United States shall be a member of either house during his continuance in office.

Section VII.   Method of Making Laws

See 1787 compromise, p. 132.

1. Money bills must originate in the House. All bills for raising revenue shall originate in the House of Representatives; but the Senate may propose or concur with amendments as on other bills.

President Nixon, more than any predecessors, "impounded" billions of dollars voted by Congress for specific purposes, because he disapproved of them. The courts generally failed to sustain him, and his impeachment foes regarded wholesale impoundment as a violation of his oath to "faithfully execute" the laws.

2. The President's veto power; Congress may override. Every bill which shall have passed the House of Representatives and the Senate, shall, before it become a law, be presented to the President of the United States; if he approve he shall sign it, but if not he shall return it with his objections to that house in which it shall have originated, who shall enter the objections at large on their journal, and proceed to reconsider it. If after such reconsideration two-thirds of that house shall agree to pass the bill, it shall be sent, together with the objections, to the other house, by which it shall likewise be reconsidered, and, if approved by two-thirds of that house, it shall become a law. But in all such cases the votes of both houses shall be determined by yeas and nays, and the names of the persons voting for and against the bill shall be entered on the journal of each house respectively. If any bill shall not be returned by the President within ten days (Sundays excepted) after it shall have been presented to him, the same shall be a law, in like manner as if he had signed it, unless the Congress by their adjournment prevent its return, in which case it shall not be a law [this is the so-called pocket veto].

3. All measures requiring the agreement of both Houses go to President for approval. Every order, resolution, or vote to which the concurrence of the Senate and House of Representatives may be necessary (except on a question of adjournment) shall be presented to the President of the United States; and before the same shall take effect, shall be approved by him, or being disapproved by him, shall be repassed by two-thirds of the Senate and House of Representatives, according to the rules and limitations prescribed in the case of a bill.

Section VIII.   Powers Granted to Congress

Congress has certain enumerated powers:

1. It may lay and collect taxes. The Congress shall have power to lay and collect taxes, duties, imposts, and excises, to pay the debts and provide for the common defense and general welfare of the United States; but all duties, imposts and excises shall be uniform throughout the United States;

2. It may borrow money. To borrow money on the credit of the United States;

3. It may regulate foreign and interstate trade. To regulate commerce with foreign nations, and among the several States, and with the Indian tribes;

For 1798 naturalization, see p. 161.   **4. It may pass naturalization and bankruptcy laws.** To establish an uniform rule of naturalization, and uniform laws on the subject of bankruptcies throughout the United States;

5. It may coin money. To coin money, regulate the value thereof, and of foreign coin, and fix the standard of weights and measures;

6. It may punish counterfeiters. To provide for the punishment of counterfeiting the securities and current coin of the United States;

7. It may establish a postal service. To establish post offices and post roads;

8. It may issue patents and copyrights. To promote the progress of science and useful arts by securing for limited times to authors and inventors the exclusive right to their respective writings and discoveries;

See Judiciary Act of 1789, p. 143.   **9. It may establish inferior courts.** To constitute tribunals inferior to the Supreme Court;

10. It may punish crimes committed on the high seas. To define and punish piracies and felonies committed on the high seas [i.e., outside the three-mile limit] and offenses against the law of nations [international law];

11. It may declare war; authorize privateers. To declare war,[1] grant letters of marque and reprisal,[2] and make rules concerning captures on land and water;

12. It may maintain an army. To raise and support armies, but no appropriation of money to that use shall be for a longer term than two years;[3]

13. It may maintain a navy. To provide and maintain a navy;

14. It may regulate the army and navy. To make rules for the government and regulation of the land and naval forces;

See Whiskey Rebellion, p. 147.   **15. It may call out the state militia.** To provide for calling forth the militia to execute the laws of the Union, suppress insurrections, and repel invasions;

---

[1] Note that the President, though he can provoke war (see the case of Polk, p. 267) or wage it after it is declared, cannot declare it.

[2] Papers issued private citizens in wartime authorizing them to capture enemy ships.

[3] A reflection of fear of standing armies earlier expressed in the Declaration of Independence.

16. It shares with the states control of militia. To provide for organizing, arming, and disciplining the militia, and for governing such part of them as may be employed in the service of the United States, reserving to the States respectively the appointment of the officers, and the authority of training the militia according to the discipline prescribed by Congress;

17. It makes laws for the District of Columbia and other federal areas. To exercise exclusive legislation in all cases whatsoever, over such district (not exceeding ten miles square) as may, by cession of particular States, and the acceptance of Congress, become the seat of government of the United States,[1] and to exercise like authority over all places purchased by the consent of the legislature of the State, in which the same shall be, for the erection of forts, magazines, arsenals, dock-yards, and other needful buildings;—and

Congress has certain implied powers:

This is the famous "Elastic Clause"; see p. 146.

18. It may make laws necessary for carrying out the enumerated powers. To make all laws which shall be necessary and proper for carrying into execution the foregoing powers, and all others powers vested by this Constitution in the government of the United States, or in any department or officer thereof.

Section IX. Powers Denied to the Federal Government

1. Congressional control of slave trade postponed until 1808. *The migration or importation of such persons as any of the States now existing shall think proper to admit shall not be prohibited by the Congress prior to the year 1808; but a tax or duty may be imposed on such importation, not exceeding $10 for each person.*

See 1787 slave compromise, p. 133.

See Lincoln's unlawful suspension, p. 420.

2. The writ of habeas corpus[2] may be suspended only in case of rebellion or invasion. The privilege of the writ of habeas corpus shall not be suspended, unless when in cases of rebellion or invasion the public safety may require it.

3. Attainders[3] and ex post facto laws[4] forbidden. No bill of attainder or ex post facto law shall be passed.

4. Direct taxes must be apportioned according to population. No capitation [head or poll tax], or other direct, tax shall be laid, unless in proportion to the census or enumeration herein before directed to be taken.[5]

5. Export taxes forbidden. No tax or duty shall be laid on articles exported from any State.

6. Congress must not discriminate among states in regulating commerce. No preference shall be given by any regulation of commerce or revenue to the ports of one State over those of another; nor shall vessels bound to, or from, one State, be obliged to enter, clear, or pay duties in another.

See Lincoln's unlawful infraction, p. 420.

7. Public money may not be spent without congressional appropriation; accounting. No money shall be drawn from the treasury, but in consequence of appropriations made by law; and a regular statement and account of the receipts and expenditures of all public money shall be published from time to time.

---

[1] The District of Columbia, 10 miles square, was established in 1791 with a cession from Virginia (see p. 144).
[2] A writ of habeas corpus is a document that enables a person under arrest to obtain an immediate examination in court to ascertain whether he is being legally held.
[3] A bill of attainder is a special legislative act condemning and punishing an individual without a judicial trial.
[4] An ex post facto law is one that fixes punishments for acts committed before the law was passed.
[5] Modified in 1913 by the 16th Amendment (see p. 630, and Amendments below).

8. Titles of nobility prohibited; foreign gifts. No title of nobility shall be granted by the United States: and no person holding any office of profit or trust under them, shall, without the consent of the Congress, accept of any present, emolument, office, or title, of any kind whatever, from any king, prince, or foreign state.

Section X.   Powers Denied to the States

Absolute prohibitions on the states:

1. The states are forbidden to do certain things. No State shall enter into any treaty, alliance, or confederation; grant letters of marque and reprisal [i.e., authorize privateers]; coin money; emit bills of credit [issue paper money]; make anything but gold and silver coin a [legal] tender in payment of debts; pass any bill of attainder, ex post facto,[1] or law impairing the obligation of contracts, or grant any title of nobility.

On contracts, see Fletcher *v.* Peck, *p. 212.*

Conditional prohibitions on the states:

2. The states may not levy duties without the consent of Congress. No State shall, without the consent of the Congress, lay any imposts or duties on imports or exports, except what may be absolutely necessary for executing its inspection laws: and the net produce of all duties and imposts, laid by any State on imports or exports, shall be for the use of the treasury of the United States; and all such laws shall be subject to the revision and control of the Congress.

Cf. Confederation chaos, p. 125.

3. Certain other federal powers are forbidden the states except with the consent of Congress. No State shall, without the consent of Congress, lay any duty of tonnage [i.e., duty on ship tonnage], keep [non-militia] troops or ships of war in time of peace, enter into any agreement or compact with another State, or with a foreign power, or engage in war, unless actually invaded, or in such imminent danger as will not admit of delay.

Article II.   Executive Department

Section I.   President and Vice-President

1. The President the chief executive; his term. The executive power shall be vested in a President of the United States of America. He shall hold his office during the term of four years,[2] and, together with the Vice-President, chosen for the same term, be elected as follows:

See 1787 compromise, p. 133.

See 1876 Oregon case, p. 461.

2. The President is chosen by electors. Each State shall appoint, in such manner as the legislature thereof may direct, a number of electors, equal to the whole number of Senators and Representatives to which the State may be entitled in the Congress; but no Senator or Representative, or person holding an office of trust or profit under the United States, shall be appointed an elector.

A majority of the electoral votes needed to elect a President. *The electors shall meet in their respective States, and vote by ballot for two persons, of whom one at least shall not be an inhabitant of the same State with themselves. And they shall make a list of all the persons voted for, and of the number of votes for each; which list they shall sign and certify, and transmit sealed to the seat of government of the United States, directed to the President of the Senate. The President of the Senate shall, in the presence of the Senate and House of Representatives, open all the certificates, and the votes shall then be counted. The person having the greatest number of votes shall be the President, if such number be a*

----

[1] For definitions, see footnotes 3 and 4 on preceding page.
[2] No reference to re-election; for anti-third term 22d Amendment, see below.

majority of the whole number of electors appointed; and if there be more than one who have such majority, and have an equal number of votes, then the House of Representatives shall immediately choose by ballot one of them for President; and if no person have a majority, then from the five highest on the list the said house shall in like manner choose the President. But in choosing the President the votes shall be taken by States, the representation from each State having one vote; a quorum for this purpose shall consist of a member or members from two-thirds of the States, and a majority of all the States shall be necessary to a choice. In every case, after the choice of the President, the person having the greatest number of votes of the electors shall be the Vice-President. But if there should remain two or more who have equal votes, the Senate shall choose from them by ballot the Vice-President.[1]

See Burr-Jefferson disputed election of 1800, p. 164.

See Jefferson as Vice-President in 1796, p. 158.

3. Congress decides time of meeting of Electoral College. The Congress may determine the time of choosing the electors and the day on which they shall give their votes; which day shall be the same throughout the United States.

4. Who may be President. No person except a natural-born citizen, *or a citizen of the United States at the time of the adoption of this Constitution,* shall be eligible to the office of President; neither shall any person be eligible to that office who shall not have attained to the age of thirty-five years, and been fourteen years a resident within the United States [i.e., a legal resident]

To provide for foreign-born like Alexander Hamilton, born in the British West Indies.

5. Replacements for President. In case of the removal of the President from office or of his death, resignation, or inability to discharge the powers and duties of the said office, the same shall devolve on the Vice-President, and the Congress may by law provide for the case of removal, death, resignation, or inability, both of the President and Vice-President, declaring what officer shall then act as President, and such officer shall act accordingly, until the disability be removed, or a President shall be elected.

Modified by Amendments XX and XXV below.

6. The President's salary. The President shall, at stated times, receive for his services a compensation, which shall neither be increased nor diminished during the period for which he shall have been elected, and he shall not receive within that period any other emolument from the United States, or any of them.

7. The President's oath of office. Before he enter on the execution of his office, he shall take the following oath or affirmation:—"I do solemnly swear (or affirm) that I will faithfully execute the office of the President of the United States, and will to the best of my ability preserve, protect and defend the Constitution of the United States."

Section II.   Powers of the President

1. The President has important military and civil powers. The President shall be commander in chief of the army and navy of the United States, and of the militia of the several States, when called into the actual service of the United States; he may require the opinion, in writing, of the principal officer in each of the executive departments, upon any subject relating to the duties of their respective offices, and he shall have power to grant reprieves and pardons for offenses against the United States, except in cases of impeachment.[2]

See Cabinet evolution, p. 142.

2. The President may negotiate treaties and nominate federal officials. He shall have power, by and with the advice and consent of the Senate, to make treaties, provided two-thirds of the Senators present concur; and he shall nominate, and by and with the advice and consent of the Senate, shall appoint ambassadors, other public ministers and consuls, judges of the Supreme Court, and all other officers of the United States, whose appointments are

---

[1] Repealed in 1804 by the 12th Amendment (for text, see Amendments below).

[2] To prevent the President's pardoning himself or his close associates, as was feared in the case of Richard Nixon. See pp. 896–897.

For President's removal power, see pp. 448–449.

not herein otherwise provided for, and which shall be established by law: but the Congress may by law vest the appointment of such inferior officers, as they think proper, in the President alone, in the courts of law, or in the heads of departments.

3. The President may fill vacancies during Senate recess. The President shall have power to fill up all vacancies that may happen during the recess of the Senate, by granting commissions which shall expire at the end of their next session.

Section III.   Other Powers and Duties of the President

For President's personal appearances, see p. 635.

Messages; extra sessions; receiving ambassadors: execution of the laws. He shall from time to time give to the Congress information of the state of the Union, and recommend to their consideration such measures as he shall judge necessary and expedient; he may, on extraordinary occasions, convene both houses, or either of them, and in case of disagreement between them, with respect to the time of adjournment, he may adjourn them to such time as he shall think proper; he shall receive ambassadors and other public ministers; he shall take care that the laws be faithfully executed, and shall commission all the officers of the United States.

Section IV.   Impeachment

See Johnson's acquittal, p. 449; also Nixon's near impeachment, pp. 896–897.

Civil officers may be removed by impeachment. The President, Vice-President and all civil officers[1] of the United States shall be removed from office on impeachment for, and on conviction of, treason, bribery, or other high crimes and misdemeanors.

Article III.   Judicial Department
Section I.   The Federal Courts

The judicial power belongs to the federal courts. The judicial power of the United States shall be vested in one Supreme Court, and in such inferior courts as the Congress may from time to time ordain and establish. The judges, both of the Supreme and inferior courts, shall hold their offices during good behavior, and shall, at stated times, receive for their services a compensation which shall not be diminished[2] during their continuance in office.

See Judicial Act of 1789, p. 143.

Section II.   Jurisdiction of Federal Courts

1. Kinds of cases that may be heard. The judicial power shall extend to all cases, in law and equity, arising under this Constitution, the laws of the United States, and treaties made, or which shall be made, under their authority;—to all cases affecting ambassadors, other public ministers and consuls;—to all cases of admiralty and maritime jurisdiction;—to controversies to which the United States shall be a party;—to controversies between two or more States;—*between a State and citizens of another State;*[3]—between citizens of different States;—between citizens of the same State claiming lands under grants of different States, and between a State, or the citizens thereof, and foreign states, citizens or subjects.

2. Jurisdiction of the Supreme Court. In all cases affecting ambassadors, other public ministers and consuls, and those in which a State shall be party, the Supreme Court shall have original jurisdiction.[4] In all the other cases before mentioned, the Supreme Court shall have appellate jurisdiction,[5] both as to law and fact, with such exceptions, and under such regulations, as the Congress shall make.

---

[1] I.e., all federal executive and judicial officers, but not members of Congress or military personnel.

[2] In 1978, in a case involving federal judges, the Supreme Court ruled that diminution of salaries by inflation was irrelevant.

[3] The 11th Amendment (see Amendments below) restricts this to suits by a state against citizens of another state.

[4] I.e., such cases must originate in the Supreme Court.

[5] I.e., it hears other cases only when they are appealed to it from a lower federal court or a state court.

3. Trial for federal crime is by jury. The trial of all crimes, except in cases of impeachment, shall be by jury; and such trial shall be held in the State where the said crimes shall have been committed; but when not committed within any State, the trial shall be at such place or places as the Congress may by law have directed.

Section III.   Treason

See Burr trial, p. 177.

1. Treason defined. Treason against the United States shall consist only in levying war against them, or in adhering to their enemies, giving them aid and comfort. No person shall be convicted of treason unless on the testimony of two witnesses to the same overt act, or on confession in open court.

2. Congress fixes punishment for treason. The Congress shall have power to declare the punishment of treason, but no attainder of treason shall work corruption of blood, or forfeiture except during the life of the person attainted.[1]

Article IV.   Relations of the States to One Another

Section I.   Credit to Acts, Records, and Court Proceedings

Each state must respect the public acts of the others. Full faith and credit shall be given in each State to the public acts, records, and judicial proceedings of every other State.[2] And the Congress may by general laws prescribe the manner in which such acts, records, and proceedings shall be proved [attested], and the effect thereof.

Section II.   Duties of States to States

1. Citizenship in one state is valid in all. The citizens of each State shall be entitled to all privileges and immunities of citizens in the several States.

This stipulation is sometimes openly flouted. In 1978 Governor Jerry Brown of California, acting on humanitarian grounds, refused to surrender to South Dakota an American Indian, Dennis Banks, who was charged with murder in an armed uprising.

2. Fugitives from justice must be surrendered by the state to which they have fled. A person charged in any State with treason, felony, or other crime, who shall flee from justice, and be found in another State, shall on demand of the executive authority [governor] of the State from which he fled, be delivered up, to be removed to the State having jurisdiction of the crime.

Basis of fugitive slave laws; see pp. 350–351.

3. Slaves and apprentices must be returned. *No person held to service or labor in one State, under the laws thereof, escaping into another, shall, in consequence of any law or regulation therein, be discharged from such service or labor, but shall be delivered up on claim of the party to whom such service or labor may be due.*[3]

Section III.   New States and Territories

E.g., Maine (1820); see pp. 209–210.

1. Congress may admit new states. New States may be admitted by the Congress into this Union; but no new State shall be formed or erected within the jurisdiction of any other State; nor any State be formed by the junction of two or more States, or parts of States, without the consent of the legislatures of the States concerned as well as of the Congress.[4]

2. Congress regulates federal territory and property. The Congress shall have power to dispose of and make all needful rules and regulations respecting the territory or other property belonging to the United States; and nothing in this Constitution shall be so construed as to prejudice any claims of the United States, or of any particular State.

---

[1] I.e., punishment only for the offender; none for his heirs.

[2] E.g., a marriage valid in one is valid in all.

[3] Invalidated in 1865 by the 13th Amendment (for text see Amendments below).

[4] Loyal West Virginia was formed by Lincoln in 1862 from seceded Virginia. This act was of dubious constitutionality and was justified in part by the wartime powers of the President. See pp. 390–391.

Section IV. Protection to the States

United States guarantees to states representative government and protection against invasion and rebellion. The United States shall guarantee to every State in this Union a republican form of government, and shall protect each of them against invasion; and on application of the legislature, or of the executive [governor] (when the legislature cannot be convened), against domestic violence.

See Cleveland and the Pullman strike, pp. 549–550.

Article V. The Process of Amendment

The Constitution may be amended in four ways. The Congress, whenever two-thirds of both houses shall deem it necessary, shall propose amendments to this Constitution, or, on the application of the legislatures of two-thirds of the several States, shall call a convention for proposing amendments, which, in either case, shall be valid to all intents and purposes, as part of this Constitution, when ratified by the legislatures of three-fourths of the several States, or by conventions in three-fourths thereof, as the one or the other mode of ratification may be proposed by the Congress; provided *that no amendments which may be made prior to the year one thousand eight hundred and eight shall in any manner affect the first and fourth clauses in the ninth section of the first article;*[1] and that no State, without its consent, shall be deprived of its equal suffrage in the Senate.

Article VI. General Provisions

This pledge honored by Hamilton, p. 143.

1. The debts of the Confederation are taken over. All debts contracted and engagements entered into, before the adoption of this Constitution, shall be as valid against the United States under this Constitution, as under the Confederation.

2. The Constitution, federal laws, and treaties are the supreme law of the land. This Constitution, and the laws of the United States which shall be made in pursuance thereof; and all treaties made, or which shall be made, under the authority of the United States, shall be the supreme law of the land; and the judges in every State shall be bound thereby, anything in the Constitution or laws of any State to the contrary notwithstanding.

3. Federal and state officers bound by oath to support the Constitution. The Senators and Representatives before mentioned, and the members of the several State legislatures, and all executive and judicial officers, both of the United States and of the several States, shall be bound by oath or affirmation to support this Constitution; but no religious test shall ever be required as a qualification to any office or public trust under the United States.

Article VII. Ratification of the Constitution

See 1787 irregularity, p. 134.

The Constitution effective when ratified by conventions in nine states. The ratification of the conventions of nine States shall be sufficient for the establishment of this Constitution between the States so ratifying the same.

Done in Convention by the unanimous consent of the States present, the seventeenth day of September in the year of our Lord one thousand seven hundred and eighty-seven and of the Independence of the United States of America the twelfth. In witness whereof we have hereunto subscribed our names.

[Signed by]

G° WASHINGTON
Presidt and Deputy from Virginia
[and thirty-eight others]

---

[1] This clause, re slave trade and direct taxes, became inoperative in 1808.

AMENDMENTS TO THE CONSTITUTION

Amendment I.   ## Religious and Political Freedom

*For background
of Bill of Rights,
see p. 143.*

Congress must not interfere with freedom of religion, speech or press, assembly, and petition. Congress shall make no law respecting an establishment of religion,[1] or prohibiting the free exercise thereof; or abridging the freedom of speech, or of the press; or the right of the people peaceably to assemble, and to petition the government for a redress of grievances.

Amendment II.   ## Right to Bear Arms

The people may bear arms. A well-regulated militia being necessary to the security of a free State, the right of the people to keep and bear arms [i.e., for military purposes] shall not be infringed.[2]

Amendment III.   ## Quartering of Troops

*See Declaration
of Independence and
British quartering
above.*

Soldiers may not be arbitrarily quartered on the people. No soldier shall, in time of peace, be quartered in any house without the consent of the owner, nor in time of war, but in a manner to be prescribed by law.

Amendment IV.   ## Searches and Seizures

*A reflection of
colonial
grievances
against Crown.*

Unreasonable searches are forbidden. The right of the people to be secure in their persons, houses, papers, and effects, against unreasonable searches and seizures, shall not be violated, and no [search] warrants shall issue but upon probable cause, supported by oath or affirmation, and particularly describing the place to be searched, and the persons or things to be seized.

Amendment V.   ## Right to Life, Liberty, and Property

*When witnesses refuse
to answer questions in
court, they routinely
"take the Fifth
Amendment."*

The individual is guaranteed certain rights when on trial and the right to life, liberty, and property. No person shall be held to answer for a capital, or otherwise infamous crime, unless on a presentment [formal charge] or indictment of a grand jury, except in cases arising in the land or naval forces, or in the militia, when in actual service in time of war or public danger; nor shall any person be subject for the same offense to be twice put in jeopardy of life or limb; nor shall be compelled in any criminal case to be a witness against himself, nor be deprived of life, liberty, or property, without due process of law; nor shall private property be taken for public use [i.e., by eminent domain] without just compensation.

Amendment VI.   ## Protection in Criminal Trials

*See Declaration
of Independence
above.*

An accused person has important rights. In all criminal prosecutions, the accused shall enjoy the right to a speedy and public trial, by an impartial jury of the State and district wherein the crime shall have been committed, which district shall have been previously ascertained by law, and to be informed of the nature and cause of the accusation; to be confronted with the witnesses against him; to have compulsory process [subpoena] for obtaining witnesses in his favor, and to have the assistance of counsel for his defense.

---

[1] In 1787 "an establishment of religion" referred to an "established church," or one supported by all taxpayers, whether members or not. But the courts have often acted under this article to keep religion, including prayers, out of the public schools.

[2] The courts, with "militia" in mind, have consistently held that the "right" to bear arms is a limited one.

Amendment VII.   Suits at Common Law

The rules of common law are recognized. In suits at common law, where the value in controversy shall exceed twenty dollars, the right of trial by jury shall be preserved, and no fact tried by a jury shall be otherwise re-examined in any court of the United States, than according to the rules of the common law.

Amendment VIII.   Bail and Punishments

Excessive fines and unusual punishments are forbidden. Excessive bail shall not be required, nor excessive fines imposed, nor cruel and unusual punishments inflicted.

Amendment IX.   Concerning Rights Not Enumerated

Amendments IX and X were bulwarks of Southern states' rights before the Civil War.

The people retain rights not here enumerated. The enumeration in the Constitution, of certain rights, shall not be construed to deny or disparage others retained by the people.

Amendment X.   Powers Reserved to the States and to the People

A concession to states' rights, p. 146.

Powers not delegated to the federal government are reserved to the states and the people. The powers not delegated to the United States by the Constitution, nor prohibited by it to the States, are reserved to the States respectively, or to the people.

Amendment XI.   Suits against a State

The federal courts have no authority in suits by citizens against a state. The judicial power of the United States shall not be construed to extend to any suit in law or equity, commenced or prosecuted against one of the United States by citizens of another State, or by citizens or subjects of any foreign state. [Adopted 1798.]

Amendment XII.   Election of President and Vice-President

1. Changes in manner of electing President and Vice-President; procedure when no presidential candidate receives electoral majority. The electors shall meet in their respective States, and vote by ballot for President and Vice-President, one of whom, at least, shall not be an inhabitant of the same State with themselves; they shall name in their ballots the person voted for as President, and in distinct ballots the person voted for as Vice-President, and they shall make distinct lists of all persons voted for as President, and of all persons voted for as Vice-President, and of the number of votes for each, which lists they shall sign and certify, and transmit sealed to the seat of government of the United States, directed to the President of the Senate;—the President of the Senate shall, in the presence of the Senate and House of Representatives, open all the certificates and the votes shall then be counted;—the person having the greatest number of votes for President shall be the President, if such number be a majority of the whole number of electors appointed; and if no person have such majority, then from the persons having the highest numbers not exceeding three on the list of those voted for as President, the House of Representatives shall choose immediately, by ballot, the President. But in choosing the President, the votes shall be taken by States, the representation from each State having one vote; a quorum for this purpose shall consist of a member or members from two-thirds of the States, and a majority of all the States shall be necessary to a choice. And if the House of Representatives shall not choose a President whenever the right of choice shall devolve upon them, before *the fourth day of March*[1] next following, then the Vice-President shall act as President, as in the case of the death or other constitutional disability of the President.

2. Procedure when no vice-presidential candidate receives electoral majority. The person having the greatest number of votes as Vice-President shall be the Vice-President, if such

Forestalls repetition of 1800 electoral dispute, p. 164.

See 1876 disputed election, pp. 460–463.

See 1824 election, pp. 223–224.

[1] Changed to January 20 by the 20th Amendment (for text, see Amendments below).

number be a majority of the whole number of electors appointed; and if no person have a majority, then from the two highest numbers on the list the Senate shall choose the Vice-President; a quorum for the purpose shall consist of two-thirds of the whole number of Senators, and a majority of the whole number shall be necessary to a choice. But no person constitutionally ineligible to the office of President shall be eligible to that of Vice-President of the United States. [Adopted 1804.]

Amendment XIII.   Slavery Prohibited

For background, see pp. 403–404.

Slavery forbidden. 1. Neither slavery[1] nor involuntary servitude, except as a punishment for crime whereof the party shall have been duly convicted, shall exist within the United States, or any place subject to their jurisdiction.

2. Congress shall have power to enforce this article by appropriate legislation. [Adopted 1865.]

Amendment XIV.   Civil Rights for Ex-slaves,[2] etc.

For background, see p. 440.

For corporations as "persons," see p. 490.

Abolishes three-fifths rule for slaves, Art. I, Sec. II, para. 3.

1. Ex-slaves made citizens; U.S. citizenship primary. All persons born or naturalized in the United States, and subject to the jurisdiction thereof, are citizens of the United States and of the State wherein they reside. No State shall make or enforce any law which shall abridge the privileges or immunities of citizens of the United States; nor shall any State deprive any person of life, liberty, or property, without due process of law; nor deny to any person within its jurisdiction the equal protection of the laws.

2. When a state denies citizens the vote, its representation shall be reduced. Representatives shall be apportioned among the several States according to their respective numbers, counting the whole number of persons in each State, excluding Indians not taxed. But when the right to vote at any election for the choice of Electors for President and Vice-President of the United States, Representatives in Congress, the executive and judicial officers of a State, or the members of the legislature thereof, is denied to any of the male inhabitants of such State, being twenty-one years of age and citizens of the United States, or in any way abridged, except for participation in rebellion, or other crime, the basis of representation therein shall be reduced in the proportion which the number of such male citizens shall bear to the whole number of male citizens twenty-one years of age in such State.

Leading ex-Confederates denied office. See p. 438.

3. Certain persons who have been in rebellion are ineligible for federal and state office. No person shall be a Senator or Representative in Congress, or Elector of President and Vice-President, or hold any office, civil or military, under the United States, or under any State, who, having previously taken an oath, as a member of Congress, or as an officer of the United States, or as a member of any State legislature, or as an executive or judicial officer of any State, to support the Constitution of the United States, shall have engaged in insurrection or rebellion against the same, or given aid or comfort to the enemies thereof. But Congress may, by a vote of two-thirds of each house, remove such disability.

The ex-Confederates were thus forced to repudiate their debts and pay pensions to their own veterans, plus taxes for the pensions of Union veterans, their conquerors.

4. Debts incurred in aid of rebellion are void. The validity of the public debt of the United States, authorized by law, including debts incurred for payment of pensions and bounties for services in suppressing insurrection or rebellion, shall not be questioned. But neither the United States nor any State shall assume or pay any debt or obligation incurred in aid of insurrection or rebellion against the United States, or any claim for the loss or emancipation of any slave; but all such debts, obligations, and claims shall be held illegal and void.

---

[1] The only explicit mention of slavery in the Constitution.
[2] Occasionally an offender is prosecuted under the 13th Amendment for keeping an employee or other person under conditions approximating slavery.

5. Enforcement. The Congress shall have power to enforce, by appropriate legislation, the provisions of this article. [Adopted 1868.]

Amendment XV.   Suffrage for Blacks

For background, see p. 442.

Black males are made voters. 1. The right of citizens of the United States to vote shall not be denied or abridged by the United States or by any State on account of race, color, or previous condition of servitude.

2. The Congress shall have power to enforce this article by appropriate legislation. [Adopted 1870.]

Amendment XVI.   Income Taxes

For background, see pp. 550, 630.

Congress has power to lay and collect income taxes. The Congress shall have power to lay and collect taxes on incomes, from whatever source derived, without apportionment among the several States, and without regard to any census or enumeration. [Adopted 1913.]

Amendment XVII.   Direct Election of Senators

Senators shall be elected by popular vote. 1. The Senate of the United States shall be composed of two Senators from each State, elected by the people thereof, for six years; and each Senator shall have one vote. The electors in each State shall have the qualifications requisite for electors of [voters for] the most numerous branch of the State legislatures.

2. When vacancies happen in the representation of any State in the Senate, the executive authority of such State shall issue writs of election to fill such vacancies: Provided, that the Legislature of any State may empower the executive thereof to make temporary appointments until the people fill the vacancies by election as the Legislature may direct.

3. This amendment shall not be so construed as to affect the election or term of any Senator chosen before it becomes valid as part of the Constitution. [Adopted 1913.]

Amendment XVIII.   National Prohibition

For background, see p. 684.

The sale or manufacture of intoxicating liquors is forbidden. 1. *After one year from the ratification of this article the manufacture, sale, or transportation of intoxicating liquors within, the importation thereof into, or the exportation thereof from the United States and all territory subject to the jurisdiction thereof, for beverage purposes, is hereby prohibited.*

2. *The Congress and the several States shall have concurrent power to enforce this article by appropriate legislation.*

3. *This article shall be inoperative unless it shall have been ratified as an amendment to the Constitution by the legislatures of the several States, as provided by the Constitution, within seven years from the date of the submission thereof to the States by the Congress.* [Adopted 1919; repealed 1933 by 21st Amendment.]

Amendment XIX.   Woman Suffrage

For background, see p. 684.

Women guaranteed the right to vote. 1. The right of citizens of the United States to vote shall not be denied or abridged by the United States or by any State on account of sex.

2. The Congress shall have power to enforce this article by appropriate legislation. [Adopted 1920.]

Amendment XX.   Presidential and Congressional Terms

Shortens lame-duck periods by modifying Art. I, Sec. IV, para. 2.

1. Presidential, vice-presidential, and congressional terms of office begin in January. The terms of the President and Vice-President shall end at noon on the 20th day of January, and the terms of Senators and Representatives at noon on the 3d day of January, of the years in which such terms would have ended if this article had not been ratified; and the terms of their successors shall then begin.

2. New meeting date for Congress. The Congress shall assemble at least once in every year, and such meeting shall begin at noon on the 3d day of January, unless they shall by law appoint a different day.

3. Emergency presidential and vice-presidential succession. If, at the time fixed for the beginning of the term of the President, the President-elect shall have died, the Vice-President-elect shall become President. If a President shall not have been chosen before the time fixed for the beginning of his term, or if the President-elect shall have failed to qualify, then the Vice-President-elect shall act as President until a President shall have qualified; and the Congress may by law provide for the case wherein neither a President-elect nor a Vice-President-elect shall have qualified, declaring who shall then act as President, or the manner in which one who is to act shall be selected, and such persons shall act accordingly until a President or Vice-President shall have qualified.

4. The Congress may by law provide for the case of the death of any of the persons from whom the House of Representatives may choose a President whenever the right of choice shall have devolved upon them, and for the case of the death of any of the persons from whom the Senate may choose a Vice-President whenever the right of choice shall have devolved upon them.

5. Sections 1 and 2 shall take effect on the 15th day of October following the ratification of this article.

6. This article shall be inoperative unless it shall have been ratified as an amendment to the Constitution by the Legislatures of three-fourths of the several States within seven years from the date of its submission. [Adopted 1933.]

Amendment XXI.   Prohibition Repealed

For background, see p. 759.

1. 18th Amendment repealed. The eighteenth article of amendment to the Constitution of the United States is hereby repealed.

2. Local laws honored. The transportation or importation into any State, Territory, or Possession of the United States for delivery or use therein of intoxicating liquors, in violation of the laws thereof, is hereby prohibited.

3. This article shall be inoperative unless it shall have been ratified as an amendment to the Constitution by conventions in the several States, as provided in the Constitution, within seven years from the date of the submission thereof to the States by the Congress. [Adopted 1933.]

Amendment XXII.   Anti-Third Term Amendment

Sometimes referred to as the anti–Franklin Roosevelt amendment.

Presidential term is limited. 1. No person shall be elected to the office of President more than twice, and no person who has held the office of President, or acted as President, for more than two years of a term to which some other person was elected President shall be elected to the office of President more than once. But this article shall not apply to any person holding the office of President when this article was proposed by the Congress [i.e., Truman], and shall not prevent any person who may be holding the office of President, or acting as President, during the term within which this article becomes operative [i.e., Truman] from holding the office of President or acting as President during the remainder of such term.

2. This article shall be inoperative unless it shall have been ratified as an amendment to the Constitution by the legislatures of three-fourths of the several States within seven years from the date of its submission to the States by the Congress. [Adopted 1951.]

Amendment XXIII.   District of Columbia Vote

Designed to give the District of Columbia three electoral votes and to quiet the century-old cry of "No taxation without representation." Yet the District of Columbia still has only one non-voting member of Congress.

1. Presidential Electors for the District of Columbia. The District constituting the seat of Government of the United States shall appoint in such manner as the Congress may direct:

A number of electors of President and Vice-President equal to the whole number of Senators and Representatives in Congress to which the District would be entitled if it were a State, but in no event more than the least populous State; they shall be in addition to those appointed by the States, but they shall be considered for the purposes of the election of President and Vice-President, to be electors appointed by a State; and they shall meet in the District and perform such duties as provided by the twelfth article of amendment.

2. Enforcement. The Congress shall have the power to enforce this article by appropriate legislation. [Adopted 1961.]

Amendment XXIV.   Poll Tax

Designed to end discrimination against blacks and other poor folk. An aspect of the civil rights crusade under President Lyndon Johnson. See p. 868.

1. Payment of poll tax or other taxes not to be prerequisite for voting in federal elections. The right of citizens of the United States to vote in any primary or other election for President or Vice-President, for electors for President or Vice-President, or for Senator or Representative in Congress, shall not be denied or abridged by the United States or any State by reason of failure to pay any poll tax or other tax.

2. Enforcement. The Congress shall have the power to enforce this article by appropriate legislation. [Adopted 1964.]

Amendment XXV.   Presidential Succession and Disability[1] (1967)

1. Vice-President to become President. In case of the removal of the President from office or of his death or resignation, the Vice-President shall become President.[2]

2. Successor to Vice-President provided. Whenever there is a vacancy in the office of the Vice-President, the President shall nominate a Vice-President who shall take office upon confirmation by a majority vote of both Houses of Congress.

Gerald Ford was the first "appointed President." See pp. 891–901.

3. Vice-President to serve for disabled President. Whenever the President transmits to the President pro tempore of the Senate and the Speaker of the House of Representatives his written declaration that he is unable to discharge the powers and duties of his office, and until he transmits to them a written declaration to the contrary, such powers and duties shall be discharged by the Vice-President as Acting President.

---

[1] Passed by a two-thirds vote of both Houses of Congress in July 1965; ratified by the requisite three-fourths of the state legislatures, February 1967, or well within the seven-year limit.

[2] The original Constitution (Art. II, Sec. I, para. 5) was vague on this point, stipulating that "the powers and duties" of the President, but not necessarily the title, should "devolve" on the Vice-President. President Tyler, the first "accidental President," assumed not only the powers and duties but the title as well.

4. Procedure for disqualifying or requalifying President. Whenever the Vice-President and a majority of either the principal officers of the executive departments or of such other body as Congress may by law provide, transmit to the President pro tempore of the Senate and the Speaker of the House of Representatives their written declaration that the President is unable to discharge the powers and duties of his office, the Vice-President shall immediately assume the powers and duties of the office as Acting President.

Thereafter, when the President transmits to the President pro tempore of the Senate and the Speaker of the House of Representatives his written declaration that no inability exists, he shall resume the powers and duties of his office unless the Vice-President and a majority of either the principal officers of the executive department [s] or of such other body as Congress may by law provide, transmit within four days to the President pro tempore of the Senate and the Speaker of the House of Representatives their written declaration that the President is unable to discharge the powers and duties of his office. Thereupon Congress shall decide the issue, assembling within forty-eight hours for that purpose if not in session. If the Congress, within twenty-one days after receipt of the latter written declaration, or, if Congress is not in session, within twenty-one days after Congress is required to assemble, determines by two-thirds vote of both Houses that the President is unable to discharge the powers and duties of his office, the Vice-President shall continue to discharge the same as Acting President; otherwise, the President shall resume the powers and duties of his office.

Amendment XXVI.   Lowering Voting Age (1971)

A response to the current revolt of youth, see pp. 884ff.

1. Ballot for eighteen-year-olds. The right of citizens of the United States, who are eighteen years of age or older, to vote shall not be denied or abridged by the United States or by any State on account of age.

2. Enforcement. The Congress shall have power to enforce this article by appropriate legislation.

Amendment XXVII.   Sex Equality (Sent to States, 1972)

See pp. 930–932 for background.

1. Women's rights guaranteed. Equality of rights under the law shall not be denied or abridged by the United States or by any State on account of sex.

2. Enforcement. The Congress shall have the power to enforce, by appropriate legislation, the provisions of this article.

3. Timing. This amendment shall take effect two years after the date of ratification.

[The original time limit on ratification was due to expire on March 22, 1979, but Congress, in a controversial move, extended the deadline to June 30, 1982. Yet ratification remained stalled on the expiration of that date, because only 35 of the necessary 38 states had given their approval.]

Growth of U.S. Population and Area

Census	Population of United States	Increase over the Preceding Census		Land Area (Sq. Mi.)	Pop. per Sq. Mi.
		Number	Percent		
1790	3,929,214			867,980	4.5
1800	5,308,483	1,379,269	35.1	867,980	6.1
1810	7,239,881	1,931,398	36.4	1,685,865	4.3
1820	9,638,453	2,398,572	33.1	1,753,588	5.5
1830	12,866,020	3,227,567	33.5	1,753,588	7.3
1840	17,069,453	4,203,433	32.7	1,753,588	9.7
1850	23,191,876	6,122,423	35.9	2,944,337	7.9
1860	31,433,321	8,251,445	35.6	2,973,965	10.6
1870	39,818,449	8,375,128	26.6	2,973,965	13.4
1880	50,155,783	10,337,334	26.0	2,973,965	16.9
1890	62,947,714	12,791,931	25.5	2,973,965	21.2
1900	75,994,575	13,046,861	20.7	2,974,159	25.6
1910	91,972,266	15,997,691	21.0	2,973,890	30.9
1920	105,710,620	13,738,354	14.9	2,973,776	35.5
1930	122,775,046	17,064,426	16.1	2,977,128	41.2
1940	131,669,275	8,894,229	7.2	2,977,128	44.2
1950	150,697,361	19,028,086	14.5	2,974,726 *	50.7
1960 †	179,323,175	28,625,814	19.0	3,540,911	50.6
1970	203,235,298	23,912,123	13.3	3,536,855	57.5
1980	226,504,825	23,269,527	11.4	3,536,855	64.0

* As remeasured in 1940; shrinkage offset by increase in water area.
† First year for which figures include Alaska and Hawaii.

Admission of States

(SEE P. 137 FOR ORDER IN WHICH THE ORIGINAL THIRTEEN ENTERED THE UNION.)

Order of Admission	State	Date of Admission	Order of Admission	State	Date of Admission
14	Vermont	March 4, 1791	33	Oregon	Feb. 14, 1859
15	Kentucky	June 1, 1792	34	Kansas	Jan. 29, 1861
16	Tennessee	June 1, 1796	35	West Virginia	June 20, 1863
17	Ohio	March 1, 1803	36	Nevada	Oct. 31, 1864
18	Louisiana	April 30, 1812	37	Nebraska	March 1, 1867
19	Indiana	Dec. 11, 1816	38	Colorado	Aug. 1, 1876
20	Mississippi	Dec. 10, 1817	39	North Dakota	Nov. 2, 1889
21	Illinois	Dec. 3, 1818	40	South Dakota	Nov. 2, 1889
22	Alabama	Dec. 14, 1819	41	Montana	Nov. 8, 1889
23	Maine	March 15, 1820	42	Washington	Nov. 11, 1889
24	Missouri	Aug. 10, 1821	43	Idaho	July 3, 1890
25	Arkansas	June 15, 1836	44	Wyoming	July 10, 1890
26	Michigan	Jan. 26, 1837	45	Utah	Jan. 4, 1896
27	Florida	March 3, 1845	46	Oklahoma	Nov. 16, 1907
28	Texas	Dec. 29, 1845	47	New Mexico	Jan. 6, 1912
29	Iowa	Dec. 28, 1846	48	Arizona	Feb. 14, 1912
30	Wisconsin	May 29, 1848	49	Alaska	Jan. 3, 1959
31	California	Sept. 9, 1850	50	Hawaii	Aug. 21, 1959
32	Minnesota	May 11, 1858			

Presidential Elections°

Election	Candidates	Parties	Popular Vote	Electoral Vote
1789	GEORGE WASHINGTON	No party designations		69
	John Adams			34
	Minor Candidates			35
1792	GEORGE WASHINGTON	No party designations		132
	John Adams			77
	George Clinton			50
	Minor Candidates			5
1796	JOHN ADAMS	Federalist		71
	Thomas Jefferson	Democratic-Republican		68
	Thomas Pinckney	Federalist		59
	Aaron Burr	Democratic-Republican		30
	Minor Candidates			48
1800	THOMAS JEFFERSON	Democratic-Republican		73
	Aaron Burr	Democratic-Republican		73
	John Adams	Federalist		65
	Charles C. Pinckney	Federalist		64
	John Jay	Federalist		1
1804	THOMAS JEFFERSON	Democratic-Republican		162
	Charles C. Pinckney	Federalist		14
1808	JAMES MADISON	Democratic-Republican		122
	Charles C. Pinckney	Federalist		47
	George Clinton	Democratic-Republican		6
1812	JAMES MADISON	Democratic-Republican		128
	DeWitt Clinton	Federalist		89
1816	JAMES MONROE	Democratic-Republican		183
	Rufus King	Federalist		34
1820	JAMES MONROE	Democratic-Republican		231
	John Q. Adams	Independent Republican		1
1824	JOHN Q. ADAMS (Min.)†	Democratic-Republican	108,740	84
	Andrew Jackson	Democratic-Republican	153,544	99
	William H. Crawford	Democratic-Republican	46,618	41
	Henry Clay	Democratic-Republican	47,136	37
1828	ANDREW JACKSON	Democratic	647,286	178
	John Q. Adams	National Republican	508,064	83
1832	ANDREW JACKSON	Democratic	687,502	219
	Henry Clay	National Republican	530,189	49
	William Wirt	Anti-Masonic	33,108	7
	John Floyd	National Republican		11
1836	MARTIN VAN BUREN	Democratic	762,678	170
	William H. Harrison	Whig		73
	Hugh L. White	Whig		26
	Daniel Webster	Whig	736,656	14
	W. P. Mangum	Whig		11
1840	WILLIAM H. HARRISON	Whig	1,275,016	234
	Martin Van Buren	Democratic	1,129,102	60
1844	JAMES K. POLK (Min.)†	Democratic	1,337,243	170
	Henry Clay	Whig	1,299,062	105
	James G. Birney	Liberty	62,300	

* Candidates receiving less than 1 percent of the popular vote are omitted. Before the 12th Amendment (1804), the Electoral College voted for two presidential candidates, and the runner-up became Vice-President. Basic figures are taken primarily from *Historical Statistics of the United States, 1789–1945* (1949), pp. 288–290; *Historical Statistics of the United States, Colonial Times to 1957* (1960), pp. 682–683; and *Statistical Abstract of the United States, 1969* (1969), pp. 355–357.

† "Min." indicates minority President—one receiving less than 50 percent of all popular votes.

Presidential Elections (Continued)

Election	Candidates	Parties	Popular Vote	Electoral Vote
1848	ZACHARY TAYLOR	Whig	1,360,099	163
	Lewis Cass	Democratic	1,220,544	127
	Martin Van Buren	Free Soil	291,263	
1852	FRANKLIN PIERCE	Democratic	1,601,274	254
	Winfield Scott	Whig	1,386,580	42
	John P. Hale	Free Soil	155,825	
1856	JAMES BUCHANAN (Min.)*	Democratic	1,838,169	174
	John C. Fremont	Republican	1,341,264	114
	Millard Fillmore	American	874,534	8
1860	ABRAHAM LINCOLN (Min.)*	Republican	1,867,198	180
	Stephen A. Douglas	Democratic	1,379,434	12
	John C. Breckinridge	Democratic	854,248	72
	John Bell	Constitutional Union	591,658	39
1864	ABRAHAM LINCOLN	Union	2,213,665	212
	George.B. McClellan	Democratic	1,802,237	21
1868	ULYSSES S. GRANT	Republican	3,012,833	214
	Horatio Seymour	Democratic	2,703,249	80
1872	ULYSSES S. GRANT	Republican	3,597,132	286
	Horace Greeley	Democratic and Liberal Republican	2,834,125	66
1876	RUTHERFORD B. HAYES (Min.)*	Republican	4,036,298	185
	Samuel J. Tilden	Democratic	4,300,590	184
1880	JAMES A. GARFIELD (Min.)*	Republican	4,454,416	214
	Winfield S. Hancock	Democratic	4,444,952	155
	James B. Weaver	Greenback-Labor	308,578	
1884	GROVER CLEVELAND (Min.)*	Democratic	4,874,986	219
	James G. Blaine	Republican	4,851,981	182
	Benjamin F. Butler	Greenback-Labor	175,370	
	John P. St. John	Prohibition	150,369	
1888	BENJAMIN HARRISON (Min.)*	Republican	5,439,853	233
	Grover Cleveland	Democratic	5,540,309	168
	Clinton B. Fisk	Prohibition	249,506	
	Anson J. Streeter	Union Labor	146,935	
1892	GROVER CLEVELAND (Min.)*	Democratic	5,556,918	277
	Benjamin Harrison	Republican	5,176,108	145
	James B. Weaver	People's	1,041,028	22
	John Bidwell	Prohibition	264,133	
1896	WILLIAM MC KINLEY	Republican	7,104,779	271
	William J. Bryan	Democratic	6,502,925	176
1900	WILLIAM MC KINLEY	Republican	7,207,923	292
	William J. Bryan	Democratic; Populist	6,358,133	155
	John C. Woolley	Prohibition	208,914	
1904	THEODORE ROOSEVELT	Republican	7,623,486	336
	Alton B. Parker	Democratic	5,077,911	140
	Eugene V. Debs	Socialist	402,283	
	Silas C. Swallow	Prohibition	258,536	
1908	WILLIAM H. TAFT	Republican	7,678,908	321
	William J. Bryan	Democratic	6,409,104	162
	Eugene V. Debs	Socialist	420,793	
	Eugene W. Chafin	Prohibition	253,840	

* "Min." indicates minority President—one receiving less than 50 percent of all popular votes.

Presidential Elections (Continued)

Election	Candidates	Parties	Popular Vote	Electoral Vote
1912	WOODROW WILSON (Min.)*	Democratic	6,293,454	435
	Theodore Roosevelt	Progressive	4,119,538	88
	William H. Taft	Republican	3,484,980	8
	Eugene V. Debs	Socialist	900,672	
	Eugene W. Chafin	Prohibition	206,275	
1916	WOODROW WILSON (Min.)*	Democratic	9,129,606	277
	Charles E. Hughes	Republican	8,538,221	254
	A. L. Benson	Socialist	585,113	
	J. F. Hanly	Prohibition	220,506	
1920	WARREN G. HARDING	Republican	16,152,200	404
	James M. Cox	Democratic	9,147,353	127
	Eugene V. Debs	Socialist	919,799	
	P. P. Christensen	Farmer-Labor	265,411	
1924	CALVIN COOLIDGE	Republican	15,725,016	382
	John W. Davis	Democratic	8,386,503	136
	Robert M. La Follette	Progressive	4,822,856	13
1928	HERBERT C. HOOVER	Republican	21,391,381	444
	Alfred E. Smith	Democratic	15,016,443	87
1932	FRANKLIN D. ROOSEVELT	Democratic	22,821,857	472
	Herbert C. Hoover	Republican	15,761,841	59
	Norman Thomas	Socialist	881,951	
1936	FRANKLIN D. ROOSEVELT	Democratic	27,751,597	523
	Alfred M. Landon	Republican	16,679,583	8
	William Lemke	Union, etc.	882,479	
1940	FRANKLIN D. ROOSEVELT	Democratic	27,244,160	449
	Wendell L. Willkie	Republican	22,305,198	82
1944	FRANKLIN D. ROOSEVELT	Democratic	25,602,504	432
	Thomas E. Dewey	Republican	22,006,285	99
1948	HARRY S TRUMAN (Min.)*	Democratic	24,105,812	303
	Thomas E. Dewey	Republican	21,970,065	189
	J. Strom Thurmond	States' Rights Democratic	1,169,063	39
	Henry A. Wallace	Progressive	1,157,172	
1952	DWIGHT D. EISENHOWER	Republican	33,936,234	442
	Adlai E. Stevenson	Democratic	27,314,992	89
1956	DWIGHT D. EISENHOWER	Republican	35,590,472	457
	Adlai E. Stevenson	Democratic	26,022,752	73
1960	JOHN F. KENNEDY (Min.)*	Democratic	34,226,731	303
	Richard M. Nixon	Republican	34,108,157	219
1964	LYNDON B. JOHNSON	Democratic	43,129,484	486
	Barry M. Goldwater	Republican	27,178,188	52
1968	RICHARD M. NIXON (Min.)*	Republican	31,785,480	301
	Hubert H. Humphrey, Jr.	Democratic	31,275,166	191
	George C. Wallace	American Independent	9,906,473	46
1972	RICHARD M. NIXON	Republican	45,767,218	520
	George S. McGovern	Democratic	28,357,688	17
1976	JIMMY CARTER	Democratic	40,828,657	297
	Gerald R. Ford	Republican	39,145,520	240
1980	RONALD W. REAGAN	Republican	**43,201,220**	489
	Jimmy Carter	Democratic	34,913,332	49
	John B. Anderson	Independent	5,581,379	0

* "Min." indicates minority President—one receiving less than 50 percent of all popular votes.

Presidents and Elected Vice-Presidents

Term	President	Vice-President
1789–1793	George Washington	John Adams
1793–1797	George Washington	John Adams
1797–1801	John Adams	Thomas Jefferson
1801–1805	Thomas Jefferson	Aaron Burr
1805–1809	Thomas Jefferson	George Clinton
1809–1813	James Madison	George Clinton (d. 1812)
1813–1817	James Madison	Elbridge Gerry (d. 1814)
1817–1821	James Monroe	Daniel D. Tompkins
1821–1825	James Monroe	Daniel D. Tompkins
1825–1829	John Quincy Adams	John C. Calhoun
1829–1833	Andrew Jackson	John C. Calhoun (resigned 1832)
1833–1837	Andrew Jackson	Martin Van Buren
1837–1841	Martin Van Buren	Richard M. Johnson
1841–1845	William H. Harrison (d. 1841) John Tyler	John Tyler
1845–1849	James K. Polk	George M. Dallas
1849–1853	Zachary Taylor (d. 1850) Millard Fillmore	Millard Fillmore
1853–1857	Franklin Pierce	William R. D. King (d. 1853)
1857–1861	James Buchanan	John C. Breckinridge
1861–1865	Abraham Lincoln	Hannibal Hamlin
1865–1869	Abraham Lincoln (d. 1865) Andrew Johnson	Andrew Johnson
1869–1873	Ulysses S. Grant	Schuyler Colfax
1873–1877	Ulysses S. Grant	Henry Wilson (d. 1875)
1877–1881	Rutherford B. Hayes	William A. Wheeler
1881–1885	James A. Garfield (d. 1881) Chester A. Arthur	Chester A. Arthur
1885–1889	Grover Cleveland	Thomas A. Hendricks (d. 1885)
1889–1893	Benjamin Harrison	Levi P. Morton
1893–1897	Grover Cleveland	Adlai E. Stevenson
1897–1901	William McKinley	Garret A. Hobart (d. 1899)
1901–1905	William McKinley (d. 1901) Theodore Roosevelt	Theodore Roosevelt
1905–1909	Theodore Roosevelt	Charles W. Fairbanks
1909–1913	William H. Taft	James S. Sherman (d. 1912)
1913–1917	Woodrow Wilson	Thomas R. Marshall
1917–1921	Woodrow Wilson	Thomas R. Marshall
1921–1925	Warren G. Harding (d. 1923) Calvin Coolidge	Calvin Coolidge
1925–1929	Calvin Coolidge	Charles G. Dawes
1929–1933	Herbert C. Hoover	Charles Curtis
1933–1937	Franklin D. Roosevelt	John N. Garner
1937–1941	Franklin D. Roosevelt	John N. Garner
1941–1945	Franklin D. Roosevelt	Henry A. Wallace
1945–1949	Franklin D. Roosevelt (d. 1945) Harry S Truman	Harry S Truman
1949–1953	Harry S Truman	Alben W. Barkley
1953–1957	Dwight D. Eisenhower	Richard M. Nixon
1957–1961	Dwight D. Eisenhower	Richard M. Nixon
1961–1965	John F. Kennedy (d. 1963) Lyndon B. Johnson	Lyndon B. Johnson
1965–1969	Lyndon B. Johnson	Hubert H. Humphrey, Jr.
1969–1974	Richard M. Nixon	Spiro T. Agnew; Gerald R. Ford
1974–1977	Gerald R. Ford	
1977–1981	Jimmy Carter	Walter F. Mondale
1981–	**Ronald Reagan**	**George Bush**

INDEX

49°

WASH.

Columbia R.

OREG.

OREGON COUNTRY
(BY AGREEMENT WITH BRITAIN, 1846)

MONT.

N. DAK.

42°

IDAHO

S. DAK.

WYO.

NEBR.

LOUISIANA PURCHASE

(FROM FRANCE, 18

NEV.

UTAH

CALIF.

MEXICAN CESSION
(1848)

COLO.

KANS.

ARIZ.

N. MEX.

OKLA

GADSDEN PURCHASE
(FROM MEXICO, 1853)

TEXAS
(INDEPENDENT REPUBLIC
ANNEXED, 1845)

TEXAS

PACIFIC

OCEAN

Rio Grande R.

Nueces R.

Territorial Growth of the United States

The Political Consolidation of Continental America, 1783-1853

THE ORIGINAL UNITED STATES
(BY TREATY WITH BRITAIN, 1783)

MASON-DIXON LINE

36° 30'

FLORIDA
(BY TREATY WITH SPAIN, 1819)

(1810)
(1813)
(SEIZED FROM SPAIN)

Lake Superior
Lake Michigan
Lake Huron
Lake Ontario
Lake Erie
St. Lawrence R.
Mississippi R.
Ohio R.

ATLANTIC OCEAN

GULF OF MEXICO

ME.
VT.
N.H.
N.Y.
MASS.
CONN. R.I.
PA.
N.J.
MD.
DEL.
W. VA.
VA.
KY.
N.C.
S.C.
GA.
TENN.
ALA.
MISS.
LA.
ARK.
MO.
WIS.
MICH.
ILL.
IND.
OHIO
NN.
OWA
FLA.

The United States and Its Possessions

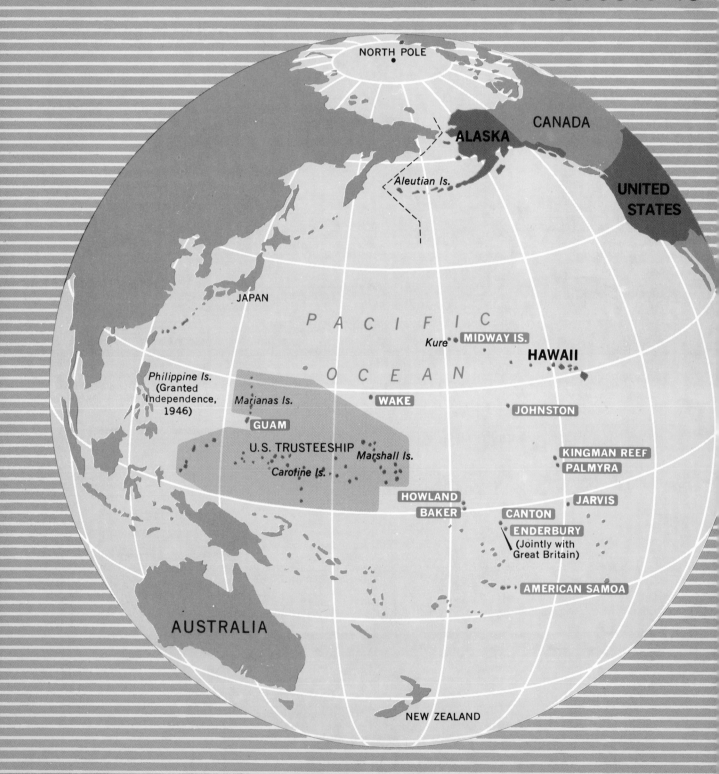

NORTH POLE

CANADA

ALASKA

UNITED STATES

Aleutian Is.

JAPAN

PACIFIC

Kure • MIDWAY IS.

HAWAII

OCEAN

Philippine Is.
(Granted
Independence,
1946)

Marianas Is.

• WAKE

JOHNSTON

GUAM

U.S. TRUSTEESHIP

KINGMAN REEF
PALMYRA

Marshall Is.

Caroline Is.

HOWLAND
BAKER

JARVIS

CANTON
ENDERBURY
(Jointly with
Great Britain)

AMERICAN SAMOA

AUSTRALIA

NEW ZEALAND

WAKE *United States Possessions*

⚓ *Bases Leased from Great Britain, 1940*

NORTH POLE

GREENLAND

ICELAND

EUROPE

CANADA

⚓ NEWFOUNDLAND

UNITED STATES

ATLANTIC

⚓ BERMUDA

MEXICO

⚓ BAHAMAS

AFRICA

OCEAN

PUERTO RICO

SWAN IS.

VIRGIN IS.

⚓ JAMAICA

⚓ ANTIGUA

CARIBBEAN SEA

CENTRAL
AMERICA

⚓ ST. LUCIA

⚓ TRINIDAD

PANAMA CANAL ZONE

⚓ BRITISH GUIANA

SOUTH

AMERICA